1906 San Francisco earthquake centennial field guides

Field trips associated with the 100th Anniversary Conference, 18–23 April 2006, San Francisco, California

Edited by

Carol S. Prentice
U.S. Geological Survey
345 Middlefield Rd., MS 977
Menlo Park, California 94025, USA

Judith G. Scotchmoor
University of California Museum of Paleontology
1101 Valley Life Sciences Building
Berkeley, California 94720-4780, USA

Eldridge M. Moores
Department of Geology
University of California
One Shields Ave
Davis, California 95616, USA

Jon P. Kiland
Dasse Design Inc.
33 New Montgomery St. Suite 850
San Francisco, California 94105, USA

THE
GEOLOGICAL
SOCIETY
OF AMERICA

Field Guide 7

3300 Penrose Place, P.O. Box 9140 • Boulder, Colorado 80301-9140 USA

2006

Published by The Geological Society of America, Inc.
3300 Penrose Place, P.O. Box 9140, Boulder, Colorado 80301-9140, USA
www.geosociety.org

Printed in the USA

A CIP catalogue record for this book is available from the Library of Congress.

ISBN 0-8137-0007-8

ISBN 978-0-8137-0007-6

Cover:
Oblique view of a digital elevation model looking northwest along the San Andreas fault (translucent pink line). Colors represent a Modified Mercalli Intensity (MMI) ShakeMap for the 1906 San Francisco earthquake (from Boatwright and Bundock, 2005; available on the web at http://pubs.usgs.gov/of/2005/1135/IntensityMaps.html). Star shows the epicenter of 1906 earthquake. The white arrow near San Juan Bautista marks the southern end of the 1906 fault rupture, and the northern white arrow marks where the surface rupture trends offshore near Point Arena. Image by Michael J. Rymer, U.S. Geological Survey. Photograph at top is San Francisco City Hall shortly after 1906 earthquake and fire (photographer unknown).

10 9 8 7 6 5 4 3 2 1

Contents

Contents

Manuel "Doc" Bonilla. Photograph by
M. Diggles, U.S. Geological Survey, 1994. To
read more about Doc Bonilla and his work, go
to www.iris.edu/seismo/quakes/1957dalycity/.

DEDICATION

This volume is dedicated to Manuel "Doc" Bonilla, U.S. Geological Survey geologist, whose pioneering work in the geological study of active faults contributed in many ways to the development of our science and to the safety of all northern Californians. His expertise and careful work are reflected directly in several of these field guides and indirectly in all of them.

ACKNOWLEDGMENTS

The editors would like to thank the conference conveners for supporting this effort, as well as the contributions of the other field trips committee members: Stephen Tobriner, John Boatwright, and Doris Sloan, in helping to put together this slate of field trips for the conference. Thanks also to all of the field trip leaders for volunteering their time toward this effort. And thanks to the many teachers and scientists who provided helpful reviews of each field guide: Thomas Brocher, Peg Dabel, Susan Garcia, Helen Hays, Scott Hays, Suzanne Hecker, Sue Hoey, Molla Huq, Anne Monk, Benjamin Pittenger, and Sue Pritchard. We are indebted to Michael Rymer, U.S. Geological Survey, for providing many of the maps and other figures, and to Lana Chan for help with the cover.

Introduction

Carol S. Prentice
U.S. Geological Survey, 345 Middlefield Rd., MS 977, Menlo Park, California 94025, USA
Eldridge M. Moores
Department of Geology, University of California, Davis, California 95616, USA

This volume consists of twenty field guides that were created to cover the diverse interests of the 100th Anniversary Conference held in San Francisco, California, to mark the centennial of the 1906 San Francisco earthquake. The guides presented here represent the interests of earth scientists, engineers, and emergency planners, and reflect the cooperation between the Seismological Society of America, the Earthquake Engineering Research Institute, and the California Governor's Office of Emergency Services, the three organizations that jointly organized this unique conference. The field guides are specifically intended to cross the boundaries between these organizations and to be accessible to the general public.

The locations of most of the field trips are shown on Figure 1, which shows the San Francisco Bay area as photographed from the International Space Station. However, the area shown on this figure is not big enough to include all of the trips: Chapters 11, 16, 19, and 20 spill over to the north, south, and east of the region shown in the figure.

The guides are geographically organized into three sections: Part I is made up of field trips within the city of San Francisco and includes trips that highlight the events of 18 April 1906 (Chapters 1, 2, and 3) as well as trips that focus on the retrofit of some of the most beautiful classic buildings in the city (Chapters 4, 5, and 6). The engineering of new buildings, built to withstand strong shaking, is highlighted in Chapter 7, and Chapters 8 and 9 are focused on the seismic safety of two of the most important elements of San Francisco's transportation infrastructure, the San Francisco–Oakland Bay Bridge and the Golden Gate Bridge. Also included in Part 1 is a trip to the San Francisco Emergency Communications Center (Chapter 10).

Part II takes the reader to locations along the San Andreas fault north and south of San Francisco, covering most of the rupture length of the 1906 earthquake. Chapters 11 and 12 cover the region north of the city, describing the fault on the north coast in Sonoma and Mendocino counties (Chapter 11) and in the Olema area in Marin County (Chapter 12). Chapters 13, 15, and 16 explore the San Andreas fault south of San Francisco, and Chapter 14 describes the effects of the earthquake on the campus of Sanford University and recent efforts to strengthen the university's older buildings.

Finally, Part III explores the larger plate boundary, including the Hayward fault (Chapter 17), the new Carquinez Strait Bridge (Chapter 18), and the Rodgers Creek and Maacama fault zones (Chapter 19). The final chapter describes a transect across the entire plate boundary and its tectonic evolution through geologic time.

1906 SAN FRANCISCO EARTHQUAKE

The 1906 San Francisco earthquake was a seminal event not only in the history of San Francisco and the state of California, but also in the history of earthquake science. The earthquake occurred at 5:18 a.m. on April 18 (Lawson, 1908). The magnitude of the earthquake is not known precisely because the number of instruments in place around the world at the time was limited. Recent studies of the archival data give magnitudes of 7.7 (Wald et al., 1993) and 7.9 (Thatcher et al., 1997). At the time of the earthquake, the relationship between faults and earthquakes had been documented, but was not well understood by most scientists. A headline from the Santa Cruz *Morning Sentinel* on 24 April 1906 well illustrates this point: "Professor George Davidson Says 'Earth Cooling,' Father Heredia Ascribes It to Vapor From Heavy Rains and Professor Larkin Says 'Typical Circular Wave Disturbance.'" None of these scientists gives the explanation that is known to almost any educated person today: that the earthquake was caused by abrupt slip on the San Andreas fault.

Prentice, C.S., and Moores, E.M., 2006 Introduction, *in* Prentice, C.S., Scotchmoor, J.G., Moores, E.M., and Kiland, J.P., eds., 1906 San Francisco Earthquake Centennial Field Guides: Field trips associated with the 100th Anniversary Conference, 18–23 April 2006, San Francisco, California: Geological Society of America Field Guide 7, p. vii–xi, doi: 10.1130/2006.1906SF(IN). For permission to copy, contact editing@geosociety.org. ©2006 Geological Society of America. All rights reserved.

Figure 1. Photograph of the San Francisco Bay area taken from the International Space Station (Mission ISS008, Roll E, frame 14841, taken 7 February 2004). Red circles show locations of field trips. Arrows indicate field trips that include stops that are outside of the area of this image.

At the time of the earthquake, a small part of the San Andreas fault had been mapped and named by Andrew Lawson, chair of the University of California, Berkeley, geology department. However, Lawson did not at the time recognize this feature as being anything particularly notable, let alone capable of producing earthquakes (Hill, 1981). However, it was Lawson who, immediately after the earthquake, recognized the need for a scientific investigation, and convinced the governor to appoint the State Earthquake Investigation Commission. The scientists appointed to this commission, as well as many additional observers, contributed to the Report of the Earthquake, edited by Lawson (volume I) and Reid (volume II), published by the Carnegie Institution, in 1908 and 1910, respectively. This report, often referred to as the Lawson Report, was the most comprehensive and thorough scientific investigation of an earthquake ever conducted at the time and remains both a model of earthquake investigations and a valuable source of data (Prentice, 1999).

Many important findings are reported in the Lawson Report. Among these is the fact that the movement on the San Andreas fault was horizontal in nature. Many photographs were taken along the fault after the earthquake, and they document this horizontal displacement in detail (Fig. 2). However, horizontal slip was not well understood at the time, and it was not until 50 years later that geologists began to understand that horizontal slip across the San Andreas fault had been occurring for many millions of years, with each earthquake contributing a small amount to this total displacement, and that cumulative slip across the fault had added up to over 300 km of horizontal offset across the San Andreas fault over geologic time (Prentice, 1999; Hill, 1981). It was not until the 1960s that a mechanism for producing this large-scale horizontal displacement was proposed: the theory of plate tectonics.

GENERAL GEOLOGY AND TECTONICS OF CALIFORNIA

The geology of California is the direct result of the action of plate tectonics. Earth's crust is composed of six major (and many smaller) plates that are in constant motion with respect to each other. There are three kinds of boundaries between these plates: (1) divergent boundaries, where plates move apart, material wells up from Earth's interior, and new crust is created; these boundaries lie mostly along Earth's major mid-oceanic ridges; (2) convergent boundaries, or subduction zones, where plates collide and one descends beneath another; as it does so, material melts and magmas (molten rock) rise and form granitic rocks (such as the Sierra Nevada granites) and volcanic features, such as the Cascade volcanoes; and (3) transform boundaries, where one plate slides past another with no creation or destruction of plate material. Some 85%–90% of the world's earthquakes occur along plate boundaries.

At present, the major geologic provinces of northern California are the active San Andreas fault system in the Coast Ranges, the Great Valley, and the Sierra Nevada mountains. To the west of the San Andreas system are mostly continental rocks that were derived from the south and transported hundreds of kilometers to the NW by movement on the San Andreas and related faults over many millions of years. The 1906 earthquake was caused by one small increment of this motion.

Although California is currently dominated by the San Andreas transform system, it was not always so. Geologic features in California make it clear that before the development of the San Andreas system, a subduction zone existed along the California margin for more than 100 million years. East of the San Andreas fault, much of the Coast Range rocks are the product of this prior tectonic environment, one in which an oceanic plate descended beneath the western California margin.

This older tectonic environment is responsible for producing the granitic rocks of the Sierra Nevada mountains, which have played a crucial role in the history of California in general, and the history of San Francisco in particular. San Francisco owes its rapid growth into a prominent city to the discovery of gold associated with the granitic rocks of the Sierra Nevada in the mid-nineteenth century. As word of this discovery spread, people flooded in from all over the world to exploit the deposits, and most of them passed through the port of San Francisco, contributing to its explosive growth. At the turn of the century, San Francisco was the most important city in western North America, serving as a major cultural and financial center, due to the geologic conditions that produced the gold in the Sierra, as well as to the geologic conditions that produced the protected San Francisco Bay, which provided one of the best harbors in the Pacific. However, these geologic forces also produced the catastrophic earthquake that devastated the city on 18 April 1906.

LIVING WITH EARTHQUAKES

Earthquakes are a fact of life in California in general and the San Francisco Bay area in particular. The lessons of the 1906 and subsequent earthquakes in major population centers worldwide make it clear that there is a price to be paid for living in earthquake country. It is essential to make certain that buildings and infrastructure are designed and built to withstand the inevitable strong shaking that will occur again and again in San Francisco. In addition, emergency management plans must be in place and constantly updated, and the general public must be educated and reminded of the importance of earthquake preparedness. As this collection of field trips strives to make clear, the problem of earthquakes is a matter to be investigated scientifically, incorporated into the design and engineering of buildings and urban infrastructure, and addressed by public policy. The centennial of the 1906 San Francisco earthquake provides an opportunity to highlight a century of progress in all three areas, as well as an opportunity to take stock of what needs to be done in order to better understand and prepare for the next major California earthquake.

Figure 2. Photographs showing the 1906 surface rupture along the San Andreas fault. (A) Offset fence located south of San Francisco (see Chapter 13 this volume). Note three fault traces indicated by red arrows that show fault motion. (B) Road between Upper and Lower Crystal Springs Reservoirs, currently Highway 92. Road and fences are offset right laterally as indicated by red arrows; fault trace is indicated by white dots (see Chapter 13). Photographs courtesy of Bancroft Library, University of California, Berkeley.

REFERENCES CITED

Hill, M.L., 1981, San Andreas fault: History of concepts: Geological Society of America Bulletin, v. 92, p. 112–131, doi: 10.1130/0016-7606(1981)92 <112:SAFHOC>2.0.CO;2.

Lawson, A.C., editor, 1908, The California earthquake of April 18, 1906: Report of the State Earthquake Investigation Commission, vol. I: Carnegie Institution of Washington Publication 87, 451 p. (reprinted in 1969).

Prentice, C.S., 1999, San Andreas Fault: The 1906 earthquake and subsequent evolution of ideas, *in* Moores, E.M., Sloan, D., and Stout, D., eds., Classic Cordilleran concepts: A view from California: Geological Society of America Special Paper 338, p. 70–85.

Reid, H.F., 1910, The mechanics of the earthquake, v. II of Lawson, A.C., chairman, The California earthquake of April 18, 1906: Report of the State Earthquake Investigation Commission: Carnegie Institution of Washington Publication 87, 192 p. (reprinted in 1969).

Thatcher, W., Marshall, G., and Lisowski, M., 1997, Resolution of fault slip along the 470-km-long rupture of the great 1906 San Francisco earthquake: Journal of Geophysical Research, v. 102, no. B3, p. 5353–5367, doi: 10.1029/96JB03486.

Wald, D.J., Kanamori, H., Helmberger, D.V., and Heaton, T.H., 1993, Source study of the 1906 San Francisco earthquake: Bulletin of the Seismological Society of America, v. 83, no. 4, p. 981–1019.

Printed in the USA

A walk along the old bay margin in downtown San Francisco: Retracing the events of the 1906 earthquake and fire

Raymond Sullivan

Department of Geosciences, San Francisco State University, San Francisco, California 94132, USA

OVERVIEW OF FIELD TRIP

The field trip covers three short walks through downtown San Francisco focusing on the events that occurred in the aftermath of the 1906 earthquake. The first walk is in the South of Market area, located on artificially filled ground of the old Mission Bay marshland. The second walk follows the path of the fire as it spread out of the South of Market area on to Market Street. The third walk is along Montgomery Street, located on the old shoreline of Yerba Buena Cove, and follows the progress of the fire as it crossed Market Street northward into the Financial District. The wetlands bordering the bay were prime real estate, and by 1906 about a sixth of the city was built on artificial fill. The highest concentration of damage to buildings by ground shaking and liquefaction caused by the earthquake occurred here. Throughout this area, water, sewer, and gas lines were ruptured, and it was the location of most of the 52 fires that flared up in the city after the earthquake. The main objective of the field trip is to evaluate the lessons we have learned from building on poorly engineered ground within a major metropolitan center in a seismically active area.

Keywords: subsidence, artificial fill, earthquake, Mission Bay marsh.

Early History

The settlement of Yerba Buena was established in the 1830s along the margin of a sheltered cove in San Francisco Bay. The port attracted settlers, and by 1847 the population had gradually increased to almost 500. Early maps drawn of the town showed the streets crisscrossing the marsh and sand dunes on the bay margins (Fig. 1). The discovery of gold in 1848 brought about a large influx of fortune seekers. In the 1850s,

the best real estate in the city was around the wharfs on the bay. Water lots, parcels located along the shore between high and low tide, were in great demand and fetched a high price. In order to reclaim the land, huge quantities of sand were removed from the dunes flanking the shore. The most accessible source of fill was from a belt of sand dunes that started near present-day Second Street and extended westward to the Civic Center. The sand was removed using steam-driven shovels known locally as "steam paddies," and dumped into Yerba Buena Cove and the Mission marshland.

The low-lying marsh in the vicinity of Mission Street between Third and First streets was known as Happy Valley, and to the south was Pleasant Valley (J.R. Smith, 2005). Rincon Hill, composed of Franciscan sandstone and shale bedrock, rose above the dunes (Fig. 2). In the late 1850s, Rincon Hill and South Park were very desirable residential parts of the city (Dobie, 1933; Shumate, 1988). This changed in 1869 when Second Street was extended by excavating a cut through Rincon Hill. The wealthy residents moved and the South of Market area went into decline. It soon became the site of working-class boarding houses, laundries, foundries, and other business premises.

A large part of the structures in the residential areas surrounding the commercial downtown center were constructed of wood. These wooden buildings were very prone to fire, and the city had experienced five major fires by 1851. In these early days, the city did not own or maintain its municipal water supply, but residences and businesses received their water from local wells and springs. A private company, the Spring Valley Water Company, was formed in the 1860s in order to improve and provide an adequate water source. The company constructed three large reservoir facilities in the hills of San Mateo County and set down large pipe conduits to bring this water into distributing reservoirs at Lake Merced and several other elevated places around the city. An intricate network of water

Sullivan, R., 2006, A walk along the old bay margin in downtown San Francisco: Retracing the events of the 1906 earthquake and fire, *in* Prentice, C.S., Scotchmoor, J.G., Moores, E.M., and Kiland, J.P., eds., 1906 San Francisco Earthquake Centennial Field Guides: Field trips associated with the 100th Anniversary Conference, 18–23 April 2006, San Francisco, California: Geological Society of America Field Guide 7, p. 1–23, doi: 10.1130/2006.1906SF(01).

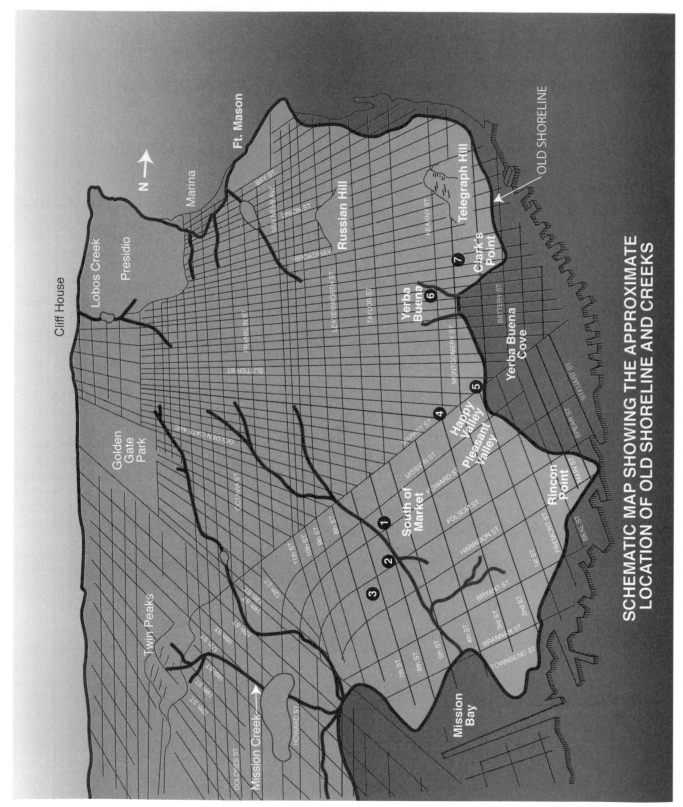

Figure 1. Approximate location of the old shoreline and creeks in San Francisco. Numbers indicate locations of stops.

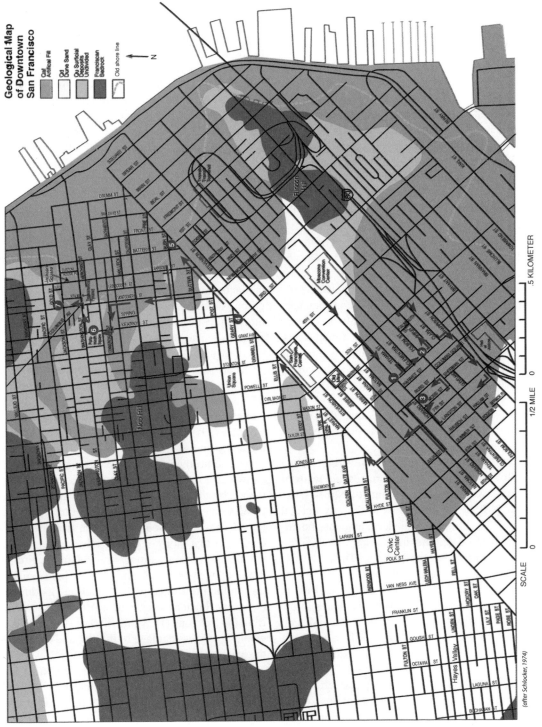

(after Schlocker, 1974)

Figure 2. Geologic map of downtown San Francisco (after Schlocker, 1974). Numbers indicate locations of stops. Arrows show route of walking tour.

pipes from the distributing reservoirs was linked to homes and businesses throughout the city (Schussler, 1906). In October 1905, the National Board of Fire Underwriters condemned San Francisco for its unpreparedness to fight a major conflagration.

The Earthquake Strikes:
Daybreak on Wednesday, 18 April 1906

The 1900 census for San Francisco and the Great Voter Register recorded that over 450,000 persons lived in the city. The South of Market area was second only to Chinatown in population density. The 7.8 moment magnitude earthquake struck at 5:12 a.m. on Wednesday, 18 April 1906, with an epicenter a few miles west of San Francisco, off the entrance to the Golden Gate Bridge. Bronson (1959), Sutherland (1959), Thomas and Witts (1971), Hansen and Condon (1989), Barker (1998), Jeffers (2003), Fradkin (2005), D. Smith (2005), Winchester (2005), and others have dramatically described the destruction of the city by the earthquake and fire.

The tremor was felt strongly throughout the city, but the damage and death toll were greatest on the filled land in the South of Market area. Filled areas on the north side of Market Street were also badly damaged, including the produce district on Washington Street and the fish market located on Merchant Street (Fig. 3). In the worst-hit areas, there was often evidence of liquefaction. Buildings were shifted off their foundations, many tilted at odd angles. Others collapsed, trapping hundreds in the lower floors of the wreckage. Debris on the streets made it difficult for vehicles to move around freely, and roads and sidewalks were buckled and fissured. Water mains and sewer lines were ruptured and spilled their contents over the streets. Electric lines were downed, and broken gas lines also posed a major hazard as fires erupted in numerous locations.

Buildings in other parts of the city were severely shaken but often only lightly damaged, although cornices and walls of some of the structures cracked or collapsed into the street. It has been estimated that 90% of the chimneys in the city needed repair after the tremor. The areas with the least amount of damage were generally located on the hills where Franciscan bedrock is at or close to the surface, and where residences were of wood frame construction. Fewer people were killed or seriously injured in these areas, and most gathered into the street as the aftershocks continued to rattle the buildings. Three aftershocks occurred within the first hour at 5:18, 5:25, and 5:42 a.m. The largest aftershock of the day occurred at 8:14 a.m. Small tremors continued into the evening and kept the residents in a constant state of alert.

The destruction of City Hall by the earthquake left Mayor Schmitz, and other municipal leaders, without a command center. The mayor, early that morning, relocated his administration to the Hall of Justice in Portsmouth Square on the north side of Market Street. One crucial member of his staff, however, was absent. Fire Chief Dennis Sullivan had been fatally injured in his apartment on the third floor of Engine House No. 3, located on Bush Street near Kearney. His leadership was sorely missed as operations designed to control the spread of fire failed, and the city was doomed to destruction (D. Smith, 2005).

Another key person who played a major role in the events associated with the earthquake and fire was General Funston, acting commander of the Army's Pacific Division. His dawn inspection of the downtown area, immediately following the tremor, indicated the likelihood of a major disaster, and the need for the authorities to maintain law and order. He sent word to Fort Mason and the Presidio, ordering troops into the downtown area to assist the police in preventing looting and to evacuate residents from districts threatened by the fire. General Funston set up his headquarters in the Phelan Building, at Market and O'Farrell, not realizing the fire was rapidly spreading and would soon threaten this street (Fig. 3). Troops from Fort Mason arrived on Market Street at around 7 a.m., and an hour later, soldiers from the Presidio were in the downtown area. Other troops were to arrive by ferry at the foot of Market Street later that morning.

All public transport ceased to operate, and downed telephone lines made it difficult for the public and authorities to assess the extent of the destruction. Communication and coordination between the administrative units was also difficult. Telegraph service was, however, maintained during the first morning and was able to alert the rest of the world that a major earthquake had struck San Francisco.

Downtown was doomed by mid-morning, when a new fire threat arose immediately west of the Civic Center (Fig. 3). This blaze has been named the "Ham and Eggs" fire by historians. It originated at 395 Hayes Street, near the intersection with Gough, about three blocks from the Civic Center (Hansen and Condon, 1989). Residents in the building attempted to cook breakfast on a damaged stove. Firemen arrived quickly at the scene and normally would have contained the blaze. However, there was no water supply in the area, and the fire soon spread, fanned by the westerly breezes. It swept eastward through the Civic Center, crossed Market Street around Ninth Street, and joined up with the South of Market area fires. When it became clear later that morning that the fires were gaining in intensity, a valiant attempt was made to contain the fire to the south of Market Street. Mayor Schmitz ordered the dynamiting of buildings in the immediate path of the fire. His other choice was to clear a perimeter to serve as a fire break some distance away from the fire zone (D. Smith, 2005). He hoped that his decision would cause less damage to the city and contain the fires along the existing broad avenues, such as Van Ness Avenue and Market Street. Dynamiting began on Eighth Street and then moved down Market to Third Street to protect the Palace Hotel and the Mint. Unfortunately, these efforts failed because of the lack of water and the poor use of explosives by inexperienced hands. By the afternoon, the fire crossed Market Street into the Financial District. Much of the city was eventually destroyed, as the blaze gradually burned through the downtown over the next three days (Fig. 3).

Figure 3. Map of San Francisco showing the areas destroyed by the 3 days of fire following the 18 April 1906 earthquake. Numbers indicate locations of stops. Arrows show route of walking tour.

WALK ONE: SOUTH OF MARKET AND THE SUBSIDENCE AREA

Significance of the Walk

The South of Market area is located on the old Mission Bay marshland (Fig. 1). Underlying fills have proven to be extremely unstable when severely shaken during a strong tremor and often have resulted in differential settlement and lateral spreading of the ground. Liquefaction potential is also high because the water table is very close to the surface. Sixth Street has been described as "ground zero" for the 1906 earthquake because it was the site of the greatest devastation and the origin of many of the fires in the downtown area (Hansen and Condon, 1989). The greatest loss of life occurred in this sector. This walk will reconstruct the events that took place along Sixth Street in the early morning of 18 April.

The walk will continue into the nearby side streets to observe the results of settlement of post-1906 buildings located on poorly engineered artificially filled ground. There is no doubt that the building subsidence has been a problem from the outset as the city expanded into this area in the 1860s. All the earlier wooden buildings were destroyed in 1906, but they were quickly replaced after the earthquake and fire. Many of the bay window homes from the reconstruction period are preserved today in the side streets in the South of Market area. These older homes are settling on the filled ground, and they are being replaced with newer structures as the area undergoes redevelopment. Damage from the Loma Prieta earthquake in 1989 accelerated the removal of many of these buildings.

Accessibility

The South of Market area is easily accessible by all the public transport systems servicing downtown. The nearest Metro and Bay Area Rapid Transit (BART) station is located at Powell and Market Street. The Golden Gate transit bus stop is located near Fifth and Mission. The AC transit bus terminus is at the Transbay Terminal near First and Mission, some five or so blocks away from the Moscone Center. Public parking is available at the Fifth and Mission garage. Restrooms are few and far between in the South of Market area, and it is a real challenge to find one open to the public. Restrooms are located at the Fifth and Mission garage. Facilities in the Chevron gas station on Sixth and Harrison and the Jiffy Lube at Seventh and Howard streets may be available on request.

STOP 1: SIXTH AND HOWARD STREETS

GPS Coordinates

The southeast corner of Sixth and Howard is 37°46.79′N, 122°24.43′W.

Directions from Moscone Center to Stop 1

The walk starts at the Moscone Center on the southeast corner at the intersection of Fourth and Howard. Walk two blocks southwest on Howard Street, crossing Fourth and Fifth streets to the southeast corner of the intersection with Sixth Street.

Stop Description

Bedrock contour maps show that a Pleistocene valley over 280 feet (90 m) deep underlies the South of Market area (Schlocker, 1974). This valley has been filled with Pleistocene and Holocene deposits composed of fluvial and dune sand and bay mud. Sand dunes covered the areas around the Moscone Center, and the walk southwest along Howard Street eventually takes us into the artificially filled marshland of old Mission Bay (Fig. 2).

The intersection of Sixth and Howard Street has changed little since 1906, although important renovations are planned. In 1906, the South of Market area was home to a large immigrant and transient population. The buildings in the area were predominantly two- to three-story wood frame hotels, rooming houses, factories, and small businesses (Fig. 4). Larger five-story boarding houses occupied corner lots, and many of them had up to 300 rooms for rent to workers and their families. On the main thoroughfares, such as Sixth Street, the lower floors of the buildings were often converted into eating houses, laundries, or grocery stores (Fig. 4).

Three boarding houses occupied the block on the northwest side of Sixth Street between Howard and Natoma (Fig. 5). On the corner was the five-story Brunswick House, and toward Market Street were the Ohio and the Lormor. Across on the southwest corner of Natoma Street was the Nevada House (Hansen and Condon, 1989; D. Smith, 2005). Most residents were asleep in the boarding houses and cheap hotels that lined these streets. Lights were on in some rooms as early risers were preparing to set out for work. Many of the eating-houses and bakeries had their stoves turned on as they prepared for the busy day ahead.

Suddenly, at 5:12 a.m. the ground started shaking violently, and buildings began to topple and collapse. The streets were buckled and filled with debris. Lights were extinguished, and in the darkness, people were calling for help. Many were trapped in the buildings. Brunswick House had collapsed into the street as the neighboring boarding houses toppled sideways into it. The total death toll in this intersection alone has been estimated to be between 150 and 300 persons. At least 23 of the 46 residents in the Nevada House died. Further up Sixth Street, between Mission and Market, the Portland House had collapsed, trapping many residents. Little was left of the lodging houses but piles of debris. People worked desperately trying to rescue those inside until fire and smoke drove them from the street. The exact death toll will never be known since little time was available to count the dead before the area had to be evacuated as fires quickly spread through the South of Market area.

Figure 4. South of Market in 1880s from Second and Howard streets. The district was composed predominately of boarding houses. The Palace Hotel is the large building in the upper right. Left in the distance is the spire of St. Patrick's Church (courtesy of San Francisco Public Library).

Figure 5. Stop 1 of the walk: looking south at the intersection of Sixth and Howard today. The one-way street at lower right is Natoma Street. The burnt and vacant apartment building in the lower left of the photograph, with the decoration of household appliances and furniture, is often referred to by the locals as the "Earthquake House." In 1906, three boarding houses stood in the block between Natoma and Howard streets. They all collapsed with a high loss of life.

STOP 2: INTERSECTION AT SIXTH AND FOLSOM STREETS

GPS Coordinates

The northeast corner of Sixth and Folsom is 37°6.72′N, 122°24.34′W.

Directions to Stop 2

From Stop 1, walk half a block southeast on Sixth Street to the intersection with Tehama Street. A short detour is recommended en route to Stop 2 to see the changes to buildings on Tehama Street as result of damage from the 1989 earthquake. The Anglo Hotel was located on the southeast corner of this intersection, and it was red-tagged after the tremor along with other adjacent buildings. The buildings on the south side of Tehama have now been replaced with modern ones. The only structure remaining in this section is located at 481 Tehama and it is easily recognizable, since it is out of line with the other building (Fig. 6). From Tehama, continue along Sixth Street to the intersection with Folsom.

Stop Description

This intersection with Folsom was a depression within the Mission Bay marsh known locally as Pioche's Lake. It was later artificially filled for housing.

The scenes that took place at the previous stop were repeated all over the South of Market area. After the earthquake, lightly clad residents poured out into the debris-covered streets and attempted to locate family and neighbors in the darkness. Smoke filled the air as small fires began to erupt. Fire had broken out down the street at Nicholas Prost's bakery on Sixth Street between Folsom and Harrison. Smoke from another large fire could be seen burning in the direction of Seventh Street. Girard House on the northwest corner of Seventh and Howard had collapsed, and a fire had started from the stove of the downstairs restaurant.

Engine No. 6 was housed close by on Sixth Street between Folsom and Shipley. The firehouse was badly damaged, and the horses used to haul their equipment were lost when they bolted out into the street. Unfortunately, the nearby fire hydrants at Sixth and Shipley and Sixth and Folsom were all ruptured, as were the sewer lines on Fourth and Sixth streets. Fire Captain Charles Cullen, in his official report, described the dilemma

Figure 6. View of the south side of Tehama Street looking toward Sixth Street near Stop 1. Buildings at this intersection were badly damaged in the Loma Prieta earthquake. The Anglo Hotel, which was located at the corner of the intersection, and the adjacent buildings have been rebuilt. One older building, at 481 Tehama Street, remains, and it is clearly out of alignment with the new structures.

when he was forced to divide his team into two groups, one to attempt to fight the fires and the other to do search and rescue. Their first rescue was in wrecked homes on either side of the firehouse, where they were able to cut their way in to free those trapped inside. They next moved to the Corona House on the northwest corner of Sixth and Folsom and rescued a man and woman in the wreckage. The fire captain estimated that some 40 residents had died that morning in the Corona House.

With fire raging all around them, the crew of Engine No. 6 covered their heads with wet sacking and hauled the equipment along Folsom Street. They stopped to check hydrants for water until they finally arrived at Fifth Street. Here they were able to locate a small supply of water in a sewer, and, for a short time, they fought the blaze. They soon had to abandon their hoses as the fire crossed Fifth and Folsom, but they hauled their engine to safety ahead of the blazing inferno. As in the case of all of the fire crews, they remained on duty for the next 55 hours.

A similar account was given by the crew of Engine No.19, which was stationed on Market near Tenth Street. Their firehouse was also badly damaged, and the horses bolted into the street. They were fortunate to recapture their horses, and they drove to Harrison and Sixth Streets, trying all the hydrants along the way. They located a small supply of water from a hydrant on Sixth Street between Folsom and Howard that had been overlooked by the crew of Engine No. 6. They fought the fires until the supply dried up. With fires raging all around, they were called away to fight yet another hot spot at Hayes and Gough streets, where the "Ham and Eggs" fire had started to burn later in the morning (Fig. 3).

STOP 3: SUBSIDENCE AREA

GPS Coordinates

The Shipley and Sixth intersection is 37°46.79′N and 122°24.30′W; the intersection of Langton and Harrison is 37°46.51′N and 122°24.42′W; and the intersection of Moss and Howard is 37°46.68′N and 122°24.53′W.

Directions

This location is not a single stop but is a walk looping around the many side streets in the subsidence area. The route is shown on Figures 2 and 3.

From Stop 2 at the intersection of Sixth and Folsom, walk half a block southeast on Sixth Street to the narrow side alley of Shipley Street, turn left (northeast), and continue to the intersection with Fifth Street.

Stop Description

The subsidence area is bounded by Fifth Street on the east and Eighth Street on the west, Mission Street to the north and Bluxome Street to the south. The walk includes many small side streets such as Jessie, Minna, Natoma, Tehama, Clemen-

tina, Shipley, Russ, Harriett, Ringold, Moss, Dore, and Langton. Another area of subsidence is found in Hayes Valley, located north of Market and west of the Civic Center (Fig. 2). Both of these areas of subsidence are situated on the artificial filled ground of the old Mission Bay marsh. The South of Market area is the focus of this walk.

Wahrhaftig (1966, 1984), Sullivan and Galehouse (1990, 1991), Steinbrugge (1969), and Youd and House (1978) have previously published some of details of the buildings in this area. All of the older buildings in the subsidence area date back to the reconstruction period following the 1906 earthquake. The district has retained most of its character over the years, with numerous two- to three-story rooming houses, apartments, small stores, and businesses. Obvious signs of subsidence along the side streets are the abandoned garages and doorways three feet or more below the present street level (Fig. 7). Because of the continuing subsidence, main roads and utilities have had to be raised periodically in order to maintain them at "official" grade level. Side alleys were raised at less frequent intervals, and often are not level with the main streets, but meet with a slope at the intersection. Some of the buildings have been deformed by differential settling and are no longer upright but lean toward a neighboring structure. Inside these buildings, doors and windows are warped, walls are cracked, and floors are not level. A recent boom in the real-estate market in San Francisco has led to repair and renovation of many of these older buildings. As a result, some of the better examples have been replaced or renovated, so that they no longer preserve the evidence of subsidence.

In both the 1906 and 1989 earthquakes, structures were damaged throughout this area as a result of differential settlement and rupturing of the ground. An insight into the kind of damage that occurred in 1906 in an adjacent section along Dore and Ninth between Bryant and Brannan streets, was described in Lawson (1908) and Youd and Hoose (1978).

Shipley Street

The subsidence walk starts at the intersection of Sixth and Shipley. Walk northeast on Shipley for one block to the intersection with Fifth Street.

The newly built loft that backs onto 254 Shipley illustrates the changes occurring in the area; this structure is very modern, with a glass exterior façade. The best examples of the effects of subsidence on older buildings can be seen at 277, 274, 258, 241–243, and 229–231 Shipley. There are many vacant lots along Shipley Street, since many older structures were removed over the years.

Clara Street

At the intersection with Fifth Street, turn right (southeast) to Clara. Continue to walk southwest down Clara back to Sixth Street.

Clara Street has changed markedly in recent years because many structures were seriously damaged in the 1989 earthquake and have been replaced with modern buildings. Other structures

R. Sullivan

Figure 7. Subsidence area: the house that was located at 278–280 Clara Street, showing the garage and entrance door below street level. The photograph was taken in February 1969. The building was renovated after the 1989 earthquake.

have undergone major renovations, and several lots that were previously vacant now contain high-priced lofts. Buildings with former garages and entrances below street level can be seen at 241 and 261 Clara. 274–276 Clara shows a typical style of building renovation of this area where the original location of the garage door is replaced with sub-basement windows. The most-photographed house in the subsidence area was located at 278–280 Clara Street (Fig. 7). It was one of homes along this street that was red tagged in 1989 and rebuilt following the tremor. The modern loft at 281 Clara was recently constructed on the site of a fenced-in vacant lot that had eventually returned to its original marsh-like setting (Fig. 8).

Langton Street

At Clara and Sixth, turn left (southeast) onto Harrison. Turn right (southwest) at intersection to walk on the north side of Harrison, passing Harriett, Columbia Square (location of a refugee camp in 1906), and Sherman streets to Seventh Street. Continue on Seventh to Langton. Turn right (northwest) and walk the two blocks of Langton.

A good example of a building in the subsidence area can be found on this mural-lined street at 182 Langton, where the former doorway of the sunken garage has been bricked up. The row of houses numbered 144–142, 140–138, 136–134, and 132–130 Langton all have stepped down entrances (Fig. 9). Subsidence features are also present at 122–120 and 73 Lang-

ton. Stop at the People's Garden on the southwest corner with Howard Street. Originally, this was an empty lot and a drug hangout. The local residents petitioned to have the site converted to a community garden.

Across the street at the intersection of Langton and Howard are examples of tilted buildings at 1122 and 1118 Howard.

Moss Street

Turn right (northeast) on Howard, crossing Seventh Street, and turn right (southeast) down Moss Street for one block to the intersection with Folsom.

Moss Street occupies a depression between Harrison and Folsom. The main roads have been paved to maintain grade so that there is a distinct elevation drop entering both ends of Moss Street. Examples of sunken buildings are best seen at 10, 14, 25, and 64–62 Moss. The apartment building at 68–72 Moss was damaged in the 1989 earthquake, and an outline of some cracks can be seen over both garages. Several lots are vacant along this street. To illustrate the real-estate boom taking place in the city, in the summer of 2005, a two-unit building at 10 Moss, built in 1907, was listed for sale at $899,000.

Russ Street

Exit Moss and turn left (northeast) on Folsom to Russ Street. Walk northwest on the one and a half blocks of Russ, crossing Howard, to Natoma.

Figure 8. Subsidence area: the vacant lot at 281 Clara Street, which had been fenced off for many years, allowing the site to return to its original marsh setting. The photograph was taken in 1976. A new building has been recently erected on this site.

Settlement affecting homes can be best seen at 155–157 and 134–132 Russ.

Natoma Street

Turn left (southwest) on Natoma Street. Natoma has the finest collection of post-1906 bay window homes, which were so widespread in the subsidence area before redevelopment (Fig. 10). Most of them show clear evidence of settlement. The best examples are in the 500 block of this street, at 554–552, 556–558, and 565–567 Natoma Street. Crossing Seventh Street, the 600 block has numerous homes with entryways and garages below street level; they include 617–619, 618, 620–622, 621, 623, 624, 632–634, 636–638, 642, 645–647, 649, and 657–659 Natoma Street. At 623 Natoma, the lower-floor entry is barely visible at street level (Fig. 11). Retrace your steps to Seventh Street. The intersection of Seventh and Natoma streets shows a marked change of grade from side alley to the main thoroughfare. The side alley has not been maintained at the "official" street level (Fig. 12).

WALK TWO: MARKET STREET FROM SEVENTH TO FIRST STREETS

Significance of the Walk

A walk along Market Street will provide a glimpse of the architecture of old, pre-1906 commercial stone buildings of the city, since the façades of most of these structures were pre-served during later reconstruction. The walk focuses on the spread of the fire into this commercial district. A stop will be made at Lotta's Fountain, where each year San Franciscans gather to honor the survivors of the earthquake and fire, and at the 1848 shoreline marker at the Mechanics Monument. Additional information about some of the buildings discussed in this section can be found in chapter 3 of this volume.

Accessibility

Parking is not allowed at any time on Market Street. The F streetcar and municipal buses run the length of Market Street. Metro and BART are located at the Civic Center, Powell Street, and Montgomery Street stations. The cable turnaround is located at Powell and California streets. A convenient Golden Gate transit bus stop is located near Fifth and Mission. The AC transit bus terminus is at the Transbay Terminal near First and Mission. The Caltrain terminal is located at Fourth and Townsend streets. Parking is available at the Fifth and Mission streets garage, and at the Sutter-Stockton garage, one block northeast of Union Square. Public garages in the downtown district have wheelchair accessible areas. Free on-street parking is available on weekends along many streets in the South of Market area. Public restrooms are available in the garages on Fifth and Mission. There are coin-operated public toilets on Market Street. Restroom facilities are also available in Embarcadero Centers 1, 2, and 3.

Figure 9. Subsidence area: many of the apartments along Langton Street have entryways below street level. This example is located at 134–136 Langton Street.

Figure 10. Subsidence area: view of older bay window homes along the 600 block of Natoma Street. Most of the residential parts of the South of Market area were composed of these attractive homes before and after the 1906 earthquake.

Figure 11. Subsidence area: this home at 623 Natoma Street is a particularly good example of the amount of subsidence that can occur in this area. Most of the first floor of this building is below street level, and the bay windows are inches from ground. The former entry door is barely visible below the street on the left-hand side of the building.

Figure 12. Subsidence area: view from Natoma Street looking northeast to Seventh Street. The automobile on the right, parked at the intersection, demonstrates the difference in grade level between the side street of Natoma and the main thoroughfare of Seventh. The new apartment building across the intersection was built after 1989 to replace structures damaged in the Loma Prieta earthquake.

Directions

On Seventh Street, turn left (northwest), crossing Mission to Market. Cross over Market to the northwest side and turn right (northeast) toward the Ferry building.

Walk Description

This walk is among historical buildings along Market Street.

Before commercial development, dunes were as high as 80 ft (26 m) in the vicinity of Market Street. Sand carried by the westerly winds from the coastal dune belt continuously blew through the area and made life unpleasant at times. Market Street started as a residential street with modest homes and wooden boardwalks. As the city grew, the character of Market Street changed from residential to commercial. Stores, banks, hotels, and business offices began to be located here in the 1860s. The 1868 earthquake had, to some degree, alerted city developers that high-rise buildings had to be solidly built using the iron or new steel-framing design. The street was finally paved with cobblestones in 1880, and the next year cable cars began to replace the old horse-drawn trolleys. The Civic Center was located at the upper end of Market in 1870, on the site of Yerba Buena Cemetery, one of 14 cemeteries located in the city. Because of the development of the Civic Center, thousands of graves had to be relocated. Old City Hall was situated at Larkin and McAllister, the site today of the Asian Art Museum (which was also formerly the old main library). It had just been completed before the earthquake at a cost of $6 million (Bronson, 1959).

The threat of fire was always foremost on the minds of city authorities. These concerns were well founded since the Baldwin Hotel, in downtown San Francisco, went up in flames in 1898. As a result, many buildings, such as the Palace Hotel and the Mint, had their own water wells and cistern system to alleviate the fire danger. In 1906, there were 52 major brick and stone buildings present in downtown San Francisco. The tallest was the 18-story Call Building. San Francisco was in the middle of a building boom, and seven new buildings were under construction when the tremor struck. It had become the major port and commercial center on the West Coast.

Corbett (1979), Waldhorn and Woodbridge (1978), Woodbridge and Woodbridge (1982), and Richards (2002) detailed the architectural history and structural design of the older buildings in the downtown area. They were not built to resist earthquakes, but had great strength and rigidity since they were designed to resist strong winds. Their massive exterior walls were generally made up of unreinforced masonry. Only six of the 52 major buildings in the downtown were so completely destroyed that it was not possible to rebuild them.

Continue on from the subsidence walk, at the northeast corner of Seventh and Mission streets is the Post Office (1905), now the Sixth Circuit Court of Appeals building. Cross over to the north side of Market; at One Jones is the Rocklin granite-faced Hibernia Bank building (1892), which is undergoing renovation (2005). Three blocks down Market, at the busy Powell Street intersection, is the James Flood building (1904) at 870 Market (Fig. 13). This was the site of the Baldwin Hotel from 1877 to 1898. Across the street is the Old Emporium (1896) at 835–865 Market. This was the original site of St. Ignatius College (University of San Francisco) between 1855 and 1880. The Old Mint is just off Market Street at 88 Fifth Street, across from the intersection with Jessie. This building, constructed in 1874, is the oldest surviving building in downtown San Francisco and the oldest government building on the West Coast. It survived with little damage thanks to the dedication of its employees, who remained on duty while fires raged around them. The financial resources housed in the Old Mint greatly helped in the reconstruction of the city following the earthquake. Between Fourth and Third streets at 785 Market is the Humboldt Bank building, which was under construction in 1906. Across the street on the north side, at 760 Market, is the Phelan building, where General Funston first established his headquarters. The present structure was built in 1908 to replace a five-story Victorian building.

STOP 4: LOTTA'S FOUNTAIN

GPS Coordinates

37°47.25′N, 122°24.19′W.

Directions

Lotta's Fountain is located at the intersection of Market, Montgomery, and Post streets.

Stop Description

Lotta's Fountain was built in 1875 on the edge of the sand dunes that covered Market Street (Fig. 3). This drinking fountain (now dry) was located in the hub of the downtown district at the busiest intersection in the city. Third Street was the through street out of town to the peninsula, and many major buildings of the city were located close by. This intersection was known as "Newspaper Angle," since the offices of the major newspapers of the city were located here. On either side of Lotta's Fountain are the old Citizens Savings building (1902) at 700 Market and the Old Chronicle building (1889) at 690 Market. Across the street at 703 Market is the site of the old Call building (1898). The Hearst building at 5 Third Street and the nearby Monadnock building at 685 Market did not survive the earthquake and fire but were rebuilt after 1906 (Fig. 3).

New Montgomery Street was originally planned as a major boulevard connecting Market Street with the south bay. As a result, two major hotels were built at the intersection. On the west corner, at 55 New Montgomery, was the deluxe Palace Hotel; when built in 1875, it was considered to be the finest hotel on the West Coast. Across the street, on the east side of

Figure 13. The Flood building at 870 Market Street was one of the old buildings along Market Street that survived the earthquake and fire. It had just been completed at the time of the earthquake.

New Montgomery at the time of the earthquake, was the very ornate, 400-room Grand Hotel, completed in 1870. The extension of New Montgomery never took place, and it has remained only two blocks long The Palace Hotel was rebuilt in 1909, but the Grand Hotel was never reconstructed.

Lotta's Fountain was always a popular meeting place in the city, and shortly after the earthquake, people gathered there seeking news of family and friends. There was little reason for them to be concerned since the area was not in any immediate danger, although smoke and fire was evident from the South of Market area. The largest fire in the area was the one near St. Patrick's Church on Jessie Street, where the San Francisco Gas and Electric Company had its station (Fig. 3). As the morning progressed, however, fire began to move through the buildings on the south side of Market Street. The Call, Monadnock, and Examiner buildings were doomed by noon (Fig. 14). Also in ruin was the nearby Grand Opera House on Mission Street where Caruso had performed the night before. The Palace Hotel became the scene of a great struggle to prevent the fire from taking hold on the north side of Market Street. When constructing the hotel, a large cistern was installed in the basement to provide a water supply in case of fire. As a result, great efforts

were made throughout the morning to save the Palace Hotel in order to have access to its water supply. The firefighters, however, diverted increasing amounts of water to other nearby buildings, and the hotel started to burn.

Lotta's Fountain is a now a National Historic Landmark. It was a gift to the city by Lotta Crabtree, a very popular actress and singer, who was born and raised in San Francisco. It is here, at 5:12 a.m. each year, on the anniversary of the 1906 earthquake, that citizens gather with the survivors to remember the events of 1906. In 2005, only six earthquake survivors attended the ceremony. The largest gathering at this site took place on Christmas Eve in 1910, when the renowned opera singer Luisa Tetrazzini gave a concert to thousands of residents who had assembled to mark the rebirth of San Francisco.

STOP 5: OLD SHORELINE MARKER AT THE MECHANICS MONUMENT (DONAHUE STATUE)

GPS Coordinates

The Mechanics Monument is located at 37°47.47′N and 122°23.96′W.

Figure 14. Market Street (stop 4). View of the Call building on the morning of the fire, 18 April 1906 (courtesy of Fireman's Fund).

Directions

From Lotta's Fountain, continue two blocks northeast on Market Street to the Mechanics Monument at the intersection of Bush and Battery streets.

Stop Description

A metal plaque denoting the location of the old shoreline of Yerba Buena Cove in 1848 is embedded in the sidewalk on the west side of the Mechanics Monument. The bronze statue was placed here in 1894 to honor Peter Donahue, an early industrialist of the city. Willis Polk designed the granite base, and James Tilden was the sculptor.

The six blocks of buildings from here to the Ferry building were built on filled land (Fig. 3). As a result, in 1855 the tidal mud flats began to be filled and protected from erosion by construction of a sea wall that extended over 3 miles (5 km) from Fort Mason along the present-day Embarcadero. In the South of Market area, construction in 1867 of a railroad causeway, the Long Bridge, helped to silt up Mission Bay.

The events of the 1906 earthquake are significant at this site because it provides an insight into the performance of high-rise structures on artificial fill during a major earthquake. Many fires originated in the warehouses and other structures along Third, Minna, Howard, Fremont, and Steuart streets in this bay-front district. One of the first reported fires was in a laundry on Howard and Hawthorne streets, just one block northeast of the current

Moscone Convention Center. Engine No. 4 was located across the street from this fire, but there was no water in any of the hydrants. Fireboats were able to protect the waterfront at the foot of Market. These South of Market fires soon merged together as a major blaze and eventually joined up with the fires from Sixth and Howard streets. Large numbers of refugees had assembled at the Ferry building but were forced to flee as the fires surrounded the ferry terminus. For a time, it was no longer possible to evacuate refugees by boat. Later that morning, the fires crossed Market Street and moved along Montgomery Street (Fig. 15).

WALK THREE: MONTGOMERY STREET TO JACKSON SQUARE

Significance of the Walk

The route along Montgomery Street follows the old shoreline of Yerba Buena Cove (Figs. 1 and 2). This street was the main thoroughfare in the Financial District in 1906. The walk follows the progress of the fire as it swept along Montgomery Street into the Financial District and Chinatown during the afternoon of 18 April. Portsmouth Square, located on the shore of Yerba Buena Cove, was the site of the original settlement established in the 1830s. Jackson Square is one of the few parts of the downtown area to survive the earthquake and fire.

Accessibility

The public transportation information listed in the Market Street walk is also applicable for this segment of the field trip. In addition, the California Street cable car line intersects Montgomery Street. Limited parking is available at St. Mary's Square garage on California Street between Kearny and Grant. Also within walking distance is Portsmouth Square garage, with an entrance on Kearney between Clay and Washington, and the Sutter-Stockton Street garage, one block northeast of Union Square. Free on-street parking is available on Sundays in the Financial District. Restroom facilities are, once more, hard to find but are available at St. Mary's Square and Portsmouth Square garages.

Directions

The walk continues from the Mechanics Monument up Bush Street for two blocks to Montgomery Street. Cross to the north side of Montgomery, and turn right (north) to its intersection with Commercial Street. Turn left (west) on Commercial to Kearney Street. Turn right (north) on Kearney to Clay Street and Portsmouth Square.

Walk Description

Gentry (1962), Delehanty (1995), Richards (2001, 2002), and others have described in some detail the historic waterfront setting of Montgomery Street. The old shoreline location can still be discerned by the abrupt increase in grade on the east-west streets as they cross Montgomery. The change in gradient represents the transition from marsh to dunes that blanketed the Franciscan bedrock hills to the west (Fig. 2).

In the1850s, this street was lined with wood shacks, warehouses, retail stores, eating places, and rooming houses (Fig. 16). Wooden wharfs stretched across the mud flats into the bay (Fardon, 1999). The area west of Montgomery is a graveyard of old abandoned ships from this period, and as many as 47 have been discovered during excavations (J.R. Smith, 2005). Montgomery Street emerged from the mud flats to become the Wall Street of the West. By the 1870s, it was part of the prosperous Financial District and contained some of the notable buildings of the city.

Intersection of Montgomery and Bush

The first couple of blocks south along Montgomery Street, between Market and Bush streets, were the locations of some small three-and four-story hotels built in the early 1860s (J.R. Smith, 2005). By the turn of the last century, they had passed their prime with the construction of larger and more deluxe hotels on Market Street and Union Square. On the west side of Montgomery Street was the Lick Hotel, opened in 1862; it occupied most of the two blocks between Bush and Post streets. This hotel suffered some minor damage in the 1865 earthquake. Across on the east side of Montgomery, between Bush and Sutter streets, was the four-story Occidental Hotel, completed in 1869. Another nearby hotel was the Russ House, which filled the entire block between Bush to Pine on the west side of Montgomery Street. The Russ House, like all the other wooden structures in the area, burned to the ground in 1906 and was replaced later by today's 31-story Russ building. On the northeast corner of Montgomery and Bush was Platte's Hall, which for 30 years had been the venue for concerts, lectures, political rallies, and sporting events. It was replaced in 1891 by the present-day Mills building at 220 Montgomery Street. The Mills building was gutted by the fire in 1906, reconstructed in 1908, and later enlarged in the 1930s to include 21-story Mills Tower.

Intersection of Montgomery and Pine

At the beginning of last century, the buildings north of the Montgomery and Bush intersection became grander and larger as the hotels and retail stores gave way to banks, steamship companies, and other business establishments. The Nevada Bank (1875–1906) stood at the northwest corner of Montgomery and Pine. Although the structure was destroyed, the vault survived in the ruins and about $3 million dollars in gold was recovered. This section of Montgomery is still crowded with banks and financial institutions.

Intersection of Montgomery and California

The Kohl building (1901), located at 400 Montgomery Street, on the northeast corner of the intersection with California Street, is one of only a few pre-1906 buildings on this street

R. Sullivan

Figure 15. Market Street: view from the Ferry building southwest up Market Street, showing the extent of the damage from the earthquake and fire (courtesy of Fireman's Fund).

to survive to the present day. Next door, at 420 Montgomery Street, is the Wells Fargo History Museum, which is open free of charge to the public. Down the street, at 465 California, at the corner with Leidesdorff Street, is the Merchant Exchange building. Built in 1903 and designed by Willis Polk, it was reconstructed after the earthquake. It was an important commercial center, and news of arriving ships was transmitted from the lookout tower on the roof to the merchants in the hall below.

Wahrhaftig (1966) described the stone used in this building and in many other buildings in the Financial District.

Two blocks up the hill from Montgomery Street, at the intersection of California Street and Grant Avenue, is Old St. Mary's Church. This brick gothic building was constructed in 1854. As in the case of many of these early brick buildings, the brick and ironwork was brought around the Horn from the East Coast. The granite blocks are from China. It was the first

Figure 16. Montgomery Street, showing the original Russ building at Montgomery and Pine streets in 1860. As the city prospered, Montgomery Street emerged as the Wall Street of the West, and the older buildings were replaced by finer ones. In this case, the Russ Hotel was constructed on this site, and it filled the entire block. The present-day 31-story Russ building was constructed after the 1906 earthquake (courtesy of Fireman's Fund).

Catholic cathedral in the western United States and at the time was located close to the administrative center of the city. As the city grew away from this area, it became incorporated into Chinatown and became surrounded by brothels and opium dens. As a warning to the local residents, the clergy posted a sign below the church clock that read, "Son, observe the time and fly from evil." The building was gutted in the fire but was later reconstructed. Today, the church still bears the same message.

Intersection of Montgomery and Sacramento Streets

A great deal of early San Francisco history is recorded at this intersection. At the southwest corner in the 1840s was a small creek that was utilized by the local Native Americans as a site for a sweathouse. On the northwest corner was the ware-house of Jacob Leese, an early resident of Yerba Buena. He used the warehouse from 1838 to 1841 to store cattle hides and other goods. Later, it became the trading post for the Hudson Bay Company from 1841 to 1846.

Intersection of Montgomery and Commercial Streets

Commercial Street, at first glance, looks like one of the many narrow side streets in the city, but from this intersection it is possible to see that the street has a unique location. Looking eastward to the bay, Commercial Street lines up with the Ferry building at the foot of Market. This street was built to lead into the Long or Central Wharf, the largest wharf in the city. The old U.S. Treasury building (Pacific Heritage Museum) erected in 1875 is located at 608 Commercial Street.

STOP 6: PORTSMOUTH SQUARE

GPS Coordinates

Portsmouth Square is located at 37°47.68′N and 122°24.31′W.

Directions

Portsmouth Square is on Kearny between Clay and Washington streets.

Stop Description

Portsmouth Square was the location of the first settlement of Yerba Buena. A partially hidden plaque at 825 Grant Street marks the site of the first residence in the settlement, belonging to William A. Richardson. The town was planned around a Spanish colonial plaza that was initially named Calle de la Fundacion. In 1846, Captain Montgomery anchored the naval sloop *USS Portsmouth* in the bay. He raised the American flag in the plaza, and this event gave the square its present name. In 1847, the year before the discovery of gold, a visit to the town center would have revealed 20–30 buildings of various kinds scattered around the plaza. The first public school in California was opened there on 3 April 1848. As the city grew, Portsmouth Square remained the administrative center until the late 1870s, when the business district gradually moved south to the new Financial District and west to Market Street.

Residents in Chinatown were abruptly awakened in the early morning of 18 April. Most of the buildings along Grant Avenue survived the tremor with moderate damage, since it is located close to Franciscan bedrock that outcrops on Nob Hill (Fig. 2). As news reached the residents in the late morning of the fire crossing Market Street, they began to pack as much of their belongings as they could carry or drag. Most were reluctant to leave, but by early afternoon it was clear that Chinatown could not be saved. They slowly left the area, with most of them heading to the Presidio.

Destruction of City Hall by the earthquake forced the administrative center to relocate, and Mayor Schmitz chose the Hall of Justice in Portsmouth Square as his command center. A gathering of prominent citizens was called to this site at 3:00 that afternoon (D. Smith, 2005). At the meeting, a committee of 50 citizens was established to help in the disaster. Even as the group met, Portsmouth Square was being threatened by fire. The meeting ended when the area was engulfed in smoke. Those gathered in the area could clearly hear the sound of dynamite explosions from nearby Leidesdorff Street, as an attempt was made to save Portsmouth Square. Dynamite supplies were by now exhausted, and the military began to resort to black powder. The use of explosives by inexperienced personnel caused sparks from the black powder explosions to spread the fire into Chinatown. Mayor Schmitz relocated his command post to Nob Hill as Portsmouth Square and Chinatown began to burn in the late afternoon and on into night.

STOP 7: JACKSON SQUARE

GPS Coordinates

The entrance to Jackson Square is at 37°47.85′N and 122°24.19′W.

Directions

Walk down Clay Street on the south side of Portsmouth Square, crossing Kearney to Montgomery Street. Walk north on Montgomery to the intersection with Washington and Columbus. This intersection marks the beginning of the Jackson Square Historic District established in 1971. This district covers a four-block area dissected by Montgomery Street. Pacific Street on the northern perimeter was the district known as the Barbary Coast.

Stop Description

The old shoreline continued along Montgomery Street to Jackson Street. This intersection was the site of a creek entering Yerba Buena Cove, and a wooden bridge was constructed in 1844 linking Clark's Point with the town. The Montgomery Street grade increases abruptly, between Jackson and Pacific streets, to mark the beginning of Clark's Point at the northern end of Yerba Buena Cove. Clark's Point was the site of the Broadway or Pacific wharf, the first one constructed out into the bay. Pacific Street is also the beginning of the infamous Barbary Coast District.

The Jackson Square Historic District starts at the intersection of Montgomery, Columbus, and Washington streets. Columbus Avenue is another street that cuts diagonally across the grid pattern. It was designed to provide easy access from the northern docks to the city's business district. Street maps in 1906 show Columbus Avenue as Montgomery Avenue. Its name was changed in 1909, along with many other streets, after the city completed its redevelopment following the earthquake. Jackson Square contains the oldest commercial buildings in the city. These structures survived, by good fortune, the three days that fires raged through the city. Jackson Square was threatened by fires that at first advanced from Market Street and then later from North Beach.

700 Block of Montgomery Street

This block contains several pre-1906 buildings. Most are located on the foundations of older buildings that were destroyed in the fire of 1851, which gutted this area. At the northeast corner of the intersection, at 700 Montgomery, is the Columbus Savings Bank, built in 1905. The old Langerman's/Belli building, at 722–724 Montgomery Street, was built in 1853 and is presently undergoing a major renovation. The Genella building at 728 Montgomery was erected in the early 1850s on the site of an 1849 building. The Golden Era building at 730–732 Montgomery dates back to 1852.

400 Block of Jackson Street

This block of Jackson Street is lined with two- and three-story warehouses, stores, and banks of the Gold Rush era. These old commercial buildings are characterized by thick, unreinforced brick walls, large heavy doors, and vaulted windows with sturdy iron shutters. Their design was an important reason that they survived the fire. Delehanty (1995) and Richards (2002) described in detail a historic walk along Jackson Street. On the north side of the street, between Montgomery and Balance streets, are clusters of buildings from the 1850s. They have a much plainer design than the more elaborate Italianate buildings of the 1860s period that dominate the south side of Jackson Street. The important buildings on this side of Jackson Street include the Lucas Turner and Co. Bank at the northeast corner of Montgomery and Jackson streets. The historical plaque indicates that it was built in 1853–1854 and is best known as the place where General William Tecumseh Sherman was bank manager. Next door is the three-story Solari building at 472–468 Jackson Street. These plain red brick structures are typical of the 1850s office buildings and stores that used to be found all over the downtown area. It was not unusual for the owner and family to live on the upper floor of the stores. Gold Street and Balance Street are service alleys located

on the north side. Balance Street, the shortest street in the city, was probably named after a ship that was buried near this site.

Across on the south side of the street is the two-story Ghirardelli Chocolate building at 415–431 Jackson. The company operated from this site between 1853 and 1894. The so-called Medico-Dental building, constructed in 1861, is next door at 435–441 Jackson. The three-story Hotaling Whiskey Warehouse, built in 1866, is on the corner at 451–455 Jackson and is recognized by its cast iron façade and tall upper windows. Around the corner, at 38–40 Hotaling Place, were the horse stables for the whiskey company. A meandering set of bricks, inset into the roadway on this service alley, depicts the location of the old shoreline (Fig. 17).

It is believed that the location of this whiskey warehouse may have played an important role in the preservation of the pre-1906 buildings along this street and the nearby Appraisers' building or Custom's House at 630 Sansome. On the first day, when fires raged through the area from Market Street, the Army was persuaded not to dynamite the building in case the barrels of volatile liquor were to explode and threaten to destroy other structures. The area was again threatened on the second day, when the fire spread in from North Beach (Fig. 3). This time, a naval relief unit saved the area by running a mile-long hose

Figure 17. Jackson Square: view down Hotaling Place. The meandering brick work in the alley is intended to depict the location of the old shoreline of Yerba Buena Cove.

from the waterfront over Telegraph Hill toward Jackson Square (Hansen and Condon, 1989). Jackson Square was again in the fire path for a third time when the blaze swept down from Telegraph Hill to the north and approached this area. It appeared likely that this island of buildings would finally be gutted, but once more providence stepped in. The wind changed direction, and Jackson Square and its whiskey distillery survived. This led to the popular query attributed to a local wit Charles K. Field, who responded to those who preached that the demise of the city was the result of its wickedness by writing, "If, as some say, God spanked the town for being over-frisky, why did He burn the churches down and spare Hotaling's Whiskey?" (Richards, 2002).

CONCLUSION

This field trip follows the events that happened on the first day of Wednesday, 18 April 1906 by walking the route of the old bay margins from the Mission Bay marshland, skirting Rincon Point, to Yerba Buena Cove, and ending near Clark's Point at the foot of Telegraph Hill (Fig. 1). There is little doubt that this land, recovered from the bay, was the site of greatest damage to structures from ground shaking, and was the origin of most of the fires. This fact has sometimes been overlooked because of the widespread destruction from the fire that followed the tremor.

As darkness fell that first day, the low-lying area around the old bay margin had been destroyed, with exception of Jackson Square. It was now the turn of the residents living close to bedrock on the slopes of Nob Hill, Russian Hill, and Telegraph Hill to witness the next stage in the destruction of the city (Fig. 3). Those living in these areas had believed, at first, that they would survive the worse of the disaster. They felt fortunate to have their homes still standing after the earthquake, and their residences were well beyond the fire zone. However, conditions deteriorated rapidly in the afternoon. Martial law was imposed throughout the city. No one entered or left the perimeter without permission. Over 250,000 people became homeless, and many fled by ferry across the bay, or were camped in Golden Gate Park or other open spaces. The fires were eventually brought under control by dawn on Saturday, 21 April 1906.

It has been estimated that ~4.7 mi^2 or 508 blocks of the city were destroyed, containing some 28,188 homes (Fradkin, 2005). The fire razed all wooden structures in its path, and only the façades of steel-framed and masonry buildings stood amid the ruins. The city set about the process of burying the dead, feeding and housing the homeless, and repairing its infrastructure as aid poured in from many parts of the world. The exact death toll from the earthquake will most likely never be known, particularly because large numbers of the dead were unaccounted for in the path of the fire. It is clear that the official number given in 1907 of 478 persons is grossly incorrect. Gladys Hansen, the former city librarian, has estimated the number at more than 3400 dead, and recently the Board of Supervisors has agreed to do a recount in order to obtain a more accurate number.

The city rapidly rose out of the debris after the disaster. Six thousand buildings had been completed by the summer of 1907, and three thousand others were under construction. The decision was made to rebuild as quickly as possible and not take advantage of the newly proposed Burnham Plan. This plan had been formulated prior to 1906, and was commissioned to enrich the city with grander boulevards and parks. It was ironic, therefore, that nature had presented the city with a unique opportunity to undertake a complete redesign of the downtown area. The opportunity was passed over as the city moved forward, as quickly as possible, with reconstruction.

ACKNOWLEDGMENTS

I wish to thank Carol Prentice, Jack Boatwright, Eldridge Moores, Judy Scotchmoor, and J.P. Kiland, who edited the manuscript and made many useful suggestions and corrections to improve it. Carol Palmer was very helpful in reviewing the paper for clerical errors. Gary Palmer provided invaluable advice and made many other contributions, including drafting the figures. My colleague, Ray Pestrong, has worked on and encouraged me regarding the South of Market study. I also gratefully acknowledge Fireman's Fund Insurance Company for providing the images from the 1906 earthquake.

REFERENCES CITED

Barker, M.E., editor, 1998, Three fearful days: San Francisco memoirs of the 1906 earthquake and fire: San Francisco, London Born Publications, 332 p.

Bronson, W., 1959, The Earth shook, the sky burned: San Francisco, Chronicle Books, 192 p.

Delehanty, R., 1995, San Francisco: The ultimate guide: San Francisco, Chronicle Books, 495 p.

Dobie, C.C., 1933, San Francisco: A Pageant: New York and London, D. Appleton-Century Company, 351 p.

Fardon, G.R., 1999, San Francisco album, photographs from 1854–1856: San Francisco, Chronicle Books, 175 p.

Fradkin, P.L., 2005, The great earthquake and firestorm of 1906: How San Francisco nearly destroyed itself: Berkeley and Los Angeles, University of California Press, 418 p.

Gentry, C., 1962, The dolphin guide to San Francisco and the Bay Area, present and past: Garden City, New York, Dolphin Books, Doubleday & Co., 240 p.

Hansen, G., and Condon, E., 1989, Denial of disaster: The untold story and photographs of the San Francisco earthquake and fire of 1906: San Francisco, Cameron and Co., 160 p.

Jeffers, H.P., 2003, Disaster by the Bay: The Great San Francisco earthquake and fire of 1906: Guildford, Connecticut, The Lyons Press, 204 p.

Lawson, A.C., chairman, 1908, The California earthquake of April 18, 1906, Report of the California State Investigation Commission: Washington, D.C., Carnegie Institute Publication 87, Land atlas, 451 p.

Richards, R., 2001, Historic San Francisco: A concise history and guide: San Francisco, Heritage House Publishers, 300 p.

Richards, R., 2002, Historic walks in San Francisco, 18 trails through the city's past: San Francisco, Heritage House Publishers, 430 p.

Schlocker, J., 1974, Geology of the San Francisco north quadrangle, California: U.S. Geological Survey Professional Paper 782, 109 p.

Schussler, H., 1906, The water supply of San Francisco, California: Before, during and after the earthquake of April 18, 1906, and subsequent conflagration: Spring Valley Water Company Report, 49 p.

Shumate, A., 1988, Rincon Hill and South Park, San Francisco early fashionable neighborhood: Sausalito, California, Windgate Press, 124 p.

Smith, D., 2005, San Francisco is burning, the untold story of the 1906 earthquake and fire: New York, Viking, Penguin Group, 294 p.

Smith, J.R., 2005, San Francisco lost landmarks: Sanger, California, Word Dancer Press, 236 p.

Steinbrugge, K.V., 1969, Seismic risk to buildings and structures on filled land in San Francisco Bay, *in* Goldman, H.B., ed., Geologic and engineering aspects of San Francisco Bay fill: California Division of Mines and Geology Special Report 97, p. 103–115.

Sullivan, R., and Galehouse, J.S., 1990, Geological setting of the San Francisco Bay area: Field trip guidebook: San Francisco, Student Chapter American Association of Petroleum Geologist Annual Convention, 82 p.

Sullivan, R., and Galehouse, J.S., 1991, Geological setting of San Francisco Bay, *in* Sloan, D., and Wagner, D.L., eds., Geologic excursions in northern California: San Francisco to the Sierra Nevada: California Division of Mines and Geology Special Publication 109, p. 1–10.

Sutherland, M., 1959, The damndest finest ruins: New York, Coward-McCann, 219 p.

Thomas, G., and Witts, M.M., 1971, The San Francisco earthquake: New York, Stein and Day, 316 p.

Wahrhaftig, C., 1966, A walker's guide to the geology of San Francisco: California Division of Mines and Geology, Mineral Information Service Special Supplement, 31 p.

Wahrhaftig, C., 1984, A streetcar to subduction and other plate tectonic trips by public transport in San Francisco: Washington, D.C., American Geophysical Union, 69 p.

Waldhorn, J.L., and Woodbridge, S.E., 1978, The Victoria legacy: Tours of San Francisco Bay area architecture: San Francisco, 101 Publications, 224 p.

Winchester, S., 2005, A crack in the edge of the world: America and the great California earthquake of 1906: New York, Harper, 462 p.

Woodbridge, S.B., and Woodbridge, J., 1982, Architecture: San Francisco the guide: San Francisco, 101 Publications, 200 p.

Youd, T.L., and Hoose, S.N., 1978, Historic ground failures in northern California associated with earthquakes: U.S. Geological Survey Professional Paper 993, 177 p.

Printed in the USA

Remnant damage from the 1906 San Francisco earthquake

John Boatwright

U.S. Geological Survey, 345 Middlefield Rd., MS 977, Menlo Park, California 94025, USA

OVERVIEW OF THE FIELD TRIP

This field trip consists of two stops at locations where it is possible to see damage from the 1906 earthquake and to gauge the intensity of the ground shaking that caused the damage. The first stop is at a cemetery in Colma, where the damage to monuments and headstones was photographed and roughly quantified in the *Report of the State Earthquake Investigation Commission*, edited by A.C. Lawson (1908), commonly referred to as the "Lawson Report." The Lawson Report represents the formal study of the earthquake and consists of a compilation of the reports of many investigators who gathered information about faulting, ground failure, and damage due to the 1906 earthquake. The second stop is at a brick office building at the southern limit of San Francisco that was damaged by the earthquake but repaired in such a fashion that the damage is still clearly evident.

Keywords: 1906 earthquake, earthquake damage, earthquake intensity, cemeteries, Lawson report.

STOP 1: THE HOLY CROSS CEMETERY IN COLMA (GPS: 37.670°N, 122.446°W)

Significance of the Site

The damage to the Holy Cross Cemetery was photographed and described ("over 75 per cent of all the monuments were either thrown down or twisted on their bases") in the 1908 Lawson Report, and can still be detected today.

Accessibility

Public, no restrooms available, ample parking.

Directions

From San Francisco, take Highway 280 south for 10 mi. Exit Serramonte Blvd. (in Colma) and turn left at the end of the off-ramp. Proceed 1 mi east on Serramonte Blvd. and turn right on El Camino Real (CA 82). Proceed 0.4 mi south and continue straight on Mission Road where El Camino Real turns to the right. Proceed another 0.6 mi and make a left at the entrance to Holy Cross Cemetery. Once past the central circular chapel, make a right and a left, and then park near the "T" in the road. The Bay Area Rapid Transit (BART) Colma station is about a mile northwest of the site on El Camino Real.

Stop Description

Because broken headstones are almost never replaced, and overturned monuments are usually reset with some misalignment, cemeteries can contain remnant damage from earthquake shaking. The southern section of the Holy Cross Cemetery, with more than an acre of pre-1906 headstones and monuments, amply demonstrates the capacity of cemeteries to act as ground motion or intensity indicators. The shaking history of the site is relatively simple: the cemetery was established in 1887; the 1906 earthquake was the first large event to damage the cemetery. The site was subsequently shaken by the **M** 5.3 (**M** = moment magnitude) Daly City earthquake in 1957 and the **M** 6.9 Loma Prieta earthquake in 1989, but Stover and Coffman (1993) estimated the intensities at this site to be less than or equal to a modified Mercalli intensity 6 (MMI). MMI 6 is described as "heavy shaking, objects moved and thrown from shelves, plaster cracked, windows broken, some chimneys and poorly braced walls damaged, bricks thrown from parapets," but is not usually strong enough to damage cemetery headstones and monuments.

Boatwright, J., 2006, Remnant damage from the 1906 San Francisco earthquake, *in* Prentice, C.S., Scotchmoor, J.G., Moores, E.M., and Kiland, J.P., eds., 1906 San Francisco Earthquake Centennial Field Guides: Field trips associated with the 100th Anniversary Conference, 18–23 April 2006, San Francisco, California: Geological Society of America Field Guide 7, p. 25–29, doi: 10.1130/2006.1906SF(02). For permission to copy, contact editing@geosociety.org. ©2006 Geological Society of America. All rights reserved.

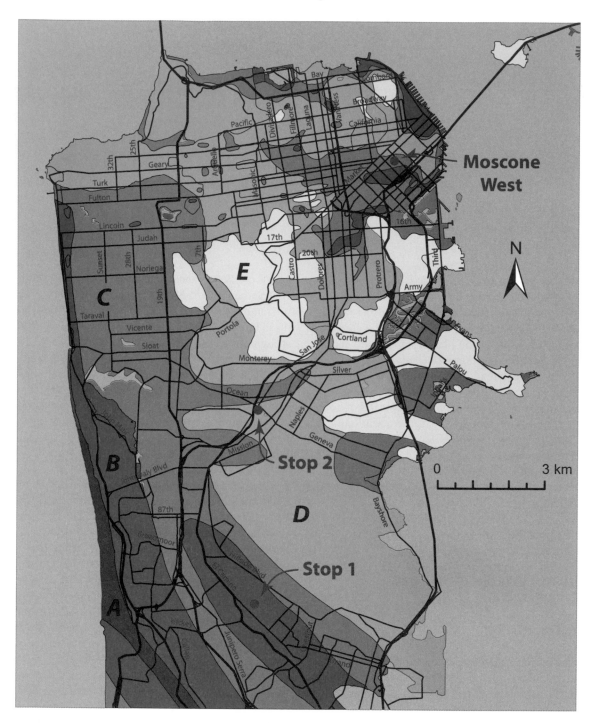

POTENTIAL DAMAGE	Light	Moderate	Moderate/Heavy	Heavy	Very Heavy
SAN FRANCISCO INTENSITY	*E*	*D*	*C*	*B*	*A*

Figure 1. Maps 19 and 21 of Lawson (1908) combined to show the intensity distribution in San Francisco, Colma, and south San Francisco. H.O. Wood's (*in* Lawson, 1908, p. 220–245) San Francisco intensity scale (A–E) corresponds to modified Mercalli intensity 10–6. The intensity distributions in Maps 19 and 21 disagree slightly in Pacifica and south San Francisco: we have followed Map 21 in these areas. The shoreline is taken from the 1906 maps, but the major roads and freeways are modern. The two stops on the tour are indicated on the map, along with the location of the Moscone West conference center.

To estimate intensity from damaged markers in cemeteries (see Boatwright and Bundock, 2005), I canvas the pre-1906 markers in a cemetery, dividing them into three categories: undamaged, chipped and/or reset, and broken. It is important to scrutinize a headstone or monument to determine if it has been reset. Characteristically, headstones will break at the bottom, where the flange fits into the footer: even if the headstone has been reset carefully, there is usually some cement showing. Similarly, if a monument such as an obelisk has been overturned and reset, it may appear undamaged: however, reset monuments are almost always slightly out of alignment.

The MMI can be estimated from the percentage of broken and chipped and/or reset headstones and monuments. At MMI 7, few or no headstones are broken or overturned; at MMI 8, 20–50% of the headstones and monuments are broken or overturned, and at MMI 9, more than 80% are broken or overturned (see Boatwright and Bundock, 2005). Cemetery markers constitute an earthquake effect intermediate between brick chimneys (MMI 6–8) and unbolted or unbraced wood-frame houses (MMI 8–9). Figure 1 combines Map 19 and 21 from Lawson (1908), using Harry Wood's San Francisco (SF) intensity scale. Comparing Wood's SF intensity scale to the modern MMI scale yields the correspondences: SF E = ~MMI 6, SF D = ~MMI 7, SF C = ~MMI 8, SF B = ~MMI 9, and SF A = ~MMI 9–10.

Figure 2 shows a photograph of damaged monuments reprinted from Lawson (1908). This photograph was located ~80 yards north of the central receiving chapel: there are now trees and grass growing where there was a carriage path in the photograph. Eugene Schmitz, the mayor of San Francisco who capably organized the city's recovery from the earthquake and fire, is buried twenty yards northeast of the photograph location. Figure 3 shows the stone railroad station, located across Mission Street from the cemetery entrance, which was damaged in the 1906 earthquake and seamlessly repaired. The old Southern Pacific right-of-way is now used by BART.

The comparison between the damaged cemetery monuments and the repaired railway station is an important one. Buildings that were damaged in the 1906 earthquake and subsequently repaired can only be detected using a photograph or a description of the damage. In contrast, damage to headstones and monuments is rarely repaired so completely that it cannot be readily detected. In general, cemeteries are more dependable indicators of earthquake damage than repaired buildings. In our last stop, however, we will see 1906 damage that has been preserved in a masonry building.

STOP 2: THE SOUTHERN PACIFIC OFFICE BUILDING AT GENEVA AND SAN JOSE AVENUES (37.720°N, 122.446°W)

Significance of the Site

An instance of 1906 earthquake damage to an unreinforced brick building that was subsequently stabilized but not demolished or repaired.

Accessibility

Public, no restrooms available, ample parking.

Figure 2. Plate 96B from Lawson (1908) showing the damage to two rows of monuments in Holy Cross Cemetery. The view is approximately south toward the present-day circular receiving chapel.

Figure 3. Plate 96A from Lawson (1908) showing the damage to the Holy Cross Station. The view looks east across the railroad right-of-way.

Figure 4. 1906 earthquake damage to the Southern Pacific office building. The view is south from Geneva Ave.; the photograph was taken in 1954. The brick wall of the second floor fell out, and the wall of the first floor was strongly cracked.

Directions

From San Francisco, take Hwy 280 south for 6 mi. Exit at Geneva Avenue and go east on Geneva. Turn right on San Jose Avenue and park. The site can also be reached by taking BART to the Balboa Park station.

Stop Description

The 1906 earthquake damaged masonry buildings throughout northern California: some of the less damaged buildings were repaired but most of the heavily damaged buildings were demolished. The repairs to the Southern Pacific office building were so marginal that it might be considered stabilized rather than repaired, although the building was used for many years after the earthquake. The damage to the building, shown in Figure 4, includes the failure of the second story wall and cracking of the first story wall. There are photographs of similarly damaged buildings throughout Lawson (1908): in particular, buildings in downtown San Francisco, Berkeley, and Los Banos. In contrast to many masonry buildings that were damaged by the earthquake, however, the Southern Pacific office building appears well-built: I would estimate the intensity to be MMI 7–8. Map 19 in Lawson (1908) grades this site as San Francisco Intensity C, which corresponds to MMI 8. Because the Southern Pacific office building was the largest building in this area at the time of the earthquake, we can assume that this intensity estimate was in part determined from the damage to this building.

ACKNOWLEDGMENTS

I would like to acknowledge Manuel "Doc" Bonilla's insightful review of this field guide; we mourn the loss of his expertise and spirit as the geologic consultant for this field trip.

REFERENCES CITED

Boatwright, J., and Bundock, H., 2005, Modified Mercalli intensity maps for the 1906 San Francisco earthquake plotted in ShakeMap format: U.S. Geological Survey Open-File Report 2005-1135, http://pubs.usgs.gov/of/2005/1135/.

Lawson, A.C., chairman, 1908, The California earthquake of April 18, 1906 (reprinted in 1969): Washington, DC, The Carnegie Institution, v. 1, 451 p.

Stover, C.W., and Coffman, J.L., 1993, Seismicity of the United States, 1568–1989 (Revised): U.S. Geological Survey Professional Paper 1527, 418 p.

Geological Society of America
Field Guide 7
2006

Downtown San Francisco in earthquake, fire, and recovery

Stephen Tobriner

Architecture Department, 232 Wurster Hall, University of California, Berkeley, California 94720-1800, USA

OVERVIEW OF FIELD TRIP

This tour includes many of San Francisco's most interesting pre- and post-1906 buildings. We will investigate these buildings in the context of their urban setting and their earthquake-resistant architecture and engineering. Many of the buildings we are going to visit were considered earthquake-resistant when they were conceived, although they might not be judged earthquake-resistant today. We will examine their histories in relation to San Francisco's struggle for safety from earthquakes and fires, and particularly the earthquake and fire of 1906. (Note: The text of this tour is excerpted from Tobriner, 2006.)

Keywords: San Francisco earthquake, architecture, engineering, earthquake damage.

Accessibility and Directions

This is an urban walking tour over level terrain covering a distance of a little over one half of a mile. Duration: a leisurely 2 hours. There are no public restrooms along the route, but restrooms are available at private establishments. The tour begins at the southwest corner of Market and New Montgomery Streets, at one of the Montgomery Street Bay Area Rapid Transit (BART) station entrances. Each stop is indicated on Figure 1, which also shows the locations of the buildings to be examined. Some of the buildings discussed herein are also discussed in chapter 1 of this volume.

STOP 1: THE PALACE HOTEL, YERBA BUENA, THE FERRY BUILDING, AUXILIARY WATER SERVICE SYSTEM

This walk starts on the southeast corner of Market and New Montgomery Streets at the corner of the present Sheraton Palace Hotel (near the BART station entrance; Fig. 1, map location B). We begin near the former shoreline of the old settlement of Yerba Buena, which in the 1840s would have been several blocks north up Montgomery Street. Everything between Battery Street (two blocks to the east [right]) and the Ferry building to the east is constructed on landfill, which can be dangerous in earthquakes.

Unless we consider the environment around us carefully, it is easy to miss the safety mitigations. Notice that there are two kinds of fire hydrants in the area, narrow white ones and others (across the street) with stout bodies and painted blue bonnets. The latter are the fire hydrants (Fig. 1, map location A) of the Auxiliary Water Service System (AWSS), which was begun in 1909 and online in 1912. It is an earthquake-resistant system of pumping stations, reservoirs, and pipes independent of the city's everyday water system that was funded by a municipal bond issue approved by San Franciscans shortly after the 1906 earthquake. Notice, too, the absence of wooden buildings in this area. This is the fire district of San Francisco, where only nonflammable decoration, and brick, stone, concrete, terracotta, and glass facades are allowed. The old fire district of the 1880s included this area as well, but in those days, many wooden structures were still present in the fire-resistant district.

In the 1870s, New Montgomery was an extension of Montgomery Street, which cut into the South of Market area grid between Second and Third Streets. The banker William Ralston had speculated on the land in the South of Market area and hoped to stimulate a real-estate boom by positioning his new Palace Hotel in this unlikely location.

The present-day Sheraton Palace Hotel is located on the corner (Fig. 1, map location B). The present building is a brick- and terracotta-clad steel-frame building designed in 1909 by George Kelham of the New York firm of Trowbridge and Livingston architects. Its low height and steel frame would have made it earthquake-resistant in the eyes of architects and engineers of the time. Its fire-resistant exterior was required in post-earthquake San Francisco. Notice the lowest part of the wall (or "water table," as it is called) is granite, above which is limestone. The black moldings are iron. Above

Tobriner, S., 2006, Downtown San Francisco in earthquake, fire, and recovery, *in* Prentice, C.S., Scotchmoor, J.G., Moores, E.M., and Kiland, J.P., eds., 1906 San Francisco Earthquake Centennial Field Guides: Field trips associated with the 100th Anniversary Conference, 18–23 April 2006, San Francisco, California: Geological Society of America Field Guide 7, p. 31–55, doi: 10.1130/2006.1906SF(03). For permission to copy, contact editing@geosociety.org.

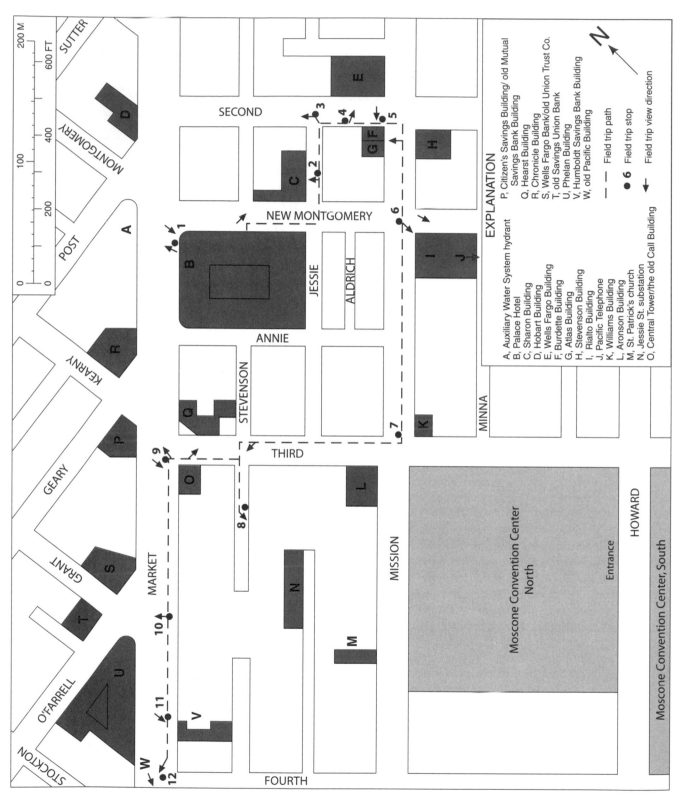

Figure 1. Map of part of downtown San Francisco, showing field-trip stops and buildings discussed in text, in relation to Moscone Center (modified from a drawing by Mike Tobriner).

the first story, the façade is brick and terracotta. Terracotta decoration became important in post-earthquake San Francisco because it was much superior to heavy, brittle stone, which performed poorly in the 1906 earthquake. Terracotta is cheap, malleable, and light. It is used here in conjunction with brick to decorate the façade. The architectural design of the Sheraton Palace is heavily influenced by the French Ecole des Beaux Arts school in decoration and plan, as a walk through the building demonstrates.

If the Market Street entrance to the hotel is open, we will walk inside (remember, this is private property). Notice the opulence of the entry hall, which cuts through the building like an indoor street (you can easily see the Jessie Street door at the end of the corridor). On the right are glass cabinets with souvenirs from the history of the building. There is usually a photograph of the old, pre-earthquake Palace Hotel on display here. Down the hall, in the center of the building, is an intersecting corridor from the main entrance on New Montgomery Street on the left and an entrance to Palm Court on the right. This strict symmetry is a hallmark of Ecole planning. The gorgeous Palm Court with its glass roof is derived from Parisian prototypes. This is where the old courtyard of the original building once stood. Before the 1906 earthquake, horse-drawn carriages entered to deposit guests in a tall, glass-covered atrium, the signature architectural feature of the old Palace Hotel.

The original Palace Hotel was designed to be earthquake-resistant by John Gaynor, a New York architect who had emigrated to San Francisco. At the time of its construction, it was one of the largest hotels in the world. Ralston, a powerful San Francisco booster, was a reckless investor but insisted that the Palace Hotel be "earthquake-proof." Gaynor used multiple brick cross walls running through the interior of the hotel, strengthened by strong cement mortar and bond iron, to tie the inside shell to the exterior of the building. According to reports, the entire building was belted together with courses of bond iron embedded every four feet in the brick walls. Combined with strong mortar and frequent cross walls, the result was an extremely innovative and strong structure.

A run on the Bank of California, which Ralston had used to finance his empire, may have led to his apparent suicide by drowning in 1875. He did not live to see that the Palace Hotel survived the earthquake of 1906 with minor structural damage. Although it had an advanced fire-fighting system, which included its own cistern, the building eventually succumbed to fire in 1906 because its water supply had been used to fight fires in neighboring buildings.

STOPS 2A AND 2B: THE SHARON BUILDING

Next, walk out the front door of the Palace Hotel and south (right) on New Montgomery to view the Sharon building (Fig. 1, map location C) across the street from the Palace Hotel (Fig. 2); this is Stop 2a. The Sharon building was designed by architect George Kelham and engineer Henry J. Brunnier

(1912). Sharon, a business partner of Ralston's, inherited all of Ralston's estate. The Sharon building is just a small piece of Sharon's real-estate empire.

Henry J. Brunnier, one of San Francisco's most famous engineers, designed the steel frame for this building. He established a reputation for designing well-braced and well-tied buildings. Having arrived in San Francisco with his wife two weeks after the earthquake, he had ample opportunity to study structural successes and failures. The burnt-out shell of the earthquake-resistant Palace Hotel deeply impressed him. Later he wrote: "The cement mortar reinforced with steel bands and with the anchors still protruding from the walls indicated that the walls had been thoroughly tied to the wood-frame floors, which, in turn, had acted as a diaphragm" (Brunnier, 1956, p. 26-2). His employees recalled that he always admonished them to tie their buildings together to act as a unit.

Brunnier opened his own office in 1908. George Kelham hired him to do the engineering for the Sharon building (1912), and the two worked together for the remainder of their professional careers. Brunnier's design for the structural system of the Sharon building called for a heavy steel frame with deep spandrel girders at each floor (Fig. 3). He tied the huge overhanging cornice, so important to the architectural character of the building, to the frame so it would never fall, as so many did during the 1906 earthquake. The building was considered a model of responsible engineering in its time and is still home to the office of H.J. Brunnier Associates.

Clearly, the building was designed to be earthquake-resistant. But what Brunnier had not figured in his calculations was the L-shape of the plan. You can see that the façade along New Montgomery has a shallow arm (Figs. 1 and 2) that reaches out to the intersection of Stevenson and New Montgomery. This shape or configuration of the plan would be hazardous in earthquakes because each leg of the L would move independently, tending to break the joint between them. Although symmetrical configurations were understood in Europe to be superior in earthquakes as early as 1783, no such understanding was present in post-earthquake San Francisco.

Next, the walk crosses New Montgomery to Jessie Street and Stop 2b. (There may be street people here—treat them with respect and caution.) Walking east on the south side of Jessie Street, look up at the brick- and terracotta-clad façade of the steel-framed Sharon building (Fig. 4). Looking carefully at the façade, ask yourself the questions: Can you see any damage from the 1989 Loma Prieta earthquake? Imagine the building moving from east to west and back again. What portion of the building would bend the most? The upper floors of the steel frame are filled with concrete, bricks, and terracotta, which help to resist lateral movement, but the first floor, with large open spaces and no such infill, is free to move. Also, in an earthquake, lateral forces, the side-to-side vibrations that occur in a building, are often strongest on the first floor. If you look carefully at the tops of the capitals of the pilasters (Fig. 5), you can still see the broken ends of the hollow terracotta. This indicates

Figure 2. The Sharon building, New Montgomery façade.

that the steel columns on the ground floor bent back and forth in the earthquake, dissipating energy. As they moved, they broke the brittle terracotta. This kind of superficial damage is unavoidable in an earthquake and has no bearing on the strength of the building, but it does highlight a problem engineers have debated. How flexible should the ground floor of a building be in order to dissipate energy but not collapse?

Can you see other signs of earthquake damage on Jessie Street? The bricks of the building on the northeast corner of Jessie at Second Street have been repaired (Fig. 6). Can you see

where they were broken along their bond joints by the Loma Prieta earthquake? On the south side of Jessie Street, to the left of the large doorway, there is a vent in a wall. Look carefully at this wall. The wall is less flexible than the columns with glass windows to the right of them. They can flex during an earthquake but the wall cannot. The only puncture in the wall is the vent. As the wall moves back and forth, shear forces crack it on the diagonal, from each corner of the vent. Although the owners have repainted the diagonal cracks, they have reemerged to record the history of the building.

Figure 3. The Sharon building, steel frame (courtesy of A.J. Brunnier Associates).

STOP 3: JESSIE AND SECOND STREET LOOKING NORTH—THE HOBART BUILDING

Next, the walk proceeds out of Jessie Street onto Second Street. On the left, at the intersection of Market and Second Streets, is the handsome Hobart building (Fig. 1, map location D; Fig. 7), designed by Willis Polk in a craggy Early Renaissance style. The steel frame of this building was designed with large knee bracing to resist earthquakes (1914).

STOP 4: SECOND STREET—THE WELLS FARGO BUILDING

Just to the right, and across Second Street, is the Wells Fargo building (Fig. 1, map location E; Fig. 8), designed by Henry Meyers in 1902. Wells Fargo stagecoaches used to deliver cargo to this building. It survived the earthquake and was restored and partially rebuilt in 1907. It was damaged

again in the Loma Prieta earthquake, after which a special steel frame was inserted in its courtyard to limit drift and provide for extra strength. Cracks in exterior stone moldings are evidence of earthquakes. The upper two stories were added after the earthquake of 1906, and the top one was occupied by the State Supreme Court for a short time after the building was remodeled.

STOP 5: SECOND AND MISSION STREETS—THE BURDETTE BUILDING, THE ATLAS BUILDING, AND THE STEVENSON BUILDING

The walk continues south on Second Street until Mission Street. On the northwest corner of Mission and Second Streets stands the most famous earthquake survivor in San Francisco, the Burdette building (Fig. 1, map location F; Figs. 9 and 10). This small, two-story, brick building survived both the earthquake and the fire undamaged. Protected by the taller buildings

Figure 4. The Sharon building, Jessie Street façade, 2005.

beside it and the intersection in front, it was the sole building in the fire district to survive with its contents intact and windows unbroken, without people on the inside or outside fighting to save it from the flames. According to a newspaper report, the owner of the building had wanted to erect an eleven-story building on the site and had therefore built a deep foundation before deciding on only two stories.

Next to the Burdette building is the Atlas building (Fig. 1, map location G; Fig. 11), at 602–606 Mission Street. Redeco-

rated as a Moderne building in the 1930s, this building was originally designed by Frank S. Van Trees in 1904 and was completed in 1906. The earthquake struck as tenants were moving into the building. This steel-frame building with brick infill had a column-beam steel frame with added knee braces (triangular stiffeners at junction of columns and beams) at each floor on the south Mission Street façade. It is hard to know whether the architect or construction engineers were thinking about earthquake resistance when they designed the building, but the knee

Figure 5. The Sharon building, detail of terracotta damage, 2005.

bracing served to limit drift (or bend) from east to west. The 1906 earthquake shook the Atlas building north to south, causing the X-shaped cracks on the east side of the building, which can still be seen from Second Street. In the Loma Prieta earthquake, the building moved from east to west, causing the X-shaped cracks that can still be seen on the south Mission Street façade and the damage to walls on the north. The worst cracks in the 1989 earthquake were on the seventh floor, the height of the cornice of the building next door: the Atlas building pounded its eastern neighbor like a castle wall hitting a battering ram. If the shaking had continued, the Atlas building would have fallen on the eastern building, but thankfully it did not.

On the southwest corner of Mission and Second Streets is the Stevenson Building, constructed in 1907 (Fig. 1, map location H). Because of damage it sustained in the Loma Prieta earthquake, engineers seismically retrofitted the building. They decided a steel frame would help to limit drift and support the floors if the ground-floor walls failed.

Figure 6. Jessie Street, detail of brick repair.

STOP 6: NEW MONTGOMERY AND MISSION LOOKING SOUTHWEST—THE RIALTO BUILDING AND PACIFIC TELEPHONE AND TELEGRAPH BUILDING

The walk turns west on Mission Street until it crosses New Montgomery. To the left is the Rialto building, at 116 New Montgomery (Fig. 1, map location I), designed by the architectural firm of Meyer and O'Brien and completed in 1902.

This steel-frame building suffered extensive damage from dynamite or a boiler explosion. The steel frame was largely rebuilt after the 1906 earthquake, but not by the original architects. The owners hired the architects Bliss and Faville to repair the façade and the steel frame in 1910. If you look carefully, you can see some of the repairs made in the corners of the window moldings in 1906 on the New Montgomery façade. Similarly, you can pick out repairs after the Loma Prieta earthquake on the Mission Street façade. The plan and elevation of

Figure 7. The Hobart building, looking north from Second Street at Jessie.

the building were typical for an up-to-date steel office building of the time.

Just to the south of the Rialto is one of San Francisco's most handsome buildings, the Pacific Telephone and Telegraph building at 134–140 New Montgomery (Fig. 1, map location J) built by Miller and Pfleuger and A.A. Cantin in 1925. The upsweep of the Moderne façade, topped by attenuated shafts and spreading vase-like capitals, is irresistible. This is a steel-frame building clad in terracotta tiles. Look for a moment at the terracotta skin. Notice that some tiles differ from others. Water seeped in between the tiles and rusted the steel frame, so tiles had to be removed to check and treat the steel. Not all the original tiles could be reused; some new ones were made that could not exactly match the old. If the building is open, we will go inside the lobby to see the beautiful Art Deco ensemble of coordinated materials and design motifs. Pfleuger was fond of Mayan and Asian decoration, which he used here on the ceiling.

Figure 8. The Wells Fargo building, Second Street.

STOP 7: MISSION AND THIRD STREETS— THE WILLIAMS BUILDING, THE ARONSON BUILDING, AND ST. PATRICK'S CHURCH

From New Montgomery, the walk goes west on Mission to Third Street, the boundary of Yerba Buena Center. On the southeast corner of Mission and Third (101–107 Third St.) is the Williams building (Fig. 1, map location K) by Clinton Day, 1907. It has been incorporated into the massive concrete building behind it (completed in 2005). Across the street, at 700 Mission, on the northwest corner of Third Street, is the Aronson building (Fig. 1, map location L) by Hemenway and Miller, 1903. This building survived the earthquake of 1906, although it was damaged in the fire. It was quickly retrofitted after the earthquake.

Down Mission Street, on the right (north) side of the street, note St. Patrick's Church (Fig. 1, map location M), which was badly damaged in 1906, but was rebuilt. Remember its location as the walk continues north on Third Street.

Figure 9. The Burdette building (below) and the Atlas building on Second Street.

STOP 8: STEVENSON STREET, WEST OF THIRD— CENTRAL TOWER, THE OLD CALL BUILDING, REAR OF JESSIE STREET, AND REAR OF ST. PATRICK'S CHURCH

At Third Street, turn right and walk north. Ahead on the left, at Market and Third, is the Art Deco Central Tower (Fig. 1, map location O; Fig. 12A). The bottom half of this building is the Call building, built in 1898 (Fig. 12B). This building survived the earthquake of 1906 and originally had a large Baroque dome (Fig. 13). On the way toward Market, turn west down Stevenson Street to Stop 8, where you will see the rear of the Jessie Street substation (Fig. 1, map location N) by Willis Polk 1905, rebuilt in 1907 and 1909. It is being incorporated into the Jewish Museum, which is being built on this site. You can also see the rear of St. Patrick's Church (Fig. 1, map location M), built in 1872. Note that its brick walls are topped by reinforced concrete walls, which were added when the church was rebuilt in 1909 minus its steeple.

Figure 10. The Burdette building and the Atlas building on Mission Street shortly after the 1989 Loma Prieta earthquake.

Figure 11. The Burdette and Atlas buildings after the 1906 earthquake and fire (courtesy of the Bancroft Library, University of California–Berkeley). Note X-shaped cracks.

There is a rare account of the 1906 earthquake near this site. Near Stevenson and Third stood the Winchester House. Looking out of the window of his fifth floor room in the Winchester House on the morning of 18 April 1906, DeWitt J. Lipe watched the nearby buildings as the earthquake struck the city (Fig. 12B.):

As I looked out on this vista, *everything was swaying*; and the first among these swaying structures to attract my particular attention was *the tall steel smokestack over the Call power plant, which toppled down within the first few seconds*, and the simultaneous *disappearance of the*

big iron water tank from the roof of the same building. That happened during the first few seconds that I was watching the effects of the quake.

Almost immediately after these incidents, *the great chimney of the San Francisco Gas and Electric Company's powerhouse*, which had been waving like a whip, broke off about the middle, and the top *went crashing down on the powerhouse itself*, which caused a terrific explosion as the debris smashed the steam pipes or boilers beneath.

About this time, *the plastering in my room began to fall in*, and the earthquake seemed to be pumping up and down with a vertical motion. It was time for me to be doing something to save myself, so I tried to dress while the place was shaking and showering plaster. While I was

Figure 12. (A) Central Tower, old Call building from Third Street, 2005.

so engaged I saw the swaying *steeple of St. Patrick's church give way and fall down <u>en masse</u>* toward Mission Street. I then heard a tremendous noise of some other falling building. Thinking it was the Call Building, I looked to my right toward Market Street; but that structure was still standing and apparently uninjured.

Then I noticed that other guests from the Winchester were crowding out on the roof of the annex, which was about on a level with the fourth-floor windows of the rear of the main building underneath me. To get out on that roof they had to jump the three-foot light well, or alley, that separated the main building from the annex. While I was *watching*

these people they were running away from the rear wall of the main building, and were looking up apprehensively toward it, and me, as though momentarily expecting the wall to fall out and crush them.

By this time I was partly dressed. The shocks had ceased, and it seemed as if the earthquake was over. *Except for fallen plaster and some disturbance of the furniture nothing seemed to be much the matter* with my room. The door was not jammed or anything. When I had hurriedly dressed myself, I went out... I ran down the stairs and saw that *the damage was far more extensive than I imagined,* and the plastering was down everywhere. (1926, p. 2)

Call Bldg.

St. Patrick's spire

Lipe's room

Call Bldg. power station

Bancroft Bldg.

Figure 12. (*conitnued*) (B) The Call building before 1906 (courtesy of the Bancroft Library, University of California–Berkeley).

STOP 9: THIRD AND MARKET STREETS: "NEWSPAPER CORNER"—THE CENTRAL TOWER (FORMERLY THE CALL BUILDING), CITIZEN'S SAVINGS BUILDING, HEARST BUILDING, AND CHRONICLE BUILDING

The walk continues up to the corner of Third and Market Streets to the old Call building, which had not collapsed, as Lipe had feared. This is "Newspaper Corner" (Fig. 14), with the *Call* Newspaper building to our left, and the Hearst *Examiner* building on the southeastern corner of Market and Third, across the street. Diagonally across Market, at Kearny, is the de Young's *Chronicle* building. More or less at the center of the intersection is Lotta's Fountain (1875), which was donated to the city by the San Francisco singer Lotta Crabtree. Every April 18 at 5:12 a.m., citizens and earthquake survivors gather at this corner to commemorate the great earthquake and fire of 1906.

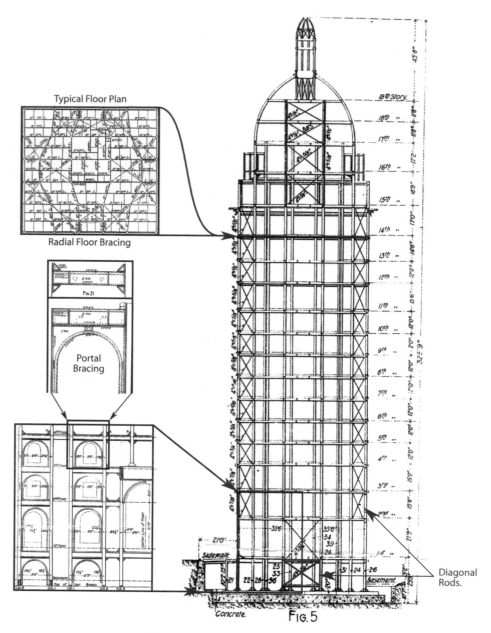

Figure 13. The Call building, steel frame.

The Call building was the most imposing of the buildings at "Newspaper Corner," and that was no accident. In 1881, the *Chronicle* began a crusade against Claus Spreckels, who had amassed a fortune by developing sugar plantations in Hawaii and shipping sugar to the San Francisco Bay area to be refined and distributed. The paper alleged, probably correctly, that the Hawaiian plantations were virtual slave camps, and went on to claim that Spreckels had swindled the stockholders of the Hawaiian Commercial and Sugar Company. So incensed was Claus Spreckels' son, Adolph, that he walked into Michael de Young's office in the Chronicle building and shot him. De Young survived and Adolph Spreckels was acquitted, but a deep and enduring enmity divided the two families. In retribution, Claus Spreckels bought the San Francisco *Call* in 1895 and set out to beat the de Youngs at their own game.

Spreckels commissioned the construction of the headquarters for the *Call* at Market and Third, across the street from the *Chronicle*. At 310 feet, the Call building would be 102 feet taller than the Chronicle building, and it had a more advanced design, which must have warmed the Spreckels' hearts. They had asked a local architectural firm, James and Merritt Reid, to design their building, but for their engineer they looked farther afield and

Figure 14. "Newspaper Corner" looking west on Market Street showing the old Call building on the left, the tower of the Humboldt Bank building, Lotta's Fountain, the old Mutual Savings building. Located directly behind this view is the old Chronicle building, 2005.

chose Charles Strobel of Chicago, one of the most famous engineers in the country. Together the Reid brothers and Strobel created an outstanding building that would outperform the Chronicle building by surviving the earthquake and fire of 1906.

Strobel's approach to the Call building was probably informed by the American Society of Civil Engineering meeting of 1892, at which members discussed the effects of wind and earthquakes on tall buildings. The sixteen-story Call building was to have a narrow tower just 75 × 75 ft and to be topped by a gracious baroque dome. A tall, narrow building like this, even though symmetrical, presented specific and difficult problems to its engineer: how could it be braced to resist the wind that blew upon its surface, or earthquakes, which would whip it back and forth from below?

To solve the problem of overturning, Strobel used a foundation of steel grillage and concrete that had already been pioneered in Chicago. He extended the two-foot-thick concrete foundation to the end of the lot lines, an area of 96 × 100 ft, even though the structure itself was only 75 × 75 ft. The foundation was laid well below street level, on wet, compact, hard sand. Two layers of fifteen-inch steel I-beams were placed at right angles to one

another and covered in concrete. On top of this, the engineer positioned twenty-eight sets of twenty-inch steel I-beams to carry the structure's columns and pedestals. The major support columns were held by cast-plate pedestals attached to the very lowest of these I-beams. The whole foundation, from concrete to grillage to column supports, acted as a unit, distributing the building's weight over the widest possible area.

Strobel attacked the problem of wind or earthquake forces with enormous ingenuity (Fig. 13). The building is a tower, its floors a series of radially symmetrical polygons within the square exterior. This costly solution, which makes for a jigsaw plan of bays of different dimensions, was obviously included to provide a very stiff diaphragm for the tower. It could be pushed from any side and the floor planes would resist distortion. Looking at the complexity of the steel work, it is hard not to think of a bridge engineer. Strobel went on to brace his steel frame with every stiffener known at the time. From the first to the third floors, he linked columns at the corners with deeply rounded fillets. These rigid portal frames, as they are called, effectively resisted lateral forces. A second series of braces, perhaps more adapted to bridges than buildings, consisted of eight bays of diagonal bracing per floor, from the foundation to the sixteenth floor, and three sets in the dome, in the form of adjustable rods. The rods, with adjustable turnbuckles, ran from the base of one column to the top of the next, forming a series of X's. This bracing method is cheaper and lighter than portal bracing but has major drawbacks. Rods cannot counter lateral forces as effectively as portal braces because they are vulnerable to bending and distorting in shear. Even if they are effective initially, after some time, or perhaps a major earthquake, they will distort and loosen, making it necessary to retune the turnbuckle. In addition to portal bracing and diagonal bracing, the main beams of the Call building were connected to the columns with knee braces. These are triangular webs riveted to columns and beams, creating a very rigid connection. Last, Strobel stabilized the center bays of the building with spandrel girders. These are deep girders that are designed to stiffen the columns of a building.

The Call building survived the 1906 earthquake and fire, while the Chronicle building survived the earthquake, but the fire collapsed its interior floors. But the Call building's success led to its eventual disfigurement. In 1938, engineers calculated that the Call building was constructed to be very stiff, with a wind resistance of 50 pounds per square foot, phenomenal for its time. B.J.S. Cahill, a local critic, called it the "handsomest tall office building in the world," which it probably was, until the owners decided, because of its strength, to remove the dome in the 1930s and add six extra stories, destroying its architectural integrity.

On the corner of Market and Third Streets, with a northern Baroque pitched roof and dormers, is the original Citizen's Savings building (Fig. 1, map location P) by William Curlett, 1902. This steel-frame, limestone-clad building survived the earthquake and was repaired and reopened in 1906. In 1964, the architects Clark and Beuttler, together with Charles Moore and Alan Morgan, created a tasteful addition to the building. Directly across the street, on the southeast corner of Third, is the Hearst building (Fig. 1, map location Q) by Kirby, Petit, and Green, built in 1909. This Mission-style building followed A.C. Schweinfurth's pre-earthquake design. It was built with special, deep sprandrel girders to be earthquake-resistant, according to the literature of the time.

The Chronicle building (Fig. 1, map location R; Figs. 15 and 16), designed by the Chicago firm of Burnham and Root, was the first seismically resistant skyscraper in San Francisco. The Chronicle building, in the heart of downtown, was an obvious bid by the paper's owner, Michael de Young, to dominate San Francisco's skyline to the same extent he had attempted to mold its public opinion. In 1888, he commissioned Burnham and Root to erect a signature building that would dwarf its neighbors and clearly indicate a center of power in the city. They responded by designing the building to take advantage of its location at the junction of Kearny, Third, and Market Streets, the busiest intersection in downtown San Francisco. The building's rusticated Richardson Romanesque stone façade rose ten stories to a clock tower which, at 218 ft, was taller than the proposed tower for the still incomplete City Hall.

It is remarkable that this first steel-and-iron-frame building in the West was not a copy of buildings constructed in New York or Chicago, but conceived as a uniquely San Franciscan structure, built specifically to resist earthquakes. The *Chronicle* explained it to its readers: "With the knowledge…that earthquakes of more or less severity may shake the city, Messrs. Burnham and Root have been obliged to make special provisions in the lofty Chronicle structure, and have thus added to the strength such features of construction as are not found in Eastern buildings of the same class" (1890, p. 2).

Like the experimental buildings going up in New York and Chicago in the late 1880s, the Chronicle building was unique; it pushed the technological envelope. Load-bearing masonry walls are extremely heavy, and, wary of adding too much weight to the ten-story building, Burnham and Root had framed the clock tower in wood. The combination of load-bearing walls and an iron-and-steel support cage was touted by the *Chronicle* as being particularly effective:

The stonework and brickwork carry but little load other than that of the walls in the construction of which they are used. The labor is divided. The steel cage, which the walls surround, carries the weight of floors and roofs, and the walls in turn afford support and protection to the upright columns of the cage, and in this way there is mutual support and protection to the upright columns of the cage, and also to an extent independence. (1890, p. 2)

In the transitional moment in which the Chronicle building was created, Burnham and Root chose the most appropriate technological solution at their disposal. How could they build the Chronicle building to resist the lateral forces of earthquakes, which up to this time had not been calculated? This took them back to the earthquake-resistant solutions of the 1870s. They seized upon bond iron and straps, both of which had proven effective in San Francisco, wrapping them around the entire exterior of the building. To further stiffen and strengthen the walls, there were four flat bands of quarter-inch steel built inside the exterior walls around the entire structure. One of these bands was five inches wide and the other three were each two inches wide. They were placed at varying heights between floor and ceiling and at varying distances horizontally from the outer surfaces of the walls, so no two straps were set directly over one another.

Having attempted to stabilize the exterior masonry wall, Burnham and Root turned their attention to the interior skeleton. The Chronicle building's footprint looked like an irregular, bent "I." They were particularly concerned that the floors of the building would lose their integrity as planes or diaphragms, and distort and collapse the skeleton. They understood, as many architects of our own time have forgotten, that asymmetrical, irregular shapes or configurations are dangerous in earthquakes because they complicate load paths and introduce torsion or twisting. They chose to stabilize the interior frame by using a system of diagonal steel straps to help the building work as a unit if swayed in an earthquake:

Figure 15. The Fidelity Savings/old Chronicle building being stripped of its sheathing, 2005.

At every floor…there is, in addition to all the steel beams and the rods necessary to this construction, a system of diagonal bracing with steel straps which find place in no other building of its class. These braces have been introduced to prevent the lateral racking and dislocation which an earthquake of great force might bring….At each intersection of one strap with another a bolt is passed through them, and at every place where a beam is crossed by a strap they are bolted together. On each floor there is thus arranged a steel net. (*San Francisco Chronicle*, 1890, p. 2)

The idea behind these experimental earthquake-resistant features, to tie the building together so it would move as a unit, was sound. But the irregular configuration (or footprint of the plan) of the Chronicle building introduced a level of complexity into the forces affecting the building that could not be corrected through strapping. Within three years, Burnham and Root themselves, along with their colleagues, would invent more effective methods for combating the problems associated with lateral forces.

The Chronicle building was already too cramped for the paper in 1906 and an addition, the Chronicle Annex, was under construction north of the original building when the earthquake struck. The Chronicle building's trademark clock tower had burned in a fire the year before. The old Chronicle building and the Annex survived the 1906 earthquake, but the fire burned

702 700 GEARY ST. KEARNY ST. CHRONICLE BUILDING, ELEVATOR 652 640 638 634 632 630 628 624

Figure 16. The Chronicle building as it appeared in 1895 (courtesy of the Bancroft Library, University of California–Berkeley).

fiercely enough to collapse the old Chronicle building's floors. The outer shell of the old building was preserved and incorporated into the new building, which included the Annex. The red brick Richardson Romanesque of the original building was matched in the Annex. The red brick contrasted with the cream and gray tile work being erected in the buildings around them. They are survivors from an earlier pre-earthquake style, far from the corporate modern aesthetic preferences of the 1950s and 1960s. Fidelity Savings, which owned the building, decided to cover this old-fashioned façade with plastic and glass sheathing which has hidden the original façade for more than thirty years. Now a new owner is stripping off the sheathing, exposing the beautifully worked stone moldings and brick walls of the structure.

STOP 10: MARKET STREET BETWEEN THIRD AND FOURTH STREETS—WELLS FARGO BANK, SAVINGS UNION BANK, AND THE PHELAN BUILDING

The walk next turns west on Market Street toward Twin Peaks in the distance. From Third to Fourth Streets, the buildings of the new, post-earthquake San Francisco can be seen on both sides of the street. Although Daniel Burnham's Parisian plan for the new San Francisco, with diagonal streets and circular hubs, failed to be implemented after 1906, the new San Francisco was an elegant collection of buildings that related to one another because they were informed by Ecole aesthetics. On the right side, at the intersection of Grant, O'Farrell, and Market Streets, is a superb ensemble of façades, all constructed

in the Ecole des Beaux Arts style and related to one another in their careful detailing, scale, and classical vocabulary. On the corner to the right, at the northeast corner of Grant Avenue, is the elegant Wells Fargo Bank (Fig. 1, map location S), originally Union Trust Co. designed by Clinton Day. Across the street is a store occupying the former Security Pacific Bank, originally Savings Union Bank (Fig. 1, map location T), designed by Bliss and Faville, 1910, and modeled on the Roman Pantheon. They are complemented by the façade of the Phelan building, on the gore (or triangular block) of Market and O'Farrell Streets at Grant.

The Phelan building (Fig. 1, map location U), a terracotta-clad, steel-frame building, was commissioned by James D. Phelan, designed by architect William Curlett and engineer Paul L. Wolfel, and erected in 1908. The triangular ground plan of the structure, on a block of Market Street between O'Farrell and Grant Streets, as well as its sand foundations and its eleven-story height, forced Phelan, Curlett, and Wolfel, of the American Bridge Company of Pittsburgh, to sink deep pile foundations and to bind the steel cage of the building together with particularly deep girders, to adequately absorb and transfer lateral forces. The asymmetrical plan of the structure called for a complicated system of cross bracing that included longitudinal tie-rods, similar in function to those in Burnham and Root's pre-earthquake Chronicle building. An article on the building states that the complicated problem of designing the structure was solved by the architect and engineer working in unison. The façade is a tour de force of shaped terracotta ornament, the perfect substitute for stone given its scarcity in California and its poor performance in earthquakes. The sheen of the terra-cotta, which destroys any illusion that the façade is stone, adds to its interest by making it bright and reflective.

STOP 11: MARKET NEAR FOURTH STREET— HUMBOLDT SAVINGS BANK BUILDING

We continue the walk west on Market Street and see to the left the tower of the Humboldt Savings Bank building, 1906–1908 (Fig. 1, map location V; Fig. 17). The architect of this building was Frederick H. Meyer, and the engineer was Christopher Snyder. This building was in construction when the earthquake struck. Its architect and engineer redesigned it because of the lessons they had learned in the earthquake and fire. Meyer, a principal in the firm Meyer and O'Brien, was a native San Franciscan who had never received a degree in architecture, and in fact had no formal education after the age of fourteen. He learned about construction by working on build-ings and about aesthetics and design through one of San Fran-cisco's architectural clubs.

Meyer was no doubt aided in making structural decisions by Christopher H. Snyder, the contracting engineer for the West Coast office of Milliken Brothers Steel Company. Snyder, a native of Illinois, designed buildings for Milliken Brothers between 1902 and 1912. Like most engineers working in San Francisco until around 1913, Snyder did not have an office of his own but worked with a steel manufacturer. Architects sent their drawings either to the manufacturer or to the local repre-sentative, who would do the calculations, design the steelwork, and then return the drawings. Snyder had attended the post-earthquake meetings of the Structural Association of San Fran-cisco and coauthored the definitive earthquake report for the American Society of Civil Engineers. He wrote several articles endorsing strong lateral bracing for steel frames. After 1912, he established his own office in the city and was one of the most prolific and influential engineers in San Francisco.

Because the Humboldt Savings Bank building was in the early stages of construction when the earthquake hit, it could have been erected without a new building permit. Here was a chance for speedy reconstruction with no intervention from city building officials. The original design of the façade remained unchanged, following Beaux Arts principles. A beautifully articulated Classical entrance led into the lobby of the narrow building, with the Humboldt Savings Bank on the left and the entrance to the office building on the right. Above the ground floor, sixteen floors of offices with repetitive windows were tied together by banded pilasters (shallow piers or rectangular columns projecting slightly from the wall), culminating in an elaborate Baroque dome. The Humboldt Savings Bank dome intentionally mimicked the larger Call building dome several blocks east on Market Street, providing a second vertical marker to establish the primacy of the street. Meyer had been very much affected by the poor performance of his earlier projects, like the Rialto building, the Monadnock building, and the Hahnemann Hospital, and he made changes in the Humboldt because of the failures he had seen.

The foundation for the Humboldt Savings Bank had been under construction on 18 April 1906, and the contractor, George Wagner, was ready to begin the steelwork. Although the foun-dation was not damaged in the earthquake, the shock and subse-quent fire altered Meyer's conception of the structure. The artistic design of the façade remained the same, but he drew large red X's over structural drawings and wrote "VOID" on them, changing many features of the original design to make the building safer. He and Snyder stiffened the building, altered its foundation, changed brick walls to concrete, and incorpo-rated many new fire-control techniques and devices. These were not casual changes, but related directly to failures in Meyer's own buildings.

The Humboldt Savings Bank building was tall (244 ft) and slender (50 ft at its smallest width, on Market Street), requiring special reinforcement. The front portion, on the Market Street side, ended in an elaborate tower topped by a dome above its seventeenth floor, while the office block behind was thirteen floors. The narrow tower was designed to be carried on a steel frame, which was braced along its width by sprandrel girders and knee braces (Fig. 18). To further strengthen the structure, the steel columns were spliced at alternate floors. These two-floor runs, it was hoped, would help the structure retain its integrity if pushed from side to side. There is no corresponding spandrel or knee bracing in the length of the building, presumably because it was felt that the reinforced concrete curtain wall, combined with the strength of the steel, could handle the load.

Originally, the narrow tower of the Humboldt Savings Bank was to be made of brick and stone, but seeing the poor performance of these two materials in the earthquake and fire, Meyer changed to concrete on the entire exterior: plain on the sides and rear, and a concrete backing for the stone and terra-cotta veneer on the front. Colusa sandstone, which proved very vulnerable to spalling—breaking off in chips—in fire, stopped at the third floor, and the terracotta veneer continued up the rest of the building.

Meyer took great care in regard to fire safety, which he often promoted through talks and articles. He used virtually every available fire-fighting precaution that could be adapted to San Francisco's situation (Fig. 19). The columns of the building were protected by concrete. The floors, originally specified to be hollow tile, were reinforced concrete. Meyer used metal trim, which was about twice the cost of first-grade oak. In fact, he took care to design all exterior surfaces to be incombustible. The exterior windows in the light court were protected by wire glass. Wire glass is exceptionally thick and incorporates a "chicken wire" membrane that ensures that if the glass cracks, it will not shatter and loosen from the frame.

Elevators are a hazard in fires because their shafts can act as flues. In successive drawings made between 31 March and 22 December 1906, Meyer progressively isolated his elevator shafts by cutting them off from the rest of the building with

Figure 17. The Humboldt Bank building tower, 2005.

automatic "underwriters' doors." Two of these tin-clad doors with heat-sensitive releases adjoined the elevator core. If fire broke out, they automatically closed, isolating the whole elevator core. The elevator core was of concrete with metal covering over all wooden surfaces. Even the draft up the isolated stairwell was reduced: a note dated 9 April 1906, directing "all risers except those of main flight from first to mezzanine and those from 17th to 18th to be perforated" was rescinded. All the risers were solid in the final drawings, so air could not filter through them and provide draft for fires (source: drawings for the Hum-

boldt Bank building, Environmental Design Archives, University of California at Berkeley).

The whole building had a system of standpipes and hoses on each floor, supplied not by gravity but by a pneumatic pump and tank in the basement. Meyer saw that standard roof tanks were dangerous in earthquakes because they sometimes fell from their supports onto the building. Even if this catastrophe were averted, they often shook loose from their connections. Meyer's solution was novel for San Francisco. He opened wells in the basement so that if the Spring Valley Water Company pipes failed, the building would have its own supply, which could be pumped directly from its wells. If the pneumatic pump failed, a special backup "underwriters' pump" could be pressed into action. These precautions were expensive, but in a sense they paid for themselves: the Humboldt Savings Bank was able to save 47% on its fire insurance because of its fireproofing and fire-fighting system.

In both its seismic design and its fire-resistant qualities, the Humboldt Savings Bank building was outstanding for its day. Despite earlier failures and a limited education, Meyer was able to rise to the expectations of his clients with a handsome, towered structure that could resist both earthquake and fire.

STOP 12: WEST FROM MARKET AND FOURTH— PACIFIC BUILDING, WEST BANK BUILDING, AND THE FLOOD BUILDING

The last section of the walk goes west on Market to the southwest corner of Market and Fourth Streets. Here is the green façade of the Pacific Building (Fig. 1, map location W, now occupied by Old Navy), purported to have been the largest reinforced concrete building in the world when it was built in 1907. The architect of the building, Charles F. Whittlesey of Los Angeles, was one of the leaders of the Mission Revival movement, inspired by the missions of California. His railroad station in Albuquerque, New Mexico, was praised by the *Architect and Engineer* as "one of the purest examples of modern mission architecture" (Corbett, 1979, p. 89). In San Francisco, however, he designed a huge concrete structure idiosyncratically decorated with rust, green, cream, and yellow tiles and decorative terracotta sculpture inspired by the work of architect Louis Sullivan. Whittlesey (1908, p. 45) justified his choice of colors in the *Architect and Engineer*: "The climate of our city is decidedly gray and this is accentuated all about town, especially in the large buildings by the use of a peculiarly gloomy stone of a disagreeable yellowish gray color that catches and absorbs much of the smudge carried on the winds."

Reinforced concrete was just being accepted as a building material in the United States when the earthquake struck in 1906. The Romans had pioneered the development of concrete and brick structures, but during the Middle Ages, the technique of making strong concrete had been lost. Only in the nineteenth century had engineers and architects reinvented concrete mixtures and made concrete more durable in tension by adding steel reinforcement, rebar. Architects and engineers were still experimenting with the correct mixtures and reinforcement of concrete when the Pacific building was constructed. The inside of the Pacific building was completely of concrete, not concrete protecting structural steel columns. Unlike some earlier concrete structures, which depended on cement and forms made in the eastern United States, the Pacific building was built of California cement. According to an article published in *Construction News* (Kenyon, 1907, p. 113), much of the construction method was devised at the job site: "The reinforcing system has

Figure 18. The Humboldt Bank building, frame (courtesy of the Bancroft Library, University of California–Berkeley).

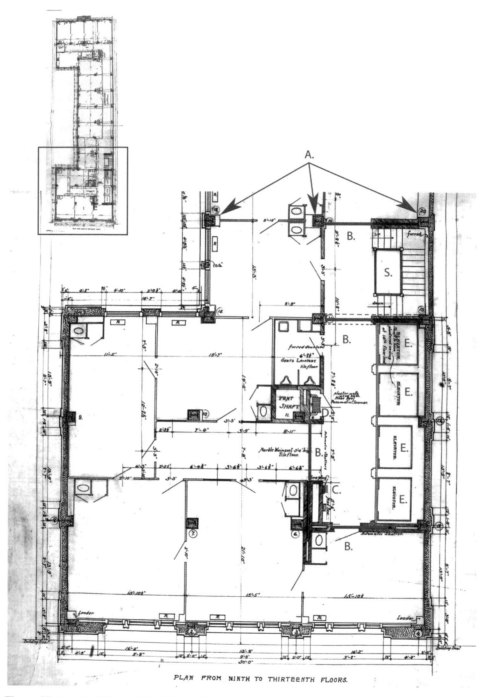

PLAN FROM NINTH TO THIRTEENTH FLOORS.

Figure 19. A typical floor of the Humboldt Bank building (courtesy of the Environmental Design Archives, University of California–Berkeley). A—concrete around steel columns; B—automatic fire doors; C—fire standpipe and plug; D—fire hose; E—elevator shafts; S—stairwells.

been devised on the spot by the builder, whose ample experience elsewhere in this class of buildings has been brought into service in the present undertaking. All of the major steel rods, three-fourths of an inch in diameter, are of the spiral twist pattern. They are twisted cold, and this process is conducted on the premises, being applied as a test to every rod used."

Using this new technology, stairs and walls could be formed into a reinforced concrete unit, cantilevers were possible without permanent underpinning, and a structure could be erected that would incorporate few burnable surfaces. The building was seen as a cast unit, a series of flexible yet integral wedded parts that could ride out an earthquake. As Whittlesey (1908, p. 45) said:

In the argument for durability, reinforced concrete is in a class by itself. As far as the elements are concerned, it is practically indestructible. It is by far the most rigid and freest from vibration of any construction known. The steel sinews forming the reinforcement give to the concrete sufficient elasticity to withstand admirably the strains produced by earthquakes, and with the ample bracket connections between columns and floor beams which this method supplies, it would require a greater shock than California has experienced since the coming of the Padres to produce in it any sign of failure. Even though it were strained to the extent of producing cracks, the strength of the structure would be but little impaired, because of the reinforcing metal.

The placement of steel rebar in the concrete and the design of the concrete members were at the heart of the strength and durability of Whittlesey's buildings. And indeed, cross sections illustrating the placement of reinforcing bars in early concrete structures, as in Whittlesey's Bartell building, indicate a solid understanding of how to design strong column and floor connections. But the concrete in this building was of varying quality, and when it was retrofitted, the engineers decided to gut the inside, replace the reinforced concrete with steel, and only save the exterior façade. Nevertheless the Pacific building, and the remodeled West Bank building (800–830 Market: across the street) of 1908, also by Whittlesey, illustrate the important part reinforced concrete played in the reconstruction of San Francisco after the earthquake of 1906.

The tour ends here. From this viewpoint, we can see many more fascinating San Francisco buildings. The Flood building by Albert Pissis, 1904, to the northwest, survived the earthquake of 1906. Cracks in the tremendous brick rear façade of the building are scars that are reminders of the earthquakes (1906, 1989) that it has survived. Looking back (east) down Market Street, the steel-frame Ferry building tower (designed by A. Page Brown, 1893–1903) survived the 1906 earthquake as well. It was designed to resist earthquakes and barely survived the 1906 earthquake. It was retrofitted with a new, seismically resistant cladding of reinforced concrete and its steel skeleton strengthened. All along the walk is evidence of how individual architects and engineers confronted both earthquakes and fires; the building community was conscious of the danger and built as safely as it could, making San Francisco architecture unique in early twentieth-century America.

REFERENCES CITED

Brunnier, H.J., 1956, Development of aseismic construction in the United States, *in* Proceedings of the World Conference on Earthquake Engineering, June 1956: Berkeley, Earthquake Engineering Research Institute, p. 26-2.

Corbett, M., 1979, Splendid survivors: San Francisco's downtown architectural heritage: San Francisco, California Living Books, 271 p.

Kenyon, W.J., 1907, Concrete in San Francisco: Construction News, v. 24 (17 August), p. 113.

Lipe, D.J., 1926, Argonaut, 10 July, p. 2.

San Francisco Chronicle, 1890, The Chronicle's new home: 22 June 1890, p. 2.

Tobriner, S., 2006, Bracing for disaster; earthquake-resistant architecture and engineering, San Francisco, 1838–1933: Berkeley, Heyday Press and the Bancroft Library, in press.

Whittlesey, C.F., 1908, Reinforced concrete construction—why I believe in it: Architect and Engineer, v. 12 (March), p. 45.

Returning a San Francisco icon to the city: The renovation of the Ferry building

Alan Kren

Rutherford & Chekene Consulting Engineers, 55 Second Street, San Francisco, California 94105, USA

OVERVIEW OF FIELD TRIP

This trip will visit the Ferry building, a classic icon of San Francisco that has recently been retrofitted to withstand the strong shaking from an earthquake. The building suffered moderate damage in the 1906 earthquake and only minor damage in the 1989 Loma Prieta earthquake.

Keywords: Historic renovation, barrel-arched truss, seismic retrofit, ferry travel.

STOP 1: FERRY BUILDING

Significance of the Site

The 1994 film "Interview with a Vampire" opens with an aerial shot east toward the Golden Gate Bridge, then rapidly travels over the San Francisco Bay before orienting west for a bird's-eye view of the city. Center-screen sits an illuminated sign mounted on the roof of a long Beaux Arts building, its tall red letters announcing that this is the Port of San Francisco. Behind the sign stands a slender tower, the clock on each face of the tower giving the time. The building, the tower, and the clocks are all parts of the Ferry building, a San Francisco icon, which ties the city to the San Francisco Bay. The Ferry building is a historic building that has recently been retrofit.

Accessibility

The Ferry building houses many shops and restaurants on the ground floor, which are publicly accessible during business hours. Parking is not readily available, but the Ferry building is accessible by Bay Area Rapid Transit (BART), by ferry, and by municipal bus.

Directions

The Ferry building is located at the eastern end of Market Street (Fig. 1). From Moscone Center, go north on Third Street, turn right on Market, and follow Market to its end.

Stop Description

History

By the last decade of the nineteenth century, San Francisco had grown into a bustling coastal city. Responding to the need to organize and improve ferry service across the bay, the citizens of the State of California passed, by a slim 900 votes, a bond initiative in 1892 to construct a ferry terminal at the base of Market Street. Architect A. Page Brown was commissioned to design the terminal and, following a research trip to Europe, he returned to California to draw up detailed concept plans (Fig. 2). His plan was accepted by the state port commission largely unchanged, though large portals at the north and south ends of the building were "value engineered" out as too expensive. Pile driving and construction of the concrete deck over the bay began in 1893, and by 1898, the building was open to the public.

The building and its ferry docks served as the hub for transport across the bay. Up until the construction of the Golden Gate Bridge and the Bay Bridge in the 1930s, the only way to cross the bay was by boat, and the ferries that crossed the bay docked at the Ferry building. Market Street at the Embarcadero bustled with activity as commuters passed through the area on their way to work. With the completion of the Bay Bridge came a decline in ferry travel, and with that, the slow decline of activity through the Ferry building. In the 1950s and 1960s, the large open interiors of the building were broken up into offices, and a third floor was inserted into the building. Concurrent to the utility conversion was the construction of the Embarcadero freeway

Kren, A., 2006, Returning a San Francisco icon to the city: The renovation of the Ferry building, *in* Prentice, C.S., Scotchmoor, J.G., Moores, E.M., and Kiland, J.P., eds., 1906 San Francisco Earthquake Centennial Field Guides: Field trips associated with the 100th Anniversary Conference, 18–23 April 2006, San Francisco, California: Geological Society of America Field Guide 7, p. 57–66, doi: 10.1130/2006.1906SF(04). For permission to copy, contact editing@geosociety.org.

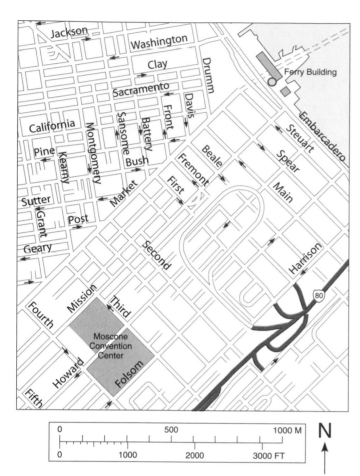

(1957), which cut off the waterfront from the city center. The building then experienced a slow decline, and by 1989 was largely forgotten and unappreciated.

Rebirth

The 1989 Loma Prieta earthquake collapsed a portion of the Cypress freeway, a "double decker" freeway with a design similar to that of other freeways around the Bay Area, including the Embarcadero freeway, the freeway that ran directly in front of the Ferry building. The Embarcadero was demolished rather than retrofitted, and where there had been a structure that divided the city from the bay, there is now a broad palm-lined boulevard. The bay is now visible to the city, and the buildings bordering it have been returned to San Francisco. But by the time this happened, the use of the waterfront had changed. Historically, the waterfront had been a working port, serving a fishing fleet and cargo ships. The fishing fleet had largely moved, and cargo ships now berthed in Oakland. The Port of San Francisco, owner of the waterfront, embarked on a process of reinvigorating and redeveloping the port, and the Ferry building was redeveloped as part of this process. Its redevelopment cleared away many years of disparate remodeling efforts and restored the building to its original character. Gone is the maze of hallways and partition walls and the stuffed-in third floor; in their place is a coherent, open building flooded with natural light from the sky-lit monitor above. The original barrel-arched trusses framing the central bay (Fig. 3) are again exposed to public view, and the grandeur of the building can again be appreciated by the public.

A Brief History of Earthquakes

Damage to the building from the great earthquake of 1906 (Fig. 4) was concentrated to the sandstone cladding the tower and the building's façade. Sandstone fell off at the base of the tower, at the juncture with the roof, and sandstone cladding the

Figure 1. Vicinity map showing the location of the Ferry building highlighted in yellow at the bottom of Market Street. The transbay Bay Area Rapid Transit tube can be seen almost bisecting the building (dashed lines).

Figure 2. An illustration of the original concept plan for the building by A. Page Brown. The large portals on each end of the building were removed from the final design because they were too expensive (courtesy of Port of San Francisco Archives).

Figure 3. The Grand Nave that runs the full 660 ft length of the building. The lightness of the barrel arch trusses is apparent, and the central sky-lit monitor illuminates the space. The diagonal members made of flat plates are tension-only plate diagonals, a few of which buckled during the Loma Prieta earthquake and were subsequently strengthened. (Photo courtesy Rutherford and Chekene Consulting Engineers).

building façade chipped, cracked, and moved out-of-plane. Photographs clearly show cladding missing from the tower, and detailed repair drawings note areas of damaged stone as concentrated in pier corners. In response, all the stone was removed from the tower and replaced with reinforced concrete. Stone at the façade was replaced or repaired.

The 1989 Loma Prieta earthquake caused limited damage to the barrel-arch trusses when shaking buckled tension-only plate diagonals temporarily loaded in compression. Buckled truss diagonals were strengthened along with a seismic retrofit to the building. A number of the concrete shear walls constructed as part of the seismic retrofit were preserved in the building's renovation.

An interesting note is the building's performance in both of these earthquakes and, in particular, the 1906 earthquake. In each case, damage was moderate and might be in part explained by the interaction, or lack of interaction, of the building with the massive concrete deck on which it sits. This is further discussed later in this paper.

Building Description

The building consists of three elements (see Fig. 5): (1) a massive double-barrel, or groined-arch, concrete deck founded on more than 5000 wooden piles driven 80 ft into bay mud; (2) a three-story steel frame with concrete-floor-slab building;

Figure 4. A classic photograph of San Francisco in flames, with the largely undamaged Ferry building in the foreground (courtesy of Bancroft Library, University of California–Berkeley).

Figure 5. Building cross section illustrating the proportions of the building elements. The long yellow elements represent wooden piers driven into bay mud capped by the groined-arch concrete deck. Above them sits the steel-frame building. Note the light trusses framing the roof. San Francisco is to the left and the bay is to the right (courtesy of Rutherford and Chekene Consulting Engineers).

and (3) a 230-ft-tall steel-framed tower. The concrete deck on which the building is perched is essentially unreinforced and relies on its mass and arching action for structural integrity. Ground-floor columns are cast iron founded on granite bases set on leveling grout. Rolled steel sections shipped from the East Coast frame the building and tower above the ground floor. The building is large in plan, measuring 152 × 660 ft, or large enough to fit two football fields plus goal posts. The tower measures 32 × 30 ft in plan, though it feels much larger in person. Light steel trusses support a wood-framed roof. The building is symmetric about its transverse axis, a gift to the structural engineer in designing a seismic force–resisting system, and to the contractor in understanding the building's construction. An interesting side note is the transbay BART tube that runs under the building (see Fig. 1). Construction of the tube in the 1960s necessitated coring through the field of wooden piles supporting the building and providing a new pile foundation system bridging the tube.

Of interest are the gravity connections (see Fig. 6) in the original construction. Connections were made without welds and employed plates, bolts, and angles in ingenious configurations to transfer gravity forces. The original lateral force–resisting system, on the other hand, was less than ideal and consisted of brick infill walls and piers located throughout the building. The numerous remodeling projects that occurred throughout the life of the building each have added their own variation to the lateral force–resisting system, resulting in a less than coherent or balanced system. One of the goals of the renovation was to provide the building with a coherent and balanced system (Fig. 7).

Historic Character

The Ferry building is on the National Historic Register as a historic building. Registration required that its renovation preserve its historic character and, therefore, that the lateral force–resisting system not appear out-of-place or disruptive to the building's character. This, the preponderance of existing brick infill walls, and the existing concrete shear walls, preserved from prior seismic upgrading, led to the use of a concrete shear-wall solution for the lateral force–resisting system.

Figure 6. Photograph illustrating gravity connection. Cabling is temporary lateral bracing installed during construction (courtesy of Rutherford and Chekene Consulting Engineers).

Arches play a significant role in the building's architecture; the regularity of their rhythm on the building exterior and interior defines much of the sense of the building. Elongated concrete wall and frame elements (see Figs. 8, 9, and 10) that provided resistance to lateral forces and preserved the openness of the archways were integrated into the length of the building interior. Finally, concrete collectors were fit into the webs of existing steel beams, in some cases requiring demolition of existing concrete fire proofing, but ultimately providing a coherent load path while preserving historic character.

Because the building is on the national register, the State Historic Building Code can be used as the governing code. This code permits two very important exceptions to the California Building Code: the first is that historic and archaic materials can be used if the structural engineer observes that they are in good condition and do not exhibit signs of distress, and the sec-ond is that the magnitude of the seismic base shear used to design the lateral force–resisting system can be reduced to 75% of "code level" shear. The first exception recognizes that the capacity of historic structural elements often cannot be calculated due to uncertainty of material properties and building construction, while the second recognizes that renovation of historic buildings to current code level is well nigh impossible without destroying the historic character and fabric of the building. It also recognizes that properly done, a historic renovation can provide life safety at reduced-force levels.

Geotechnical Considerations

The San Francisco Bay Area is widely known as a seismically active region, and two major faults, the San Andreas fault and the Hayward fault, lie ~9.5 mi to the west and east of this site, respectively. Ground shaking from these two faults and from the Calaveras fault, 21.5 mi to the east, presents the most significant earthquake hazards at the site. Treadwell and Rollo Geotechnical Engineers developed a site-specific elastic design response spectrum for the site for a maximum probable earthquake and a maximum credible earthquake. These spectra served as the basis for the seismic design.

Bay water moves freely under the deck of the Ferry building, which shouldn't be surprising considering that the building original served as a ferry terminal, which required that it be built out into the bay. Soil under the water consists of ~100 ft of very soft clay known as bay mud. Underlying the bay mud is a layer of dense sand, ~20 ft thick, and under that lays a thick, stiff clay layer. The deck is founded on more than 5000 Douglas fir piles that extend ~80 ft into the bay mud. The piles were found to be in excellent condition due to the anaerobic conditions of the bay mud.

Building Behavior

The three distinct building elements (massive deck, building, and tower) posed the question of how these elements interacted, and a dynamic analysis provided the answer. The deck is massive in comparison to the building and the tower; its weight accounts for more than 75% of the combined weight of the three, and it is founded on wood piles in bay mud. The piles in fact do not reach down to stiff sands, but by virtue of their numbers they have supported all of the structure for more than 100 years. The building is short and stiff, and the tower is tall and relatively stiff due to being clad in concrete. The dynamic analysis revealed that the deck had a fundamental period of vibration of 2.2 s, the building had a fundamental period of vibration 0.2 s, and the tower had a fundamental period of vibration of 0.7 s. In essence, the three elements could be considered separately: the building and tower responded to the movement of the deck, while the deck responded to the movement of the earth. The dynamic analysis also provided the relative magnitude of accelerations at the building floors and, unsurprisingly, revealed that they were somewhat different than a code distribution.

A. Kren

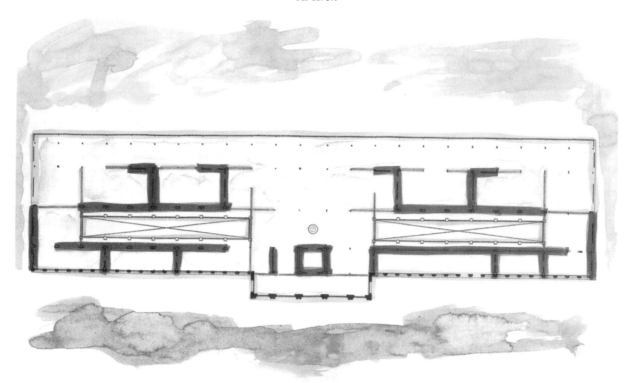

Figure 7. Diagrammatic plan of the first floor. Shear walls and wall frames are shown in pink; collector elements are shown in yellow. North is to the left, and the Embarcadero is below. Note how the near symmetry of the lateral force–resisting system matches the building's symmetry. The base of the tower is the square at the center front of the building. The main entrances to the building flank the tower (courtesy Rutherford and Chekene Consulting Engineers).

Figure 8. Illustration of the concrete wall frames located along the Grand Nave and configured to preserve the building's historic character (courtesy of Rutherford and Chekene Consulting Engineers).

Figure 9. Reinforcement for a concrete wall frame. Note the existing steel framing intersecting the top of the pier. Reinforcement for concrete collector beams can be seen at the top of the photo. Collector beams were built into the web of existing steel wide flanges. The golden brick arches of the third floor are the finished faces of the wall-frame elements (courtesy of Rutherford and Chekene Consulting Engineers).

At this point, the seismic retrofit became three different tasks:

1. Check that the piles supporting the deck could undergo the lateral translations resulting from the maximum credible earthquake without failing. Their movement was extracted from the dynamic analysis, and their capacity to withstand the resulting moments and shears was calculated using their ultimate material capacities. (An extensive condition assessment and material testing program had been undertaken by the port in the 1980s, and the results from this program, as well as a testing program undertaken at the time of the project, were used throughout the life of the project.) Fortunately, the piles could withstand the translation, because it was not economically feasible to correct such a deficiency.

2. Design a retrofit of the building as if the building were founded on the earth using a static analysis of the building, but with the relative magnitude of the story forces based on the results of the dynamic analysis.

3. Design a retrofit of the tower as if the tower were founded on the earth using a dynamic analysis of the building.

In order to limit damage and interaction between the deck and surrounding piers, an expansion joint surrounds the building on three sides. It can be seen as the flat metal plate between the building and the surrounding piers on the north, south, and east sides of the building.

Design and Construction Challenges

The fundamental difference between design and construction of new buildings versus the renovation of existing buildings is that in new buildings the designer decides what is required and designs it, while at existing buildings the designer decides what is required and then designs something that can be built given all of the existing structural and nonstructural elements already in place (Fig. 11). This challenge can lead to interesting or unusual solutions, such as using a #3 reinforcing bar when doweling into the edge of a four inch concrete slab to ensure there is sufficient edge distance, because a hole for a larger bar might well blow out the slab edge. At times, capacity design principles are used to ensure that preferred yielding mechanisms occur. Both of these strategies (and others) were employed in the renovation; the latter was used when strengthening existing roof trusses to act as collectors. The force level used to strengthen the trusses was determined based on the capacity of the wooden diaphragm delivering force to the trusses, and the trusses were strengthened to elastically transfer this load. This is a very useful design method, as the designer can ensure that the gravity-supporting roof truss will not fail when acting as part of the seismic force–resisting system.

As mentioned previously, renovation of historic buildings presents further challenges in that structural intervention must be compatible with the historic fabric of the building. Design is often governed not by what is structurally most advantageous, but what can be built within the framework of historic preservation. What might seem an otherwise undesirable detail is the only acceptable detail as it preserves historic fabric (Figs. 12 and 13). And finally, it should be mentioned that renovation can involve a tremendous amount of demolition, so much so that the structural engineer is left wondering exactly what is holding the building up during construction. It is at such times that the skills of the shoring engineer are greatly appreciated (Fig. 14).

CONCLUSIONS

While renovation of historic buildings presents unique challenges to the structural engineer, the real key to a successful project is teamwork on the part of all the design and construc-

Figure 10. The brick-faced arches at the upper level highlight concrete wall-frame elements, which are part of the lateral force–resisting system. These wall-frame elements continue to the foundation level. When walking along the Grand Nave, you are also walking over bay water (courtesy of SMWM Architects).

Figure 11. Existing construction can complicate details. In this photo, an existing steel beam is engulfed by concrete collector reinforcement. This beam was an unusual condition, and it was necessary to design around it in order to maintain continuity in the collector alignment, as well as work within the space allotted to the structure by the architect (courtesy of Rutherford and Chekene Consulting Engineers).

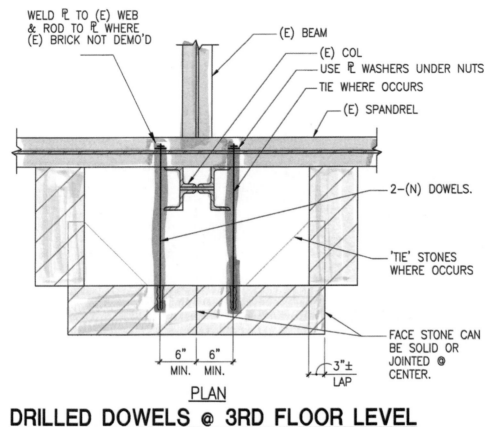

WELD ℞ TO (E) WEB
& ROD TO ℞ WHERE
(E) BRICK NOT DEMO'D

(E) BEAM

(E) COL

USE ℞ WASHERS UNDER NUTS

TIE WHERE OCCURS

(E) SPANDREL

2-(N) DOWELS.

'TIE' STONES
WHERE OCCURS

FACE STONE CAN
BE SOLID OR
JOINTED @
CENTER.

6" MIN.   6" MIN.

3"±
LAP

PLAN

DRILLED DOWELS @ 3RD FLOOR LEVEL

Figure 12. Plan detail of stone-cladding anchorage. This detail was developed to anchor the stone cladding to the building without the anchorage being visible from outside the building (courtesy of Rutherford and Chekene Consulting Engineers).

Figure 13. Compare the actual installation of the stone-cladding anchorage to the detail. What appears a neat and clean installation on paper requires a tremendous amount of effort (courtesy of Rutherford and Chekene Consulting Engineers).

Figure 14. This photo illustrates the amount of demolition that was required to renovate the building. Building remodeling in the 1960s had transformed this elevation into an almost-blank concrete wall. The concrete was removed in order to reconstruct the exterior into something in keeping with the historic character of the building. Lateral stability was provided through as system of interior cross braces made of cables. Figure 6 shows the top of one such cable looped around the top of a column (courtesy of Rutherford and Chekene Consulting Engineers).

tion disciplines. In this, the project was extremely fortunate, as all members of the design and contractor teams worked well together (Fig. 15). Problems that arose due to unforeseen conditions, and there are many unforeseen conditions in renovation, were worked out collaboratively with concerns of all parties considered and addressed. The final product of this effort can be seen in the building today.

ACKNOWLEDGMENTS

Wilson Equity Office: Developer; Wilson Meany: Developer; SMWM: Architect; Baldauf Catton Von Eckartsberg: Retail Architect; Page and Turnbull: Preservation Architect; Rutherford and Chekene: Structural Engineer; Olivia Chan: Civil Engineer; Plant Construction: Contractor.

Figure 15. Photograph of the crew and design team. The pride in their work can be sensed from their attention to the photographer. (Photo courtesy of Rutherford and Chekene Consulting Engineers.)

Geological Society of America
Field Guide 7
2006

Ninth District U.S. Court of Appeals, San Francisco, California

Peter Lee
Skidmore, Owings & Merrill LLP, One Front Street, San Francisco, California 94111, USA

OVERVIEW OF FIELD TRIP

This field trip consists of one location stop and a building tour of the 1996 historic rehabilitation and seismic retrofit of the Ninth District U.S. Court of Appeals building in San Francisco. This field guide provides an overview of the building's significant historic features, a brief presentation on the history of the facility, and a summary of the historic rehabilitation and seismic retrofit.

Keywords: seismic retrofit, federal buildings, base isolation, architecture, National Register of Historic Places.

STOP 1: SEVENTH AND MISSION STREETS, SAN FRANCISCO

Significance of the Site

With over 100 years of history, the court facility is one of the most beautiful buildings in America (Fig. 1) but has a troubled history that combines extraordinary architecture and damaging earthquakes. Built in 1905, the building withstood the 1906 Great San Francisco Earthquake with some damage, and is now listed on the National Register of Historic Places. The building is one of the best examples of so-called American Renaissance architecture as an expression of the Beaux Art style of architecture. The building is owned and operated by the U.S. General Services Administration (GSA) and houses federal court and law library facilities. While the building was closed due to minor damage following the 1989 Loma Prieta earthquake, the 1996 seismic retrofit and facility upgrade included a seismic base-isolation system to protect this invaluable historic structure from major damaging earthquakes. Additionally, the GSA and the U.S. Geological Survey (USGS; www.usgs.gov) collaborated to install a program of seismic instrumentation in the retrofitted building to provide vital data on the performance of the seismic base-isolation system and the response of the superstructure during future earthquakes.

Accessibility of the Site

The building is a public building; however, security screening and identification are required. Restrooms are available, and there is limited on-site and metered off-site parking and a tour-bus drop-off point. Public tours are available: go to www.ca9.uscourts.gov/ for a schedule and additional information.

Location

The Ninth District U.S. Court of Appeals building is located at 95 Seventh Street, San Francisco, California 94103-1518, USA.

GPS Coordinates

Latitude: 37.7881°N; longitude: 122.3907°W.

Directions

From the Moscone Convention Center at Fourth Street and Howard Street, head southwest on Howard Street, go three blocks, turn right at Seventh Street, and go one block to Mission Street and Seventh Street (Fig. 2). The entrance to the Ninth District U.S. Court of Appeals building is on Seventh Street at the southwest corner of the block. A guarded on-site parking entrance is on Mission Street at the rear of the building.

Stop Description

The guided tour by facility management and tour-guide personnel will include historic features, selected courtrooms, chambers, the law library, and typical seismic isolator and foundation conditions. Many of these areas are not normally open to the public without special arrangements.

Lee, P., 2006, Ninth District U.S. Court of Appeals, San Francisco, California, *in* Prentice, C.S., Scotchmoor, J.G., Moores, E.M., and Kiland, J.P., eds., 1906 San Francisco Earthquake Centennial Field Guides: Field trips associated with the 100th Anniversary Conference, 18–23 April 2006, San Francisco, California: Geological Society of America Field Guide 7, p. 67–77, doi: 10.1130/2006.1906SF(05). For permission to copy, contact editing@geosociety.org. ©2006 Geological Society of America. All rights reserved.

Figure 1. Ninth District U.S. Court of Appeals building (1905–1933), San Francisco, California (photo courtesy Skidmore, Owings & Merrill LLP).

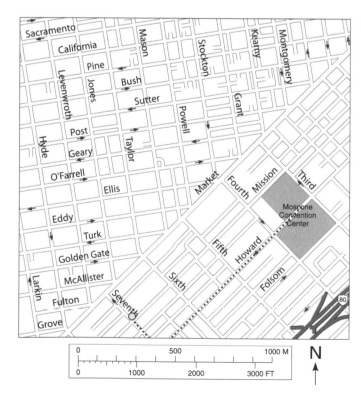

Figure 2. Map of downtown San Francisco showing the route from the Moscone Center to the Ninth District U.S. Court of Appeals (courtesy of the U.S. Geological Survey).

Brief Summary of the Historical Significance and Chronology

The land was purchased in 1891 for US$1.04 million. The building was envisioned and designed in the late 1890s, and original construction was started in 1897. It opened in the summer of 1905 (cost of construction: US$2.5 million). In April 1906, it was damaged by, yet survived, the Great Earthquake of 1906. The building was rebuilt and reopened in 1910 (cost of repairs: US$295,000), and the east wing was added during the Great Depression in 1933 (US$625,000). It was listed on the National Register of Historic Places in 1971. The building was damaged and closed following 1989 Loma Prieta earthquake and was reopened in 1996 following historic rehabilitation (US$91 million).

Original U.S. Court of Appeals and Post Office Building (1905)

The architect of the original building was James Knox Taylor, Chief Architect of the U.S. Treasury Department. He took a personal interest in making the building one of the most ornate and embellished works in the United States after the Library of Congress in Washington, D.C. (Figs. 3 and 4). The building became known as the U.S. Post Office and Federal Court House.

1933 East Wing Addition

The architect of the east wing addition was George Kelham, a local San Francisco and Ecole des Beaux Arts–trained leading

U. S. POST OFFICE AND FEDERAL COURT HOUSE, SAN FRANCISCO, CALIFORNIA   2

1905

Figure 3. The U.S. Post Office and Federal building (1905) (courtesy National Archives).

Post Office construction, about 1904

Figure 4. The U.S. Post Office and Federal building under construction (1905) (courtesy National Archives).

architect of the period. The 1933 addition (Fig. 5) consisted of a four-story addition at the east wing enclosure of the post office, with a total construction cost of US$625,000. While the exterior replicated the original 1905 construction, the interiors were much more restrained, reflecting the economics and aesthetics of the Great Depression era.

1996 GSA Seismic Retrofit and Historic Rehabilitation

The architect and structural engineer for the 1996 GSA seismic retrofit and historic rehabilitation was Skidmore, Owings & Merrill LLP, San Francisco, California, led by architect Craig Hartman and structural engineer Navin Amin. The project manager for the GSA was Sara Delgado.

The Great San Francisco Earthquake of 18 April 1906

During the 1906 San Francisco earthquake, the city was devastated; however, the court building and post office facility was left standing (Figs. 6 and 7). Although the exterior granite and interior finishes suffered extensive damage, the building was restored and reopened four years later.

Loma Prieta Earthquake of 17 October 1989

Following the 1989 Loma Prieta earthquake, in which the building experienced minor damage, the building was vacated and evaluated by current standards and found deficient to withstand future earthquakes without significant damage and loss to

the historical and irreplaceable value of the architecture. The GSA hired Skidmore, Owings & Merrill LLP to implement an historical rehabilitation, facility upgrade, and seismic retrofit of the building structure that would protect it from future damaging earthquakes.

As noted, the U-shaped original building designed by James Knox Taylor was built in 1905, with a fourth wing

Bush St., Powell to Mason showing Post Office in center of photograph

Figure 6. City devastated; post office left standing (courtesy California Historical Society, San Francisco).

Figure 7. Liquefaction and ground failure at Seventh and Mission Streets (courtesy California Historical Society, San Francisco).

Figure 5. The four-story addition at the east wing enclosure of the post office (1933) (courtesy National Archives).

designed by George Kelham added in 1933. The exterior façades facing the streets are primarily white Sierra ashlar granite on the exterior, backed on steel frames with riveted connection joints. The exterior façades facing the interior courtyard are primarily terracotta with tile detail. This is the most ornate federal building west of the Mississippi River. The superstructure gravity framing consists typically of built-up steel columns, steel beams, and girders supporting a concrete floor. Figures 8, 9, and 10 illustrate the overall building section, typical plan, and interior courtyard central addition.

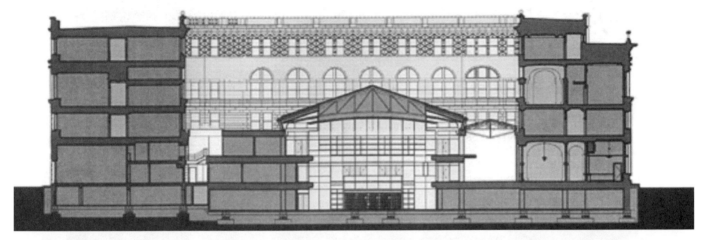

Figure 8. Section at 1905 and 1933 of wings including central addition (image courtesy Skidmore, Owings & Merrill LLP).

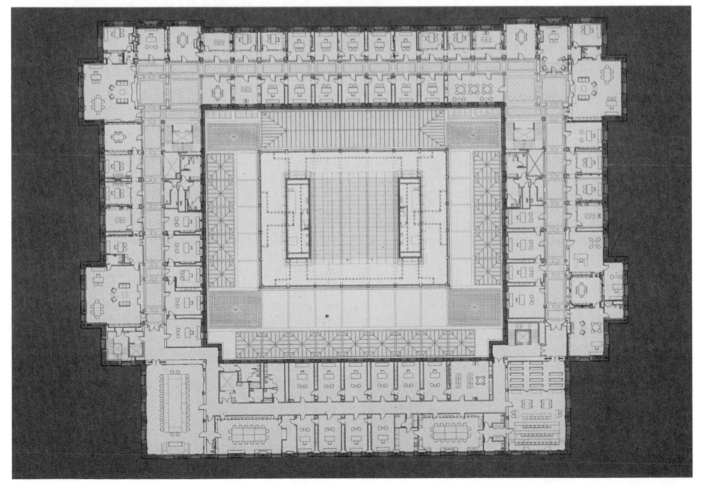

Figure 9. Plan view of level 2 (image courtesy Skidmore, Owings & Merrill LLP).

Figure 10. Model view of central addition (image courtesy Skidmore, Owings & Merrill LLP).

1996 GSA Seismic Retrofit and Historic Rehabilitation

The 1996 upgrade of the U.S. Court of Appeals building was the Federal Government's first seismic base-isolation retrofit project and posed many special challenges. The size (350,000 square feet) and weight (60,000 tons) of the building made the issues of cost versus seismic performance critical to the feasibility of the project. At the same time, the architectural significance of the building made the issues of seismic performance and impact on the historic building equally critical. To optimize the cost and performance issues, the structural design focused on three primary, yet related issues: (1) selection of where to locate the plane of seismic isolation bearings to allow for the best response of the superstructure during earthquake ground shaking, while integrating the layout of the isolators with architectural programming requirements; (2) selection between three available seismic isolation system designs, which included elastomeric lead-rubber, high-damping rubber, and Friction Pendulum steel sliding bearings; and (3) determination of the amount of superstructure strengthening required that would minimize disruption to historical details of the building.

The overall seismic performance objective of the design of the seismic isolation retrofit was to withstand a major earthquake, defined as a design basis earthquake with a 10% probability of exceedance in 50 years (a 475-year return period) resulting in only minor damage. To utilize the strength and stiffness of the existing building's granite and masonry walls to resist seismic

forces, analytical studies and in situ forced-vibration testing of the existing building (Fig. 11) was undertaken during the design phases of the project. The resulting test data were used to correlate observed minor damage during the 1989 Loma Prieta earthquake with the measured dynamic characteristics of the existing superstructure. The design goal was to limit damage in the retrofitted building when subjected to future major earthquakes with a seismic isolation system.

Based on extensive evaluations and investigations of the existing building, coupled with an assessment of future court facility requirements, a strategy that incorporated functionality integrated with architectural, mechanical, and electrical system requirements was devised. A seismic isolation system was implemented with base isolators, and the plane of seismic isolation was located above existing foundation footings. This approach made available ~80,000 square feet of useable space in the one basement structure. In consideration of all cost and functionality issues, the seismic isolation system selected was a steel sliding system consisting of a total of 256 Friction Pendulum System (FPS™) seismic isolators. The FPS isolation system was developed and manufactured by Earthquake Protection Systems, Inc. (www.earthquakeprotection.com). Figure 12 shows the typical complete installation of the isolators at existing columns along the interior courtyard perimeter. Figure 13A shows a construction detail of a typical isolator including the location of temporary hydraulic jacks to support column verti-

Figure 11. Forced-vibration testing of existing building (photo courtesy Skidmore, Owings & Merrill LLP).

Figure 12. Installation of isolators at the courtyard perimeter (photo courtesy Skidmore, Owings & Merrill LLP).

P. Lee

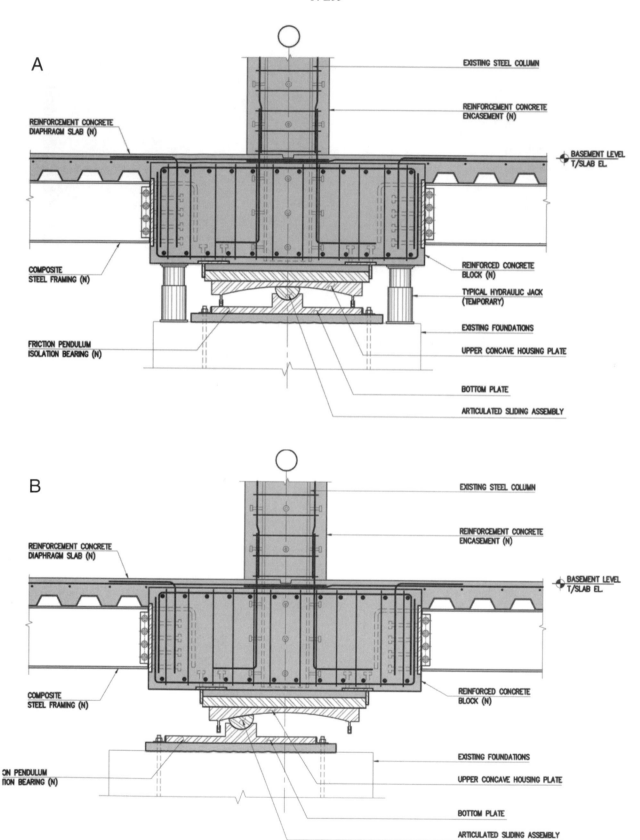

Figure 13. (A) Typical Friction Pendulum System (FPS™) bearing installation detail. (B) Typical isolator and column in displaced position. (Images courtesy Skidmore, Owings & Merrill LLP.)

cal loads during installation; Figure 13B shows a typical detail of the isolator and column in a displaced position as a result of horizontal seismic excitation of the building.

The 77-inch radius-of-curvature bearings, with a pendulum period of vibration of 2.75 s and displacement capacity of up to 14 inches, were placed facing upward to minimize forces transmitted to existing foundations during peak earthquake response. Additional savings were realized by not dropping the pile foundation in the 1933 wing to accommodate other isolation systems in order to maintain required headroom. The forced-vibration tests conducted to assess the building's dynamic characteristics further aided to limit the amount of superstructure shear-wall strengthening required.

Further structural economy and architectural program functionality were achieved by demolishing and removing the existing central post office structure and replacing it with a state-of-the-art law library with a natural-skylight central courtyard.

During construction, it was important to rehabilitate both the exterior and interior historic finishes of the building. Examples of the restored finishes are shown in Figures 14, 15, and 16 for a typical exterior entrance, interior hallway, and courtroom number one, respectively.

To install the seismic isolators above each foundation footing, existing columns and connecting floor diaphragms were strengthened to allow for stability even if the building were to be displaced up to 14 inches during lateral earthquake shaking. Innovative lifting mechanisms were devised to install the isolation bearings using economical concrete jacking blocks at each of the existing steel columns.

This technically innovative approach had never before been used and led to a four-times-faster construction schedule and associated cost savings. The Friction Pendulum bearings were designed and installed in 1994 in only six months. Each bearing was tested to verify bearing properties prior to installation. Additionally, a full-scale bearing was tested on a shake table at the University of California–Berkeley. The tests and evaluations helped to validate and provide correlation with structural analysis and design assumptions.

Seismic Instrumentation Program (USGS/GSA)

The historic rehabilitation and seismic retrofit of the base-isolated building also included a seismic instrumentation program to record data in future earthquakes. During the retrofit, the USGS and the U.S. General Services Administration (GSA) cooperated in the installation of a total of 36 sensor

Figure 14. Exterior white Sierra ashlar granite and (A) lanterns (photo courtesy Skidmore, Owings & Merrill LLP) and (B) solid bronze doors (photo courtesy of William A. Porter).

Figure 15. Irreplaceable Venetian mosaics and white marble corridor (photos courtesy of William A. Porter).

Figure 16. Courtroom Number One, Ninth District U.S. Court of Appeals (photo courtesy Skidmore, Owings & Merrill LLP).

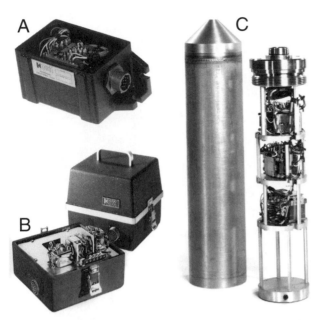

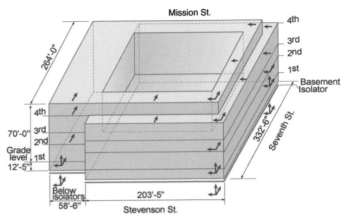

Figure 18. Ninth District U.S. Court of Appeals building diagram of sensor locations (courtesy Mehmet Celebi, U.S. Geological Survey).

Figure 17. Typical force-balance accelerometers (courtesy of Kinemetrics, Inc.): (A) Uniaxial, FBA-11. (B) Triaxial, FBA-13. (C) Downhole, FBA-13DH.

channels incorporating force-balance accelerometers with state-of-the-art digital recording capability (operational as of 1998). Typical uniaxial, triaxial, and downhole accelerometers are shown in Figure 17. During future earthquakes, the dense array of recorders will provide vital data on the performance of the isolators and the response of the superstructure. Figure 18 illustrates a building diagram with sensor layout and location. A free-field station was also deployed close to the building to provide key input data for evaluation of structures in the proximity of the Ninth District U.S. Court of Appeals building and contribute to the assessment of the variation of ground motion within downtown San Francisco. Additional information on the seismic instrumentation of buildings with an emphasis on federal buildings (Celebi, 2002) can be found at www.usgs.gov.

A Tribute

As noted in the GSA's 2003 publication, *United States Court of Appeals Building for the Ninth Circuit* (p. 55):

Strengthened to withstand the force of nature and restored to its original splendor, this beautiful building stands as a testament to the people who built it. The American taxpayers at the end of the 19th century gave us a building worth saving. Those at the end of the 20th century have continued the legacy by preserving this architectural treasure for future generations.

Design Awards

In recognition of design creativity, efficiency, and cost and time savings on this project, Skidmore, Owings & Merrill LLP was presented with the GSA's 1995 National Award for Engineering, Technology, and Innovation. The project has received additional design awards, including the following: GSA National Honor Design Award, 1994, from the U.S. General Services Administration; Structural Engineers Association of Illinois (SEAOI) Most Innovative Structure Award, 1995; Outstanding Structural Engineering Excellence Award, 1996, from the Structural Engineers Association of California (SEAOC); and the Design Award for Historic Preservation and Restoration, 1996, from the U.S. General Services Administration.

REFERENCES CITED

Celebi, M., 2002, Seismic instrumentation of buildings: Menlo Park, California, United States Geological Survey, GSA/USGS project no. 0-7460-68170, 94025.
U.S. General Services Administration, 2003, United States Court of Appeals Building for the Ninth Circuit: Washington, D.C., U.S. General Services Administration, p. 55.

Web References and Further Reading

Earthquake Protection Systems Inc.: www.earthquakeprotection.com.
National Park Service, Southeast Archaeological Center: www.cr.nps.gov/seac/building.htm.
Skidmore, Owings & Merrill LLP: www.som.com.
U.S. Court of Appeals for the Ninth District: www.ca9.uscourts.gov.
U.S. Geological Survey home page: www.usgs.gov.
U.S. General Services Administration, U.S. Court of Appeals, Ninth Circuit, Statement of Significance, http://w3.gsa.gov/web/p/interaia.nsf/1fd3e688294c3a74852563d3004975f4/b3184f421a8b98398525672a0079611e?OpenDocument.

San Francisco Civic Center

Simin Naaseh

Forell/Elsesser Engineers, Inc., 160 Pine Street, Suite 600, San Francisco, California 94111, USA

OVERVIEW OF FIELD TRIP

San Francisco's Civic Center (Figs. 1 and 2) is on the National Register of Historic Places because it includes a magnificent collection of nineteenth and twentieth century Revival and Beaux Arts architecture and exemplifies the finest manifestation of the "City Beautiful" movement in the United States. The Civic Center is known as one of the most important national and international historic sites, as it is the birth place of the United Nations and has witnessed the drafting and signing of post World War II peace treaties with Japan. Major government and cultural buildings surround the Civic Center Plaza, including San Francisco City Hall, the Asian Art Museum, the new Main Library, the Bill Graham Civic Auditorium, as well as the State Supreme Court building. This trip will visit both the San Francisco City Hall and the Asian Art Museum to explore their recent seismic retrofits as well as their histories.

Keywords: National Register of Historic Places, San Francisco City Hall, Asian Art Museum, Beaux Arts architecture, earthquake.

STOP 1: SAN FRANCISCO CITY HALL

Significance of the Site

The San Francisco City Hall (SFCH) is a national historic landmark building, designed in 1912 to replace its predecessor, which was destroyed in the 1906 earthquake (Fig. 3A). This historically significant building was seismically upgraded in 1999 with a base isolation system to protect it from future earthquakes.

Accessibility

This site is open to the public, but not all spaces within the building are publicly accessible.

Directions

From Moscone Center, go southwest on Howard toward Fourth Street. Turn right on Ninth Street, cross Market Street, and bear left on Hayes Street, then turn right onto Van Ness Avenue. City Hall is east of Van Ness, between Grove and McAllister (Fig. 1).

Stop Description

The SFCH is recognized as one of the most important historic buildings in the United States and represents a notable example of neoclassical architecture in the country. This monumental five-story building occupies two city blocks, and is crowned with a dome topped by a lantern that extends 310 ft above the base (Fig. 3B). The building's most historically significant feature is its ornately clad granite exterior.

City Hall was designed by Bakewell and Brown Architects and Christopher Snyder, structural engineer. The building, with its rectangular plan, has dimensions of ~300 ft × 400 ft (Fig. 4A). The 90-ft-diameter grand rotunda area creates a focal point to the center of the building (Fig. 4B). Two rectangular open areas at the north and south sides flank the main floor of the rotunda. Immediately above these open areas are two large light courts, which are open to the sky above the second floor (Fig. 4B and 4C). Together, the rotunda and the court areas serve as ceremonial spaces during official visits by dignitaries from around the world, as exhibit spaces, and for cultural events, public ceremonies, and weddings. As such, the public enjoys the grand, public spaces in City Hall on many occasions. The rotunda and the surrounding public spaces are ornately clad with richly detailed limestone and plaster. The light courts above the second floor allow ample natural light to the rotunda area.

The building structure is composed of a complete steel frame with concrete slabs (Fig. 5). Towering above the central rotunda space is its central dome, a multi-tiered steel structure supported on concentric circles of columns, support girders,

Naaseh, S., San Francisco Civic Center, *in* Prentice, C.S., Scotchmoor, J.G., Moores, E.M., and Kiland, J.P., eds., 1906 San Francisco Earthquake Centennial Field Guides: Field trips associated with the 100th Anniversary Conference, 18–23 April 2006, San Francisco, California: Geological Society of America Field Guide 7, p. 79–91, doi: 10.1130/2006.1906SF(06). For permission to copy, contact editing@geosociety.org. ©2006 Geological Society of America. All rights reserved.

Figure 1. Map showing the Moscone Convention Center and field trip stops 1 and 2.

Figure 2. Aerial view of San Francisco Civic Center.

and four towers located at the corners of the rotunda. The foundation system is shallow footings. The exterior granite walls are backed with unreinforced masonry (URM). Many of the infill partition walls are constructed with hollow clay tile (HCT).

City Hall was designed and built following the 1906 San Francisco earthquake that caused the collapse of its predecessor. As such, at the time this building was designed, there was much awareness about earthquakes and their impact on structures. Specifically, the behavior of domed buildings was of much concern, as the former City Hall was also a domed building that shed all of its massive granite cladding during the 1906 earthquake (Fig. 3A). However, in 1912, there were no established guidelines for design of seismic-resistant buildings. The structural engineer for City Hall, nevertheless, had an ingenious idea about designing this building in such a manner that the

Figure 3. (A) City Hall in ruins after 1906 earthquake. (B) The new City Hall, built in 1925 (photographer: Robert Canfield).

building would dissipate earthquake energy at the main floor, and consequently not transmit the damaging earthquake energy up to the dome, hence protecting the dome and its drum support structure. To accomplish this, he intentionally designed a "soft story" at the main floor, counting on the flexibility of this floor to dissipate the earthquake energy. This was done by discontinuing the brick light court walls, as well as discontinuing the dome support concrete walls at the main floor, and instead transitioning to HCT walls (Fig. 6A and B). The height of the main floor as well as the open spaces also helped with this design intent of "flexibility" at this floor.

While this idea was conceptually attractive, the materials that were used in the main floor and their design and detailing did not allow for sufficient ductility and resilience to endure many large cycles of ground shaking without severe damage and potential for collapse in a major earthquake. The design, however, did work for the moderate 1989 Loma Prieta earthquake with only a few seconds of strong shaking. The building was extensively damaged in the Loma Prieta earthquake, but remained stable. Much of the damage was concentrated at the main floor, as envisioned by the original engineer. There was extensive damage at the dome/drum area as well. However, the dome remained stable. The 1989 damage, along with concerns regarding the reduced strength of the building against future earthquakes, prompted efforts to repair and seismically upgrade the building.

Several retrofit schemes were developed and evaluated based on the building's seismic performance, functional needs, and preservation of its historic fabric. From these alternatives, a base isolation scheme combined with some superstructure strengthening was selected as the most appropriate and cost effective solution.

Base isolation is a state of the art seismic protection technology that started with very few applications in United States in the 1980s. Isolators are devices that are installed under the building to help decouple the building from the shaking ground beneath. Isolators are designed to dissipate earthquake energy in a controlled and predictable manner. An isolated building is designed to move several inches at the isolation interface in the event of a large earthquake, while the rest of the building above the isolators moves essentially as a rigid body, protecting the structure and the non-structural elements from damage that is caused in conventionally designed buildings by inter-story displacements (Fig. 7A and 7B).

City Hall's unique original dome and flexible drum structure has the characteristics of amplifying the dynamic response of the building at the dome area, making the dome especially vulnerable to earthquake damage in the event of a large earthquake, similar to its predecessor that was destroyed in the 1906 earthquake. Base isolation alters the dynamic response of the building, providing protection for the dome structure. No conventional retrofit solution could offer the same protection for the dome. Conventional solutions would have required virtual dismantling of the dome to provide strengthening, whereas base isolation required an easily installed three-dimensional space truss above the vaulted ceilings directly below the dome, representing a significant cost savings while preserving the building's historic fabric. In addition, base isolation reduces the relative floor-to-floor deformations substantially, thus making it more tolerable for the brittle structural and non-structural historic elements.

Although base isolation substantially reduces the seismic forces the building will experience, some lateral resistance elements were required to stiffen and strengthen the superstructure (Fig. 8). The building's seismic upgrade system includes shoring and cutting of the building's existing steel columns and perimeter brick walls for installation of isolators above the existing foundations and additional lateral force resisting elements to stiffen and strengthen the superstructure (Fig. 9). The superstructure strengthening included concrete shear walls

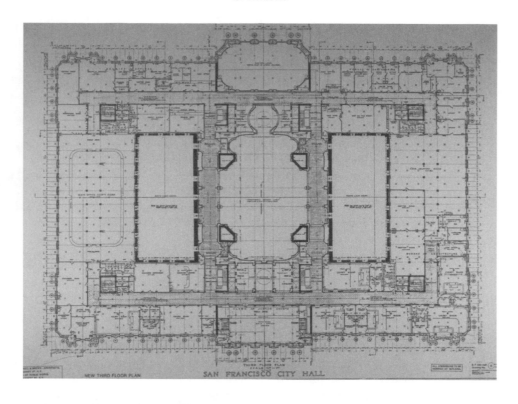

Figure 4. (A) Floor plan for City Hall. (B) Rotunda ceiling (photographer: Robert Canfield). (C) Ceremonial stairs in rotunda, inside City Hall (photographer: Robert Canfield).

Figure 5. City Hall under construction.

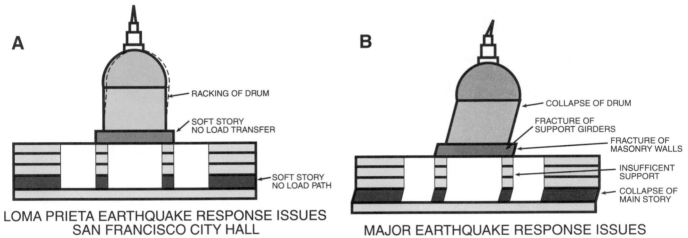

A

RACKING OF DRUM

SOFT STORY
NO LOAD TRANSFER

SOFT STORY
NO LOAD PATH

**LOMA PRIETA EARTHQUAKE RESPONSE ISSUES
SAN FRANCISCO CITY HALL**

B

COLLAPSE OF DRUM

FRACTURE OF
SUPPORT GIRDERS

FRACTURE OF
MASONRY WALLS

INSUFFICENT
SUPPORT

COLLAPSE OF
MAIN STORY

MAJOR EARTHQUAKE RESPONSE ISSUES

Figure 6. (A–B) Structural characteristics of City Hall.

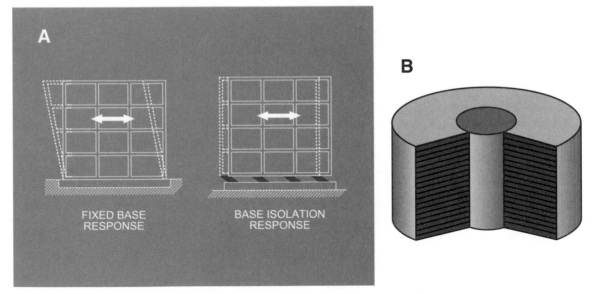

A

FIXED BASE
RESPONSE

BASE ISOLATION
RESPONSE

B

Figure 7. (A) Fixed base versus base isolation response. (B) Lead-rubber isolator like the ones installed at San Francisco City Hall to mitigate future earthquake damage.

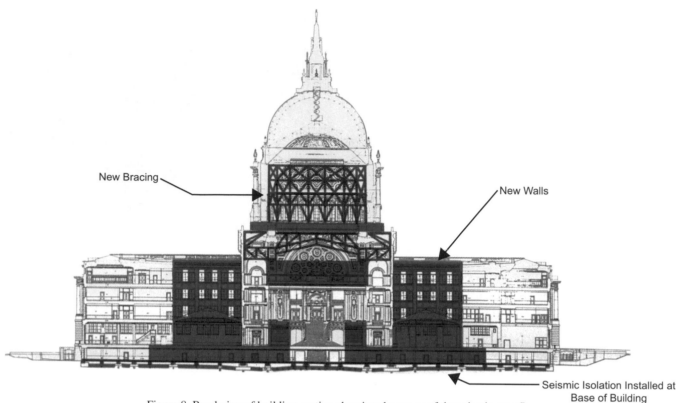

New Bracing

New Walls

Seismic Isolation Installed at
Base of Building

Figure 8. Rendering of building section showing the scope of the seismic retrofit.

around the light courts, reinforcing of the rotunda tower walls and installation of steel braces and shotcrete walls at various levels of the dome and drum. The isolation system is installed below the lowest floor level, and light court shear walls and transfer trusses are "invisible," hidden within cavity walls and above vaulted ceilings.

The construction of this seismic retrofit scheme was extremely complex and required special sequencing of the work. The potential vulnerability of the building during construction was given serious consideration, as the construction involved intricate shoring, jacking, and partial removal of over 500 columns and nearly 1400 linear feet of massive brick walls at their base, in order to install the isolators. Each column was supported by a temporary shoring frame, to allow cutting of the column and installation of the base isolators. The base isolation seismic retrofit allowed preservation of this national treasure and the rebirth of a City Hall that would last for at least another century (Fig. 10).

To monitor the building's response in future earthquakes, the building is instrumented by the California Geological Survey, with seismic accelerometers at multiple locations throughout. These monitoring devices record real-time response data at various locations in the building. The data will be available shortly after any earthquake that generates ground shaking at the city hall site. This information can be used to evaluate the response of the building after an earthquake and compare that with the analytically projected response. The instrumentation is a valuable tool to provide data regarding the seismic response of the building at various earthquake scenarios, allowing engineers to refine their analytical methods and tools and be better equipped to design seismic-resistant buildings in the future. While our understanding of earthquakes and the response of buildings have improved tremendously since the 1906 earthquake, there are still limitations that preclude engineers from the ability to precisely project the seismic behavior of structures.

STOP 2: ASIAN ART MUSEUM

Significance of the Site

The city of San Francisco's Old Main Library, a 1917 historic building constructed of structural steel and unreinforced brick masonry, was renovated, seismically upgraded, and transformed into the new Asian Art Museum in 2004 (Fig. 11). This building is one of the most notable examples of Beaux Arts architecture in the United States. The seismic design must protect not only the building but also the invaluable collection within from damage in future earthquakes.

Accessibility

This site is public-access with the purchase of a ticket.

Figure 9. (Top) Photograph showing column jacking in progress (photographer: Robert Canfield). (Bottom) Photograph showing column cutting in progress (photographer: Robert Canfield).

Figure 10. Photograph of San Francisco City Hall at night (photographer: Robert Canfield).

Figure 11. The Asian Art Museum (Stop 2).

Directions

The museum is located only one block east of City Hall, on Larkin between Fulton and McAllister (Fig. 1).

Stop Description

The museum houses an irreplaceable collection of Asian art and artifacts, including immensely valuable, brittle Ming Dynasty vases, and represents the largest non–real-estate asset in the city of San Francisco, with an estimated value of US$5 billion. The adaptive reuse of the 180,000-square-foot building was orchestrated by the Milanese architect, Gae Aulenti, FAIA, known for her adaptive reuse of the Gare D'Orsay, a Parisian train station, into the internationally renowned Musee D'Orsay. HOK was the local architect of record.

The new Asian Art Museum is a monumental building located in the San Francisco Civic Center Historic District and is recognized as one of the most notable examples of Beaux Arts architecture in the United States. The building was originally designed in 1915 by the architect George W. Kelham and structural engineer H.J. Brunnier to compliment the new City Hall building under construction. The ultimate goal of city planners was to establish a civic center district with government, judicial, library, and arts components. With a new library commissioned and constructed within the district in the late 1990s, the renovation of the old library to become a world-class museum completed the founding planner's goal.

The seismic design criteria for the project were certainly to protect the brittle and vulnerable historic fabric and structure of the building. However, the primary objective was to protect the art collection on display and in storage. For both "moderate"

and "severe" earthquakes, the goal was to suffer no loss in collection value.

The museum structure and the collection were seismically protected by a combination of base isolation and superstructure reinforcement (Fig. 12). The isolation bearings were placed over a reinforced mat foundation system below the original slab on grade. A new suspended floor, above the isolation plane, supports basement loads. Reinforced concrete shear walls, from the top of the basement floor to the roof level, provided a complete and rigid lateral load path for all sections of the building. Floor diaphragm reinforcement and collector lines tied the existing and new floors into the shear walls.

Base isolation combined with superstructure reinforcement provided the most reliable protection available to the artifacts stored and displayed in the museum. Base isolation allowed architectural freedom to manipulate the floor plate in a manner that optimized gallery space and light distribution. The seismic demands imposed on displayed artifacts were reduced to a level at which conventional artifact bracing methods could be effective (Fig. 13).

Performance goals for property protection govern many parts of the design. These goals are as follows:

- In a "moderate" earthquake of Modified Mercalli Intensity (MMI) VI, similar to a repeat of the ground shaking of the Loma Prieta earthquake experienced at the site, the goal is to suffer no loss in collection value.
- In a "major" earthquake of MMI VII–VIII, similar to the ground shaking expected from a Magnitude 7 earthquake on the mid-peninsula segment of the San Andreas fault or one of the East Bay faults (the closest point of fault rupture ± 18 km from the site), the goal is to suffer no loss in collection value.

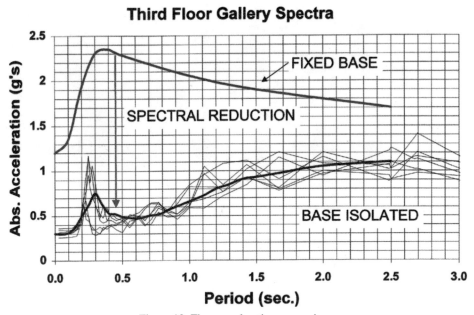

Figure 12. Floor acceleration comparison.

Figure 13. New exhibit space in the Asian Art Museum. Priceless treasures are protected from future damaging earthquakes by the seismic retrofit completed in 2004.

• In a "great" earthquake of MMI IX+, intended to represent a repeat of the 1906 San Francisco earthquake on the northern segment of the San Andreas fault (the closest point of fault rupture ± 12 km from the site), the goal is to have no loss in collection value in storage and a loss of less than 1% of collection value on display.

The museum is seismically protected by a combination of base isolation and superstructure reinforcement (Fig. 14). The base isolation bearings were placed over a reinforced foundation system below the current slab on grade. A new suspended basement floor was constructed above the isolation bearings. Reinforced concrete shear walls were con-

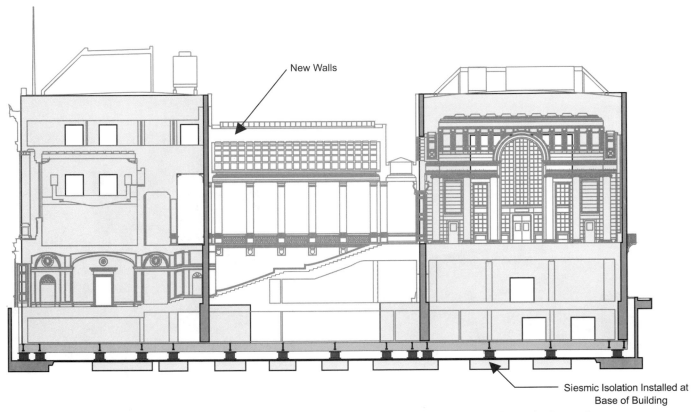

New Walls

Siesmic Isolation Installed at
Base of Building

Figure 14. Rendering of the Asian Art Museum building section showing the scope of the seismic retrofit.

structed from the top of the basement floor to the roof level to provide a complete and rigid lateral load path for all sections of the building. Floor diaphragm reinforcement and collector lines were used to tie the existing and new floors into the new shear walls.

A majority of the isolators were installed directly beneath steel columns. To facilitate the installation, the shoring contractor engaged the load in each column to allow column cutting and isolator installation (Fig. 15A–D).

- Step 1—The existing slab on grade and fill were removed to expose the sides of the existing footings. The new infill mat was dowelled to the existing spread footings. The new combined mat was designed to resist future vertical and seismic loads as well as jacking point loads during construction.
- Step 2—Shoring members with carefully controlled hydraulic jacks were used to transfer the vertical load from the column onto the new foundation mat.
- Step 3—The existing column was cut and new steel cruciform weldment was installed to allow the attachment of bearing to the column and infill framing. The bearings were placed and flatjacks were used to preload the system. A flat-

jack is a sheet metal bladder that is pressure inflated with long pot life, low heat output epoxy.
- Step 4—The shoring haunches were removed and infill framing and walls were constructed.

It took ~14 days to install a bearing from the time the shoring hardware was placed until it was removed.

Site seismicity and stringent artifact protection goals made base isolation the only viable retrofit option (Fig. 16). Although base isolation significantly reduced the lateral loads on the superstructure, shear wall and collector strengthening were also required to prevent art damage. The tower walls braced the various segmented wings and allowed for long, expansive gallery diaphragms. Base isolation allowed architectural freedom to manipulate the floor plate in a manner that optimized gallery space and light distribution.

The reduction in seismic demand allowed for conventional art anchorage methods to be employed. Rigid casework and cabinetry were designed to support the museum's irreplaceable collection. Existing historical fabric was refurbished and braced in place, preserving the architecture of the former Old Main Library for generations (Fig. 17).

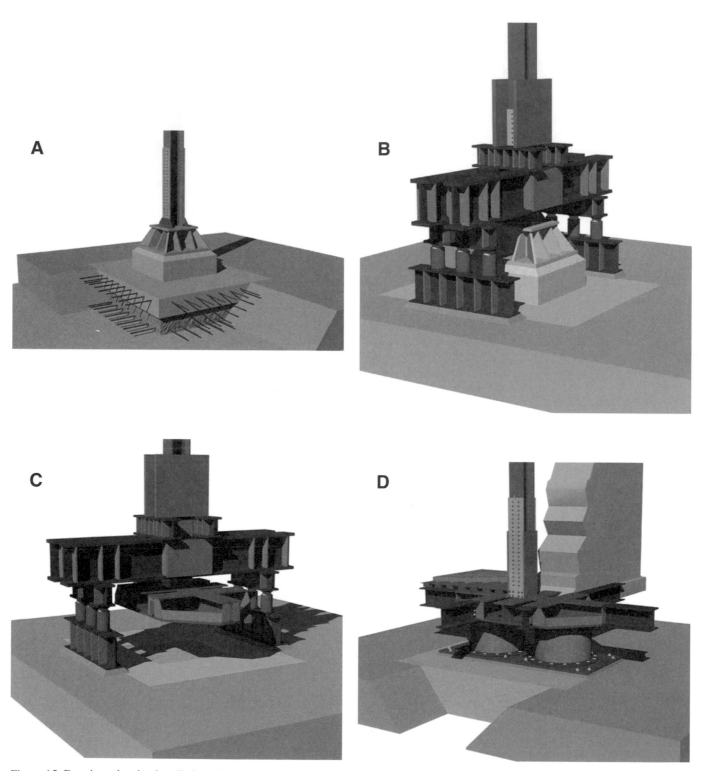

Figure 15. Drawings showing installation of the base isolation system. (A) Column and its footing dowelled to new infill mat. (B) Shored column. (C) Cut column and cruciform installation. (D) Base isolator bearings installed.

Figure 16. Photograph of retrofit construction in progress (photographer: Robert Canfield).

Figure 17. Photograph of the San Francisco Asian Art Museum.

Printed in the USA

Geological Society of America
Field Guide 7
2006

Twenty-first century high-rises

Neville Mathias
Jennifer Kimura
Peter Lee
Skidmore, Owings, and Merrill, LLP, 1 Front Street, San Francisco, California 94111, USA

OVERVIEW OF FIELD TRIP

This five-building walking tour (Fig. 1) provides an overview of significant tall buildings in San Francisco that were constructed in the first few years of the twenty-first century and gives insight into the modern design and seismic innovations of today's skyscrapers in high seismic zones. The St. Regis Tower (42 story), 101 Second Street (26 story), the JP Morgan Chase Building (31 story), the Paramount (39 story), and the Four Seasons Hotel (40 story) will be surveyed in this tour. These buildings showcase a variety of important structural designs and use of materials including (1) reinforced concrete framed dual system, (2) structural steel framed dual system, (3) steel frame with sloped boxed columns and offsets, (4) precast hybrid moment resistant frame, and (5) steel framed dual system with nonlinear viscous damping.

Keywords: San Francisco, architectural engineering, seismic retrofit, reinforced concrete, steel frame, dual system, moment-resistant architecture, high rise architecture.

STOP 1: ST. REGIS MUSEUM TOWER, 125 THIRD STREET

Significance of the Site

Winner of the American Concrete Institute's (ACI) 2004 Construction Award and the ACI 2004 Structural Award, the St. Regis Museum Tower is currently the tallest concrete structure in the United States within Seismic Zone 4 (the zone of strongest shaking). The existing adjacent historic "Williams Building" has been retrofitted and incorporated to act integrally with the tower.

Accessibility

This is a private building with no public restrooms available, and there is limited off-site metered parking.

GPS Coordinates

Latitude: 37.7859290; longitude: −122.4014820.

Directions

From the Moscone Center, head northeast on Howard Street, and turn left on Third Street. Continue two blocks to 125 Third Street (Fig. 2).

Stop Description

Owner: Carpenter & Company and Starwood Lodging
Architect and Structural Engineer: Skidmore, Owings and
    Merrill LLP
General Contractor: Webcor Builders

Construction of the St. Regis Museum Tower project was completed in 2005, and incorporates a cast-in-place reinforced concrete superstructure and an architectural precast concrete and glass exterior wall system (Fig. 3A and 3B). The building is a 42-story tower that houses a five-star hotel in the lower 20 floors and condominiums in the upper floors. The Museum of the African Diaspora occupies part of the first three stories above grade. There is a four-level subterranean garage below the building. The project consists of 750,000 total square feet and sits on San Francisco Redevelopment Agency property at Third and Mission, adjacent to the Museum of Modern Art and across from

Mathias, N., Kimura, J., and Lee, P., 2006, Twenty-first century high-rises, *in* Prentice, C.S., Scotchmoor, J.G., Moores, E.M., and Kiland, J.P., eds., 1906 San Francisco Earthquake Centennial Field Guides: Field trips associated with the 100th Anniversary Conference, 18–23 April 2006, San Francisco, California: Geological Society of America Field Guide 7, p. 93–106, doi: 10.1130/2006.1906SF(07). For permission to copy, contact editing@geosociety.org. ©2006 Geological Society of America. All rights reserved.

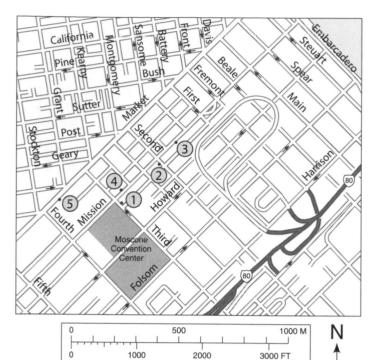

Stop 1: St Regis Museum Tower
125 3rd St. (& Mission)

- Completed 2005
- Mixed-use building
- Current tallest concrete structure in seismic zone 4
- Innovative seismic retrofit
- Concrete dual system

Stop 2: 101 Second St
Mission St. & 2nd St.

- Completed in 2000
- Commercial Office building
- "Dogbone" moment connections
- Steel dual system

Stop 3: JP Morgan Chase Building
560 Mission St (& 2nd)

- Completed 2002
- Office building
- Plaza & urban park: features bamboo grove and stone fountain
- Steel dual system

Stop 5: Four Seasons Hotel
757 Market St. (& 4th)

- Completed 2001
- Mixed-use building
- First significant use of nonlinear viscous dampers
- Steel dual system

Stop 4: The Paramount
680 Mission St. (& 3rd)

- Completed 2004
- Residential Building
- Tallest pre-cast concrete building in a high seismic zone
- First significant application of Precast Hybrid Moment Resisting Frames (PHMRF)

Figure 1. Map showing locations of the five field trip stops in relation to Moscone Center and photographs of each of the five buildings covered in the field guide, with a summary of information for each stop (map drafted by Michael Rymer, U.S. Geological Survey). Stop 1: Photo courtesy of Skidmore, Owings & Merrill LLP; photographer, Mark Schwettmann. Stop 2: Photo courtesy of Skidmore, Owings & Merrill LLP, photographer, Nick Merrick. Stop 3: Photographer: Tim Griffith, Esto Photographics, Inc. Stop 4: Photographer: Bernard André, Bernard André Photography. Stop 5: Photographer: Tim Griffith, Tim Griffith Photography.

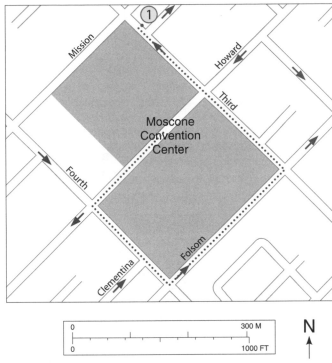

Figure 2. Map showing the location of Stop 1 (St. Regis Tower) in relation to Moscone Center (map drafted by Michael Rymer, U.S. Geological Survey).

the Moscone Convention Center. The seismic design includes a lateral system, which is a "dual system" consisting of special moment-resisting perimeter frames and a shear-wall "box" core. The Williams Building (adjacent to the tower) retrofit primarily consists of an internal skin of shotcrete on the masonry walls and floor diaphragms tied at aligning floors to those of the new tower, ensuring that the two buildings will move as a unit during strong shaking. In addition, a new mat foundation was constructed to alleviate liquefaction concerns.

STOP 2: 101 SECOND STREET

Significance of the Site

Construction of the 101 Second Street tower project was completed in 2000, and incorporates a structural steel superstructure and an architectural limestone and glass exterior wall system. The project consists of a 26-story office building with a public enclosed art exhibition space at its base and entry. The building towers to a total height of 353 feet 6 inches with a total of 369,000 square feet of rentable office space. Individual floors range from 13,500 to 17,000 rentable square feet with an additional 9,500 square feet of ground-floor restaurant and retail spaces. The basement level includes 52 valet-served parking stalls.

Figure 3. (*this and following page*) (A) Photograph of St. Regis Tower (Stop 1).

Figure 3. (*continued*) (B) Panorama of St. Regis Tower and vicinity. Photos courtesy of Skidmore, Owings & Merrill LLP; photographer, Mark Schwettmann.

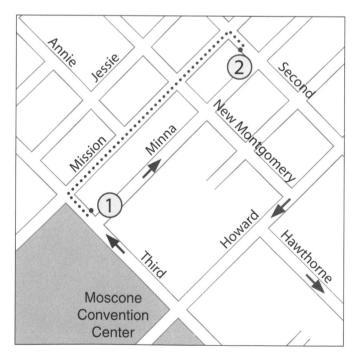

Accessibility

This is a private building with no public restrooms available, and there is limited off-site metered parking.

GPS Coordinates

Latitude: 37.7880280; longitude: −122.3996820.

Directions

From the St Regis Tower at 125 Third Street, head northwest on Third, turn right on Mission Street, and turn right on Second Street (Fig. 4).

Stop Description

Owner: Hines Interests Limited Partnership
Developer: Myers Development Company
Architect: Skidmore, Owings and Merrill LLP
Structural Engineer: Middlebrook and Louie
General Contractor: Hathaway Dinwiddie Construction Company

Figure 4. Map showing the location of Stop 2 (101 Second Street) in relation to Stop 1 (map drafted by Michael Rymer, U.S. Geological Survey).

Figure 5. (*this and the following two pages*) (A) Photograph of 101 Second Street (Stop 2). Photos (A–B) courtesy of Skidmore, Owings & Merrill LLP; photographer: Nick Merrick.

In a neighborhood of modestly scaled buildings in San Francisco's South of Market area, 101 Second Street was designed by the architect to be contextually sympathetic, while avoiding traditional historic forms (Fig. 5A and 5B). The building steps down, in a series of vertical slabs, to the height of its neighbors (Fig. 5C). This approach conforms to the city's zoning code without resorting to conventional "wedding-cake" massing, and creates an elegant silhouette that emphasizes the building's height.

101 Second Street's material palette expresses the tower's basic structural and programmatic concept. The tower's central core is clad in limestone panels, with windows articulated as punched openings to emphasize its solidity. This central slab is flanked by lighter glass volumes, which contain the tower's lease space and provide the building's primary views.

The building demonstrates a public spirit at its base and top. At the street corner, the tower steps down toward a glass art pavilion (Fig. 5C), a public art exhibition space that doubles as the building's entrance. At the top, a glass veil encloses the building's mechanical equipment. Designed to capture the sun as it moves throughout the day, the translucent crown transforms the building's roof into a glowing beacon.

Figure 5. (*continued*) (B) Detail of the 101 Second Street building showing its step-down design. Photos (A–B) courtesy of Skidmore, Owings & Merrill LLP; photographer: Nick Merrick.

The superstructure seismic lateral force resisting system consists of structural steel dual system frames made up of interior core braced frames and perimeter special moment resisting frames utilizing "dogbone" ductile-type connection detailing. Typical floor framing construction consists of 3 inch metal decking with 3-1/4 inch lightweight concrete fill supported on steel wide flange beams and girders spanning from the building core to the perimeter. All beams and girders are connected to the floor slab via welded shear studs acting as composite members.

The foundation and substructure system consists of reinforced concrete pile caps and grade beams supported on pre-cast, pre-stressed concrete driven piles and cast-in-place "Fundex" type piles. Perimeter basement walls are constructed of reinforced concrete.

STOP 3: JP MORGAN CHASE BUILDING, 560 MISSION STREET

Significance of the Site

Construction of the JP Morgan Chase Building was completed in 2002. This is a 31-story, class A office building. The 789,701-square-foot building also features two levels of under-

Figure 5. (*continued*) (C) The art pavilion at the entrance to 101 Second Street, night view.

ground parking and a large ground-level plaza. The building is 100% leased to JP Morgan Chase and Co. and is their West Coast headquarters. The project is owned by National Office Partners Limited Partnership, a joint venture between Hines and the California Public Employees' Retirement System.

Accessibility

This is a private building with no public restrooms available, and there is limited off-site metered parking.

GPS Coordinates

Latitude: 37.7890280; longitude: −122.3983820.

Directions

From 101 Second Street, head northwest on Second, and turn right on Mission Street (Fig. 6).

Stop Description

Owner: National Office Partners Limited Partnership (NOP)
Developer: Hines Interests Limited Partnership

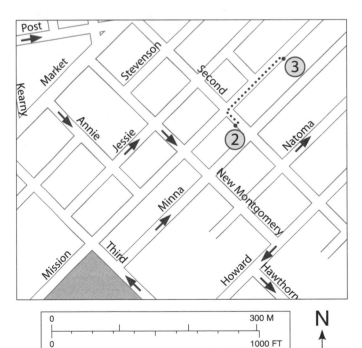

Figure 6. Map showing the location of Stop 3 (JP Morgan Chase building) in relation to Stop 2 (map drafted by Michael Rymer, U.S. Geological Survey).

Figure 7. (*this and the following two pages*) (A–B) Two exterior views of the JP Morgan Chase Building. Photographer: Tim Griffith, Esto Photographics, Inc.

Architect: Pelli Clarke, Pelli Architects (formerly Cesar Pelli and Associates)
Executive Architect: Kendall Heaton Associates
Structural Engineer: CBM Engineers
General Contractor: Turner Construction

The design of 560 Mission Street is both modern and classical. It is an elegant, delicately proportioned tower of glass and aluminum (Fig. 7A and 7B). The aluminum, painted a deep, rich green, forms a tapestry of lines on the glass wall. The changes in densities of this play of lines recall San Francisco's Hallidie building, the first "glass curtain wall" building in the western United States.

The project includes a plaza and urban park that features a bamboo grove and stone fountain. The fountain serves as the backdrop for a kinetic sculpture by artist George Rickey titled "Annular Eclipse" (Fig. 7C). The project received the American Society of Landscape Architects Award in 2003.

The structural system consists of a steel dual system of special moment-resisting frames and concentric braced frames to resist seismic forces. The structural design incorporates architectural features of the building including slop-

Figure 7. (*continued*) (C) a view of the plaza and urban park. Photographer: Tim Griffith, Esto Photographics, Inc.

ing box columns and 10-foot column offsets supporting the top four stories and, again, at the building base at levels eight and below.

STOP 4: THE PARAMOUNT, 680 MISSION STREET

Significance of the Site

Construction of the Paramount building was completed in 2004, and was the tallest precast concrete building in Seismic Zone 4, as well as the tallest precast, pre-stressed concrete framed structure in any region of high seismic hazard. The Paramount, located in the South of Market area of downtown San Francisco, won the Harry H. Edwards Industry Award in 2002 from the Precast Construction Institute for its innovative use of a structural frame as an exterior skin. The Paramount also received the 2004 (Structural Engineering Association of California) SEAOC Award Nomination for Best Use of New Technology in New Construction, as well as the 2004 SEAOC Award for Excellence in Structural Engineering. Significant schedule and cost savings were achieved on the project by the integration of the lateral force resisting system and building exterior façade into the same precast elements. The seismic design also includes a Precast Hybrid Moment Resistant Frame (PHMRF) system, and represents the first significant use of the PHMRF system.

Accessibility

This is a private building with no public restrooms available, and there is limited off-site metered parking.

GPS Coordinates

Latitude: 37.7866670; longitude: −122.4014320.

Directions

From the JP Morgan Chase Building, head southwest on Mission Street (Fig. 8).

Stop Description

Owner/Developer: The Related Companies
Design Architect: Elkus Manfredi Architects
Executive Architect: Kwan Henmi Architecture and Planning
Structural Engineer: EngleKirk Partners
General Contractor: Pankow Residential Builders Ltd.

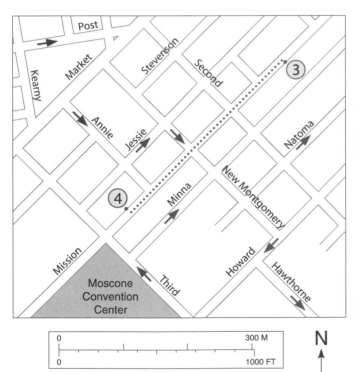

Figure 8. Map showing the location of Stop 4 (the Paramount building) in relation to Stop 3 (map drafted by Michael Rymer, U.S. Geological Survey).

This 39-story, 420-foot-tall residential tower's 660,000 square feet include 460,000 square feet of residential space and 200,000 square feet in the eight-level parking garage and retail shops (Fig. 9A and 9B). Overlooking San Francisco's Yerba Buena Center at Third and Mission Streets, the building contains 486 apartment units, commercial retail on the first two levels, an athletic club and business center for the residential tenants, and a 355-car parking structure.

Figure 9. (*this and following page*) (A–B) Photographs of the Paramount Building (Stop 4). Photographer: Bernard André, Bernard André Photography.

The superstructure consists of a cast-in-place reinforced concrete shear wall system and a precast and cast-in-place moment resisting frame system utilized from the mat foundation to the 8th floor. The shear walls terminate at the 8th floor. Above this level, a PHMRF system has been utilized to provide lateral resistance to seismic forces. The innovative PHMRF frame provides lateral support in both the longitudinal and transverse directions.

STOP 5: FOUR SEASONS HOTEL, 757 MARKET STREET

Significance of the Site

Opened in January 2001, this is one of the first completed skyscrapers of the twenty-first century in San Francisco. This 40-story, 398-foot-tall building contains the Four Seasons Hotel, with 277 guest rooms, 142 luxury condos, and retail stores.

Accessibility

This is a private building with no public restrooms available, and there is limited off-site metered parking.

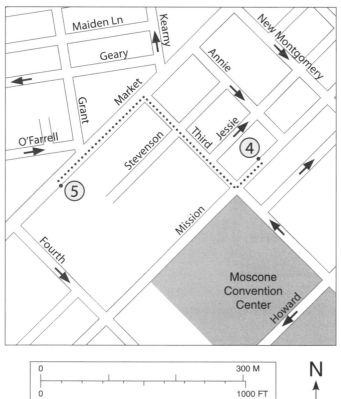

Figure 10. Map showing the location of Stop 5 (Four Seasons Hotel) in relation to Stop 4 (map drafted by Michael Rymer, U.S. Geological Survey).

Figure 9. (*continued*) (A–B) Photographs of the Paramount Building (Stop 4). Photographer: Bernard André, Bernard André Photography.

Figure 11. (*this and following page*) (A–B) Photographs of the Four Seasons Hotel (Stop 5). Photographer: Tim Griffith, Tim Griffith Photography.

GPS Coordinates

Latitude: 37.7866670; longitude: −122.4014320.

Directions

From the Paramount Building, head southwest on Mission Street, turn right on Third Street, and turn left on Market Street (Fig. 10).

Stop Description

Owner/Developer: Millennium Partners MDA Associates, Inc.
Construction Management: Bovis Lend Lease, Inc.
Architect: Gary Edward Handel + Associates; Del Campo and Maru Architects
Structural Engineer: DeSimmone Engineers

With construction completed in 2001, the Four Seasons Hotel and Residences mixed-use project on Market Street houses the 277-room Four Seasons hotel, 142 luxury residential condominiums, and the amenities of a state-of-the-art 100,000 square foot Sports Club/LA Fitness and spa facility (Fig. 11A and 11B). The building facility includes 80,000 square feet of retail space and 25,000 square feet of outdoor restaurant and café space along a connecting pedestrian corridor. The Four Seasons Hotel and Residences is located in close proximity to San Francisco's Financial District and Union Square, as well as the South of Market area adjacent to Sony Metreon, the Yerba Buena Gardens, and the Moscone Convention Center.

The steel-framed superstructure includes a structural steel dual system consisting of a concentrically braced core, and special moment resisting frames with proprietary ductile girder to column moment resisting connections. The core-braced frames also incor-

Figure 11. (*continued*) (A–B) Photographs of the Four Seasons Hotel (Stop 5). Photographer: Tim Griffith, Tim Griffith Photography.

porate innovative use of nonlinear fluid viscous dampers to further dissipate energy due to lateral wind and seismic forces.

ACKNOWLEDGMENTS

The authors want to thank the following people for information essential in the tour guide preparation: Dr. Ronald M. Polivka, managing principal at DeSimone Consulting Engineers (Four Seasons Hotel); Dr. P.V. Banavalker, President of Ingenium, Inc. (J.P. Morgan Chase Building); Dr. Edward Qi, Associate Principal at Middlebrook + Louie (101 Second Street); Tony Ghodsi, Principal at Englekirk Partners (The Paramount); Glenn Rescalvo, partner in charge, and Lauren Hlavenka, marketing associate, at Handel Architects, LLP (Four Seasons Hotel); and Edward Dionne, senior associate at Pelli Clarke Pelli Architects (J.P. Morgan Chase Building).

FURTHER READING

Banavalker, P.V., and Parikh, V., 2001, Change in trend of structural systems for high-rise building in seismic regions: Trends in Tall Building, September, p. 1–14.

DeSimone, S., and Bongiorno, S., 2002, The seismic solution: Modern Steel Construction, December, p. 1–5.

Englekirk, R.E., 2002 Design-construction of the Paramount—A 39-story precast prestressed concrete apartment building: PCI Journal, July/August, p. 56-71.

The San Francisco–Oakland Bay Bridge

Charles Rabamad

Governor's Office of Emergency Services, Response and Recovery Division, 3650 Schriever Avenue, Mather, California 95655, USA

OVERVIEW OF THE FIELD TRIP

This field trip consists of a 30-minute presentation by the California Department of Transportation (Caltrans) about the ongoing construction of the new, seismically upgraded Bay Bridge, followed by a guided boat tour of the ongoing bridge construction.

Keywords: Seismic design, San Francisco Bay Bridge, earthquake engineering, bridge safety.

STOP 1: CALTRANS FIELD OFFICE AND BOAT TOUR OF NEW BAY BRIDGE CONSTRUCTION

Significance of the Site

The San Francisco–Oakland Bay Bridge provides a vital transportation link from San Francisco to the East Bay region. During the 1989 Loma Prieta earthquake, part of the bridge failed (Fig. 1), and subsequent studies concluded that a new bridge, designed to withstand strong earthquakes, would be the best way to ensure the bridge's future safety.

Accessibility

This field trip is provided courtesy of Caltrans by special arrangement and is not normally available to the public.

Directions

From Moscone Center, take Highway 80 eastbound across the San Francisco–Oakland Bay Bridge. Merge onto Highway 880 southbound. Take the West Grand–Maritime exit, turn right onto Maritime Avenue, and turn right onto Burma Road. The offices are located at the end of the street, at 345 Burma Road, Oakland (Pier 7) (Fig. 2).

Stop Description

In 1924, government engineers investigated the possibilities of building the San Francisco–Oakland Bay Bridge and determined that it would be impractical due to earthquake faults and the difficulty of finding a solid anchorage on the muddy bottom. However, President Herbert Hoover, an engineer, took an interest in the idea and in October 1929, with California Governor C.C. Young, appointed the Hoover-Young San Francisco Bay Bridge Commission. The Commission submitted its report in August 1930, concluding that not only was the bridge necessary to the development of the area, but that it was "entirely feasible from economic and construction viewpoints." Hoover expedited War and Navy Department approvals and promised financial support through his Reconstruction Finance Corporation. Contracts for the first construction were awarded in April 1933.

The San Francisco–Oakland Bay Bridge, built for a total cost of US$77.6 million, opened to vehicular traffic on 12 November 1936. Tolls paid off the government loan within twenty years. Upon its completion, the Bay Bridge was recognized as the greatest bridge in the world for its length, cost, weight, depth, amount of steel and concrete used, number of piers, and versatility of engineering. On 17 October 1989, the tremors of the Loma Prieta earthquake signaled the beginning of the end for the eastern span of the San Francisco–Oakland Bay Bridge. The magnitude 6.9 earthquake severely damaged the 1930s-era double-deck truss structure, knocking down a portion of the upper deck, killing one motorist and exposing the span's weakness (Fig. 1).

With the bridge out of service for a month, Caltrans inaugurated a study to determine if the bridge could withstand another earthquake. Seismic experts say a major temblor is likely to occur in the next 30 yr—an ominous fact for the bridge, considering it lies only a few miles from both the San Andreas and Hayward faults.

Rabamad, C., 2006, The San Francisco–Oakland Bay Bridge, *in* Prentice, C.S., Scotchmoor, J.G., Moores, E.M., and Kiland, J.P., eds., 1906 San Francisco Earthquake Centennial Field Guides: Field trips associated with the 100th Anniversary Conference, 18–23 April 2006, San Francisco, California: Geological Society of America Field Guide 7, p. 107–109, doi: 10.1130/2006.1906SF(08). For permission to copy, contact editing@geosociety.org. ©2006 Geological Society of America. All rights reserved.

Figure 1. Aerial view of roadbed collapse of the San Francisco–Oakland Bay Bridge. View northwestward. Photograph by C.E. Meyer, U.S. Geological Survey (Nakata et al., 1999).

Caltrans determined that while the western side of the bridge from San Francisco to Yerba Buena could be retrofitted to withstand a major quake, it would be far more cost-effective in the long-run and safer to build a new eastern span rather than retrofit it. Built according to 1930s codes, the bridge was designed for what today are merely minimal seismic impacts. The wooden timbers on which the bridge piers stand leave the bridge increasingly vulnerable over time. To bring the bridge up to modern standards would be relatively too expensive, unreliable, and extremely difficult given today's traffic levels.

The initial proposal for the eastern span was to build an elevated viaduct, which was criticized by many as being merely a "freeway on stilts" and was not well received by the public. Subsequently, a design contest was held and the search for a "signature span" was held. One of the many unique and innovative proposals was selected.

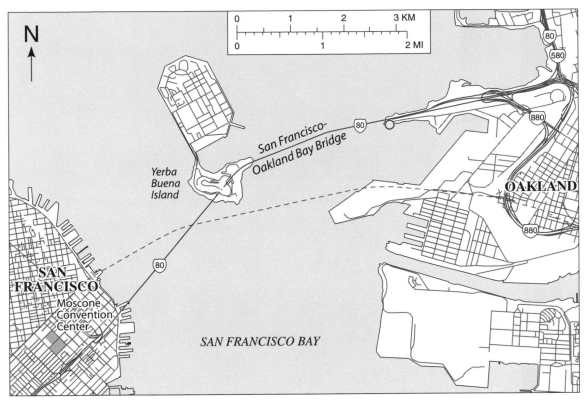

Figure 2. Map showing San Francisco–Oakland Bay bridge and Caltrans field offices (yellow dot) at 345 Burma Road (map by M. Rymer, U.S. Geological Survey).

Finally, the design went out for bid, and the results were surprising. Only one bid was returned and its cost was considerably higher than expected. The entire project is projected to cost US$6.2 billion (as of July 2005), a substantial increase over the 1997 estimate of US$1.1 billion for the original simple viaduct plan, and US$2.6 billion for a tower span.

In late 2004, California's governor decided to scrap the signature bridge idea, and decided to go back to the original simple viaduct plan. However, this produced a great deal of controversy. The governor did not think that the entire state should contribute to the cost of the new bridge; he believed it to be a local Bay Area problem. Eventually, midway through 2005, a compromise was reached and an agreement was made to build the signature span and to fund it with an increase in the bridge toll. The delay precipitated by the governor's decision to go back to the simple viaduct is estimated to have added an additional US$350 million to the overall cost. The entire project is scheduled to be completed in 2012 at a total cost of US$6.3 billion.

REFERENCES CITED

Nakata, J.K., Meyer, C.E., Wilshire, H.G., Tinsley, J.C., Updegrove, W.S., Peterson, D.M., Ellen, S.D., Haugerud, R.A., McLaughlin, R.J., Fisher, G.R., and Diggles, M.F., 1999, The October 17, 1989, Loma Prieta, California, earthquake—Selected photographs: U.S. Geological Survey Digital Data Series, DDS-29, http://pubs.usgs.gov/dds/dds-29/.

Geological Society of America
Field Guide 7
2006

Golden Gate Bridge field guide

Moh Huang
Strong Motion Instrumentation Program, California Geological Survey,
801 K Street, MS 13-35, Sacramento, California 95814-3531, USA
Jerry Kao
Golden Gate Bridge, Highway and Transportation District,
P.O. Box 9000, Presidio Station, San Francisco, California 94129-0601, USA

OVERVIEW OF THE FIELD TRIP

This field trip consists of stops in four locations (Fig. 1) that provide insight into the seismic retrofit and strong motion instrumentation of the Golden Gate Bridge (Figs. 2 and 3). Only one of the four stops is normally open to the public (Stop 3a). The first stop at the Golden Gate Bridge Highway and Transportation District (GGBHTD) office board room will include an introduction to the bridge history and presentation of the seismic retrofit schemes, strong motion instrumentation of the bridge, and the data products available from the California Strong Motion Instrumentation Program (CSMIP) of the California Geological Survey (CGS). At the second stop, participants will see a free-field instrument in the maintenance area.

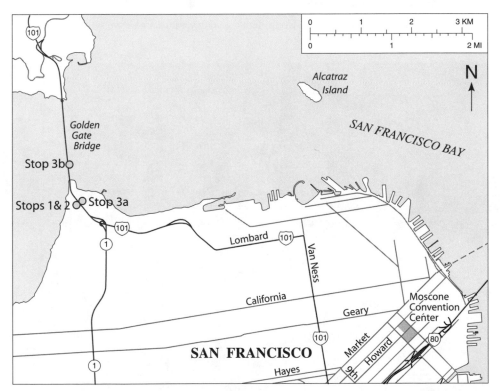

Figure 1. Map showing locations of field trip stops in relation to Moscone Center (map drafted by Michael Rymer, U.S. Geological Survey).

Huang, M., and Kao, J., 2006, Golden Gate Bridge field guide, *in* Prentice, C.S., Scotchmoor, J.G., Moores, E.M., and Kiland, J.P., eds., 1906 San Francisco Earthquake Centennial Field Guides: Field trips associated with the 100th Anniversary Conference, 18–23 April 2006, San Francisco, California: Geological Society of America Field Guide 7, p. 111–122, doi: 10.1130/2006.1906SF(09). For permission to copy, contact editing@geosociety.org. ©2006 Geological Society of America. All rights reserved.

Figure 2. Photograph of the Golden Gate Bridge looking northward from near the southern anchorage.

Figure 3. Aerial view looking down on the south anchorage of the Golden Gate Bridge. Stops 1–3a are visible in this view.

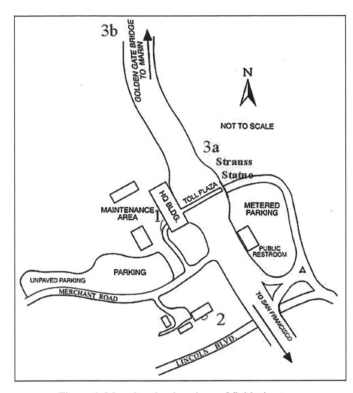

Figure 4. Map showing locations of field trip stops.

At the third stop, we will observe retrofit work under way (in 2006) from a public overlook area. At the fourth stop, we will see the seismic sensors and instrumentation installed on the bridge. The locations of these four stops (Stops 1, 2, 3a, and 3b) are shown in Figure 4.

Keywords: Golden Gate Bridge, seismic retrofit, strong motion instrumentation, ShakeMap.

STOP 1: BRIDGE DISTRICT OFFICE BOARD ROOM

Significance of the Site

The board room at the district office provides a convenient location for an introduction to the Golden Gate Bridge and the design of its seismic retrofit. Bridge District personnel will introduce the history of the bridge and give an overview of the seismic retrofit schemes for the bridge. A representative from the California Geological Survey will present an overview of the California Strong Motion Instrumentation Program, its products (including ShakeMaps and data available at the Engineering Data Center on the internet), and the instrumentation placed on the bridge.

Accessibility

The lectures provided in the board room must be pre-arranged with the Bridge District.

Directions

From Moscone Center, follow Howard Street southwest. Turn right onto 9th Street. Turn left on Hayes immediately after crossing Market Street. Turn right on Van Ness, and follow signs to the Golden Gate Bridge. Exit at "Last San Francisco Exit" immediately before the toll plaza, following the sign to the "Golden Gate National Recreation Area View Area." Bear left, crossing under the bridge to a stop sign, then continue into the public parking lot.

Stop Description: Overview of Golden Gate Bridge Seismic Retrofit

The following description for Stop 1, through the information about Phase 3 of the retrofit, is reprinted with permission from the GGBHTD Web site at http://goldengatebridge.org/projects/retrofit.php (updated October 2005).

It was a bone rattling, concrete crushing, nerve-racking 15 seconds. At 5:04 p.m. on Tuesday evening, October 17, 1989, the 6.9 magnitude Loma Prieta earthquake caused 68 deaths, at least 3,700 injuries, and an estimated dollar loss of $6 billion to $7 billion. The earthquake reminded the world that the San Francisco Bay region remains vulnerable. Although the Golden Gate Bridge suffered no observed damage from the Loma Prieta earthquake (the epicenter was located some 60 miles to the south), the earthquake became a catalyst for the extensive seismic retrofit program that the historic structure is undergoing today.

Perhaps the most impressive statistic resulting from research conducted since the Loma Prieta earthquake is the conclusion by the U.S. Geological Survey (USGS) and other scientific organizations that there is a 62 percent probability of at least one magnitude 6.7 or greater earthquake, capable of causing widespread damage, impacting the San Francisco Bay region by 2032.

The Golden Gate Bridge represents a vital transportation link to the San Francisco Bay area, serving more than 40 million vehicles a year. The bridge is recognized by the American Society of Civil Engineers as one of seven civil engineering wonders of the United States. The bridge is a national treasure known and admired around the world. Spanning 1.7 miles from abutment to abutment, the Golden Gate Bridge consists of six main structures (Fig. 5):

1. San Francisco (south) approach viaduct;
2. San Francisco (south) anchorage housing and pylons S1 and S2;
3. Fort Point Arch;
4. Main suspension bridge;
5. Marin (north) approach viaduct;
6. Marin (north) anchorage housing and pylons N1 and N2.

Immediately following the Loma Prieta earthquake, the Golden Gate Bridge Highway and Transportation District, San Francisco, California, the owner and operator of the Golden

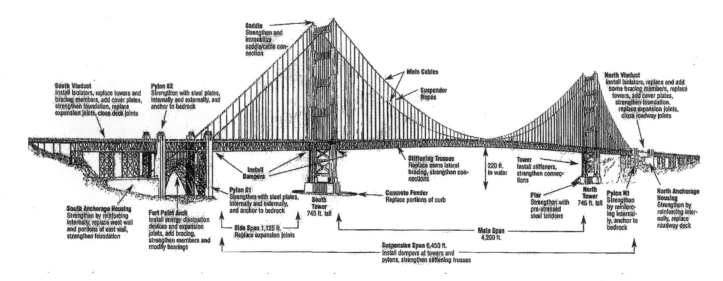

Golden Gate Bridge Seismic Retrofit Measures

Figure 5. Drawing of the Golden Gate Bridge showing seismic retrofit measures.

Gate Bridge, engaged a team of consultants to conduct a seismic vulnerability study. The conclusion of the study was that under a Richter magnitude 7.0 or greater earthquake with an epicenter near the bridge, it would experience severe damage that could close this important transportation link for an extended period of time. If a Richter magnitude 8.0 or greater earthquake occurred near the bridge, there would be a substantial risk of collapse or impending collapse of the San Francisco and Marin approach viaducts and the Fort Point Arch, and extensive damage to the remaining bridge structures, including the main suspension bridge.

It was also determined that retrofitting the bridge would be more cost effective than replacing it. In 1992, the Golden Gate Bridge Highway and Transportation District hired engineering consultants to develop seismic retrofit design criteria. As part of this task, the site-specific design ground motions associated with different magnitudes of earthquakes and expected performance levels were defined as the basis for the bridge retrofit design. The site-specific, moderate earthquake was defined as one having a 10% chance of being exceeded in a 50-year period and producing an acceleration of 0.46 g at the bridge. The site-specific, maximum credible earthquake was defined as one having a return period of 1000 yr or having an acceleration of 0.65 g, which is equivalent to an earthquake of magnitude 8.3 on the Richter scale.

Because of financial constraints, the Highway and Transportation District proceeded with the construction of the seismic retrofit in phases reflecting the degree of structural vulnerabilities.

In 1996, the three construction phases were established as follows: Phase 1 (completed 2002): retrofit the Marin (north) approach viaduct. Phase 2 (scheduled completion, middle

2006): retrofit the San Francisco (south) approach viaduct, San Francisco (south) anchorage housing, Fort Point Arch, and pylons S1 and S2. Phase 3 (awaiting funding): retrofit main suspension bridge and Marin (north) anchorage housing.

The total estimated steel and concrete quantities for the entire retrofit project are as follows: structural steel: 22.3 million pounds; structural concrete: 24,000 cubic yards; reinforcing steel: 5.3 million pounds.

A schematic of retrofit measures for the Golden Gate Bridge is shown in Figure 5.

Phase 1—Completed in 2002

On 27 June 1997, the Board of Directors of the Highway and Transportation District awarded a contract to Balfour Beatty Construction, Inc., El Dorado Hills, California, for the first phase of seismic retrofit construction. It also organized a construction administration team made up of district staff and consultants. HNTB Corporation, St. Louis, Missouri, was selected to provide construction management and inspection of the project. HNTB's subconsultants included Towill, Inc., for surveying; Thomas Jee and Associates, Inc., for steel bridge engineering and inspection; Kennedy/Jenks for hazardous materials (hazmat) technical support; and Al Gok Consultants, Inc., for construction safety.

The seismic retrofit measures applied to the bridge structures consisted of various methods of structural upgrades and included both the strengthening of structural components and the modification of structural response of the structures, so they can better respond to strong motions without damage. The cost of phase 1 totaled $71 million, which was funded using Golden Gate Bridge tolls.

The major strengthening measures implemented on the Marin (north) approach viaduct include the following: (1)

strengthening of the existing foundations; (2) total replacement of the four supporting steel towers and strengthening of bent N11; (3) replacement and addition of top and bottom lateral bracing and strengthening of vertical truss members and truss connections; and (4) modification of the structural system to minimize the effects of ground motions on the structure by connecting five, simply supported truss spans into a continuous truss, installing seismic expansion joints at the north and south ends of the viaduct truss, and installing isolator bearings atop the new steel support towers at the pylon N2 support and at bent N11.

The scope of retrofit within the viaduct truss was significantly reduced through the installation of lead-core-rubber–type isolator bearings. These bearings enable displacements of the truss relative to its supports, thereby significantly reducing the transfer of seismic forces onto the truss.

The maximum credible earthquake is predicted to create up to 12-inch displacements of the truss. To prevent the truss from crushing against the Marin (north) abutment and pylon N2, seismic expansion joints were constructed at these locations by removing a section of the orthotropic steel deck of the viaduct at pylon N2 and removing and reconstructing the Marin abutment back wall. These joints enable truss displacements of up to 15 inches, thereby preventing damage that could jeopardize the integrity of the structure.

A primary challenge of phase 1 was to construct the retrofit measures under continuous traffic. The construction inspection team closely monitored the structure throughout the complex process of installing temporary bracing, constructing and loading temporary supports for replacement of the towers, removing and replacing members, and strengthening members and connections.

The first work undertaken was to connect the viaduct spans to create a continuous superstructure capable of distributing lateral forces to prescribed points while the structure underwent tower replacements. Bent N11 near the Marin (north) abutment was substantially strengthened to substitute for temporary loss of longitudinal stiffness at the removed supporting towers. Before the individual towers could be replaced, the retrofit sequence required that truss members directly above each of the towers be replaced and truss panel points be strengthened.

The contractor retrofitted the tower foundations in a two-stage operation. The first stage was constructed with the existing towers still in place, which allowed them to schedule this work outside of the project critical path.

During the first stage, cast-in-drilled-hole (CIDH) piling and pile caps were added around the perimeter of the original foundation pedestals. The new concrete to existing concrete interfaces were strengthened with post-tensioning of monostrands, clamping the new footings to the pedestals of the existing foundations. The existing grade beams between the foundation pedestals were also substantially strengthened, and additional grade beams were constructed.

After the existing tower was removed, the second stage of the foundation retrofit proceeded. First, the remaining upper portions of the existing pedestals were demolished. Then, new upper pedestals were constructed and closure pours placed to incorporate these elements into the entire foundation system. The erection of a new tower followed.

The most visually dramatic Phase 1 work was the complete removal and replacement of the four steel support towers with footprints of 50 feet by 75 feet and heights of up to 150 feet. The contractor sequentially replaced the existing towers with new ones that very closely imitated the appearance of the original towers.

Jacking of the superstructure continuously under traffic was an interesting aspect of the tower removal and replacement operation. Once erection of the temporary supports was completed on the sides of the original tower, a series of synchronized jacks lifted the superstructure from the six original tower bearings by loading the six temporary support bearings. The temporary supports and jack were located 25 feet away from the adjoining original tower. At the jacking points, the superstructure had to be lifted by up to 1 1/2 inches to provide for up to 1/4-inch of lift at the existing bearings. This separation was sufficient for the contractor to proceed with removal of the original bearings, which was followed by demolition of the tower below.

The synchronous lift system used by the contractor was controlled at an electronic central control panel that was capable of raising the individual jack rams in precise increments of 0.2 inch and of shutting down the individual jacks once the superstructure was raised the prescribed height.

A total of six jacking points were used per tower; each point consisting of a cluster of four 200 ton jacks. Each jack cluster was tied to a single manifold, such that all four jacks received the same hydraulic and electronic signals from the controller. This system included highly accurate (up to 0.04 inch) sensors, which were attached to the superstructure to control its position. Aside from this means of displacement monitoring, a licensed land surveyor was also deployed on a nearby hillside to monitor structure location prior to, during, and after the jacking operations so as to detect any unplanned movement. Locking collars were placed on the jacks as a means of providing redundancy in the event of a hydraulic failure of the jacking system. Workers monitored the existing tower bearings and reported on their status via radio.

The overall jacking operations typically required approximately half an hour, the majority of which was spent checking and monitoring the status of the lift, with frequent instrument readings and status verifications.

Phase 2—To Be Completed Mid-2006

On 10 October 2000, the district began soliciting for bids for phase 2 of the Golden Gate Bridge Seismic Retrofit Project. On 11 May 2001, the Board of Directors of the district authorized award of the phase 2 construction contract to Shimmick Construction Company, Inc./Obayashi Corporation, a Joint Venture, Hayward, California.

In June 2001, the second construction phase began; it is the most complex part of the project in terms of design and construction. Federal, state, and regional funds totaling $171 million were aggressively sought and authorized to complete this phase. This phase, set to be completed in 2006, encompasses the retrofit of several different types of structures associated with the south approach: the south approach viaduct, south anchorage housing, Fort Point Arch, and south pylons. Retrofit measures developed for each of these structures reflect their individual behavior under seismic ground motions and their interaction at points of interface while accommodating their already-in-place historic configuration.

Without closing the Golden Gate Bridge to traffic, the steel support towers and bottom lateral bracing of the south approach viaduct is being entirely replaced, and seismic isolation bearings and joints are being installed at the roadway level. The west wall of the south anchorage housing is being replaced, and massive internal shear walls are being constructed. Five million pounds of external and internal steel plating are being added to south pylon walls. The historic architectural appearance of the external surfaces of the pylons will remain unchanged with the addition of a new external concrete cover on top of the new plating.

The Fort Point Arch is being retrofitted with new arch bearings and energy dissipation devices, and isolation joints are being installed. Steel members throughout the entire arch are undergoing extensive strengthening.

Not only were immense challenges presented in the design and engineering of this phase of retrofit construction, but the construction site itself presents very unique project limitations. The construction site is located in a very compact area bounded on the west by the Pacific Ocean and on the east by very steep slopes. Severe weather, including strong wind and high waves, is nearly constant. Access consists of two narrow roads that must be shared with thousands of tourists visiting the Golden Gate Bridge and the Historic Fort Point Site located directly below the Fort Point Arch structure of the bridge. Construction on the arch is limited to four days per week to allow limited visitation to the Historic Fort Point Site. The small construction staging areas available near the work site further restrict the logistics of the construction operations.

Phase 3—Remains Unfunded (January 2006)

The $160 million third and final phase of construction is planned to retrofit the main suspension span, the two main towers, and the north anchorage and pylon N1. The district continues to work diligently at the state and federal levels to assure funding for this phase and has secured $5 million toward this project to date. Once funding is available, the project can be completed in approximately 4 years.

Strong Motion Instrumentation of the Golden Gate Bridge

Instrumentation of the Golden Gate Bridge was planned by the California Geological Survey and California Strong Motion Instrumentation Program (CSMIP) and the Golden Gate Bridge Highway and Transportation District in cooperation with an appointed seismic instrumentation advisory panel in 1992. A total of 76 sensors (including 72 accelerometers and 4 relative displacement sensors) were installed in 1995 prior to retrofitting the bridge. Specifically, the numbers of sensors installed at each structure are: 15 at the north viaduct and north anchorage housing; 33 on the suspension bridge; 22 at the south viaduct, south anchorage housing, and Fort Point Arch; 3 at the south free-field; and 3 at the downhole geotechnical array near south viaduct.

The locations of these 76 sensors are shown in Figures 6–9. The purpose of the pre-retrofit instrumentation was to measure the response of the various bridge structures to ground motions. In the main suspension bridge, the instrumentation was designed to measure three-dimensional motions of the towers, plus vertical, longitudinal, transverse, and torsional motions of the suspended trusses. These measurements were accomplished mainly with accelerometers (for example, a sensor as shown in Fig. 10). Additional instrumentation with relative displacement sensors measure relative displacements across the expansion joints at the south tower and pylon S1, and uplift due to rocking at the base of the tower shafts.

After completion of the retrofit for the north viaduct, 18 additional sensors were installed (Fig. 11). In addition, a downhole geotechnical array was installed near the north viaduct. When the retrofit of south viaduct is completed in 2006, 25 more sensors will be added. The total then will be 119 sensors.

ShakeMaps

A ShakeMap is a graphical representation of the intensity, or the amount of ground shaking, at a particular place due to an earthquake. The information it presents is different from the earthquake magnitude because it focuses on the effect of the earthquake, the ground shaking, rather than on how much energy was released at the earthquake source. Magnitude (for example 5.1 for the Napa earthquake illustrated in Fig. 12) reflects the energy released in the earthquake. In contrast, intensity indicates how the ground shook at a particular site. While an earthquake has only one magnitude and epicenter, it causes varying shaking severity throughout a region. The intensity (which varies with distance to the earthquake, site geology, and other factors) indicates the potential damage. The purpose of ShakeMap is to quickly provide a picture of the intensity of ground shaking after an event.

The California Integrated Seismic Network (CISN, a partnership of CGS, the U.S. Geological Survey, Caltech and the University of California at Berkeley) produces ShakeMaps after significant earthquakes in California. Critical to improving emergency response, ShakeMaps require the measured data from many stations, and these agencies began pooling their data after the 1994 Northridge earthquake, a project that was encouraged by the Office of Emergency Services (OES) and Federal

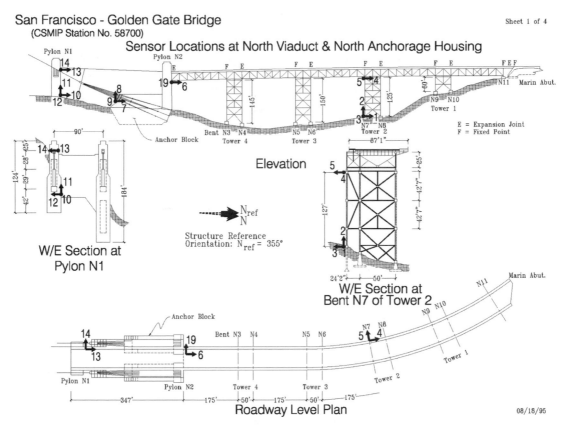

Figure 6. Drawing showing locations of strong motion instrumentation near north anchorage of the Golden Gate Bridge.

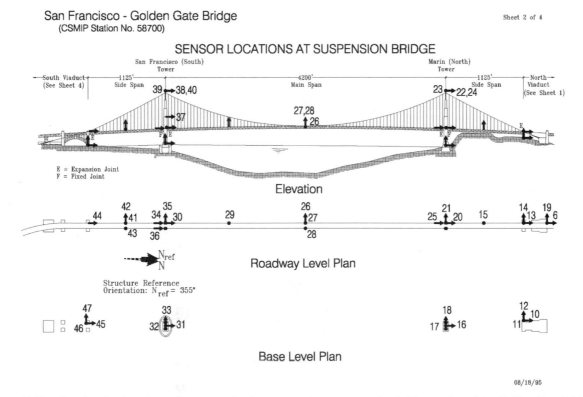

Figure 7. Drawing showing locations of strong motion instrumentation on suspension bridge section of the Golden Gate Bridge.

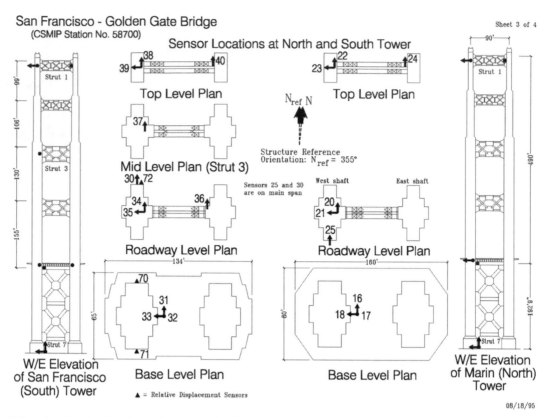

Figure 8. Drawing showing locations of strong motion instrumentation near north and south towers of the Golden Gate Bridge.

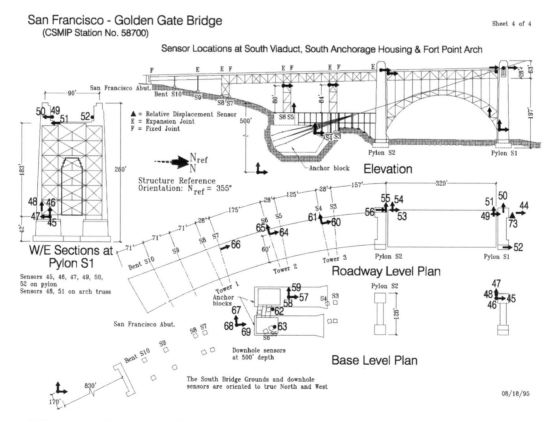

Figure 9. Drawing showing locations of strong motion instrumentation near south anchorage of the Golden Gate Bridge.

Figure 10. Photograph of accelerometer installed as part of instrumentation of the Golden Gate Bridge.

Emergency Management Agency (FEMA). Rapid-response ground motion maps (ShakeMaps) are generated automatically after earthquakes for use by emergency responders, the media, and the public. The maps use the recorded ground motions to calculate local shaking levels and areas of likely damage distribution. ShakeMaps are computed and posted within minutes of the occurrence of the earthquake (www.cisn.org/shakemap.html). Maps are updated as additional data become available. Currently, ShakeMaps are available for instrumental intensity, peak ground acceleration, peak ground velocity, and spectral response.

A measuring station on the grounds at the south end of the Golden Gate Bridge is one of many CGS/CSMIP stations that record the ground shaking for use in producing ShakeMaps.

ShakeMaps are valuable for postearthquake response in many applications, for example: (1) conducting damaged building and safety inspections; (2) for use at hospitals and other emergency response facilities; (3) assessing the impact on status of utility systems and transportation networks (see Fig. 13 for an example); (4) estimating shelter needs from housing loss projections; (5) evaluating hazardous material release and debris from collapsed structures; (6) preliminary estimation of economic loss (cities, counties); and (7) management of insurance claims.

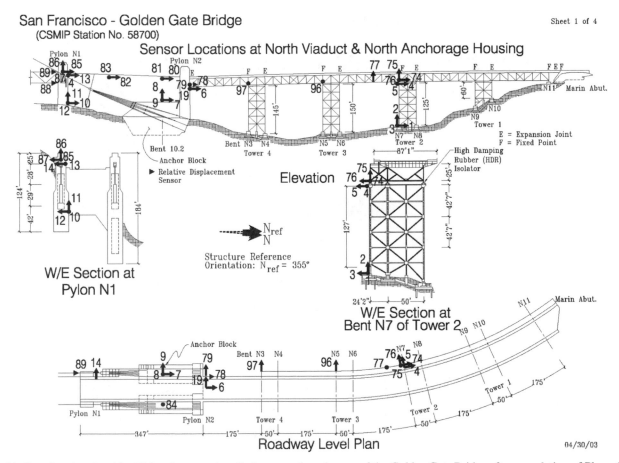

Figure 11. Drawing showing 18 additional sensors installed near north anchorage of the Golden Gate Bridge after completion of Phase 1 of the seismic retrofit project.

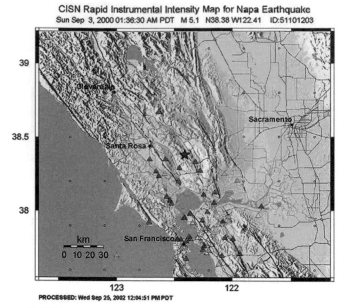

CISN Rapid Instrumental Intensity Map for Napa Earthquake
Sun Sep 3, 2000 01:36:30 AM PDT   M 5.1   N38.38 W122.41   ID:51101203

PROCESSED: Wed Sep 25, 2002 12:04:51 PM PDT

PERCEIVED SHAKING	Not felt	Weak	Light	Moderate	Strong	Very strong	Severe	Violent	Extreme
POTENTIAL DAMAGE	none	none	none	Very light	Light	Moderate	Moderate/Heavy	Heavy	Very Heavy
PEAK ACC.(%g)	<.17	.17-1.4	1.4-3.9	3.9-9.2	9.2-18	18-34	34-65	65-124	>124
PEAK VEL.(cm/s)	<0.1	0.1-1.1	1.1-3.4	3.4-8.1	8.1-16	16-31	31-60	60-116	>116
INSTRUMENTAL INTENSITY	I	II-III	IV	V	VI	VII	VIII	IX	X+

The CISN Engineering Data Center

Information on the instrumented bridges and other stations and the sensor locations on the structures are available at the Engineering Strong Motion Data Center (EDC; http://www.quake.ca.gov/cisn-edc) of the California Integrated Seismic Networks (CISN) (see the CGS home page at http://www.quake.ca.gov for more links). The strong motion data recorded are also available at the EDC. Internet Quick Reports (IQR) at the EDC list strong motion records immediately after a significant earthquake. IQR use internet technology as a means to provide engineers access to processed strong motion data and spectral information, as well as information about the structures and sites, very rapidly after an earthquake.

Users of the EDC have direct access to the processed strong motion data from previous earthquakes and detailed information on instrumented structures. The users can also download all the records from a specific station. The EDC increases the ability of earthquake engineers and emergency managers to respond knowledgeably and rapidly after earthquakes.

Figure 12. Example of a ShakeMap, produced by the California Integrated Seismic Network (CISN) for the 3 September 2000 M 5.1 Napa earthquake (courtesy California Geological Survey, www.cisn.org/shakemap/nc/shake/51101203/intensity.html).

9/28/2004 Parkfield, California Earthquake

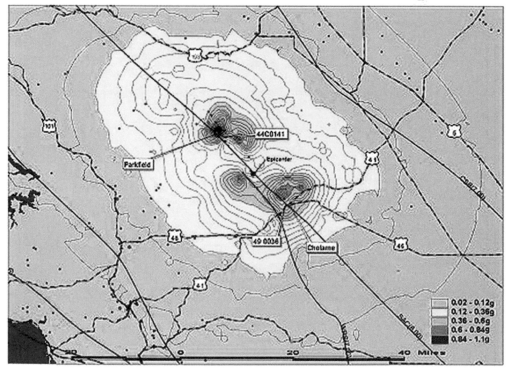

▨	0.02 - 0.12g
▨	0.12 - 0.36g
▨	0.36 - 0.6g
▨	0.6 - 0.84g
▨	0.84 - 1.1g

Figure 13. Map showing contours of peak ground acceleration for the 28 September 2004 Parkfield earthquake. This is an example of the application of ShakeMap to rapidly assess the impact of this earthquake on the status of utility systems and transportation networks; g—force of gravity.

STOP 2: FREE-FIELD STATION IN THE MAINTENANCE AREA

Significance of the Site

This is one of the strong motion instruments that measures the shaking produced during large earthquakes.

Accessibility

This area is not open to the public.

Directions

From the district office building, cross Merchant Road to the instrument location shown on Figure 4.

Stop Description

The group will view the free-field instrument located on a rock outcrop in the maintenance area south of the district office. This instrument measures three components of ground motion on the south end of the Golden Gate Bridge. The measured ground motion is incorporated into the ShakeMaps routinely generated after a significant earthquake. In addition, instruments are installed on the north side of the bridge, in a downhole geotechnical array near the south viaduct, and at the bases of both towers. Measurements from these instruments will provide information on the input ground motions to the bridge superstructure.

STOP 3A: FORT POINT OVERLOOK AREA

Significance of the Site

This is a short walking tour that will visit a display about the details of the bridge construction and then proceed to an overlook of the bridge.

Accessibility

This is a public-access site; see http://goldengatebridge.org/visitors/whattodo.php for additional information.

Directions

From Stop 2, cross under the bridge to Strauss Statue. Follow the brick sidewalk located behind the Strauss Statue and continue to follow the bricks to the right until they join an asphalt overlook.

Stop Description

The tour group will visit the Strauss Statue located on the southeast side of the bridge and view a display of a cross section of one of the bridge's main cables behind the statue. The tour group will then take a short walk to the Fort Point overlook from the southeast parking lot. At the overlook, the participants will view the seismic retrofit work under way or completed at the south viaduct and the Fort Point Arch (Fig. 14).

Figure 14. Photograph of the Golden Gate Bridge undergoing Phase 2 of the seismic retrofit project.

Figure 15. Photograph of San Francisco Tower.

STOP 3B: THE SAN FRANCISCO TOWER

Significance of the Site

The instruments located at this stop record the strong ground motion during large earthquakes.

Accessibility

Pedestrians are normally not allowed on the west sidewalk; however, the east sidewalk is open to pedestrians. The west sidewalk is normally only open to cyclists.

Directions

From the Fort Point overlook, follow the bridge sidewalk to San Francisco Tower.

Stop Description

The group will walk on the west sidewalk to the San Francisco Tower (Fig. 15). The participants will be able to view the seismic recorders and sensors.

WEB REFERENCES

California Geological Survey: http://www.conscrvation.ca.gov/cgs; http://www.quake.ca.gov.
California Integrated Seismic Networks: http://www.cisn.org.
CISN Engineering Data Center: http//www.quake.ca.gov/cisn-edc.
Golden Gate Bridge, Highway and Transportation District, http://www.goldengatebridge.org.

The San Francisco Emergency Communications Center

Doug Sandy

Disaster Preparedness Division, Office of Emergency Services and Homeland Security,
1011 Turk Street, San Francisco, California 94102, USA

OVERVIEW OF FIELD TRIP

This field trip consists of a visit to the site of one of the 1906 earthquake relief camps and the City and County of San Francisco Emergency Communications Center facility, located at 1011 Turk Street in San Francisco.

Keywords: San Francisco, disaster response, emergency communications, response coordination.

Significance of the Site

Jefferson Square Park served as a refugee encampment after the 1906 earthquake. Across the street, the modern San Francisco Emergency Communications Center will be a major factor in coordinating the emergency response to the next earthquake or other natural disaster to strike San Francisco.

GPS Coordinates

37.781N, 122.426W.

Accessibility

Jefferson Square Park is a public park. The emergency communications center facility is a secure, restricted access building. Visitors must have prior approval for entry and must provide government-issued identification (a driver's license or passport). The facility does not have public parking, but some limited on-street parking may be available on side streets (parking in front of the facility is restricted). The facility is handicapped-accessible and has restrooms available for visitors.

Directions

The communications center is located at 1011 Turk Street, across from Jefferson Square Park, between Gough and Laguna Streets (Fig. 1). From the Moscone Convention Center, walk north on Fourth Street five blocks to Market Street, turn left, and walk less than a block to the Powell Street Bay Area Rapid Transit (BART) station. Take the BART train from the Powell Street station one stop to the Civic Center station. After taking the escalator up from the station, walk straight ahead to Hyde Street and turn north (right), walking two blocks to Golden Gate Avenue, then proceed west five blocks to Gough Street. Turn north (right) and walk one block to Turk Street. Turn west on Turk (left) and walk two blocks to 1011 Turk Street. The center is also accessible by cab or MUNI bus #31, which runs east-west on Eddy Street (one block north of Turk).

Stop Description

Jefferson Square Park functioned as a housing and feeding site for people left homeless by the 1906 earthquake (Fig. 2). The Emergency Communications Center now sits directly across the street from the park (Fig. 3). The building, which was completed in 1999, was designed to critical facility building standards, including a base-isolation system, back-up power and cooling systems. The 34,000-square-foot center houses the police, fire, and emergency medical services (911) dispatch center and the Office of Emergency Services and Homeland Security. The facility also serves as the primary emergency operations center for the City and County of San Francisco. The building houses the control system for the recently completed Emergency Outdoor Warning System, which will be utilized to warn the public of an emergency, such as a tsunami or earthquake.

Sandy, D., 2006, The San Francisco Emergency Communications Center, *in* Prentice, C.S., Scotchmoor, J.G., Moores, E.M., and Kiland, J.P., eds., 1906 San Francisco Earthquake Centennial Field Guides: Field trips associated with the 100th Anniversary Conference, 18–23 April 2006, San Francisco, California: Geological Society of America Field Guide 7, p. 123–125, doi: 10.1130/2006.1906SF(10). For permission to copy, contact editing@geosociety.org. ©2006 Geological Society of America. All rights reserved.

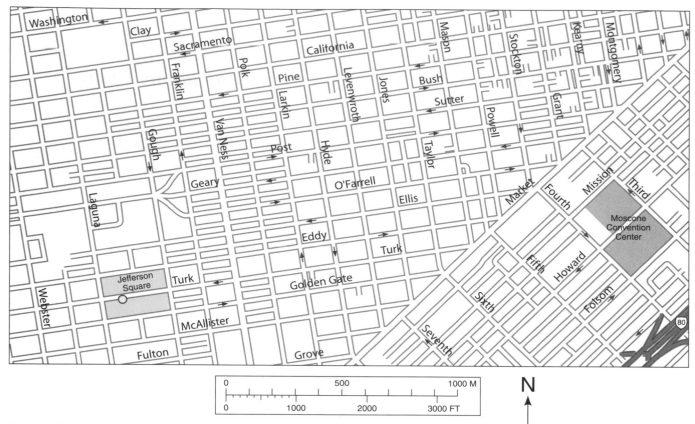

Figure 1. Map showing locations of San Francisco Emergency Communications Center (yellow dot on Turk between Laguna and Gough) and Jefferson Square Park in relation to the Moscone Center.

Figure 2. Photograph of 1906 refugee encampment in what is now Jefferson Square Park.

Figure 3. Photograph of San Francisco Emergency Communications Center, situated across the street from Jefferson Park.

Geological Society of America
Field Guide 7
2006

The San Andreas fault in Sonoma and Mendocino counties

Carol S. Prentice
U.S. Geological Survey, 345 Middlefield Rd., MS 977, Menlo Park, California 94025, USA
Keith I. Kelson
William Lettis & Associates, Inc., 1777 Botelho Drive, Walnut Creek, California 94596, USA

OVERVIEW OF THE FIELD TRIP

This two-day trip explores the northern San Andreas fault in the Gualala area between Fort Ross and Point Arena (Fig. 1). The first stop overlooks the Golden Gate Bridge and includes a discussion of its in-progress seismic retrofit. Several subsequent stops are at paleoseismic sites on the San Andreas fault. The stop at Annapolis Road includes a short hike along the fault through the redwood forest. This section of the fault is locked and has not moved since the 1906 earthquake. Additional stops visit Quaternary marine terraces and include discussion of associated tectonic deformation.

Keywords: San Andreas fault, paleoseismology, Gualala block, 1906 earthquake.

DAY 1: MOSCONE CENTER IN SAN FRANCISCO TO GUALALA, CALIFORNIA

Stop 1: Golden Gate Bridge Vista Point

Significance of the Site
The Golden Gate Bridge is a critical transportation link for the San Francisco Bay area. Built in the 1930s, it does not currently meet modern criteria for seismic safety, and is now undergoing a seismic retrofit to bring it up to modern seismic performance standards.

Accessibility
This site is a public area; restrooms are available, and there is a large parking area.

GPS Coordinates
37.84672°N, 122.37881°W.

Directions
Exit from northbound Highway 101 at Vista Point (1.8 mi from the south end of the bridge).

Stop Description
From this vantage point we can see the Golden Gate Bridge, a symbol of California as well as a vital transportation link for the San Francisco Bay area. The bridge was completed in 1937 and was considered a milestone in engineering (see Chapters 9 and 12, this volume). However, techniques for protecting bridges from strong seismic shaking have developed a great deal in the last several decades, and a comprehensive study conducted after the Loma Prieta earthquake in 1989 indicated that the Golden Gate Bridge would not be able to withstand a repeat of the 1906 earthquake. The second phase of the three-phase seismic retrofit is still in progress as of January 2006. However, the third phase, to strengthen the bridge span itself, has not yet been funded. Details of the seismic retrofit are described in Chapter 9 of this volume.

Stop 2: Mill Gulch

Significance of the Site
The offset of Mill Gulch, combined with a study of paleoseismic excavations and data collected after the 1906 earthquake, provide a slip rate across the fault averaged over the past 5000 yr. The fault rupture was photographed and mapped in detail in this area after the 1906 earthquake.

Accessibility
This property is part of Fort Ross State Historic Park, and is publicly accessible.

GPS Coordinates
38.50191°N, 123.21913°W.

Prentice, C.S., and Kelson, K.I., 2006, The San Andreas fault in Sonoma and Mendocino counties, *in* Prentice, C.S., Scotchmoor, J.G., Moores, E.M., and Kiland, J.P., eds., 1906 San Francisco Earthquake Centennial Field Guides: Field trips associated with the 100th Anniversary Conference, 18–23 April 2006, San Francisco, California: Geological Society of America Field Guide 7, p. 127–156, doi: 10.1130/2006.1906SF(11). For permission to copy, contact editing@geosociety.org. ©2006 Geological Society of America. All rights reserved.

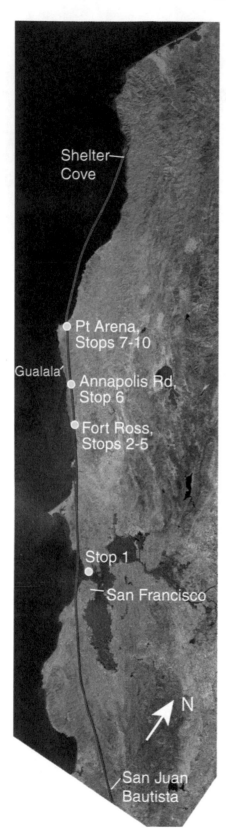

Figure 1. Landsat satellite image showing 1906 rupture trace of the northern San Andreas fault and field trip stops (image produced by M. Rymer, U.S. Geological Survey).

Directions

From Stop 1, continue northward on Hwy 101 to Petaluma. Exit at East Washington, turning left at the end of the exit ramp. Follow East Washington through the town of Petaluma and west toward Bodega Bay. East Washington becomes Hwy 1. Follow Hwy 1 north through Jenner and continue for 10 mi to pullout on the left side of the highway (Fig. 2). From here cross the fence and walk northward along the small ridge adjacent to the parking area for a view of Mill Gulch. Distance from Stop 1 is 79 mi.

Stop Description

Stop 2 is just north of where the San Andreas fault intersects the coastline north of the Russian River (Fig. 2). Visible from Stop 2 is Mill Gulch, a deeply incised stream that is offset 80–100 m across the San Andreas fault (Fig. 3). An abandoned channel of Mill Gulch is visible on Figure 3, north of Stop 2. Progressive offset of Mill Gulch over time created a situation in which the stream had to flow a long distance northwest along the fault before meeting the sea. Eventually, the stream cut a new, shorter, and more favorable path straight across the fault to the ocean, leaving its former channel abandoned. Since that time, the new channel of Mill Gulch has been offset by 80–100 m. Figure 4A shows the offset of the modern Mill Gulch. Figure 4B shows the mouth of the abandoned channel. The size of the

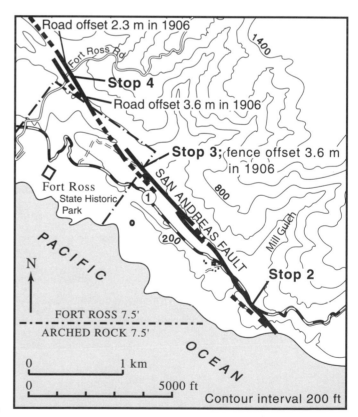

Figure 2. Map showing field trip Stops 2–4. Modified from Prentice et al., 1991. Offset values from Lawson, 1908.

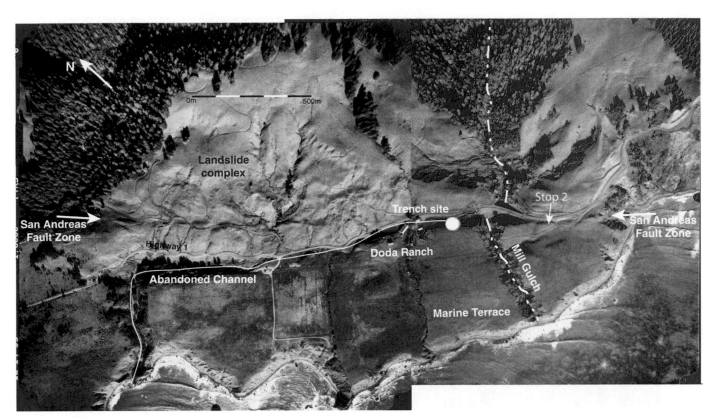

Figure 3. Aerial photograph (1999) of Mill Gulch area (Stop 2) showing offset of Mill Gulch and the abandoned channel where trench was excavated to determine how long ago abandonment occurred.

valley shown in Figure 4B is much too large for the small amount of discharge from its current headwaters; so little water flows in this stream today that there is a campground in the valley where Mill Gulch used to flow. Also note on Figure 4B that the mouth of the abandoned channel is above sea level. Since the channel was abandoned, the stream flow has been insufficient to incise the valley to keep up with coastal uplift.

We excavated trenches in the abandoned channel (trench site shown in Fig. 3) and collected charcoal samples from pre- and post-abandonment sediments to estimate the age of the 80–100 m offset. Radiocarbon analyses of these samples provide minimum ages that range from 4290–4520 to 4890–5290 cal yr B.P., and a single maximum age of 5040–5320 cal yr B.P. These data suggest a slip rate of 19 ± 4 mm/yr (best estimate of 18 ± 3 mm/yr) (Prentice et al., 2000, 2001; Muhs et al., 2003a).

Photographs taken in this area in 1906 after the earthquake illustrate the nature of the fault rupture (Fig. 5). In addition, F.E. Matthes made a detailed topographic map along this part of the fault (Fig. 6) (Lawson, 1908). We have superimposed the old map onto the aerial photographs (Fig. 7A) in order to precisely locate the 1906 fault rupture (Fig. 7B). Hiking to the south end of the area of the surveyed map, one can find the locations of several of the photographs taken in 1906 (Fig. 8).

Stop 3: Offset Fence and Marine Terrace Overlook

Significance of the Site

This location affords a view of the marine terraces of the Gualala block. In addition, there is a fence that was offset 3.6 m in 1906. This fence was surveyed in 1907 and is discussed in the Lawson Report (Lawson, 1908). Very few of the fences offset in 1906 remain. This is a rare example of an original offset fence.

Accessibility

The fence marks the boundary between Fort Ross State Historic Park property on the north and private property on the south. This part of the state park is normally not accessible to the public without permission. Beware of poison oak growing along the fence!

GPS Coordinates

Gate: 38.51491°N, 123.23986°W; offset fence: 38.5144°N, 123.23211°W.

Directions

From Stop 2, continue north on Hwy 1 for 1.5 mi. Turn right on the dirt road. The gate at the end of the road is locked; permission is needed to access this part of the state park. Con-

Figure 4. (A) Oblique aerial view looking eastward up Mill Gulch (1999). (B) Oblique aerial view of abandoned channel. Note contrast in stream morphology and elevations of stream mouths.

Surface Rupture

Figure 5. Photograph of 1906 surface rupture taken looking southward from a point south of Mill Gulch. See Figure 7B for approximate camera location. Courtesy of Bancroft Library, University of California–Berkeley (call number 1957.007.255, Series I). Photograph by A.C. Lawson.

tinue on the dirt road 0.5 mi to the top of a hill near some water tanks. Park near the water tanks and walk south to the fence. The view of the terraces is from the top of the hill. Walk east along the fence to the offset.

Stop Description

From this location, the view toward the ocean shows the flight of Pleistocene marine terraces present along the coast of the Gualala block. On rising crustal blocks, such as most of coastal California, interglacial high stands of the sea leave a stair-step flight of marine terraces. Mapping and detailed survey measurements of these terraces are under way to improve understanding of tectonic rates in the region. The most useful geomorphic features associated with the terraces are the former shorelines (Fig. 9). The shoreline angle provides an approximation of the location of sea level at the time the terrace was formed. The former shorelines can be used to estimate horizontal motion across the San Andreas fault where they intersect the fault near Point Arena (Stop 9), in addition to providing estimated rates of coastal uplift (Lajoie et al., 1991).

An old picket fence offset by the 1906 earthquake is still visible, though the modern wire fence that parallels the old fence currently marks the property boundary. Although many of the old fence posts have fallen, enough remain standing in 2006 to see the 1906 offset. The survey of this fence shown in Lawson (1908) shows that the total offset of 3.7 m was distributed

over a distance of 126 m, with only 2.3 m occurring where the main fault crosses the fence (Fig. 10). Historical research shows that Esper Larsen did the original survey between 20 January and 3 February1907, about a year after the earthquake (Prentice, 1989; Muhs et al., 2003a). Re-surveys of this fence in 1985 and 1999 show virtually no change since the 1907 survey. This indicates that no measurable afterslip occurred on this fault between February 1907 and 1999, consistent with re-surveys of other offset fences along the San Francisco peninsula (R.E. Wallace, U.S. Geological Survey, 1994, personal commun.).

The survey of this fence (and others offset by the fault surface rupture) is significant for mitigation and/or design of engineered structures, such as petroleum pipelines, railroad tracks, or water conveyance pipelines or canals that cross active faults. Based on the survey of this fence by Lawson (1908) and more recent surveys of similar features in Turkey by Rockwell et al. (2002), a model of fault deformation has been constructed for use in engineering design (Bray and Kelson, 2006). These studies suggest that ~85% of the total lateral deformation is typically accommodated across the primary surface-rupture trace, with the remaining 15% of deformation occurring in two zones bordering the primary fault. In conjunction with paleoseismic and geologic information across a given fault zone, these relationships can be used to help design mitigation strategies for fault-rupture damage to gas pipelines (Hart et al., 2004; Kelson et al., 2004) or transportation viaducts (William Lettis & Associates, 2003).

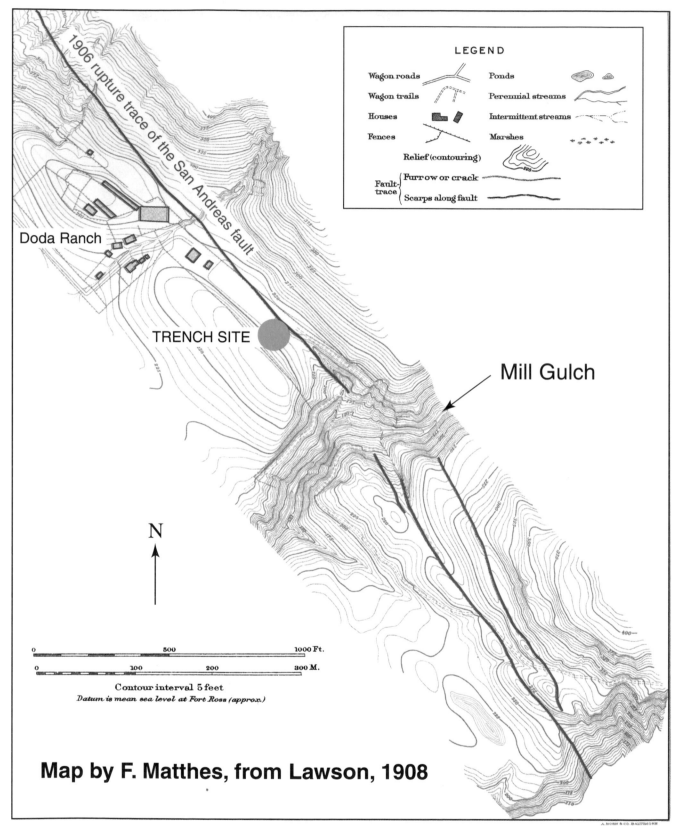

Figure 6. Part of detailed topographic map made by Matthes of this part of the surface rupture in 1906 (*in* Lawson, 1908). Note offset of Mill Gulch, which is easy to measure from this map, made before construction of Hwy 1 disrupted the area. Contour interval is 5 ft.

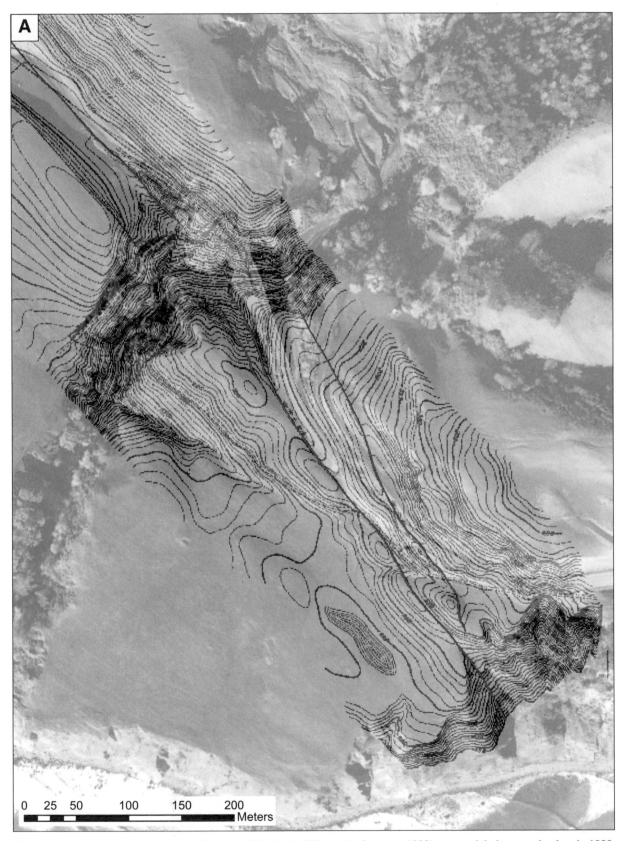

Figure 7. (*this and following page*) (A) Overlay of Matthes' 1906 map (*in* Lawson, 1908) onto aerial photograph taken in 1999.

Figure 7. (*continued*) (B) 1906 fault rupture traces mapped by Matthes superimposed on aerial photograph. Approximate camera locations of Figures 5 and 8 are shown.

Figure 8. (*this and following page*) Photographs of San Andreas fault surface rupture taken in 1906 in vicinity of Stop 2. (A) View looking southward at surface rupture on edge of bluff. Rocks in ocean are visible today from this location. Courtesy of Bancroft Library, University of California–Berkeley (call number 1957.007.256, Series I). (B–C) Views looking northward along surface rupture. Doda Ranch visible in distance. See Figure 7B for approximate camera locations. Courtesy of Bancroft Library, University of California–Berkeley (call numbers 1957.007.260 and 1957.007.259, Series I). Photographs by A.C. Lawson.

Figure 8. (*continued*)

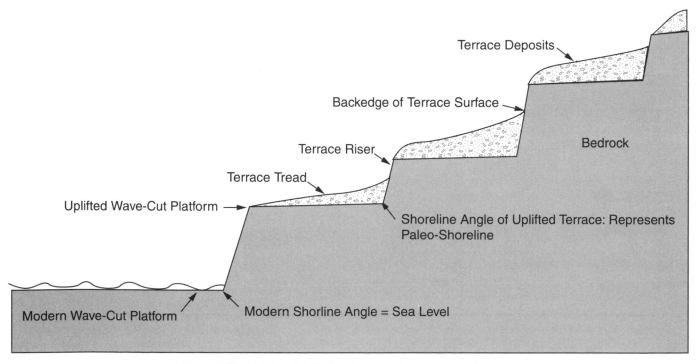

Figure 9. Sketch of typical flight of terraces showing terrace features.

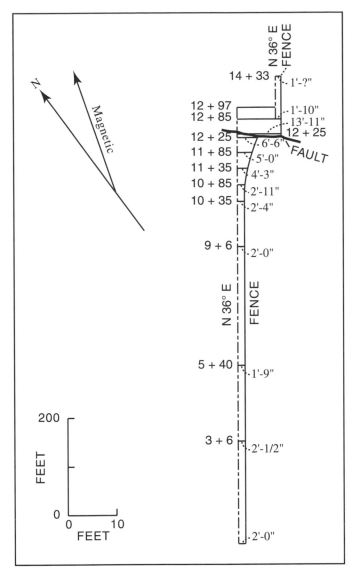

Figure 10. Survey of fenceline done in 1907 (Lawson, 1908). Fence posts still visible at Stop 3 in 2006.

Approximately 200 m northwest of the fence along the fault is a paleoseismic site known as the Archae Camp site. Trenches excavated across the fault here in the 1990s provided some of the earliest information about prehistoric earthquakes on this part of the San Andreas fault. These studies provide broad constraints on the timing of the past four surface ruptures on the North Coast segment (Noller et al., 1993; Simpson et al., 1996; Noller and Lightfoot, 1997). Two trenches excavated in 1992 showed the presence of three pre-1906 deposits interpreted to be scarp-derived colluvial deposits, and provided limited radiometric, obsidian-hydration, and archaeologic data to address event timing (Noller et al., 1993). Two trenches excavated in 1994 showed a series of slope deposits that also were interpreted to be related to surface-rupture events (Simpson

et al., 1996). Table 1 provides age estimates of surface ruptures based on our reanalysis of the age estimates from this site using the OxCal program, as well as the recently developed event chronology from the Fort Ross Orchard site (Stop 4). In general, the rupture chronology interpreted from the Archae Camp and Orchard sites are in agreement (Table 1) and generally agree with earlier work done at Point Arena (Prentice, 1989). Based on the combined record from Fort Ross Orchard and Archae Camp, we interpret the occurrence of four late Holocene surface ruptures on the North Coast segment of the San Andreas fault within the past ~1100 yr (Fig. 11).

Stop 4: Fault Rupture through the Russian Orchard at Fort Ross State Historic Park

Significance of the Site

The San Andreas fault in this part of the park traverses an orchard planted by Russian colonists during their stay between 1812 and 1842. The fault has had a prominent influence on the site topography, and recent trenching studies have used these fault-related features to assess the timing of several pre-1906 earthquakes on the San Andreas fault. The site provides paleoseismic information that will help address whether or not this section may generate moderate magnitude earthquakes in addition to large 1906-type earthquakes.

Accessibility

This is part of Fort Ross State Historic Park and is open to the public. No restrooms are available, and there is limited parking space on Fort Ross Road.

GPS Coordinates

38.52353°N, 123.24120°W.

Directions

From Stop 3, return to Hwy 1 and continue northward 0.7 mi. to the intersection with Fort Ross Road (Fig. 2). Turn right (east) on Fort Ross Road toward Seaview. Continue for 0.5 mi. to a small turnout on the northwest side of Fort Ross Road. Walk southeast through a gate in the wooden fence and then through a chain-link gate to the orchard enclosure. Walk eastward to a narrow topographic trough that marks the trace of the San Andreas fault.

Stop Description

Fort Ross Road borders the northwestern side of the Fort Ross Orchard and experienced 2.3 m of right-lateral offset on the main fault strand during the 1906 rupture, and probably additional slip as secondary deformation. Lawson (1908) also documented 3.6 m of offset across a road at the southern end of the orchard (Fig. 2). The site contains a prominent northeast-(uphill-) facing fault scarp that has helped trap colluvial sediments derived from the scarp and the adjacent hillslope to the northeast (Figs. 12 and 13). The orchard itself contains several

TABLE 1. SUMMARY OF AGE ESTIMATES FOR RECENT SURFACE-RUPTURING EARTHQUAKES
ON THE SAN ANDREAS FAULT AT THE FORT ROSS ORCHARD AND ARCHAE CAMP SITES

Fort Ross Orchard (2-sigma range)	Archae Camp (Simpson et al., 1996)	Archae Camp (revised) (2-sigma range)	Fort Ross Orchard and Archae Camp (2-sigma range)
A.D. 1906	(Event Z) A.D. 1906	A.D. 1906	A.D. 1906
(Event 2) A.D. 1660 to 1830		(Event 2) A.D. 1570 to 1906	(Event 2) A.D. 1660 to 1812*
(Event 3) A.D. 1220 to 1380	(Event Y) A.D. 1170 to 1650	(Event 3) A.D. 1220 to 1560	(Event 3) A.D. 1220 to 1380
(Event 4) A.D. 1040 to 1190	(Event X) A.D. 920 to 1285	(Event 4) A.D. 920 to 1230	(Event 4) A.D. 1040 to 1190
	(Event W) A.D. 555 to 950	(Event 5) A.D. 600 to 880	(Event 5) A.D. 555 to 950

Note: Table modified from Kelson et al. (2006). Age ranges represent uncertainty levels estimated by the OxCal analytical program (Ramsey, 2003).
*Timing of Event 2 truncated at A.D. 1812 based on lack of evidence in Ft. Ross historical records since arrival of Russian colonists (Lightfoot et al., 1991).

fruit trees planted by the Russian colonists who lived at Fort Ross between 1812 and 1842. The small (~50 × 150 m) orchard includes olive, pear, cherry, apple, and other fruit trees, although only a few original Russian-planted trees remain. Unfortunately, there does not appear to be any linear arrangements of the original trees that could be used as a piercing line to measure offset across the fault. The orchard likely was not being maintained during the 1906 surface rupture, and the site has undergone little cultural modification since the departure of the Russians in early 1842.

Paleoseismic trenching within the orchard provides data on the earthquake history of the North Coast segment of the northern San Andreas fault within the past 1100 yr (Kelson et al., 2003, 2005a, 2005b, 2006). Trenches across the northeast-facing fault scarp at the site provide stratigraphic and structural evidence of the 1906 earthquake and three pre-1906 surface ruptures. These trenches show the presence of scarp-derived colluvial deposits, possible fissure-fill deposits, and tentative upward fault truncations that provide evidence of three possible surface ruptures prior to 1906 (Fig. 14). Coarse-grained scarp-derived colluvial sediments shed from the scarp after individual surface-rupturing earthquakes pre-date the 1906 rupture and constrain the timing of the past four surface ruptures at the site, which occurred in A.D. 1906, between A.D. 1660 and 1812, between A.D. 1220 and 1380, and between A.D. 1040 and 1190 (Fig. 15). Our reanalysis of radiocarbon ages from the nearby Archae Camp site (see Stop 3) are consistent with these dates and further constrain the earliest of these events to have occurred between A.D. 555 and 950 (Table 1; Fig. 11).

The time windows for late Holocene ruptures at Fort Ross are consistent with results from several other sites on the North Coast segment of the fault, although published paleoseismic data are, at present, insufficient to address the long-term behavior of the entire northern San Andreas fault. The behavior of the northern San Andreas fault probably involves a mix of large, long ruptures like the 1906 event and smaller ruptures along shorter segments of the fault (Kelson et al., 2005a, 2005b, 2006).

Stop 5: Shoreline Angle View Point

Significance of the Site

View of an unusually well exposed shoreline angle associated with the oxygen isotope stage 5a (ca. 80,000 yr B.P.) marine terrace.

Accessibility

This site is part of Fort Ross State Historic Park and is a publicly accessible parking area.

GPS Coordinates

38.52478°N, 123.26696°W.

Directions

From Stop 4, return to Hwy 1 and continue north for 1.3 mi to a large pullout on the left (west) side of Hwy 1, just south of the Fort Ross Lodge. Park and walk to the southern edge of the parking area (Fig. 16).

Stop Description

The broad bench on which we are parked is a marine terrace that was cut by wave action when this area was below sea level. Uplift of the California coast since then has brought the

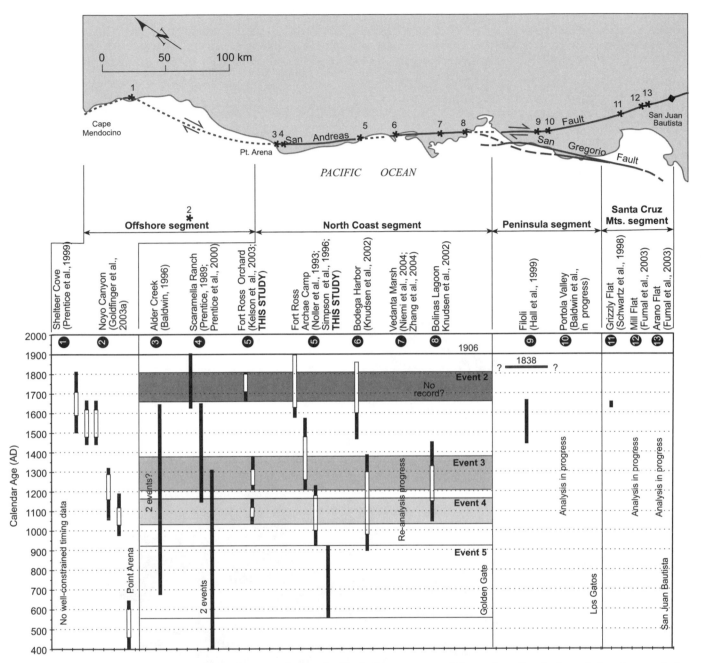

Figure 11. Summary of earthquake chronology interpreted along the North Coast segment of the northern San Andreas fault and event-timing data from sites on adjacent fault segments. Additional analyses of timing data for the Vedanta Marsh, Portola Valley, Mill Canyon, and Arano Flat sites are in progress and may result in revisions to this interpreted chronology. Open bars show 1-sigma confidence limits; solid bars show 2-sigma confidence limits. Shaded horizontal bands show interpreted time windows for ruptures on the North Coast segment based on data from the Fort Ross Orchard site. From Kelson et al. (2006).

marine terrace to its current position above sea level. A view of the former shoreline at the time this terrace was formed is visible looking south across the cove (Fig. 17). This is an outstanding (and rare) example of an exposure of a shoreline angle (Fig. 9). The elevation of this feature is 26 m above mean sea level. This is the lowest marine terrace in this area, and our mapping suggests it is correlative with the Point Arena terrace, which is

dated to the ca. 80,000 yr B.P. (marine isotope substage 5a) sea-level high stand (Muhs et al., 1994, 2002, 2003b). Estimates of the elevation of sea level 80,000 yr ago vary widely, from approximately -20 m to ~0 m below today's sea level (Muhs et al., 2003b). Therefore, the former shoreline has been uplifted between 26 and 46 m in 80,000 yr, or at an average rate of between 0.3 and 0.6 mm/yr.

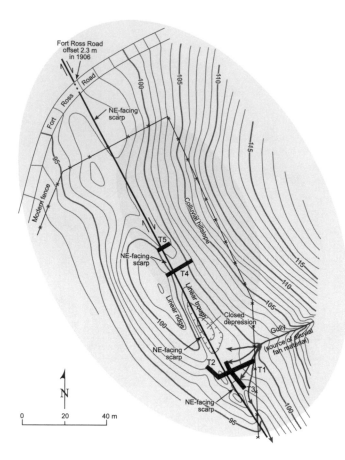

Figure 12. Detailed topographic map of the Fort Ross Orchard site, showing the San Andreas fault trace and trenches T1 to T5. Map developed from total station electronic survey; contour interval of 1 m uses arbitrary site datum. From Kelson et al. (2006).

Figure 13. Photograph looking southwest across the northern San Andreas fault at the Fort Ross Orchard site, showing trenches 4 and 5 (Kelson et al., 2006).

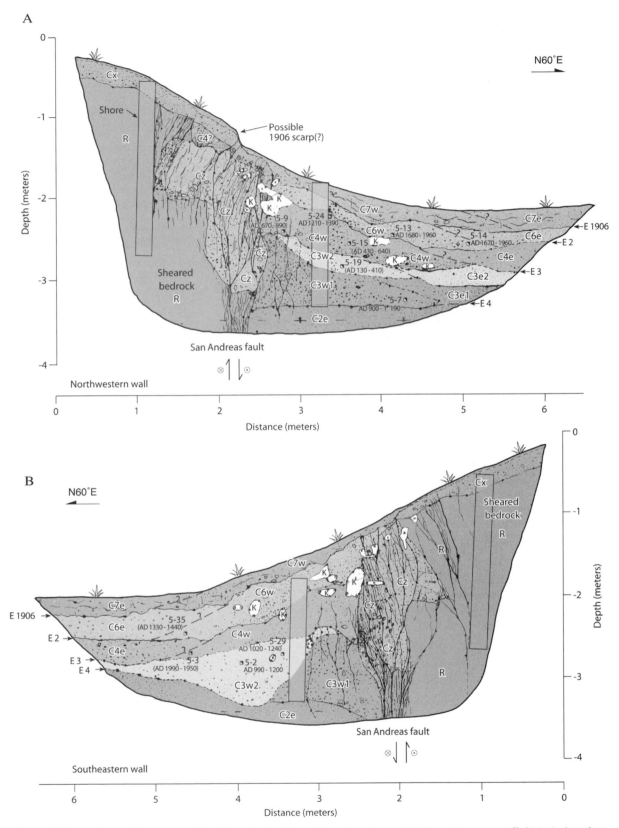

Figure 14. Maps of trench 5 exposures, Fort Ross Orchard site; (A) northwestern wall, (B) southeastern wall. Unit designations: C—colluvium; numbered with younger deposits having higher numbers; w—derived from western source; e—derived from eastern source. From Kelson et al. (2006).

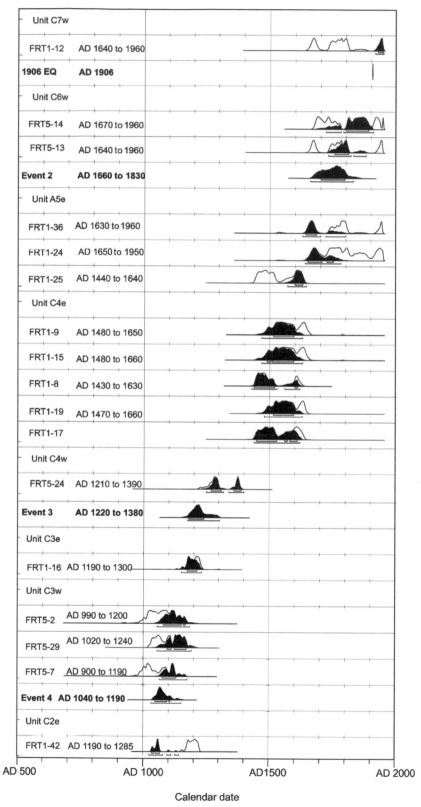

Figure 15. Summary of analytical results from stratigraphic ordering using OxCal v3.9 (Ramsey, 2003), showing probability density functions for radiocarbon samples and rupture events. Unshaded areas represent original probability density function (PDF) for calibrated ages; shaded areas show revised PDFs based on OxCal stratigraphic ordering model. Horizontal bars beneath each shaded PDF show 1-sigma and 2-sigma age ranges (Kelson et al., 2006).

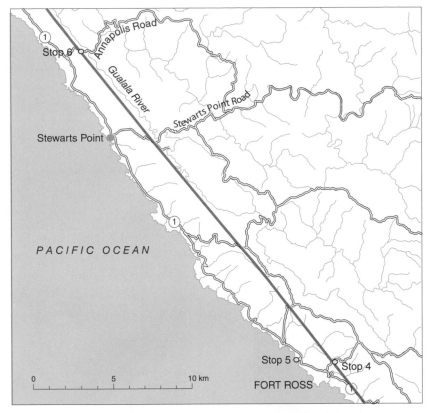

Figure 16. Map showing locations of Stops 5 and 6.

Figure 17. Photograph of well-exposed shoreline angle associated with stage 5a (ca. 80 ka) marine terrace visible from Stop 5. Photograph taken in 2005 by Christopher Crosby.

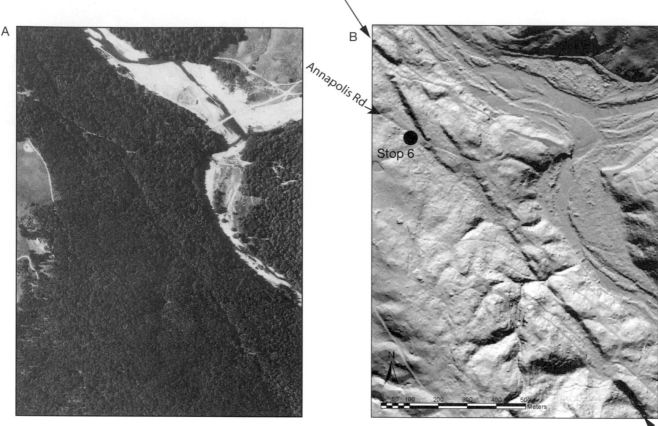

Figure 18. Comparison between 1996 aerial photograph (A) and 2003 LiDAR image of same area (B). Ground surface beneath forest canopy is revealed by LiDAR imaging technique, allowing more accurate mapping of fault traces.

Stop 6: Annapolis Road: Fault Geomorphology in the Redwood Forest

Significance of the Site

This stop provides an excellent example of the San Andreas fault within the redwood forest. A prominent scarp and sag pond are present.

Accessibility

Parking along the side of the county road is limited. Property to the north and south of the road is privately owned, at the time of this writing by Gualala Redwoods, and permission is needed to walk along the fault. However, the fault is clearly visible from the public road, and can be seen especially well on the north side of the road. No restrooms are available.

GPS Coordinates

38.70050°N, 123.42180°W.

Directions

From Stop 5, continue north on Hwy 1 for 16.8 mi. Turn right (east) on Annapolis Road. The fault crosses the road 0.9 mi from the intersection with Hwy 1 (Fig. 16).

Stop Description

The difficulty of accurately mapping the active traces of the San Andreas fault in detail in the redwood forest is well demonstrated by the aerial photograph shown in Figure 18A. Aerial photographs do not clearly show the ground surface beneath the forest canopy. However, a new imaging technique, known as LiDAR (light detection and ranging; also known as ALSM for airborne laser swath mapping), allows the forest to be virtually removed. The result is shown in Figure 18B, which shows exactly the same region as Figure 18A, without the forest cover. Our new mapping using LiDAR data is providing a much more detailed and accurate map of this part of the San Andreas fault than has been produced previously (Prentice et al., 2003, 2004; Brown and Wolfe, 1972). The part of the fault between Fort Ross and Point Arena is the first part of the San Andreas to be imaged using this new technique.

The fault at this location is one of two prominent fault traces, the eastern of which is ~150 m farther down Annapolis Road (Fig. 18B). The uphill-facing scarp clearly visible on the north side of the road at this location is very typical of this section of the fault. If you have permission from the landowner, you can walk to the northwest along the fault for ~50 m to another very typical feature along this section of the fault: a pond formed against the uphill-facing scarp resulting from the disruption of the local drainages by both horizontal and vertical offset across the fault. These ponds are called sag ponds and occur along most strike-slip faults, but their size and abundance along this section of the North Coast San Andreas is remarkable. This sag pond, though only ~10–20 m wide, is ~200 m long.

Approximately 8 km (5 mi) southeast of this location, where the fault crosses Stewarts Point Road (Fig. 16), Matthes reported a zone consisting of two lines of "strong" faulting and several lines of "dim" faulting, over which ~2.4 m (8 ft) of offset were distributed in 1906 (Lawson, 1908). The fact that two lines of faulting were reported by Matthes only 8 km (5 mi) to the south, coupled with the geomorphically fresh appearance of both faults mapped across Annapolis Road, suggests that both traces were active here in 1906, though no direct observations were reported from this location.

End of Day 1. Overnight in Gualala, California. From Stop 6, return to Hwy 1 and continue north 7.1 mi to Gualala (Fig. 1).

DAY TWO: GUALALA TO POINT ARENA AND ALDER CREEK; RETURN TO SAN FRANCISCO

Stop 7: Thrust Fault on Marine Terrace

Significance of the Site

Deformation is occurring off the main trace of the San Andreas fault, and is well expressed at this location where Miocene bedrock is thrust over late Pleistocene marine terrace deposits.

Accessibility

This site is on U.S. Bureau of Land Management (BLM) property and is open to the public. Parking near the entrance gate is limited. No restrooms are available.

GPS Coordinates

BLM gate: 38.94038°N, 123.72969°W; exposure of thrust fault: 38.93340°N, 123.72630°W.

Directions

From Gualala, continue north on Hwy 1 for 16.1 mi. Turn left (west) onto Lighthouse Road. The BLM access gate is on the left, 0.8 mi from the intersection with Hwy 1. Walk through the gate and hike southward along the marine terrace ~0.6 mi to the sea cliff and sinkhole exposures of the fault (Fig. 19).

Stop Description

At this location the Point Arena terrace is well expressed geomorphically. Sea cliff exposures reveal two Quaternary thrust faults that have been active since the time this terrace formed (Prentice, 1989; Prentice et al., 1991; Muhs et al., 2003a). The first of these exposures is illustrated in Figures 20 and 21. Miocene bedrock has been thrust over deposits that overlie the ca. 80,000 yr B.P. wave-cut platform. Several other exposures in this vicinity show similar relationships. Two nearby sea cliff exposures reveal a thrust fault that soles into a bedding plane within the Miocene bedrock. Faulted terrace deposits are also well exposed in a

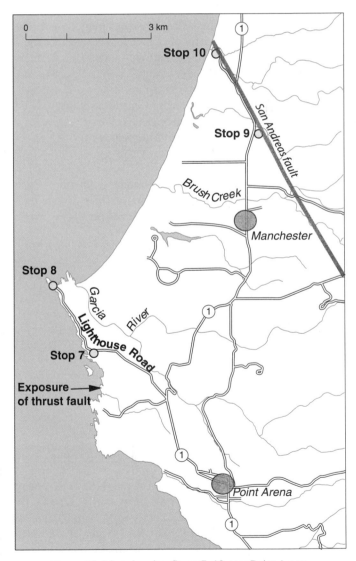

Figure 19. Map showing Stops 7–10 near Point Arena.

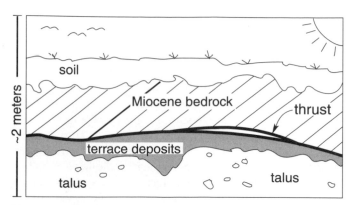

Figure 20. Sketch of sea-cliff exposure of thrust fault juxtaposing Miocene bedrock over late Pleistocene marine terrace deposits. Modified from Prentice, 1989.

nearby sinkhole. These relations indicate Quaternary compression along the plate boundary in this area, and demonstrate that ongoing deformation is not confined to the San Andreas fault. Whether this fault system is capable of producing earthquakes independently of the San Andreas fault, or whether it moves sympathetically during some large San Andreas events, is unknown.

Stop 8: Point Arena Lighthouse: Marine Terraces

Significance of the Site

This site provides an excellent vantage point from which to view the coastal marine terraces and the difference in their elevation north and south of the San Andreas fault.

Accessibility

The lighthouse is an historic site that is open to the public. Fees are charged for entry. Restrooms are available.

GPS Coordinates

Gate: 38.95121°N, 123.73742°W.

Directions

From Stop 7, continue northwest on Lighthouse Road. The entrance to Point Arena lighthouse is at the end of Lighthouse Road, 0.1 mi.

Stop Description

The Point Arena lighthouse is situated on the Point Arena marine terrace. At this location, fossils were collected and studied by Kennedy (1978), Kennedy et al. (1982), Kennedy and Armentrout (1989), and Muhs et al. (1990, 1994). U-series analyses of marine terrace corals from Point Arena are ca. 76,000 yr B.P. and ca. 88,000 yr B.P. (Muhs et al., 1990, 1994). A more recent and more precise mass-spectrometric

U-series analysis of a single *Balanophyllia* coral from the lowest terrace at Point Arena has an apparent age of 83,000 ± 800 yr B.P. (Muhs et al., 2002) and is therefore broadly consistent with the earlier ages. These analyses make this terrace the best-dated marine terrace in northern California north of San Francisco. Fossils are rarely preserved in marine terrace deposits, but they are crucial in understanding the ages of the terraces, and therefore in using the terraces to understand Quaternary tectonics.

The flight of coastal marine terraces changes abruptly, as does the overall topography, across the San Andreas fault (Fig. 22). From this vantage point, the elevation change is obvious when looking northwest. Our correlations of marine terraces across the fault imply that rates of coastal uplift are much higher NE of the fault. Mapping the terraces north to the town of Mendocino suggests that the rates of uplift gradually decrease northward along the coast.

Stop 9: Marine Terrace Risers and The San Andreas Fault

Significance of the Site

Marine terrace risers intersect the San Andreas fault. The offset of the terrace risers allows us to estimate the slip rate across the fault averaged over the past ~100,000 yr.

Accessibility

This site is on private property, and permission is needed to park inside the fence. The terrace risers can be viewed from the public highway, but there is little room to park. No restrooms are available.

GPS Coordinates

38.98670°N, 123.68479°W.

Directions

From Stop 8, return to Hwy 1. Continue 4.8 mi north on Hwy 1 through the town of Manchester, and turn right (east) onto a dirt road. Cross the cattle guard and park along the side of the dirt road (Fig. 19).

Stop Description

From this location, we look across the San Andreas fault at two marine terrace risers (old sea cliffs) that are truncated on the NE side of the San Andreas fault (Figs. 23 and 24), and we see a prominent marine terrace riser on the SW side of the fault. Because right-lateral strike slip has occurred across the San Andreas fault since the time these terraces formed, the riser SW of the fault at this location cannot correlate to either of the risers NE of the fault. The only potential correlative to the risers on the NE side of the fault is located SW of the San Andreas fault and is right-laterally offset 1.3–1.8 km (0.8–1.1 mi)

Figure 21. Photograph of thrust fault illustrated in Figure 20. Arrows point to fault plane. Photograph by M. Rymer, U.S. Geological Survey.

(Fig. 24, not visible from Stop 9). The prominent riser at this location on the SW side of the fault must also have a correlative NE of the fault. The risers on the NE side of the fault visible from Stop 9 (Figs. 23 and 24) are both unlikely candidates because right-lateral movement on the San Andreas fault would have displaced the correlative feature to the SE (Fig. 24). The best candidate for a correlative is located NE of the fault, and is right-laterally offset 2.3–3.2 km (1.4–2 mi) (Fig. 24). Estimates of the ages of these former shorelines (ca. 80,000 yr, ca. 100,000 yr, and ca. 120,000 yr, or substages 5a, 5c, and 5e) suggest average late Pleistocene slip rates of 16–24 mm/yr (Prentice, 1989; Prentice et al., 2000; Muhs et al., 2003a), consistent with slip rates estimated from study of Holocene features.

Stop 10: Mouth of Alder Creek

Significance of the Site

The San Andreas fault trends offshore at this location. The fault rupture was photographed and described here after the 1906 earthquake.

Accessibility

This site is within Manchester State Park and is a publicly accessible. Parking is available, but there are no restrooms.

GPS Coordinates

39.00415°N, 123.69418°W.

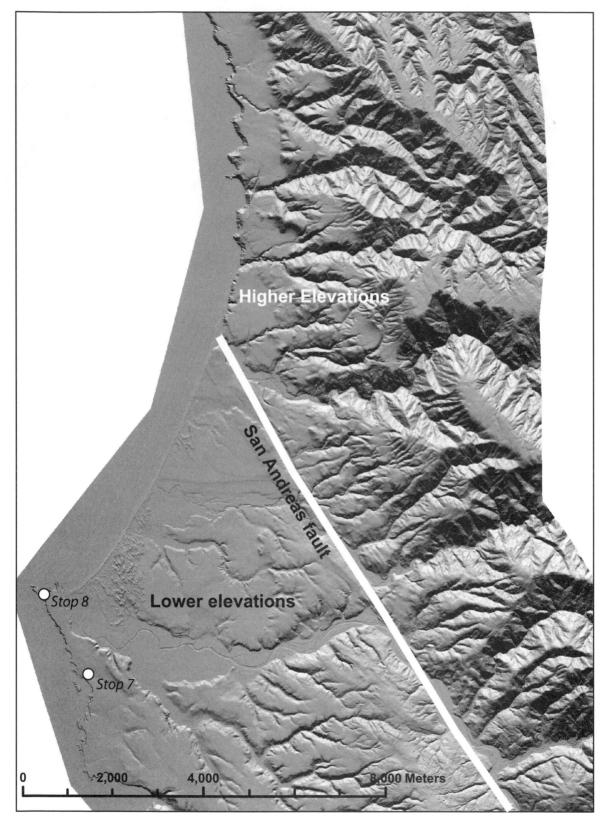

Figure 22. LiDAR image of Point Arena region showing pronounced difference in elevations of marine terrace north and south of San Andreas fault.

Figure 23. Photograph of terrace risers intersecting San Andreas fault near Stop 9.

Directions

From Stop 9, continue north on Hwy 1 for 0.6 mi. Turn left (west) onto a road indicated by a coastal access sign. Follow the road to its end (0.7 mi) and park (Fig. 19).

Stop Description

The San Andreas fault northwest of this location is under the waters of the Pacific Ocean for almost the entire remainder of its course to the northwest (Fig. 1). Alder Creek itself has been offset ~650–900 m by repeated motion across the San Andreas fault (Fig. 19) (Prentice, 1989). Matthes wrote about this location after the 1906 earthquake:

The fault-trace enters the shore less than half a mile north of the mouth Alder Creek and crosses with a course of S.28° E. the bench-land, or wave-cut terrace, to the banks of the creek about 500 feet in from its mouth. Over the surface of the bench it is marked by characteristic rending and heaving of the sod. At the point where it reaches Alder Creek, the stream bank is rocky and steep, and the course of the crack can be traced down the rocky bluff, tho [*sic*] somewhat obscured by talus. (F.E. Matthes *in* Lawson, 1908).

Matthes made a sketch map showing these features (Fig. 25). He also took several photographs that illustrate his description of the fault. Figure 26A shows the fault in 1906 on the rocky bank of Alder Creek opposite the parking area. Figure 26B shows the same feature in 2005. Figure 27A shows "the rending and heaving of the sod" that Matthes refers to between the bank of Alder Creek and the modern sea cliff. Figure 27B was taken in the same area as Figure 27A in 2005. Figure 28 shows the ruined bridge across Alder Creek at this location, which was destroyed by fault offset. A remnant of the old road that led to this bridge is still visible across the creek. A new bridge was built to take its place, and part of the abutment of that bridge (destroyed by the floods of 1964) remains on the stream bank between the parking lot and the creek. At times of low flow, the fault zone in bedrock is visible along the stream bank northwest of the old bridge abutments and is expressed as a zone of highly sheared rock known as fault gouge.

If the water level in Alder Creek is low enough to cross, it is instructive to walk northward along the beach to see where

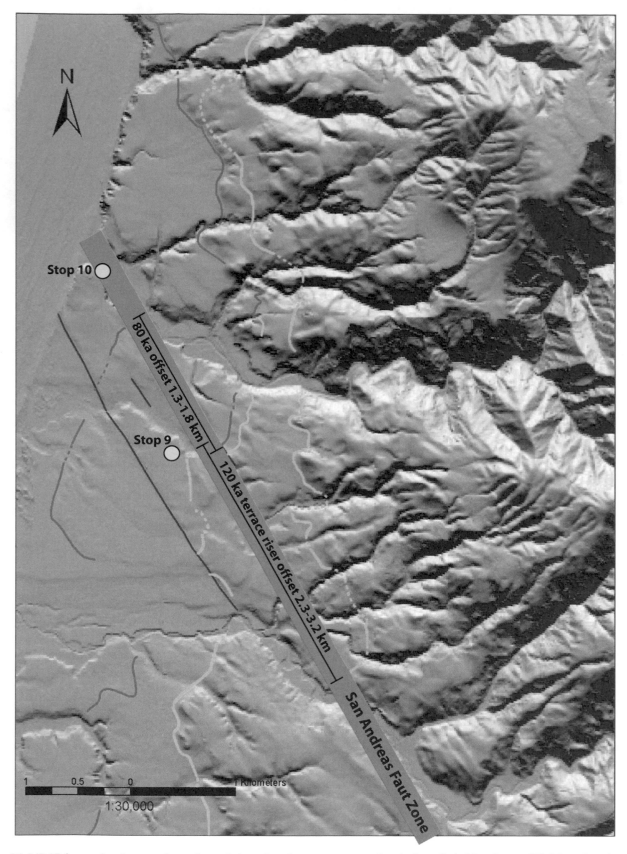

Figure 24. LiDAR image showing mapping and correlation of marine terraces across San Andreas fault. Mapping modified from Prentice, 1989.

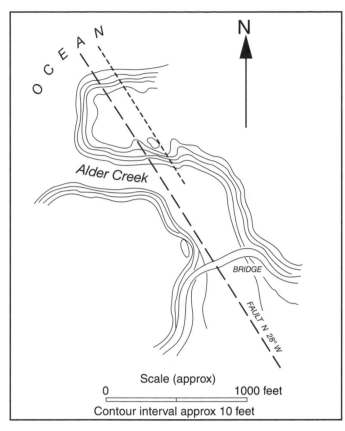

Figure 25. Sketch map made of area near Stop 10 by Matthes in 1906 (*in* Lawson, 1908).

the fault zone intersects the modern sea cliff. The bedrock exposed in the sea cliff is profoundly sheared and a wide zone of fault gouge and broken up blocks of rock is exposed in the cliffs (Fig. 29). This is the result of millions of years of motion across the fault, one earthquake at a time every few hundred years. It is also possible to climb up to the top of the bluff to the region where the photographs in Figure 27 were taken. Figure 30 shows the view from the top of the bluff looking southward along the San Andreas to Stop 10.

ACKNOWLEDGMENTS

This research was supported, in part, by the U.S. Geological Survey (USGS), Department of the Interior, under USGS award numbers 00-HQ-GR-0072 and 02-HQ-GR-0069. The views and conclusions contained in this document are those of the authors and should not be interpreted as necessarily representing the official policies, either expressed or implied, of the U.S. Government. The California Department of Parks and Recreation graciously provided permission to conduct trenching investigations within Fort Ross State Historic Park. Thanks especially to California Department of Parks and Recreation personnel Bill Walton, Heidi Horvitz, Breck Parkman, and Dan Murley. We thank Gualala Redwoods as well as Ralph Bean for access to their property. Thanks to Christopher Crosby for help with scouting the stops and creating several figures. We also thank reviewers Tom Brocher and Jack Boatwright for very helpful reviews of the manuscript.

Figure 26. (A) Photograph taken near Stop 10 by Matthes in 1906. Courtesy of Bancroft Library, University of California–Berkeley (call number 1957.007.338, Series I). (B) Photograph of same feature in 2005.

Figure 27. (A) Photograph taken looking northward along surface rupture on bluff on north side of Alder Creek. This illustrates the "rending and heaving of the sod" described by Matthes at this location (*in* Lawson, 1908). Photograph taken in 2005 in same area as (A), looking northwest along the eastern fault trace.

Figure 28. Photograph of bridge destroyed by fault offset in 1906. Courtesy of Bancroft Library, University of California–Berkeley (call number 1957.007.387, Series I). Photograph by F.E. Matthes.

Figure 29. Photograph taken in 2005 of sea-cliff north of Alder Creek showing wide shear zone and fault gouge. Eastern trace of 1906 rupture was near the north end of shear zone (arrow).

Figure 30. View to southeast along the San Andreas fault from bluff north of Alder Creek.

REFERENCES CITED

Bray, J.D., and Kelson, K.I., 2006, Observations of surface fault rupture from the 1906 earthquake in the context of current practice: Spectra, Special Volume on the 1906 Earthquake Centennial: Earthquake Engineering Research Institute (in press).

Brown, R.D., and Wolfe, E.W., 1972, Map showing recently active breaks along the San Andreas fault between Point Delgada and Bolinas Bay, California: U.S. Geological Survey Miscellaneous Geological Investigations, Map I-692, scale 1:24,000.

Hart, J.D., Zulfiqar, N., Lee, C.-H., Dauby, F., Kelson, K.I., and Hitchcock, C.S., 2004, A unique pipeline fault crossing design for a highly focused fault: International Pipeline Conference 2004, Calgary, Alberta, October 4–8, paper IPC04-0212, 8 p.

Kelson, K.I., Koehler, R.D., and Kang, K.-H., 2003, Initial evaluation of paleo-earthquake timing on the northern San Andreas fault at the Fort Ross Orchard site, Sonoma County, California: Final Technical Report submitted to the U.S. Geological Survey National Earthquake Hazard Reduction Program, Award No. 00HQGR0072, 29 p.

Kelson, K.I., Hitchcock, C.S., Baldwin, J.N., Hart, J.D., Gamble, J.C., Lee, C.-H., and Dauby, F., 2004, Fault rupture assessments for high-pressure pipelines in the southern San Francisco Bay Area, California: Proceedings of International Pipeline Conference 2004, Calgary, Alberta, October 4–8, paper IPC04-0102, 8 p.

Kelson, K.I., Streig, A., and Kochler, R.D., 2005a, Preliminary Evaluation of Paleoearthquake Timing, northern San Andreas Fault, Fort Ross, California [abs.]: Geological Society of America Abstracts with Programs, v. 37, no. 4, p. 77.

Kelson, K.I., Streig, A., and Koehler, R.D., 2005b, Preliminary evaluation of paleoearthquake timing, northern San Andreas fault, Fort Ross, California: Final technical report submitted to the U.S. Geological Survey National Earthquake Hazard Reduction Program, Award No. 00HQGR0072, 29 p.

Kelson, K.I., Streig, A., and Koehler, R.D., 2006, Timing of late Holocene paleo-earthquakes on the northern San Andreas Fault, Fort Ross Orchard site, Sonoma County, California: Bulletin of the Seismological Society of America (in press).

Kennedy, G.L., 1978, Pleistocene paleoecology, zoogeography and geochronology of marine invertebrate faunas of the Pacific Northwest Coast (San Francisco Bay to Puget Sound) [Ph.D. thesis]: Davis, University of California, 824 p.

Kennedy, G.L., and Armentrout, J.M., 1989, A new species of chimney-building *Penitella* from the Gulf of Alaska (Bivalvia: Pholadidae): The Veliger, v. 32, p. 320–325.

Kennedy, G.L., Lajoie, K.R., and Wehmiller, J.F., 1982, Aminostratigraphy and faunal correlations of late Quaternary marine terraces, Pacific Coast, USA: Nature, v. 299, p. 545–547, doi: 10.1038/299545a0.

Lajoie, K.R., Ponti, D.J., Powell, C.L. II, Mathieson, S.A., and Sarna-Wojcicki, A.M., 1991, Emergent marine strandlines and associated sediments, coastal California: A record of Quaternary sea-level fluctuations, vertical tectonic movements, climatic changes, and coastal processes, in Morrison, R.B., ed., Quaternary nonglacial geology: Conterminous U.S.: Boulder, Colorado, Geological Society of America, The Geology of North America, v. K-2, p. 190–203.

Lawson, A.C., 1908, The California earthquake of April 18, 1906: Report of the State Earthquake Investigation Commission (Reprinted 1969): Carnegie Institution of Washington Publication 87, v. 1, 451 p. and atlas.

Lightfoot, K., Wake, T., and Schiff, A.M., editors, 1991, The archaeology and ethnohistory of Fort Ross, California: Contributions of the University of California Archaeological Research Facility, v. 1, no. 49.

Muhs, D.R., Kennedy, G.L., and Rockwell, T.K., 1994, Uranium-series ages of marine terrace corals from the Pacific coast of North America and implications for last-interglacial sea level history: Quaternary Research, v. 42, p. 72–87, doi: 10.1006/qres.1994.1055.

Muhs, D.R., Kelsey, H.M., Miller, G.H., Kennedy, G.L., Whelan, J.F., and McInelly, G.W., 1990, Age estimates and uplift rates for late Pleistocene marine terraces: Southern Oregon portion of the Cascadia forearc: Journal of Geophysical Research, v. 95, p. 6685–6698.

Muhs, D.R., Simmons, K.R., Kennedy, G.L., Ludwig, K.R., and Groves, L.T., 2002, A cool eastern Pacific Ocean at the close of the last interglacial period, ca. 80,000 yr B.P.: Geological Society of America Abstracts with Programs, v. 34, no. 6, p. 130.

Muhs, D.R., Prentice, C.S., and Merritts, D.J., 2003a, Marine terraces, sea level history and Quaternary tectonics of the San Andreas fault on the coast of California, in Easterbrook, D.J., ed., Quaternary Geology of the United States, International Quaternary Association (INQUA) 2003 Field Guide Volume, Desert Research Institute, Reno, Nevada, p. 1–18.

Muhs, D.R., Wehmiller, J.F., Simmons, K.R., and York, L.L., 2003b, Quaternary sea-level history of the United States: Developments in Quaternary Science, v. 1, p. 147–183.

Noller, J.S., and Lightfoot, K.G., 1997, An archaeoseismic approach and method for the study of active strike-slip faults: Geoarchaeology: International Journal, v. 12, p. 117–135.

Noller, J.S., Kelson, K.I., Lettis, W.R., Wickens, K.A., Simpson, G.D., Lightfoot, K., and Wake, T., 1993, Preliminary characterizations of Holocene activity on the San Andreas fault based on offset archaeological sites, Ft. Ross State Historic Park, California: Final Technical Report submitted to the U.S. Geologic Survey National Earthquake Hazards Reduction Program, Award no. 14-08-0001-G2076, 17 p.

Prentice, C.S., 1989, Earthquake geology of the northern San Andreas fault near Point Arena, California [Ph.D. thesis]: Pasadena, California, California Institute of Technology, 252 p.

Prentice, C.S., Niemi, T.M., and Hall, N.T., 1991, Quaternary tectonics of the northern San Andreas fault, San Francisco Peninsula, Point Reyes, and Point Arena, California, in Sloan, D., and Wagner, D.L., eds., Geologic

excursions in northern California: San Francisco to the Sierra Nevada: California Department of Conservation, Division of Mines and Geology, Special Publication 109, p. 25–34.

Prentice, C.S., Langridge, R., and Merritts, D.J., 2000, Paleoseismic and Quaternary tectonic studies of the San Andreas fault from Shelter Cove to Fort Ross, in Bokelmann, G. and Kovach, R.L., eds., Proceedings of the Third Conference on Tectonic Problems of the San Andreas System: Stanford, California, Stanford University Publications, p. 349–350.

Prentice, C.S., Prescott, W.H., Langridge, R., and Dawson, T., 2001, New geologic and geodetic slip rate estimates on the North Coast San Andreas Fault: Approaching agreement?: Seismological Research Letters, v. 72, p. 282.

Prentice, C.S., Crosby, C.J., Harding, D.J., Haugerud, R.A., Merritts, D.J., Gardner, T., Koehler, R.D., and Baldwin, J.N., 2003, Northern California LiDAR data: A tool for mapping the San Andreas fault and Pleistocene marine terraces in heavily vegetated terrain [abs.]: Eos (Transactions, American Geophysical Union), v. 84, no. 46 (Fall Meeting Supplement), Abstract G12A-06.

Prentice, C.S., Koehler, R.D., III, Baldwin, J.N., and Harding, D.J., 2004, Evaluation of LiDAR Imagery as a tool for mapping the northern San Andreas Fault in heavily forested areas of Mendocino and Sonoma Counties, California [abs.]: Eos (Transactions, American Geophysical Union), v. 85, no. 47 (Fall Meeting Supplement), Abstract G11B-07.

Ramsey, C.B., 2003, Radiocarbon calibration and analysis of stratigraphy: The OxCal Program v3.10: http://www.rlaha.ox.ac.uk/O/oxcal.php.

Rockwell, T.K., Lindvall, S., Dawson, T., Langridge, R., and Lettis, W.R., 2002, Lateral offsets on surveyed cultural features resulting from the 1999 Izmit and Duzce earthquakes, Turkey: Bulletin of the Seismological Society of America, v. 92, p. 79–94, doi: 10.1785/0120000809.

Simpson, G.D., Noller, J.S., Kelson, K.I., and Lettis, W.R., 1996, Logs of trenches across the San Andreas fault, Archae Camp, Fort Ross State Historic Park, Northern California: Final Technical Report submitted to the U.S. Geologic Survey National Earthquake Hazards Reduction Program Award No. 1434-94-G-2474, 1 plate.

William Lettis & Associates, Inc., 2003, Geologic evaluation of the Hayward fault crossing, BART Warm Springs Extension, Fremont, California: unpublished report prepared for Parsons Brinkerhoff Quade & Douglas, Inc., San Francisco, California, dated June 27, 2003, 61 p.

Geological Society of America
Field Guide 7
2006

The 1906 earthquake rupture trace of the San Andreas fault north of San Francisco, with stops at points of geotechnical interest

Tina M. Niemi
University of Missouri–Kansas City, Department of Geosciences,
5110 Rockhill Road, Flarsheim Hall 420, Kansas City, Missouri 64110-2499, USA
N. Timothy Hall
3586 Spirit Lane, Pollock Pines, California 95726, USA
Alexander Dahne
University of Missouri–Kansas City, Department of Geosciences,
5110 Rockhill Road, Flarsheim Hall 420, Kansas City, Missouri 64110-2499, USA

OVERVIEW OF FIELD TRIP

The main destination of this field trip is the San Andreas fault in Marin County, where the ground rupture of the 1906 earthquake is well preserved within the boundaries and easements of Point Reyes National Seashore. In addition to three stops along the fault, the field guide also describes stops to view the Golden Gate Bridge and White's Hill slide on Sir Francis Drake Boulevard near the town of Fairfax, and it discusses the geology along the way. Figure 1 shows the location of the stops for this field trip. Excellent online fieldtrip guides to the geology of Point Reyes peninsula, the Marin Headlands, and the San Andreas fault are available on the Internet (Stoffer, 2005; Elder, 2005).

The great San Francisco earthquake of 18 April 1906 was generated by rupture of at least 435 km of the northern San Andreas fault (Lawson, 1908). The earthquake produced maximum horizontal offsets of 16–20 ft (5–6 m) along the San Andreas fault north of San Francisco and smaller offsets south of the city. In Marin County, there has been very little urbanization along the fault. Prior to the establishment of the National Seashore in 1962, most of the region was used for dairy farming and cattle ranching. Because the region remains largely as it was in the late nineteenth century, conditions are ideal for investigating how the morphology of the rupture has changed in the 100 years since the earthquake. Furthermore, this section of the San Andreas fault continues to yield important data about dates of prehistoric earthquakes and the slip rate of the fault.

Two fundamentally different types of bedrock underlie Marin County (Fig. 2). Right-lateral shear along the San Andreas transform plate boundary during the late Cenozoic has juxtaposed Franciscan subduction zone rocks on the east against the Salinian terrane of Point Reyes peninsula to the west. The Franciscan Assemblage (Complex) is a highly deformed, lithologically heterogeneous sequence of metamorphosed volcanic and sedimentary rocks accreted to western North American during subduction of the Farallon plate in the Mesozoic. The Salinian terrane is a displaced fragment of continental crust that consists of Cretaceous plutonic and older metamorphic rock overlain by lower Eocene to Pliocene marine sedimentary rocks (Clark and Brabb, 1997). In between the Franciscan and Salinian terranes lies a valley created by the San Andreas fault zone that is characterized by Quaternary deposition and low ridges and depressions elongated parallel or subparallel to the fault.

Along the route of this field trip on our way to the San Andreas fault, road cuts expose the world-famous, Franciscan Accretionary Complex rocks including oceanic pillow basalts (greenstone) overlain by radiolarian chert, graywacke sandstone, and "mélange" (from the French word for "mixture"), with inclusions of greenstone, chert, serpentinite, and graywacke. Isolated outcrops or knobs of erosion-resistant rocks within a surrounding matrix of highly sheared shale of the mélange typify the topography of grass-covered slopes of eastern Marin County. During the trip we will also travel through a forest of redwood trees near Samuel Taylor State Park en route to the Douglas-fir–covered Point Reyes peninsula.

Keywords: San Francisco earthquake, rupture morphology, San Andreas fault, Franciscan Complex; Point Reyes.

Niemi, T.M., Hall, N.T., and Dahne, A., 2006, The 1906 earthquake rupture trace of the San Andreas fault north of San Francisco, with stops at points of geotechnical interest, *in* Prentice, C.S., Scotchmoor, J.G., Moores, E.M., and Kiland, J.P., eds., 1906 San Francisco Earthquake Centennial Field Guides: Field trips associated with the 100th Anniversary Conference, 18–23 April 2006, San Francisco, California: Geological Society of America Field Guide 7, p. 157–176, doi: 10.1130/2006.1906SF(12). For permission to copy, contact editing@geosociety.org. ©2006 Geological Society of America. All rights reserved.

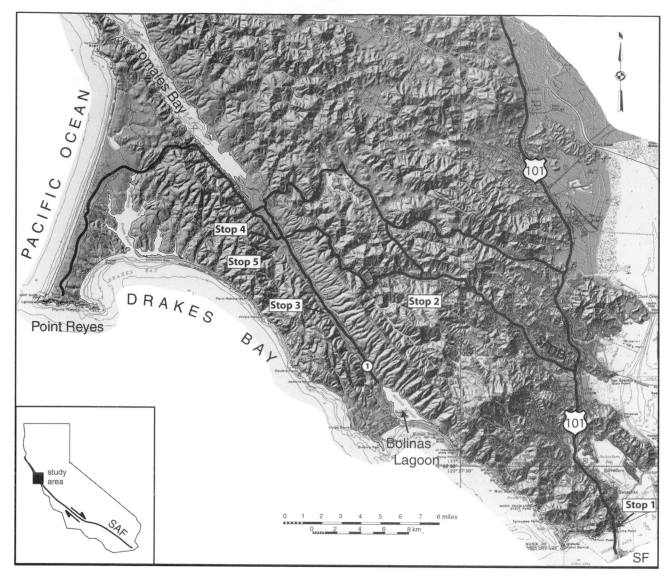

Figure 1. Shaded relief map showing the fieldtrip route and field stops (Map modified from Graham and Pike, 1997). SFDB—Sir Francis Drake Blvd. Inset map: Location of study area in California; SAF—San Andreas fault.

STOP 1: GOLDEN GATE BRIDGE AT VISTA POINT

Significance of the Site

This is an excellent location to view the Golden Gate Bridge and the rocks of the Marin headlands.

Accessibility

Vista Point has public parking and restrooms.

GPS Coordinates

37°50.803′N, 122°28.729′W.

Directions

Exit northbound Highway 101 at Vista Point (1.8 mi from the south end of the bridge).

Site Description

Vista Point, located at the northern end of the Golden Gate Bridge, is built over rocks of the Marin headlands terrane (Blake et al., 1984), which is a slice of ancient Jurassic oceanic crust. Excellent exposures of rocks that represent ancient seafloor (an ophiolitic rock sequence) are found along Highway 101 and Alexander Avenue (the first exit north of the Golden Gate Bridge). Fog permitting, Vista Point affords a spectacular

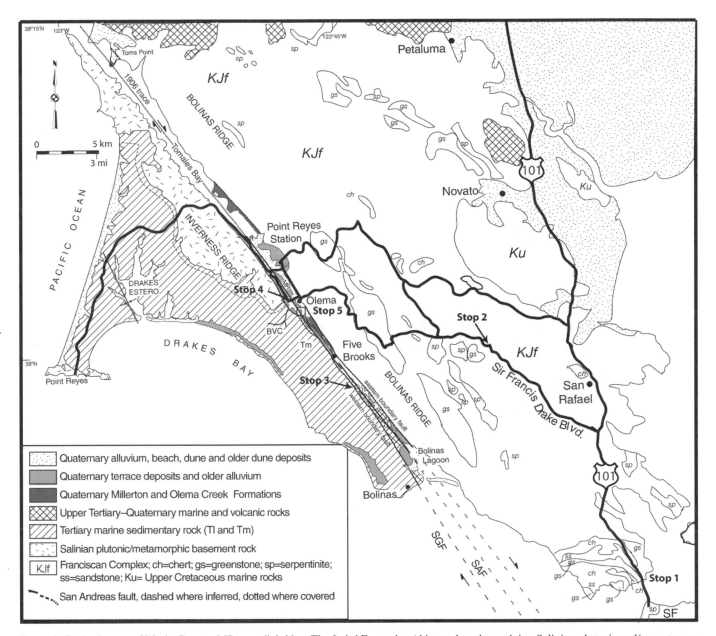

Figure 2. Geologic map of Marin County. MR—medial ridge; Tl—Laird Formation (thin sandy unit overlying Salinian plutonic and/or metamorphic basement rock); Tm—Monterey Formation (extensive siliceous shale unit on Inverness Ridge west of study area); BVC—Bear Valley Creek drainage; SGF—San Gregorio fault; SAF—San Andreas fault. (Map modified from Galloway, 1977; Kleist, 1981; Clark and Brabb, 1997; Grove and Niemi, 2005).

view of one of California's most famous and beautiful landmarks—the Golden Gate Bridge. Connecting San Francisco and peninsula cities to Marin County and counties farther to the north of San Francisco Bay, the bridge is a vital transportation link in the Bay Area's economic engine (Fig. 3). More than 40 million vehicles cross this span every year!

First opened on 27 May 1937, the bridge was designed to overcome formidable environmental obstacles that include challenging meteorologic, hydrographic, geologic, and seismic conditions. Builder and Chief Engineer Joseph Strauss presented the first blueprints of the proposed bridge to the city of San Francisco in 1921 and estimated it would cost twenty-five million dollars to build, a figure that at the time was equal to two-thirds of all appraised property value in the entire city! With financial help from A.P. Giannini (Bank of America), the technical genius of engineers Charles Ellis and Leon Moisseiff, and the architectural design contributions of Irving Morrow, the bridge became a reality.

Figure 3. Golden Gate Bridge viewed to the northeast from the south approach toward the Marin headlands. Stop 1, Vista Point, is a scenic turn out, viewing facility, and parking area located near the north approach to the bridge. Photograph by Alexander Dahne, July 2005.

Here are some important design statistics:

• Including both approaches, the bridge is 1.7 miles (2.8 km) long;
• The main suspension span (distance between towers) is 4200 ft (1300 m);
• Clearance of the deck above mean higher high water is 220 ft (67 m);
• The total weight of bridge, anchorages, and approaches (after deck replacement in 1985) is 887,000 tons;
• The diameter of each main cable is 36 3/8 inches (91.8 cm); and
• The total length of wire used in both cables is 80,000 miles (130,000 km), or enough to circle Earth more than three times!

To accommodate wind loads, the center span of the bridge can deflect up to 27.7 ft (8.45 m). Severe winds in December have forced closure of the span only three times: 1951 (69 mph), 1982 (70 mph), and 1983 (75 mph). The span rippled in 1951, and steel girders were subsequently added to stiffen and add support to the roadway. The bridge is also designed for a maximum

downward deflection of 10.8 ft (3.3 m) and is able to support a live load (vehicles and people) of 4000 pounds per linear foot.

The bridge spans a bedrock canyon that is more than 300 ft (90 m) deep and is swept clean of sediment by strong tidal currents with an average flow of 2.3 million cubic feet per second at velocities that range from 4.5 to 7.5 knots. One sixth of the volume of San Francisco Bay, or an estimated 390 billion gallons, flows through the Golden Gate four times a day! The canyon was carved into Franciscan Assemblage bedrock during the last glacial period (Pleistocene), when sea level was 400 ft (120 m) lower than present and the combined flow of the Sacramento and San Joaquin rivers eroded into the continental shelf. These rivers join in the delta near Stockton, flow through a drowned valley (now occupied by San Francisco Bay) to the Pacific Ocean, draining 40% of the land surface of California. As recorded in the Merced Formation south of San Francisco, a shallow marine basin that developed along the San Andreas fault, sediment from the Sierra Nevada first reached the Bay Area coast ca. 0.6 Ma (Hall, 1965; Clifton et al., 1988). This date undoubtedly reflects the opening of the Carquinez Strait near Vallejo and might also mark the opening of the Golden Gate.

The north anchorage and tower of the bridge are founded in a relatively coherent slab of oceanic crust consisting of massive pillowed greenstone that is overlain by contorted red chert and bedded graywacke. The south anchorage and tower are underlain by California's state rock—serpentinite—pervasively sheared mantle material not highly regarded for its structural soundness. A professorial controversy over the stability of the south tower between Stanford's Bailey Willis and Berkeley's Andrew Lawson was eventually resolved after divers, using black powder bombs and hydraulic hoses, created a smooth platform 110 ft (34 m) below the ocean surface. After observing this surface in an inspection well, geology Professor Lawson declared, "The rock of the entire area is compact, strong serpentine remarkably free from seams. ... When struck with a hammer, it rings like steel" (pbs.org, 2004).

In addition to the daily challenges of fog, wind, tidal currents, and traffic, this engineering wonder faces inevitable severe ground motions that will be generated by future earthquakes within the San Andreas fault system. The main San Andreas fault lies just offshore, ~6 mi (10 km) west of the Golden Gate. Within this offshore area between Daly City and Bolinas Lagoon, the 1906 earthquake nucleated and ruptured in both directions: southeastward to San Juan Bautista and northwestward to Shelter Cove in Humboldt County (Bolt, 1968; Boore, 1977; Zoback et al., 1999). Reid's (1910) original investigation into the mechanics of the 1906 earthquake concluded that there were two closely spaced shocks: a foreshock centered off the Golden Gate, and a main shock centered near Olema (Stops 4 and 5 on this trip). However, more recent studies place the epicenter off the Golden Gate (Lomax, 2005).

Consultants hired by the Golden Gate Bridge district concluded that a repeat of the 1906 earthquake would pose a substantial risk of collapse, or impending collapse, of the San

Francisco and Marin approach viaducts and the Fort Point Arch and extensive damage to the main suspension span and other bridge components. In 1996, three construction phases for the seismic retrofit of the bridge were established (see Chapter 9 of this volume, for more detail about the retrofit).

- Phase 1: Retrofit the Marin approach viaduct, completed in 2002;
- Phase 2: Retrofit the San Francisco approach viaduct, Fort Point Arch, and pylons S1 and S2, scheduled for completion in 2005; and
- Phase 3: Retrofit the main suspension span and the north and south towers, a four-year project that is presently unfunded.

As we proceed northward up the grade beyond the bridge and approach the Rainbow Tunnel, note the different slopes excavated into the Franciscan graywacke. A dip slope on the left (west) has a relatively low angle because the slope direction and the direction of tilt of the rock layers are in the same direction. The steeper slope on the right (east) has a higher angle because the rock layers tilt in the opposite direction to the excavated slope. Once through the tunnel, immediately look to the left to see greenstone pillows exposed in a near vertical cut. As we descend the Waldo grade, we cross an ancient fault separating the relatively coherent Marin Headlands slab of Franciscan bedrock from pervasively sheared and landslide-prone Franciscan mélange on the north.

STOP 2: WHITE'S HILL–SIR FRANCES DRAKE BOULEVARD MILEPOST 9.25

Significance of the Site

This site features the exposure of a landslide.

Accessibility

This site is at a roadside turnoff along Sir Francis Drake Boulevard; no facilities.

GPS Coordinates

38°00.567′N, 122°37.046′W.

Directions

This stop is on Sir Frances Drake Boulevard, 7.9 mi northwest of the intersection of Highway 101 and Sir Frances Drake Boulevard.

Description of Site

Landslides, including slumps, earth flows, and debris flows, are common throughout the San Francisco Bay Area. In an effort to mitigate potential land slope failures and to provide digital maps and plotable map databases, the U.S. Geological Survey has produced Internet-accessible landslide hazard maps (Wentworth et al., 1997, http://wrgis.wr.usgs.gov/open-file/of97-745/madl.html). Our second stop will be along Sir Frances Drake Boulevard at a site near the town of Fairfax with a well-identified landslide (Figs. 1 and 2).

The major landslide located at milepost 9.25 has caused continued settlement and lateral movement of the outer or northbound lane of Sir Francis Drake Boulevard. Downslope-facing concave "smiles" enclosing down-dropped sections of pavement were typical features of the White's Hill grade. Highway crews maintained the pavement in a passable condition by adding successive asphalt concrete overlays to build up the roadbed across the side area. Recent subsurface investigations by Harlan Tait Associates (HTA), a Bay Area geotechnical consulting firm, found 34 ft (10 m) of fill had been placed on the actively moving landslide mass. The maximum thickness of asphalt concrete overlays found by HTA was 19 ft (5.8 m). If Nicholas Steno was correct in his stratigraphic law of superposition, here is an event-by-event record of latest Holocene landslide activity!

Completed in September 1938, the current alignment of Sir Francis Drake Boulevard was located unknowingly across the milepost 9.25 landslide. However, the landslide soon became obvious as the road fill began to fail. HTA found that the slope reentrant here has the classic morphology of a colluvium-filled swale (a long, narrow and shallow trough filled with a mixture of sediment of various sizes, all moving downslope by gravity) that was already a rotational slump–debris flow that had failed long before construction of the highway. The margins of the swale are underlain by well-bedded sandstone and shale of the Franciscan Assemblage, rock units that are clearly visible in cuts at the top of the White's Hill grade.

The ancient slide mass within the swale consists primarily of pervasively sheared Franciscan Assemblage mélange (predominantly shale) and colluvium, and is over 700 ft (200 m) long, ~50 ft (15 m) thick, and descends ~350 ft (110 m) vertically from near the summit of White's Hill to the channel of Fairfax Creek. HTA estimated that ~200 ft (60 m) of this ancient slide mass was inadvertently reactivated as a rotational slump with some lateral translation (downslope movement) by the construction of Sir Francis Drake Boulevard.

Typically, there are four types of solutions available to engineers to mitigate active landslides. The first is to consider sliding as a maintenance issue and do nothing but patch the road (and/or make other repairs) after sliding has occurred. The second is to eliminate the problem area by removing the entire slide mass. The third is to try to stabilize the landslide by various means including removing water from the slide mass, regrading the head of the slide to reduce the driving force, and/or stabilizing the slide mass and over-steepened slope or scarp by means of buttress fills or retaining structures. A fourth potential solution would be to avoid the landslide entirely by going around, over, or under it.

The first approach (often favored by the California Department of Transportation [Caltrans]) was used by the county of Marin for decades, but apparently became increasingly expensive and occasionally left the road in a hazardous condition. The second approach would involve massive grading, which in environmentally and fiscally conscious Marin County would not be politically feasible. The third approach was, in fact, recommended by HTA and prior consultants. A system of drains and hydroaugers (nearly horizontal drainage elements drilled into the ground in order to minimize groundwater) were installed in the milepost 9.25 slide in 1988, but failed to stop the downslope movement. In 2000, HTA recommended construction of a soldier pile or a retaining wall with steel-beam uprights with concrete crossbeams along the outer edge of the pavement to stabilize the roadbed. Marin County, however, has opted to "avoid" the active slide issue altogether and built a bridge across it! At the very least, it will be interesting to monitor the ongoing geomorphic evolution of this rather typical coastal California hillside.

STOP 3: PACIFIC COAST SCIENCE AND LEARNING CENTER (BONDIETTI RANCH)

Significance of the Site

This site provides a view of the 1906 earthquake rupture trace.

Accessibility

This is federal land; facilities are available by prior arrangement. Contact the headquarters of the Point Reyes National Seashore.

GPS Coordinates

37°58.245′N, 122°43.856′W.

Directions

This site is on Highway 1, 5.8 mi (9.3 km) south of the intersection of Sir Francis Drake Boulevard and Highway 1.

Description of the Site

Sir Francis Drake Boulevard intersects with California Highway 1 in the little town of Olema. Crowned the epicenter of the 1906 San Francisco earthquake by Reid (1910), Olema has changed little since the time of the earthquake (except for the addition of the Point Reyes Seashore Lodge in 1998). We will travel south on Highway 1 to our third stop at the Point Reyes National Seashore's Pacific Coast Science and Learning Center located on the old Bondietti Ranch.

Highway 1 follows the 45-km-long, northwest-southeast oriented linear depression that formed along the San Andreas

fault zone (Fig. 4). The north and south portions of the fault zone are submerged beneath the waters of Tomales Bay and Bolinas Lagoon, respectively. Most of the subaerial portion of the San Andreas fault lies within the open space of the Point Reyes National Seashore Park, the Golden Gate National Recreation Area, and the Vedanta Retreat. This is one of the longest, undisturbed, publicly accessible tracts of the San Andreas fault in northern California.

The 1906 San Andreas fault trace lies within Quaternary deposits (Hall and Hughes, 1980) in the center of the valley, whose edges are defined by additional faults that Galloway (1977) named the eastern and western boundary faults (Fig. 2). These boundary faults probably extend the length of the valley, although in places they are obscured by streams, landslide deposits, vegetative cover, and an apron of sediment deposited at the edge of the mountains (alluvial fans). As we travel south on California Highway 1, many classic examples of fault-related landforms, including depressions or sag ponds, scarps, hillside benches, linear ridges, and other geomorphic features indicative of active faulting, appear both on the 1906 trace of the fault as well as on the eastern boundary fault (Brown and Wolfe, 1972).

The narrowest part of the San Andreas fault valley, at Five Brooks Horse Stables, is the north end of a topographic and structural high where Franciscan Complex basement is exposed at the land surface and overlain to the south by the Plio(?)-Pleistocene Merced Formation, a sequence of fine-grained, shallow-marine sandstones and siltstones (Blake et al., 1974; Clifton et al., 1988). North of Five Brooks, basement is mostly covered by a suite of upper Quaternary sediments of the Olema Creek Formation and other younger alluvial deposits that accumulated in the San Andreas fault zone during a time of climate fluctuation and fault-related deformation (Grove et al., 1995; Grove and Niemi, 2005). Erosional remnants of these Quaternary sediments form low ridges within the fault valley, including the so-called medial ridge (Hall and Hughes, 1980).

Unlike some sections of the 1906 earthquake rupture, the Marin County section was very well documented by Grove Karl Gilbert. As pointed out by W.W. Rubey in the introduction to the 1969 reprint of the Carnegie Institution Publication 87 (p. ix), *California Earthquake of April 18, 1906* (Lawson, 1908), none of the members of the State Earthquake Investigation Commission were "students of earthquakes" except G.K. Gilbert and H.F. Reid. Gilbert described damage and superbly surveyed offsets along the surface rupture of the fault in Marin County between the towns of Point Reyes Station and Bolinas beginning one week after the earthquake. In addition to the Carnegie publication (Lawson, 1908), Gilbert's observations of the 1906 earthquake are published in two places—in a popular book edited by David Starr Jordan of Stanford University titled *The California Earthquake of 1906* (Gilbert, 1907a) and in U.S. Geological Survey Bulletin 324 (Gilbert, 1907b).

It was not until after the 1906 earthquake that the full length of the San Andreas fault and the nature of its slip were

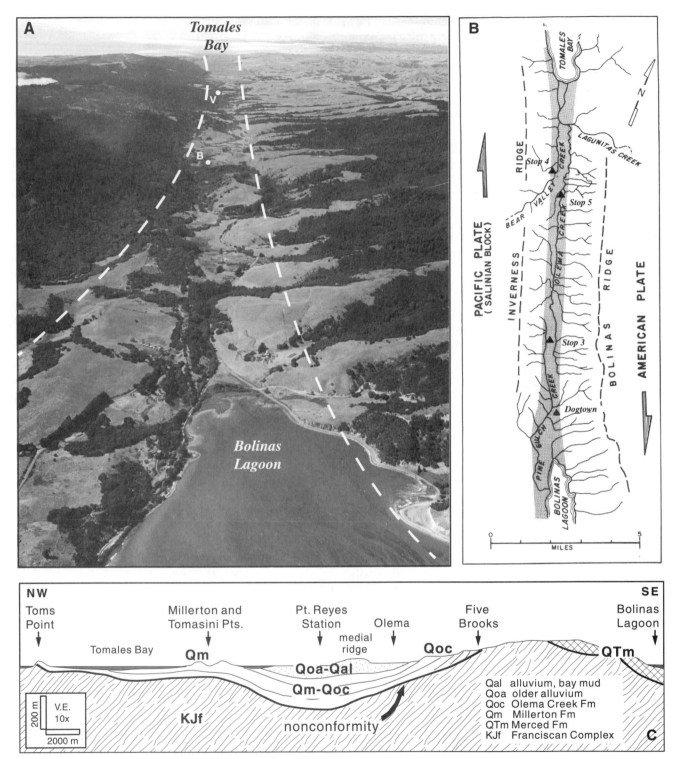

Figure 4. (A) Aerial view (looking northwest) of the San Andreas fault zone in Marin County from Bolinas Lagoon in the foreground to Tomales Bay. Dashed lines show the approximate limits of the fault zone. B—Bondietti Ranch stop; V—Vedanta trench site stop. Photography by R.E. Wallace (U.S. Geological Survey). (B) Drainage map of the San Andreas fault zone in Marin County showing Olema, Bear Valley, and Pine Gulch creeks. Shaded area indicates the approximate limits of fault zone morphology. Dashed lines show the crests of the bounding ridges. Stops 3 and 4 and the Vedanta paleoseismic sites (Stop 5) are marked with triangles. (Modified from Lawson, 1908, p. 31). (C) Interpretation of subsurface geology along the length of the San Andreas fault valley east of the fault. Constraints are surface geology, an oil well log at the latitude of Point Reyes Station, water well logs in the valley between Point Reyes Station and Five Brooks, and gravity data between Point Reyes and Olema (After Grove and Niemi, 2005).

recognized. G.K. Gilbert's field investigation of the fault rupture between Bolinas Lagoon and Tomales Bay helped confirm the large, right-lateral, essentially instantaneous slip of the fault. This section of the fault was also visited and photographed by other well-known geologists, including John C. Branner, Harold O. Fairbanks, and Rutliff S. Holloway. James Macelwane also visited the 1906 rupture along this section of the San Andreas fault in 1923 and took photographs that were included in his book, *When the Earth Quakes* (1947).

The Beisler and Bondietti ranch sites lie in the San Andreas fault zone ~5 mi (8 km) northwest of the town of Bolinas and 6.5 mi (11 km) south of Olema. The Bondietti ranch buildings are still extant, while all traces of the Beisler ranch, with the exception of a row of Monterey cypress trees, have been removed.

In his study of the 1906 earthquake in Marin County, G.K. Gilbert references several of his field observations and photographs to these two ranches.

Bondietti Ranch—11 May 1906 (G.K.G. Notebook No 108, p. 31–32):

Bondietti's is E. of main crack 20 rods. House shifted 3′ toward the fault. Barn tilts. Men milking the cows thrown from the fault. Secondary cracks run through ponds. Bondietti infers that there were earthquakes before. This theory I verify by visiting a pond which is margined by the main fault. The up throw of earlier faults like this one has interrupted a drainage hollow and dammed the water. The catchment is small and a pond is the result. So this faulting is on an old line, recently used. I see 3 other lakes on the same line and am told of 4 more. They are features of a faulted valley on the slope of a hill.

Bondietti and Beisler ranches—30 April 1907 (G.K.G. Notebook No 110, p. 35–37):

Lunch at Bondietti's. He has lived here 17 years and has felt several noteworthy quakes. On one occasion a store was so shaken the loss from breakage was considerable—about 7 years ago. Several times milk in pans had been spilt.

The Bondietti and Beisler ranch sites lie on a structurally complex, dissected medial ridge within the San Andreas fault zone valley. This ridge is flanked on the southwest by Pine Gulch Creek, which drains southeastward into Bolinas Lagoon, and on the northeast by Olema Creek, which flows to the northwest into Tomales Bay. The topographic expression of the active fault traces is very clear along this section of the San Andreas fault and the photographic coverage of the 1906 activity by G.K. Gilbert is extensive and excellent (Fig. 5). With the exception of a substantial increase in vegetation, which made relocation of Gilbert's photo stations very difficult, this area has remained essentially unchanged since 1906. Figure 6 shows four relocated historical photographs of the 1906 earthquake ground rupture.

G.K. Gilbert's account of Bondietti having experienced several earthquakes in the years prior to 1906 is very noteworthy. Growing seismological evidence suggest that the 1906 earthquake had a profound effect on Bay Area seismicity. While a large number of earthquakes occurred on numerous Bay Area faults prior to the 1906 earthquake (Toppozada et al., 1981; 2002), a period of seismic quiescence followed the earthquake (the "stress shadow" of Harris and Simpson, 1998). These data suggest a regional earthquake cycle may be controlled by 1906-type earthquakes. Bufe and Varnes (1993) modeled the Bay Area seismicity, computed a recurrence of 1906-type earthquakes of 269 ± 50 yr, and estimated that the previous great earthquake occurred around 1637. Schwartz et al. (1998) surveyed available paleoseismic data from the northern San Andreas fault and suggested that a mid-seventeenth century earthquake may have occurred along the entire 1906 rupture length. These data were used to support the "concept that long strike-slip faults can contain master rupture segments that repeat in both length and slip distribution" (Schwartz et al., 1998, p. 17,985). However, the presently available stratigraphic and age resolution of the paleoseismic data at the Vedanta site (Stop 5) suggest that coseismic slip and recurrence intervals vary over time.

STOP 4: POINT REYES NATIONAL SEASHORE HEADQUARTERS AND BEAR VALLEY VISITOR CENTER

Significance of the Site

The Point Reyes National Seashore features the Earthquake Trail, which is posted with interpretive signs and includes spots to view the rupture trace of the 1906 San Francisco earthquake.

Accessibility

This is a National Park; Bear Valley Visitor Center is open Monday–Friday, 9 a.m.–5 p.m., and weekends and holidays, 8 a.m.–5 p.m. The Earthquake Trail is wheelchair accessible. Public restrooms and picnic tables are available.

GPS Coordinates

38°02.475′N, 122°47.988′W.

Directions

Drive 0.1 mi north on Highway 1 from the intersection with Sir Francis Drake Boulevard in Olema. Turn west on Bear Valley Road and drive 0.5 mi to the entrance of the Point Reyes National Seashore Headquarters and the Bear Valley Visitor Center on your left. Drive west and park at either the visitor center or across the drive near the Earthquake Trail.

Site Description

The Point Reyes National Seashore Headquarters and Bear Valley Visitor Center are located on the site that was the Skinner Ranch at the time of the 1906 earthquake. The Point Reyes

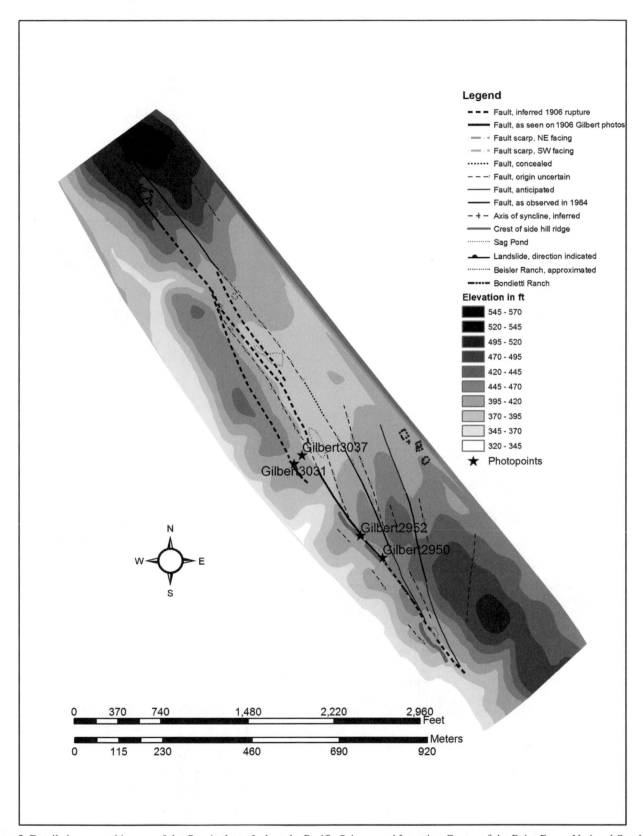

Figure 5. Detailed topographic map of the San Andreas fault at the Pacific Science and Learning Center of the Point Reyes National Seashore. At the time of the 1906 San Francisco earthquake this was the site of the Beisler and Bondietti ranches. The location of historical photographs of the ground rupturing taken by G.K. Gilbert are shown on the map and in Figure 6. (Map modified from Hall et al., 1986).

Figure 6. Relocation of four historic photographs of the 1906 rupture of the San Andreas fault on the Bondietti Ranch. See Figure 5 for photo locations. Photographs courtesy of the U.S. Geological Survey.

National Seashore is also one of the 30 most visited parks in the National Park system. Because of the easy accessibility of the park to the greater Bay Area population, Point Reyes National Seashore is one of the best publicly owned sites to view the essentially unmodified fault rupture of the 1906 San Francisco earthquake. The park is also ideally situated to provide the public with information about the geologic hazards posed by earthquakes and specific information about earthquake pre-paredness. At this stop, we will walk the Earthquake Trail and view the "moletrack," or furrow, caused by rupture of the San Andreas fault in the 1906 San Francisco earthquake. The original Earthquake Trail and interpretative exhibits (Hall, 1974; 1976) have recently been replaced with new signs to help commemorate the centennial of the 1906 earthquake. Figure 7 shows an aerial photograph and sketch map of the location of Stops 4 and 5.

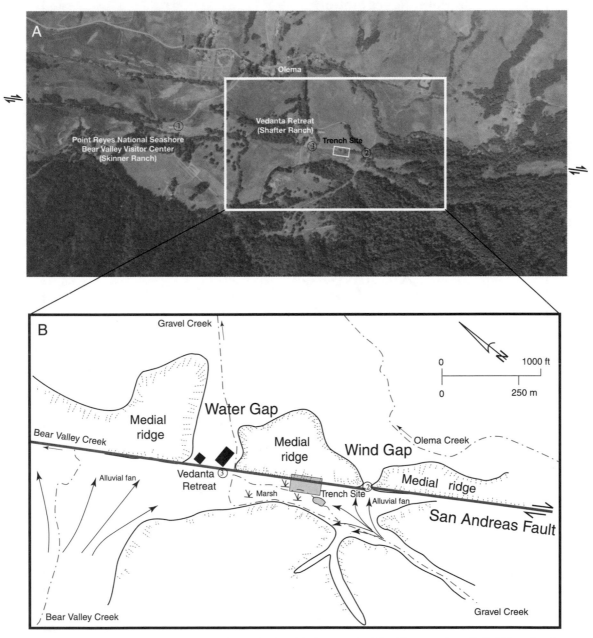

Figure 7. (A) This image shows a portion of a vertical aerial photograph of the Olema region. (1:20,000 scale, photo number 6-19 taken 6 June 1974, courtesy of Point Reyes National Park). Sites with historical measurements of 1906 surface displacements are marked 1, 2, and 3. (B) Sketch map of the Vedanta paleoseismic site on the Vedanta Retreat showing various physiographic features and location of trenches. Note how both Bear Valley Creek and the Gravel Creek drainages are deflected to the northwest along the San Andreas fault.

A lateral offset that shifted structures nearly 15–16 ft (5 m) to the right across the San Andreas fault was measured in firm ground at the Skinner Ranch. G.K. Gilbert measured four displaced cultural features at this site (Fig. 8)—a row of raspberry bushes (4.4 m), a path to the house (4.6 m), the southeast corner of the cow barn (4.9 m), and a fence (4.7 m) (Lawson, 1908).

All but the southeastern corner of the Skinner Ranch barn pictured in the background of Figure 9 was situated west of the active San Andreas fault trace. When the fault moved in 1906, the barn remained intact but the southeastern corner slid off its foundation. In 1940, the original barn was replaced by a similar structure on the same site.

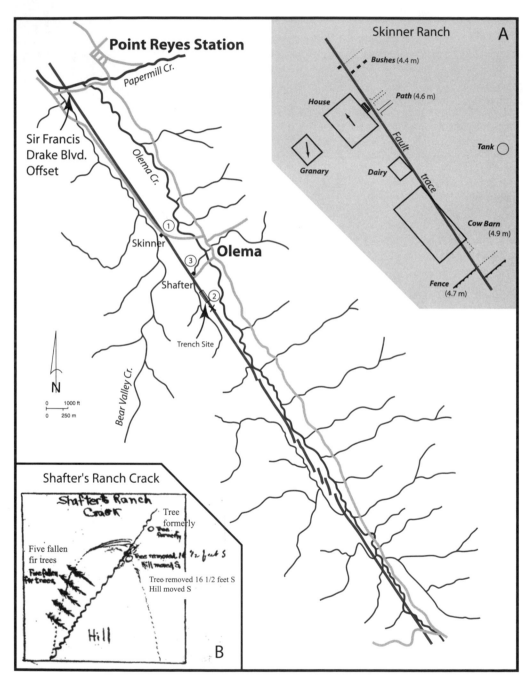

Figure 8. Map of 1906 fault trace and drainage systems in Olema Valley (1, 2, and 3 are the same as in Fig. 7) (Modified from Figure 16 of Lawson, 1908). (A) Sketch map showing displaced cultural features measured by G.K. Gilbert at location 1. The broken lines show the positions of the feature before the earthquake in relation to the same objects to the west of the fault. (Modified from Figure 22 of Lawson, 1908). (B) D.S. Jordan's sketch map of the 1906 fault trace and offset tree at the Wind Gap site on the Shafter Ranch (now the Vedanta Retreat). Location 2 marked on the map.

Figure 9. View northwest along the moletrack of the 1906 earthquake on the Skinner Ranch (now the Point Reyes National Seashore). The southeast corner of the barn in the background was shifted 4.9 m off its foundation. Photograph courtesy of the U.S. Geological Survey. The lower photograph shows the same view ~100 years later. The original barn was removed and reconstructed in 1940. The blue posts mark the 1906 trace of the San Andreas fault.

G.K. Gilbert recorded some other effects of ground shaking at the Skinner Ranch. Men and cows were thrown down while a ten-foot-high (3-m) wooden water tank that was one-third full and that stood only 100 ft (30 m) east of the fault neither moved on nor damaged its light frame. The ranch house shifted to the northwest on its foundation, despite the fact that the ground under it also moved in the same direction. By contrast, the granary that stood 100 ft (30 m) west of the house shifted 3 ft (1 m) in a southerly direction. The arrows drawn on these buildings in Figure 8 show their directions of movement. None of the original offset cultural features have survived. However, the sidehill bench of the 1906 fault trace and a reconstruction of an offset fence can be seen along the Earthquake Trail (Fig. 9). Historic photographs at this location show that a fence once stood at this location, but the coseismic offset was never recorded.

The maximum measured offset of the 1906 earthquake was a 20–21 ft (6–6.1 m) offset measured across Sir Francis Drake Boulevard (Levee Road) (Lawson, 1908). This road was built across the head of Tomales Bay, 0.8 km west of Point Reyes Station (Fig. 8). This measurement was deemed too large by G.K. Gilbert as he wrote in his letter to A. Lawson on 21 May 1906: "As the horizontal throw here is greater than at any other point, I am disposed to ascribe it in part to the flow of the soft alluvial formation" (Bancroft Library Archives, University of California, Berkeley).

STOP 5: PALEOSEISMIC SITE ON THE VEDANTA RETREAT

Significance of the Site

This site serves as a research location for slip rate and other data on the history of earthquakes generated on the San Andreas fault before 1906.

Accessibility

This is private land owned by the Vedanta Society of Northern California. Inquire at the green barn between 9 a.m. and 5 p.m. for access.

GPS Coordinates

38°02.476′N, 122°47.988′W.

Directions to the Site

The Vedanta Retreat is on Highway 1 in Olema (0.2 mi [0.3 km] south of the intersection of Sir Francis Drake Boulevard and Highway 1).

Description of the Site

The key objective of paleoseismology is to determine the characteristics of prehistoric earthquakes as a means of antici-

pating the future behavior of the causative fault. Geologists who pursue paleoseismic investigations typically attempt to establish credible values for the timing, displacements, and magnitudes of late Holocene earthquakes by interpreting both the surface morphology and the stratigraphic record at favorably situated sites where an event-by-event record of prior slip on the subject fault is likely to have been preserved. This stop at the Vedanta Retreat is the site of intense paleoseismological research of the San Andreas fault over the past decade and a half. The objectives of this research are to document the late Holocene slip rate, determine a high-resolution paleoearthquake chronology, and to measure the slip per event in pre-1906 earthquakes.

The Vedanta Retreat is a Hindu religious and meditation center owned and operated by the Vedanta Society of Northern California. The Vedanta Retreat, established before the national park, has allowed public access to the property via the Rift Valley Trail. This trail follows close to the 1906 trace of the San Andreas fault. We will examine the location of paleoseismic trench excavations that are on the private land portion of the Vedanta Retreat. Prior permission is needed to access these locations.

Century-old eucalyptus and cypress trees line the drive to the Vedanta Retreat. On the way down the drive, we cross a bridge built over Olema Creek, a drainage that flows northwestward into Tomales Bay. The entrenchment of Olema Creek several meters into its floodplain deposits is apparently historical (Niemi and Hall, 1996). South of the driveway is the late Holocene floodplain of the once meandering Olema Creek. At the end of the tree-lined drive, within a water gap in the low-lying medial ridge of late Quaternary sediment, is the large colonial house built in 1869, the residence of judge and cattleman Payne Shafter, who once owned nearly all of Point Reyes peninsula.

The following are excerpts from Gilbert's field notes written during his visits to the 1906 ground ruptures near the Vedanta research area:

Skinner and Shafter Ranches—9 May 1906, (G.K.G. Notebook 108, p. 25):

At Skinners' … it (the mole track) passes under a large cow barn which held to the SW land and was dragged over the NE … 16 feet. At Payne J. Shafter's place there is a similar offsetting estimated by Mrs. Shafter at 25 feet, but I could not verify … The shear zone in the firm ground of the hill is 5–15 feet wide, with straggling side cracks. There is also a vertical component, the west side rising a few feet.

Shafter Ranch—12 October 1906 (G.K.G. Notebook 109, p. 17):

From Shafter's Ranch southward for about 1.5 miles the rift follows the west side of a ridge. At first the ridge is broad and borders a swamp—gradually changing to flat meadow—and the fault line is exactly occupied by a road. Then there is a narrow break in the ridge, and beyond this break it becomes steep sided; the meadow is replaced by a slope which grows steeper.

Shafter Ranch—29 March 1907 (G.K.G. Notebook 110, p. 23–24):

Just south of Shafter's the sag is flat bottomed and with sedge, rushes and cattails. The cattails are largely on the west side, indicating that before the quake the west side was the lower. Now the east side is lower. There is a lane of water along the east edge (faultline)—besides standing water over much of it. Mr. Shafter says that just after the shock water ran south till the sunken tract was filled—the flow being reversed. He had drained this tract and now it is water covered again. All of which shows that here vertical throw was on the west ... There is another very low col 1/4 miles south of Shafter's. The creek could be diverted by raising its water 2 feet.

Shafter Ranch—28 April 1907 (G.K.G. Notebook 111, p. 17):

Mr. Shafter said there was no water along the line of the fault (south of his house) before the quake. Now there is two feet in a lane 10–15 rods long and 15 feet wide.

From the G.K. Gilbert descriptions of the location of the 1906 rupture and geomorphic change that occurred on the Shafter Ranch at the time of the earthquake, we learn several important facts. The San Andreas fault is a single strand within a secondary zone of cracking 3–4.5 m wide that closely follows the eastern side of a marsh. Local subsidence during the earthquake caused water to pond to at least a depth of 70 cm along the fault trace. In fact, Gilbert notes that Shafter had been trying to drain the marsh. A historic photograph of this fault rupture and the water ponded along the fault is shown in Figure 10A. At the south end of the marsh, the 1906 trace shifted from the base of the ridge to a side hill bench southeast of a gap in the ridge (Lawson, 1908).

Gilbert's description of the fault location and geomorphic expression ("another very low col") is consistent with and probably describes the wind gap site (Fig. 10B). The wind gap at the Vedanta Retreat is a site where the northern San Andreas fault is crossed at nearly right angles by a former stream. For this reason, we chose this site for a detailed trench investigation with a high potential to yield a Holocene geologic slip rate from offset channel deposits. In the wind gap area, we excavated six trenches perpendicular to and several trenches parallel to the trend of the fault (Fig. 10B). We estimated the slip rate of the San Andreas fault by matching offset segments of a buried late Holocene stream channel. Stream deposits from 1800 ± 78 yr B.P. are offset 42.5 ± 3.5 m across the active (1906) fault trace, which yields a minimum late Holocene slip rate of 24 ± 3 mm/yr (Niemi and Hall, 1992; Niemi, 1992). The similarity of the late Pleistocene rates to the Holocene slip rate indicates that the rates may not have changed over the past 30 k.y., and perhaps the past 200–400 k.y. (Grove and Niemi, 2005).

Field notes of D.S. Jordan (Stanford University Archives) describe an oak tree that was translated 16.5 ft (5 m) to the south, where it hit a ridge (Fig. 8). D.S. Jordan wrote:

At the Shafter Ranch ... A gateway which formerly led to a road by the side of the barn is now practically blocked up by the barn itself, having moved 16 1/2 feet further south. A little south of the Shafter Ranch a large chestnut oak tree about two feet through stood at the very edge of the crack and this had been violently shoved 16 1/2 feet further south, where it is pushed into the side of a hill, along the margin of which the crack goes.

We have interpreted the location of the sketch to be the wind gap on the Vedanta Retreat based on the description, the map, and by relocation of historic photographs of the fallen trees that are on the sketch. Several historic photographs of large downed Douglas fir trees that have fallen from the medial ridge toward the west match this location. Therefore, the 16.5 ft (5 m) offset measurement is the closest coseismic slip measurement to the Vedanta marsh paleoseismic site.

The Vedanta marsh paleoseismic site is located just northwest of the wind gap (Fig. 7). This site is an exceptional paleoseismic resource because it is a location where predominately fine-grained, organic-rich deposition has continuously buried the fault trace during the late Holocene. The Vedanta site along the San Andreas fault occupies a marsh with both standing and running surface water. The Vedanta paleoseismic site has all of the elements that promise to provide a high-resolution paleo-earthquake chronology for the past >2000 yr. The fault zone is wide with multiple fractures and is underlain by definable event stratigraphy. The layers deposited across the fault contain abundant in situ organic materials that provide radiocarbon age control. The margins of channel deposits, downed Douglas fir trees, and the margins of landslide debris lobes detected in trench exposures also provide piercing points that can be matched across the fault in order to estimate paleoslip.

Four field seasons of excavation have recently been conducted at the Vedanta paleoseismic site during 2001, 2002, 2004, and 2005 (Niemi et al., 2002; Zhang et al., 2003a, 2003b; Zhang, 2006). The success of these current research efforts is attributable to a new strategy to dewater the site. In August 2001, we used a track-mounted excavator to open a 20-m-long, 4-m deep ditch with sloped sides (hereafter referred to as the V-ditch). In addition to the V-ditch, eight other backhoe trenches were excavated across the fault (Fig. 10C), logged, sampled in great detail, and the results carefully evaluated.

A photographic log of the V-ditch exposure is shown in Figure 10D. The main fault zone consists of a 2-m-wide zone of upward-branching fault splays within the marsh stratigraphy. A secondary, predominantly dip-slip fault is located 5 m to the east of the main fault (Fig. 10C) and juxtaposes older sediment (>25 ka) against colluvium in apparent down-to-the-west normal separation. The exposed 4-m-thick section consists of six major peat layers interbedded with fluvial gravel and marsh clay. These layers interfinger eastward with colluvial gravels derived from the medial ridge. A clear, vertical transition from predominantly fine-grained marsh deposits to coarse-grained sediment occurs ~1 m below the ground surface. The shift toward coarse clastic sedimentation at this location signals an environ-

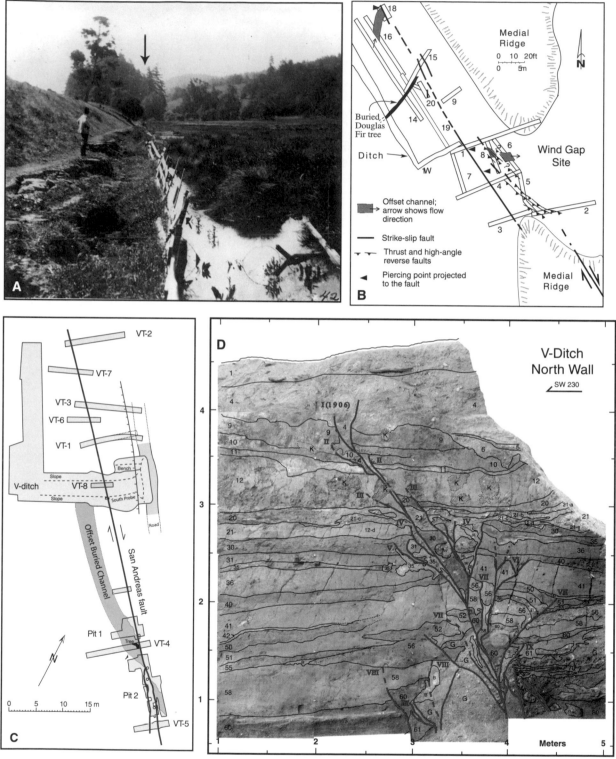

Figure 10. (A) J. Branner photograph of the 1906 rupture at the Shafter Ranch (Vedanta Retreat), showing slump failure of the road, tilted fence, and a lane of water along the rupture in the marsh. Arrow marks the location of the 1906 rupture trace south of the marsh and wind gap where it takes a side hill bench position. (Courtesy of Stanford University Archives). (B) Sketch map of the wind gap site (location B on Fig. 7) showing the location of trenches, faults, and buried offset channel used to estimate the late Holocene slip rate for the San Andreas fault at this site (Niemi and Hall, 1992). (C) Map of paleoseismic trench locations in the Vedanta marsh. See Figure 7 for the location of the trench site. (D) Trench log of the north wall of the V-Ditch showing evidence for eleven earthquakes over the past 2500 years.

mental change possibly triggered by the regional deforestation and denudation caused by the arrival of European settlers and loggers in the mid-nineteenth century. Efforts to drain the marsh over the past 150 yr have also lowered the water table ~1.5 m (Niemi, 1992). Historical erosion, channel incision, and increased sedimentation rates have been documented for this region (Niemi and Hall, 1996).

Accelerator mass spectrometry radiocarbon dating of samples of peat, macrofossils (cones, leaves, pine needles, and branches), and charcoal collected throughout the section indicate that the base of the exposed section is ca. 2500 yr B.P. We recognize evidence for a minimum of ten earthquakes using outward-splaying faults, upward fault terminations, and the vertical succession of fissure fills. Slip accompanying the 1906 earthquake displaces a portion of the upper gravel and a possible late nineteenth century road fill. Deformation within each of the laterally correlative, upper three peat layers deposited ca. 300, 700, and 1100 yr B.P. exposed in all the trenches provide age constraints on the timing of four pre-1906 earthquakes. Earlier events were exposed in the one deep excavation and are confined within the stratigraphic section dated to ca. 1000 A.D. to 900 B.C. Most of the event horizons terminate in or near major in situ peat layers that provide excellent organic material for radiocarbon analysis. Our data indicate a variation in the length of recurrence intervals between paleoearthquakes, which suggests that the characteristic earthquake model may not be appropriate for the slip behavior of the northern San Andreas fault.

During the 2004 and 2005 field seasons, we conducted three-dimensional excavations on both sides of trench 4 along the fault trace in order to accurately document the cumulative displacement of an offset paleochannel (Zhang et al., 2004). The exposed 3-m-wide paleochannel has a cumulative right-lateral offset of 7.8–8.3 m that was produced by coseismic slip during the 1906 earthquake and the earthquake prior to it (the penultimate earthquake) (Fig. 10C). Several 1906 coseismic slip measurements made near (both north and south of) the excavation site indicate ~4.4–5 m of right-lateral slip. Trench excavation and paleogeographic reconstruction also support that ~5 m of coseismic slip occurred at the trench site in the 1906 earthquake. These data suggest that prior to 1906, the paleochannel may have been offset by only 2.8–3.3 m during the penultimate earthquake dated to the late seventeenth to early eighteenth century (based on analyses of existing radiocarbon dates and stratigraphic event horizons). This interpretation of the data suggests that the San Andreas fault at this location north of San Francisco may produce earthquakes with a smaller magnitude than the 1906 earthquake. These data have major implications for the rupture behavior model used for the San Andreas fault in probabilistic seismic hazard assessments.

ROAD LOG

This field trip log begins at the northernmost point in the city of San Francisco—the south end of the Golden Gate Bridge. Proceed northward on Highway 101 across the Golden Gate Bridge and get into the curb lane before reaching Marin County.

Cumulative
mi   (km)

1.8   (2.9) Turn right to Vista Point and park. There are restrooms and ample parking.

Stop 1: Golden Gate Bridge at Vista Point (View of the Golden Gate Bridge, San Francisco and central San Francisco Bay) (37°50.803′N, 122°28.729′W)

Cumulative
mi   (km)

2.0   (3.2) Complete the circle at Vista Point and return to Highway 101 north.

3.2   (5.1) Note the difference in the steepness of the road cut in the Franciscan graywacke sandstone. The slope on the west (left) is an anti-dip slope that is stable at a much steeper angle than the dip slope on the right (east), the steepness of which is limited by the dip of bedding.

9.6   (15.2) Get into the lane for the San Anselmo exit. At 10.0 mi (15.9 km), exit right toward San Anselmo and proceed west on Sir Francis Drake Boulevard. Here you will encounter several communities and suburban traffic congestion. Stay on Sir Francis Drake Boulevard all the way to Point Reyes National Seashore.

13.9   (22.1) Red Hill on the right—site of a major landslide in the middle of the last century. The headwall scarp is still visible.

15.5   (24.6) Town of Fairfax.

17.3   (27.5) Base of White's Hill grade. Note the steep topography and the condition of the pavement where the road crosses gullies in the steep, east-facing slope.

17.9   (28.4) Park on the right shoulder at the south end of the bridge located just below the top of the grade. There is ample room for parking here, but no restrooms are available.

Stop 2: White's Hill–Sir Francis Drake Boulevard, Milepost 9.25 (38°00.5672′N, 122°37.046′W)

Walk down the steep steps adjacent to the southeastern abutment of the bridge to access the ground beneath the bridge. Here you will see a display of modern American art, active landslide scarps, and a variety of earth materials in the east-facing slope including artificial fill and asphalt concrete overlying landslide debris. The original road grade is well preserved along the west side of the bridge and makes an excellent strain gauge for monitoring active slope processes. Cuts near the southwestern abutment of the bridge reveal slope-parallel joints that have influenced the steepness of the local slopes.

Cumulative
mi   (km)

22.3   (35.4)   Town of Lagunitas. The creek in this area, Lagunitas Creek, drains into the south end of Tomales Bay at the town of Point Reyes Station. This creek was known as Papermill Creek in 1906.

23.5   (37.3)   Enter Samuel P. Taylor State Park, deep in a coastal redwood forest.

26.9   (42.7)   Leave Samuel P. Taylor State Park and enter the Golden Gate National Recreation Area.

~29.2   (47.5)   Cross the crest of Bolinas Ridge, which is underlain by rocks of the Franciscan Assemblage.

30.2   (47.9)   Intersect Highway 1 at a three-way stop in the town of Olema. Welcome to Point Reyes National Seashore and the San Andreas fault zone! Turn left on Highway 1 and proceed to the southeast along the fault zone. Look for topographic features indicative of geologically young faulting. The 1906 rupture typically lies off to the right of Highway 1 just beyond the western edge of the grassy meadows.

30.4   (48.3)   The road to Vedanta Retreat is on the right. (We will return here for our last stop of the day.)

32.1   (50.9)   Note the sag along a fault at the eastern boundary of the San Andreas fault zone. The major stream in this area is Olema Creek, which flows to the northwest along the fault zone and also drains into the southern end of Tomales Bay near Point Reyes Station.

36.0   (57.1)   Turn right (west) on the dirt road toward the Pacific Coast Science and Learning Center. Go 0.1 mi (0.16 km) and park. There is ample parking here and restrooms are available by prior arrangement.

Stop 3: Pacific Coast Science and Learning Center (Bondietti Ranch) (37°58.245′N, 122°43.856′W)

Cumulative
mi   (km)

36.2   (57.5)   Return to Highway 1 and turn left (northwest) to return to the town of Olema. At Olema (42.0 mi [66.7 km]), proceed to the north (after stopping at the intersection, of course).

42.1   (66.8)   Turn left onto Bear Valley Road and proceed toward the headquarters entrance of Point Reyes National Seashore.

42.6   (67.6)   Turn left into the visitors center and immediately cross the 1906 trace of the San Andreas fault. It is marked by blue posts and passes beneath

the far lefthand (southeast) corner of the red barn on your left. Proceed west to the visitors center and park. Restrooms are available. Be certain to see the movie that the Discovery Channel prepared and donated to the National Seashore.

Stop 4: Point Reyes National Seashore Headquarters (38°02.475′N, 122°47.988′W)

Cumulative
mi   (km)

43.0   (68.3)   Return to Bear Valley Road, turn right and retrace your steps to Highway 1 and turn right to the town of Olema. Continue straight through Olema (after stopping) to the road leading to the Vedanta Retreat.

43.8   (69.5)   Turn right toward Vedanta Retreat (marked by a wooden sign) and proceed down a gravel lane bordered by eucalyptus and cypress trees that are more than 120 years old. The white house on the right was built in the late 1860s and belonged to Payne Shafter at the time of the 1906 earthquake. The 1906 rupture lies just beyond the house and barn complex. Park by the green barn and ring the visitor's bell for permission to enter the site. This is a private religious retreat and restrooms are not available. Reservations to visit this site must be made in advance with the Vedanta Society of Northern California.

Stop 5: Paleoseismic Site on the Vedanta Retreat (38°02.476′N, 122°47.988′W)

Cumulative
mi   (km)

44.4   (70.5)   Return to Highway 1 and turn left toward Olema. At the three-way stop, turn right onto Sir Francis Drake Boulevard and retrace your steps back to the Golden Gate Bridge and the City of San Francisco. Round trip mileage to the south end of the Golden Gate Bridge = 74.6 mi (118.4 km).

ACKNOWLEDGMENTS

This research was supported by grants from the U.S. Geological Survey (USGS) National Earthquake Hazards Reduction Program award numbers 14-08-0001-G1777, 01HQGR0194, 03HQGR0015, and 05HQGR0165 to Niemi and award number 14-08-0001-G514 to Hall and others. The views and conclusions contained in this document are those of the authors and should not be interpreted as necessarily representing the official policies, either expressed or implied, of the U.S. government.

Several University of Missouri–Kansas City students have provided field assistance and mapping, including Hongwei Zhang, Shari Generaux, Alivia Allsion, Nasser Mansoor, Christian Gierke, Janice McCabe, Jamie Thomason, and Jennifer Goucher, for which we are very grateful. Recent collaborations and discussions with Karen Grove (San Francisco State University) and Tom Fumal (USGS) have also been very helpful. We are especially thankful to the Vedanta Society of Northern California and the members of the Vedanta Retreat for granting us permission to conduct research on their property in Olema, California. The Point Reyes National Seashore superintendents (John Sansing and Don Neubacher) and their staff have also supported and facilitated this research. We thank Ben Becker, director of the Point Reyes National Seashore Pacific Science and Learning Center, for providing logistical support.

ONLINE RESOURCES

Clark, J.C., and Brabb, E.E., 1997, Geology of Point Reyes National Seashore and vicinity, California: A digital database: U.S. Geological Survey Open-File Report 1997-456, http://wrgis.wr.usgs.gov/open-file/of97-456/.

Elder, W.P., 2005, The geology of the Golden Gate Headlands: National Park Service, www.nps.gov/prsf/geology/geology.htm.

Point Reyes National Seashore, 2001, Point Reyes National Seashore official Web site: Point Reyes National Seashore, http://www.nps.gov/pore/visit.htm.

Stoffer, P.W., 2005, The San Andreas fault in the San Francisco Bay Area, California: A geology fieldtrip guidebook to selected stops on public lands: U.S. Geological Survey Open-File Report 2005-1127, http://pubs.usgs.gov/of/2005/1127/.

Stoffer, P., and Phillip, E., 2003, Point Reyes National Seashore: A 3-D tour featuring park geology: U.S. Geological Survey Western Earth Surface Processes Team, http://3dparks.wr.usgs.gov/ptreyes/.

U.S. Geological Survey, 1997, San Francisco Bay region, California, landslide folio: U.S. Geological Survey Report 97-745, http://wrgis.wr.usgs.gov/open-file/of97-745/.

REFERENCES CITED

Blake, M.C., Jr., Bartow, J.A., Frizzell, V.A., Jr., Schlocker, J., Sorg, D., Wentworth, C.M., and Wright, R.H., 1974, Preliminary geologic map of Marin and San Francisco counties and parts of Alameda, Contra Costa and Sonoma counties, California: U.S. Geological Survey Miscellaneous Field Studies Map MF-574, scale 1:62,500.

Blake, M.C., Jr., Howell, D.C., and Jayko, A.S., 1984, Tectonostratigraphic terranes of the San Francisco Bay Region, *in* Blake, M.C., Jr., ed., Franciscan geology of northern California: Society for Sedimentary Geology (SEPM) Pacific Section Book 43, p. 5–22.

Bolt, B.A., 1968, The focus of the 1906 California earthquake: Bulletin of the Seismological Society of America, v. 50, no. 1, p. 457–471.

Boore, D.M., 1977, Strong-motion recordings of the California earthquake of April 18, 1906: Bulletin of the Seismological Society of America, v. 67, no. 3, p. 561–577.

Brown, R.D., and Wolfe, E.W., 1972, Map showing recently active breaks along the San Andreas fault between point Delgada and Bolinas Bay, California: U.S. Geological Survey Miscellaneous Geological Investigation Map I-692, scale 1:62,500, 2 sheets.

Bufe, C.G., and Varnes, D.J.., 1993, Predictive modeling of the seismic cycle of the greater San Francisco Bay region: Journal of Geophysical Research, v. 98, p. 9871–9883.

Clark, J.C., and Brabb, E.E., 1997, Geology of Point Reyes National Seashore and vicinity: a digital database: U.S. Geological Survey Open-File Report 97-456, scale 1:48 000, 1 sheet, 17 p., http://wrgis.wr.usgs.gov/open-file/of97-456/.

Clifton, H.E., Hunter, R.E., and Gardner, J.V., 1988, Analysis of eustatic, tectonic, and sedimentologic influences on transgressive and regressive cycles in the upper Cenozoic Merced Formation, San Francisco, California, *in* Paola, C., and Kleinspehn, K.L., eds., New perspectives of basin analysis: New York, Springer-Verlag, p. 109–128.

Elder, W.P., 2005, The geology of the Golden Gate Headlands: National Park Service, www.nps.gov/prsf/geology/geology.htm (Accessed 26 Jan. 2006).

Galloway, A.J., 1977, Geology of the Point Reyes peninsula, Marin County, California: California Division of Mines and Geology Bulletin 202, 72 p.

Gilbert, G.K., 1907a, The investigation of the California earthquake of 1906, *in* Jordan, D.S., ed., The California earthquake of 1906: San Francisco, A.M. Robertson, p. 215–256.

Gilbert, G.K., 1907b, The earthquake as a natural phenomenon, *in* The San Francisco earthquake and fire of April 18, 1906, and their effects on structures and structural materials: U.S. Geological Survey Bulletin, v. 324, p. 1–13.

Graham, S.E., and Pike, R.J., 1997, Shaded relief map of the San Francisco Bay region, California: U.S. Geological Survey Open-File report 97-745B, http://wrgis.wr.usgs.gov/open-file/of97-745/of97-745b.html.

Grove, K., and Niemi, T.M., 2005, Late Quaternary deformation and slip rates in the northern San Andreas fault zone at Olema Valley, Marin County, California: Tectonophysics, v. 401, no. 3–4, p. 231–250, doi: 10.1016/j.tecto.2005.03.014.

Grove, K., Colson, K., Binkin, M., Dull, R., and Garrison, C., 1995, Stratigraphy and structure of the Late Pleistocene Olema Creek formation, San Andreas fault zone north of San Francisco, California, *in* Sangines, E., Andersen, D., Buising, A., eds., Recent geologic studies in the San Francisco Bay area: Society for Sedimentary Geology (SEPM) Pacific Section Book 76, p. 55–77.

Hall, N.T., 1965, Late Cenozoic stratigraphy between Mussel Rock and Fleishhacker Zoo, San Francisco peninsula: International Association for Quaternary Research, VII Congress, Guidebook I: Northern Great Basin and California, p. 151–158.

Hall, N.T., 1974, The Earthquake Trail at Point Reyes National Seashore: California Geology, v. 27, no. 4, p. 87–89.

Hall, N.T., 1976, Earthquake Trail revisited: California Geology, v. 29, no. 9, p. 206–207.

Hall, N.T., and Hughes, D.A., 1980, Quaternary geology of the San Andreas fault zone at Point Reyes National Seashore, Marin county, California, *in* Streitz, R., and Sherburne, R., eds., Studies of the San Andreas fault zone in northern California: California Division of Mines and Geology Special Report 140, p. 71–87.

Hall, N.T., Hay, E.A., and Cotton, W.R., 1986, Investigation of the San Andreas fault and the 1906 earthquake, Marin County, California: National Earthquake Hazards Reduction Program Final Technical Report, Contract #14-08-0001-21242, 3 maps, scale 1:1200.

Harris, R.A., and Simpson, R.W., 1998, Suppression of large earthquake by stress shadows: a comparison of Coulomb and rate-and-state failure: Journal of Geophysical Research, v. 103, p. 24,439–24,451, doi: 10.1029/98JB00793.

Kleist, J.R., ed., 1981, The Franciscan Complex and the San Andreas fault from the Golden Gate to Point Reyes, California: Pacific Section, American Association of Petroleum Geologists, Field Trip Guidebook, v. 51, 31 p.

Lawson, A., 1908, The California earthquake of April 18, 1906; Report of the State Earthquake Investigation Commission: Washington, Carnegie Institute Publication 87, 451 p. (Reprinted 1969).

Lomax, A., 2005, A re-analysis of the hypocentral location and related observations for the great 1906 California earthquake: Bulletin of the Seismological Society of America, v. 91, p. 861–877.

Macelwane, J.B., 1947, When the Earth quakes: Milwaukee, The Bruce Publishing Company.

Niemi, T.M., 1992, Late Holocene slip rate, prehistoric earthquakes, and Quaternary neotectonics of the northern San Andreas fault in Marin County, California [Ph.D. thesis]: Stanford, California, Stanford University, 6 Plates, 199 p.

Niemi, T.M., and Hall, N.T., 1992, Late Holocene slip rate and recurrence of great earthquakes on the San Andreas fault in northern California: Geology, v. 20, p. 195–198, doi: 10.1130/0091-7613(1992)020<0195:LHSRAR>2.3.CO;2.

Niemi, T.M., and Hall, N.T., 1996, Historical changes in the tidal marsh of Tomales Bay and Olema Creek, Marin County, California: Journal of Coastal Research, v. 12, no. 1, p. 90–102.

Niemi, T.M., Zhang, H., Generaux, S., Fumal, T., and Seitz, G., 2002, A 2500-year record of great earthquakes along the northern San Andreas fault at Vedanta marsh, Olema, California: Geological Society of America Abstracts with Programs, v. 34, no. 5, p. A-86.

PBS.org, 2004, People & Events: Underwater construction at the Golden Gate Bridge: http://www.pbs.org/wgbh/amex/goldengate/peopleevents/e_divers.html (Accessed 26 Jan. 2006).

Reid, H.F., 1910, California earthquake of April 18, 1906: Report of the state Earthquake Investigation Commission: Washington, DC, Carnegie Institution, Volume II: Mechanics of the Earthquake, 192 p.

Schwartz, D.P., Pantosti, D., Okumura, K., Powers, T.J., and Hamilton, J.C., 1998, Paleoseismic investigation in the Santa Cruz Mountains, CA—Implications for recurrence of large magnitude earthquakes on the San Andreas fault: Journal of Geophysical Research, v. 103, B8, p. 17,985–18,001, doi: 10.1029/98JB00701.

Stoffer, P.W., 2005, The San Andreas fault in the San Francisco Bay Area, California: A geology fieldtrip guidebook to selected stops on public lands: U.S. Geological Survey Open-File Report 2005-1127, 133 p., http://pubs.usgs.gov/of/2005/1127/.

Toppozada, T.R., Real, C.R., and Parke, D.L., 1981, Preparation of isoseismal maps and summaries of reported effects for pre-1906 California earthquakes: California Division Mines and Geology Open-File Report 81-11, 182 p.

Toppozada, T.R., Branum, D.M., Reichle, M.S., and Hallstrom, C.L., 2002, San Andreas fault zone, California: M ≥ 5.5 earthquake history: Bulletin of the Seismological Society of America, v. 92, no. 7, p. 2555–2601, doi: 10.1785/0120000614.

Wentworth, C.M., Graham, S.E., Pike, R.J., Beukelman, G.S., Ramsey, D.W., and Barron, A.D., 1997, Summary distribution of slides and earth flows in Marin county, California: U.S. Geological Survey Open-File Report 97-745C, http://wrgis.wr.usgs.gov/open-file/of97-745/madl.html.

Zhang, H., 2006, Paleoseismic studies of the northern San Andreas fault at Vedanta Marsh site, Olema, California [Ph.D. thesis]: Kansas City, University of Missouri-Kansas City, 334 p.

Zhang, H., Niemi, T.M., Generaux, S., and Fumal, T.E., 2003a, Earthquake events and recurrence interval on the northern San Andreas fault at Vedanta marsh site, Olema, California: North-Central Section Meeting, Geological Society of America, Kansas City, Missouri: Geological Society of America Abstracts with Programs, v. 35, no. 2, p. A-58.

Zhang, H., Niemi, T.M., Generaux, S., Fumal, T.E., and Seitz, G., 2003b, Paleoseismology of the northern San Andreas fault at Vedanta marsh site, Olema, CA: The XVI International Quaternary Association Congress: Reno, Nevada, International Union for Quaternary Research, Abstracts with Programs, p. 107.

Zhang, H., Niemi, T.M., Allison, A.J., and Fumal, T.R., 2004, Noncharacteristic slip on the northern San Andreas fault in Olema, CA: American Geophysical Union, American Geophysical Union Meeting, San Francisco, California, Dec. 13–17, 2004, abstract no. T13C-1395.

Zoback, M.L., Jachens, R.C., and Olson, J.A., 1999, Abrupt along-strike change in tectonic style: San Andreas fault zone, San Francisco peninsula: Journal of Geophysical Research, v. 104, B5, p. 10,719–10,742, doi: 10.1029/1998JB900059.

Geological Society of America
Field Guide 7
2006

The San Andreas fault on the San Francisco peninsula

Carol S. Prentice
U.S. Geological Survey, 345 Middlefield Rd., MS 977, Menlo Park, California 94025, USA
Greg Bartow
San Francisco Public Utilities Commission, 1145 Market Street, San Francisco, California 94103, USA
N. Timothy Hall
3586 Spirit Lane, Pollock Pines, California 95726, USA
Michele Liapes
San Francisco Public Utilities Commission, 1155 Market Street, San Francisco, California 94103, USA

OVERVIEW OF THE FIELD TRIP

This field trip consists of stops in four locations that provide insight into the San Andreas fault along the San Francisco peninsula. The first two stops provide an overview and close-up look at the fault where no urbanization has occurred. The last two stops are examples of areas where urbanization occurred directly over the fault prior to current regulations. The field trip also addresses the history of, and seismic hazard issues related to, an important part of the San Francisco Public Utilities Commission's (SFPUC) water-supply system, which is located along the San Andreas fault.

Keywords: San Andreas fault, 1906 earthquake, seismic hazard, San Francisco water-supply system, earthquake geology, San Francisco peninsula.

STOP 1: OVERLOOK OF THE SAN ANDREAS FAULT FROM REST AREA EAST OF HIGHWAY 280

Significance of the Site

The San Andreas fault is the primary fault that contributes to the earthquake hazard for northern California and is what caused the 1906 San Francisco earthquake. This fault carries a significant fraction of the motion between the Pacific and North America plates. From this site, the prominent valley created by the San Andreas fault is visible, along with the reservoirs that serve as the terminus of the Hetch Hetchy Water System, located within this valley. The 72-year-old system transports Sierra Nevada mountain drinking water 167 mi to the Bay Area, serving 2.4 million people in San Francisco and three neighboring counties. The Upper and Lower Crystal Springs reservoirs have a working volume of 17.2 billion gallons, and the San Andreas reservoir has a working volume of 3.2 billion gallons.

Accessibility

This is a public area; restrooms are available, and there is ample parking.

GPS Coordinates

37.53855°N, 122.36354°W.

Directions

From San Francisco, take Highway 280 southbound ~10 mi and exit at Bunker Hill Drive (in Hillsborough). Turn left at the end of the off-ramp and left again toward Bunker Hill Drive. Go over Highway 280 and turn left onto 280 northbound. After 1 mile, exit at the rest area, park, and walk up the path south of the restrooms to the statue of Junipero Serra (Fig. 1). Note that the exit off of Highway 280 for the rest area is not available from the southbound lanes, only from the northbound lanes.

Stop Description

The San Andreas fault zone is geomorphically expressed along this part of the San Francisco peninsula as a prominent linear valley (Fig. 1B), visible (on a clear day!) from the Stop 1 vista point. The San Francisco earthquake of 18 April 1906 is the most recent large earthquake to rupture the entire northern San Andreas fault, including the section that can be seen from

Prentice, C.S., Bartow, G., Hall, N.T., and Liapes, M., 2006, The San Andreas fault on the San Francisco peninsula, *in* Prentice, C.S., Scotchmoor, J.G., Moores, E.M., and Kiland, J.P., eds., 1906 San Francisco Earthquake Centennial Field Guides: Field trips associated with the 100th Anniversary Conference, 18–23 April 2006, San Francisco, California: Geological Society of America Field Guide 7, p. 177–192, doi: 10.1130/2006.1906SF(13). For permission to copy, contact editing@geosociety.org. ©2006 Geological Society of America. All rights reserved.

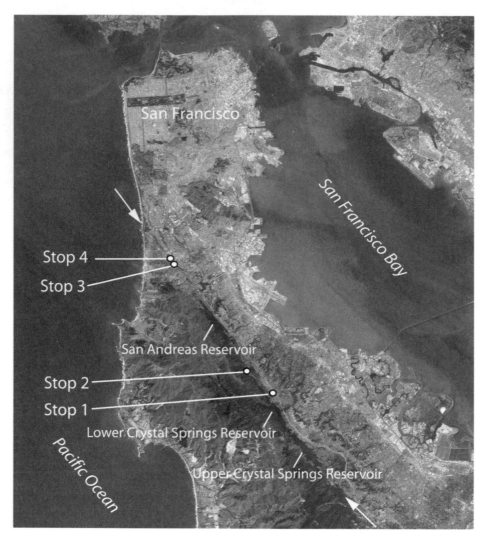

Figure 1. (*this and following page*) (A) Landsat satellite image showing the San Francisco peninsula and locations of field-trip stops (satellite image processed by M. Rymer, U.S. Geological Survey [USGS]).

this vista point (Fig. 2). Surface rupture associated with this earthquake was reported along ~435 km of the fault, from near San Juan Bautista to several km northwest of Shelter Cove, ~120 km NW of Point Arena (Fig. 3) (Lawson, 1908; Prentice, 1999). Due to its proximity to the San Francisco urban area, the San Francisco peninsula section of the fault is one of the most potentially hazardous segments along the entire length of the San Andreas fault. However, it remains one of the most poorly studied in terms of slip rate and earthquake recurrence. One study site, known as the Filoli site, is situated at the southern end of Crystal Springs reservoir (Fig. 1). Geologic studies at this site show that the fault moves at an average rate of 17 ± 4 mm/yr over geologic time (Hall et al., 1999). The fault has not moved since the 1906 earthquake, but eventually it will slip several meters all at once as it did in 1906, causing another large earthquake and catching up to its average slip rate.

SFPUC Water System and the 1906 Earthquake

The San Andreas fault traverses the peninsula watershed, which has been an important source of water for San Francisco since the 1860s, when the city's local creeks and lakes were no longer sufficient for the growing population's needs. The SFPUC reservoirs visible from this site (Upper and Lower Crystal Springs Reservoirs and the San Andreas Reservoir) were created in the 1870s and 1880s by the Spring Valley Water Company. The active trace of the San Andreas fault runs through these reservoirs (Fig. 1A), but they survived the earthquake. However, the water distribution system was severely damaged, which contributed to the difficulty in stopping the fire that followed the earthquake in San Francisco. Fault slip destroyed one of the three main pipelines and fractured the two others, though the dams survived (Figs. 4 and 5) (Schussler,

Figure 1. (*continued*) (B) Oblique aerial view of the San Andreas fault looking north-west from the south end of Crystal Springs Reservoir (Robert Wallace, USGS).

1906). The ground shaking also caused the rupture of mains and pipelines throughout the city itself (Lawson, 1908), which contributed to the three days of fires that claimed about four square miles of land and some 28,000 buildings. The fire destroyed the Spring Valley Water Company's downtown headquarters, which housed all water system plans, drawings, and specifications (Figs. 6, 7, and 8). The fact that the company's visionary

engineer, Hermann Schussler, was able to recall pipeline layout and locations from memory alone greatly expedited the restoration of the city's water supply.

San Andreas Reservoir is the northernmost of the SFPUC's reservoirs south of San Francisco. The earthen dam impounding this reservoir was built in 1870 and has a height of 105 ft (32 m) with a crest length of 960 ft (293 m). The San Andreas fault

Figure 2. Panorama of three overlapping photographs showing view of the San Andreas fault from Stop 1. Arrows indicate the linear valley associated with San Andreas fault. Highway 280 is visible in the foreground; Crystal Springs Reservoir is visible in middle-ground.

passes under the eastern abutment of the dam, and, although there was a 9-ft (2.7-m) shearing movement across the fault at this location during the 1906 earthquake, there was no significant damage to the dam. The dam embankment did not fail because shearing along the San Andreas fault was confined to the bedrock ridge that forms the eastern abutment of the dam (Hall, 1984). The brick waste weir tunnel below San Andreas dam was displaced right-laterally 9 ft (2.7 m) in the earthquake. One of the three outlets from San Andreas Reservoir was plugged with 50 ft (~15 m) of concrete in 1983 to eliminate any possibility of a destructive, uncontrolled flow in the event of a severe earthquake or other disaster.

Upper Crystal Springs Reservoir is impounded by an earthen dam with a puddle-clay core, 520 ft (159 m) long and 70 ft (21 m) high, built in 1876. Since 1923, the dam has supported the roadbed for State Highway 92 to the city of Half Moon Bay, which was already an important transportation link, even in 1906 (Fig. 9). Originally, the first outlet for Upper Crystal Springs Reservoir was a brick-lined, horseshoe-shaped tunnel, 6 ft (2 m) high, 5.5 ft (~1.67 m) wide, and 775 ft (236 m) long, on the east side of the dam. A 90-ft-deep (27.5 m), brick-lined shaft at mid-tunnel gave access to a 42 inch (1.1 m) regulating gate, which controlled the water from the reservoir. The original outlet tunnel was damaged during the 1906 earthquake when some 20 ft (6.1 m) of the line fractured by a lateral earth movement of 5.5 ft (~1.67 m). A 22 inch (0.6 m) pipe was then laid through the concrete culvert at the west end of the dam to siphon water into the lower lake. The earthquake damage was ultimately repaired, and on 28 August 1924, the original tunnel was restored to provide unregulated flow between the upper and lower reservoirs.

Lower Crystal Springs Dam was built in 1888. In 1911, it was raised to its present height of 154 ft (47 m). The dam is 176 ft (54 m) wide at the base and 600 ft (183 m) long at the crest. The gravity-type, arched dam is built of interlocking concrete blocks formed and poured in place. It was the largest dam of its kind at the time of its construction. While the dam withstood the 1906 San Andreas and 1989 Loma Prieta earthquakes, it is in need of major upgrades to satisfy spillway capacity increases under the probable maximum flood criteria as required by the California Division of Safety of Dams. The agency has ordered that the maximum water surface elevation be lowered by 8 ft (2.4 m) until the upgrades are completed.

The Beginnings of the Hetch Hetchy Water System

The experience of losing their entire city to three days of fires for lack of water spurred San Francisco officials to revitalize a decades-old campaign to secure ongoing delivery of moun-

Figure 3. Landsat satellite image of part of northern California showing San Andreas fault rupture segment (red line) associated with the 1906 San Francisco earthquake. White rectangle shows area of Figure 1 (satellite image processed by M. Rymer, U.S. Geological Survey).

Figure 4. Photograph of 1906 San Andreas fault surface rupture within peninsula watershed (courtesy of San Francisco Public Utilities Commission).

tain water for a growing population. Work began on the Hetch Hetchy Water System in 1914 under the leadership of another master engineer, the newly appointed Michael O'Shaughnessy, who attracted some of the best engineering talent of the time. Construction went on day and night to complete the linear system of tunnels, pipelines, dams, and reservoirs that would convey water by gravity alone from the Sierra Nevada Mountains to the coast (Fig. 10A). On 28 October 1934, a cheering crowd gathered at Pulgas Water Temple, the aqueduct's terminus on the southern edge of Crystal Springs Reservoir, to witness the first mountain waters pouring into the San Francisco distribution system (Fig. 10B) (SFPUC, 2005a).

Hetch Hetchy System Today

The Hetch Hetchy Water System consists of over 280 miles of pipelines, more than 60 miles of tunnels, 11 reservoirs, 5 pump stations, and 2 water treatment plants. Its water comes

Figure 5. (A) Damage due to fault rupture to pipeline that carried water from San Andreas Dam to San Francisco (courtesy of Bancroft Library, University of California at Berkeley). (B) The Lock's Creek Flume, a quarter of a mile south of the San Andreas Dam on the peninsula watershed, also collapsed. This artificial channel diverted water to the San Andreas Reservoir (16 June 1906) (courtesy of San Francisco Public Utilities Commission).

Figure 6. The earthquake fractured water mains throughout San Francisco, including this one—which sank 16 ft—shown under repair on Market Street at Spear (6 September 1907) (courtesy of San Francisco Public Utilities Commission).

from two primary sources: nearly 85% is from the upper Tuolumne River watershed in the Sierra Nevada Mountains within Yosemite National Park, and the remaining ~15% comes from surface water in two local watersheds: Alameda watershed in the East Bay and the peninsula watershed. The system is storage-poor, meaning that it is heavily dependent on a steady flow of water from the Sierra Nevada Mountains. In summer months, when water demand is highest, the water stored in local reservoirs plays a crucial role in meeting water demands.

Seismic Vulnerability

The Hetch Hetchy Water System pipelines cross three major earthquake faults—Calaveras, Hayward, and San Andreas—and two lesser-known ones—the Greenville and Great Valley faults (SFPUC, 1999). The peninsula reservoirs are located in the San Andreas fault zone, and the Calaveras fault runs very near the Calaveras Reservoir in the Alameda watershed. Also, after more than seven decades of service, portions of the aqueduct are nearing the end of their useful life (SFPUC, 2005b).

Figure 7. Fire hydrants, including this one on the northeast corner of Mission and Main Streets, were dry due to damage associated with the earthquake shaking (6 June 1906) (courtesy of San Francisco Public Utilities Commission).

Figure 8. The city-wide fires claimed the Spring Valley Water Company's pipe storage yard on Bryant Street (5 May 1906) (courtesy of San Francisco Public Utilities Commission).

SFPUC Water System Improvement Program

The SFPUC regularly inspects the dams and has conducted full-scale investigations of safety aspects, including the geology and seismology of the area, as well as conducting analyses of the structure of the dams themselves. However, seismic upgrades to dam appurtenances and pipelines are planned. To ensure a reliable flow of drinking water for its customers, the SFPUC, together with its 28 wholesale partners, has launched a $4.3 billion water-system improvement program to repair, replace, and seismically upgrade the Hetch Hetchy system's aging pipelines, tunnels, reservoirs, and dams (SFPUC, 1999, 2005b). Projects include installation of crossover and isolation valves at regular intervals throughout the pipelines, and at crucial fault crossings, plus reinforcement and upgrades to certain sections of these pipelines; seismic retrofits on San Francisco city reservoirs; and the creation of crucial system redundancies that will allow for ongoing maintenance of critical facilities, providing a potential backup if a pipeline rupture should occur due to an earthquake or any other cause.

Figure 9. Offset of fence and road across Upper Crystal Springs Reservoir dam in 1906. Offset of 8 ft was measured at this location (23 July 1906) (courtesy of San Francisco Public Utilities Commission).

Figure 10. (A) Photograph of O'Shaughnessy Dam, located in Yosemite National Park, under construction, night view (ca. 1920). Construction of the future Hetch Hetchy Water System went on day and night. City Engineer O'Shaughnessy's 24-hour schedule was an innovation at the time. (B) To the cheering crowd at Pulgas Water Temple, the first mountain waters rushing into Crystal Springs Reservoir represented the security of reliable water delivery into the future (28 October 1934) (courtesy of San Francisco Public Utilities Commission [SFPUC]).

STOP 2: OFFSET CYPRESS TREES, FENCE, AND STREAM CHANNEL

Significance of the Site

This part of the San Andreas is unique along the San Francisco peninsula because it is largely undisturbed. A fence and tree line that were both offset by the 1906 fault rupture remain well preserved. A stream that has been offset by many earthquakes over thousands of years shows that the fault has not changed location significantly in recent geologic time.

Accessibility

Permission is needed from San Francisco watershed 30 days in advance, fees are charged, and the maximum group size is 25. The key must be picked up and returned the day of entry. Contact San Francisco Water Department, 1000 El Camino Real, P.O. Box 730, Millbrae, California 94030, USA, +1-650-872–5900, for more information. There are no restrooms here, but there is parking available.

GPS Coordinates

Parking area: 37.65°N, 122.47°W; offset fence: 37.56°N, 122.4°W.

Directions

From northbound Highway 280, exit Trousdale Boulevard (in the city of Millbrae), turn left at the end of the off-ramp, and left again at the stop sign. Cross under Highway 280, and continue straight to the paved parking area in front of Trousdale Gate. (Note this is a locked gate; the key is available through the San Francisco Water Department.) The sign on the gate reads "San Andreas Rd." Go through the gate and continue ~1 mi to the parking area near the houses. From here, continue on foot down the dirt road (~0.5 mi to site from parking spot) through another gate to a fence line. Follow the fence line downhill to the San Andreas fault (Fig. 1).

Stop Description

The best-surviving features offset during the 1906 earthquake on the San Francisco peninsula are a fence and a row of cypress trees near Crystal Springs Reservoir. Here, right-lateral displacement of 9 ft (2.7 m) is still clearly visible. This locality was photographed in 1906 and is shown in plate 61B of Lawson (1908) (reproduced here as Fig. 11). Note that the displacement is distributed over a zone several meters wide. Note also the excellent preservation of delicate geomorphic features that show the nature and exact location of the surface rupture (seen in Fig. 11 to the right of the person standing in the middleground of the photograph).

North of the offset fence, the 1906 trace of the San Andreas fault lies in a trough and is marked by a small, closed depression, both of which are typical along strike-slip faults. The fault trace can be followed to the northwest, where prior fault movements have offset a stream channel between 170 and 285 ft (52–87 m). This offset represents the sum of 19–32 earthquakes comparable in slip to that of 1906, suggesting that the active trace has not changed location significantly for thousands of years (Hall, 1984).

STOP 3: URBAN SAN ANDREAS FAULT, CORNER OF WESTBOROUGH BOULEVARD AND FLEETWOOD DRIVE, SAN BRUNO

Significance of the Site

The San Andreas fault along this part of the peninsula is covered by urban development. Many houses were built on top of the fault, creating a significant seismic hazard. At this location, an overlook of the subdivision combined with predevelopment photographs show where the fault has been urbanized.

Accessibility

This is a public-access site, but there are no restrooms, and there is only limited parking on residential streets.

GPS Coordinates

37.64°N, 122.46°W.

Directions

From northbound Highway 280, exit onto Skyline Boulevard. In 3.5 mi, at the fourth stop light, turn right onto Westborough Boulevard. Turn right on Fleetwood Drive (0.1 mi) and park. Walk to the vacant lot on the east side of Fleetwood Drive at the intersection with Westborough Boulevard.

Stop Description

The urban development in this area (Fig. 12) occurred prior to enactment of the California law that prohibits such construction directly on top of an active fault (Alquist-Priolo Earthquake Fault Zoning Act, 1972). The fault was once well expressed through the area and was visible looking to the east of this vacant lot, but construction has entirely obliterated the geomorphic features, such as sag ponds and shutter ridges, that once marked the active trace. Using photographs taken of the rupture after the earthquake in 1906 and analysis of predevelopment aerial photographs, a detailed geographic information system (GIS) analysis of the best estimate of precisely where the fault broke in 1906 through this area is being developed by the U.S. Geological Survey (Prentice and Hall, 1996). A photograph taken in 1906 shows a

Figure 11. 1906 photograph showing surface rupture, offset fence, and tree line at Stop 2. CT—cypress trees. Man (circled) standing on fault trace is shown for scale (courtesy of Bancroft Library, University of California at Berkeley).

fence offset by three fault strands, a main trace with just under 2 m of right-lateral offset, and two smaller, parallel breaks (Fig. 13A). This 1906 fence offset was still visible in 1956, when M.G. Bonilla of the U.S. Geological Survey took the picture shown in Figure 13B at the same location and the photograph shown in Figure 13C from Stop 3. However, the fence was gone by 1962, when he took the photograph shown in Figure 13D. Our mapping indicates that a number of the houses visible from this location are located directly on top of the 1906 rupture trace.

STOP 4: URBAN SAN ANDREAS FAULT, MYRNA LANE, SOUTH SAN FRANCISCO

Significance of the Site

The San Andreas fault along this part of the peninsula is covered by urban development. Many houses were built on top of the fault, creating a significant seismic hazard. This stop is a short walk through one such neighborhood.

Accessibility

This is a public-access site, but there are no restrooms, and there is only limited parking on residential streets.

GPS Coordinates

37.65°N, 122.47°W.

Directions

From the intersection of Westborough Boulevard and Fleetwood Drive (Stop 3), turn right (eastward) onto Westborough Boulevard. In 0.2 mi, at the first stoplight, turn right onto Callan Boulevard. In 0.2 mi, at the first stop sign, turn left onto Dunhollow Way (to the right is Greendale Drive). In 0.2 mi, at the first stop sign, turn right onto Carter Drive. In 0.1 mi, turn right onto Cromwell Row. In 0.1 mi, turn right on Myrna Lane and park in the cul-de-sac (or wherever possible).

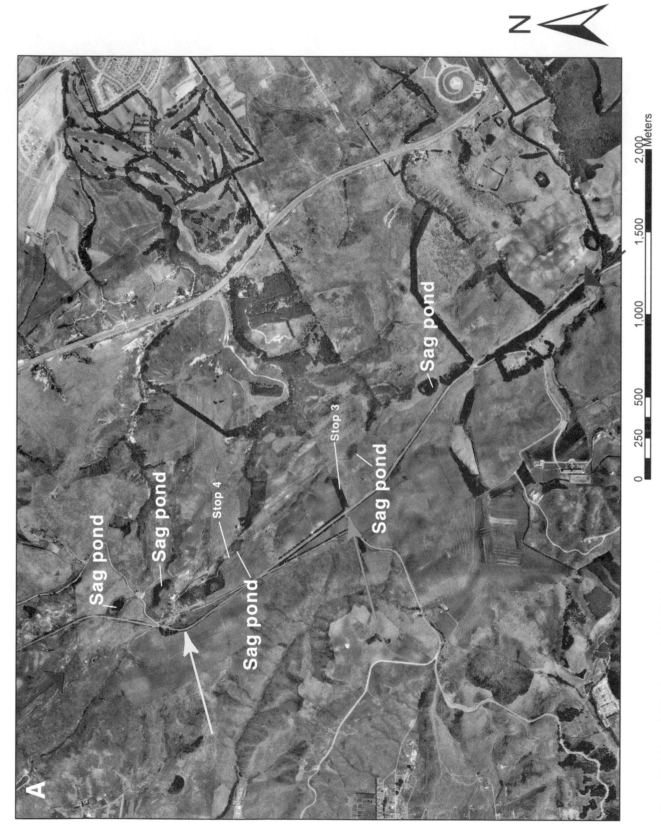

Figure 12. (*this and following page*) (A) 1946 aerial photograph showing locations of Stops 3 and 4. Yellow and green arrows show corresponding points in A and B. Yellow arrow points to bend in Skyline Boulevard, and green arrow points to intersection of Skyline Boulevard and Westborough Road. Red arrows show San Andreas fault.

Figure 12. *(continued)* (B) 1992 aerial photograph of same region shown in A, showing urban development across San Andreas fault zone.

Figure 13. (*this and following page*) (A) 1906 photograph showing off-set fence displaced by three traces of the San Andreas fault. Main trace is marked by white line; red arrows point to secondary traces. Note man for scale (courtesy of Bancroft Library, University of California at Berkeley). (B) Photograph showing same offset fence in 1956. Offset at main trace is still plainly visible (Manuel Bonilla, U.S. Geological Survey). (C) Photograph from location of Stop 3 taken in 1956 looking along offset fence shown in A and B. Red arrow shows offset at main trace. White arrow points to adobe building seen in D. (D) Photograph from same location (Stop 3) in 1962 showing the beginning of urban development across the fault (Manuel Bonilla, U.S. Geological Survey). Note that hill associated with San Andreas fault seen in C has been obliterated. White arrow points to adobe building seen in C.

C

D

Stop Description

This development (Fig. 12), constructed prior to the Alquist-Priolo Act, is built over the 1906 fault rupture. The developers in this instance apparently tried to keep homes off the fault by keeping a green belt and a road over the area where they believed the fault came through; however, many of these structures appear to be directly on top of the 1906 rupture trace (Fig. 12B).

ACKNOWLEDGMENTS

The authors gratefully acknowledge the contributions of photographer Katherine Du Tiel, who provided high-quality reproductions of historic images from San Francisco Public Utility Commission (SFPUC) archives, and Watershed Resources Manager Joe Naras, who facilitated access to the fault on SFPUC watershed lands. We also wish to thank reviewers Judy Scotchmoor, Tom Brocher, and John Boatwright for insightful and helpful comments on an earlier version of this manuscript.

REFERENCES CITED

Hall, N.T., 1984, Holocene history of the San Andreas fault between Crystal Springs Reservoir and San Andreas Dam, San Mateo County, California: Seismological Society of America Bulletin, v. 7, p. 281–299.

Hall, N.T., Wright, R.H., and Clahan, K.B., 1999, Paleoseismic studies of the San Francisco peninsula segment of the San Andreas fault zone near Woodside, California: Journal of Geophysical Research, v. 104, p. 23,215–23,236, doi: 10.1029/1999JB900157.

Lawson, A.C., chairman, 1908, The California earthquake of April 18, 1906: Washington, D.C., Carnegie Institute, Report of the State Earthquake Investigation Commission, Carnegie Institute Publication 87, 451 p.

Prentice, C.S., 1999, San Andreas fault: The 1906 earthquake and subsequent evolution of ideas, *in* Moores, E.M., Sloan, D., and Stout, D., eds., Classic Cordilleran concepts: A view from California: Geological Society of America Special Paper 338, p. 70–85.

Prentice, C.S., and Hall, N.T., 1996, Using historical research to locate the 1906 rupture of the San Andreas fault on the San Francisco peninsula: Geological Society of America Abstracts with Programs, v. 28, no. 7, p. 102.

San Francisco Public Utilities Commission (SFPUC), 1999, Water reliability partnership and EQE, Facilities Reliability Program Phase II—Regional system overview, hazard events and maps: San Francisco, SFPUC.

San Francisco Public Utilities Commission (SFPUC), 2005a, A history of the municipal water department and Hetch Hetchy System: San Francisco, SFPUC, 56 p.

San Francisco Public Utilities Commission (SFPUC), 2005b, The Water System Improvement Program: San Francisco, SFPUC, http://sfwater.org/main.cfm/MC_ID/7/MSC_ID/6 (Accessed 25 Oct. 2005).

Schussler, H., 1906, The water supply of San Francisco, California, before, during, and after the earthquake of April 18, 1906: New York, Marthin B. Brown Press, 103 p.

Geological Society of America
Field Guide 7
2006

The effects of the 1906 earthquake on the Stanford University campus

Clayton T. Hamilton
School of Earth Sciences, Dean's Office, Stanford University, 397 Panama Mall, Stanford, California 94305, USA
Laura L. Surma
School of Humanities and Sciences, Stanford University, Stanford, California 94305, USA
Anne E. Egger
Department of Geological and Environmental Sciences, School of Earth Sciences,
Stanford University, 450 Serra Mall, Building 320, Stanford, California 94305, USA

OVERVIEW

Leland Stanford (president of the Central Pacific Railroad and former governor of California) and his wife Jane established Stanford University in 1885 as a memorial to their only child, Leland Jr., who died from typhoid fever contracted while vacationing in Florence in 1884. In 1906, fifteen years after opening, the university had just completed an aggressive building program and was poised to refocus its attention on academics when, at 5:12 a.m. on 18 April, those plans were radically changed. The first shock waves of the earthquake did not cause immediate alarm, but the continued shaking intensified as the peninsula segment of the San Andreas fault, only a few miles away, ruptured. Several of the buildings, only recently completed, disintegrated. Chimneys in both the men's and women's dorms buckled and fell, carrying sections of floors down with them. Remarkably, there were only two fatalities on campus, a student and a university employee. In response to the damage, university President David Starr Jordan cancelled classes for the remainder of the year and closed the university. It was soon realized, however, that only the showier buildings built after Leland Stanford's death were badly damaged; the main buildings of the Quad were still functional. The university would reopen and resume classes on their normal schedule in the autumn.

The 1906 earthquake prompted awareness at Stanford that its location so close to an active fault is no place for seismically unsafe monumental architecture. Over subsequent years, the university would not only build safer buildings, but would research earthquakes and engineering methods for withstanding earthquakes. In contrast to 1906, no Stanford buildings were destroyed in the 1989 earthquake (much smaller than that of 1906, but nonetheless a significant earthquake), and campus was closed for only one day.

This field guide describes a walking tour (about one hour) of the Stanford campus showing selected effects of both the 1906 and 1989 earthquakes and describing how the Stanford community responded to the subsequent challenges. The tour is on paved paths and is accessible to pedestrians, bicyclists, and wheelchairs (Fig. 1).

Keywords: Stanford University, earthquake damage, life safety fix, stock farm monocline, retrofit, volt meter.

DIRECTIONS TO THE STANFORD UNIVERSITY CAMPUS

From San Francisco, take I-280 south. Exit at Sand Hill Road, following signs east to Menlo Park and Stanford. Turn right on Junipero Serra, then left onto Campus Drive West. Follow Campus Drive around to Palm Drive and turn right onto Palm Drive. Park in the Oval (at the end of Palm Drive) or turn right onto Museum Way and park in one of the lots near the museum. Note that Stanford permit parking is enforced Monday–Friday, 8 a.m.–4 p.m., in most lots; on weekends, you do not need a permit to park in these spots. Visitor (pay) parking is located in the Oval, in front of the Museum, or in the parking garage next to the museum; these spots should be used while permit parking is enforced.

STOP 1: THE QUAD AND THE CAMPUS PLAN

Significance of the Site

Memorial Arch once towered above the entrance to the Quad but was damaged beyond repair in the 1906 earthquake. Other components of campus planning were also altered significantly at this time.

Hamilton, C.T., Surma, L.L., and Egger, A.E., 2006, The effects of the 1906 earthquake on the Stanford University campus, *in* Prentice, C.S., Scotchmoor, J.G., Moores, E.M., and Kiland, J.P., eds., 1906 San Francisco Earthquake Centennial Field Guides: Field trips associated with the 100th Anniversary Conference, 18–23 April 2006, San Francisco, California: Geological Society of America Field Guide 7, p. 193–213, doi: 10.1130/2006.1906SF(14). For permission to copy, contact editing@geosociety.org. ©2006 Geological Society of America. All rights reserved.

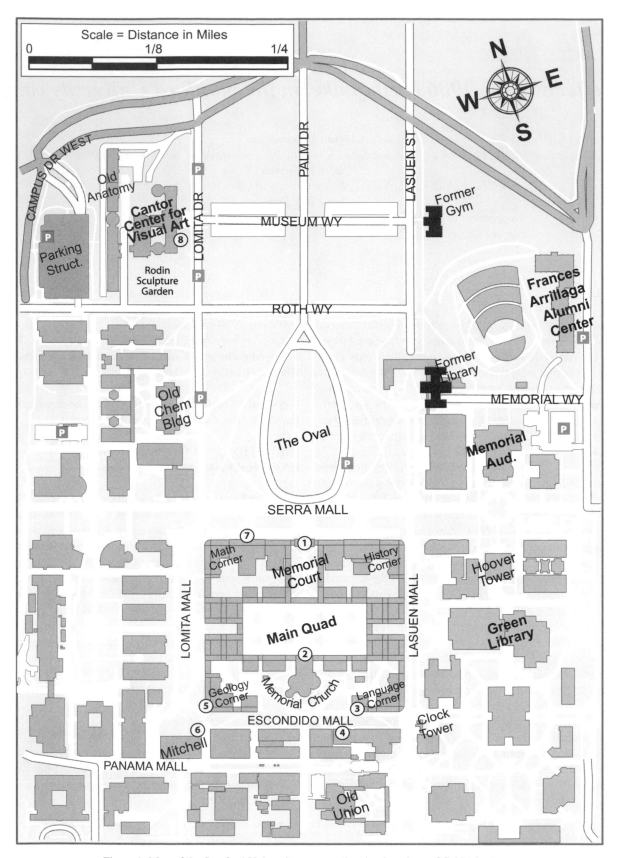

Figure 1. Map of the Stanford University campus showing locations of field-trip stops.

Accessibility

This is a public site.

GPS Coordinates

E0573360; N4142718 (UTM).

Directions

Walk to the main entrance of the Quad and Memorial Court.

Stop Description

The entrance to the Quad hasn't always been the open, understated entry it is today, but was once framed by the towering Memorial Arch (Fig. 2). Completed in 1902 and dedicated to Leland Stanford Jr., Memorial Arch was designed to be a focal point of the Quad and was of great symbolic importance to the Stanfords (Turner, 1975). The arch was essentially a stone shell with stairways leading up the interior to an observation platform. There was no reinforcement to help withstand sideways shaking (called shear forces), so it crumbled during the earthquake (Fig. 3). The cost to repair and reinforce this massive hollow structure proved to be prohibitive, so the university dismantled it down to the bases, which were capped with red tile roofs. Although the choice was based on economics, it is generally agreed that this alteration improved the strength of the architectural ensemble of the Quad.

Memorial Arch had been part of a larger campus plan. Leland and Jane Stanford had asked renowned landscape architect Frederick Law Olmsted (famous as the designer of Central Park in New York City) to design the campus of their new university. The resulting plan represented a compromise between the naturalistic, low-key Olmsted style and the more monumental tastes of the Stanfords: a long approach on a palm-lined drive, a massive arch at the entrance to the Quad, a towering church spire at the back of the Quad, and planned academic buildings to be housed in lateral arcaded Quads extending out on either end from the Main Quad (Fig. 4) (Turner, 1975). Rising behind it all are the steep Coast Ranges. Based on this design, the inner Quad buildings were constructed, and the university opened in October of 1891. Less than two years later, in 1893, Leland Stanford died.

After Leland's death, the terms of his will and the original grant of endowment gave Jane Stanford almost complete control over the university, which was faced with a severe financial crisis due to problems with Leland's estate (Turner et al., 1976). The next five years of financial struggle meant that no new buildings were constructed, even though the Olmsted plan was far from completion. In 1898, funds finally became available to Jane, and a new construction boom began. Stanford's

Figure 2. The original Memorial Arch, completed in 1902. Photo ca. 1905 (courtesy of Stanford University Archives).

Figure 3. Memorial Arch showing extensive damage after the 1906 earthquake. Photo by Dane M. Greer, April 1906 (courtesy of Stanford University Archives).

Figure 4. Perspective drawing of the design for the university, ca. 1888 (courtesy of Stanford University Archives).

first President, David Starr Jordan, would later call this "Stanford's Second Stone Age" (Davis and Nilan, 1989). Jane directed the completion of the outer Quad buildings, Memorial Arch, and Memorial Church per the original plan. She then began a series of buildings along Palm Drive, which were a complete departure from the Olmsted plan: the chemistry building, the gym, and library were initially intended for Olmsted's lateral Quads but now lined the drive toward Palo Alto (Fig. 5).

Besides relocating the buildings, Jane had her architects design them in a style different from the "Richardsonian Romanesque" architecture of the Quad. The gym was a neo-Palladian design (Fig. 6) and the library was a loose copy of a building at the Philadelphia Centennial Expo of 1876 (Fig. 7). These buildings sat near the museum, which had already been built outside the Quad in a neoclassical style, copying the National Museum of Athens (Turner et al., 1976).

Figure 5. The library and gym under construction along Palm Drive, ca. 1905 (courtesy of Stanford University Archives).

Figure 6. Approach to the gym along what is now called Museum Way, ca. 1906 (courtesy of Stanford University Archives).

Unlike Leland, Jane had little experience with contractors and relied heavily on builders, architects, and her brothers to oversee the projects. These men would prove to be less competent than the original university builders, with disastrous consequences. In the rush to finish the gym and the library, one catastrophic decision was to use shallow foundations without wide footings, (unlike the inner Quad buildings). Jane, who died in 1905, thankfully never saw the consequences of this decision.

At the time of the earthquake, neither the gym nor the library had yet been occupied, but the university had accepted them from the contractors. Both buildings were completely destroyed by the earthquake: the gym collapsed in on itself (Fig. 8), while the library appeared to disintegrate (Fig. 9). A Commission of Engineers later found the collapse of these buildings to be "caused by ignoring structural principles in design ... the constructive details and important parts of their integrity" (Schulz et al., 1906, p. 3).

In the Quad, a striking pattern emerged from the earthquake damage: buildings constructed before Leland's death (the inner Quad) fared well, while those built after his death (the outer Quad) were almost all destroyed or rendered unusable. An investigative report by the engineering commission stated, "Our

Figure 7. View of the completed library across the Oval, ca. 1906 (courtesy of Stanford University Archives).

Figure 8. The collapsed gym after the earthquake. Photo by James H. Polhemus, April 1906 (courtesy of Stanford University Archives).

opinion is that a large percentage of the sum total of damage was caused by and was the direct result of the disregard of simple constructive principles, both of design and workmanship" (Schulz et al., 1906). Repairs to the inner Quad were mostly done by the time 1906–1907 classes started, while repairs to the outer Quad continued into 1908. Academics once again took a back seat to architecture and President David Starr Jordan mourned, "There is now nothing to do but to go over it again, with the same rigid economies that have marked the whole history of the University" (Elliott, 1937).

In 1906, the university was composed of 42 buildings, nearly all of which needed some work after the earthquake. President Jordan initially estimated the loss at US$2.8 million (US$57.5 million adjusted to inflation, 2005) (Elliott, 1937). In actuality, the total cost to restore all the buildings, including the replacement of most of the lost space and functionality of the destroyed buildings, would cost just over US$2 million. By comparison, after the 1989 earthquake, The Federal Emergency Management Agency (FEMA) assessed the damage to 200 of Stanford's 678 major buildings at US$67 million. The univer-

Figure 9. The ruins of the library after the earthquake, ca. April 1906 (courtesy of Stanford University Archives).

sity ultimately paid US$300 million to repair damaged structures, seismically strengthen over a hundred other buildings, and restore cherished historical buildings.

STOP 2: MEMORIAL CHURCH

Significance of the Site

The response of Memorial Church's bell tower to the ground shaking in the 1906 earthquake illustrates the need to tie building elements together. Considered the "heart of the Quad" and the "soul of Stanford," the church alone received special treatment after both the 1906 and 1989 earthquakes.

Accessibility

This is a public site.

GPS Coordinates

E057331; N4142570 (UTM).

Directions

Enter the Main Quad through Memorial Court. If the front doors to the church are open, visitors may enter. The church is used as a place for quiet contemplation, so please exit the church before resuming conversation.

Stop Description

Memorial Church was built between 1899 and 1903 and dedicated to the memory of Leland Stanford. The design was loosely based on H.H. Richardson's Trinity Church in Boston (Turner et al., 1976), but included the rough-hewn stonework, low arches, round turrets, and heavy red tile roofs characteristic of the rest of the Quad. Topping the structure was an 80-ft bell tower that stood out as monumentally as the massive Memorial Arch (Fig. 10). Entirely covering the façade of the church were mosaics not called for in the original design, perhaps the first of Jane's decisions to depart from the design principles laid out in Olmsted's university plan.

During the 1906 earthquake, the primary source of damage to the church was the movement of the crossing structure. The crossing structure is the arched square area where the transepts intersect the nave; large mosaic archangels look down from each corner. This structure had an internal steel frame (originally designed to support clockwork and bells) that swayed and flexed in response to shaking—actually one of the advantages of steel construction. The surrounding stone walls, however, flexed very little in response to shaking, and since the crossing structure was not strongly attached to these stone walls, it swayed independently from the rest of the building during the earthquake. Holes were gouged in surrounding roofs and the nave roof was pushed forward, helping to knock off the mosaic façade. The bell tower plummeted almost straight down into the chancel (Fig. 11).

Figure 10. Memorial Church before the earthquake, ca. 1904 (courtesy of Stanford University Archives).

Figure 11. Memorial Church after the earthquake, showing the gouged roofs and unharmed organ. Photo by Carl Breer, April 1906 (courtesy of Stanford University Archives).

The dust settled slowly and revealed a terrible sight. The high steeple of the Church had collapsed and ... broken through the roof of the building on all sides... The great bells of the tower went through the floor. The works of the clock stood in their house poised on the truncated tower ... The concussion of air in the body of the Church burst out the front wall ... leaving unharmed the great organ ... It is a magnificent wreck, as it was a magnificent structure in life. It is the one thing the earthquake did that we cannot forgive. (Personal letter from President Jordan's secretary, George A. Clark, 27 April 1906.)

Memorial Church was integral to the identity of the young university, so the reconstruction effort that began in 1908 was aimed at restoring the church to its original grandeur and preventing future damage. Workers laboriously dismantled the structure and catalogued each stone (Fig. 12); the crossing structure was left intact due to the apparent lack of damage. Concrete walls were then poured over a rebar framework, and the original stone was reapplied. Because many of the mosaics were damaged (except the archangels), the original artisans from Venice returned in 1914 to create new ones. Meanwhile, finding a seismically safer design to replace the bell tower continued to puzzle the Stanford trustees, so they decided to leave reconstruction for future generations (Durand et al., 1908). The crossing structure was topped with a simple skylight. The cost for reconstructing Memorial Church was nearly as much as the more than US$650,000 spent on repairing all the remaining damaged campus buildings (except the arch, gym, library, and museum additions) (Elliott, 1937). By comparison, the inner Quad had been constructed for US$537,000.

The reconstruction after 1906 protected much of the church during the Loma Prieta earthquake in 1989. During Loma Prieta, the movement of the central crossing structure caused interior stones to fall, and the four mosaic archangels began to peel off

Figure 12. The dismantling of Memorial Church with the intact connecting structure left standing, ca. 1909 (courtesy of Stanford University Archives).

from their structural backing. Had the earthquake lasted longer or been more powerful, the crossing structure would have flexed more and perhaps ripped apart adjacent roofs or even been destroyed. It was clear that this central component needed to be stabilized, so the church was once again closed for reconstruction.

The seismic retrofitting that took place in the early 1990s required workers to pass steel and concrete through a three foot opening in the exterior wall and into spaces only two feet wide. The whole crossing structure was tied together and stabilized, enabling it to be an anchor for the wings. The entire building was then brought up to modern earthquake codes, ensuring both safety and longevity, and ornamental elements like the four archangels were strengthened (Surma, 2005, personal commun.). Incidentally, the chimes from the original clockwork were saved and are now in the glass case beneath the clock tower.

Because Memorial Church is a nonacademic building, funds for its 1990s reconstruction had to be covered entirely by donations. Alumni were eager to support the project and a campaign to raise US$8.5 million for construction expenses plus an additional US$1.5 million for an endowed preservation fund exceeded its goals. A portion of the 1,800 donations even came from undergraduate students, showing that affection for the church hasn't changed with the generations (Surma, 2005, personal commun.).

STOP 3: ARCADE COLUMNS

Significance of the Site

More than anything else, Stanford's arcades impart an impression of the California mission influence. They also show how skilled engineers have become at reinforcing even decorative elements.

Accessibility

This is a public site.

GPS Coordinates

E0573373; N4142466 (UTM).

Directions

Walk to the back of the church on the left side and head toward the columned arcade on the left.

Stop Description

The use of arcaded passageways to link buildings around a courtyard is one of the most obvious influences of California mission architecture found at Stanford. Significantly, this is the one major element in the original campus plan that had the approval of all involved parties from the beginning.

Unfortunately, the columns and arches of the arcades are also the most structurally vulnerable components of the Quad, and they were heavily damaged in the 1906 earthquake (Fig. 13). In fact, a free-standing arcade once stretched from Language Corner to Geology Corner, but it completely collapsed during the 1906 earthquake (Fig. 14). Though the Quad columns were repaired after 1906, it wasn't until the 1989 earthquake that they were reengineered. One of the tasks of retrofitting the Quad after 1989 was to replace damaged sandstone columns and exterior elements with seismically safer look-alikes. The job was extremely well done, and most visitors to Stanford now assume that everything is still made of sandstone. Look closely at the columns and at the walls, however. Notice that the material that makes up the columns has obvious bubbles and consists of many-colored grains in a tan matrix. In the sandstone, the grains are mostly clear; they are packed together rather than embedded in a matrix, and there are no bubbles. Most of the arcade columns are now reinforced concrete rather than stone, though not all. Columns that do not stand alone (such as those adjacent to walls) were largely left intact and can generally be distinguished from afar because they are crumbling at the base due to weathering and the wear and tear of campus life.

STOP 4: POWERHOUSE

Significance of the Site

During the 1906 earthquake, a recording volt meter in Stanford's powerhouse behaved like a modern seismograph, recording not only the main shock, but also large aftershocks.

Accessibility

This is a public site.

GPS Coordinates

E0573373; N4142466 (UTM).

Directions

The former powerhouse site is located directly across Escondido Mall from the end of the Language Corner arcade and Stop 3.

Stop Description

Stanford supplied its own power in 1906, just as it does today. The old powerhouse with its 100-ft smokestack was located next to the engineering buildings (Fig. 15). According to the night watchman, the University fireman, Otto Gerdes, was in the powerhouse when the earthquake struck. He started to run for the door, then wheeled around and raced back to the main electrical power switch, yelling, "They'll all be on fire." He cut electricity to the campus, but was killed by the collaps-

Figure 13. Damage to the arcade columns in the Quad, ca. April 1906 (courtesy of Stanford University Archives).

Figure 14. The collapsed arcade behind Memorial Church, looking from Language Corner toward Geology Corner. Photo by W.C. Mendenhall, April 1906 (courtesy of the U.S. Geological Survey).

Figure 15. The university powerhouse behind Memorial Church, ca. 1905 (courtesy of Stanford University Archives).

ing smokestack as he tried to escape; he was one of only two casualties in the earthquake (the other was a student in Encina Hall, the men's dormitory). President Jordan credited Gerdes with saving the campus from fire (Breer, 1963).

Interestingly, a Bristol recording volt meter that was housed in the powerhouse to track generated voltage behaved like a modern seismograph during the 1906 earthquake. This device consisted of a clockwork mechanism with a circular chart that was changed daily. A pen, restricted to one axis, recorded the voltage on the chart.

Up to 5:12 a.m. on 18 April, the recording pen traced the voltage as usual (Fig. 16). At that point, the shaking caused the pen to move rapidly for 53 s, after which the power was broken. The clockwork mechanism remained intact after the collapse of the smokestack, and the pen continued to record the aftershocks, showing major aftershocks at 10:48 a.m. and 2:28 p.m. Finally, the clockwork mechanism ran down and the volt meter stopped recording at around 6:40 p.m.

We can compare the volt-meter reading with a partial recording made by the Ewing Three-Component Seismograph at the Lick Observatory on Mount Hamilton, California (Fig. 17). This seismograph was obviously a much more sensitive piece of equipment, but the volt meter is notable for recording similar information. It is interesting to note that the amplitude of the shock caused both pieces of equipment to exceed their recording range. Meanwhile, the shock that the volt meter recorded at

10:48 a.m. is a bit of a mystery as there are no recorded reports of aftershocks felt at that time. The 2:28 p.m. aftershock was widely reported, however (Meltzner and Wald, 2002).

STOP 5: GEOLOGY CORNER

Significance of the Site

Geology Corner is the only corner of the Quad still being used for its original purpose. This usage influenced how it could be repaired after the 1989 earthquake. It also is where geologist J.C. Branner worked on the Lawson Report.

Accessibility

This is public site, with public restrooms.

GPS Coordinates

E0573164; N4142508 (UTM).

Directions

Walk northwest down Escondido Mall (away from the clock tower). Geology Corner is the corner of the outer Quad past the church.

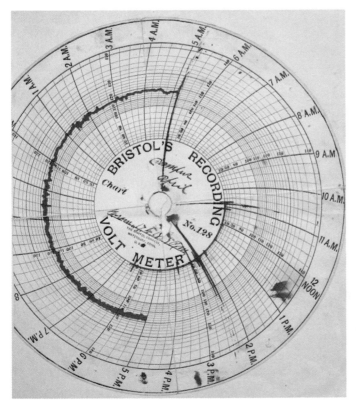

Figure 16. The 17–18 April 1906 volt-meter recording from the power-house (courtesy of Stanford University Archives).

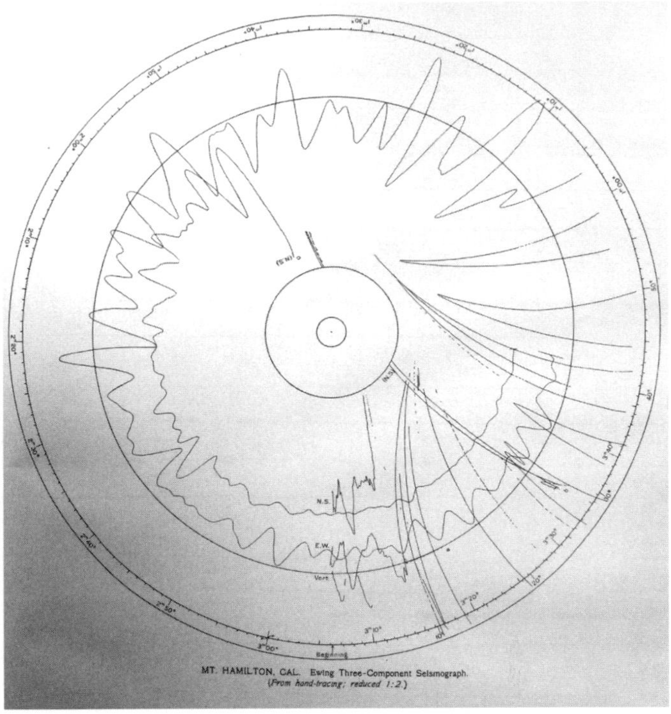

Figure 17. Circular seismograph from Lick Observatory, as printed in the Lawson Report Atlas (courtesy of Branner Earth Sciences Library and Maps Collection, Stanford University).

Stop Description

All of the outer Quad buildings needed significant repair and retrofitting after 1906 (Fig. 18), with most work completed by 1908. Retrofitting began again in the 1960s to bring the buildings up to more modern standards. Math Corner was retrofitted first using the expensive "gut and stuff" approach, in which massive bracing was put up on the outside of the building, the interior was removed, and then a new building with additional floors was built on the inside of the existing masonry walls. History Corner (see map, Fig. 1) was retrofitted in the 1980s and remained virtually unscathed during Loma Prieta. Concrete floors replaced wooden ones, and the building was internally braced (Surma, 2005, personal commun.). Language and Geology Corners were never retrofitted, and they both suffered significant damage in 1989.

The reconstruction of these two buildings after the earthquake was approached very differently. Language Corner also received the gut-and-stuff treatment that Math Corner had, but Geology Corner received the much cheaper Life Safety Fix, in which the building was stabilized so that people inside would be safe during an earthquake, but the possibility of damage to the building still existed. Cost was obviously one of the issues in choosing this approach, but so was the building's history. Geology Corner is the only corner of the outer Quad still being used for its original purpose and with essentially its original

layout. It therefore fell under FEMA guidelines on how federal funds could subsidize the repair of a historical building (Ernst, 2005, personal commun.). Specifically, the building had to be maintained in its original state rather than being redesigned to create more classroom space. Whereas an additional floor was added to Language Corner, the original high-ceilinged architecture of Geology Corner was preserved while the building was stabilized, leaving this corner of the Quad most representative of an original outer Quad building.

Geology Corner's first occupant was geologist John Casper Branner, the first professor hired at Stanford in 1891, its first librarian, and second president. After the earthquake, Branner's colleague, geologist Andrew Lawson at the University of California, Berkeley, lost no time in establishing a commission of renowned scientists to study the massive rupture (Fradkin, 2005). The State Earthquake Investigation Commission included such luminaries as G.K. Gilbert (U.S. Geological Survey), Harry Fielding Reid (Johns Hopkins), as well as Lawson and Branner. They attempted to map and record as much detail as possible along the San Andreas fault rupture (Lawson, 1908). Little noticed at the time, the Lawson report would become quite famous by 1969, with some saying that most modern earthquake science owes its origins to what was published by that group of scientists (Fradkin, 2005). Besides valuable observations, the report led to Reid's formulation of "elastic rebound

Figure 18. Damage to the Geology Corner of the Quad, ca. April 1906 (courtesy of Stanford University Archives).

theory" (which describes how earthquakes release energy), Lawson's recognition of the San Andreas fault as a fault zone stretching down to near Los Angeles, and descriptions of how building design and local geology determine structural damage during an earthquake (Fig. 19).

STOP 6: THE MITCHELL BUILDING AND STOCK FARM MONOCLINE

Significance of the Site

The hump that the Mitchell building sits on runs through campus and is a reminder of how tectonic activity influences the landscape around Stanford. The Mitchell building has obvious shear walls that have been retrofitted on the building's exterior.

Accessibility

This is a public site.

GPS Coordinates

E0573147; N4142489 (UTM).

Directions

Walk toward the patio of the Mitchell building, which is located diagonally up the hill from Geology Corner.

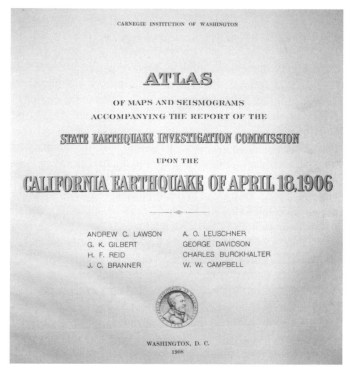

Figure 19. Cover page to the Lawson Report Atlas (courtesy of Branner Earth Sciences Library and Maps Collection, Stanford University).

Stop Description

As you walk from Geology Corner southwest to the Mitchell building, you'll notice that it sits quite a bit higher than the Quad, but if you look east down Escondido Mall, you'll see that the hill tapers off. This hill is a surface expression of a geologic feature known as the Stock Farm monocline, a small fold in the unconsolidated sediments that Stanford sits on, which has been mapped by Stanford geologists (Fig. 20; Page, 1993, and references therein). This fold and others in the Santa Clara Valley run parallel to the San Andreas fault (located only a few miles west of the campus), which suggests that they are directly related. While they are indeed related, the folds result from a slightly different process than the fault. The San Andreas fault represents the boundary between the North American and Pacific plates and is roughly followed by I-280 west of campus. Along this boundary, the Pacific plate is moving northward relative to the North American plate, but the plates do not move exactly parallel to each other—they are also moving slightly toward each other, or converging, which results in the uplifted hills west of campus. The Stock Farm monocline is also a result of that convergent motion. Although no surface deformation was recorded in either 1906 or 1989 on the monocline, it is regarded as capable of minor movement in association with an earthquake on the San Andreas fault, or perhaps another, related fault concealed at depth beneath the campus (Page et al., 1996).

The old buildings aren't the only ones on campus that needed retrofitting. If you look at the corner columns on Mitchell Earth Sciences building, you see that the concrete in the middle of the closely spaced uprights looks different. There were originally two smaller columns that have been joined together with a wall, called a shear wall, which extends from the roof all the way down to the basement and is an example of a retrofit that brought an older building up to modern code (Surma, 2005, personal commun.). When Mitchell building was built in 1969, California's building codes regarding seismic safety weren't nearly as rigorous as they are today. Building codes are informed by two types of ongoing research at universities like Stanford; engineers model how buildings respond to ground movement and develop materials and designs that can better withstand earthquake shear forces, while seismologists investigate how seismic waves move through different types of sediment and rock. As new and better understandings are reached through research, building codes are updated to improve public safety.

During the 1989 earthquake, Mitchell building performed well, but when the university reanalyzed buildings using dynamic engineering models rather than static models (computers were much better in the 1990s!), the engineers learned that a different type of earthquake could render the building unusable (Surma, 2005, personal commun.). The retrofitted shear walls have improved the building's ability to withstand a wider variety of earthquake forces.

The Mitchell retrofit is an example of how Stanford takes a proactive approach to emergency preparedness and response.

Stanford's program of retrofitting campus structures is motivated not by law but according to three overall institutional goals: to protect life safety for the Stanford community, to secure critical infrastructure and facilities, and to reduce interruption in teaching and research (Surma, 2005, personal commun.). While Stanford had already been retrofitting campus structures, the 1989 Loma Prieta earthquake spurred a lot of activity stimulating the university's preparedness, response, and recovery program, even though damage had only closed the campus for one day. This program is designed to provide Stanford with a 36–72 hour window of self-sufficiency without regional resources. Current assessments predict that the university would be reasonably able to cope with a 1906-type earthquake (Surma, 2005, personal commun.).

STOP 7: AGASSIZ STATUE

Significance of the Site

The statue of Agassiz, head buried in the concrete, is an iconic image from the 1906 earthquake.

Accessibility

This is a public site.

GPS Coordinates

E0573293; N4142752 (UTM).

Directions

Walk back toward the Oval on Lomita Mall. Turn right at the front of the Quad. The Agassiz statue is mounted above the entrance to Building 420.

Stop Description

The marble statue of Louis Agassiz, famed naturalist and geologist, fell off the front of the zoology building during the 1906 earthquake (Fig. 21). The images of him with his head stuck in the sidewalk are the most famous of all images related to Stanford's damage and have spawned a number of legends. David Starr Jordan credited Dr. Frank Angell (psychology) with probably one of the most famous quotes, "Agassiz was great in the abstract but not in the concrete" (Jordan, 1922). Carl Breer, 1909, later wrote, "Many stories were told about Agassiz' natural instinct that when the earthquake came he decided to stick his head underground to find out what was going on in the earth below" (Breer, 1963). Despite smashing through the sidewalk, Agassiz suffered only a broken nose and was returned to his pedestal, the only statue on the University front to have fallen. The statue is now securely attached to its base and the building wall.

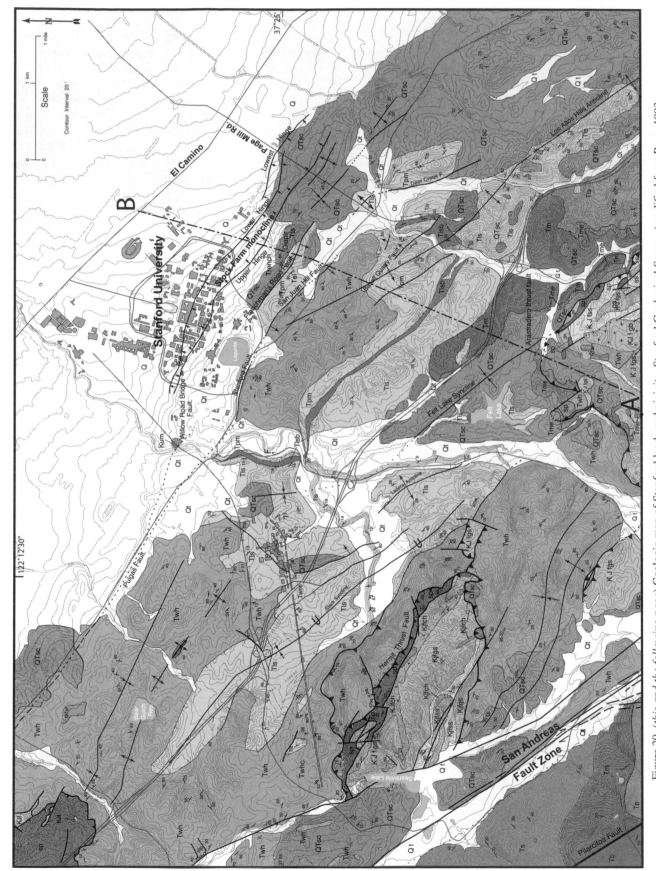

Figure 20. *(this and the following page)* Geologic map of Stanford lands and vicinity, Stanford Geological Survey (modified from Page, 1993, and references therein). Abbreviations: cgl—conglomerate, ss—sandstone.

Map legend

Rock Units

Quaternary

Q Alluvium

QTsc Santa Clara Formation *non-marine cgl & ss*

Tertiary

Tme Merced Formation *marine sandstone*

Tp Purisima Formation *marine sandstone*

Tm Monterey Formation *siliceous shale*

Tls / Tlsi Ladera sandstone (Tlsi = porcellanite)

Tpm / Tlsb Page Mill Basalt (Tlsb = bioclastic unit)

Twh / Twhc Whiskey Hill Sandstone (Twhc = chaotic)

Tb Butano Sandstone

Ts Butano equivalent (east of Pilarcitos fault)

Tel Unnamed marine claystone

Cretaceous

Kum Unnamed marine mudstone

Jurassic - Cretaceous

Kjf Franciscan Formation

gs greenstone
ch chert
ss greywacke

bs blueschist
+ + + / + + + gabbro
s p serpentine

m melange

FAULTS

High angle (dip)

Thrust

Strike slip

Decollement surface

FOLDS

Syncline overturned

Anticline

Syncline

Monocline hinge

Strike and Dip of beds. (20)

⊕ Flat lying beds

A ——·——·——· B Cross-section line

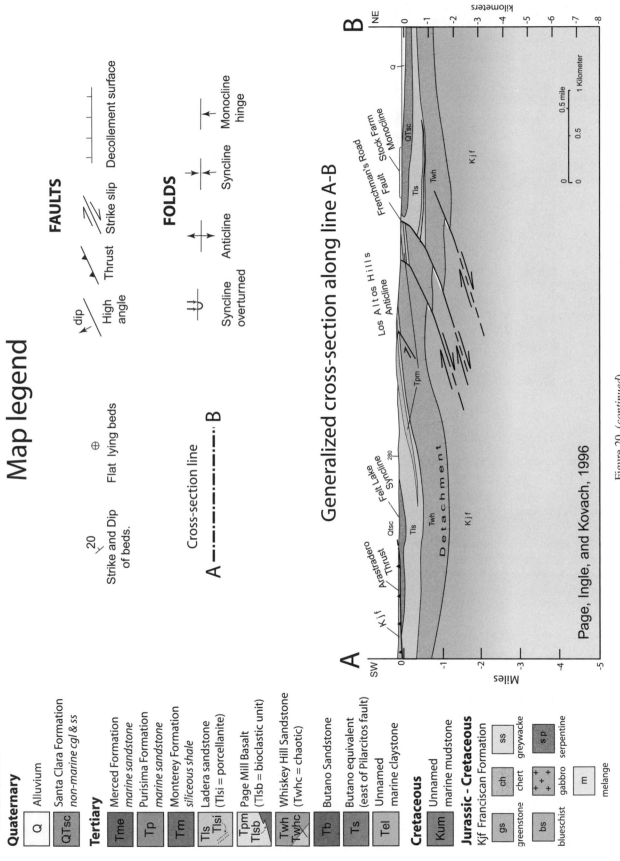

Generalized cross-section along line A-B

Page, Ingle, and Kovach, 1996

Figure 20. *(continued)*

Figure 21. The statue of Louis Agassiz head-down in the sidewalk. Photo by W.C. Mendenhall, April 1906 (courtesy of the U.S. Geological Survey).

STOP 8: THE CANTOR ARTS CENTER AND OLD CHEMISTRY BUILDING

Significance of the Site

After an earthquake, institutions like Stanford need to decide the fate of damaged buildings. The Cantor Arts Center and the old chemistry building show contrasting results of these decisions from both the 1906 and 1989 earthquakes.

Accessibility

This is a public site, with restrooms available and ample parking.

GPS Coordinates

E0573328; N4143196 (UTM).

Directions

Walk to the end of Museum Way, to the front of the Cantor Arts Center. Take note of the old chemistry building, which lies along Lomita Drive toward campus and is surrounded by a green construction fence (in 2006).

Stop Description

The main entrance to the Cantor Art Center is one of the original buildings of the university. Initially called the Stanford Museum, it was composed of a main building built with reinforced concrete and twisted iron (a new technique at the time that made for quicker construction) and two long wing additions built with brick (Fig. 22). In 1906, only the original building made of concrete survived, while the brick additions were notable for their complete collapse (Fig. 23).

Not surprisingly, the collections were substantially damaged (Fig. 24). The main building reopened in 1909, but due to the lack of educational ties to the university and consequent disinterest, the collapsed wings were never rebuilt, and the diminished collection received little attention (Joncas and Casper, 1999). In fact, other departments began to be housed in the building, and pieces from the remaining collection "disappeared." The museum was closed in 1945. In the 1960s, after it had reopened, the chair of the art department revived interest in the museum by strengthening its academic ties, and it came to be seen as an important part of the university's educational mission (Joncas and Casper, 1999). After the 1989 Loma Prieta earthquake, Stanford seized the opportunity to reinvent the museum, seismically retrofitting the older building and designing new wings honoring both the original building and the

Figure 22. The Stanford Museum with wing additions under construction, ca. 1905 (courtesy of Stanford University Archives).

Figure 23. Damage to the museum wing additions, ca. April 1906 (courtesy of Stanford University Archives).

Figure 24. Damage to the museum collections, ca. April 1906 (courtesy of Stanford University Archives).

various transformations it has undergone. Today, the Cantor Arts Center has become an integral part of campus for both visitors and students.

By comparison, the old chemistry building that stands near the museum has suffered a different fate. Completed in 1903 (Fig. 25), it performed fairly well in 1906. Many chimneys collapsed, and a portion of the front façade fell, but otherwise it was in relatively good shape (Fig. 26).

By the 1940s, the department of chemistry had outgrown the building, and the first of the Stauffer Laboratories was built behind it (Hutchinson, 1977). Renovation projects in the main building in the early 1960s included structural reinforcements in the large lecture hall and library but did not prevent the third floor of the building from being condemned a few years later, obligating the university to seal it off. By that time, many of the laboratory facilities were in the additional Stauffer Laboratories, and the construction of the Mudd Building in the 1970s rendered the old chemistry building largely useless. Damage from the 1989 earthquake left the building in limbo, prompting the question: do its historic value and the needs of the university justify its repair costs? It was not in use at the time of the 1989

Figure 25. The old chemistry building, ca. 1904 (courtesy of Stanford University Archives).

Figure 26. Damage to the old chemistry building, ca. April 1906 (courtesy of Stanford University Archives).

earthquake, and thus has not received priority for repair. It is one of the few major buildings still closed due to the Loma Prieta earthquake; the old anatomy building, directly west of the Cantor Arts Center, is another.

Although reuses have been suggested for the old chemistry building, including various arrangements of offices, classrooms, laboratories, or even as a library, funding sources have yet to be identified, so no renovation project is scheduled.

ACKNOWLEDGMENTS

The authors would like to thank the Stanford 1906 Centennial Committee, Judy Scotchmoor, and Tom Brocher for their helpful comments, as well as Margaret Kimball, Stanford Archivist, for her wealth of knowledge and assistance with photographs.

REFERENCES CITED

Breer, C., 1963, The earthquake story of Stanford: Photograph albums 1906–1964: Stanford, California, Stanford University Archives, v. 1, unpaginated.

Clark, G.A., 1906, Personal correspondence: Stanford, California, Stanford University Archives.

Davis, M., and Nilan, R., 1989, The Stanford album: A photographic history, 1885–1945: Stanford, California, Stanford University Press, 302 p.

Durand, W.F., Marx, C.D., and Wing, C.B., 1906–08, Papers of the Stanford University Commission of Engineers: Stanford, California, Stanford University Archives, unpaginated.

Elliott, O.L., 1937, Stanford University: The first twenty-five years: Stanford, California, Stanford University Press, 624 p.

Fradkin, P.L., 2005, The great earthquake and firestorms of 1906: How San Francisco nearly destroyed itself: Berkeley, University of California Press, 432 p.

Hutchinson, E., 1977, The Department of Chemistry, Stanford University, 1891–1976: A brief account of the first eighty-five years: Stanford, California, Department of Chemistry, Stanford University, 122 p.

Joncas, R., and Casper, G., 1999, Building on the past: The making of the Iris & B. Gerald Cantor Center for Visual Arts at Stanford University: Stanford, California, Stanford University, 143 p.

Jordan, D.S., 1922, The days of a man, being memories of a naturalist, teacher, and minor prophet of democracy: Yonkers-on-Hudson, New York, World Book Co., v. 2, 906 p.

Lawson, A.C., 1908–1910, The California earthquake of April 18, 1906: Report of the State Earthquake Investigation Commission: Washington, D.C., Carnegie Institution, 2 p.

Meltzner, A.J., and Wald, D.J., 2002, Felt reports and intensity assignments for aftershocks and triggered events of the great 1906 California earthquake: U.S. Geological Survey Open-File Report 02-37, 301 p.

Page, B.M., 1993, Geologic map of Stanford lands and vicinity: Stanford, California, Stanford Geological Survey, scale 1:25,500.

Page, B.M., Ingle, J.C., and Kovach, R.L., 1996, Quaternary diaper of claystone in faulted anticline, Stanford, California: California Geology, v. 49, no. 3, p. 55–67.

Schulz, H.A., Galloway, J.D., and Leonard, J.B., 1906, Report on condition of buildings constituting Leland Stanford Junior University, California, and damages resulting thereto from the effects of the earthquake of April 18th, 1906: Stanford, California, Stanford University Archives, 35 p.

Turner, P., 1975, Architecture as memorial: The design of Stanford: The Stanford Magazine, v. 1, no. 3, p. 50–56.

Turner, P., Vetrocq, M.E., and Weitze, K., 1976, The founders and the architects: The design of Stanford University: Stanford, California, Stanford University, 96 p.

Geological Society of America
Field Guide 7
2006

Earthquake Trail, Sanborn County Park:
A geology hike along the San Andreas fault

Phillip W. Stoffer

U.S. Geological Survey, 345 Middlefield Rd., MS 973, Menlo Park, California 94025, USA

OVERVIEW OF THE FIELD TRIP

On the southern part of the San Francisco Peninsula, the San Andreas fault traverses the actively uplifting Santa Cruz Mountains. The field guide is comprised of a hiking tour along the fault in Sanborn County fault, a visit to a winery and vineyards traversed by the fault, and visits to two wineries that provide vistas of the San Andreas Rift Valley and surroundings.

Keywords: fault zone, geomorphology, deflected drainages, landscape evolution, fault scarps, mass wasting.

STOP 1: SANBORN COUNTY PARK

Significance of the Site

Sanborn County Park straddles a section of the San Andreas fault zone where it passes through the Santa Cruz Mountains in Santa Clara County, California (Fig. 1). This stop entails a hike along the Sanborn Earthquake Trail, a moderately strenuous hiking route that is 2.5 mi (4 km) long and leads through hilly terrain covered with a mixed redwood, Douglas fir, oak woodlands, and grasslands within the park and on other public land. The park area experienced strong earthquake shaking during the magnitude 7.9 1906 San Francisco earthquake and the magnitude 6.9 1989 Loma Prieta earthquake. The trail provides access to a variety of geomorphic features associated with the fault zone, including offset streams, shutter ridges, sag ponds, fault scarps, and other fault-related landforms. Most of these landscape features are developed on an old alluvial fan system along streams draining from a high ridgeline eastward into the rift valley along the San Andreas fault zone. Other ongoing surface processes affecting the forested landscape include landslides, debris flows, floods, giant tree falls, and other forms of mass wasting and erosion, as well as both prehis-

toric and modern human activity that have left an imprint on the landscape. The route follows established park trails including the route of the biology-oriented Sanborn Nature Trail.

Accessibility

This is a public, county park; entrance fees are charged, restrooms are available, and there is ample parking.

Directions

From San Francisco, take I-280 south toward San José. Exit to California Highway 85 south and proceed 3.5 mi (6 km) to the De Anza Boulevard exit. Bear right onto De Anza Boulevard and proceed south 4 mi (7 km) to the intersection of Route 9 in downtown Saratoga. From the south (San José), take California Highway 85 north and then take Route 9 west to the town of Saratoga. Proceed west on Route 9 (also called Big Basin Way or Congress Springs Road) through downtown Saratoga and proceed up Saratoga Canyon for ~3 mi (5 km). Turn left on Sanborn Road. Proceed 1 mi (1.6 km) to the entrance to Sanborn County Park on the right. A day-use fee ($5) is required for each vehicle entering the park. After passing the entrance station, follow the main park road uphill to the RV campground parking area. If day-use parking spaces are not available in the RV area, use the day-use parking lot just below the RV campground. The hike begins near the trailhead to the walk-in campground near the RV campground restroom facility.

Warnings for Hikers

Please be aware that poison oak, ticks, rattlesnakes, mountain lions, or other natural hazards can be encountered in the park (as anywhere in the Santa Cruz Mountains). Rattlesnakes are generally harmless unless provoked (Fig. 2). Simply take

Stoffer, P.W., 2006, Earthquake Trail, Sanborn County Park: A geology hike along the San Andreas fault, *in* Prentice, C.S., Scotchmoor, J.G., Moores, E.M., and Kiland, J.P., eds., 1906 San Francisco Earthquake Centennial Field Guides: Field trips associated with the 100th Anniversary Conference, 18–23 April 2006, San Francisco, California: Geological Society of America Field Guide 7, p. 215–235, doi: 10.1130/2006.1906SF(15). For permission to copy, contact editing@geosociety.org. ©2006 Geological Society of America. All rights reserved.

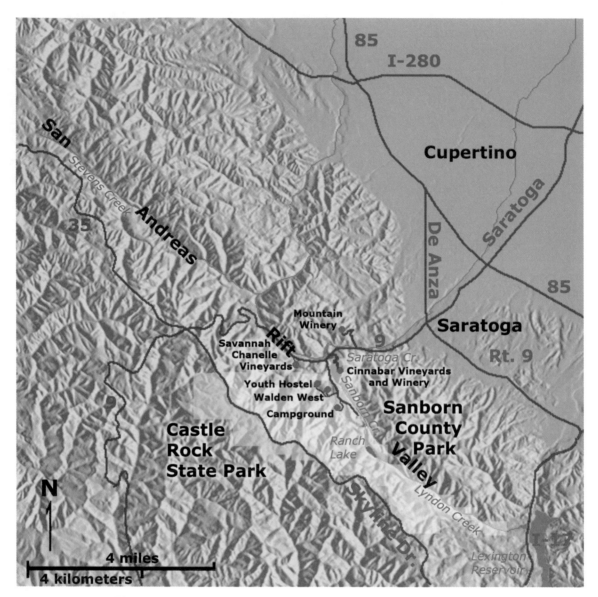

Figure 1. Map of the Sanborn County Park vicinity near Saratoga, California.

Figure 2. A western diamondback rattlesnake warms itself in the morning sun on a Sanborn County Park trail.

another route if you encounter one, and warn others in the area to be aware. Rattlesnakes are most likely to be seen near water sources on hot summer days. All wildlife in the park is protected. Slick trails, falling branches from trees, and stream flooding may be potential hazards during storms. Pets and smoking are not allowed on park trails. Bring some water on the hike.

Stop Description

This stop comprises several hikes that can be taken individually or linked together to make a longer hike. Please stay on the trails. Park trial maps and guides that describe these hikes are available at the Park's Nature Center (YSI on Fig. 3) and at the park headquarters (HQ on Fig. 3). The complete field trip hike described below typically takes 4–5 hours with a mixed group of people of all ages. This includes time for discussion and a picnic in the park after the walk.

Sanborn Earthquake Hike—Geology Field Trip Route

Figure 3 shows the route of the recommended hike. Numbered and lettered dots on the map show the general location where stops for observation are located. However, field trip participants should be on the lookout for wildlife and additional natural features not mentioned in the text.

Stop A is located near several large sandstone boulders ~100 ft (30 m) downhill of the intersection of two paved trails near the RV campground restroom facility. This first stop is located at the edge of the large field that provides one of the best views of the park vicinity. Landscape features visible from this location include the following:

The San Andreas fault. It may not be evident to most people who visit Sanborn County Park that they are, in fact, in the San Andreas fault zone. The fault passes through this portion of the Santa Cruz Mountains in and around Sanborn Park. The San Andreas fault extends from great depths estimated from seismic

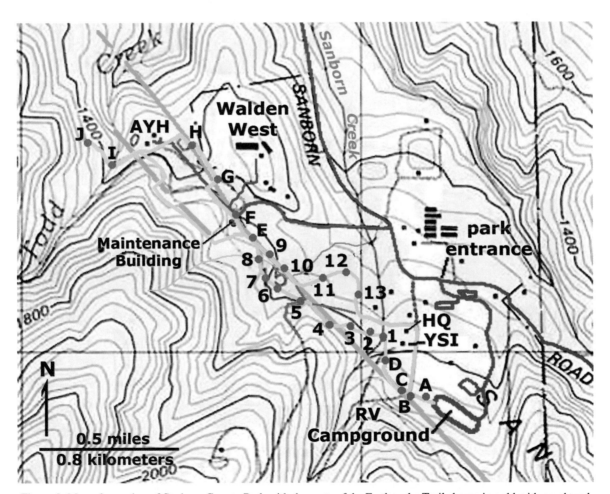

Figure 3. Map of a portion of Sanborn County Park with the route of the Earthquake Trail shown in gold with numbered and lettered stops in orange. Stops are organized as both letters (A–J) and numbers (1–13). The letter stops of the Earthquake Trail were added to incorporate the preexisting numbered stops of the already established Sanborn Nature Trail. Each of the stops is marked by a lettered or numbered trail-stop post. The trace of the San Andreas fault is shown in green. Park access roads are shown in red. The base map is a U.S. Geological Survey topographic map showing elevation contour lines in feet. The hike begins at a kiosk with park rules and regulations near the RV campground restrooms.

data to be in the range of ~9–12 mi (15–20 km) under the Santa Cruz Mountains (Jachens and Griscom, 2004). As the fault zone approaches the surface it splays into a complex system of both parallel and interconnecting faults. The San Andreas, Hayward, Calaveras, and other earthquake faults are all part of the greater San Andreas fault system (Fig. 4). In the San Francisco Bay region, the San Andreas fault system displays a total offset of ~286 mi (460 km), but only ~87 mi (140 km) of this offset occurred along the San Andreas fault in the central Santa Cruz Mountains; the rest of the offset occurred on the Hayward and Calaveras faults in the East Bay region and on other regional faults (Dickinson, 1997; Graymer et al., 2002).

The San Andreas fault is not perfectly straight. In places, such as in the Santa Cruz Mountains, the fault trace bends slightly to the left. This bend causes uneven forces throughout the crust and results in the ongoing uplift of the Santa Cruz Mountains. Gradual changes in elevation are occurring continuously throughout the Coast Ranges, both upward and downward with the build-up of pressure and its release during episodic earthquakes. Fission track studies and other data demonstrate that rock in the Santa Cruz Mountains has risen ~2 mi (3.2 km) over the past 4.7 million years (a rate of ~0.6 mm/yr) (Bürgmann et al., 1994). Since the highest elevations in the Santa Cruz Mountains are only slightly higher than

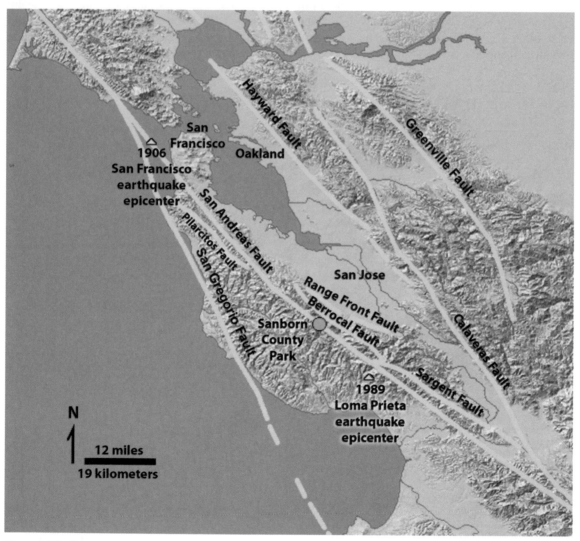

Figure 4. The San Andreas fault system in the San Francisco Bay region. The San Andreas fault is a relatively new geologic feature in the San Francisco Bay region. It began forming in south-central California ~28 million years ago but propagated through the Bay Area only ~10–6 million years ago (Elder, 2001). Prior to the San Andreas fault, a completely different continental margin configuration existed in California. Traditionally, the San Andreas fault has been used to separate the North American plate on the east and the Pacific plate on the west in California. The offset along the San Andreas fault is a strike-slip fault with right-lateral offset, such that the west side (the Pacific plate) is moving northward relative to the east side (the North American plate). (A U.S. Geological Survey publication, *This Dynamic Earth*, provides an introduction to plate tectonics theory; it is available online at http://pubs.usgs.gov/publications/text/dynamic.html.)

0.63 mi (1 km), the rate of erosion of the mountain uplands is therefore ~0.4 mm/yr. However, uplift and erosion factors are complex, and they are neither uniform nor synchronous throughout the Santa Cruz Mountains.

The San Andreas Rift Valley. Sanborn Creek is a headwaters tributary of the greater Saratoga Creek watershed that drains along Route 9 into Saratoga. Over time, streams have carved a canyon that follows the zone of crustal weakness associated with the San Andreas fault zone. The combination of stream erosion and movement along different faults near the surface has resulted in the formation of the San Andreas Rift Valley; it is both a "geologic-structural" valley and a "surface-erosional" valley. The landscape is a reflection of two totally different geologic processes—(1) tectonic forces affecting Earth's crust below ground and raising the land surface, and (2) the combination of erosional and depositional processes occurring at the land surface. However, the structural forces are, in part, controlling how and where erosion and deposition occur in the park area. The combined headwater valleys of Sanborn Creek, Lyndon Creek (to the south), and Saratoga and Stevens Creek define the trace of the San Andreas Rift Valley in the central Santa Cruz Mountains (see Fig. 1).

The gap in the hills to the south of the campground marks the location of the active trace of the San Andreas fault. The steep slope above the RV campground is a fault line scarp. However, in most places on the steep slope, the fault is covered by colluvium and does not show an obvious surface expression to point to its exact location on the slope. Note that the exact fault location is not always easy to see. In most places, the surface expression of the San Andreas fault is complex. Slumping and landsliding occur along the fault in many areas where it crosses slopes. In addition to the main (or active) trace of the San Andreas fault, there are many other faults in the area, some of which display evidence of recent movement.

Bedrock geology. Figure 5 is a portion of a geologic map showing the Sanborn County Park area (Brabb et al., 2000). The bedrock west of the San Andreas fault consists of Tertiary-age sedimentary rocks (roughly 40–30 million years old) that probably overlie more ancient Salinian granitic basement rocks at depths of ~4 mi (6 km) below Castle Rock Ridge. On the hillsides to the east of the San Andreas Rift Valley (toward Saratoga) the bedrock consists of oceanic basement rocks and associated younger sedimentary rocks (Coast Range Ophiolite and Franciscan Complex, roughly 165–120 million years old). With the uplift of the Santa Cruz Mountains, erosion of bedrock on the mountainsides on both sides of the San Andreas fault contributed sediments that partially filled in the San Andreas Rift Valley. Figure 6 is a generalized geologic cross section across the park area between two mountain ridges that border the rift valley—Castle Rock Ridge on the west and El Sereno on the east.

Alluvial fans. The sloping fields in the main park area are part of a system of alluvial fans associated with streams draining from Castle Rock Ridge to the west. Over thousands of years, sediments eroded from the steep slopes above were deposited on the more level slope in the valley below. Alluvium is unconsolidated material on the land surface, including soil, boulders, and sediments deposited by wind and water. An alluvial fan is a wedge-shaped accumulation of stream-deposited sediments that spreads out into a valley from a canyon source area, such as in a valley along a fault-bounded highland area. Where many alluvial fans join together along a mountain front, the result is a broad, apron-like, sloping, alluvium-covered surface called a bajada. Much of Sanborn Park is located on an old alluvial fan complex (or bajada) that is currently being incised by streams. The surface of the fan is highly irregular from stream erosion and from offset along the San Andreas fault, which cuts across the alluvial surface.

Stop B is located at the intersection of trails near a park information kiosk just north of the campground restrooms. Note the abrupt change in slope near the kiosk and trail-intersection area. This break-in-slope at the top of the alluvial fan is the fault-line scarp of the San Andreas fault. Three low pyramid-topped posts with red bands just south of the Stop B post mark the most likely location of the San Andreas fault. Whether or not there was surface rupture here from the 1906 earthquake is uncertain because no reports from 1906 were made at this location. However, there almost certainly was surface rupture, if not exactly where the posts are, then very close by. Without a recent major earthquake, or trenching, the exact locations of faults in this area are not clearly visible. Surface erosional processes have erased evidence of surface rupture along the fault trace. There could be more than one seismically active strand of the fault in this valley.

The amount of surface rupture in the southern Santa Cruz Mountains caused by the Great San Francisco Earthquake of 18 April 1906 is uncertain but probably varied between 3 and 10 ft (1–3 m) of right-lateral offset. The best reported observation was 5 ft (1.5 m) of right-lateral offset in Wrights Tunnel (south of Lexington Reservoir) (Prentice and Schwartz, 1991); however, analysis of historical documents shows that the tunnel was offset a total of at least 5.6–5.9 ft (1.7–1.8 m) (Prentice and Ponti, 1997); the main trace of the San Andreas fault has been mapped east of the trail entrance (McLaughlin et al., 2002). Many of the ground ruptures in the southern Santa Cruz Mountains found after both the 1906 and 1989 earthquakes were a result of landslides induced by ground shaking (Prentice and Schwartz, 1991). Nearly all the trails, roads, and manmade structures in the park area were constructed after the 1906 earthquake.

The greatest offsets reported after the 1906 earthquake occurred north of the San Francisco Bay region, with 16 ft (5 m) of right-lateral offset well documented near Point Arena, and 20 ft (6 m) reported near Point Reyes, but the measurement near Point Reyes is uncertain, and may include nontectonic displacement due to ground shaking and lateral spreading. Southward into the Santa Cruz Mountains, the amount of offset reported after the 1906 earthquake diminished to ~1.2 m (4 ft) near Watsonville, to almost nothing observable on the surface south of San Juan Bautista, although tremendous seismic shak-

P.W. Stoffer

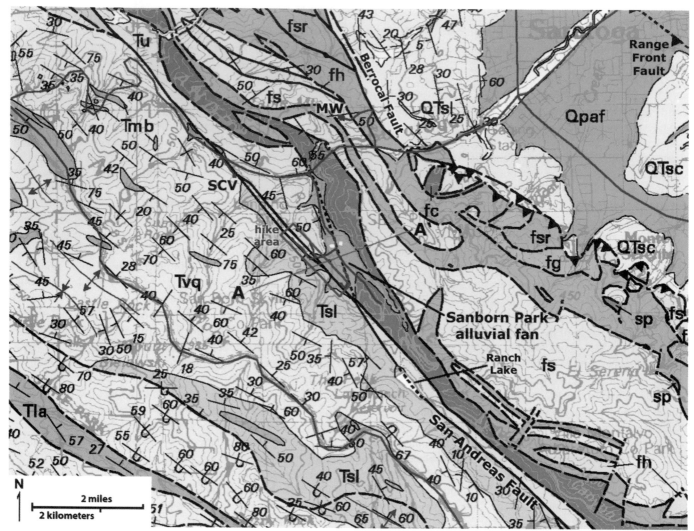

Figure 5. Geologic map of the area encompassing Sanborn County Park (from Brabb et al., 2000). The dark blue box at the center of the figure shows the Earthquake Hike field area in Sanborn County Park. SCV—Savannah-Chanelle Vineyards; MW—Mountain Winery. Map units include Qpaf—Quaternary (Pleistocene) alluvial fan deposits; QTsc—Santa Clara Formation (gravel, sand, and mud of Pliocene and early Quaternary age); and QTsl—lake beds. Franciscan Complex (undivided) and other rocks east of the San Andreas fault include fsr—sheared rock (mélange); fg—greenstone; fh—argillite and shale, some sandstone; fs—sandstone; fc—chert; sp—serpentinite; db—diabase and gabbro (Coast Range Ophiolite); and Tu—unnamed Tertiary mudstone, shale, argillite and sandstone (Eocene?). Tertiary marine sedimentary rocks west of the San Andreas fault include Tla—Lambert Shale (lower Miocene and Oligocene); Tmb—Mindego Basalt and related volcanic rocks (lower Miocene and Oligocene); Tvq—Vaqueros Sandstone (lower Miocene and Oligocene); and Tsl—San Lorenzo Formation (Oligocene and upper and middle Eocene), which consists of mostly shale and mudstone. A to A′ shows the location of a geologic cross section illustrated in Figure 6. Line symbols with associated numbers represent the strike direction and dip angle of mapped rock units. Map modified from Brabb et al., 2000.

ing was reported over a much greater region extending far to the south in the vicinity of Pinnacles National Park. Subsurface rupture along the fault probably extended well beyond the region of surface rupture (http://quake.wr.usgs.gov/info/1906/offset.html; Gilbert et al., 1907; Lawson, 1908).

Stop C marks the beginning of a narrow path that leads downhill along the escarpment of the San Andreas fault into the drainage of Sanborn Creek. The escarpment marks the west side of the San Andreas fault. On the east side of the fault near the trail intersection is a large water tank constructed by the

Santa Clara County Water District that was built for irrigation and emergency purposes in the park. The tank was constructed in 2003 on a small hill on the east side of the fault.

This undeveloped section of the trail is inaccessible when wet. If the trail is closed, proceed down and pick up the route at the Visitor Center–Youth Science Institute (YSI) and continue on the hike from there.

The trail leads several hundred feet downhill through a grove of small redwoods. The ecosystem around Sanborn Park includes redwood and Douglas fir forests in the cooler, wetter

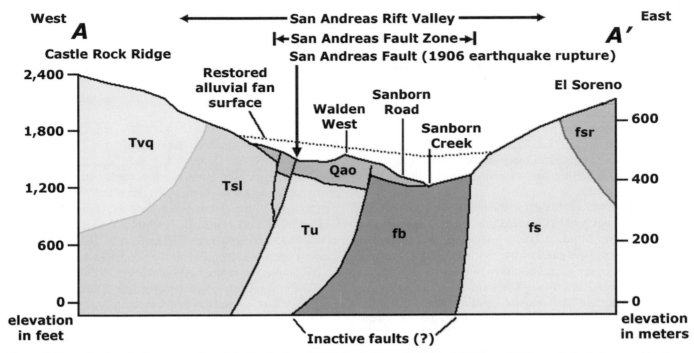

Figure 6. Generalized geologic cross section of the San Andreas Rift Valley between Castle Rock Ridge and El Sereno (ridge). Cross section location is shown as A to A′ on Figure 5. The subsurface character of the faults and bedrock are inferred from mapped features in the surrounding area. The diagram also illustrates the differences in the use of the terms San Andreas fault, San Andreas fault zone, and San Andreas Rift Valley.

valleys and north- and east-facing slopes, whereas chaparral and shrub oak dominate the higher, dry, west-facing slopes. Large redwood stumps along the trail and throughout the park show that the area was heavily lumbered in the late nineteenth century.

Keep looking to the north through the gaps in the forest to where Sanborn Creek descends off of the escarpment of the San Andreas fault. Just north of an "artificial" waterfall created by a pipe diversion of Sanborn Creek, the natural stream makes a sharp turn and flows northwestward along the fault for some distance before turning again to resume its initial eastward course in its incised valley. The bend in the stream formed due to stream capture as the western (uphill) side of the San Andreas fault moved northward relative to the alluvial fan (downhill) side of the fault. Over time, the stream has continued to flow in its current channel, resulting in a dog-leg shaped path of the stream channel called a *deflected drainage*. This zigzag-shaped bend shows that the course of Sanborn Creek has been affected by the right-lateral relative motion along the San Andreas fault. Much of the landscape geomorphology in Sanborn Park is related to the formation of offset drainages and stream capture along the San Andreas fault.

Continue downhill to a wet area near the intersection of several trails. Stop D is located near some very large boulders where the narrow path intersects a larger park trail. Some springs are located nearby in a low area to the south of the stream. Springs are common along fault zones because faults and fractures serve as fluid-migration pathways. Whether these springs are related to a fault is uncertain.

How did the large boulders get here? The boulders are derived from the Vaqueros Sandstone or the San Lorenzo Formation. Both of these sedimentary rock formations occur as bedrock in the hillsides to the west and above Sanborn Park. The Vaqueros Sandstone is the dominant cliff-forming unit in Castle Rock State Park, located along the ridge west of Sanborn Park. These large blocks of sandstone were carried downslope onto the alluvial fan by rock falls, landslides, or debris flows from the upland areas to the west. If they were transported by a landslide or debris flow, the smaller rock fragments and mud would have surrounded these boulders, but must have long since eroded away. Large boulders are a typical occurrence on the upper portion of alluvial fans. Another possible explanation is that the huge boulders were dislodged during a large earthquake on the San Andreas fault and rolled down the steep slope and across the fault.

The Vaqueros Sandstone (lower Miocene and Oligocene, roughly 20–30 million years old) consists of light-gray to buff, fine- to medium-grained, locally coarse-grained arkosic (feldspar mineral-bearing) sandstone interbedded with olive- and dark-gray to red and brown mudstone and shale. Sandstone beds are commonly from 1 to 10 ft (0.3–3 m) thick, and mudstone and shale beds are as much as 10 ft (3 m) thick. In this region, the Vaqueros Sandstone varies from several feet to as much as 2300 ft (700 m) in thickness (Brabb et al., 2000). The formation consists of sediments that were probably deposited in a shallow marine shelf environment, offshore of a river mouth that was probably far to the south (possibly in southern California). These sediments, now rock, where transported northward to their present location by movement along the San Andreas fault system.

The San Lorenzo Formation (Oligocene and upper and middle Eocene, roughly 30-to-50 million years old) consists of dark-gray to red and brown shale, mudstone and siltstone, with local interbedded layers of sandstone, and is ~1800 ft (550 m) thick. Within the upper part of this formation are large, elongate carbonate concretions. The presence of shale indicates that the formation represents materials deposited in somewhat deeper water, a setting farther offshore than the younger Vaqueros sediments.

Volcanic rocks are present in the hillsides west of the fault with outcrops and boulders scattered throughout the Santa Cruz Mountains. The Mindego Basalt (Miocene and Oligocene) includes both extrusive and intrusive volcanic rocks that range in color from dark-gray to orange-brown to greenish-gray breccia, tuff, pillow lavas, and flows. The intrusive rocks tend to be coarsely crystalline. Radiometric dates of selected samples yielded an age of ~20.2 (± 1.2) million years (Brabb et al., 2000).

Along the San Andreas fault, these rock units are highly fractured and mixed together. Cobbles and boulders of basalt can be found in the alluvial sediments along streams in the park area. Fossils are not common in either the Vaqueros or San Lorenzo formations locally. Collectively, the rocks on the west side of the fault in Sanborn Park are between 20 and 50 million years old, whereas the rocks on the east side of the fault are much older. The latter belong to the Franciscan Complex, a mix of ancient marine sediments and oceanic crustal rocks that formed in the mid- to late-Mesozoic era, roughly between 200–100 million years ago (Elder, 2001). Franciscan rocks are not exposed along this field trip route.

Continue downhill and then bear to the right, avoiding the private residence (a post with an arrow marks the route). Proceed downhill; once you get to the paved road, take the wooden bridge across a small pond and then proceed uphill to the left to the Visitor Center (Youth Science Institute building near the Park Office).

Local legend says that the shaking caused by the 1906 earthquake caused much of the water to splash out of the pond in this area. Note that much of the landscape here has been modified since the earthquake. A significant portion of the water in Lake Ranch Reservoir (at the south end of the park) was also reported to have splashed out during the earthquake. The reservoir lies in a modified natural sag pond along the San Andreas fault in the natural upland saddle between the drainages of Sanborn Creek (on the north) and Lyndon Creek (canyon to the south).

Nature Center–Youth Science Institute (YSI)

Park maps and brochures are available at the Nature Center–YSI. Several displays highlighting local Native American (Ohlone) culture and history are located on the outside patio area of the Nature Center. A number of artifacts are on display. Other exhibits include live animals that populate the Santa Cruz

Mountains, earthquake and geology displays, an insect zoo, and a garden featuring native plants and plants used by Native Americans. The YSI is an educational institution that conducts a variety of pre-kindergarten to high school and teenage group programs, after school science classes, and summer science camps (with similar programs at Vasona and Alum Rock County Parks).

Geology along the Sanborn Nature Trail

From the Nature Center–YSI, follow the route of the Sanborn Nature Trail. Nature-trail brochures are available at the park office and at the Nature Center–YSI. Near the Visitor Center, a sign points to "Peterson Memorial Trail, San Andreas Trail, and Walden West." Follow the trail downhill past some big blocks of sandstone to a recently renovated stage area. The bridge across Sanborn Creek is at Stop 1 on the Nature Trail route.

At Stop 1, the nature trail is devoted to a coastal redwood, the California state tree. Coastal redwoods can grow more than 320 ft (100 m) high and can live more than 2000 years. The red bark of the redwoods contains a resin that helps protect them from fire. They also are able to reproduce through their root system when cut down or damaged by fire. Most of the redwoods in the park are younger than a century because the area was heavily lumbered in the late 1800s. The remnants of old logging trails are still visible in many places. These road scars can now serve as a measure of landscape change and forest recovery over time, and many now serve as hiking trails through the park.

At the wooden bridge, note the incised character of the stream valley (Sanborn Creek, a tributary of Saratoga Creek along Route 9). Also note the abundance of large sandstone boulders in the creek bed. Signs describe the creek bed area as a "restoration area" to repair damage from past heavy foot traffic off the trails. The small stream has cut down into an older surface of the alluvial fan. Note that near Stop 1 a narrow flood plain forms the floor of this stream gorge and that the small stream is limited to an irregular channel incised into this flood plain. The floodplain can be completely covered during floods or especially when debris flows occur.

Proceed steeply uphill from the bridge along the Nature Trail to Stop 2, which is located on a flat area (a stream terrace) above the incised valley of Sanborn Creek. This stop in the Sanborn Nature Trail guide points out the differences between a redwood and a Douglas fir. Both trees are used for lumber. However, Douglas firs are also currently farmed as Christmas trees throughout the Santa Cruz Mountains.

Continue along the trail uphill to Stop 3, a good area to examine the character of the old alluvial fan surface. Note the gentle slope to the east and the abundance of rock material on the surface between the trees. All the material beneath the surface is poorly consolidated alluvium deposited by stream processes, landslides, slumps, debris flows, rockfalls, and creep from the hill slope above before the modern forest developed. Erosion has removed most of the finer sediment from around the largest boulders, resulting in their concentration on the surface of the old alluvial fan.

Stop 4 is located where the trail approaches the steep escarpment at the top of the alluvial fan. Note, however, that there is no stream at the head of the fan! The source of the alluvial fan sediments has been displaced to the northwest by motion on the San Andreas fault. The fault probably crosses the trail at a notch on the south side where the park has posted a sign designating an area closed for restoration. While walking along the trail beyond this point, note how some of the small drainages were abandoned as the streams' headwater areas moved northwestward over time relative to the alluvial fan. Past great earthquakes in this area have produced surface displacements measurable in many feet. Such shifts in ground motion assist "stream capture" and the development of new drainages and the abandonment of others.

Stop 5 is located at the intersection of the Nature Trail and the Peterson Memorial Trail. In the Nature Trail guide, Stop 5 is a good location to learn to differentiate blackberry plants from poison oak. Both plants have leaves with three rounded or oak-like leaflets. However, poison oak is an upright shrub or climbing vine with drooping leaves. Small white flowers in the spring give way to white berries in loose clusters along the stem in the summer to fall seasons. In the fall, the leaves can turn bright red. Blackberries and other berries are easy to confuse with poison oak because they are also shrub size and have leaves consisting of three leaflets. However, berries have stiff, protective hairs on the leaves, stems, and branches, and some have thorns. A simple phrase to remember the difference between the two plants is "Leave of three, let it be. If it's hairy, it's a berry."

Poison oak is abundant everywhere in the Santa Cruz Mountains. Although the plant foliage is the most toxic, the barren branches, fallen leaves in winter months, and soil around the plants still can cause serious reactions in some people. Smoke from burning brush can carry the toxic resins. Simply washing laundry may not be enough to remove toxic resins from clothing, although for most people this is sufficient. The best solution to the poison oak problem is to learn to recognize and avoid the plant in all seasons.

In the vicinity of the trail intersection, note that the Peterson Memorial Trail to the right (downhill) follows an incised valley that does not have an actively flowing stream (Fig. 7). This valley is an example of an abandoned stream channel—cut off from its headwater area due to motion along the fault.

Figure 7. A park trail near Stop 4 follows a beheaded stream channel formed by right-lateral fault motion and stream capture. Unlike at Stop 1, there is currently no active stream channel to match the size of this valley. The escarpment of San Andreas fault is to the right.

Follow the Patterson Memorial Trail uphill a short distance to where the Nature Trail continues on the right. After the trail intersection, the Nature Trail traverses part of the fault scarp of the San Andreas fault. Although most of the relative displacement along the fault is horizontal, right-lateral, strike-slip motion, part of the motion is also vertical in this area (contributing to the uplift of the Santa Cruz Mountains). In general, for every 10 ft the west side of the fault moves northward, the Santa Cruz Mountains also rise ~1 ft. It is also important to note that relative motion is not uniform everywhere along the fault (or faults), which adds to the complexity of the evolving landscape. In most places, the exact trace of the fault is not easy to see, except relatively soon after a major earthquake when surface rupture along the fault is commonly visible. Erosion and shifting surface sediments typically mask the traces of surface rupture within a few years.

Stop 6 is at a massive stump of a redwood harvested in the 1800s (Fig. 8). This tree was ~1000 yr old and probably ~260 ft (80 m) high when it was cut. During its lifetime, the tree probably experienced several major earthquakes, and in the course of its lifetime the land it occupied probably moved as much as 56 ft (17 m) northwestward relative to the opposite side of the fault! (This estimate is based on right-lateral slip rates along the local section of the San Andreas fault by McLaughlin et al., 1999.)

Stop 7 is near the location of a large Douglas fir that fell during a storm in 1995. Note the abundance of rock material tangled in its decaying roots. This fallen tree is a testament to the erosional forces created by biological activity. The hummocky character of the forest landscape is partly a result of tree falls in the past. Other forces affecting the hillside are the constant seasonal wetting and drying, causing clays in the soil to expand and contract and gradually causing materials to creep downslope. During colder periods in the past, freezing and thawing of the land surface probably also generated significant amounts of ground movement and supply of sediment to the alluvial fan. Combined with the force of gravity, weathered rock and soil migrates downslope over time. These processes are collectively called mass wasting.

Stop 8 is by a small wooden bridge over another small stream that crosses a strand of the San Andreas fault. Many of

Figure 8. Stump of a great redwood harvested in the late nineteenth century. Note the offspring of the original tree on the uphill side of the stump. The tree was probably ~1000 years old when it was harvested. Three youngsters for scale.

the small streams in this area tend to dissipate as they approach and cross the fault. The flat area downslope is in part an ephemeral sag pond. A sag pond is a fault-related low area where water may accumulate because (1) sedimentation cannot keep pace with the tectonic forces warping the landscape downward, or (2) erosion cannot keep pace with uplift blocking a drainage outlet. Between Stop 8 and the next stop (Stop E), notice the abundance of large boulders scattered on the surface throughout the forest. These massive boulders were transported downslope by rock falls, landslides, or debris flows from the eastern mountain front of Skyline Ridge and deposited on the alluvial fan surface.

Northern Sanborn County Park Area

At the trail intersection beyond Stop 8, leave the Nature Trail temporarily. Turn left and proceed northward along the trail toward Walden West and the American Youth Hostel (Welch Hurst House). From this point, the trail basically follows the trace of the San Andreas fault. (**Note:** Do not follow the "San Andreas Trail"—this trail does not follow the San Andreas fault, but instead leads uphill to the Skyline Boulevard area near Castle Rock State Park; a lower section of this trail is part of an optional return route after Stop J described below).

Stop E is located near two large "fairy rings" on the right side of the trail (Fig. 9). These circular groves of redwoods formed when a large "parent" tree died (or was cut) and a ring of new trees sprouted around the base of the missing tree. Also note the low, rocky linear ridge along the right side of the trail as you approach the park maintenance buildings (on the left). This is a "shutter ridge" formed by strike-slip motion along the San Andreas fault (Fig. 10).

Stop F is located at the intersection of the trail with the paved road. The road splits here to the park maintenance area, Walden West, and continues northwestward to the American Youth Hostel. The San Andreas fault passes through this vicinity. Take time to look at the stone walls and stream culverts in this area. One of the pillars just downhill of the intersection displays a date of 1955 with a geology pick commemorating Vernon Pick, a successful Utah uranium prospector who temporarily owned this land.

Look for recent cracks, fractures, and right-lateral offsets in the stone walls that may be a result of earthquake damage (an example is shown in Fig. 11). However, not all damage to the walls and culverts in this area may be from earthquakes; some could be from slumping, tree-root breakage, or other causes related to gravity-driven "mass-wasting creep." Earthquake

Figure 9. A fairy ring of redwoods at Stop E. After a mature redwood dies or is cut down, offspring chutes may sprout from the parent tree's roots. The original stump gradually rots away, leaving a ring of trees around the perimeter of the parent tree. There are several large and developing fairy rings along the trail route.

Figure 10. The trail follows a shutter ridge along the San Andreas fault between Stops E and F near the Sanborn County Park maintenance facility. The shutter ridge is on the right side of the trail. The slope to the left is part of the old alluvial fan along the mountain front of Castle Rock Ridge.

shaking typically causes ground ruptures that are not directly related to fault slip. This segment of the San Andreas fault is considered "locked" since the 1906 earthquake, unlike other faults in the region that show evidence of slow movement or "creep." Different segments of the regional fault system are "locked" or "creeping" and although all fault segments are potential sites for large, damaging earthquakes, the locked segments are locations where pressure will be released in potentially large, damaging earthquakes in the future (as has often occurred in the past). The Sanborn County Park area experienced heavy shaking during the 1989 Loma Prieta earthquake, but no fault surface rupture was observed in the vicinity.

Pick named the land Walden West and for a time developed an underground uranium ore testing facility and bomb shelter farther up the road (this underground structure was later abandoned and sealed off for public safety concerns). Local legend says that shortly after building his laboratory, Pick chose to abandon his homestead to seek tax-exempt freedom outside of the United States. The county then purchased the land in 1977 for inclusion in Sanborn County Park. Walden West is an outdoor education and summer day camp under the direction of the Santa Clara County Department of Education.

Downhill from the intersection, the road follows a stream valley that was once the channel of Todd Creek—another case of an abandoned channel and stream capture due to offset along the fault. Because of stream capture, Todd Creek now drains north of the large field below Walden West (located on the hilltop on the right). The broad field area was once the floodplain of Todd Creek, and in the past was partially occupied by a natural sag pond that has been modified and enlarged (Fig. 12). Since the 1906 earthquake, this field was drained and used as an orchard. The intersection at the south end of the field basically marks a stream divide between headwater areas of Sanborn Creek (to the south) and Todd Creek (to the north). As you will see as you continue the hike, Todd Creek has captured the stream drainage around this former sag pond area.

Stop G is in the field along the road leading to the American Youth Hostel. Follow the dirt trail from the Stop G sign-post out to a line of three red pyramid-topped posts. The three posts mark the known location of the San Andreas fault.

An exploratory trench was dug in this location by the U.S. Geological Survey to help characterize past earthquake activity of the San Andreas fault. Although the trench exposed the trace of the fault, unfortunately, agricultural activity in the

Figure 11. This culvert built by Vernon Pick in 1955 displays fractures that could be associated with ground shaking or other geologic processes. The arrows on this image show where to look for fractures. Fractures and traces of offset are visible at both ends of the culvert.

field in the last century had disrupted the surficial deposits that might have provided information about the frequency of earthquakes in this area over the past few centuries. This information can be used to make judgments about the frequency of future earthquakes along the fault. The difference between a "fault" and an "earthquake fault" or "active fault" is that the latter shows evidence of fault movement during the Holocene (the current geologic epoch that began roughly 11,500 yr ago following the last ice age of the Pleistocene Epoch). Not all faults in the San Francisco Bay area are considered active faults.

Stop H is located farther down the trail at an intersection with another trail connecting the playing fields at Walden West to a pond surrounded by a redwood forest. Note the drop from the field to the creek below. Although this area has been heavily modified over the years, it still reflects the character of the natural sag pond that existed here in the past. The trace of the San Andreas fault runs through this pond area. The Stop H area provides a reasonable view to the north across the valley of Saratoga Creek and northwest along the trend of the San Andreas Rift Valley toward Table Mountain and the more distant grass-covered peak of Black Mountain located within the

Monte Bello Open Space Preserve. Note the abundance of chaparral growing on the south-facing slopes of Table Mountain.

Continue along the trail around the pond. Turn right on the paved road toward the American Youth Hostel. This Youth Hostel is a log-style house with a large hexagonal central room. It was originally named Welch-Hurst House and was built in 1908 as a summer home for the Honorable Judge James Welch and his family. In 1955, the Welch-Hurst House and surrounding lands were sold to Vernon Pick. When the house and land were later sold to the county, renovation costs were considered too high and the house was slated for demolition. However, the Santa Clara Valley hostelling club saved and renovated the building through a grassroots collective effort beginning in 1979. The Sanborn Park Hostel is now listed on the National Registry of Historic Places (www.sanbornparkhostel.org/about.html).

A large fairy ring of redwood trees is the location of a picnic ground in front of Welch-Hurst House. The building is made of native sandstone from the Vaqueros and San Lorenzo formations. Note the large round concretions used as monument caps near the front door of the house. Concretions are abundant in the San Lorenzo Formation. Also note the large prehistoric mortar hole carved in the large sandstone slab incorporated into

Figure 12. The trace of the San Andreas fault runs through an abandoned field near Walden West. In the past, the field was a sag pond that was drained and used as an orchard. In the more distant past, Todd Creek drained across this area before stream capture occurred and altered the stream's path to its modern drainage to the north of the field. The headwater valley of Todd Creek can be seen in the top of this image.

the front right side of the path leading to the front of the house. Other mortar holes used for grinding acorns and other food products by Native Americans are present in several of the large boulders along a short trail behind the hostel building.

Continue around the left (west) side of the hostel building. Follow the stairs or path down to the low, flat area next to the building, which is currently used as a volleyball court. Note that the hostel building is built on a low, straight ridge covered with blocky alluvium. The building is situated on an old terrace of Todd Creek just west of the trace of the fault. The low, flat area occupied by the volleyball court represents an old stream meander of Todd Creek after being captured in its current drainage configuration, but before the incision of the modern gorge north of the Welch-Hurst House.

Continue west across the flat area and follow the old road downhill (to the west). Stop I is located at a bridge over Todd Creek. Todd Creek has a steep drainage profile relative to Sanborn Creek. The creek has rapidly carved into the older alluvial fan deposits that once accumulated in this portion of the San Andreas Rift Valley. Note the size of the large boulders in the creek and exposed in the steep hillsides along the creek and the

road (Fig. 13). These blocks are not bedrock, but rather, are materials that moved down the slope by mass movement in the past (landslides, rockfalls, debris flows, creep, etc.). Some of the large boulders near the bridge contain concretions.

Continue west along the trail for a couple hundred feet to the next stop. Stop J is located near a precipitous drop-off where a landslide has taken away part of the old road. The poorly consolidated sediments of the alluvial fan are prone to landslides in areas of steep stream incision. Use caution when approaching the escarpment! From the trail above the slump escarpment, it is possible to see the layered beds of alluvial sediments. Note the tree roots exposed in the surface soil profile. The lack of trees in the landslide area reflects that much of this hillside fell away in a massive landslide event that happened during the particularly wet winter of 1995. Also note that very little sediment remains in the toe area of the landslide. Much of the landslide material probably moved downstream in the form of a debris flow. Numerous other slumps and landslides occur throughout the hillsides in this vicinity.

Return along the old road (trail) to the intersection with the paved road. Bear to the right, and then bear to the left past the

Figure 13. Colluvium (boulders and soil) partly held in place by tree roots along the trail by Todd Creek near Stop I. The colluvium is derived from older alluvial deposits that are being exhumed by erosion along the eastern flank of Castle Rock Ridge.

gate onto the route of the San Andreas Trail. Follow this trail back to the vicinity of the park maintenance building near Stop 8 on the Sanborn Nature Trail.

Along the San Andreas Trail, look for landscape features that might display evidence of faulting and stream offset. The San Andreas fault zone is complex; in many places it is represented by multiple parallel and interconnecting faults. The landscape features, including linear scarps and the sag ponds, suggest that there may be several active fault traces within the vicinity. Note that although the landscape has been heavily modified by recent human activity, it still reflects the geomorphic profile of an alluvial fan, similar to the area near the RV campground area. It is likely that these flat areas were once aligned but have since been offset by movement along the fault.

Sanborn Nature Trail (continued)

The San Andreas Trail descends off an elevated portion of the alluvial terrace and follows a small stream downhill to an intersection with the Nature Trail near Stop E. Turn right on the Nature Trail (south toward park headquarters). Bear to the right and continue along the Nature Trail to Stop 9. The trail follows the trace of the San Andreas fault southward. Note the

sag area along the trail on the right (the sag area is typically dry in the summer).

Stop 9 is near what appears to be an abandoned stream cut through the shutter ridge along the San Andreas fault on the east side of the trail. At Stop 9, the Sanborn Nature Trail guide discusses how the leaves, flowers, and fruit of the California buckeye are poisonous to humans and animals. However, buckeye nuts were prepared as food by the Ohlone Indians when acorn supplies were low. Buckeye nuts are rich in starch, but are not suitable for food because they contain a poisonous glucoside, aesculin, which can cause severe gastroenteritis, depression, hyperexcitability, dilated pupils, and coma. The Native Americans roasted the nuts among hot stones, peeled and mashed them, and leached them with water for several days. This treatment apparently removed the toxic aesculin. Buckeyes can be particularly hazardous to pets (especially to dogs that chew sticks of buckeye wood).

Stop 10 is located near another gap in the shutter ridge. This one, however, looks like it was modified by human activity. Stop 10 provides an opportunity to examine the curved trunks of trees along the offset stream drainage. The trees are adjusting to the slow creep of surface materials down the slope into the creek bed. Just south of the trees with curved trunks, the stream curves to the left and cuts through the shutter ridge (Fig. 14). The Nature Trail crosses a small bridge and then bears to the left at a trail intersection.

Stop 11 in the Sanborn Nature Trail guide is a location to examine a Pacific madrone tree. Unfortunately, the specimen to be examined is now dead, but there are many others in the vicinity. Madrone trees have a multitude of uses. The fruit (berries) are an important food source for many species of mammals and birds. The Ohlone Indians ate the berries both raw and cooked. Early European settlers preferred to use charcoal derived from madrone wood in the manufacture of gunpowder. Both Native Americans and early settlers used tea brewed from the bark, leaves, and roots of the madrone tree as relief for stomachaches and treatment for colds; this tea was also used topically as an astringent (useful against inflammation and to stop bleeding). Today, madrone is primarily used as an evergreen ornamental plant. Its hard wood resembles black cherry and is used as furniture paneling, flooring, tobacco pipes, and other novelties, in addition to firewood.

Stop 12 is a large boulder (locally called "Ghost Rock") along the Sanborn Nature Trail that displays tafoni-style weathering (Fig. 15). Tafoni forms on rocks exposed at the surface for long periods of time, such as these boulders resting on an old surface of the alluvial fan. When precipitation soaks into porous sandstone, some of the mineral cement dissolves. As the rock dries out, capillary action brings moisture along with dissolved minerals to the surface. As the water evaporates, the minerals precipitate. In this manner, the rocks actually break down from the inside out as this weathering process removes the mineral cement below the surface. The wind and rain help to sculpt away the softer rock, leaving the more resistant, tightly cemented surface rock behind. Tafoni-style weathering is responsible for the unusual character of the massive Vaqueros Sandstone outcrops in Castle Rock State Park on the ridge west and above Sanborn County Park and along Skyline Boulevard. Local legend is that Ghost Rock may have been set up to appear as it does. The two "eyes" look similar to small grinding mortars elsewhere in the park area.

Stop 13 in the Sanborn Nature Trail guide describes the dusky-footed woodrat, a common pack rat in woodland and chaparral habitats throughout California. Woodrats gather litter from the forest floor to build small lean-to–style middens, typically under brush or in the pockets of tree stumps. Woodrats will gather whatever catches their eye, including garbage, and incorporate it into their middens. The hiking trail ends near restrooms near the park office area and lower parking area.

Figure 14. View along the Nature Trail between Stops 10 and 11. A small stream channel follows the trace of the San Andreas fault before it cuts through the shutter ridge on the east side of the fault. Note the curved trunks of the large Ponderosa pines in the distance near a small bridge over the creek. The trees in the foreground are redwoods.

STOP 2: SAVANNAH-CHANELLE WINERY AND VINEYARDS

Significance of the Site

The driveway and parking area associated with the winery and the wine tasting room are built right within the San Andreas fault zone, and geomorphic features associated with active faulting are well developed (Fig. 16). A good view of the grounds is possible from a picnic area a short walk uphill from the parking lot. This vista point provides a view along the trace of the fault to the south toward Sanborn County Park.

Accessibility

This is a privately owned business, open to the public during business hours. Wine tasting and vineyard tours are offered for a fee. The tasting room is open 11 a.m. to 5 p.m. daily. For additional information, see the Savannah-Chanelle Web site, www.savannahchanelle.com/index.html.

Directions

From Stop 1, return to Sanborn Road and turn left. At Highway 9 (Congress Springs Road), turn left (westward) and continue to the entrance to Savannah-Chanelle Vineyards on the left. A sign indicating the entrance is on the right. Turn into the vineyards and proceed to the parking area in front of the tasting room.

Stop Description

The San Andreas fault crosses Highway 9 near the driveway to the Savannah-Chanelle Vineyards (Figs. 1 and 16). The large home associated with the vineyard is built on top of a shutter ridge associated with the fault. The trace of the fault follows a hillside bench along Sanborn Creek Valley along the lower eastern flank of Castle Rock Ridge (to the west). The bedrock in the hills consists of Eocene- and Oligocene-age marine sandstone and shale, whereas Quaternary alluvial-fan deposits underlie the bench and lowlands in the valley along

Figure 15. "Ghost Rock" is located at Stop 12 along the Nature Trail. The "mouth" is a typical example of taphoni-style weathering. The two "eyes" may be Native American grinding mortar holes in a rock that was later set upright into its current position.

Sanborn Creek. Rocks of Mesozoic age underlie the forests on El Sereno Ridge on the opposite side of the valley (east of the San Andreas fault).

STOP 3: CINNABAR VINEYARDS AND WINERY

Significance of the Site

This stop provides excellent views of the San Andreas Rift Valley to the west and to the Santa Clara Valley to the east.

Accessibility

This is a privately owned business that is open to the public only for special events. However, special arrangements can be made for groups to visit. See the Cinnabar Web site, www.cinnabarwine.com, for more information.

Directions

From Stop 3, return to Highway 9 (Congress Springs Road) and turn right. Proceed eastward on Highway 9, past the intersection with Sanborn Road, and turn left onto the driveway and entrance to the vineyards and winery at 2300 Congress Springs Road.

Stop Description

Cinnabar Vineyards and Winery is located on the north end of El Sereno Ridge on the east side of the San Andreas Rift Valley near Sanborn County Park. The mountaintop setting provides spectacular views of Santa Clara Valley around San José to the east and the rift valley and Castle Rock Ridge to the west (Fig. 17). Unobstructed views extend to the south where the San Andreas fault passes beneath Lake Ranch Reservoir in the saddle

Figure 16. The Savannah-Chanelle Vineyards straddles the San Andreas fault north of Sanborn County Park. The fault line passes through the parking area at the wine tasting room. The yellow dashed line in this image shows the approximate location of the fault. This view is looking southeast from the winery's picnic area across the trace of the fault and the valley of Sanborn Creek (within the San Andreas Rift Valley). The mixed redwood and Douglas pine forest on the right is along McElroy Creek. McElroy Creek drains off of Castle Rock Ridge and displays displacement by stream capture where it crosses the fault near the vineyard. The grape vineyards in the foreground on the left are on a shutter ridge on the east side of the fault. The Cinnabar Vineyards are on El Soreno Ridge in the distance on the east side of the San Andreas Rift Valley.

between upper Sanborn Creek Valley and Lyndon Creek Valley. The fault zone near Walden West and the Savannah-Chanelle Vineyards are clearly visible. To the north, a stark vegetation contrast highlights the difference of soil, bedrock, and climate conditions on opposite sides of the rift valley in the vicinity of Saratoga Gap where the San Andreas fault crosses a low saddle between the Saratoga Creek and upper Stevens Creek drainages.

It should be noted that despite the name "Cinnabar," there are no mercury mines or ore deposits associated with the vineyard, even though North America's largest historic mercury mining district is located only a few miles south in the New Almaden region of the eastern foothills of the Santa Cruz Mountains. The label name Cinnabar was established to honor the traditional mission of alchemy—to miraculously transform ordinary metals into silver and gold with the help of the mineral cinnabar.

STOP 4: THE MOUNTAIN WINERY

Significance of the Site

This stop provides vistas of the San Andreas Rift Valley, southern San Francisco Bay, and the Berrocal fault.

Accessibility

This is a privately owned business open to the public for special events and by arrangement. For more information, see the Mountain Winery Web site, www.mountainwinery.com.

Directions

From Stop 3, return to Highway 9 (Congress Springs Road) and turn right. After 0.3 mi (0.5km), turn left onto Pierce Road, and continue 0.2 mi (0.3km) to the entrance gate on the left.

Stop Description

Paul Masson purchased a scenic mountaintop near Saratoga in 1901 and began clearing the land for vineyards and construction of what would become the historic Paul Masson Winery building. The Great San Francisco Earthquake of 1906 caused considerable damage to the new winery and widespread destruction throughout the communities in the South Bay. Paul Masson salvaged a twelfth century Spanish front portal from St. Patrick's Cathedral in San José that was destroyed in the 1906 earthquake. He incorporated the arched doorway into the rebuilt winery building (now part of the concert stage). During the Prohibition Era, most wineries in California were closed, but Paul Masson's Mountain Winery survived with a permit for production of sacramental wines. A music series titled "Music at the Mountain Winery" began in 1958 and has become a well-known tradition that has continued to the present. The winery building became a California Registered Historic Landmark and was placed on the National Registry of Historic Places in 1960. The facility was purchased by its current owners in 1999 and is now used to host summer concert series, weddings, banquets, wine tasting, meetings, and a variety of special events. The mountaintop setting of the facilities provides spectacular views of the surrounding region, including the South Bay region.

Figure 17. This view from the Cinnabar Winery shows part of the rift valley of the San Andreas fault at Sanborn County Park. Open fields around Walden West (WW) are on a low ridge on the east side of the San Andreas fault (SAF). The modern drainage of Todd Creek (TCm) drains down a steep canyon off of Castle Rock Ridge (CRR). In the past, Todd Creek (TCa) flowed south before cutting through the shutter ridge at Walden West and draining into Sanborn Creek Valley (SCV). The driveway leading to Walden West follows the beheaded-stream valley (bsv) of ancestral Todd Creek.

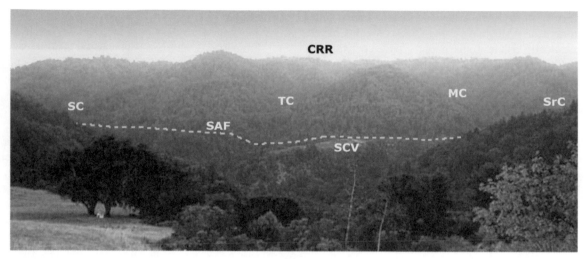

Figure 18. This view is looking west from the Mountain Winery parking area toward Castle Rock Ridge (CRR) and the rift valley of the San Andreas fault (SAF). The Savannah-Chanelle Vineyards (SCV) is near the center of the image. On the east flank of the ridge, McElroy Creek (MC) drainage is to the right of the vineyard. Todd Creek (TC) is to the left of center, and Sanborn Creek (SC) is to the far left (south). Saratoga Creek (SrC) comes in from the upper right and drains to the lower left.

The mountaintop setting of the Mountain Winery also provides views to the west of the San Andreas Rift Valley around Sanborn County Park (Fig. 18). The view looking west from the lower parking area of the Mountain Winery provides a good orientation to the vicinity of the Hike route of Stop 1. The geomorphology associated with the San Andreas fault is highlighted by the vineyards of the Savannah Chanelle Winery and the grass-covered fields around Walden West School. The upland drainages of Sanborn and Todd Creeks are also visible on the steep, forested, eastern escarpment of Skyline Ridge.

The view looking to the east from both the lower parking area and the Mountain Winery's patio dining area encompasses the South Bay region including the nearby eastern foothills to the Santa Cruz Mountains near Saratoga. A straight valley and adjacent ridge roughly 0.6 mi (1 km) east of the Mountain Winery follows the trace of the Berrocal fault (see Figs. 4 and 5). A thrust fault system known as the Range Front fault (or Monte Vista fault) runs along the base of the foothills near Interstate 280 and California Highway 85 in Saratoga. These faults are part of the San Andreas fault system and may actually merge with the main fault zone at depth. Both the Berrocal and the Range Front fault systems are considered to be potential earthquake-generating faults. The foothills around Saratoga are structurally complex, having numerous faults and folds that cut both older bedrock and younger, overlying alluvial sediments.

ACKNOWLEDGMENTS

Special thanks to James S. Moore (Eagle Scout, Boy Scouts of America, Skyline Council, Troop 5, Palo Alto, California), Tom Borra (Sanborn County Park Ranger, County of Santa Clara, Environmental Resources Agency, Los Gatos, California), and Carol Prentice (U.S. Geological Survey, Earthquake Hazards Team) for their help in developing this field trip.

REFERENCES CITED

Brabb, E.E., Graymer, R.W., and Jones, D.L., 2000, Geologic map and map database of the Palo Alto 30¢ × 60¢ Quadrangle, California: U.S. Geological Survey Miscellaneous Field Studies Map MF-2332, 2 sheets, scale 1:100,000, http://pubs.usgs.gov/mf/2000/mf-2332/.

Bürgmann, R., Arrowsmith, R., Dumitru, T., and McLaughlin, R., 1994, Rise and fall of the southern Santa Cruz Mountains, California, from fission tracts, geomorphology, and geodesy: Journal of Geophysical Research, v. 99, no. B10, p. 20,181–20,202, doi: 10.1029/94JB00131.

Dickinson, W.R., 1997, Overview: Tectonic implications of Cenozoic volcanism in coastal California: Geological Society of America Bulletin, v. 109, p. 936–954, doi: 10.1130/0016-7606(1997)109<0936:OTIOCV> 2.3.CO;2.

Elder, W., 2001, Geology of the Golden Gate Headlands, *in* Stoffer, P.W. and Gordon, L.C. eds., Geology and natural history of the San Francisco Bay Area—A field-trip guidebook: U.S. Geological Survey Bulletin 2188, p. 61–86, http://geopubs.wr.usgs.gov/bulletin/b2188/.

Gilbert, G.K., Humphrey, R.L., Sewell, J.S., and Soul, J.F., 1907, The San Francisco earthquake and fire of April 18, 1906, and their effects on structures and structural materials: U.S. Geological Survey Bulletin 324, 170 p.

Graymer, R.W., Sarna-Wojcicki, A.M., Walker, J.P., McLaughlin, R.J., and Fleck, R.J., 2002, Controls on timing and amount of right-lateral offset on the East Bay fault system, San Francisco Bay region, California: Geological Society of America Bulletin, v. 114, no. 12, p. 1471–1479, doi: 10.1130/0016-7606(2002)114<1471:COTAAO>2.0.CO;2.

Jachens, R.C., and Griscom, A., 2004, Geophysical and geologic setting of the earthquake, inferred from gravity and magnetic anomalies, *in* Wells, R.E., ed., The Loma Prieta, California, earthquake of October 17, 1989, geologic setting and crustal structure: U.S. Geological Survey Professional Paper 1550-E, p. F49–E80.

Lawson, A.C., chairman, 1908, The California earthquake of April 18, 1906; Report of the State Earthquake Investigation Commission: Carnegie Institution of Washington Publication 87, 2 volumes.

McLaughlin, R.J., Langenheim, V.E., Schmidt, K.M., Jachens, R.C., Stanley, R.G., Jayko, A.S., McDougall, K.A., Tinsley, J.C., and Valin, Z.C., 1999, Neogene contraction between the San Andreas Fault and the Santa Clara Valley, San Francisco Bay region, California: International Geology Review, v. 41, p. 1–30.

McLaughlin, R.J., Clark, J.C., Brabb, E.E., Helley, E.J., and Colón, C.J., 2002, Geologic maps and structure sections of the southwestern Santa Clara Valley and southern Santa Cruz Mountains, Santa Clara and Santa Cruz Counties, California: U.S. Geological Survey Miscellaneous Field Studies Map MF–2373, 5 sheets, scale 1:24,000, http://geopubs.wr.usgs.gov/map-mf/mf2373/.

Prentice, C.S., and Schwartz, D.P., 1991, Re-evaluation of 1906 surface faulting, geomorphic expression, and seismic hazard along the San Andreas Fault in the southern Santa Cruz Mountains: Bulletin of the Seismological Society of America, v. 81, no. 5, p. 1424–1479.

Prentice, C.S., and Ponti, D.J., 1997, Coseismic deformation of the Wrights tunnel during the 1906 San Francisco earthquake: A key to understanding 1906 fault slip and 1989 surface ruptures in the southern Santa Cruz Mountains, California: Journal of Geophysical Research, v. 102, p. 635–648, doi: 10.1029/96JB02934.

Geological Society of America
Field Guide 7
2006

A field guide to the central, creeping section of the San Andreas fault and the San Andreas Fault Observatory at Depth

Michael J. Rymer
Stephen H. Hickman
Philip W. Stoffer
U.S. Geological Survey, 345 Middlefield Road, Menlo Park, California 94025, USA

OVERVIEW OF FIELD TRIP

This field trip is along the central section of the San Andreas fault and consists of eight stops that illustrate surface evidence of faulting, in general, and features associated with active fault creep, in particular. Fault creep is slippage along a fault that occurs either in association with small-magnitude earthquakes or without any associated large-magnitude earthquakes. Another aspect of the trip is to highlight where there are multiple fault traces along this section of the San Andreas fault zone in order to gain a better understanding of plate-boundary processes.

The first stop is along the Calaveras fault, part of the San Andreas fault system, at a location where evidence of active fault creep is abundant and readily accessible. The stops that follow are along the San Andreas fault and at convenient locations to present and discuss rock types juxtaposed across the fault that have been transported tens to hundreds of kilometers by right-lateral motion along the San Andreas fault. Stops 6 and 7 are examples of recent studies of different aspects of the fault: drilling into the fault at the depth of repeating magnitude (M) 2 earthquakes with the San Andreas Fault Observatory at Depth (SAFOD) and the geological, geophysical, and seismological study of M 6 earthquakes near the town of Parkfield.

Along with the eight official stops on this field trip are 12 "rolling stops"—sites of geologic interest that add to the understanding of features and processes in the creeping section of the fault. Many of the rolling stops are located where stopping is difficult to dangerous; some of these sites are not appropriate for large vehicles (buses) or groups; some sites are not appropriate for people at all. We include photographs of or from many of these sites to add to the reader's experience without adding too many stops or hazards to the trip.

An extensive set of literature is available for those interested in the San Andreas fault or in the creeping section, in particular. For more scientifically oriented overviews of the fault, see Wallace (1990) and Irwin (1990); for a more generalized overview with abundant, colorful illustrations, see Collier (1999). Although the presence of small sections of the San Andreas fault was known before the great 1906 San Francisco earthquake, it was only after that event and subsequent geologic investigations reported in Lawson (1908) that showed the fault as a long structure, extending all the way from east of Los Angeles into northern California. Prentice (1999) described the importance of the 1908 "Lawson report" and how it pivotally influenced the understanding of the San Andreas. Hill (1981) presented a wonderful introduction to the evolution of thought on the San Andreas. Geologic maps and maps of the most recently active fault trace in the creeping section, or large parts of it, include those by Brown (1970), Dibblee (1971, 1980), and Wagner et al. (2002); detailed geologic maps are discussed at various stops in this guide. Various aspects of the creeping section of the San Andreas fault have been the focus of many geologic field trips in the past few decades. Guidebooks for some of those trips include those by Gribi (1963a, 1963b), Brabb et al. (1966), Rogers (1969), Bucknam and Haller (1989), Harden et al. (2001), and Stoffer (2005).

The creeping section of the San Andreas fault zone lies between areas that experienced large-displacement surface breakage during great earthquakes in 1857 and 1906 (Fig. 1, inset). Burford and Harsh (1980) divided the creeping section into three segments: (1) a northwest section where the creep rate increases to the southeast in step-like increments, (2) a central section where the creep rate is relatively constant at a maximum value of ~30 mm/yr (~1.2 in/yr), and (3) a southeast section where the creep rate decreases to the southeast (Fig. 2).

Rymer, M.J., Hickman, S.H., and Stoffer, P.W., 2006, A field guide to the central, creeping section of the San Andreas fault and the San Andreas Fault Observatory at Depth, *in* Prentice, C.S., Scotchmoor, J.G., Moores, E.M., and Kiland, J.P., eds., 1906 San Francisco Earthquake Centennial Field Guides: Field trips associated with the 100th Anniversary Conference, 18–23 April 2006, San Francisco, California: Geological Society of America Field Guide 7, p. 237–272, doi: 10.1130/2006.1906SF(16). For permission to copy, contact editing@geosociety.org. ©2006 Geological Society of America. All rights reserved.

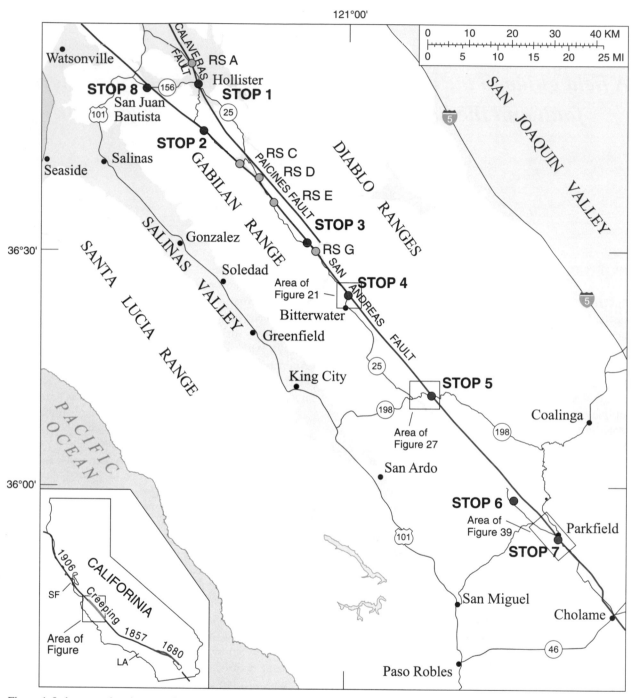

Figure 1. Index map showing creeping section of the San Andreas fault (from Cholame northwestward to San Juan Bautista), southern section of the Calaveras fault, and location of field trip stops (red dots) and rolling stops (yellow dots; labeled 'RS' in this figure and in Figs. 21, 27, and 38). Yellow—alluvium in valleys. Only selected faults, roads, and towns included for reference. Location of creeping section and surface rupture associated with great earthquakes, with dates, along San Andreas fault shown in inset.

The rate of slip along the creeping section of the fault zone has been measured using creepmeters, alignment arrays, and laser distance-measuring devices. The aperture of measurements over which these measurements are made ranges from 10 m (~33 ft) (creepmeters) to 100 m (~330 ft) (alignment arrays) to kilometers and tens of kilometers (laser measuring devices).

Creepmeter and alignment-array measurements are here termed "near-fault" measurements; laser measurements over distances of 1–2 km (~0.6–1.2 mi) are termed "intermediate-scale" measurements; laser measurements over tens of kilometers (miles) are termed "broadscale" measurements. Comparisons among near-fault, intermediate-scale, and broadscale measure-

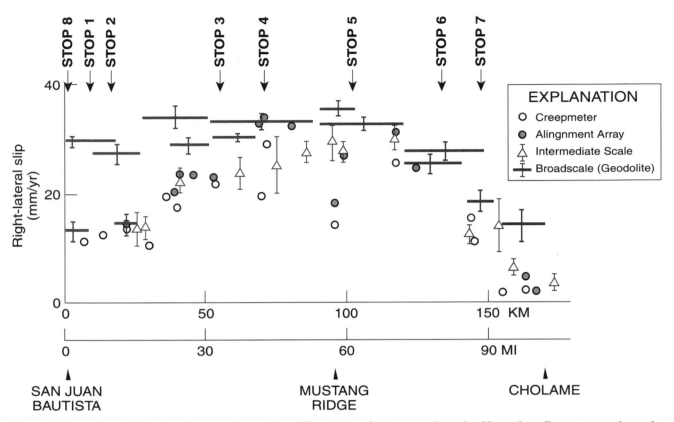

Figure 2. Comparison of slip rates along creeping section of San Andreas fault zone as determined by various distance-measuring techniques (modified from Lisowski and Prescott, 1981). Geodetic measures at northern end of creeping section of San Andreas fault are significantly greater than creepmeter and alignment array measures because the longer line lengths include slip on the Calaveras fault. Location of stops in this field guide marked with arrows at top.

ments and geologic maps show that the northwest part of the creeping section of the fault is composed of two narrow zones of active deformation, one along the San Andreas fault and one along the Calaveras-Paicines fault, whereas the central and southeast sections are both composed of a single relatively narrow zone of deformation. The southeast section is transitional to a locked zone southeast of Cholame; a locked fault is one that slips only in association with a moderate to large earthquake. Throughout the creeping section of the San Andreas fault zone, broadscale measurements generally indicate more deformation than near-fault and intermediate-scale measurements, which are in reasonably close agreement except at Monarch Peak (Mustang Ridge), near the center of the creeping section and our Stop 5 (Figs. 1 and 2).

Features that we see on this trip include offset street curbs, closed depressions (sag ponds), fault scarps (steep slopes formed by movement along a fault), a split and displaced tree, offset fence lines, fresh fractures, and offset road lines (Fig. 3 is a sketch showing some of the landforms that represent deformation by an active fault). We also see evidence of long-term maturity of the San Andreas fault, as indicated by fault features and displaced rock types (Fig. 4). Finally, we will visit sites of ongoing research into the processes associated with earthquakes

and their effects. Discussions include drilling into the San Andreas fault at the SAFOD drill site and the 2004 Parkfield earthquake and its effects and implications.

Keywords: San Andreas fault, creeping section, SAFOD, fault structure, Hollister, Parkfield.

STOP 1: EVIDENCE OF FAULT CREEP ALONG THE CALAVERAS FAULT, DUNNE PARK, HOLLISTER

Significance of the Site

Evidence of fault creep along the southern section of the Calaveras fault is readily abundant in Hollister. The Calaveras fault carries a significant fraction of the motion between the Pacific and North America plates in central California; slip is partitioned from the San Andreas fault northeastward onto the Calaveras fault, such that the Calaveras fault in and near Hollister moves at an average rate of ~12–14 mm/yr (~0.5–0.6 in/yr) (Rogers, 1969; Lisowski et al., 1991). Many houses and roads were constructed on top of the fault, creating an opportunity for viewing evidence of creep displacement of manmade features.

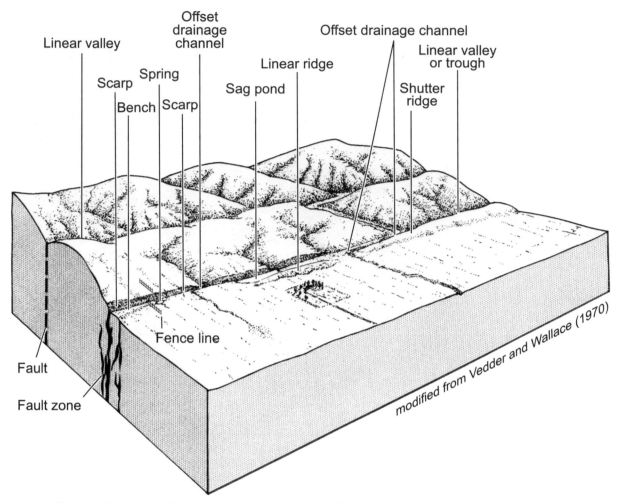

Figure 3. Common landforms along an active strike-slip fault (modified from Vedder and Wallace, 1970).

Accessibility

This site is publicly accessible, restrooms are available, and there is ample parking.

Directions

From San Francisco, take Hwy 101 southbound ~70 mi. Exit Hwy 25 (south of the city of Gilroy), turn left at the end of the off-ramp, and drive southeast, toward Hollister. Go past the intersection of Hwy 156 and drive into the city of Hollister; turn right onto Seventh Street, and drive 2 1/2 blocks to Dunne Park (Fig. 5).

Rolling Stop A

View the southwest-facing scarp along Calaveras fault; at the intersection of Hwy 25 and 156, ~2 mi (~3 km) north of town, the road crosses through a fault stepover to where the Calaveras fault forms a sag pond and a northeast-facing scarp. See Stoffer (2005).

Here we suggest that common courtesy be granted the residents of Hollister. As visitors to fault features, we are intrigued by evidence of faulting and implications of the faulting processes; the residents may be less enthusiastic or may not want crowds standing on their property. Please do not point or gawk at the setting. As visitors here to learn about the effects of faulting, we wish to remain welcomed by the community.

Stop 1 Description

Creep activity along the Calaveras fault in some developed parts of the city of Hollister (Fig. 5) provides the opportunity to see displaced cultural features. We concentrate on features in and around Dunne Park, between Sixth and Seventh Streets, so as to minimize disruption to the community on residential streets away from the public park. However, evidence of fault creep is also ample farther to the north, especially between Locust Avenue and Fifth Street (for example, see Fig. 6). Between Sixth and Seventh Streets, we see offset sidewalks, curbs, and short retaining walls, along with a low, linear slope along the fault in

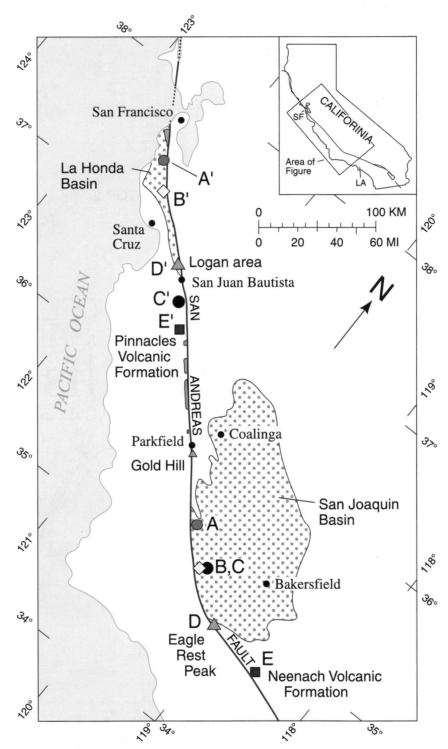

Figure 4. Locations of some pre-Quaternary features offset by the San Andreas fault in the California Coast Ranges. The La Honda Basin is an offset segment of the San Joaquin sedimentary basin (Stanley, 1987). A–A′—Butano Sandstone and Point of Rocks Sandstone Member (of Kreyenhagen Formation), representing offset parts of an Eocene deep-sea fan (Clarke and Nilsen, 1973) and steeply southwest-dipping slopes of the San Joaquin and La Honda Basins during late Zemorrian time (Stanley, 1987); B–B′—deepest parts of the San Joaquin and La Honda Basins adjacent to the San Andreas fault during Saucesian time (Stanley, 1987); C–C′—unusual clasts in upper Miocene conglomerate in the Temblor Range east of fault and their postulated source area in the Gabilan Range west of fault (Huffman, 1972); D–D′—bedrock exposures of unusual quartz-bearing mafic rocks at Logan, Gold Hill, and Eagle Rest Peak (Ross, 1984); E–E′—locations of the Pinnacles and Neenach Volcanic Formations (Matthews, 1976). Dark green polygons—outcrops of Jurassic and Cretaceous Franciscan Complex rocks within 10 km (6 mi) distance southwest of the San Andreas fault. Modified from Irwin (1990).

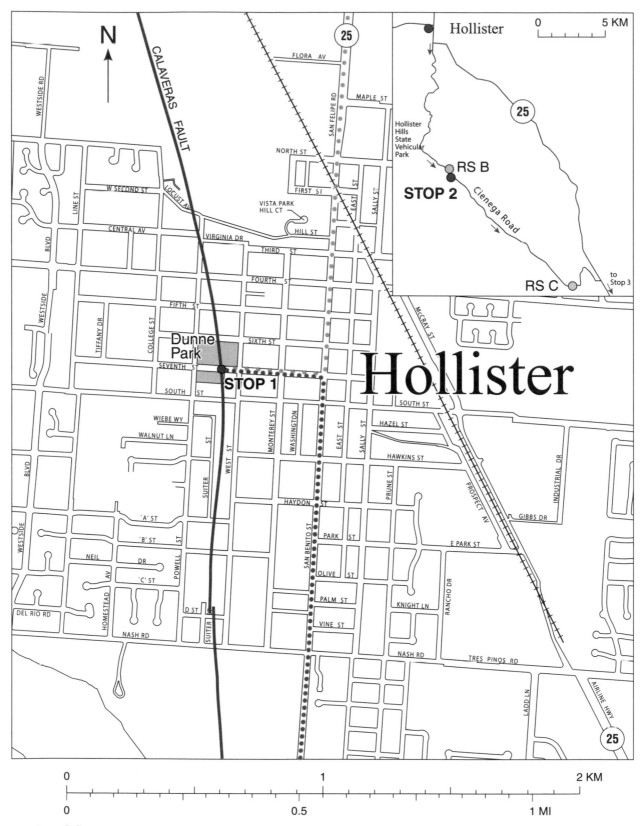

Figure 5. Street map of Hollister, California, with location of active strand of the Calaveras fault and Stop 1. Widely spaced green dotted line—path to Stop 1; closely spaced gray dotted line—path out of town and toward Stop 2. Base modified from City of Hollister (not all streets labeled); fault trace from Rogers (1969).

Figure 6. Fence and sidewalk right-laterally offset by incremental creep along the Calaveras fault on the north side of Fifth Street, Hollister, California. View eastward; photograph taken June 1989.

grass-covered sections of the park (Figs. 7–10). Figure 7 shows an offset sidewalk along the north side of Sixth Street. This view is lined up with the north (left) side of the sidewalk in the distance so as to gauge the amount of offset of the sidewalk in the foreground, on the opposite side of the fault. Here, as is common elsewhere along the Calaveras and other faults, the fault shows a broad zone (width of ~15 m [~49 ft]; Rogers, 1969) of warping and offset. Figure 8 compares offset of a curb joint on the north side of Sixth Street with photographs taken 36 years apart. Measurement of the amount of offset of the curb by Rogers (1969) and us (in 2005) indicates an offset in that period of ~14 cm (5.5 in)—this implies a creep rate of only ~4–5 mm/yr 0.16–0.20 in/yr). However, as stated above and seen in other features (including Figs. 6, 7, and 9), creep is distributed in a broad zone; thus, offset of the curb in Figure 8 represents only a fraction of the total creep offset. Continuing offset of another curb, along the south side of Seventh Street, is shown in similar views in Figure 9. The roadway in these views has been repaved at least once, but the curb and gutter are the same, although with greater offset in time. Within Dunne Park, a small fault scarp (up on the east) is expressed along this section of the Calaveras fault (Fig. 10). Presence of this scarp does not necessarily imply sig-

nificant local vertical slip along the fault; rather, there is likely a small vertical component of slip but with dominant right-lateral motion along the fault.

STOP 2: DEROSE WINERY—DEFORMED WALLS AND OFFSET CONCRETE DRAINAGE CHANNEL

Significance of the Site

This site along the San Andreas is easily accessible and includes walls and a drainage channel built across the creeping section of the fault. Also, this is one of the locations of earliest detection and monitoring of creep displacement across the San Andreas fault (Steinbrugge and Zacher, 1960; Tocher, 1960).

Accessibility

This is private property, but there are restrooms, and ample parking is available.

Directions

From Stop 1, drive east on Seventh Street. Turn right onto San Benito Street and drive 0.7 mi (1.1 km) south on San Benito to the intersection with Nash Road. Continue straight at the light, following signs to the Hollister Hills State Vehicular Recreation Park (see Fig. 5 and inset). At 1.6 mi (2.6 km) after leaving Seventh Street, turn right (west) onto Union Road at the stop sign. Cross over the bridge spanning the San Benito River. At 1.7 mi (2.7 km), immediately after crossing the bridge, turn left (south) onto Cienega Road. At 3.2 mi (5.1 km), there is a stop sign. Continue to the right on Cienega Road. The road winds uphill. At 6.5 mi (10.4 km), cross Bird Creek, then at 7.0 (11.2 km), turn left (southeast) onto Cienega Road. At 8.1 mi (13.0 km) is Vineyard School, on the right, which was built on the San Andreas fault. At 8.8 mi (14.1 km), there is a sag pond along the fault on the left. The sag pond is the topic of Rolling Stop B (Fig. 5, inset; see also Fig. 11). A local oral history account is that this pond drained after the 1906 San Francisco earthquake. At 9.0 mi (14.4 km) is Stop 2—DeRose Winery. Park here.

Stop 2 Description

The winery at Stop 2 was built on the San Andreas fault and is slowly being torn apart by ongoing fault creep. The general setting of the site is shown in Figures 11 and 12. Figure 11 is an oblique aerial view of the San Andreas fault, with the DeRose Winery about in the middle of the view. Figure 12 is a sketch map of the winery showing the location of the San Andreas fault and locations where more detailed inspections of the effects of fault creep are evident in the winery walls and a concrete drain. Ongoing creep has displaced the lower, concrete part of the wall on the northwest side of the winery; creep has warped and bowed the wooden, upper part of the wall (Fig. 13).

Figure 7. Sidewalk and short retaining wall right-laterally offset by creep along the Calaveras fault on the north side of Sixth Street, Hollister. View eastward; photograph taken July 2005.

Figure 8. Curb with right-lateral offset on the north side of Sixth Street. (A) Photograph of curb and offset taken in 1969 (Rogers, 1969). (B) Photograph of the same curb, with greater offset, taken in July 2005. View is eastward in both photos.

Figure 9. Curb with right-lateral offset along the south side of Seventh Street. (A) Photograph of curb and offset taken in June 1989. (B) Photograph of the same curb, with greater offset, taken in June 2005. View is westward in both photos.

Figure 10. Fault scarp along Calaveras fault in Dunne Park. The east (left) side of the fault is slightly higher than the west side; these relations are common along the Calaveras fault for several blocks in Hollister and indicate a small, local vertical component of slip within the predominant right-lateral slip along the fault. Lawn mower for scale. View is southward, approximately centered on fault trace (black arrows); photograph taken June 2005.

Inspection of other walls and columns within the winery reveal additional evidence of fault creep and its effects on man-made features astride the fault.

A concrete drainage channel on the southeast side of the winery also shows evidence of deformation due to ongoing creep displacement and warpage. Comparison of photographs taken of the drainage channel 41 years apart graphically reveal evidence of fault creep (Fig. 14A and 14B). Both of these photographs also indicate that along with the brittle failure right at the fault, there is distributed warpage of the drainage channel spread over a distance of ~6–8 m (20–26 ft).

STOP 3: SAG POND, OFFSET FENCE, FAULT MORPHOLOGY, AND DISPLACED ROCK TYPE

Significance of the Site

This site along the San Andreas offers views of a number of various fault features visible from a single location. A fence

that is offset by fault creep is well preserved. This site also has views of closed depressions (sag ponds) along the San Andreas fault and lithologic evidence of long-term migration of the San Andreas fault.

Accessibility

Ample parking is on northeast side of road, but there are no restrooms. The features are visible from the parking location. Note that the parking area is on the left side of the road as we drive south and on a turn; therefore, all due caution should be used in crossing possible oncoming traffic.

Directions

From the DeRose Winery, drive southeastward on Cienega Road (see Fig. 5, inset). Drive to the Airline Highway (Hwy 25); turn right onto Hwy 25. Stay on Hwy 25. Turn left into parking area (pullout) on left side of road (see cautionary note, above).

Figure 11. Oblique aerial view of San Andreas fault and DeRose Winery (in center), which is the location of Stop 2. The fault is marked with white arrows; S—sag pond and Rolling Stop B. View is northwestward; photograph taken before 1966 by R.E. Wallace.

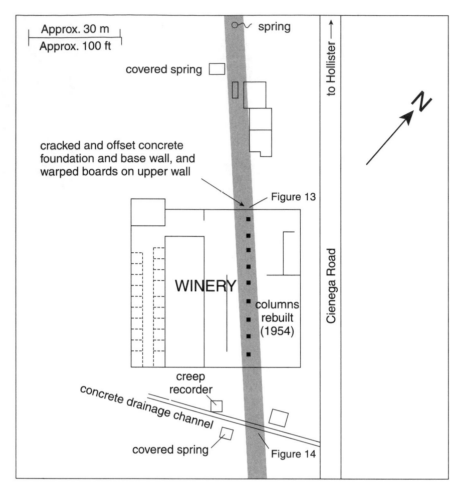

Figure 12. Sketch map of the DeRose Winery and location of Stop 2. Winery is cut by the San Andreas fault; creep along fault gradually offsets rigid features. Locations of Figures 13 and 14 shown on northwest and southeast sides of winery. (Slightly modified from Tocher, 1960; Harden et al., 2001).

Rolling Stop C (Fig. 1; Fig. 5, inset)

Cienega Road here crosses the main trace of the San Andreas fault. Often (depending on the recency of road repair), there are fresh cracks across the road due fault creep.

Rolling Stop D (Fig. 1)

Along Hwy 25, landslides are locally abundant. The local hills consist of poorly consolidated gravel and sand that commonly slide downhill when saturated with water. Landslides here are very well expressed.

Rolling Stop E

Here (Fig. 1) the Airline Highway (Hwy 25) crosses the main trace of the San Andreas fault. This site is on a curve in a narrow section of the road and thus is not recommended as a place to stop or stand.

Pass the turnoff to the west (right) to the Pinnacles National Monument. We do NOT diverge from Hwy 25 here, even though this is a worthy stop for those with time to see one of the key litho-

logic markers for total displacement along the San Andreas fault. Volcanic rocks exposed within Pinnacles National Monument are mineralogically and chemically identical to volcanic rocks on the other side of the San Andreas fault, but are located ~315 km to the southeast (Matthews, 1976; Ross, 1984; Irwin, 1990; see Fig. 4). Stop 3 is ~2.5 mi southeast of the Pinnacles turnoff.

Stop 3 Description

This stop includes a road-cut exposure of rocks of the Franciscan Complex that most commonly are located only on the northeast side of the San Andreas fault (there are some exceptions). Conventional thought is that rocks of the Franciscan Complex (summarized in Bailey et al., 1964) are restricted to the northeast side of the San Andreas (see Irwin, 1990, for a summary). However, here at Stop 3 is an outcrop of Franciscan greenstone (altered oceanic basalt; Fig. 15) exposed ~160 m (520 ft) southwest of the San Andreas. The presence of such rocks indicates that there is likely another fault farther to the west

Figure 13. Northwest wall of DeRose Winery showing evidence of incremental creep (fault slip) along the San Andreas fault. View is to the southwest; photograph taken November 2005.

Figure 14. Concrete drainage channel at DeRose Winery showing evidence of incremental creep (slip) along the San Andreas fault. (A) View to the southwest showing small amount of right-lateral displacement in a broad zone of warpage; photograph taken by Stanley Skapinsky (San José State University), April 1961. (B) Approximately same view as in (A) but with greater right-lateral displacement and similar broad zone of warpage; photograph taken November 2005.

Figure 15. Greenstone (altered oceanic volcanic rocks) of the Franciscan Complex exposed ~200 m (~790 ft) southwest of the San Andreas fault. View is southwestward; photograph taken June 2005.

of here that transported such rocks along its eastern side. Movement along such a fault has since transferred to the San Andreas fault. We will see other, similar, features later on this trip.

The San Andreas fault along this part of the creeping section is expressed by sag ponds and fault scarps, geomorphic features that indicate active faulting. While standing at the northwestern end of the pullout for Stop 3 (at a private gate), we can see features associated with the active nature of the San Andreas fault. Figure 16 reproduces a view from this spot that shows a large southwest-facing scarp along the fault and a fence line that is offset part way up the scarp. Notice that the fence line is offset where there is a side-hill bench (a common fault-related feature; marked with white arrows in Fig. 16) that extends diagonally along the scarp (see also Fig. 17 for another view of the same area). Also visible from the same pullout is a series of sag ponds along the San Andreas fault, located to the northeast side of the road (Fig. 17).

STOP 4: CREEP OFFSET OF ROAD, FAULT SCARP, AND STRUCTURAL COMPLEXITY, BITTERWATER VALLEY

Significance of the Site

The San Andreas fault in this part of the creeping section is well expressed with fresh fractures in road paving, fault scarps, and an offset fence line. Long-term structural complexity in the

fault is indicated by geomorphic features; structural complexity is further revealed by subsurface studies associated with the local Bitterwater oilfield.

Accessibility

This site is publicly accessible, but there are no restrooms. There is ample parking in the pullout on right side of road.

Directions

From Stop 3, drive southeast on Hwy 25 (Fig. 1). Turn right at stop sign and park on the right.

Along Hwy 25 between Stops 3 and 4, there are three places where the road crosses the San Andreas fault (Rolling Stops F, G, and H), and just before the stop sign and turn to Stop 3 is a site with a good view of a fault scarp (Rolling Stop I).

Rolling Stop F

About 200 m (1/8 mi) southeast of Stop 3, the road crosses the San Andreas fault. This site is located in a turn on a slope and thus is a dangerous place to stop or stand. The presence of the fault is indicated by fractures in the road paving; look for fractures (or feel them) as you drive along the road. This location is immediately off the bottom right of Figure 17.

Figure 16. Fence line (marked with diagonal black arrows) right-laterally offset across San Andreas fault (marked with vertical white arrows). Trace of San Andreas fault marked by side-hill bench about half way up fault scarp. View is northward; photograph taken June 2005.

Rolling Stop G

Hwy 25 again crosses the San Andreas fault (Fig. 18). Here, at least as revealed in the summer of 2005, the fault shows up as a single fracture that crosses the road at an acute angle.

Rolling Stop H

Hwy 25 crosses the San Andreas fault, near the southeast end of Rabbit Valley, where the creep along the fault shows up as a zone of parallel, left-stepping fractures with a width of ~14 m (46 ft) (Fig. 19).

Rolling Stop I

From this location, there is a good view to the southeast of a well-developed scarp along the San Andreas fault in Bitterwater Valley; however, given little room for parking, and the presence of a slope and a turn, this is a dangerous place to stop. The view in Figure 20 shows a northeast-facing scarp along the fault. (We stop and park a short distance below this rolling stop.)

Stop 4 Description

This stop is on the northeastern edge of Bitterwater Valley, the shape of which is controlled by the San Andreas fault zone. As at rolling stops F, G, and H, Hwy 25 here crosses the active trace of the San Andreas fault and is offset by continued creep

(Figs. 21 and 22). Creep (fault) fractures across the road are expressed en echelon and show right-lateral offset of the paint centerline (Fig. 22). Similarly, right-lateral offsets are noticeable ~0.8 mile (1.3 km) to the southeast, where an old fence line is offset across the fault (Figs. 23 and 24). (The fence shown in Figure 24 is on private property and should not be visited without permission; views are available from the county road to the north [see Figs. 21 and 24]). Another feature at Stop 4 is the Bitterwater oilfield (Fig. 25), which is structurally controlled by movement along the San Andreas fault. The oilfield, along with surface and subsurface studies of the local structural controls of oil migration and traps, indicate the presence of faults in addition to the main San Andreas fault (Figs. 21 and 26).

STOP 5: THE SAN ANDREAS FAULT ON MUSTANG RIDGE—FAULT FEATURES AND ROCK TYPES

Significance of the Site

The San Andreas fault along this part of the creeping section is expressed in a wide zone of abundant sag ponds and springs and other geomorphic features suggestive of active faulting. There is also a split tree. This stop also includes discussion of ongoing faulting on secondary faults that are part of the process of fault straightening and increasing fault maturity.

Figure 17. Oblique aerial photograph of the San Andreas fault (large oblique arrows) and pull out ("P") for Stop 3. Small vertical arrows mark location of fence line shown in Figure 16. Note evidence for presence of several sag ponds (labeled "S," dry at the time of year in this image) along multiple fault strands of the San Andreas fault. Rolling Stop F is just off the bottom right of image, where the road crosses the San Andreas fault. View is northwestward; photograph taken September 1979.

Figure 18. Road centerline right-laterally offset where it crosses the San Andreas fault at Rolling Stop G, ~0.5 km (0.3 mi) southeast of Stop 3 (see Fig. 1 for location). View is southward; photograph taken August 2005.

Figure 19. Fresh echelon cracks in road where road crosses San Andreas fault at Rolling Stop H (see Fig. 21 for location). Notebook in left lane for scale. View is southwestward; photograph taken June 2005.

Figure 20. Photograph of San Andreas fault and prominent northeast-facing fault scarp (marked with arrows), as viewed from Rolling Stop I and near Stop 3 (see Fig. 21 for location). San Andreas fault is ~20 m (~65 ft) to the right of road in this view. View is southeastward; photograph taken July 2005.

Accessibility

This is a private site; there are no restrooms. There is limited parking in the pullout on the north (left) side of the road.

Directions

Along Hwy 25, drive south from the Bitterwater Valley to Hwy 198 (Figs. 1 and 27). Turn east (left) and drive uphill, up the flanks of Mustang Ridge. From the intersection of Hwys 25 and 198, drive ~3 1/2 mi (~5.6 km) to Stop 5, a small pull-out and gate on top of the ridge (Fig. 27); if necessary, a larger pullout is located on the left side of the road ~1/8 mi (~0.3 km) farther east.

Rolling Stop J

While driving uphill onto Mustang Ridge, you will pass a large block of greenstone from the Franciscan Complex. Apparently, erosion undercut the greenstone block to a point below the middle of its mass, such that the block has since moved from near the top of the Mustang Ridge to partway down its slope, coming to rest on top of the Pliocene Pancho Rico Formation.

Rolling Stop K

As you drive up the hill, note the contact between sandstone of the Pliocene Pancho Rico Formation and serpentinite. This contact is due to downhill motion of the serpentinite in a landslide. Landslides are common along both northeast and southwest flanks of Mustang Ridge, and locally are as wide as ~1 km (0.6 mi).

Stop 5 Description

Mustang Ridge is a terrific place to examine the San Andreas fault because of the wide range of features and inferences on abundant faulting processes. First, Mustang Ridge is atypical of strike-slip fault settings in that the San Andreas fault zone extends along a ridge crest instead of along a linear trough (see Figs. 3, 27, and 28). Second, the San Andreas fault zone on Mustang Ridge is ~1.5–3 km wide, with a main trace, secondary faults, and northeast and southwest boundary faults (Fig. 27). Geologic mapping of the fault zone (Rymer, 1981) revealed secondary faults on the northeast side of the main trace that extend for ~7 km (4.2 mi) parallel to the fault. Youthful geomorphic features and comparison of

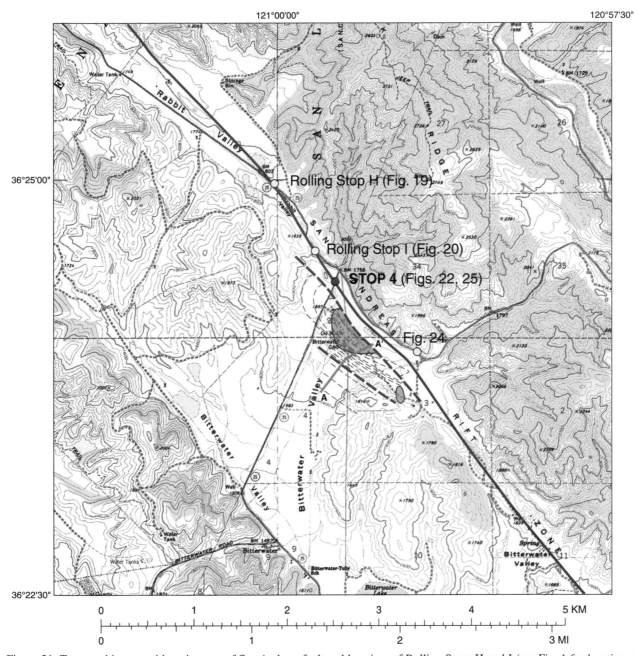

Figure 21. Topographic map with main trace of San Andreas fault and locations of Rolling Stops H and I (see Fig. 1 for location of map). Contours on top of O'Connor Member of the Brickmore Canyon Formation and inferred fault southwest of San Andreas main trace from Gribi (1963a).

short-range and intermediate-range distance measurements indicate that the secondary faults are active, taking up about one third of the right-lateral displacement in the fault zone (Rymer et al., 1984). The zone of secondary faults slips such that it transfers motion through a structural stepover in the main trace; eventually, the San Andreas fault here will be straighter and smoother.

Some of the features discussed above, but that we will not visit on this field trip, include the views in Figures 29 and 30.

Figure 29 shows part of the southwest boundary fault, where much older Franciscan Complex rocks have been thrust up such that they now lie structurally on top of young rocks of the Pliocene and Pleistocene Paso Robles Formation (Rymer, 1981). Figure 30 shows a scarp along one of the secondary faults on top of Mustang Ridge. Included in this view is a sag pond; on Mustang Ridge about half of the sag ponds and ~70% of springs lie along secondary faults and not the main trace of the San Andreas fault (Rymer, 1981).

Figure 22. Road centerline right-laterally offset where it crosses the San Andreas fault at Stop 4 (see Fig. 21 for location). View is southwestward; photograph taken June 2005.

We take a short hike to the north along the ridge, where we will see other features related to active faulting. One of those features is a smallish oak tree that is partially split by creep offset along the San Andreas main trace (Fig. 31). The tree spans only part of the zone of shear and thus is splitting apart right-laterally rather slowly, with enough time to grow and partially heal part of the tear. A short distance to the northwest along the fault we will visit a sag pond (Fig. 32) with steep sides and a sill height of several meters. Also present along Mustang Ridge are abundant rocks of the Franciscan Complex that are remnants of ocean-floor processes and later subduction (collision of oceanic crust with continental crust; in this case, where the oceanic crust was thrust beneath the North America plate). Figure 33 shows a blueschist block that contains metamorphic minerals that formed under high pressures but low temperatures. This block of blueschist now rests adjacent to the main trace of the San Andreas fault.

STOP 6: THE SAN ANDREAS FAULT OBSERVATORY AT DEPTH (SAFOD)—DRILLING INTO THE FAULT

Significance of the Site

The San Andreas Fault Observatory at Depth (SAFOD) is a comprehensive project to better understand the physics of faulting and earthquake generation by drilling into the fault at the depth of repeating M ~2 earthquakes (~3.2 km [1.9 mi]). This stop is a visit to the drill site (Fig. 34); although the drill rig is no longer present, the discussion below presents initial drilling results and very briefly summarizes ancillary geological and geophysical studies.

Accessibility

Normally, no access is available to this site; visits may be made ONLY THROUGH ORGANIZED SCIENTIFIC TOURS. Please respect the privacy and rights of the landowners.

Stop 6 Description

The SAFOD drill site is located 1.8 km (1.1 mi) southwest of the surface trace of the San Andreas fault, such that the inclined borehole passes through the fault at seismogenic depths (Fig. 35). Phase 1 of SAFOD, rotary drilling to 2.5 km (1.5 mi) vertical depth and to within 700 m (~2300 ft) of the surface trace of the San Andreas, was carried out during the summer of 2004. Phase 2 of the project was conducted during the summer of 2005 and involved rotary drilling through the entire fault zone while collecting nearly continuous cuttings and mud gas samples, spot cores, and a comprehensive suite of geophysical logs. Initial results indicate greater fault

Figure 23. Oblique aerial photograph of San Andreas fault, northeast-facing fault scarp (in foreground, marked with small, oblique black arrows) and structural step over near Stop 4. Right-lateral offset of fence line along driveway to ranch in midground shown in Figure 24 (marked with red arrow). View is southeastward; photograph taken September 1979.

Figure 24. Fence along ranch driveway (private road) right-laterally offset where fence and driveway cross the San Andreas fault (red arrow; see Fig. 23 for location). View is southward; photograph taken from county road in June 2005.

Figure 25. Storage tanks and oil pumps that are part of the Bitterwater oilfield and within the San Andreas fault zone (see Fig. 21 for location). View is southward; photograph taken June 2005.

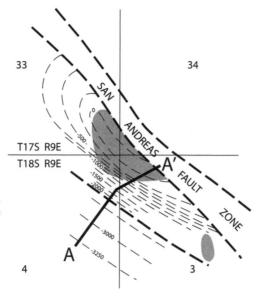

Figure 26. Structure section along section A–A′ that crosses anticline and fault in the Bitterwater oil field (from Gribi, 1963a). (See Fig. 21 for location).

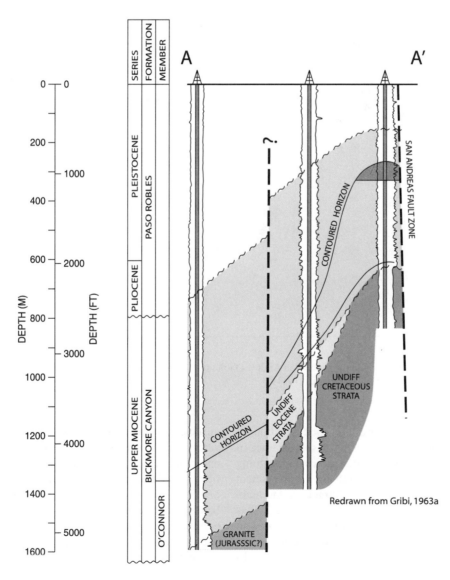

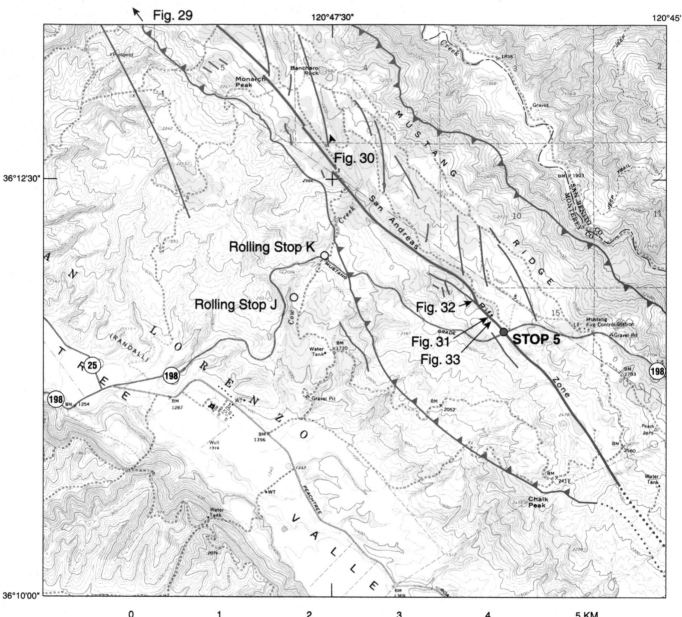

Figure 27. Topographic map with traces of faults in the San Andreas fault zone, location of Stop 5, and locations of Rolling Stops J and K (see Fig. 1 for location of map). Fault mapping from Rymer (1981).

complexity than anticipated and a long-term rock-type boundary located ~600 m (~2000 ft) southwest of the surface trace of the fault. Locations of the M 2 target earthquakes and ongoing fault creep measured in the borehole will be used to select intervals in which to continuously core sidetracks to the main SAFOD borehole in the summer of 2007, during Phase 3. This will permit scientists to compare the mineralogy, physical properties, and deformational behavior of fault rocks that fail primarily through creep against those that fail during earth-quakes. Construction of the multi-component SAFOD obser-vatory is now under way with a seismometer and tiltmeter now operating at depths of 1 and 2.5 km (0.6 and 1.5 mi) and a fiber-optic laser strainmeter cemented behind casing at a depth of 1.5 km (0.9 mi). After Phase 3 is complete, the borehole will be instrumented with an array of downhole sensors to monitor earthquakes, deformation, fluid pressure, and temperature within and adjacent to the fault zone through multiple earth-quake cycles.

Figure 28. Oblique aerial photograph of San Andreas fault zone on Mustang Ridge, Stop 5, and abundant sag ponds (some marked with S). View is northwestward; photograph taken September 1979.

Figure 29. Photograph of Franciscan Complex rocks (KJf) structurally overlying Pliocene and Pleistocene Paso Robles Formation gravels (QTp) on the southwest flank of Mustang Ridge (see Fig. 27 for location). View is northwestward; photograph taken April 1980.

Figure 30. Photograph of sag pond and west-facing scarp along secondary fault on Mustang Ridge (see Fig. 27 for location). View is northward; photograph taken April 1980.

Figure 31. Oak tree with right-lateral offset at its base (see Fig. 27 for location). Slip along the San Andreas fault (creep) apparently is distributed across a broad zone (~15–20 m wide [48–64 ft])—some of the distributed slip is ripping the tree apart. Pocket knife for scale. View is southeastward; photograph taken May 1979.

Figure 32. Sag pond along main trace of the San Andreas fault (see Fig. 27 for location). View is northwest-ward; photograph taken May 2005.

Figure 33. Block of blueschist (high-pressure, low-temperature metamorphic rock) along main trace of the San Andreas fault (see Fig. 27 for location). Photograph taken May 2005.

Figure 34. Drill rig at San Andreas Fault Observatory at Depth site that was used to drill through the San Andreas fault to a depth of 3.2 km (~1.9 mi) in the summer of 2005. Photograph taken August 2005.

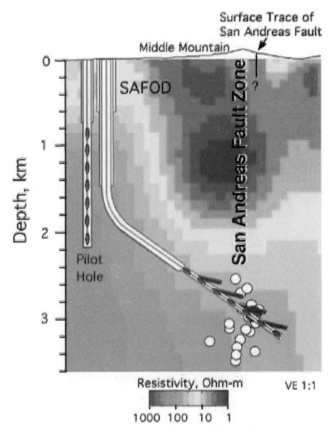

Figure 35. Cross-sectional view of drilling associated with the San Andreas Fault Observatory at Depth (SAFOD) experiment. Pilot hole drilled to ~2.2 km (~1.4 mi) depth below the surface; main hole drilled to ~3.2 km (~1.9 mi) depth below the surface. Background represents resistivity profile from a magnetotelluric survey by Unsworth and Bedrosian (2004); earthquake locations from Thurber et al. (2004).

In preparation for SAFOD, a 2.2-km-deep (1.3-mi-deep) pilot hole was drilled in 2002 (Fig. 35), and an extensive suite of geological, geophysical, and seismologic site investigations were conducted around the drill site and across the San Andreas fault zone (see Hickman et al., 2004, and papers therein). New geologic mapping to characterize the SAFOD drill site indicates that the fault zone here is composed of many faults—at least three of which are significant. Southwest of the San Andreas fault is the Buzzard Canyon fault that ~2 km (1.2 mi) to the north includes Franciscan Complex rocks. The presence of Franciscan Complex rocks, normally found only on the east side of the San Andreas fault, suggests that the Buzzard Canyon fault may have been a significant—possibly even a plate-boundary—fault in earlier geologic times (Catchings et al., 2002; Rymer et al., 2003). Another significant local fault is the northern extension of the Gold Hill fault (see Fig. 36). The Gold Hill fault juxtaposes rock between it and the current San Andreas fault that has affinities to rock in the southern Sierra Nevada and northern Gabilan Range (see Fig. 4).

The SAFOD site is ~15 km (~9.3 mi) northwest of Parkfield (Fig. 1). The San Andreas fault at this location is creeping at the surface at ~20 mm/yr (0.8 in/yr), with most of the fault

displacement localized to a zone no more than 10 m (32 ft) wide. Numerous microearthquakes occur along the San Andreas fault near SAFOD at depths of 2.5–12 km (1.5–7.2 mi). SAFOD lies just north of the rupture zone of the 1966 M_S 6.2 Parkfield earthquake, but south of the northern end of the rupture zone of the 2004 M_W 6 Parkfield earthquake (Langbein et al., 2005; Rymer et al., 2005), the most recent in a series of events that have ruptured the fault seven times since 1857.

STOP 7: THE PARKFIELD BRIDGE ASTRIDE THE SAN ANDREAS FAULT—DISCUSSION OF INSTRUMENTATION FOR THE PARKFIELD EARTHQUAKE EXPERIMENT AND EFFECTS OF THE 2004 PARKFIELD EARTHQUAKE

Significance of the Site

Much of the interest in moderate earthquakes in the Parkfield section of the San Andreas fault has been driven by the Parkfield Earthquake Experiment (see Bakun et al., 2005). At this stop, we will discuss the goals of the experiment, some of

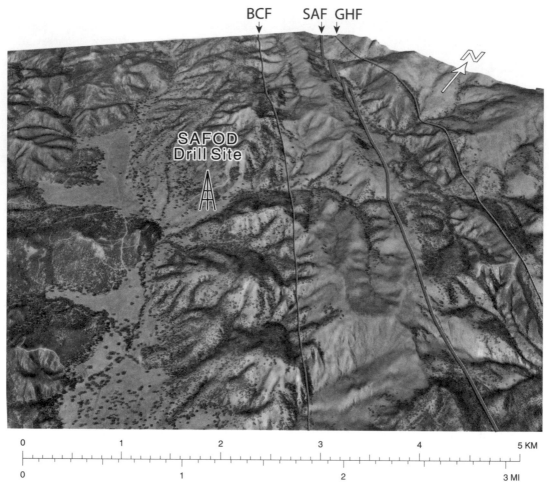

Figure 36. Oblique virtual view of San Andreas Fault Observatory at Depth (SAFOD) site and three prominent faults in the fault zone (Buzzard Canyon, San Andreas, and Gold Hill faults; labeled BCF, SAF, and GHF, respectively). Bar scale appropriate at distance of SAFOD drill site only. View is northwestward.

the instrumentation installed to record the earthquake and its effects, and the results of such measurements before, during, and after the 2004 Parkfield earthquake.

Accessibility

This is on a public road with parking on the shoulder of the road. There are no restrooms.

Directions

From the center of Parkfield, drive south ~1/2 mi (0.8 km) to the Parkfield Bridge.

Stop 7 Description

This stop provides the opportunity to discuss the Parkfield Earthquake Experiment, the anticipated earthquake itself, and some of the results of earthquake studies. At this site, we can walk (with a bit of climbing) below the bridge and see where surface slip and afterslip associated with the 2004 Parkfield earthquake moved the bridge supports relative to the bridge span.

Parkfield Bridge

The San Andreas fault passes beneath the bridge, near its western end (Figs. 37–39). An older version of the bridge had been continually offset by fault creep. The current bridge is a rebuilt version of the former, with the reconstruction only on the columns and supports beneath. Surface fractures and afterslip associated with the 2004 Parkfield earthquake displaced the ground beneath the bridge near its western end. This slippage also moved the supports and parts of the bridge.

Rolling Stop L

The Parkfield-Cholame Road crosses, and was offset by, the San Andreas fault at four places in the 4 miles (6.4 km) southeast of Stop 7. Depending on the timing of road repairs and the amount

Figure 37. Oblique aerial photograph of the San Andreas fault, town of Parkfield, Stop 7 (marked with red dot), and abundant geomorphic evidence for the presence of an active fault. View is northeastward; photograph taken March 2003.

of recent afterslip and/or creep, the presence of the fault can be seen as fractures across the road, or felt as bumps in the road.

STOP 8: SAN JUAN BAUTISTA MISSION, STATE PARK, AND THE SAN ANDREAS FAULT

Significance of the Site

This site along the San Andreas fault provides an opportunity for visitors to enjoy a historic site (Mission San Juan Bautista), which is situated adjacent to the San Andreas fault (Fig. 40).

Accessibility

This site is now a state park and therefore is publicly accessible; there are restrooms and ample parking.

Directions

From Hwy 101 (see Fig. 1), exit onto Hwy 156. Drive east for ~3 mi (4.8 km). Exit Hwy 156 onto Muckelemi Street, and proceed east to 2nd Street. Turn right (east) and drive two blocks. Here is the San Juan Bautista Historical Park and Stop 8.

Stop 8 Description

The first church built at this site was completed in 1798 and was significantly damaged by earthquake shaking in 1800. The present structure of Mission San Juan Bautista was completed in 1812, which, in turn, was heavily damaged in the 1906 San Francisco earthquake. During the 1906 earthquake, parts of the outer walls collapsed (see, for example, Photo 8 from the Harry Downie collection in Brabb et al., 1966).

San Juan Bautista was approximately the southeastern end of surface faulting associated with the 1906 earthquake (Lawson, 1908); the community is also near the northwestern end of the central, creeping section of the fault (Figs. 1 and 2). Figure 40 is an oblique aerial view to the northwest of the San Andreas fault and San Juan Bautista. The mission was built right above a scarp along the San Andreas fault (the fault scarp is located between the mission and the oval, a rodeo grounds, in Fig. 40—the rodeo grounds are now removed). From the grassy square on the southeast side of the mission, one can appreciate the setting of the mission with its elevation-enhanced view of the San Juan Valley, even if the mission is located right above the scarp of the San Andreas fault (Figs. 40 and 41).

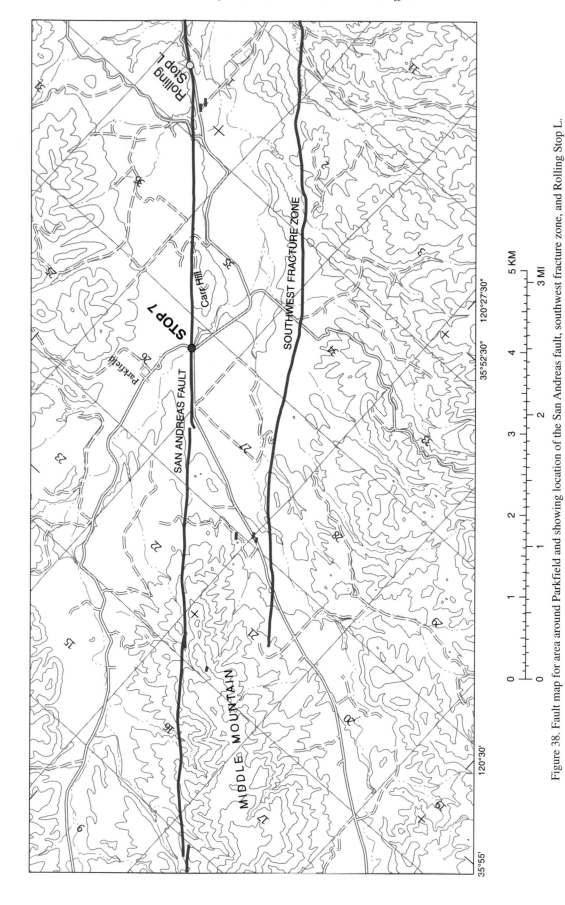

Figure 38. Fault map for area around Parkfield and showing location of the San Andreas fault, southwest fracture zone, and Rolling Stop L.

Figure 39. Oblique aerial view of the San Andreas fault and Parkfield (in midground); location of Stop 7 is at bridge (Parkfield Bridge) in lower right. View is northeastward; photograph taken in 1984 by W.H. Bakun.

Figure 40. Oblique aerial view of the San Andreas fault (between white arrows) and city of San Juan Bautista. Location of Stop 8 is at Mission San Juan Bautista (San Juan Bautista Historical Park). View is northwestward; photograph taken before 1966 by R.E. Wallace.

Figure 41. Mission San Juan Bautista and location of Stop 8. San Andreas fault is located downslope immediately to the right of this view of the mission. View is northward; photograph taken November 2005.

REFERENCES CITED

Bakun, W.H., Aagaard, B., Dost, B., Ellsworth, W.L., Hardebeck, J.L., Harris, R.A., Ji, C., Johnston, M.J.S., Langbein, J., Lienkaemper, J.J., Michael, A.J., Murray, J.R., Nadeau, R.M., Reasenberg, P.A., Reichle, M.S., Roeloffs, E.A., Shakal, A., Simpson, R.W., and Waldhauser, F., 2005, Implications for prediction and hazard assessment from the 2004 Parkfield earthquake: Nature, v, 437, p. 969–974, doi: 10.1038/nature04067.

Bailey, E.H., Irwin, W.P., and Jones, D.L., 1964, Franciscan and related rocks, and their significance in the geology of western California: California Division of Mines and Geology Bulletin 183, 177 p.

Brabb, E.E., Maddock, M.E., and Wallace, R.E., 1966, Guide to San Andreas fault from San Francisco to Hollister, field trip C, *in* Geology of Northern California: California Division of Mines and Geology Bulletin 190, p. 453–464.

Brown, R.D., Jr., 1970, Map showing recently active breaks along the San Andreas and related faults between the northern Gabilan Range and Cholame Valley, California: U.S. Geological Survey Miscellaneous Geological Investigations Map I-575, scale 1:62,500.

Bucknam, R.C., and Haller, K.M., 1989, Examples of active faults in the western United States: A field guide: U.S. Geological Survey Open-File Report 89-528, 140 p.

Burford, R.O., and Harsh, P.W., 1980, Slip on the San Andreas fault in central California from alinement array surveys: Bulletin of the Seismological Society of America, v. 70, p. 1233–1261.

Catchings, R.D., Rymer, M.J., Goldman, M.R., Hole, J.A., Huggins, R., and Lippus, C., 2002, High-resolution seismic velocities and shallow structure of the San Andreas fault zone at Middle Mountain, Parkfield, California: Bulletin of the Seismological Society of America, v. 92, p. 2493–2503.

Clarke, S.H., Jr., and Nilsen, T.H., 1973, Displacement of Eocene strata and implications for the history of offset along the San Andreas fault, central and northern California, *in* Kovach, R.L., and Nur, A., eds., Proceedings of the conference on tectonic problems of the San Andreas fault system: Stanford, California, Stanford University Publications in the Geological Sciences, v. 13, p. 358–367.

Collier, M., 1999, A land in motion: California's San Andreas fault: Berkeley, University of California Press, 118 p.

Dibblee, T.R., Jr., 1971, Geologic map of the Parkfield quadrangle, *in* Geologic maps of seventeen 15-minute quadrangles (1:62,500) along the San Andreas fault in the vicinity of King City, Coalinga, Panoche Valley, and Paso Robles, California, with index map: U.S. Geological Survey Open-File Report, 17 sheets, scale 1:62,500.

Dibblee, T.R., Jr., 1980, Geology along the San Andreas fault from Gilroy to Parkfield, *in* Streitz, R., and Sherburne, R., eds., Studies of the San Andreas fault zone in northern California: California Division of Mines and Geology Special Report 140, p. 3–18.

Gribi, E.A., 1963a, Bitterwater oil field, San Benito County, California, *in* Payne, M.B., ed., Guidebook to the geology of Salinas Valley and the San Andreas fault: Pacific Sections, American Association of Petroleum Geologists and Society of Economic Paleontologists and Mineralogists, Annual Spring Field Trip, p. 74–75.

Gribi, E.A., Jr., 1963b, The Salinas basin oil province, *in* Payne, M.B., ed., Guidebook to the geology of Salinas Valley and the San Andreas fault: Pacific Sections, American Association of Petroleum Geologists and Society of Economic Paleontologists and Mineralogists, Annual Spring Field Trip, p. 16–27.

Harden, D.R., Stenner, H., and Blatz, I., 2001, The Calaveras and San Andreas faults in and around Hollister, *in* Stoffer, P.W., and Gordon, L.C., eds., Geology and Natural History of the San Francisco Bay Area—A fieldtrip guidebook: U.S. Geological Survey Bulletin 2188, p. 145–164, http://geopubs.wr.usgs.gov/bulletin/b2188/.

Hickman, S., Zoback, M., and Ellsworth, W., 2004, Introduction to special section: Preparing for the San Andreas Fault Observatory at Depth: Geophysical Research Letters, v. 31, L12S01, doi: 10.1029/2004GL020688.

Hill, M.L., 1981, San Andreas fault: History of concepts: Geological Society of America Bulletin, v. 92, p. 112–131, doi: 10.1130/0016-7606(1981)92 <112:SAFHOC>2.0.CO;2.

Huffman, O.F., 1972, Lateral displacement of upper Miocene rocks and the Neogene history of offset along the San Andreas fault in central California: Geological Society of America Bulletin, v. 83, no. 10, p. 2913–2946.

Irwin, W.P., 1990, Geology and plate-tectonic development, *in* Wallace, R.E., ed., The San Andreas fault system, California: U.S. Geological Survey Professional Paper 1515, p. 61–80, http://education.usgs.gov/california/pp1515/chapter3.html.

Langbein, J., Borcherdt, R., Dreger, D., Fletcher, J., Hardebeck, J.L., Hellweg, M., Ji, C., Johnston, M., Murray, J.R., Nadeau, R., Rymer, M.J., and Treiman, J.A., 2005, Preliminary report on the 28 September 2004, M 6.0 Parkfield, California earthquake: Seismological Research Letters, v. 76, no. 1, p. 10–26.

Lawson, A.C., compiler, 1908, The California earthquake of April 18, 1906: Report of the State Earthquake Investigation Commission, vol. I: Carnegie Institution of Washington Publication 87, 451 p.

Lisowski, M., and Prescott, W.H., 1981, Short-range distance measurements along the San Andreas fault system in central California, 1975 to 1979: Bulletin of the Seismological Society of America, v. 71, p. 1607–1624.

Lisowski, M., Savage, J.C., and Prescott, W.H., 1991, The velocity field along the San Andreas fault in central and southern California: Journal of Geophysical Research, v. 96, p. 8369–8389.

Matthews, V., III, 1976, Correlation of Pinnacles and Neenach volcanic formations and their bearing on San Andreas fault problem: American Association of Petroleum Geologists Bulletin, v. 60, no. 12, p. 2128–2141.

Prentice, C.S., 1999, San Andreas fault: The 1906 earthquake and subsequent evolution of ideas, *in* Moores, E.M., Sloan, D., and Stout, D.L., eds., Classic Cordilleran concepts: A view from California: Geological Society of America Special Paper 338, p. 79–85.

Rogers, T.H., 1969, A trip to an active fault in the City of Hollister: Mineral Information Service, v. 22, p. 159–164.

Ross, D.C., 1984, Possible correlations of basement rocks across the San Andreas, San Gregorio-Hosgri, and Rinconada–Reliz–King City faults, California: U.S. Geological Survey Professional Paper 1317, 37 p., http://pubs.er.usgs.gov/pubs/pp/pp1317.

Rymer, M.J., 1981, Geologic map along a 12 kilometer segment of the San Andreas fault zone, southern Diablo Range, California: U.S. Geological Survey Open-File Report 81-1173, scale 1:12,000., http://pubs.er.usgs.gov/pubs/ofr/ofr811173.

Rymer, M.J., Lisowski, M., and Burford, R.O., 1984, Structural explanation for low creep rates on the San Andreas fault near Monarch Peak, central California: Bulletin of the Seismological Society of America, v. 74, p. 925–931.

Rymer, M.J., Catchings, R.D., and Goldman, M.R., 2003, Structure of the San Andreas fault zone as revealed by surface geologic mapping and high-resolution seismic profiling near Parkfield, California: Geophysical Research Abstracts, v. 5, p. 13,523.

Rymer, M.J., Tinsley, J.C., Treiman, J.A., Arrowsmith, J.R., Clahan, K.B., Rosinkski, A.M., Bryant, W.A., Snyder, H.A., Fuis, G.S., Toké, N., and Bawden, G.W., 2006, Surface fault slip associated with the 2004 Parkfield, California, earthquake: Bulletin of the Seismological Society of America (in press).

Stanley, R.G., 1987, New estimates of displacement along the San Andreas fault in central California based on paleobathymetry and paleogeography: Geology, v. 15, no. 2, p. 171–174, doi: 10.1130/0091-7613(1987) 15<171:NEODAT>2.0.CO;2.

Steinbrugge, K.V., and Zacher, E.G., 1960, Creep on the San Andreas fault: Fault creep and property damage: Seismological Society of America Bulletin, v. 50, no. 3, p. 389–396.

Stoffer, P.W., 2005, The San Andreas fault in the San Francisco Bay area, California: A geology fieldtrip guidebook to selected stops on public lands: U.S. Geological Survey Open-File Report 2005-1127, 133 p., http://pubs.er.usgs.gov/pubs/ofr/2005/1127.

Thurber, C., Roecker, S., Zhang, H., Baher, S., and Ellsworth, W., 2004, Fine-scale structure of the San Andreas fault zone and location of the SAFOD target earthquakes: Geophysical Research Letters, v. 31, L12S02, doi: 10.1029/2003GL019398.

Tocher, D., 1960, Creep on the San Andreas fault—Creep rate and related measurements at Vineyard, California: Bulletin of the Seismological Society of America, v. 50, p. 396–404.

Unsworth, M., and Bedrosian, P.A., 2004, Electrical resistivity at the SAFOD site from magnetotelluric exploration: Geophysical Research Letters, v. 31, L12S05, doi:10.1029/2003GL019405.

Vedder, J.G., and Wallace, R.E., 1970, Map showing recently active breaks along the San Andreas and related faults between Cholame Valley and Tejon Pass, California: U.S. Geological Survey Miscellaneous Geologic Investigations Map 1-574, scale 1:24,000.

Wagner, D.L., Greene, H.G., Saucedo, G.J., Pridmore, C.L., Watkins, S.E., Little, J.D., and Bizzarro, J.J., 2002, Geologic map of the Monterey 30′ × 60′ quadrangle and adjacent areas, California: A digital database: California Geological Survey CD, v. 2002-04.

Wallace, R.E., ed., 1990, The San Andreas fault system, California: U.S. Geological Survey Professional Paper 1515, 283 p., http://education.usgs.gov/california/pp1515/copyright.html.

The Hayward fault

Coordinators
Doris Sloan
Department of Earth and Planetary Science, University of California, Berkeley, California 94720, USA
Donald Wells
Geomatrix Consultants, Inc., 2101 Webster Street, 12th Floor, Oakland, California 94612, USA

Contributors: ***Glenn Borchardt,*** *Soil Tectonics, P.O. Box 5335, Berkeley, California 94705, USA;* ***John Caulfield,*** *Jacobs Associates, 465 California Street, Suite 1000, San Francisco, California 94104-1824, USA;* ***David M. Doolin,*** *Earthquake Engineering Research Center, 1301 South 46th Street, Building 451, University of California–Berkeley, Richmond, California 94804, USA;* ***John Eidinger,*** *G&E Engineering Systems Inc., 6315 Swainland Rd, Oakland, California 94611, USA;* ***Lind S. Gee,*** *Albuquerque Seismological Laboratory, U.S. Geological Survey, P.O. Box 82010, Albuquerque New Mexico 87198-2010, USA;* ***Russell W. Graymer,*** *U.S. Geological Survey, 345 Middlefield Rd, MS 975, Menlo Park, California 94025, USA;* ***Peggy Hellweg,*** *Berkeley Seismological Laboratory, University of California, Berkeley, California 94720, USA;* ***Alan Kropp,*** *Alan Kropp & Associates, 2140 Shattuck Avenue, Suite 910, Berkeley, California 94704, USA;* ***Jim Lienkaemper,*** *U.S. Geological Survey, 345 Middlefield Rd, MS 975, Menlo Park, California 94025, USA;* ***Charles Rabamad,*** *Office of Emergency Services, 3650 Schriever Ave, Mather, California 95655, USA;* ***Nicholas Sitar,*** *Department of Civil and Environmental Engineering, Earthquake Engineering Research Center, University of California, Berkeley, California 94720, USA;* ***Heidi Stenner,*** *U.S. Geological Survey, 345 Middlefield Rd, MS 975, Menlo Park, California 94025, USA;* ***Stephen Tobriner,*** *Architecture Department, University of California, Berkeley, California 94720, USA;* ***David Tsztoo,*** *Special Projects Division, East Bay Municipal Utility District, 375 11th Street, M.S. 303, Oakland, California 94607, USA;* ***Mary Lou Zoback,*** *U.S. Geological Survey, 345 Middlefield Rd, MS 975, Menlo Park, California 94025, USA*

OVERVIEW OF FIELD TRIP

This field guide consists of eleven stops at sites that illustrate the geological, geophysical, geographic, and engineering aspects of the Hayward fault in the East Bay. Section I (Stops 1–4) consists of stops that are part of the University of California at Berkeley (UC-Berkeley), including research facilities, retrofit of campus buildings, and geomorphic features along the fault. Section II (Stops 5 and 6) consists of stops along the Hayward fault north of the UC-Berkeley main campus, and Section III (stops 7–11) consists of stops related to the Hayward fault south of the UC-Berkeley main campus (Fig. 1). Stops are designed to illustrate geomorphic features of the fault, the effects of fault creep on structures sited on the fault, and retrofit design of structures to mitigate potential future deformation due to fault rupture.

Keywords: Hayward fault, seismic retrofit, fault creep, fault displacement, shake table, Seismic Simulator, paleoseismology.

SECTION I: THE HAYWARD FAULT AT UC-BERKELEY

The UC-Berkeley campus is located on the eastern alluvial plain rising from San Francisco Bay, at an elevation between 300 and 500 feet and abutting the Oakland-Berkeley Hills. The Hayward fault is located along the topographic interface between the gently sloping plain and the hills (Fig. 1), and poses a significant ground-rupture and seismic shaking hazard to the UC-Berkeley campus (Fig. 2).

The location of the Hayward fault across the Berkeley campus is known from interpretation of pre-development geomorphic features observed on topographic maps and photographs, from fault trenching studies, and from observations of fault creep-related deformation to man-made structures. Distinct right-lateral offsets of Hamilton, Blackberry, and Strawberry Creeks, and an ancient landslide in the area of the Greek Theater, indicate the general location of the fault. In addition, two former (and now dry, "beheaded") channels of Strawberry Creek cross the Berkeley

Sloan, D., Wells, D., Borchardt, G., Caulfield, J., Doolin, D.M., Eidinger, J., Gee, L.S., Graymer, R.W., Hellweg, P., Kropp, A., Lienkaemper, J., Rabamad, C., Sitar, N., Stenner, H., Tobriner, S., Tsztoo, D., and Zoback, M.L., 2006, The Hayward fault, *in* Prentice, C.S., Scotchmoor, J.G., Moores, E.M., and Kiland, J.P., eds., 1906 San Francisco Earthquake Centennial Field Guides: Field trips associated with the 100th Anniversary Conference, 18–23 April 2006, San Francisco, California: Geological Society of America Field Guide 7, p. 273–331, doi: 10.1130/2006.1906SF(17). For permission to copy, contact editing@geosociety.org.

Figure 1. Map of the Hayward fault and stops.

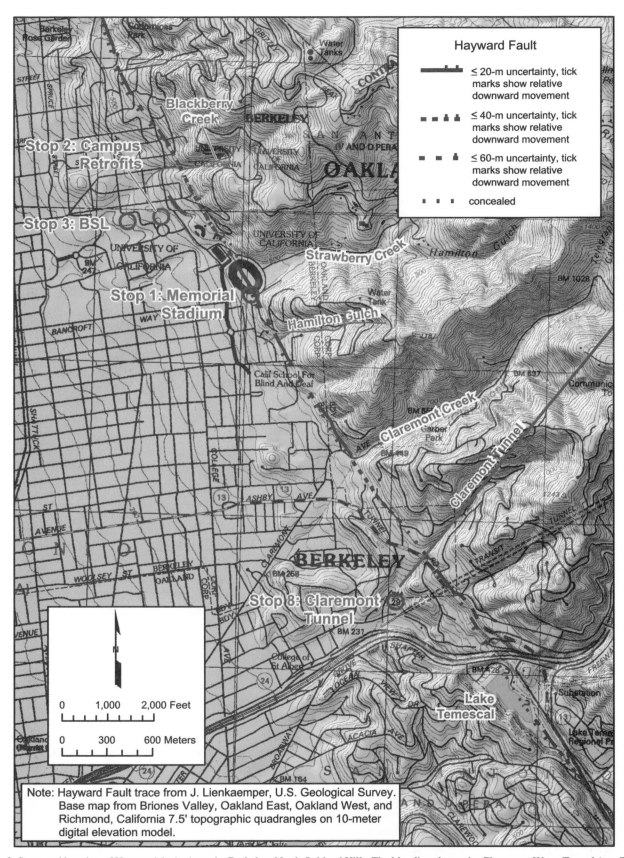

Figure 2. Stops and location of Hayward fault along the Berkeley–North Oakland Hills. The blue line shows the Claremont Water Tunnel (see Stop 8).

campus: one flowed through the East Gate and beneath the site of the Mining Circle (Fig. 3). An older channel flowed down Hearst Avenue. Fault trenching studies in the area of the Foothill Housing complex, Bowles Hall, Memorial Stadium, and the Smyth-Fernwald housing complex have identified primary and secondary traces of the Hayward fault. Right-lateral offsets of curbs, culverts, walkways, and buildings across the campus indicate the location of the creeping trace of the fault.

Stop 1: Memorial Stadium (Donald Wells, Nicholas Sitar, and David M. Doolin)

Significance of the site

Memorial Stadium (Fig. 4) was built in 1923 as a tribute to World War I heroes. It sits directly astride the creeping trace of the Hayward fault, at the base of Strawberry Canyon where Strawberry Creek exits the Berkeley Hills. The university is currently developing plans to renovate the stadium, including improvements to mitigate fault rupture hazard to the structure.

Accessibility

This is University of California at Berkeley property; restrooms are available, and there is limited parking in the surrounding neighborhood (very difficult when school is in session). Accessible from AC Transit Bus No. 51 and from downtown Berkeley Bay Area Rapid Transit (BART) station. From BART, walk east one block to campus.

GPS Coordinates

South Entrance to Stadium: 37.8700°N, 122.2504°W.

Directions

From San Francisco, take Highway 80 east (Bay Bridge) to Ashby Avenue exit (first Berkeley exit). Continue east 2 mi on Ashby Avenue to Telegraph Avenue, and turn left. Follow Telegraph Avenue north (0.6 mi) to Dwight Way and turn right. Continue east on Dwight Way to Piedmont Avenue (0.5 mi). Continue on Dwight Way one block to Prospect Street and turn left. Follow Prospect Street two blocks (0.25 mi) north to the south end of the stadium.

Stop Description

Memorial Stadium (Fig. 4) is an integral part of the UC-Berkeley campus. The stadium hosts football games, houses the athletic department offices, and is eligible for inclusion in the National Register of Historic Places. At the time of construction, the presence and youthful activity of the Hayward fault was known, but the earthquake hazard was not appreciated. Although the last major earthquake on the Hayward fault occurred in 1868, within the memory of residents still alive at the time Memorial Stadium was constructed, this earthquake did not produce surface rupture along the fault in Berkeley.

Prior to construction of the stadium, a faulted linear ridge, referred to as a shutter ridge, extended across the mouth of Strawberry Creek, forming a natural bowl at the mouth of the canyon. Strawberry Creek flowed westward to the mouth of the canyon, was deflected northward ~1100 ft along the shutter ridge, and resumed a westward flow around the end of the shutter ridge (Fig. 3). The stadium was constructed across the shutter ridge, natural bowl, and edge of the Berkeley Hills. The northeast side of the stadium is founded on a cut-slope in Cretaceous Great Valley Sequence sandstone; the west side is founded on dense alluvium-colluvium on the shutter ridge; and the north end, south end, and southeast side of the stadium are founded on fill placed in the creek channel and natural bowl. Strawberry Creek was buried in a culvert beneath the stadium and the area where Kleeberger Athletic Field was later constructed on the north side of the stadium. A second culvert was later constructed beneath Stadium Rim Way, crossing the hill north of the stadium and continuing beneath Kleeberger Field to carry excess flow from Strawberry Creek (Fig. 5). The creek now emerges from the culverts behind the Women's Faculty Club near the intersection of Centennial Drive and Gayley Road.

The position of the shutter ridge, location of changes in channel morphology of Strawberry Creek, and locations of fault creep in the area of the stadium show that the main creeping trace of the Hayward fault bisects the stadium from the south end through the north end (Fig. 3). The stadium structure has been deformed as a result of ongoing fault creep. As much as 15 inches (38 cm) of creep may have occurred beneath the stadium since it was built, assuming an average creep rate of ~4.7 mm/yr (Galehouse, 2002). Creep on the Hayward fault has resulted in cracking and separation of exterior and interior walls and joints, tilting of interior columns, and offset of expansion joints along the stadium's rim.

From the Prospect Court parking lot, climb the outside stairs along the south side of the stadium. Note the diagonal fractures extending along the south wall of the stadium. About halfway up the stairs, the fractures change orientation from down-to-the-west to down-to-the-east (Section LL, bottom profile on Fig. 6). This transition is consistent with the projected location of the creeping trace of the fault as identified inside the stadium. A similar inversion in the direction of fracturing occurs on the north exterior wall of the stadium, east of the north access tunnel (Section A, top profile on Fig. 6). Although there is extensive fill under the north and south ends of the stadium, the zone of extensive fracturing is localized and does not extend across the area where the thickest fill occurs below the stadium walls. Therefore, because of the orientation and localized nature, the zone of extensive fracturing does not appear to be the result of settlement of fill. In addition, and in contrast to the extensive fracturing in the exterior walls at the north and south ends of the stadium, only a few, short vertical fractures occur along the western exterior wall of the stadium (Section C on top profile, and Sections HH–K on lower profile of Fig. 6). Examples of the types of fractures and inferred mechanism for the origin of these fractures in the exterior stadium walls are shown on Figure 6 and in Doolin et al. (2005).

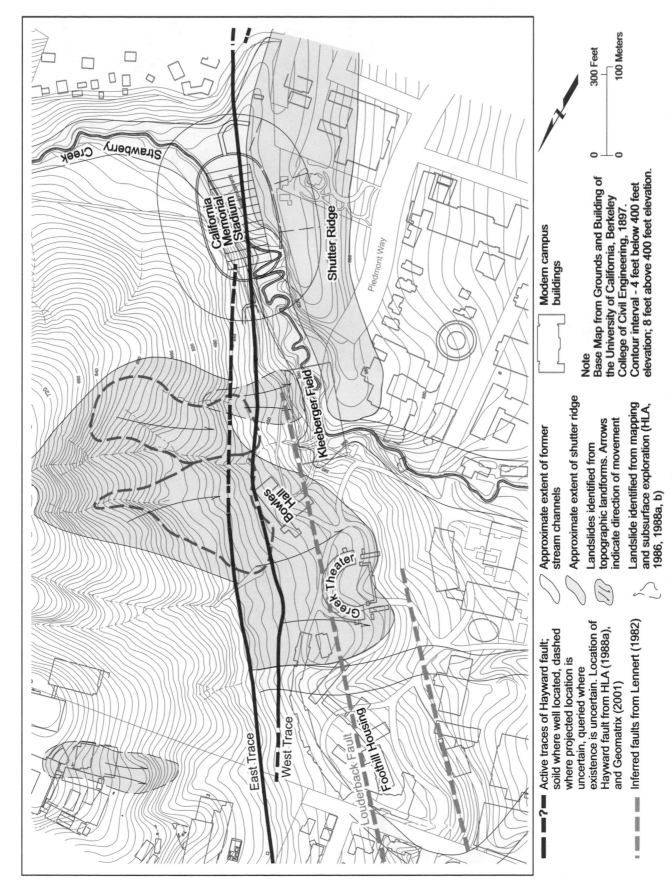

Figure 3. Geomorphic features and location of Hayward fault at the University of California, Berkeley. Modified from Geomatrix Consultants (2001).

Figure 4. Memorial Stadium on the University of California–Berkeley campus. Kite photograph by Charles Beuton, University of California–Berkeley.

Return to the parking lot level. There is an expansion joint on the west side of the first entryway in the stadium. The stadium was originally built in two halves, to allow motion on the Hayward fault during a large earthquake. Apparently, it was thought that in such an event, the stadium structure would just gently separate along the junction. The walls of the stadium have tilted, forming about a 6-inch-wide gap at the top that is covered by a metal plate. The ~15 inches of fault creep occurring since construction of the stadium are accommodated in part by fracturing of the exterior wall along the stairs and by slip and rotation of the stadium walls along the expansion joint.

Enter the stadium through the archway at the base of the stairs. Note the tall interior columns supporting the stadium seating deck. The columns are progressively tilted around the south end of the stadium, from east (near the tunnel to the south end of the field) to west at the expansion joint (at the double columns). The creeping trace of the fault is constrained to pass between the first vertical column (on the east) and the first tilted column on the west, near the entrance of the tunnel to the field (Fig. 7). The tilting of the columns occurs because the stadium seating deck at the top of the columns is founded on fill east of the fault and is effectively cantilevered to the west across the creeping trace of the fault. Thus, the bases of the columns west of the fault are moving northwest, past the tops of the columns, which are attached to the stadium seating deck. The cantilevered deck section extends westward to the expansion joint. On the north side of the stadium, the orientation and locations

of tilted columns indicate that the portion of the seating deck on the west (founded on the shutter ridge) is cantilevered eastward across the creeping trace of the fault.

Continue through the mezzanine level to the seats. Walk up the steps to the rim of the stadium to view the displacement at the top of the expansion joint (Sections K–KK). Walk down the steps to the field level to see deformation in the seating area. Note the separation of the stairs and the concrete footing for the seating decks and the minor cracking in the small wall around the field at the base of the steps (Sections KK–L-LL). Similar deformation is observed in Sections XX–X-WW at the north end of the stadium (Fig. 7). A series of fractures is also present on the east wall of the north access tunnel. Outside the north tunnel entrance, extensive fracturing occurs in the wall extending up the exterior stairs to the east (top profile on Fig. 6). The interior staircase up to the mezzanine level, which is accessed through the first entryway east of the tunnel, also is fractured due to fault creep (Fig. 7A). These features show that creep displacement on a narrow fault trace is accommodated across a wider zone within the stadium structure above the fault.

Logging of fault trenches extending from the curb at the parking lot and up the hill directly north of the exterior stairs revealed weakly defined shearing (attributed to creep in the soil) and several small faults in the young colluvium along the lower portion of the hill (Fig. 3). Fault creep deformation identified in the Strawberry Creek culverts (beneath the hillslope north of the trenches and beneath the stadium playing

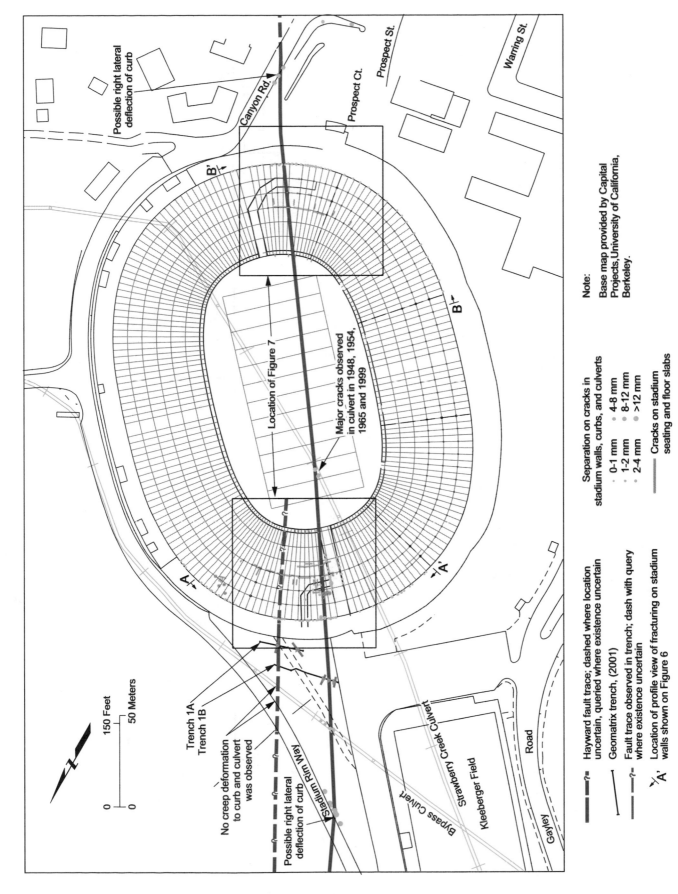

Figure 5. Plan map of Memorial Stadium area showing location of creep-related deformation. Modified from Geomatrix Consultants (2001).

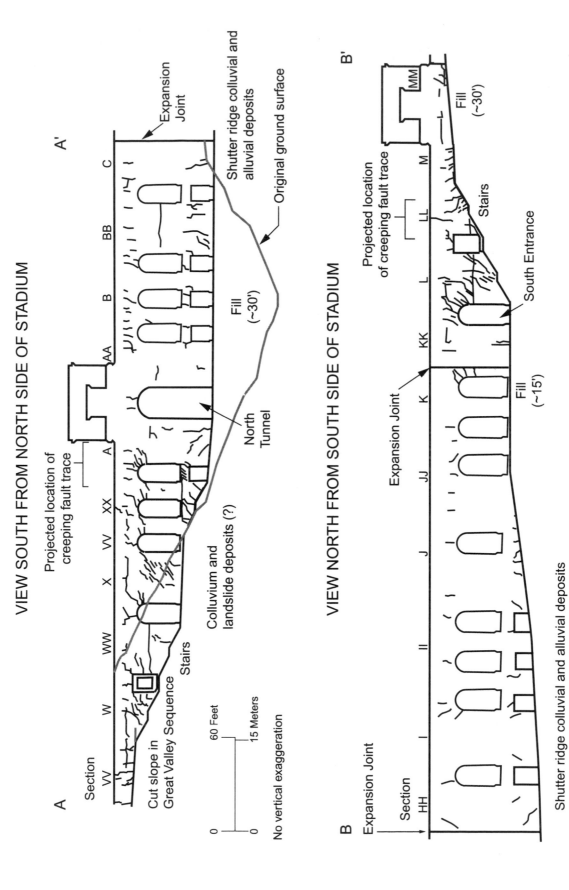

Figure 6. Elevation views of the northern (B, at bottom above) and southern (A, at top above) ends of Memorial Stadium. The diagonal, vertical, and horizontal fractures are interpreted as fault related, settlement induced, and construction induced, respectively. Modified from Geomatrix Consultants (2001).

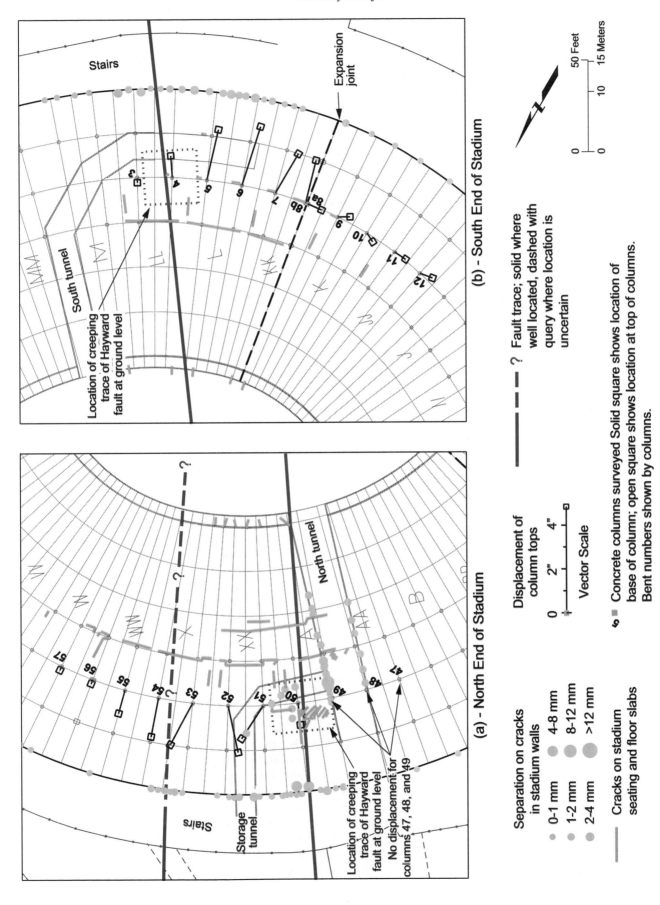

(a) - North End of Stadium

(b) - South End of Stadium

Figure 7. Enlarged plan views of the northern (a, top left) and southern (b, top right) ends of the stadium. Modified from Geomatrix Consultants (2001).

field) and in the curb on Stadium Rim Way north of the stadium align with the zone of shearing observed in the trenches, and with the location of inversion of fracturing in the north and south stadium walls. The alignment of these features observed at or below ground level, along with the deformation to the columns inside the stadium, constrains the location of the creeping trace of the Hayward fault. The extent of shearing and faulting in the trenches and the width of fracturing in the stadium (attributed to fault creep) is used to infer a wider zone through the stadium where fault rupture may occur (Geomatrix Consultants, 2001).

The university and the athletic department are currently developing a plan to renovate the stadium. The plan is to preserve the historic character of the stadium while creating a first-rate facility that improves life safety, enhances the game-day experience for fans, and provides the football team and twelve other men's and women's intercollegiate teams with space for a state-of-the-art training and development and coaching center. The university and its consultants also are developing plans to improve the seismic safety of the stadium and to mitigate the surface rupture hazard. These plans are in the early stages of development but may involve reconstructing portions of the stadium above the fault zone on a mat foundation. The reconstructed sections would be connected to the eastern and western sections of the stadium across a series of seismic joints that would accommodate fault creep and fault displacement in the event of an earthquake. Specific considerations that may be addressed in mitigating the fault rupture hazard are the likely fault displacement during an earthquake on the Hayward fault, the amount of deformation that may propagate through the fill above the fault, and the width of the zone of deformation at the foundation level.

Additional information on Memorial Stadium, the Hayward fault, and the geology of the campus is found on "The Geology of Bear Territory" Web site at http://seismo.berkeley.edu/geotour/, and in Doolin et al. (2005), Borchardt et al. (2000), and Hirschfeld et al. (1999).

Stop 2: Seismic Retrofits on the UC-Berkeley Campus (Stephen Tobriner)

Significance of the Site

The Hayward fault cuts across the eastern end of the UC-Berkeley campus; this trip will examine seismic retrofits to buildings on the campus. The buildings illustrate different retrofit strategies, each designed to solve the specific seismic problem posed by the particular building. These buildings represent only a portion of the scores of buildings retrofitted on the UC-Berkeley campus. The retrofitted buildings on this tour include historic South Hall, built in 1870; the Hearst Mining Building, designed by John Gale Howard and completed in 1907; Hildebrand and Latimer Halls, designed by Ansen and Allen in 1960; and Wurster Hall, designed by Esherick, Olsen, DeMars and completed in 1964.

Accessibility

BART, Berkeley Station; AC Transit; public restrooms are available; parking on street or in the University Hall West Lot, Addison and Oxford Streets; Martin Luther King Jr. Student Union Garage, Bancroft below Telegraph.

GPS Coordinates

South Entrance to Memorial Stadium: 37.8700°N, 122.2504°W (WGS84/NAD83); Campanile 37.8720°N, 122.2578°W (WGS84/NAD83).

Directions

See the directions under Stop 1 to reach the UC-Berkeley campus. Walk to the grassy area west of the Campanile and look west at South Hall (see Fig. 8, map of campus).

Stop Description

Our tour of seismically retrofitted buildings on the UC-Berkeley campus (Fig. 8) begins southwest of the Campanile, facing west toward the façade of present-day South Hall (A, Fig. 8). Surrounding this area are campus buildings shaped and reshaped by seismic engineering. Chief among them are the oldest buildings of the group, South Hall (1870–1873) and the Campanile (1914–1916). These two buildings were designed from the outset to be earthquake-resistant: South Hall in reaction to the earthquake of 1868 and the Campanile in reaction to the earthquake of 1906. The retrofit programs of the university have also been prompted by earthquakes. The Santa Barbara earthquake of 1925 and the Long Beach earthquake of 1933 prompted a seismic retrofit for Stephen's Hall, the old student union, just to the left (southeast). The San Fernando earthquake of 1971 stimulated the university to reevaluate its building stock in relation to earthquake danger in 1978. Finally, the Loma Prieta earthquake of 1989 forced the university to confront the problems of seismic safety. With some retrofits already completed, university officials and California law makers saw what could happen as they witnessed tremendous losses in the 1994 Northridge earthquake in Southern California and the 1995 Kobe earthquake in Japan. The Hayward fault, as you shall see on this tour, runs through the campus, making UC-Berkeley one of the most seismically hazardous university campuses in the world.

After scattered retrofits, the university began in earnest to make the entire campus earthquake-resistant in one of the most ambitious programs, not only in California, but in the world. Usually, retrofits and seismic upgrades occur after a great disaster. UC-Berkeley's program is a mitigation program, confronting damage before it occurs. In the late 1990s, the university imaginatively combined a one-time grant from the Federal Emergency Management Agency (FEMA), funds for seismic upgrading from California Proposition 122, and university money into a single fund to support a new program called the Seismic Action Plan for Facilities Enhancement and Renewal (SAFER), committed to invest $20 million per

MAP OF CAMPUS

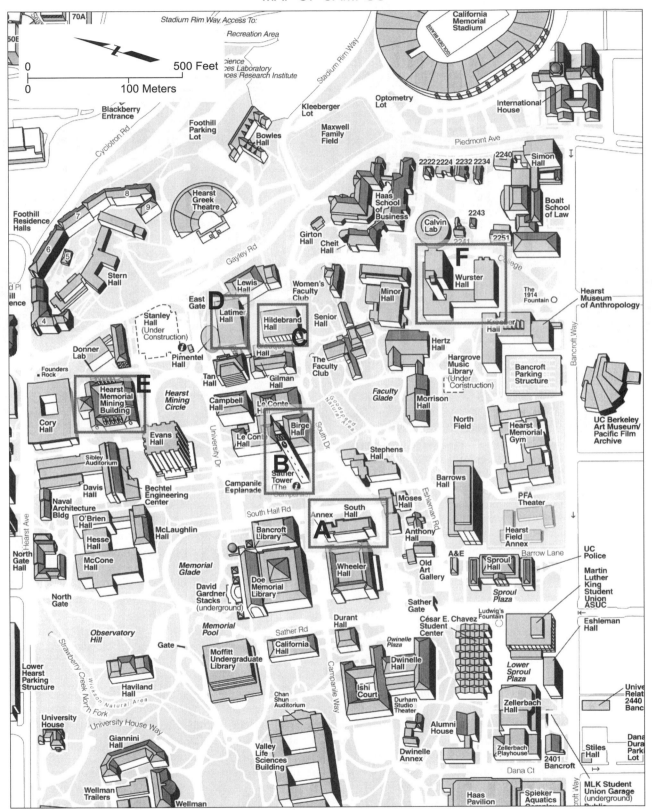

Figure 8. Map of the campus, showing retrofitted buildings described in the field guide. A—South Hall; B—The Campanile; C—Hildebrand Hall; D—Latimer Hall; E—Hearst Memorial Mining Building; F—Wurster Hall.

Figure 9. South Hall, 1873. Diagram of reinforcement in South Hall. A—bond iron courses through masonry; B—iron pilasters held in place by bond iron; C—the position of floor anchors in masonry; D—the position of internal iron girders.

year over 20 years to make the campus safe during earthquakes. The UC-Berkeley program is a model for seismic mitigation. Each building has been retrofitted using a system uniquely adapted to it, so each is different. Today we will examine just a few of the buildings that have been retrofitted on this campus.

On our tour we are going to see a strange phenomenon, best represented by South Hall: Even buildings originally constructed to be seismically resistant sometimes have to be retrofitted. Because seismic engineering has progressed since it was first built in the 1870s, South Hall was gutted and reinforced to be an even more effective earthquake-resistant building in the 1980s. Likewise, sometimes modern buildings, like Doe Library or the Bancroft Library (to your right), were not built strongly enough to resist earthquakes, so they have to be retrofitted. Unfortunately, the retrofits on campus will not make these buildings "earthquake-proof." Engineers never use that term because they cannot guarantee buildings they construct will be earthquake proof, but *earthquake-resistant*. These retrofits are designed primarily to save the lives of the students, staff, and professors.

South Hall

South Hall (Fig. 9), the oldest building on campus, was initially designed to be earthquake-resistant in 1870 because the university regents had seen building failures in San Francisco in the earthquakes of 1865 and 1868. The regents understood that wood buildings resisted seismic forces more effectively than brick masonry, and they considered having South Hall constructed of wood. The problem with wood is that it burns and is less monumental than brick. So they decided on brick, but they stipulated that the new building had to be earthquake-resistant.

Let us take a minute to try to understand the problems inherent in making a brick building earthquake resistant. Buildings are designed to support static or vertical loads. These include the weight of the materials in the walls, floors, and roof (dead loads), and whatever rests on the floors and can be moved, like people and furniture, as well as whatever falls on the roof, like snow (live loads). These loads are usually applied to the structure slowly and evenly, pressing down vertically.

However, the waves generated by an earthquake create dynamic forces that vibrate the structure and change rapidly. As the building vibrates in response to seismic ground motion, inertial forces are created within it. When it is pushed to one side, it rebounds, but because of inertial forces, it continues past its former resting position to bend in the opposite direction. Because buildings are primarily designed to resist vertical forces, sidewise (lateral) forces are the most dangerous in earthquakes.

Imagine South Hall in an earthquake. Think of it moving up and down and side to side in relation to ground shaking. Can you visualize what would happen if you pushed it strongly to the left or right? Lateral forces are transferred from the ground through walls to diaphragms, like floors and roofs, and then back to the ground again through the walls. The forces acting upon the walls are called shear forces. Shear forces, which tend to distort the shapes of walls, occur when lateral forces push a wall along its length. If a brick wall is pushed sideways by lateral forces, it will resist until the bond breaks between the bricks, or the bricks themselves break. A diagonal crack, called a shear crack, will appear, or sometimes an X-shaped crack. When you push against a wooden pencil, it can bend. Because stone and bricks are brittle, they can't bend, so they crack and eventually break.

Even in an extensive uninterrupted brick wall, bricks are problematic in earthquakes. The greater the mass—the heavier the wall—the greater the inertial forces an earthquake will create within it. In accordance with Newton's Second Law of Motion, $F = M \times A$, inertial force (F) is equal to the mass of the building (M, equivalent to its weight at ground level) times the acceleration (A). When shaken side to side, a properly braced, square, wooden, three-story structure on a sound foundation with well-tied diaphragms will bend because of wood's ductility and elasticity. A similar masonry building is heavier, stiffer, and more brittle, and instead of bending to dissipate energy, the brittle masonry will crack, or the walls may rupture and collapse.

Engineers and architects in the San Francisco of the 1860s were alarmed by this problem of brittle brick masonry, and they tried to solve it by designing buildings that included more flexible materials to hold them together. They also understood, as do modern engineers, that a building must be tied together to act as a unit in an earthquake.

South Hall as a Seismically Resistant Structure, 1870

South Hall was designed by David Farquharson (of Knitzer and Farquharson architects) probably using the ideas of the first design for the building by John Wright. Farquharson's seismic system was an architectural composite; it depended upon a building's brick walls, wood supports, wood diagonal sheathing, wood floors, iron tie-bars, iron anchors, and iron columns working together. He considered how every part of the structure, from its foundation to its chimneys, could be tied together. He believed that a building's structure, as well as its decoration, could aid in its seismic resistance. His use of seismically resistant ornament heralded a new style of architecture that was beautiful because of its frank expression of purpose.

South Hall is bound together by ribbons of iron called bond iron (Fig. 10), and the brickwork and lime mortar are exceptionally strong, even by modern standards. Pieces of bond iron measuring two and a half inches by three-eighths of an inch were worked through the brick above and below the apertures on each story and at the joist level. These pieces of iron were spliced together with two bolts at each joint to form a continuous belt around the whole structure. As each belt of bond iron approached an end wall of the structure, it was forged into a threaded rod. Depending upon their position, these rods either entered heavy corner impost blocks or went directly through the wall of the building to be bolted to iron pilasters on the exterior. This network was clearly intended to hold the whole structure together should the bricks begin to fail.

A second line of defense can be seen on the building's exterior, which is decorated with vertical ornamental panels made of cast iron. They appear at the corners and sides of the building, often with the threaded rods of the bond iron protruding through them. The rods are secured to the panels by decorative bolts that form a regular pattern, appearing even where no rods are present. Rather than securing the panels (which are held in place by special iron hooks), these bolts unite the bond iron from one side of the building to the other. This linking suggests that Farquharson hoped to form a sort of exoskeleton.

Farquharson seems to have taken great care to make sure the floors functioned as diaphragms, tying the exterior walls to them and thus helping the building move as a unit. South Hall is an I-shaped building with a corridor running down the middle. Farquharson lapped every other 4 × 16-inch joist over the top of the corridor, effectively tying the building together. Every joist in the structure was either nailed to a hanger or extended out into the brick walls. Large, round iron anchors are buried three widths into the brick exterior walls, bolted to the end of huge iron angles attached to the joists.

If the brickwork began to break up, vertical iron Ts implanted in the north and south walls of each the large lecture halls on the wings of South Hall would provide support (Fig. 11). Two great iron girders spanned the north and the south lecture halls, supporting 4 × 16-inch wooden joists. The vertical iron Ts supported the iron girders on each side of the room, creating a redundant brick and iron wall support; the iron would probably have buckled without brick around it. Farquharson's construction points to the significance of redundancy, another important idea in earthquake-resistant construction.

The Retrofit of South Hall, 1980s

When engineers examined South Hall in the 1980s, it was classed as an unreinforced masonry building (URM). The engineering firm of Rutherford and Chekene decided they could not depend on Farquharson's solutions because of certain design flaws in the building. There were notable weaknesses. For example, the horizontal planes in the building—floors and roofs—were intended to act as diaphragms, distributing loads to the exterior walls. But the roof structure was poorly con-

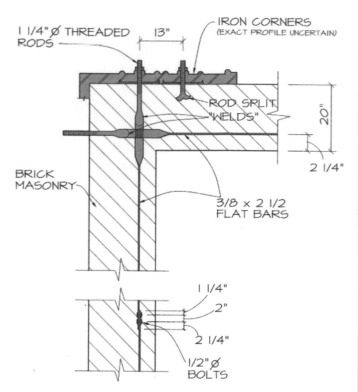

Figure 10. Diagram of bond iron in walls and attachment to external iron pilasters in South Hall.

ceived and badly built. The entire roof assembly needed to be rebuilt and many of its members replaced. The engineers also felt the many windows and fireplace flues in the façades weakened the wall planes to such an extent that they might fail in shear, that is, "in-plane." Because of these problems, they gutted the interior and tied the backs of the bricks to a reinforced concrete wall of sprayed shotcrete, which they built on the back side of the original wall. In order to do the work, they dismounted (and subsequently remounted) all the decorative woodwork and plaster on the walls. They also installed new floors to work more effectively as diaphragms, and tied the building together vertically by running reinforcement rods through its walls and the fireplace flues. When they were through with the interior, they removed the chimneys and substituted plastic replicas. The retrofit was done so carefully that both the interior and exterior of South Hall are remarkably similar in appearance to the original building.

The Jane K. Sather Campanile

To the right is the Campanile (B, Fig. 8), designed in 1914 by John Galen Howard, engineer Erle L. Cope, and consulting engineer Charles Derleth Jr. A professor of civil engineering, Derleth was the designer of the structural system that was intended to resist earthquakes. Walk up to the walls of the Campanile and look at the corners. Look at the sides of the tower and the canopy over the front door. Why do you suppose that

Figure 11. South Hall wall in demolition. Iron T-shaped columns (B) hold up girders (A) with bond iron in outside walls. Note one row of bricks has been removed.

there appear to be subtle barriers of plants and the canopy around the tower?

Derleth designed the tower to be both strong and flexible. He studied how towers failed in San Francisco in 1906 and decided his would never fail. One of the strategies he decided upon was to build a steel frame and use reinforced concrete as a backing for the granite veneer on the exterior. In order to make the tower strong and stiff, but also flexible enough to bend, he staggered the braced floors with unbraced floors. If you are here when the tower is open, go into the lobby and look at the plans. Then take the elevator to the top, not just to see the view, but to examine the structure of the tower, which is easy to see. Derleth made sure his tower would rock back and forth in an earthquake slowly enough as to be out of resonance with the earthquake. To be in resonance would be very dangerous. When we instinctively kick our feet while on a swing, we are attempting to put ourselves in resonance with the arc of the swing. When buildings are in resonance with earthquakes, as in the Mexico City earthquake of 1985, they can shake themselves to pieces.

Have you solved the problem of the planting? The corners tell the story. It wasn't shaking, but expansion and contraction caused by heat gain, combined with minute movements of the tower and decaying anchorage of the granite that contributed to its cracking. In the 1950s, while the problem was under investigation, the university erected the canopy to protect the entrance and the planting to keep us at a safe distance from the tower. In 1976, the granite was repaired and recaulked, but still the barriers remain. Unfortunately, seismic retrofits require more than planting and canopies.

Walk east on the road next to Strawberry Creek, passing Le Conte and Gilman Halls on our left, until we see a concrete and brick building hovering in front of us. Walk up to it and stand at the southeastern corner of its façade.

Hildebrand Hall

In the 1960s, the university began work on three buildings that would make up the core of its chemistry department, Latimer (1960–1963), Hildebrand Hall (1963–1966), and the huge, oval Pimentel Hall auditorium (1963–1964). The architects were Anshen and Allen, who in this case wanted to fashion handsome scientific buildings in the corporate mold of the day. The engineer of one of these buildings, Hildebrand Hall (C in Fig. 8; Fig. 12), was the famous T.Y. Lin (1912–2003). Although earthquake forces were specified in the building codes, no powerful earthquake had yet tested the engineering aesthetic of the day, which focused on economy and invention. T.Y. Lin was known internationally as the "father of pre-stressed concrete," a technology that fundamentally broadened the possibilities of architecture, engineering, and construction. Although pre-stressing technology was first invented in the 1940s, T.Y. Lin was the first to make it practical, economical, and popular. He enthusiastically recognized its enormous potential, not only for saving money but also for bringing a new freedom to architecture. Hildebrand Hall exemplifies the potentialities of pre-stressed concrete.

Reinforced concrete derives its strength from embedding steel, which is extremely strong in tension, in concrete, which is strong in compression but weak in tension. In a conventional reinforced concrete slab or beam, the normal bending forces put the bottom portion into tension, causing cracking at the bottom part of the beam. In a pre-stressed slab or beam, an initial tension is applied to the reinforcing steel prior to the pour. After the concrete cures, the steel tendons are released, causing the entire slab to go into compression, thus eliminating the tension stress at the bottom portion of the concrete and increasing the capacity of the slab. Pre-stressed slabs and beams can therefore be much thinner than conventional reinforced concrete, decreasing the weight and cost of each element and allowing for more innovative designs. The savings can approach 50% in concrete weight and 20% in steel weight.

Hildebrand Hall lies adjacent to the south side of Latimer Hall. A system of underground passageways connects the two buildings and other adjacent labs. Hildebrand Hall consists of two partially underground floors and a three-story tower that rises from the plaza level. You can actually walk underneath Hildebrand to a small courtyard and up two curving stairs to Latimer. (If this passage is closed, it is possible to walk around the left side of the Hildebrand façade and upstairs to the plaza.)

On the plaza, turn to the southeast to look at Hildebrand (Fig. 13). The first level of the tower houses the chemistry library, whereas the two lower floors and the two upper floors contain labs, workshops, and storage spaces. The top two floors cantilever dramatically over the glazed library level. The building's site slopes equally dramatically to the south, exaggerating the effect of the cantilever. Designed to achieve architectural harmony with the adjacent buildings, the materials palette included concrete, glass, and terracotta.

Remember the problem of shear? Shear-resisting elements are absent here to a degree almost shocking by today's standards. The concrete stair and elevator enclosures provided the only lateral force resistance in the building. These enclosures shared the gravity loads with eight interior columns and a series of box and fin columns at the edge of the first floor. Precast panels were hung from the cantilevered second and third floors to create a façade. In earthquake country, this design was a disaster waiting to happen. As in South Hall, engineers and architects were innocent of how to design appropriately for earthquakes. But there is a difference: Farquharson had tried to use redundancy and multiple systems. T.Y. Lin was more intent on a single, light, cheap, beautiful system.

In 1997, Forell/Elsesser, Rutherford and Chekene and Degenkolb Engineers completed a joint seismic analysis of Hildebrand Hall. The analysis predicted that the interior columns would punch through the floor slabs, causing widespread structural collapse on all three floors of the tower. The precast panels' connections to the second and third floor slabs were expected to break due to lateral motion, and the library mezzanine was expected to collapse due to a lack of lateral resistance.

Anshen and Allen and Forell/Elsesser investigated numerous retrofit strategies for Hildebrand Hall and finally decided to use unbonded braces, which were a very new and promising addition to anti-seismic technology. You can see these braces on the plaza floor of the building (Fig. 14). Unbonded braces work in a simple and elegant manner. In a traditional steel cross brace, lateral forces are resisted axially by each cross-member. An applied lateral force will stretch one cross-member in tension and shorten the other in compression. Unbonded braces are made of both steel—which is strong in tension—and concrete—which is strong in compression, enabling the braces to exhibit nearly identical properties in both tension and compression. In addition to the braces, new concrete shear walls, providing lateral support, were added to the two lowest stories, and on the east and west side a portion of the shear walls extend up to the roof. The walls around the stair cores were strengthened and reinforcement was

Figure 12. Hildebrand Hall seen from the southwest.

added to the column-to-slab connections, mitigating the threat of punching shear by the columns. The connections between the precast panel hangers and the roof and floor slabs were strengthened as was the mezzanine level of the library.

Turn around; on the north side of the Plaza is Latimer Hall.

Latimer Hall

Architects Anshen and Allen also designed Latimer Hall (D in Fig. 8; Fig. 15). However, instead of T.Y. Lin, the engineer chosen for Latimer was Henry Degenkolb (1913–1989), a world-renowned expert in earthquake engineering. Despite the

difference in the engineers' expertise, both buildings were found to be seismically unfit in a 1997 review and in 2001 both received extensive retrofits as part of the university's SAFER program. The fact that both buildings needed retrofits is a testament to the dramatic growth in the body of knowledge regarding earthquake engineering in the past four decades.

Henry Degenkolb graduated with a degree in civil engineering from UC-Berkeley in 1936. Special attention to seismic concerns comprised one of the major differences between the work of Degenkolb's firm and those of conventional offices. In professional practice, Degenkolb was one of the few offices in

Figure 13. Hildebrand Hall from the plaza.

Figure 14. Hildebrand Hall: unbonded braces.

Figure 15. Latimer Hall.

the country that set the standard for seismic safety. Although Degenkolb had been practicing for over two decades by 1960, when Latimer Hall was designed, the industry's knowledge of building performance in earthquakes was still nascent compared to what we know today. A string of earthquakes—in Alaska in 1964, Caracas in 1967, and San Fernando in 1971—spurred a period of intensive investigation of earthquakes and revision of building codes. When Degenkolb designed Latimer Hall, the code was a very thin document compared to today, but he recognized the threat of earthquakes and, like many engineers in California, designed beyond the code.

In addition to two basement stories, the 184,000-square-foot building has nine stories above ground in a rectangular tower that accommodates 831 laboratory stations and 213 fume hoods. The building's program required a floor plan that was unimpeded by walls and columns to allow for a flexible laboratory layout. The volume and complexity of the building program and needed services substantially influenced the design of the building. To develop an architectural solution that successfully addressed all of the project's challenges, Anshen and Allen worked closely with Degenkolb Engineers. To provide the main structure of the building, the project team used exterior concrete box columns. These large, hollow columns visibly line the exterior of the north and south sides of the

building. They are like large, square donuts, 7 ft-3 inches wide, spaced 27 ft apart and constructed of 14-inch-thick walls of poured concrete heavily reinforced with steel rebar. These columns provide major structural support for the building and house the large ducts that drain the laboratory fume hoods, leaving each floor with an open plan that allows for easy rearrangement with nonstructural partitions. Openings in the columns at each floor made access for maintenance or modification relatively easy. The columns also provide a highly visible architectural expression of the building's structural and mechanical systems, announcing, as a series of exterior fume hoods would, the activities taking place within.

These concrete box columns, along with the floor diaphragms connecting them, provided the lateral force resistance in the longitudinal direction. Short shear walls at the stair and elevator cores also provided longitudinal shear strength. Lateral force resistance in a transverse direction was supplied by large concrete shear walls capping the east and west ends of the building, aided by the walls around the elevator core. Gravity loads were shared by the perimeter box columns, the elevator and stair cores, and 12 steel columns in the interior of the building.

In April of 1997, UC-Berkeley enlisted Degenkolb Engineers to do a preliminary seismic evaluation of Latimer Hall as part of its newly instituted SΛFER program. This brief review of the building determined that in the case of a "rare" earthquake (one with a 10% chance of occurring within 50 years) the building would perform with a "poor," or near collapse, rating. This performance expectation was due mainly to deficiencies in the longitudinal lateral force resisting system. The box columns, and the floor slabs spanning the distance between them, were designed to act as moment frames that resisted applied shear force. However, the floor slabs were not continuous through the box columns, and their attachment to the columns was insufficient for the system to behave like a true frame in the event of a strong lateral load. The other longitudinal walls were too slender to add significant lateral support. Other deficiencies were also noted in the transverse direction; namely, that the stress in the transverse shear walls would exceed capacity and that openings at the first level of these walls weakened them.

The "poor" rating of the building and the chemistry department's size and importance to the university made Latimer Hall a high priority for a seismic retrofit. The university applied for and received a large grant from FEMA, nominally under the "Preventative Medicine Test Cases" program, and began the retrofit in 2000. Anshen and Allen once again acted as architects and Forell/Elsesser Engineers were hired as the structural engineers.

The architects and engineers worked together to find a retrofit solution that would not block light into the lab spaces.

Rather than introducing a new structural system to the building, the selected strategy strengthened the building's existing system. This scheme essentially consisted of adding more reinforced concrete to the existing columns, beams, and walls at the building's exterior. You can see this by looking at the concrete balconies between the columns. Notice the different color of the concrete. These balconies were added along the longitudinal side of the building to strengthen it. Increased strength in the transverse direction was achieved by thickening and reconfiguring the shear walls at the east and west façades and improving their connections to the ground. The building continues to express its structural and mechanical systems on its exterior, now with a new layer that serves as a testament to the quickly changing field of earthquake engineering.

Now walk north again through Latimer Hall if it is open, or around it if not, passing the round to the Mining Circle and past the newly constructed Stanley Hall (the original Stanley Hall was demolished because it was a seismic hazard). In front and across the circle is the Hearst Memorial Mining Building.

The Hearst Memorial Mining Building

The Hearst Memorial Mining Building (E in Fig. 8; Fig. 16) was designed by John Galen Howard and completed in 1907. Phoebe Apperson Hearst, widow of Senator George R. Hearst,

Figure 16. Hearst Mining Building.

provided the funding for the building, which was to be a memorial to her late husband, who made his fortune in mining. The exterior is one of the most beautiful examples of the French Ecole des Beaux Arts style on campus. Step up to the façade and look at the detailing. Here the ideals of the Ecole, symmetry regularity and hierarchy, are married to an elegant Renaissance Revival–Mission style. As you walk inside, you are greeted by a magnificent open atrium (Fig. 17), the design for which was inspired by Henri Labrouste's reading room (1862–1868) of the Bibliotheque Nationale in Paris. Behind the vestibule was a tremendous open nave, which was designed to hold working mining machinery. Today, this space is occupied by classrooms and offices.

Walk in the door and admire the soaring atrium (Fig. 17). Read the bronze plaque with the dedication to George Hearst. Opposite the front door are double doors leading into the former nave which housed the mining machines. Facing the double doors are photographs of the building being retrofitted.

The building is a four-story steel and unreinforced masonry building with exterior cladding of granite masonry. The struc-

Figure 17. Hearst Mining Building interior.

tural system consists of brick bearing walls with a very thin steel skeleton that was found to be inadequate to support the high gravity loads. An unreinforced concrete and brick foundation supports the steel frame columns, the unreinforced brick masonry walls, and the concrete floors. Modifications were made in 1947 when the central nave was destroyed to create additional levels. In 1949 and 1959, other open galleries were closed in.

In a 1990 study conducted by the engineering firm Rutherford and Chekene and the architectural firm Esherick, Homsey, Dodge and Davis, several seismic construction deficiencies were found in the Hearst Memorial Mining Building. The masonry brick walls were overstressed in the shear; a number of the slabs were neither tied together nor tied to the masonry brick walls; the front façade did not adequately resist lateral loads; and chimneys, terra cotta, tile ceilings, and stone ornamentation were seen as falling hazards.

How could this building be made safe without destroying its beauty and historical character? After much discussion, it was decided by the engineers and the Chancellor's Seismic Review Committee that to bring the building from a "very poor" rating to a "good" rating, it would be necessary to use one the most expensive earthquake resistant systems: base isolation. In base isolation, a building's foundations are decoupled from the lateral motions of the earth. The Hearst Memorial Mining Building's base isolation system consists of 134 steel and rubber laminated composite columns, called base isolators, which can move 28 inches in any horizontal direction, allowing the building to safely ride out earthquakes. Because of the reinforcing steel plates, these bearings are very stiff in the vertical direction but are soft in the horizontal direction, so they can move sideways. The Hearst Memorial Mining Building's seismic retrofit not only strengthened the building, but it also allowed for significant upgrades. Additional space was created underground to house mechanical equipment, and two new three-story buildings were added at the north face. The scheme included the preservation of the building façades and restoration of many of its interior features.

Unfortunately, there are no pictures of the base isolators in the photographic display facing the double doors, and you can't see them inside the building without special permission. But if you walk out of the building, stand on the steps, and look down at its foundation, you will see that it is encircled by what appear to be dark gray paving blocks. These blocks cover the moat that runs around the entire building and are designed to move if the building pushes them. The stairs you are standing on and the entire building are supported by the base isolators.

Retrace your steps, walking south between Le Conte and Gilman Halls and crossing the footbridge over Strawberry Creek to lovely Faculty Glade. Walk up the hill, passing the music building. Before looking at the last retrofit on the tour, walk straight ahead to the new Jean Gray Hargrove Music Library by Mack Scogin Merrill Elam architects (2004). This is a steel building clad in panels of slate. Look at the doorway.

You can see that part of the lateral resistant system for the building is being used as decorative feature. Have you seen a version of this system before? (Yes, in Hildebrand. This is an unbonded brace.)

If you turn around and look east, you'll see Wurster Hall. It is hard to miss.

Wurster Hall

William Wilson Wurster, the man who established the basic design parameters, picked the architects, and approved or vetoed their every decision, was pleased when he saw the nearly complete Wurster Hall (F in Fig. 8; Fig. 18) in 1964: "I wanted it to look like a ruin that no regent would like … It is absolutely unfinished, uncouth, and brilliantly strong. …This is the way architecture is best done. What I wanted was a rough building, not a sweet building. …The regents like cutie-pie and slick things…" Wurster succeeded in his wish that no regent would like the building. None did. William Wurster, the dean of the new College of Environmental Design, had a specific goal in mind when he chose the architects and interrupted their process time and time again. Like a proud father setting his sons to work, he continued to influence them. Don Olsen, one of Wurster Hall's architects, called him their "godfather"; when he was not present, he was "God hovering [over] the whole thing." Wurster wanted a particular look to the school. For him, the incomplete and the rough in architecture were physical manifestations of his philosophy of architectural education. He knew he was setting one architect against another to unleash "controlled chaos" when he chose architecture faculty members Vernon DeMars, Joseph Esherick, Donald Olsen, and Donald Hardison to design the future Wurster Hall. He wanted "strong people, each with a different slant."

After a series of attempts to create a combined design for the new College of Environmental Design (CED), Joe Esherick took over the decision-making process and set his office to work on the drawings, which did in fact incorporate some of the ideas of his partners. The building was to be as flexible in its floor plan as possible, a huge loft building, a giant concrete factory where architects, artists, craftspeople, city planners, and landscape architects would be free to explore new possibilities. The entire building is developed on the module of 4'8", which was the area required for the surface of a drawing desk. It was to be environmentally sensitive, using special sun shades, "brise soleil," popularized by Le Corbusier. It was to be a product of the here and now, built of concrete, and as Wurster insisted, without any silly tile roofs (like those on every other UC building of the period). It was to be cheap and durable, made of reinforced concrete. Not only was reinforced concrete economically feasible, it also offered the sculptural quality that the designers desired.

The construction of the building included a combination of cast-in-place concrete with precast elements. The floors and roof were poured in place, while the exterior columns and sunshades were precast. The structural engineer, Isadore Thomp-

Figure 18. Wurster Hall, western façade.

son, invented the precast elements, which were sidewalls and brise soliel attached to mast-like fins poured elsewhere and lifted into place on the façade. If you look carefully at the façade, you can see how fins and their sidewalls are combined to create the façade. The interior of Wurster Hall was left unfinished to expose the various building systems (Fig. 19). All of the mechanical and electrical systems were suspended from the ceiling for the aesthetic effect and also because imbedding them in the concrete slab would render maintenance impossible.

UC-Berkeley architecture professors Mary Comerio and Stephen Tobriner became very concerned about the building in the 1990s. Tobriner examined the plans and found the building lacked sufficient lateral resistance systems. It would pancake in a major earthquake. As a member of the Seismic Review Committee, he asked the university to study the building. When the study was concluded, Wurster Hall, one of the largest and most heavily populated buildings on campus, was found to be a collapse hazard. In his analysis, engineer Ephriam Hirsch found that the 10-story tower had practically no bracing in the east-west direction, and that the tower's existing shear walls were discontinuous. As a result, the tower was likely to collapse during a major seismic event. Additionally, Wurster Hall's U-shaped plan with deep reentrant corners has the potential for high lateral stresses at the intersection of the north and south legs.

During a major seismic event, severe damage was likely to occur at the corners where the north and south towers join the building. In order to strengthen the building, a building committee was convened in the fall of 1997 to review the retrofit process. The committee interviewed a number of potential teams to complete the retrofit project and selected the architectural firm of Esherick, Holmes, Dodge and Davis (EHDD) with the structural engineering firm of Rutherford and Chekene. Another committee was formed to work with the architect and engineer to develop a creative, cost-effective, and functional solution. Members of the CED wanted the retrofit not only to solve the poor seismic condition, but to enhance the existing structure as well.

Walk up to Wurster Hall and walk through and up the stairs to the courtyard. Look over to the tower for the most obvious retrofits (Fig. 20).

The project committee selected a design that involved adding a tube-like structure on the east of the tower and installing more continuous shearwalls on the west side of the tower, essentially creating two tubes. These tubes would brace the tower and provide lateral support. The tube scheme also included adding new shear walls and foundations to help resist lateral forces, minimizing potential displacement of the tower. Collector beams in the diaphragm were designed to tie the new

Figure 19. Wurster Hall interior.

shear walls together with the existing structure, and two new foundations supported by drilled piers were added under the tubes. One tube, to the east, is clearly visible from the court yard. Walk back into the building and peer in a few offices: notice the steel columns. To strengthen the fin columns, steel columns were added on the interior of the façade to transfer the vertical loads.

Walk over to the entrance of the Environmental Design Library. If you look inside, you can see a lovely two-story atrium in the reading room, the location of the former stacks, which were seismically hazardous. It is heartening that in the best of seismic retrofits, the functioning and the aesthetics of a building can be improved as well. Such was the case in Wurster Hall.

Stop 3: Berkeley Seismological Labs (Lind S. Gee and Peggy Hellweg)

Significance of the Site

Seismology has a long tradition at UC-Berkeley. In 1887, seismometers were installed at the Student Observatory (on the knoll opposite the entrance to McCone Hall) and at Lick Observatory on Mount Hamilton by Edward S. Holden, professor of astronomy and president of the university. From these two observatories, the seismic network at UC-Berkeley has grown over the last century to include nearly 50 sites in California and southern Oregon. Today, the Berkeley Seismological Laboratory (BSL) is involved in a wide range of geophysical monitoring and research.

Accessibility

The BSL is open for tours by appointment only. Certain displays are accessible to the public during normal business hours. Restrooms are available in McCone Hall. Street parking is difficult, but the campus is easily accessible by BART and AC Transit. Parking is available on the street and on Level 2 of Lower Hearst Garage (entrance on Scenic Ave at Hearst Ave).

GPS Coordinates

Latitude: 37:52:27N (37.8742); Longitude 122:15:35W (−122.2598).

Directions

The BSL is located on the second floor of McCone Hall, on the north side of the UC-Berkeley campus. From the intersection of Euclid and Hearst, enter the campus at the North Gate. McCone Hall is the second building on your left, a five-story structure. Walk or take the elevator to the second floor; the BSL suite is located at the north end of the building.

Figure 20. Wurster Hall Tower from the courtyard looking north.

Stop Description

Visitors to the BSL will learn about the history of the lab and the role of the UC-Berkeley faculty and staff in studying the 1906 earthquake—now and then. Historical instrumentation, as well as current earthquake information, is on display. The tour includes examples of modern seismic sensors and information about the BSL's role in the California Integrated Seismic Network and earthquake monitoring.

Although much of the data collection now takes place invisibly on computers, several historical instruments are on display. A Wiechert seismometer with a 160 kg inverted pendulum stands in the ground floor lobby of McCone Hall. BSL acquired this seismometer in 1911 with funds donated by William Randolph Hearst after the 1906 earthquake to improve our capabilities to monitor seismicity in California. It and others like it were operated until the early 1970s, although new instruments were regularly added to stations as they were invented. Several examples of the Wood-Anderson seismometer are on display in the hall cases on the second floor near the entrance to BSL's suite. This small seismometer was fundamental to the development of the local or Richter magnitude scale in the late 1920s and early 1930s. Before, each seismograph station was likely to be equipped with a different instrument from others around it. Thus, each record of an earthquake was

unique and could not be directly compared with those from other stations. This changed with the advent and installation of a standardized seismograph, the Wood-Anderson, at many locations in both northern and southern California. The hall displays also showcase maps of current seismicity, California faults and their associated hazards, as well as examples of current research directions at BSL. Within the BSL suite, the floors and doors are a reminder of the range of seismology. The floor shows a seismogram recorded at the BSL station CMB in Sonora, California, on 11 July 1995. It shows Rayleigh waves, a type of seismic surface wave, generated by a moment magnitude (M_W) 6.8 earthquake that occurred over 12,000 km away in the Myanmar-China Border Region. When an earthquake is strong enough, the waves will travel around the earth several times. The seismogram on the floor shows six such passages. The office doors display the seismogram of a local magnitude (M_L) 4.2 earthquake, which occurred on the Hayward fault at 1:24 a.m. local time on 26 June 1994, just 7 km away from here. This recording was made at BSL's station in the Berkeley Hills, BKS. Within the BSL suite computers display current seismicity, the digital data as it arrives from the seismometer stations of the network. A rotating drum recorder, called a helicorder, produces paper records using data from the station BKS.

Stop 4: Berkeley Laboratories of the Earthquake Simulator and Network for Earthquake Engineering Simulation at the University of California Richmond Field Station (Nicholas Sitar)

Significance of the Site

The earthquake simulator, or "shake table," was the first of its kind ever built in the world and is still the largest in the United States.

Accessibility

Restrooms are available on site; there free parking on site; no permit is required for entrance during regular business hours.

GPS Coordinates

37.9160°N, 122.3320°W.

Directions

From San Francisco or Oakland: Take I-80 East (toward Sacramento). Immediately following the Gilman Ave. exit, take the I-580 West exit (toward the San Rafael Bridge). Exit the freeway at the Bayview Ave. exit (the 2nd exit after merging onto I-580W). Turn left at the end of the off-ramp and continue straight onto Meade after stopping at the stop sign. Turn left at S. 47th St. (the 2nd street on the left), then immediately turn right (before entering the new Business Park) onto Seaver and enter the Richmond Field Station. Stop at the security kiosk. If a guard is on duty, tell him or her that you are visiting the Seismic Simulator in Building 420. At the first intersection, turn left and look for Building 420 on your left. You may park in the parking lot in front of the building.

Stop Description

The Seismic Simulator is located in Building 420, a separate, specially designed structure. The 40-ft-high, 60-ft-wide, 120-ft-long building is serviced by a 10-ton bridge crane and houses the earthquake simulator with its control and data acquisition facilities, an electronic maintenance room, and a suite of offices.

The central feature of the laboratory is the 20 × 20-foot shaking table. The table is configured to produce three translational components of motion: one vertical and two horizontal. These three degrees of freedom can be programmed to reproduce any wave forms within the capacities of force, velocity, displacement, and frequency of the system. It may be used to subject structures weighing up to 100,000 lbs to horizontal accelerations of 1.5 Gs. The concrete shaking table is heavily reinforced both with ordinary reinforcement and with post-tensioning tendons.

The University of California at Berkeley Network for Earthquake Engineering Simulation (NEES) site, known as nees@berkeley, features a 60 × 20-ft-strong floor, 40-ft clearance, a reconfigurable reaction wall, a 4-million-pound axial loading capacity, several large static and dynamic actuators, new instrumentation and a 128 channel high-speed data acquisition system, and advanced hybrid simulation capability that enables testing of large and complex structures. Real-time tests at actuator speeds up to 0.5 m/s are possible, and the digital controller can control up to eight independent degrees of freedom. The facility became operational on 30 September 2004.

SECTION II: THE NORTHERN HAYWARD FAULT

Stop 5: Hayward Fault Exposures at Point Pinole (Glenn Borchardt)

Significance of the Site

The northern end of the Hayward fault is at Point Pinole Regional Shoreline, a beautiful, relatively undeveloped 2000-acre oasis where tectonics, landslides, and global warming interact to form an earth scientist's dream (Fig. 21). Just outside the park lies a planner's nightmare: houses built in 1950 right on top of the fault without so much as a query about the strange white streak that appeared in aerial photos taken a decade earlier (Fig. 22). Within the park, two petroleum-laden pipelines lie buried along the railroad track near the entrance: one suspended in a 12-ft culvert designed to survive anything, and one built, like the railroad, without an inkling that the fault creeps 5.6 mm/yr below (Fig. 23). This field trip is a short introduction to a full-day trip that entails a 4-mi-hike (7-km) around the shoreline at Point Pinole (Borchardt and Seelig, 1991). In addition to the infrastructural items, we will examine the tectonic geomorphology of the Hayward fault, which includes a prominent fault scarp, benches, linear troughs, and an active, offset landslide. All this is on a backdrop of great crustal stability in which we can observe the effects of today's increasing sea level on top of evidence for the last time the bay was 20 feet higher than at present.

Accessibility

There are public restrooms available and ample parking.

GPS Coordinates

37.9915°N; –122.3553°W.

Directions

From San Francisco, cross the Bay Bridge and take I-80 east toward Vallejo/Sacramento. Exit at Richmond Parkway and turn left. Continue on Richmond Parkway, turn right at Atlas Road, turn left at Giant Highway, and turn right at Point Pinole Regional Shoreline.

Stop Description

Point Pinole Regional Shoreline is the park preserved by dynamite, having once been known as the "powder capitol of the west." Due to its relatively remote location, explosives were manufactured here from 1881 to 1960. Rare bricks found in the tidal marsh are said to be evidence of occasional mishaps. The park district bought the land from U.S. Steel in 1972 and has been "undeveloping" it ever since. Seismic

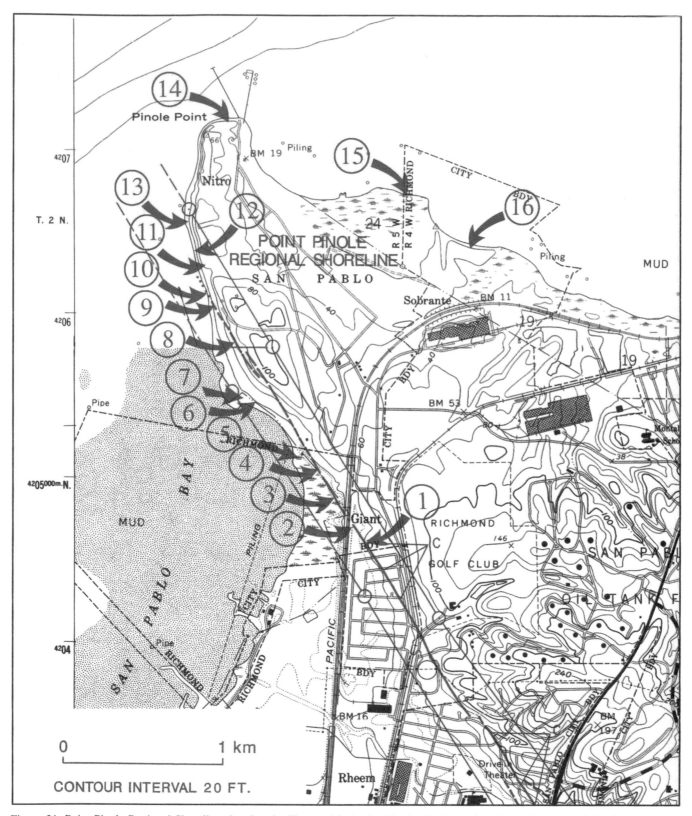

Figure 21. Point Pinole Regional Shoreline showing the Hayward fault, the Alquist-Priolo earthquake fault zone, and the field trip stops described in Borchardt and Seelig (1991). We will be visiting the first eight stops on the Borchardt and Seelig trip. C indicates the creeping section of the fault. The housing development between the railroad tracks south of the park is Parchester Village, which was built in 1950, before the fault-zoning act was passed.

Figure 22. 1939 aerial photo showing the white linear feature that marks the location of the Hayward fault through what became Parchester Village in 1950. The white streak is the result of cultivation and erosion of an "E" soil horizon, which formed as a result of the water barrier produced by the fault. Most of the buildings seen here have been removed from the park.

Figure 23. 1978 aerial photo of the Hayward fault as it passes through Parchester Village, offsets two pipelines and the Union Pacific railroad tracks, and then forms the linear scarp along the tidal marsh.

studies within the park have continued since the first U.S. Geological Survey (USGS) alignment array was emplaced in 1968. (Note: creep rates in the following are given in millimeters per year [mm/yr]. One mm = 0.039 inches; 3 mm = ~1/8 inch.)

Location 1 (0 mi [0 km])—USGS Alignment Array and Creep Meter

After bisecting several houses, streets, and curbs (Fig. 24) in Parchester Village at 5.6 mm/yr since 1950 (Lienkaemper,

Borchardt, and Lisowski, 1991), the Hayward fault crosses the southern boundary of the park (Fig. 23). The fault is delineated here by a small SW-facing scarp associated with a prominent white linear feature on 1939 air photos (Fig. 22). A series of benchmarks placed perpendicular to the fault by the USGS in 1968 underwent ~2.5″ (65 mm) of aseismic displacement between 1968 and 1980 (5.3 mm/yr; Harsh and Burford, 1982). A real-time creep station was installed across the fault in 1996, yielding steady creep measurements of 4.8 mm/yr in a 50-ft-wide (15 m) zone from 1996 to 2004 (Bilham, 2005).

Location 2 (~325 ft [0.10 km])—Offset Wave-Cut Platform

The Hayward fault generally forms the boundary between the East Bay Hills and the alluvial plain formed along San Francisco Bay, but at this site, the fault is up to ~650 ft (200 m) from the range front (Figs. 21 and 22). This area is nearly flat because bay waters reached elevations up to 13 ft (4 m) higher than this location the last time global warming caused sea level to be higher than at present—~122,000 yr ago (Edwards et al., 1987). Wave action leveled the surface of the fault into a feature called a wave-cut platform. Despite the fan-shaped landform on the other side of the railroad tracks, none of the seismic trenches dug here in 1987 and 1994 uncovered stream alluvium that would provide a geologic slip rate for the fault. The nearest stream crosses the fault 2260 ft (690 m) to the south, so the geologic slip rate here appears to be <6 mm/yr since the bay waters receded ~114,000 yr ago.

The strong linear feature on 1939 aerial photos (Fig. 22) was shown during seismic trenching to be a light gray "E" hori- zon (a soil horizon depleted of organic matter and iron oxides) formed in response to the water barrier formed by the fault (compare Figs. 25 and 26) (Borchardt, 1988a). The shallow water table helped to preserve spectacular slickensides at the 13-ft (4-m) depth (Fig. 27). The area is still nearly level today because vertical slip along the fault diminishes as it steps over to the Rodgers Creek fault to the northwest.

An earthquake on the northern Hayward fault probably would impact the Union Pacific railroad and the fuel lines lying just northwest of here (Steinbrugge et al., 1987). The U-shaped parallel lines east of the tracks (arrows, Fig. 28) are the result of fill settlement on either side of a 300-ft-long 12-ft culvert buried in 1975 (Fig. 28). A 16″ pipeline suspended within the culvert will provide an uninterruptible fuel supply from the Chevron refinery on the west side of the fault to power plants on the east side of the fault. Unfortunately, an older 12″ fuel line lies buried alongside the tracks and could rupture at any time due to the stresses already introduced by creep along the fault.

Figure 24. Right-lateral curb offset at 704 Phanor Drive due to aseismic slip in Parchester Village that was 150 mm (6 inches) by 21 March 1985. More precise techniques found 214 mm of offset in a wider span of the northwestern curb on Banks Drive in 1988 (Lienkaemper et al., 1991). By now, the offset should be about twice as much as shown here. Gene Kelley, Colorado State University, for scale.

Figure 25. Moderately strong soil developed on the SW side of the Hayward fault in Trench DMG-E (Borchardt, 1988a).

*Location 3 (~1000 ft [0.30 km])—Tidal Marsh
and Fault Scarp*

A prominent SW-facing scarp forms an abrupt boundary between the tidal marsh and the uplands north of the railroad tracks. This linear scarp strikes N30W—on trend with the Hayward fault seen on air photos and in seismic excavations to the SE. We studied a small embayment here that contains late Holocene surficial estuarine deposits overlying the projection of the fault. The white patches in this area (Fig. 28) were studied for evidence of paleoliquefaction—there was none (Borchardt, 1988b). No evidence for catastrophic ground rupture was found in the park.

Figure 26. Light gray "E" horizon developed on the NE side of the Hayward fault in Trench DMG-E, a few meters from the soil profile in Figure 25 (Borchardt, 1988a).

Figure 27. Slickensides from Trench DMG-E excavated across the Hayward fault in 1987 (Borchardt, 1988a).

Location 4 (~1300 ft [0.40 km])—Peat and Crustal Stability

A 1300-yr-old black sedimentary peat containing sand-size flakes of vermiculite (flakes of weathered biotite mica sometimes mistaken for gold in Sierra streams) lies buried in the tidal marsh southwest of the fault (Figs. 29 and 30). Examination of the salt marsh cliff and probings throughout the marsh revealed that the base of this distinctive peat layer exists at depths between 14″ and 30″ (36 and 75 cm) and that it varies in thickness from 4″ to 11″ (10–27 cm). Its depth and age are what would be expected in a crustally stable part of the world such as Micronesia (Bloom, 1970). Global sea level rise has been ~0.4 mm/yr during the past 4000 years, but measurements at the

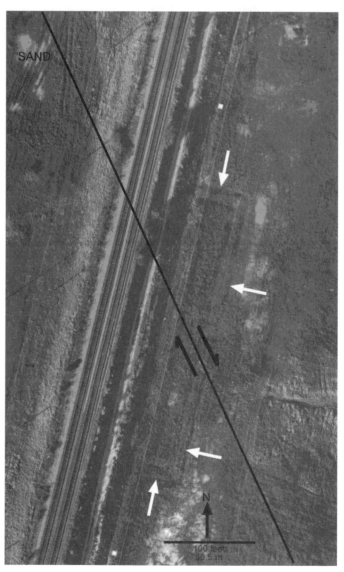

Figure 28. 1978 aerial photo showing a close-up of the point at which the fault crosses the railroad track. White arrows show the location of two parallel fill-settlement lines that mark the location of a special 12-ft culvert offset containing a suspended petroleum line built in 1975. The beginning and end of the installation is marked by two white squares that are 500 ft apart (Borchardt, 1988a).

Golden Gate show a rise of 2 mm/yr between 1857 and 1975. In addition, this implies that the 6.5-ft-high (2-m) scarp is a result of uplift on the NE rather than subsidence on the SW. No definite offsets were observed in boring transects and trenches across the fault projection (Fig. 29).

Location 5 (0.3 mi [0.55 km])—Bay Mud Cliff

Modern plant remains of the type found in the dated peat layer may be seen here mixed with vermiculite particles at the edge of the mud flat (Fig. 30). At low tide, the peat layer is exposed within the bay mud deposits along the full length of the salt marsh cliff. Bay mud is of mixed clay mineralogy and normally contains only clay and silt. Sand, if any, is brought in locally from nearby upland drainages.

Location 6 (0.6 mi [1.00 km])—Paleosol Section P2

This paleosol (fossil soil) section, like most of the others along the shoreline, was exposed as a result of erosion produced by rising sea level in San Pablo Bay (Figs. 31 and 32). Note that the young trees at the shoreline are being rapidly undermined.

The modern soil has traces of gravel and a moderately developed B horizon (a soil horizon in which clay and iron oxides have accumulated) overlying a zone of mangan (black manganese oxide coatings) development.

The development in the lower paleosol here is particularly striking (Fig. 31). This paleosol has a 35″-thick (88-cm) B horizon with strong blocky structure and clay films that extend into the BC horizon (a transitional soil horizon less weathered than the B horizon) for at least another 18″ (45 cm). At a depth of 131–140″ (333–355 cm), the base of the paleosol contains moderately dense, 2″-diameter (5-cm) calcite (calcium carbonate) nodules. The mechanism by which these nodules could form in soils and paleosols of the Bay Area is not well understood. In California, most calcareous soil horizons are found in the semiarid and arid regions. Calcium carbonate nodules, however, have been reported in borings in east-west cross sections across the southern San Francisco Bay. ^{230}Th-^{234}U analysis of two of these nodules resulted in an age of 26,000 yr. This was confirmed by a ^{14}C date of 21,000 yr B.P. (yr B.P. of 1950), coral-corrected to 26,000 calendar years. The modern

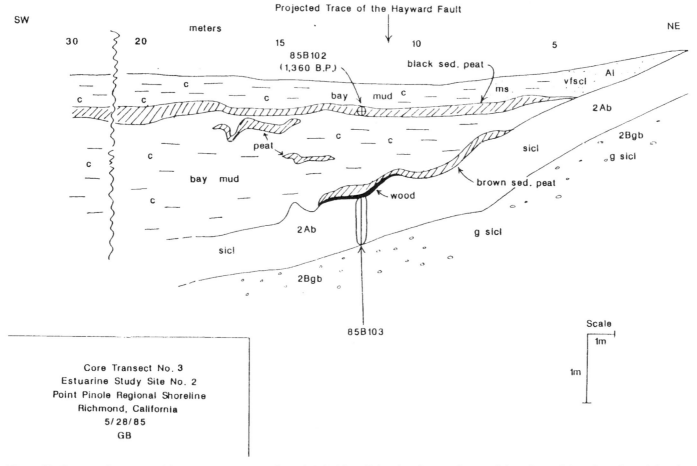

Figure 29. Cross section prepared from a core transect at Location 4 of Stop 5 showing the peat, bay mud deposits, and the paleosol overlying the projected trace of the Hayward fault (from Borchardt, 1988a).

Figure 30. Bay mud cliff showing the younger bay mud and the pervasive sedimentary peat at the base that was dated at 1300 calendar years old.

wave-cut platform ~328 ft (100 m) northwest of this site is presently cutting through an arcuate zone of calcite nodules that dips SW.

Location 7 (0.7 mi [1.10 km])—Landslide Toe

Modern as well as ancient landslides exist along the Hayward fault as it crosses the SW side of the ridgeline (Fig. 32). A water pipeline has been displaced ~30 ft (10 m) downslope by a major landslide that crosses the Hayward fault. Landslide deposits "rumple" the landscape, producing closed depressions as well as raised topography. The soils within such deposits are typically multicolored, having both oxidized and reduced zones that are indicated by changes in iron mineralogy. The slides are triggered by extremely active erosion at the bay cliff, where there are excellent exposures of the toes and slide planes.

Location 8 (0.8 mi [1.35 km])—Landslide–Fault Complex

Heading uphill, cross a series of benches and linear depressions that are parallel to the Hayward fault (Fig. 32). It is likely that some of the downslope depressions are the oldest and were produced during early Holocene earthquakes. These may contain "faults" that are no longer active. A trench at this site was dug across this prominent linear depression in a bench along the mapped trace of the fault. The trench exposed a cross section through a block of NE-dipping Tertiary bedrock that had slid across the fault and was subsequently displaced. The soil SW of the fault is only 3.3 ft thick (1 m), whereas the soil NE of the fault is up to 13 ft (4 m) thick. The lower 3.3 ft (1 m) of the deep soil was devoid of modern rootlets and yielded a soil carbon age of 4200 yr.

Figure 31. Paleosol (fossil soil) at the base of soil profile P2 at Point Pinole Regional Shoreline. The white nodules are calcium carbonate dated at 26,000 yr old (Borchardt et al., 1988; Borchardt and Seelig, 1991).

Stop 6: Fault-Related Landslide at Cragmont School (Alan Kropp)

Significance of the Site

An elementary school has recently been reconstructed in an area of active landsliding as well as adjacent to the active Hayward fault. Extensive studies were required to meet safety requirements for the new buildings.

Accessibility

This is a public site, but there are no restrooms and only on-street parking.

GPS Coordinates

37.89349°N, 122.26785°W.

Directions

From the University of California Memorial Stadium, head north on Gayley Road. Turn left (west) on Hearst Avenue and proceed five blocks to Spruce Street. Turn right (north) on Spruce

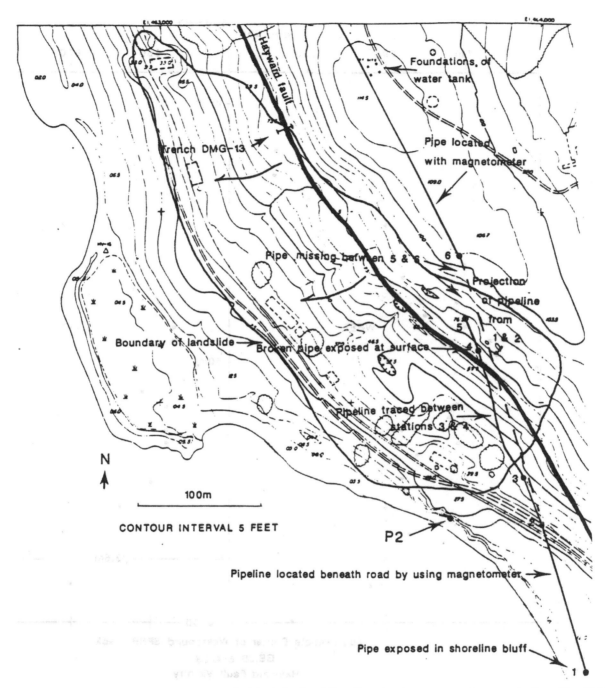

Figure 32. Active landslide along the Hayward fault at Point Pinole Regional Shoreline, showing a survey of a water pipeline offset 30 ft by landsliding since 1920. P2 is the location of a soil profile having two paleosols "fossil soils" in addition to the modern surface soil.

Street and proceed ~10 blocks. After passing Santa Barbara Road, look for parking along the street. Get out of your vehicle and walk to the intersection of Spruce Street and Marin Avenue.

Stop Description

The Cragmont School site is located on the northern corner of Spruce Street and Marin Avenue (Fig. 33). This parcel lies about halfway up a southwest-facing hill slope along the north-

west-trending Berkeley Hills. The site is at an elevation of ~600 ft and is bounded along its southeast border by Marin Avenue; this street extends linearly up the hillside at an average inclination of ~5:1 (horizontal to vertical).

The oldest widespread rocks in this region are highly deformed sedimentary and volcanic rocks of the Mesozoic-age Franciscan Complex. These materials are in fault contact with the somewhat younger Mesozoic-age Great Valley Complex (which

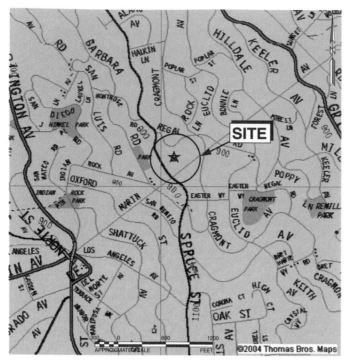

Figure 33. Site location map.

includes both the Coast Range Ophiolite and the Great Valley Sequence). These materials are, in turn, overlain by a diverse sequence of Tertiary sedimentary and volcanic rocks. Since deposition, the Mesozoic and Tertiary rocks have been extensively deformed by repeated episodes of folding and faulting.

The general geologic setting of the area is illustrated on Figure 34 (taken from the Stop 5 field trip guide notes in Ponce et al. [2003]). The caption from the Ponce field trip guide has been included with this figure because it illustrates a geologic understanding that has undergone a number of shifts over the past 20 yr. The Northbrae Rhyolite has recently been determined to be a deformed Miocene volcanic rock, whereas an earlier understanding indicated the rhyolite was part of the Jurassic silicic volcanics within the Coast Range Ophiolite (Jones and Curtis, 1991) (although before that, they were believed to be Miocene in age). A large extruded exposure of the rhyolite is present on the northeast side of Santa Barbara Avenue ~100 ft northwest of Marin Avenue. This exposure is also visible in the historic photograph (Fig. 35).

Historically, published maps of this area have shown several traces of the Hayward fault (Bishop, 1973; Case, 1963; Radbruch-Hall, 1974). The 1982 Alquist-Priolo Fault Map (California Division of Mines and Geology, 1982) indicated the primary trace passed ~300 ft southwest of the site, approximately at the intersection of Santa Barbara Road and Marin Avenue. However, other traces are truncated ~1500 ft to the southeast and 1000 ft to the northwest, which, if extended, might pass through the school site. Lienkaemper (1992) mapped the recent active traces of the Hayward fault and indi-

cated the active trace passed along the northeast side of Spruce Street, at the school's southwest border.

Offset from the Hayward fault in the area is obscured by landslide movements and various repeated construction activities. However, right-lateral offset due to the Hayward fault can generally be seen in the curb lines on both sides of Marin Avenue, just uphill of Spruce Street (these features are cited by Lienkaemper, 1992). While looking up Marin Ave. from Spruce Street (and avoiding the traffic on this heavily-traveled road), a broad left-lateral offset can be seen near Cragmont Avenue due to landslide displacement of the roadway.

Landsliding in this area is well known, and an historic photograph of the area shows the hummocky topography that existed before most construction occurred (Fig. 35). Published maps have varied widely in interpretations of the extent of the landslides, however. In fact, in his mapping of the Quaternary faulting of the Hayward fault, Herd (1978) indicated the entire hillside area from just north of the University of California campus to the southern portion of El Cerrito was one massive landslide complex. Other maps, such as Nilsen (1975) and Dibblee (1980), showed discreet landslides, especially in the area of Cragmont School, but these maps varied widely in their interpretation regarding landslide limits. As a result, starting in 1985, the author began preparing maps of deep-seated, slow moving "active" and "potentially active" landslides for local distribution. (Active landslides were defined as landslides that moved recently enough to damage cultural features, whereas potentially active landslides were slide deposits that were very young but did not significantly damage cultural features.) An example of a 1995 version of this map is presented as Figure 36. More recent delineation of the boundaries of these landslides based on InSAR data has been presented in Hilley et al. (2004).

Since there are both an active fault and active landslide deposits in this area, a number of studies have been performed in an attempt to separate movements from these two sources. The most prominent of these studies are Hoexter et al. (1982, 1992), Lennert (1982), and Waterhouse (1992). Lennert focused on the offset between sections of concrete pavement in Spruce Street just southeast of Marin Avenue to help understand the mechanism. These slab sections were offset in a right-lateral sense and he attributed this movement to creep of the Hayward fault (unfortunately, these slabs were recently covered by asphaltic concrete when Spruce Street was repaved). In the Hoexter studies, surveys were extended along the southeast curbline of Marin Avenue from "the Circle" at Arlington Avenue up the hill past the school to Grizzly Peak Boulevard. Several feet of right lateral offset was recorded between Santa Barbara Road and Spruce Street, much of which was attributed to fault creep but a portion of which was attributed to landslide movement. An additional left lateral offset of ~5 ft over a very broad zone between Spruce Street and Cragmont Avenue was also recorded; this was attributed to the oblique component of the active landslide movement. Hoexter also attributed most of the concrete slab offset in Spruce Street to landslide movement.

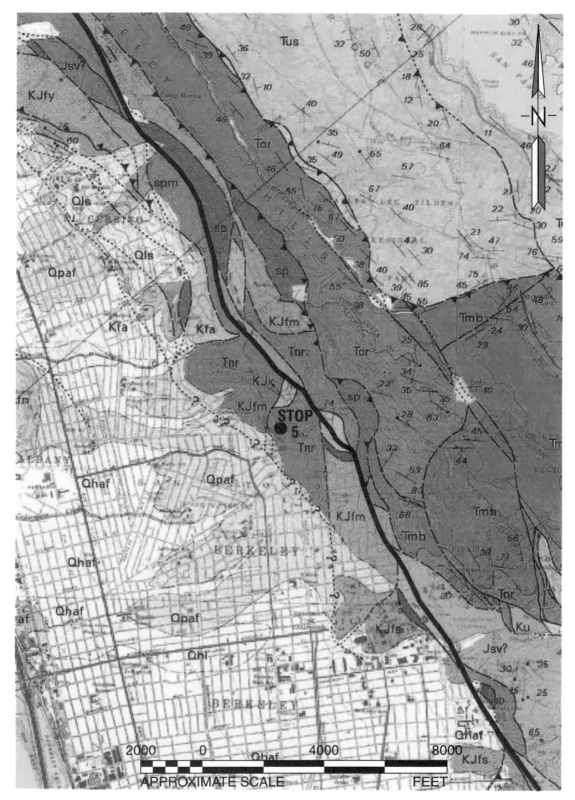

Figure 34. "Geologic map of the Berkeley area (modified from Graymer, 2000) showing the distribution of the Northbrae rhyolite (Tnr). The through-going mapped active strand of the Hayward fault is shown as a thick black line; the field trip stop location is shown as a black dot. Note that the Northbrae rhyolite has no apparent offset along the mapped active strand of the Hayward fault, although the outcrops of questionably identified silicic volcanics of the Coast Range Ophiolite (Jsv?) could be correlative with the Northbrae rhyolite, which would indicate an ~4 km offset" (figure and caption from Ponce et al., 2003, their Stop 5, Figure 5-1).

Figure 35. Photograph taken in late 1800s from Los Angeles and Mariposa Avenues. Marin Avenue was later built immediately beyond (northwest) the creek channel. Farm and saloon buildings in approximate area where Cragmont School later constructed (Berkeley Historical Society).

The subject site at the northern corner of Marin Avenue and Spruce Street has been in use for a lengthy period as a public elementary school location. Portable school buildings were placed on the Cragmont school site early in the twentieth century, and the first permanent buildings were built as the entire site was developed in 1927. "Modern" concrete buildings replaced the earlier structures in 1966, and additional buildings were constructed in 1975. Unfortunately, structural evaluations after the 1989 Loma Prieta earthquake indicated concerns about the seismic performance of the "modern" concrete buildings and these structures were closed. In light of the active fault and active landslide concerns, extensive studies were performed by Harding Lawson Associates and William Cotton and Associates in the early 1990s (Harding Lawson Associates, 1991; Cotton, W., and Associates 1993, 1995) to help characterize the site-specific geologic framework present and indicate whether new school buildings could be built that would avoid the landslide and fault concerns.

The investigations by William Cotton and Associates concluded the entire school site was located within landslide deposits of various ages (1993). The active landslide materials were shown to encompass the southeastern portion of the site (roughly parallel to Marin Avenue), with a dormant lobe of the same landslide encroaching further into the site. The remainder of the site was underlain by sheared and fractured bedrock units,

which were believed to possess a low potential for reactivation; these materials were classified as a static (ancient) landslide. In relation to the Hayward fault, no subsurface exploration on the site encountered evidence of active faulting, and it was concluded no active trace of the fault was within the school site, but an active trace might be present immediately downhill based on a preponderance of other data. Therefore, as shown on Figure 37, William Cotton and Associates (1995) recommended new buildings be constrained by setbacks beyond the active and dormant portions of the landslide, as well as a projection of the nearest possible active fault trace. The new school campus has subsequently been reconstructed using these setback requirements.

SECTION III: THE SOUTHERN HAYWARD FAULT

The Hayward fault lies along a narrow rift valley along Highway 13 (Warren Freeway) that extends over a distance of 5 mi from the Berkeley-Oakland border at Lake Temescal, south to the intersection of Highway 13 with Highway 580. At the north end of the rift valley, the fault apparently passes along the east bank of Lake Temescal, through the dam, and beneath Highway 24, as described in Borchardt et al. (2000). The fault continues through a residential area to Tunnel Road, and along Tunnel Road toward the Claremont Resort in Berkeley. The fault passes

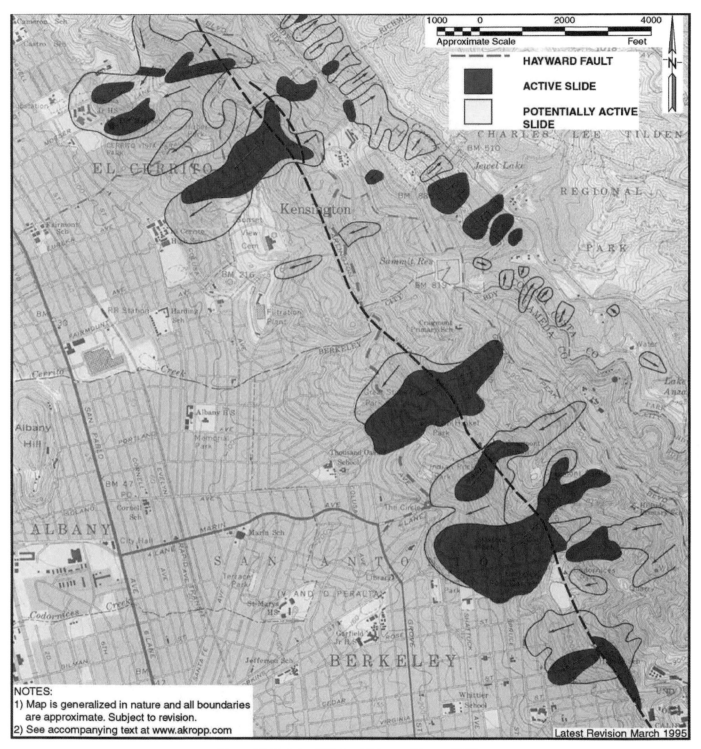

Figure 36. Berkeley Hills landslide map (Kropp, 1995).

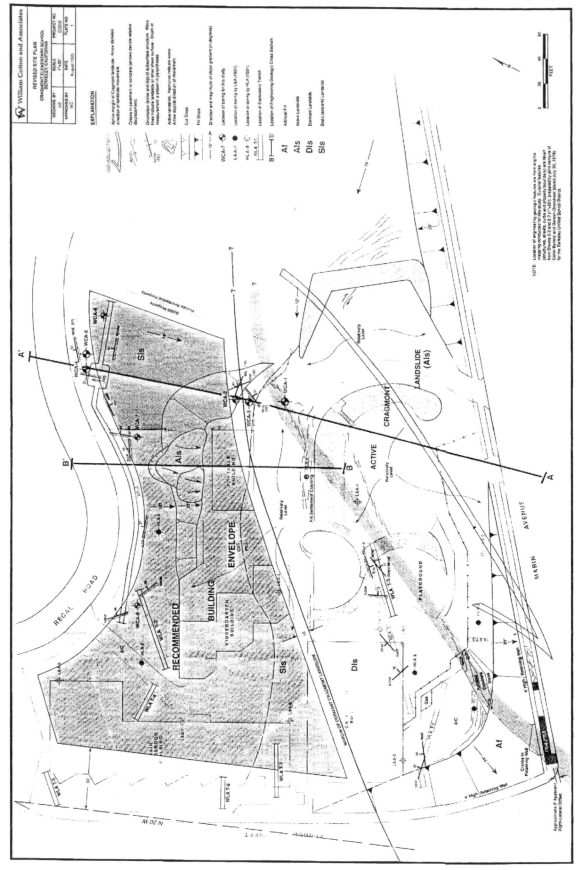

Figure 37. Site map that guided school reconstruction (Cotton and Associates, 1995).

through the East Bay Municipal Utility District's (EBMUD's) Claremont Water Tunnel and Bay Area Rapid Transit (BART) tunnel in the area directly north of Highway 24 (Fig. 2).

Stop 7: Oakland City Hall Base Isolation (Charles Rabamad and Donald Wells)

Significance of the Site

Constructed in 1914 in the Beaux Art style, and currently registered as a National Historic Landmark, this building is 18 stories tall. It consists of a 3-story podium, a 10-story office tower, and a 2-story clock tower base that supports a 91-ft ornamental clock tower (Fig. 38). The total height of the building is 324 feet, and the total square footage is 153,000 sq. ft. The structural system is a riveted steel frame with unreinforced masonry perimeter in-fill walls clad with granite veneer and terra cotta ornamentation (DIS Inc., 2005).

The Oakland City Hall, which was severely damaged in the 1989 Loma Prieta earthquake, was retrofitted (1992–1994) to withstand earthquake ground shaking through the installation of a seismic base isolation system. The first high-rise building in California to be base isolated, it served as a model for design-

Figure 38. Photograph of Oakland City Hall (from Steiner and Elsesser, 2004).

ers and resulted in the acceptance of base isolation as a cost-beneficial method of seismic risk reduction for historic buildings. The successful installation of the base isolation system led the way for funding for seismic isolation of other public buildings damaged by the Loma Prieta earthquake.

GPS Coordinates

37.8052°N, 122.2725°W.

Accessibility

This site is not accessible to the public. Parking: Nearby parking is available at the following locations: Dalziel Building (250 Frank H. Ogawa Plaza) Parking Garage (entrance on 16th Street at Clay Street); Clay Street Garage (entrance on Clay Street between 14th and 15th Streets, behind City Hall); City Center Garage (entrance on 11th Street between Clay Street and Broadway; also entrance on 14th Street).

Directions

From San Francisco: Take I-80 East toward the Bay Bridge. Take the I-580 East/Downtown Oakland (CA-24) exit toward Hayward/Stockton. Merge onto I-580 East. Take the MacArthur Blvd/San Pablo Ave exit. Continue on W. MacArthur Blvd. Turn Right on San Pablo Avenue, and bear right on City Hall Plaza/Frank H. Ogawa Plaza (Fig. 39).

Stop Description

The Oakland City Hall (Fig. 38) suffered significant damage in the October 1989 Loma Prieta earthquake, forcing the city to move all operations out of the building. The city hired a project team, headed by VBN Architects, to undertake a detailed feasibility study to quantify the building's lateral capacity and to examine alternative repair and strengthening schemes. The decision to install a seismic base isolation system as the most cost-effective solution was reached after eight alternative repair systems were compared and analyzed. A significant factor in the selection of base isolation as the most cost-effective approach was the limited strength of the building as constructed. To minimize the amount of new construction, the existing structure was given credit for the strength it exhibited during the Loma Prieta earthquake. This performance-based approach required less strengthening than conventional, code-based design, which ignores the existing capacity of the building.

A total of 42 lead-rubber and 69 rubber base isolators were placed under the building columns during 1992–1994 (Fig. 40). The isolators are 29–39 inches in diameter and 19 inches high. The columns supporting the office tower portion of the building carry extremely high loads (3000 kips dead load and more than 4100 kips for combined live and dead loads), requiring two to four isolators for each of these columns (Steiner and Elsesser, 2004). The foundation thickness above the seismic isolators

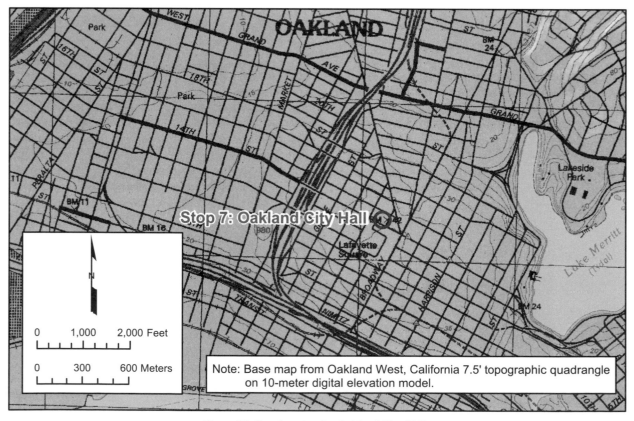

Figure 39. Stop location for Oakland City Hall.

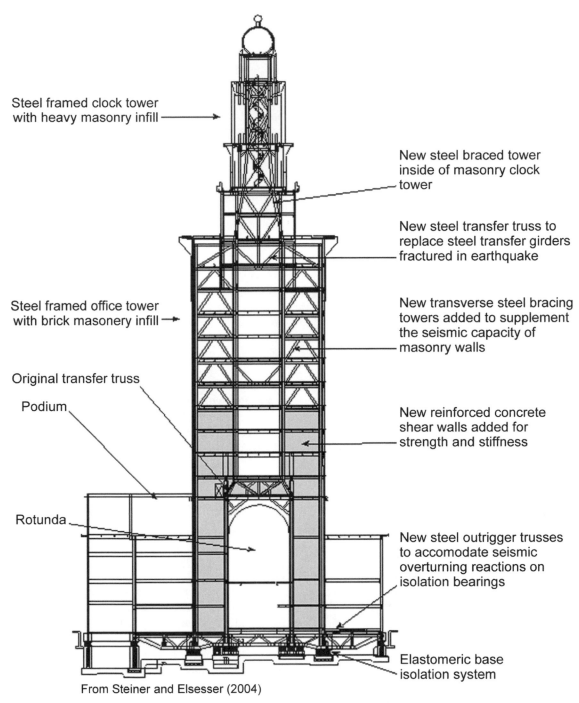

Steel framed clock tower
with heavy masonry infill ──→

New steel braced tower
inside of masonry clock
tower

New steel transfer truss to
replace steel transfer girders
fractured in earthquake

Steel framed office tower
with brick masonery infill ──►

New transverse steel bracing
towers added to supplement
the seismic capacity of
masonry walls

Original transfer truss

Podium

New reinforced concrete
shear walls added for
strength and stiffness

Rotunda

New steel outrigger trusses
to accomodate seismic
overturning reactions on
isolation bearings

Elastomeric base
isolation system

From Steiner and Elsesser (2004)

Figure 40. Diagram of seismic retrofit components at Oakland City Hall.

was increased by adding new concrete around the perimeter of all footings. The interaction between old and new concrete was improved by installation of special tendons (32 mm DYWIDAG Transverse Bar Tendons [THREADBAR®]) that passed through holes cored through the concrete.

Strengthening to the building included installation of a new steel-braced tower inside the masonry clock tower, a new steel transfer truss at the base of the clock tower to replace steel trans-fer girders cracked during the earthquake, new traverse steel bracing in the office tower to supplement the seismic capacity of the masonry walls, addition of reinforced concrete shear walls at the base of the office tower and through the core of the podium, and new steel trusses to accommodate overturning reac-tions on the isolation bearings (Steiner and Elsesser, 2004).

At the time of the retrofit work, it was the tallest seismi-cally isolated building in the world.

Stop 8: Claremont Water Tunnel Portal (Donald Wells, John Caulfield, and David Tsztoo)

Significance of the Site

The Claremont Water tunnel, which is owned by the East Bay Municipal Utility District (EBMUD), is a critical lifeline facility that supplies water to more than 800,000 customers west of the Oakland-Berkeley Hills. The tunnel crosses the Hayward fault ~850 ft in from the west portal. EBMUD is constructing a bypass tunnel that incorporates several innovative design measures to mitigate the potential for service loss due to fault rupture through the tunnel during a major earthquake on the Hayward fault. The BART tunnel also crosses the Hayward fault, ~900 feet south of the Claremont Tunnel. Information on the fault crossing and construction issues for BART is described in Borchardt et al. (2000).

Accessibility

There is limited parking at the Rock La Fleche School or on Chabot Road. The Claremont Tunnel Portal is visible through the chain link fence on the north side of the parking lot at the school. Entrance to EBMUD property is not allowed except by prior permission.

GPS Coordinates

37.8519°N, 122.2390°W.

Directions

From Oakland City Hall, follow San Pablo Avenue 0.3 mi northeast, turn left onto 19th Street, and continue on to 18th Street 0.2 mi to intersection of Castro Street at Highway 980. Turn right onto the ramp for Highway 980 then continue on to Highway 24 east toward Walnut Creek for 3.2 mi. Exit right onto Keith Avenue toward Broadway Avenue (0.2 mi), keep right on Broadway under the highway (0.1 mi), and keep left on Patton Street. Continue 0.2 mi and turn right onto Chabot Avenue. Continue 0.3 mi to the intersection with Golden Gate Avenue. Follow Golden Gate Avenue ~250 ft, and turn right up the hill into the parking lot for Rock La Fleche School. The Claremont Center Tunnel Portal is located directly north of the driveway and parking lot for the school.

Alternate Directions

From Memorial Stadium on the Berkeley campus, drive south on Prospect Street (0.25 mi), turn right on Dwight Way, and make an immediate left turn to continue south on Waring Road (past the Clark Kerr Campus). Turn left on Derby and right on Belrose, continuing on Claremont Blvd. to Ashby Avenue (0.8 mi from Dwight Way). Turn left (east) on Ashby Avenue, which becomes Tunnel Road, passing the Claremont Resort on the left. Continue on Tunnel Road to the divided section of road (0.4 mi), and turn right on The Uplands. Follow The Uplands for 0.3 mi (around to the right to a large intersection), and continue left 0.2 mi down the hill (south) on Roanoke Road to the bottom at Chabot Elementary School. Turn left on Chabot Road and continue 0.2 mi to the intersection with Golden Gate Avenue. Follow Golden Gate Avenue ~250 ft, and turn right up the hill into the parking lot for Rock La Fleche School. The Claremont Center Tunnel Portal is located directly north of the driveway and parking lot for the school.

Stop Description

The Claremont Water Tunnel was excavated and constructed between 1926 and 1929, is 9 ft in diameter, and extends 3.4 mi from the Claremont Center Portal through the Oakland-Berkeley Hills to the Orinda Water Treatment Plant. The tunnel routinely carries 110 million to 175 million gallons per day (mgd). Most of the tunnel is constructed of unreinforced concrete. Inspection of the tunnel showed that the tunnel is cracked and deformed due to creep on the Hayward fault and that voids are present between the existing concrete liner and the surrounding rock throughout the tunnel. Prior to retrofitting, the primary concern for operation of the tunnel was the potential for fault offset during a major earthquake on the Hayward fault, which could have effectively blocked the tunnel, resulting in loss of service for up to six months, a reduction in fire-fighting capacity, and associated economic losses for East Bay communities.

As part of a system-wide seismic improvement program, EBMUD and its consultants developed a solution to retrofit the tunnel that will allow for sustained operation following a major earthquake on the Hayward fault. The seismic retrofit includes constructing a 1570-ft bypass tunnel across the fault zone, with a 480-ft access tunnel driven parallel to the existing tunnel (Fig. 41A and 41B). Use of the access tunnel allows construction of the bypass tunnel without interruption in service of the existing tunnel. When completed, the bypass tunnel will tie into the existing tunnel on both sides of the Hayward fault zone, and the existing tunnel between the tie-ins will be backfilled with cellular grout and abandoned. Elsewhere in the existing tunnel, structural repairs will be completed where needed, and the concrete walls will be strengthened with grout injected into gaps between the walls and the rock around them. The contact grouting is necessary to improve interaction between the ground and liner, and will significantly reduce the potential for damage to the liner due to ground shaking. A major constraint on the bypass tunnel construction and repairs to the existing tunnel is that shutdown of the water flow and retrofit work in the existing tunnel is constrained to a three-month window between December and February due to water system demands. Specific concerns for construction of the bypass tunnel include areas of squeezing ground, groundwater flow, and the presence of naturally occurring methane gas and petroleum.

Three major types of geologic conditions have been identified along the existing tunnel near the Hayward fault zone and west portal. Franciscan Complex mélange, including sheared shale, sandstone, altered volcanic rocks, serpentinite, silica carbonate, and some blocks of chert and blueschist, occur west of the Hayward fault zone (extending ~800 ft east from the west portal). Silica carbonate rock and serpentinite, with some

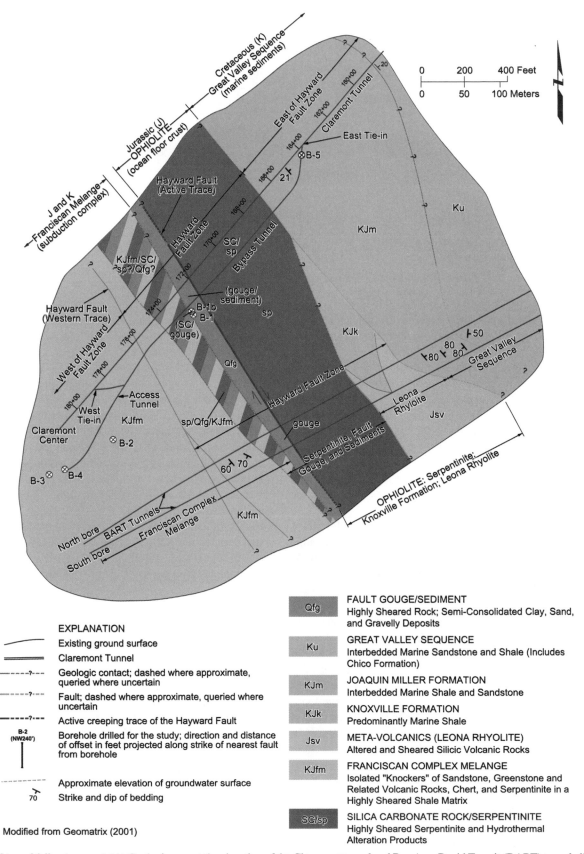

EXPLANATION

	Existing ground surface
	Claremont Tunnel
----?---	Geologic contact; dashed where approximate, queried where uncertain
----?---	Fault; dashed where approximate, queried where uncertain
----?-•-	Active creeping trace of the Hayward Fault
B-2 (NW240')	Borehole drilled for the study; direction and distance of offset in feet projected along strike of nearest fault from borehole
	Approximate elevation of groundwater surface
70	Strike and dip of bedding

Modified from Geomatrix (2001)

Qfg	**FAULT GOUGE/SEDIMENT**	Highly Sheared Rock; Semi-Consolidated Clay, Sand, and Gravelly Deposits
Ku	**GREAT VALLEY SEQUENCE**	Interbedded Marine Sandstone and Shale (Includes Chico Formation)
KJm	**JOAQUIN MILLER FORMATION**	Interbedded Marine Shale and Sandstone
KJk	**KNOXVILLE FORMATION**	Predominantly Marine Shale
Jsv	**META-VOLCANICS (LEONA RHYOLITE)**	Altered and Sheared Silicic Volcanic Rocks
KJfm	**FRANCISCAN COMPLEX MELANGE**	Isolated "Knockers" of Sandstone, Greenstone and Related Volcanic Rocks, Chert, and Serpentinite in a Highly Sheared Shale Matrix
SC/sp	**SILICA CARBONATE ROCK/SERPENTINITE**	Highly Sheared Serpentinite and Hydrothermal Alteration Products

Figure 41. (*this and following page*) (A) Geologic map at the elevation of the Claremont tunnel and Bay Area Rapid Transit (BART) tunnel alignment.

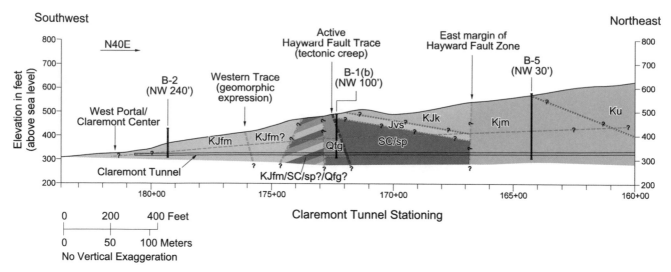

Figure 41. (*continued*) (B) Geologic profile along the Claremont tunnel alignment.

clayey gouge, and Great Valley Sequence sandstone with interbedded shale and siltstone occur east of the Hayward fault zone (Fig. 41A).

In the bypass tunnel, the Hayward fault zone includes two distinct zones: (1) the primary fault zone, which is composed of ~6 inches to 1 ft of dark gray to black, stiff, highly plastic clay (gouge) with sand-size to fine gravel-size inclusions of light-green crushed serpentine; and (2) the clay gouge associated with fault parallel zones of pervasively sheared and crushed serpentinite up to several feet wide. Immediately east of the fault zone, bedrock is serpentinite with inclusions of metabasalt. The serpentinite becomes blocky and less deformed away from the fault zone.

Immediately west of the fault zone, bedrock includes Mesozoic (~200 million to 65 million yr B.P.) Franciscan mélange (serpentinite and sheared greenstone) and silica carbonate rock. Semi-consolidated middle to late Quaternary age (~750,000 yr to 10,000 yr B.P.) alluvial and colluvial sediments also are exposed in the tunnel west of the Hayward fault (Fig. 41A and 41B). The alluvial and colluvial materials are stratified, are gravelly to clayey, and contain rounded pebbles and cobbles and large wood fragments. These materials were deposited on an erosional surface developed on the Franciscan mélange and silica carbonate rock. The alluvial and colluvial materials are interpreted to have been deposited in a depression along the fault, such as in the area of a possible extensional bend in the fault at Lake Temescal to the south (Geomatrix Consultants, 2001). Sediments accumulated in the depression along the fault; as the fault moved by creep and by sudden slip during earthquakes, these sediments were transported northward along the west side of the fault to the area of the Claremont Tunnel.

The location, width, and potential amount of fault displacement are critical factors for the design of the bypass tunnel. Geologic investigations performed for the project identified a design-level primary fault displacement of 7.5 ft horizontally

and 9 inches vertically, which was estimated to occur within a 60-ft reach to be identified during tunnel inspections and excavation of the bypass tunnel (Geomatrix Consultants, 2001). Galehouse (2002) notes that in this area, the fault creeps at ~0.18–0.25 inch per year. The primary fault zone is located within a wider secondary faulting zone extending for 920 ft, where additional fault displacement of up to 2.25 ft (30% of the slip in the primary zone) may occur.

The performance goal of the seismic improvements to the Claremont Tunnel includes maintaining a minimum flow of 130 mgd without significant decrease in water quality for a period of 60–90 days following a major earthquake on the Hayward fault. Inspection of and any necessary repairs to the tunnel would be initiated following the post-earthquake period of high water demand and following repairs to other critical components of the water system. The tunnel also is designed to accommodate fault creep of up to 0.25 inch/yr over a design lifetime of 50 yr.

The seismic design measures used in construction of the bypass tunnel include the following:

- Construction of an enlarged tunnel structure through the entire zone of potential fault offset to accommodate potential fault displacement without blockage of the tunnel;
- Construction of backfill concrete side drifts surrounding the tunnel through the zone of primary fault displacement (Fig. 42);
- Installation of a structural steel carrier pipe within the tunnel across the zone of primary faulting (Fig. 43); and
- Construction of gaps in the final concrete lining reinforcement through the zone of primary fault displacement to permit shear failure between adjacent liner segments.

The enlarged tunnel section has a 2.25-ft-thick concrete liner, which will serve to accommodate any secondary fault displacement. In the area where primary fault rupture of up to

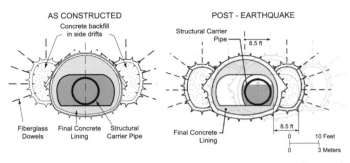

Figure 42. Cross section of oversized tunnel section before and after 8.5 ft (2.6 m) of discrete fault offset. Modified from Kieffer et al., 2004.

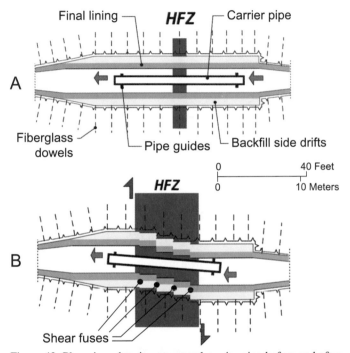

Figure 43. Plan view showing structural carrier pipe before and after 8.5 feet (2.6 m) of distributed fault offset (HFZ—Hayward fault zone). Modified from Kieffer et al., 2004.

7.5 ft is expected to occur, the concrete side drifts will mitigate the potential for faulted ground entering the tunnel and polluting the water supply (Fig. 42). The structural carrier pipe will prevent blockage of and will allow for the required minimum flow through the tunnel should the tunnel crown collapse due to fault rupture. The steel carrier pipe is lightly restrained within the surrounding tunnel so that it is essentially free to rotate and shift as fault displacement occurs (Fig. 43A). The gaps (referred to as shear fuses) in the liner consist of isolated locations without longitudinal steel reinforcement to permit the liner to displace segments while minimizing the potential for significant collapse of the lining (Fig. 43B). Additional details on the measures to mitigate the potential for loss of service due to fault rupture are presented in Kieffer et al. (2004).

Stop 9: City of Hayward Fault Creep
(Russell W. Graymer)

Significance of the Site

Here we can see evidence of creeping and non-creeping strands of the Hayward fault. We will look at the effect of fault creep on various structures, including the old City Hall. We will look at the effect of the fault on San Lorenzo Creek, and the possibility that the creeping strand is only one of the active strands of the fault here.

Accessibility

This is a public site; public restrooms are nearby, and there is easy on-street parking

GPS Coordinates

36.67079°N, 122.08117°W.

Directions

From the Claremont Tunnel Portal, get on Highway 13 South. Merge onto Interstate 580 East. Exit at Hayward–Foothill Blvd. Go straight ahead onto Foothill Blvd. Turn right onto C Street. Go two blocks to Mission Blvd. and park near the old City Hall (see map, Fig. 44).

Stop Description

Start by looking through the glass doors on the old Hayward City Hall (now unused). Note the large cracks and other evidence of structural distress. This building was unfortunately built directly on the creeping strand of the Hayward fault. A creeping fault strand is one that slowly but continuously moves at the surface in response to the same forces that generate earthquakes. This creeping strand moves right (if you look across the fault, the other side is moving to the right) at ~6 mm/yr (Lienkaemper et al., 2001). That is only 0.0000000004 (4 ten-billionths) miles per hour, so don't try to see it go. However, over years and decades that continuous sliding adds up.

From City Hall, walk northwest along Mission Blvd, parallel to the creeping strand. Note that there is a little hill to the east. In addition to sliding right, the Hayward fault is also pushing its east side up ~0.5–1 mm/yr (Gilmore, 1992; Kelson and Simpson, 1995; Lienkaemper and Borchardt, 1996). Half a block past B Street, turn right into the City of Hayward parking lot. Here look for evidence of the creeping strand on the pavement, curbs, and nearby buildings (Fig. 45).

Does surface creep mean that the fault is not building up the stress to generate a future earthquake? Unfortunately, probably not. Because the rate of surface creep is less than the long-term rate of fault offset, geologists believe that deep in the earth where large earthquakes are generated the fault is stuck tight and building up stress (Simpson et al., 2001). The last time this fault released that stress was in 1868, when it produced a severe earthquake that caused major regional damage (Fig. 46).

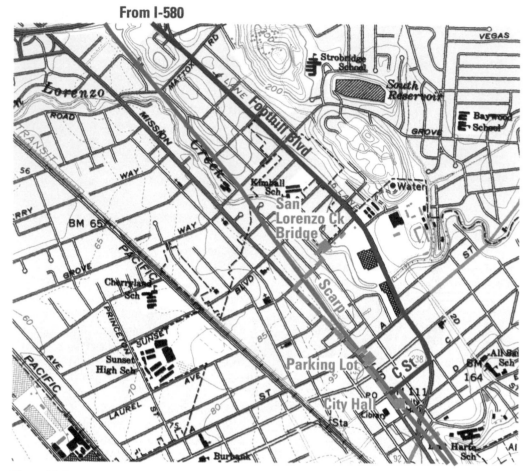

Figure 44. Topographic map of downtown Hayward and north. The driving route is shown in blue; the walking route and the features mentioned in text are shown in green. The creeping strands of the Hayward fault are shown in orange.

From the parking lot, continue northwest on Mission Blvd two blocks past A Street to Simon Street. Turn right and climb up the steep hill pushed up by the Hayward fault. A steep hillside like this is called a scarp. Just over the top of the hill, turn briefly left on Main Street, then immediately right onto Hazel Street and go to the bridge over San Lorenzo Creek. Note that the creek here is running northwest, parallel to the creeping strand (Fig. 44). Where creeks and streams cross active faults, they are frequently deflected by the long-term offset of the fault (Wallace, 1990). Looking at the map of San Lorenzo Creek, you can see that it is deflected to the right in two places, here and on the other side of the hill to the northwest, although neither of those deflections is directly along the creeping strand (Lienkaemper, 1992). That means that there are probably two more strands of the Hayward fault in this area that pulled the stream into its current shape (Fig. 47). Are these strands part of the active Hayward fault? Geologists do not know. Unfortunately, scientific studies that were undertaken after the 1868 earthquake have been lost, so we don't now know if either of the strands that offset the creek broke the

Figure 45. Photograph of evidence of right lateral creep on the mapped active strand of the Hayward fault. This offset curb is in the parking lot between A and B streets in downtown Hayward.

ground during that quake. However, geologists do know that long-term offset on the Hayward fault has taken place on several strands and that here the creeping strand has taken up at most 5% of the total offset over the fault's geologic history (Graymer et al., 1995; Graymer, 1999). Radiometric dating of offset rocks suggest that the fault has a total offset of ~100 km or 60 mi in the past 12 million years (Graymer et al., 2002), but only at most 3 mi (5 km) can have occurred on the creeping strand because that strand runs right through an only slightly offset rock body. Perhaps the creek-deflecting strands are now-abandoned old strands, or perhaps they are still-active strands that aren't creeping. We are still learning about how the complicated Hayward fault works.

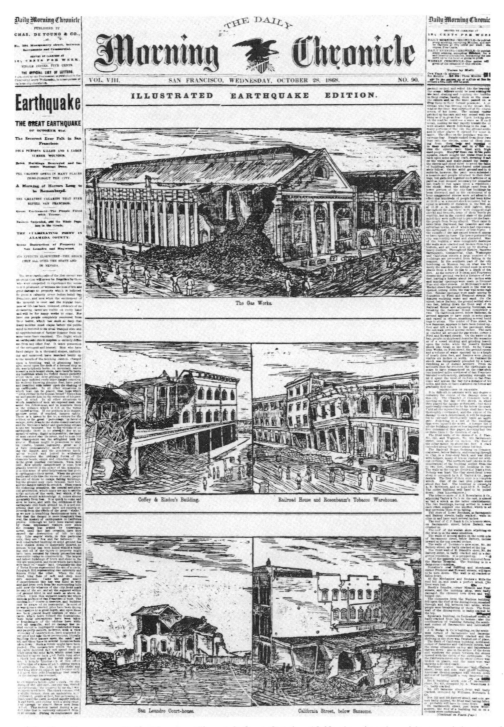

Figure 46. Front page of the *San Francisco Daily Morning Chronicle* from October 1868, showing the widespread damage from the earthquake generated by rupture of the Hayward fault. This earthquake was known as the Great San Francisco Earthquake until 1906.

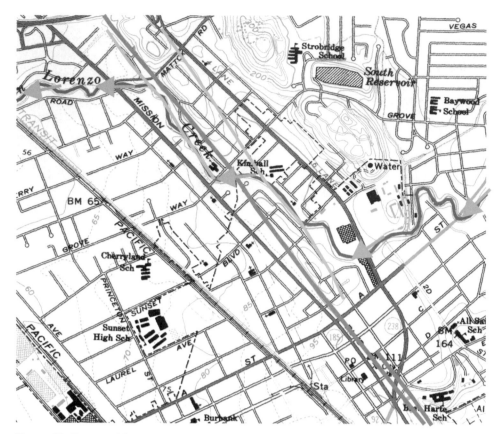

Figure 47. Topographic map of downtown Hayward and north. The mapped active trace of the Hayward fault is shown as a thick orange line, San Lorenzo Creek is shown by the blue line, and the double right-step in San Lorenzo Creek is illustrated by the blue arrows. The non-creeping strands of the Hayward fault that probably caused the double right-step are shown in green.

Stop 10: Fault Trench Exhibit at Fremont Central Park (Heidi Stenner, Jim Lienkaemper, and Mary Lou Zoback)

Significance of the Site

The Hayward fault has been studied and trenched extensively in Fremont's Central Park to help locate new civic structures away from active fault traces and to evaluate the safety of existing structures in and near the fault. The 1868 earthquake on the Hayward fault broke the earth's surface at this location. A trench excavated in 1987 represented a particularly clear example of the active Hayward fault trace. This trench will be reopened for two months in 2006 as an exhibit to show the public what an active fault looks like beneath the surface (to depths of 10–15 ft) and to explain how it produces earthquakes.

Accessibility

This exhibit is on City of Fremont property and has ample parking and public restrooms nearby. Wheelchairs can access the site.

GPS Coordinates

37.549205°N, 121.968917°W.

Directions

From the City of Hayward, take I-880 South. Exit to the Northeast onto Stephenson Boulevard. You will be heading toward the East Bay hills. Turn right onto Paseo Padre Parkway. Turn left onto Sailway Road into Central Park. The Trench Exhibit will be northwest of the parking area. Signs will guide you.

Stop Description

Do earthquakes tend to repeat at regular intervals? If so, knowing when they have happened in the past may tell us when to expect the next one. Many earthquakes happened long before people were recording history, so how can we discover what happened so long ago?

Geologists look for evidence by digging into the ground to study the layers of earth that accumulate, one on top of the other, over time. Like the pages of a history book, each layer records what was happening at that time. A layer of round rocks can indicate an ancient river, whereas a layer of mud can be from an ancient flood. Layers also record earthquakes. The ground can shift several feet or much more during an earthquake, disrupting the layers (and "tearing" the pages of Earth's history book). In the years after an earthquake, new layers of rock and soil may blanket the area and bury the broken layers below.

To go back in time, geologists dig trenches up to 20 ft deep and 10 ft wide and then walk in to observe the layers. If there has been a large quake, the sediment will be disrupted along the fault. Any layers that are not disturbed and that rest on top of the faulted layers were laid down after the earthquake. Then, if we can figure out when the layers formed, we can date the earthquake. Geologists look for plant or animal remains, like sticks or shells, in the buried layers and date them using the same tools used by archaeologists.

With the information gathered in the trenches, geologists can tell how often earthquakes occur and even how large past quakes were. The more scientists know about a fault's past, the better they are able to suggest what may happen in the future.

This fault trench exhibit in Fremont's Central Park (Fig. 48) consists of an open pit that exposes the Hayward fault in a locality where the steep fault ruptured in 1868 and is easily observed in the different types of sediment (Fig. 49). The Fig. 49 photo comes from a trench located where the exhibit is today, ~150 feet north of the front of the former library (now the teen center). The public can observe the fault from the ground surface as well as walk down into the pit for a closer look. Visitors can also see where slow and constant creep along the fault is

deforming the parking lot. A series of explanatory posters and exhibit material and brochures cover what happened during the earthquake here in 1868, a description of the City of Fremont's response to dealing with the hazard posed by the Hayward fault, as well as general information on earthquake preparedness and mitigation.

The exhibit is open for two months, beginning in April 2006 and concluding in May 2006, and is open both during the week (by appointment, primarily for school groups) as well as on the weekend for individuals and families. Volunteer docents will staff the exhibit during operating hours. The exhibit includes a rectangular open pit roughly 10–15 ft deep with gently sloped sides and stair access to the bottom. The fault trace is exposed on two walls of the pit and is highlighted with surface markers to help explain it.

Stop 11: Bay Division Pipeline Crossing, Fremont (Donald Wells and John Eidinger)

Significance of the Site

The Bay Division Pipelines Nos. 1 and 2 are owned by the San Francisco Public Utilities Commission (SFPUC) and supply drinking water from the Sierra Nevada Mountains and local watersheds to customers in four Bay Area counties. These

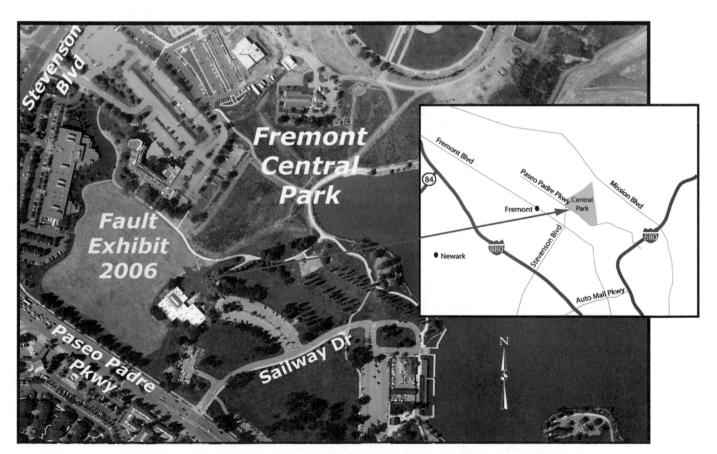

Figure 48. An aerial view of Central Park in Fremont with an inset of a road map showing its location.

pipelines, along with Bay Division Pipelines Nos. 3 and 4 located ~4 mi south, are a critical lifeline facility that supplies most of the water to the 2.4 million people in San Francisco, San Mateo, Santa Clara, and Alameda counties either directly or through wholesale customers. These four pipelines all cross the southern reach of the Hayward fault. The San Francisco Public Utilities Commission and its consultants have evaluated the fault rupture hazard and have developed and implemented mitigation measures to minimize the potential for damage and loss of service to the pipelines due to surface fault rupture along the Hayward fault.

Accessibility

There is parking along north side of Grimmer Boulevard at the intersection of Paseo Padre Parkway. The Bay Division Pipelines 1 and 2 cross beneath Paseo Padre Parkway ~400 ft southeast of the intersection with Grimmer Boulevard, continuing west beneath Grimmer Boulevard ~500 ft west of the intersection with Paseo Padre Parkway.

GPS Coordinates

37.5408°N, 121.9050°W.

Directions

From the parking lot at Fremont Civic Center–Lake Elizabeth, return to Paseo Padre Parkway, and turn left. Continue 1.0 mi south to intersection with Grimmer Boulevard. Turn right on Grimmer Boulevard, and park in the dirt area on right side of road. Walk across Grimmer Boulevard to the sidewalk and dirt area at the corner of Paseo Padre Parkway and Grimmer Boulevard.

Stop Description

The Bay Division Pipelines (BDPL) Nos. 1 and 2 extend ~21 mi from the Irvington Tunnel in Fremont westward under San Francisco Bay to the Pulgas Tunnel near Redwood City. BDPL No. 1 is a 60-inch, riveted steel pipeline constructed in 1925. BDPL No. 2 is a 66-inch, welded steel pipeline constructed in 1935. The pipelines run parallel in an 80-ft-wide right-of-way and cross the Hayward fault in the vicinity of Paseo Padre Parkway and Grimmer Boulevard in Fremont (Fig. 50). The pipelines are buried in the area of the Hayward fault, except for a 200-ft-long above-ground, pedestal-supported reach located west of the fault.

In the Central Park area of Fremont, the Hayward fault is characterized by a well-located creeping fault, designated as the western trace, and a discontinuous eastern trace that bound a low knoll at the Fremont Civic Center and a depression at Tule Pond north of Lake Elizabeth (Fig. 51). The average horizontal creep rate on the western fault trace over the past ~20 years is ~5 mm/yr in the area of Lake Elizabeth (Galehouse, 2002). At Lake Elizabeth, the western trace of the Hayward fault bounds a series of low, rounded hills on the west from a low-lying area on the east (Fig. 51). The low-lying area was formerly called Stivers Lagoon; this lagoon was modified by the City of Fremont to develop Central Park and the Lake Elizabeth recreation

Figure 49. (*this and following page*) (A) Photograph of the Hayward fault exposure in a trench opened in 1987 on City of Fremont property (photo courtesy of San Jose Mercury News). The fault is a sharp boundary between fine-grained gray silt and light-colored sandy gravels.

area. Borchardt et al. (2000) present a summary of the development history of the Fremont Civic Center site. The extent of the eastern trace south from the Civic Center knoll along Lake Elizabeth is uncertain.

Inspection of the BDPL 1 and 2 in the early 1990s by the SFPUC revealed that the pipes were distressed due to fault creep and that expansion couplings originally outfitted on both sides of the fault had accommodated some of the slip due to fault creep (Eidinger, 2001). The SFPUC determined that these pipelines, as well as BDPL 3 and 4 (located 4 mi south of BDPL 1 and 2), could fail due to ongoing fault creep or rupture of the Hayward fault. Although the SFPUC has raw water storage facilities along the peninsula, the system is dependent upon a steady of flow of drinking water through the Bay Division Pipelines to service their customers, particularly during peak demand. Thus, failure of these pipelines would result in significant reduction in water service to the South Bay and Peninsula customers. The SFPUC initiated a program to evaluate and mitigate the potential for loss of service to these four pipelines.

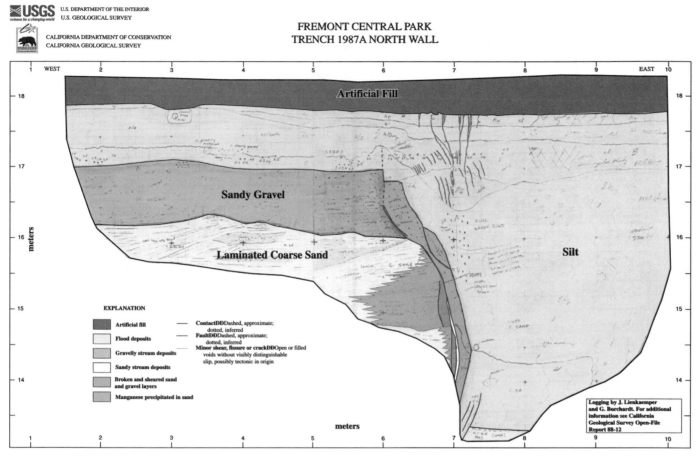

Figure 49. (*continued*) (B) Geologic log of the opposite wall of the trench with a 2-ft grid superimposed.

Geomatrix Consultants (1999) conducted detailed investigations at the BDPL 1 and 2 to locate the western (creeping) trace of the Hayward fault, to assess the evidence for an eastern trace of the Hayward fault, and to define the width of the fault zone and the expected displacement during future earthquakes. Fault trenching showed that the pipelines traverse the main active trace of the Hayward fault along the projected location of the main creeping trace of the fault. The zone of active creep and major deformation is ~20 ft wide, and zones of subsidiary faulting and folding extend 15–30 ft on each side of the primary zone of creep and faulting (Fig. 52). The eastern fault trace observed to the north at the Civic Center knoll was not observed in the fault trenches and does not extend to the BDPL. The trenching investigation also showed that the expansion couplings installed during construction of the pipeline to span the fault zone were mislocated to the east of the main creeping trace of the fault.

The SFPUC design team considered two levels of fault displacement for the design of retrofit measures for BDPL 1 and 2. The displacements were based on a probabilistic distribution of maximum magnitudes for rupture of the Hayward fault and empirical relationships between magnitude and fault displacement (Geomatrix, 1999). The "probable earthquake" was selected at the 84th percentile nonexceedance level, corresponding to a horizontal displacement of 5 ft; a "maximum earthquake" displacement of 10 ft also was considered, which corresponds to about a 95th percentile nonexceedance level.

BDPL 1 and 2 intersect the Hayward fault at an angle of ~70°, such that right-lateral movement on the fault produces net tension in the pipes (Fig. 53). Detailed surveying of the pipelines also showed that fault creep was accommodated by slip only out of the westernmost expansion joint and that continued creep could result in failure of the pipeline by about the year 2010 or sooner. The design team considered several design options to replace the pipelines at the fault crossing. These options were based on a nonlinear structural model of the pipeline developed using three-dimensional nonlinear pipeline elements and suitable nonlinear soil springs (Eidinger, 2001).

The selected mitigation was the "rapid anchorage" design, which used new, thick, welded pipes set in pea gravel for 90 ft across the fault zone and in controlled low-strength material (CLSM) beyond the fault zone extending to Grimmer Boulevard and Paseo Padre Parkway (Fig. 54). Native soil was com-

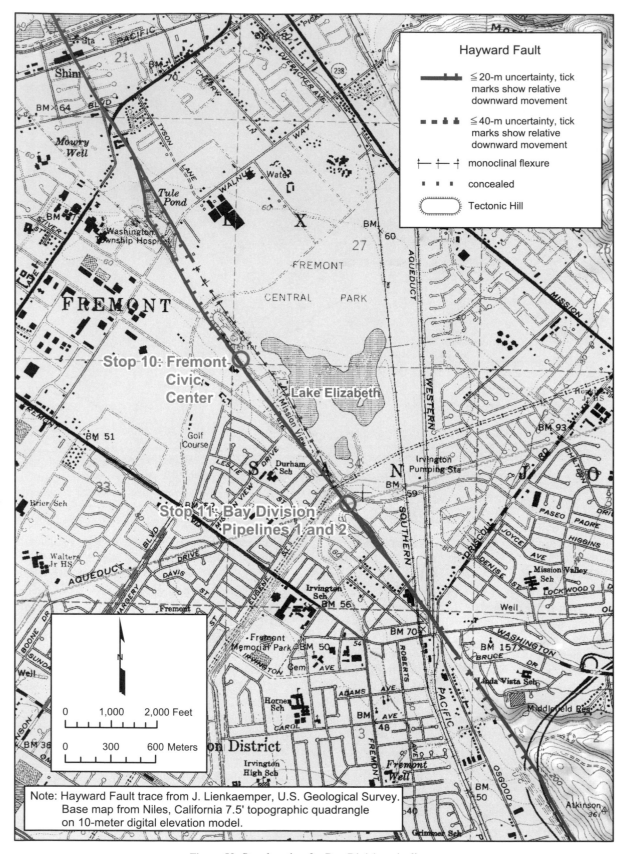

Figure 50. Stop location for Bay Division pipelines.

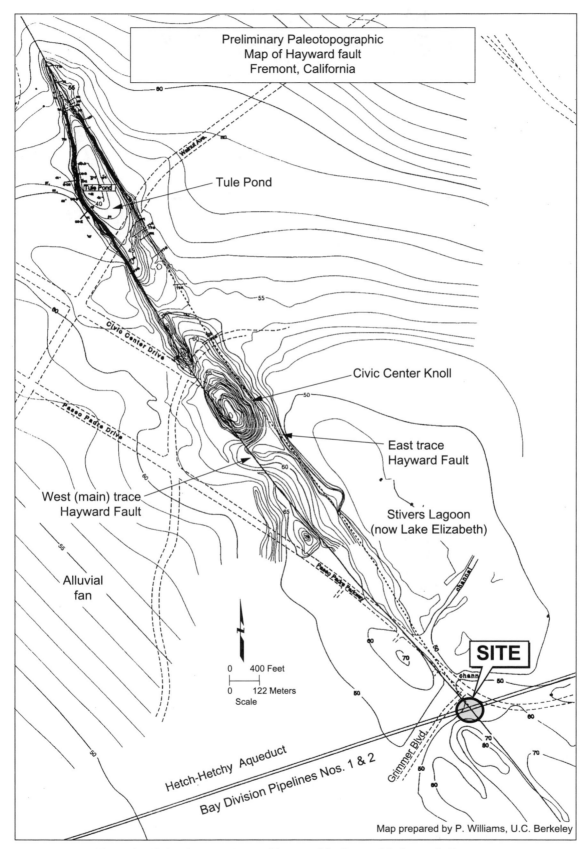

Preliminary Paleotopographic
Map of Hayward fault
Fremont, California

Tule Pond

Civic Center Knoll

East trace
Hayward Fault

West (main) trace
Hayward Fault

Stivers Lagoon
(now Lake Elizabeth)

Alluvial
fan

0   400 Feet
0   122 Meters
Scale

SITE

Hetch-Hetchy Aqueduct

Bay Division Pipelines Nos. 1 & 2

Map prepared by P. Williams, U.C. Berkeley

Figure 51. Predevelopment topographic map of the Hayward fault zone in Fremont.

HAYWARD FAULT ZONE

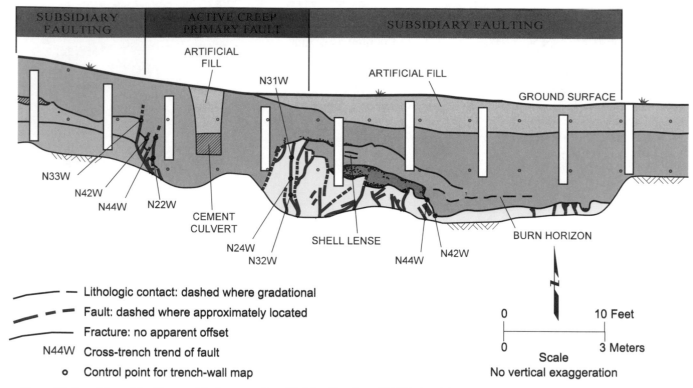

Figure 52. Trench log of the Hayward fault zone at Bay Division Pipelines (BDPL) 1 and 2 crossing. From Geomatrix Consultants (1999).

pacted to grade overlying the pea gravel and CLSM. The pea gravel was designed to permit flexure of the pipeline in the event of rupture on the Hayward fault. New welded steel pipelines were slip-lined and grouted in place through the existing pipelines beneath Grimmer Boulevard and Paseo Padre Parkway; the slip-line pipe reaches were connected to the existing pipe beyond the roads using a butt strap joint. This option was selected in part because this method would not require trenching across the city streets adjacent to the site. Other considerations in this design option included:

- Selecting a hard, epoxy-type corrosion protection to promote transfer of strain into the pipeline section anchored in the CLSM;
- Adding straps (lugs) to the pipeline to improve anchorage in the CLSM and to minimize transfer of strain to the adjacent original pipeline sections;
- Installing new seismic isolation valves ~650 ft away from the fault;
- Installing 24″ bypass pipelines with a manifolds designed for use with six 12″ flexible hoses; and
- Constructing a retaining wall to stabilize sloping ground adjacent to the pipelines.

The hydraulically actuated isolation valves can be closed remotely without the need for an additional power source.

Bypass pipeline manifolds are located on both sides of the fault zone, such that flex hoses could be installed across the fault to restore water flow in the unlikely event of failure of the pipelines between the valves. The performance objective of the bypass pipeline is to restore most of the water supply across the Hayward fault within 24 hours in the event of pipeline failure.

Mitigation options for BDPL 3 and 4 were developed using a cost-benefit analysis (discussed in Eidinger, 2001), and implementation of the selected option(s) has recently been initiated.

ACKNOWLEDGMENTS

The authors wish to thank the following organizations for permission to visit the sites and facilities described in this guidebook: The University of California at Berkeley, East Bay Municipal Utility District, San Francisco Public Utilities Commission, and the cities of Pinole, Berkeley, Oakland, Hayward, and Fremont. The support of Geomatrix Consultants for Donald Wells and the extensive work by Javier Chalini, David O'Shea, and Steve Wessels of the Graphics Design Group of Geomatrix Consultants in preparing illustrations for several of the stops is greatly appreciated. We also appreciate the use of several original illustrations provided by the Earthquake Engineering Research Institute, Oakland, California.

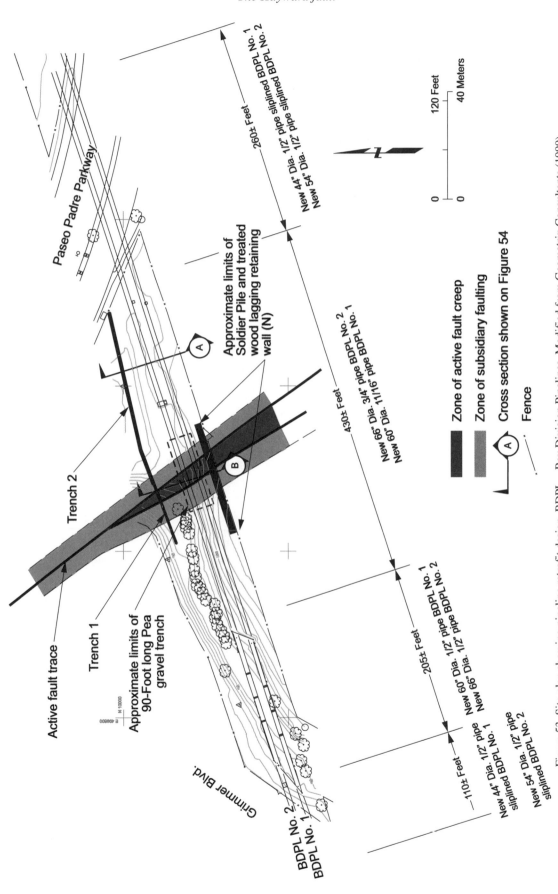

Figure 53. Site plan showing pipeline retrofit design. BDPL—Bay Division Pipelines. Modified from Geomatrix Consultants (1999).

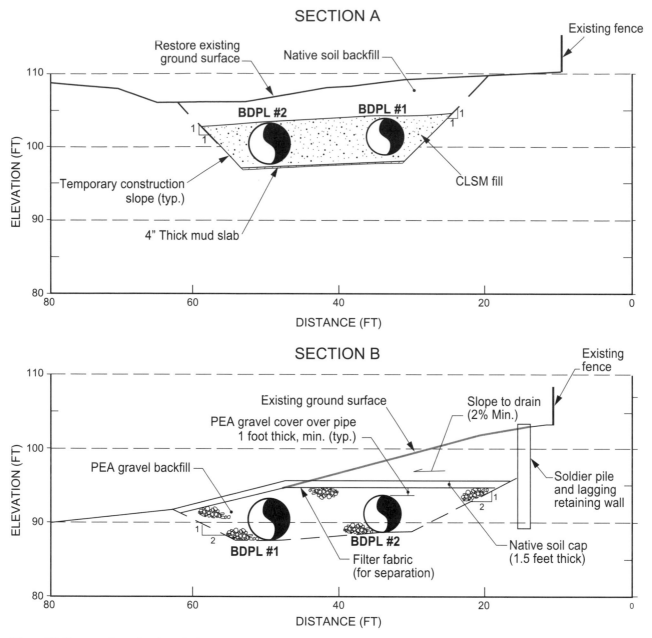

Figure 54. Cross sections showing pipeline retrofit design. (A) Cross section through fault zone reach. (B) Cross section outside fault zone reach. BDPL—Bay Division Pipelines. From Geomatrix Consultants (1999).

REFERENCES CITED

General References for the Hayward Fault

Ponce, D.A., Bürgmann, R., Graymer, R.W., Lienkaemper, J.J., Moore, D.E., and Schwartz, D.P., 2003, Proceedings of the Hayward Fault Workshop, Eastern San Francisco Bay Area, California, September 19–20, 2003: U.S. Geological Survey Open-File Report 2003-485, 71 p. URL: http://pubs.usgs.gov/of/2003/of03-485/.

U.S. Geological Survey, "Browse the Hayward fault map": http://quake.wr.usgs.gov/research/geology/hf_map/HF_index.html.

Stop 1: Memorial Stadium

Borchardt, G., Taylor, C.L., Rogers, J.D., Wells, D.L., Shastid, T., Yiadom, A., Ortiz, J., and Williams, P.L., 2000, Engineering for surface ground rupture on the Hayward fault: *in* Alvarez, L., ed., AEG-GRA 2000 Field Trip Guidebook, From the Pacific Ocean to the Sierra Nevada: Taming Shaky Ground: Association of Engineering Geologists and Groundwater Resources Association, Chap. 6, 25 p.

Doolin, D.M., Wells, D.L., and Williams, P.L., 2005, Assessment of fault-creep deformation at Memorial Stadium, University of California, Berkeley, California: Environmental & Engineering Geoscience, v. 11, no. 2, p. 125–139, doi: 10.2113/11.2.125.

Galehouse, J.S., 2002, Data from theodolite measurements of creep rates on San Francisco Bay region faults, California: 1979–2001: U.S. Geological Survey Open-File Report 02-225, http://geopubs.wr.usgs.gov/open-file/of02-225/.

Geomatrix Consultants, Inc., 2001, Fault rupture hazard evaluation, California Memorial Stadium: Report prepared for Capitol Projects, University of California, Berkeley, October.

Harding Lawson Associates, 1986, Geologic and Fault Hazard Investigation Phase I, Foothill Student Housing, University of California, Berkeley: Report Prepared for O'Brien-Kreitzberg and Associates, San Francisco, 13 November, 3 p., 28 plates.

Harding Lawson Associates, 1988a, Geologic and Fault Hazard Investigation Phase II, Foothill Student Housing, University of California, Berkeley: Report Prepared for O'Brien-Kreitzberg and Associates, San Francisco, 12 January, 31 p., 48 plates.

Harding Lawson Associates, 1988b, Supplemental Fault Hazard Investigation, "Louderback Trace," Foothill Student Housing Project, University of California, Berkeley: Report Prepared for O'Brien-Kreitzberg and Associates, San Francisco, 22 June.

Hirschfeld, S.E., Borchardt, G., Kelson, K.I., Lienkaemper, J.J., and Williams, P.L., 1999, The Hayward Fault—Source of the next big Quake? *in* Wagner, D.L., and Graham, S.A., eds., Geologic Field Trips in Northern California: California Geological Survey Special Publication 119, p. 150–159.

Lennert, B.J., 1982, Accurate location of the active trace of the Hayward fault between Ashby and Marin Avenues in Berkeley, with proposed models of stress-strain conditions from creep and rapid offset, *in* Hart, E.W., Hirschfeld, S.E., and Schulz, S.S., eds., Proceedings, Conference on Earthquake Hazards in the Eastern San Francisco Bay Area: California Division of Mines and Geology Special Publication 62, p. 45–54.

Stop 4: UC Richmond Field Station

George E. Brown Jr. Network for Earthquake Engineering Simulation (NEES): University of California at Berkeley, http://nees.berkeley.edu

Pacific Earthquake Engineering Research Center (PEER): University of California at Berkeley Richmond Field Annex maps: http://peer.berkeley.edu/PEERCenter/Contact/maps.html.

Stop 5: Point Pinole

Bilham, R., 2005, Creepmeters on the San Andreas fault system: http://cires.colorado.edu/~bilham/creepmeter.file/creepmeters.htm.

Bloom, A.L., 1970, Paludal stratigraphy of Truk, Ponape; and Kusaie, Eastern Caroline Islands: Geological Society of America Bulletin, v. 81, p. 1895–1904.

Borchardt, G., 1988a, Soil development and displacement along the Hayward fault, Point Pinole Regional Shoreline, Richmond, California, *in* Borchardt, Glenn, ed., Soil development and displacement along the Hayward fault (Volume II): Point Pinole, California, California Division of Mines and Geology Open-File Report DMG OFR 88-13, p. 95–161.

Borchardt, G., 1988b, Estuarine deposition and its relationship to the Hayward fault, Point Pinole Regional Shoreline, Richmond, California, *in* Borchardt, Glenn, ed., Soil development and displacement along the Hayward fault (Volume II): Point Pinole, California, California Division of Mines and Geology Open-File Report DMG OFR 88-13, p. 163–220.

Borchardt, G., and Seelig, K.A., 1991, Soils, paleosols, and Quaternary sediments offset along the Hayward fault at Point Pinole Regional Shoreline, Richmond, California, *in* Sloan, Doris, and Wagner, D. L., eds., Geologic excursions in northern California: San Francisco to the Sierra Nevada, California Department of Conservation, Division of Mines and Geology Special Publication 109, p. 75–83.

Borchardt, G., Seelig, K.A., and Wagner, D.L., 1988, Geology, paleosols, and crustal stability at Point Pinole Regional Shoreline, Contra Costa County, California, *in* Borchardt, G., ed., Soil development and displacement along the Hayward fault (Volume II): Point Pinole, California, California Division of Mines and Geology Open-File Report DMG OFR 88-13, p. 3–94.

Edwards, R.L., Chen, R.H., Ku, T.-L., and Wasserburg, G.J., 1987, Precise timing of the last interglacial period from mass spectrometric determination of Thorium-230 in corals: Science, v. 236, p. 1547–1553.

Harsh, P.W., and Burford, R.O., 1982, Alinement-array measurements of fault slip in the eastern San Francisco Bay area, California, *in* Hart, E.W., Hirschfeld, S. E., and Schulz, S.S., eds., Proceedings of the Conference on Earthquake Hazards in the Eastern San Francisco Bay Area, California Division of Mines and Geology Special Publication 62, p. 251–260.

Lienkaemper, J.J., Borchardt, G.R., and Lisowski, M., 1991, Historic creep rate and potential for seismic slip along the Hayward fault, California: Journal of Geophysical Research, v. 96, no. B11, p. 18,261–18,283.

Steinbrugge, K.V., Bennett, J.H., Lagorio, H.J., Davis, J.F., Borchardt, G.R., Toppozada, T., Degenkolb, H.J., Laverty, G.L., and McCarty, J.E., 1987, Earthquake planning scenario for a magnitude 7.5 earthquake on the Hayward fault in the San Francisco Bay area, California Department of Conservation, Division of Mines and Geology Special Publication 78, 243 p.

Stop 6: Cragmont School

Bishop, C.C., 1973, Geological and geophysical investigations for tri-cities seismic safety and environmental resources study: California Division of Mines and Geology Preliminary Report 19, 44 p.

California Division of Mines and Geology, 1982, Special Study Zones, Richmond 7.5-minute Quadrangle, 1:24,000.

Case, J.E., 1963, Geology of a portion of the Berkeley and San Leandro Hills, California [PhD. dissertation]: Berkeley, University of California, 216 p.

Cotton, W., and Associates, June 1993, Engineering Geologic and Geotechnical Engineering Investigation, Cragmont Elementary School, Berkeley, California, AP#2602.

Cotton, W., and Associates, September 1995, Supplemental Fault Investigation, Cragmont Elementary School: Berkeley, California, AP#2602.

Dibblee, T.W., Jr., 1980, Preliminary geologic map of the Richmond quadrangle, Alameda and Contra Costa Counties, California: U.S. Geological Survey Open-File Report 80-1100, scale 1:24,000.

Graymer, R.W., Jones, D.L., and Brabb, E.E., 1995, Geologic map of the Hayward fault zone, Contra Costa, Alameda, and Santa Clara Counties, California: A digital database: U.S. Geological Survey Open-File Report 95-597, http://wrgis.wr.usgs.gov/open-file/of95-597/.

Graymer, R.W., 2000, Geologic map and map database of the Oakland metropolitan area, Alameda, Contra Costa and San Francisco Counties, California: U.S. Geological Survey Miscellaneous Field Studies MF-2342, http://geopubs.wr.usgs.gov/map-mf/mf2342/.

Harding Lawson Associates, 1991, Fault and Landslide Hazard Evaluation, Cragmont School, Berkeley, California: unpublished consultant report no. 3874,034.03 to the Berkeley Unified School District, 20 p.

Herd, D.G., 1978, Map of Quaternary faulting along the northern Hayward Fault Zone; Mare Island, Richmond, Briones Valley, Oakland West, Oakland East, San Leandro, Hayward, and Newark 7–1/2′ Quadrangles, California: U.S. Geological Survey Open-File Report 78-308, scale 1:24,000.

Hilley, G.E., Burgman, R., Ferretti, A., Novali, F., and Rocca, F., 2004, Dynamics of slow-moving landslides from permanent scatter analysis: Science, v. 304, p. 1952–1955, doi: 10.1126/science.1098821.

Hoexter, D.F., Knudsen, K., Hecht, B., Laduzinsky, D., and Fielder, G., 1992, Creep and downslope movements in the Hayward fault zone in North Berkeley: Ten years later, *in* Second Conference, Earthquake Hazards in the Eastern San Francisco Bay Area: California Division of Mines and Geology Special Publication 113, p. 121–127.

Hoexter, D.F., Levine, C.R., Hecht, B., and Collier, G., 1982, Deformation along the Hayward fault zone, North Berkeley: Fault creep and landsliding, *in* Hart, E.W., Hirschfeld, S.E., and Schulz, S.S., eds., Proceedings, Conference on Earthquake Hazards in the Eastern San Francisco Bay Area: California Division of Mines and Geology Special Publication 62, p. 1–10.

Jones, D.L., and Curtis, G.H., 1991, Guide to the geology of the Berkeley Hills, central Coast Ranges, California, *in* Sloan, D., and Wagner, D.L., eds., Geologic Excursions in Northern California: San Francisco to the Sierra Nevada: California Division of Mines and Geology Special Publication 109, p. 63–74.

Kropp, A., and Associates, 1995, Landslides of the Berkeley Hills: Berkeley, Alan Kropp and Associates, unpublished consultant's map, scale 1:24,000.

Lennert, B.J., 1982, Accurate location of the active trace of the Hayward fault between Ashby and Marin Avenues in Berkeley, with proposed models of stress-strain conditions for creep and rapid offset: California Division of Mines and Geology Special Publication, v. 62, p. 45–54.

Lienkaemper, J.J., 1992, Map of recently active traces of the Hayward fault, Alameda and Contra Costa Counties, California: U.S. Geological Survey Miscellaneous Field Studies Map MF-2196, 13 p., 1 sheet, scale 1:24,000.

Nilsen, T.H., 1975, Preliminary photointerpretive map of landslide and other surficial deposits of the Richmond 7.5-minute quadrangle, Contra Costa and Alameda Counties, California: U.S. Geological Survey Open-File Report 75-227-47, scale 1:24,000.

Ponce, D.A., Burgmann, R., Graymer, R.W., Lienkaemper, J.J., Moore, D.E., and Schwartz, D.P., 2003, Proceedings of the Hayward Fault Workshop, Eastern San Francisco Bay Area, California, September 19–20, 2003: U.S. Geological Survey Open File Report 03-485, 71 p.

Radbruch-Hall, D.H., 1974, Map showing recently active breaks along the Hayward fault zone and the southern part of the Calaveras fault zone, Cali-

fornia: U.S. Geological Survey Miscellaneous Geologic Investigations Map I-813, scale 1:24,000.

Waterhouse, G.V., 1992, The Hayward fault and deep-seated landsliding in the Northern Berkeley Hills, *in* Hart, E.W., Hirschfeld, S.E., and Schulz, S.S., eds., Proceedings, Conference on Earthquake Hazards in the Eastern San Francisco Bay Area: California Division of Mines and Geology Special Publication 62, p. 1–10.

Stop 7: Oakland City Hall

DIS, Inc., 2005, Oakland City Hall project brief: http://www.dis-inc.com/oakbrief.htm.

Steiner, F., and Elsesser, E., 2004, Design decision, methods, and procedures: Oakland City Hall repair and upgrades: Earthquake Engineering Research Institute Report DS-4, 29 p.

Stop 8: Claremont Water Tunnel Portal

Borchardt, G., Taylor, C.L., Rogers, J.D., Wells, D.L., Shastid, T., Yiadom, A., Ortiz, J., and Williams, P.L., 2000, Engineering for surface ground rupture on the Hayward fault, *in* Alvarez, L., ed., AEG-GRA 2000 Field Trip Guidebook, from the Pacific Ocean to the Sierra Nevada: Taming shaky ground: Association of Engineering Geologists and Groundwater Resources Association, Chap. 6, 25 p.

Galehouse, J.S., 2002, Data from theodolite measurements of creep rates on San Francisco Bay region faults, California: 1979–2001: U.S. Geological Survey Open-File Report 02-225, http://geopubs.wr.usgs.gov/open-file/of02-225/.

Geomatrix Consultants, 2001, Preliminary geologic interpretive report for the Claremont Tunnel Seismic Upgrade Project: Report for East Bay Municipal Utility District, Oakland, California, 54 p.

Kieffer, D.S., Caulfield, R.J., and Tsztoo, D.F., 2004, Seismic retrofit of the Claremont Tunnel, Proceedings of the EUROCK 2004 and 53rd Geomechanics Colloquium: International Society of Rock Mechanics Regional Symposium, Salzburg, Austria, October 7–9, 6 p.

Stop 9: City of Hayward Fault Creep

Gilmore, T.D., 1992, Historical uplift measured across the eastern San Francisco Bay region, *in* Borchardt, G., et al., eds., Proceedings of the Second Conference on Earthquake Hazards in the Eastern San Francisco Bay Area: California Division of Mines and Geology Special Publication 113, p. 55–62.

Graymer, R.W., 1999, Offset history of the Hayward fault zone, San Francisco Bay region, California: Geological Society of America Abstracts with Programs, v. 31, no. 6, p. 59.

Graymer, R.W., Jones, D.L., and Brabb, E.E., 1995, Geologic map of the Hayward fault zone, Contra Costa, Alameda, and Santa Clara Counties, California: A digital database: U.S. Geological Survey Open-File Report 95-597, http://wrgis.wr.usgs.gov/open-file/of95-597/.

Graymer, R.W., Sarna-Wojcicki, A.M., Walker, J.P., McLaughlin, R.J., and Fleck, R.J., 2002, Controls on timing and amount of right-lateral offset on the East Bay fault system, San Francisco Bay region, California: Geological Society of America Bulletin, v. 114, p. 1471–1479, doi: 10.1130/0016-7606(2002)114<1471:COTAAO>2.0.CO;2.

Kelson, K.I., and Simpson, G.D., 1995, Late Quaternary deformation of the southern East Bay Hills, Alameda County, California: American Association of Petroleum Geologists Bulletin, v. 79, p. 590.

Lienkaemper, J.J., 1992, Map of recently active traces of the Hayward Fault, Alameda and Contra Costa Counties, California: U.S. Geological Survey Miscellaneous Field Studies Map MF-2196, scale 1:24,000, 1 sheet, 13 p.

Lienkaemper, J.J., and Borchardt, G., 1996, Holocene slip rate of the Hayward Fault at Union City, California: Journal of Geophysical Research, v. 101, p. 6099–6108, doi: 10.1029/95JB01378.

Lienkaemper, J.J., Galehouse, J.S., and Simpson, R.W., 2001, Long-term monitoring of creep rate along the Hayward fault and evidence for a lasting creep response to 1989 Loma Prieta earthquake: Geophysical Research Letters, v. 28, p. 2265–2268, doi: 10.1029/2000GL012776.

Simpson, R.W., Lienkaemper, J.J., and Galehouse, J.S., 2001, Variations in creep rate along the Hayward fault, California, interpreted as change in depth of creep: Geophysical Research Letters, v. 28, p. 2269–2272, doi: 10.1029/2001GL012979.

Wallace, R.E., 1990, Geomorphic expression, *in* Wallace, R.E., ed., The San Andreas fault system, California: U.S. Geological Survey Professional Paper 1515, p. 15–58.

Stop 11: Fremont Pipeline Crossing

Borchardt, G., Taylor, C.L., Rogers, J.D., Wells, D.L., Shastid, T., Yiadom, A., Ortiz, J., and Williams, P.L., 2000, Engineering for surface ground rupture on the Hayward fault: *in* Alvarez, L., ed., AEG-GRA 2000 Field Trip Guidebook, From the Pacific Ocean to the Sierra Nevada: Taming shaky ground: Association of Engineering Geologists and Groundwater Resources Association, Chap. 6, 25 p.

Eidinger, J.M., 2001, Seismic retrofit of the Hetch Hetchy Aqueduct at the Hayward fault: *in* Castronova, J.P., ed., Pipeline 2001: Advances in Pipelines Engineering & Construction, American Society of Civil Engineers Conference, San Diego, California, July 15–18, 2001, 10 p.

Galehouse, J.S., 2002, Data from theodolite measurements of creep rates on San Francisco Bay region faults, California: 1979–2001: U.S. Geological Survey Open-File Report 02-225, http://geopubs.wr.usgs.gov/open-file/of02-225.

Geomatrix Consultants, Inc., 1999, Phase III Engineering Report on Geotechnical and other Specialized Engineering Services, Seismic Upgrade for Bay Division Pipeline Nos. 1 and 2: Report prepared for San Francisco Utilities Engineering Bureau, UEB Contract No. CS-458, May 1999.

Geological Society of America
Field Guide 7
2006

The new Carquinez Strait Bridge

Mark A. Ketchum
OPAC Consulting Engineers, 315 Bay Street, 2nd Floor, San Francisco, California 94133, USA
Donald Wells
Geomatrix Consultants, Inc., 2101 Webster Street, 12th Floor, Oakland, California 94612, USA

OVERVIEW OF FIELD TRIP

The Carquinez Strait (Alfred Zampa Memorial) Bridge (Figs. 1 and 2) is the first new toll bridge in California built to the stringent post-1989 performance-based design standards. This field trip consists of two stops that provide opportunities to observe the bridge site and discuss details of the design of the structure. The first stop on the south overlook of the strait provides an overview of the site. The second stop on the north side of the strait will start on the bicycle and pedestrian path plaza and will continue across the bridge.

Keywords: suspension bridge, seismic design, performance-based design, geologic hazards, geotechnical engineering, foundation design.

STOP 1: CARQUINEZ STRAIT SCENIC OVERLOOK PLAZA, SAN PABLO AVENUE, CROCKETT, CALIFORNIA

Significance of the Site

From this location, the Carquinez Strait Bridge, the Sacramento River channel that the bridge spans, and the site geological formations can be observed. Both structurally and architecturally, the Carquinez Strait Bridge is a modern interpretation of a classic suspension bridge. Completed in November 2003, it incorporates many firsts in U.S. suspension bridge design and construction, including drilled shaft foundations, reinforced concrete cellular towers, and an aerodynamically streamlined steel box girder roadway structure with orthotropic deck (Fig. 2). This stop provides an opportunity to observe and discuss the issues leading to the bridge-type selection, as well as its design and construction.

Accessibility

This is a public site with ample parking.

Directions

From San Francisco, take I-80 eastbound ~24 mi and exit Cummings Skyway (in Crockett), turn left at the end of the off-ramp onto Cummings Skyway, and then turn right at the end of Cummings Skyway onto San Pablo Avenue. Travel about 0.5 mi northbound on San Pablo Avenue to the strait overlook, which is on the left side of the highway.

Stop Description

The Carquinez Strait carries the waters of the Sacramento River into San Pablo Bay. The Carquinez Strait Bridge is at the mouth of the strait, at a headlands site where there are different geologic conditions and development patterns on each side of the river. The strait is currently spanned by two steel truss bridges, built in 1927 and 1958, and the new suspension bridge, which provide a vital links on the Interstate Highway 80 corridor.

The site has long been a transportation link between the Bay Area and Sacramento. Ferry service was initiated here in 1917. The first Carquinez Strait Bridge was completed in 1927, owned and operated by the private American Toll Bridge Company. University of California (UC) at Berkeley Dean of Engineering Charles Derleth Jr. was chief engineer and D.B. Steinman was the designing engineer. The State of California took over the bridge in 1940. The second Carquinez Strait Bridge was completed in 1958 as part of the interstate highway system, designed by the California Division of Highways. It is similar in layout to the first bridge, but incorporates many advancements, including the use of welded high-strength steel.

Ketchum, M.A., and Wells, D., 2006, The new Carquinez Strait Bridge, *in* Prentice, C.S., Scotchmoor, J.G., Moores, E.M., and Kiland, J.P., eds., 1906 San Francisco Earthquake Centennial Field Guides: Field trips associated with the 100th Anniversary Conference, 18–23 April 2006, San Francisco, California: Geological Society of America Field Guide 7, p. 333–338, doi: 10.1130/2006.1906SF(18). For permission to copy, contact editing@geosociety.org. ©2006 Geological Society of America. All rights reserved.

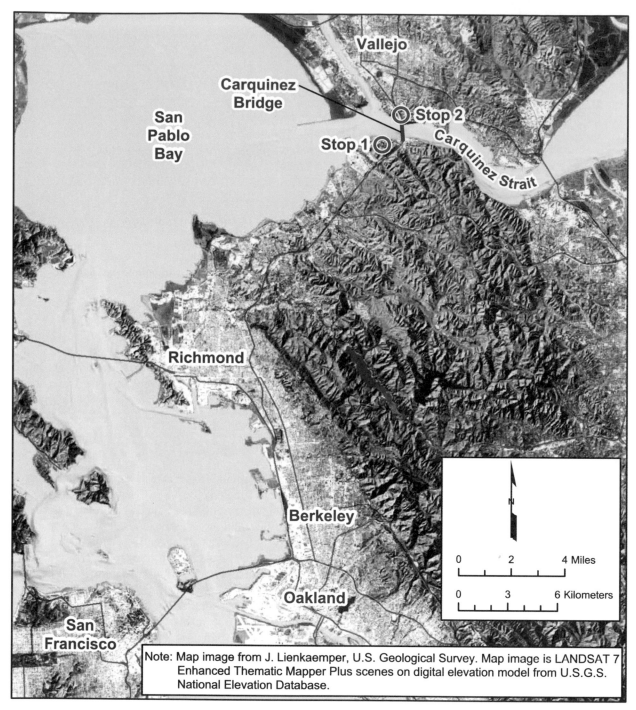

Figure 1. Location of Carquinez Strait Bridge.

Increasing traffic and deteriorating structural condition prompted funding for replacing the 1927 bridge to be included in Regional Measure 1, a 1988 ballot measure that was approved by the Bay Area electorate. The replacement schedule was accelerated when seismic studies identified a high retrofit cost for the aging structure.

Initial California Department of Transportation (Caltrans) studies for the replacement bridge included cable-stayed, arch, and truss alternatives, each with two main spans, similar in layout to the existing bridges. A suspension alternative was added, based on a concept developed independently by OPAC Consulting Engineers. In these initial studies, an orthotropic steel deck

Figure 2. Photograph of new Carquinez Strait (Alfred Zampa Memorial) Bridge.

suspension bridge and a concrete deck cable-stayed bridge were identified as the preferred alternatives.

Final type selection studies were performed under Caltrans supervision by the De Luew-OPAC-Steinman joint venture, which was engaged by Caltrans to design the bridge. The suspension alternative was selected for final design and construction, based on superior seismic performance, shorter construction schedule, less risk of ship impact due to fewer number of piers in the water, less maintenance required on the cable system, better aesthetics, and smaller construction risk. Projected construction costs for the alternatives were similar.

Geologic and Geotechnical Conditions for Foundation Design

The Carquinez Strait is a narrow channel that the Sacramento River has incised through the Central California Coast Ranges (Fig. 1). In this area, the late Cretaceous–age (ca. 100–65 Ma) Panoche Formation has been uplifted and folded, forming a generally northwest-trending ridge composed of steeply dipping, soft to hard, fine-grained marine sandstone, siltstone, and claystone (shale) (Fig. 3). These sedimentary rocks underlie the bluffs that define the strait. Young alluvial deposits and bay mud overlie bedrock along the margins of and along the channel between the bluffs.

An extensive geologic and geotechnical investigation was completed by Geomatrix Consultants and Earth Mechanics (1999) to characterize the subsurface conditions for the bridge foundation. The foundation elements included the north anchorage, north tower, south tower, south transition pier, and south anchorage, and during the design process, each of these

elements was evaluated for stability under both service and seismic loads. The seismic loads were based on a design earthquake of moment magnitude (M_W) 6.2 occurring on the Franklin fault, which lies ~1 km south and west of the bridge site (Fig. 3). A scouring analysis was performed to characterize three geologic conditions for the two towers, including existing conditions, maximum scour, and 50% of maximum scour, for use in stability analyses. The anchorages were analyzed for sliding and overturning forces based on the three-dimensional geometry of the foundation and the rock mass. A range of strength tests were performed on rock samples from each of the foundation sites to develop bearing capacities, lateral passive resistance pressure, lateral earth pressures, and side shear resistance of the rock sockets.

The north anchorage, located at the top of the bluff at an elevation of ~50 m, is underlain by thin soil deposits overlying relatively soft rock that has an average shear-wave velocity of ~550 m/s to a depth of ~90 m. The field and subsurface investigations revealed the rock to be highly weathered and extensively fractured. Field exploration also revealed a series of small northeast-trending shear zones and faults at the anchorage; these features correspond to the location of a possible eroded head scarp of an ancient landslide complex. The inferred head scarp of the landslide complex appeared to extend ~1.5 km northwest along Interstate Highway 80 from the strait, and the slide plane would extend west to the Mare Island Strait. Because the landslide mass appeared to be several tens of thousands to hundreds of thousands of years old, and because no evidence for recent movement on the inferred deep slide plane was observed, the potential for displacement on these structures

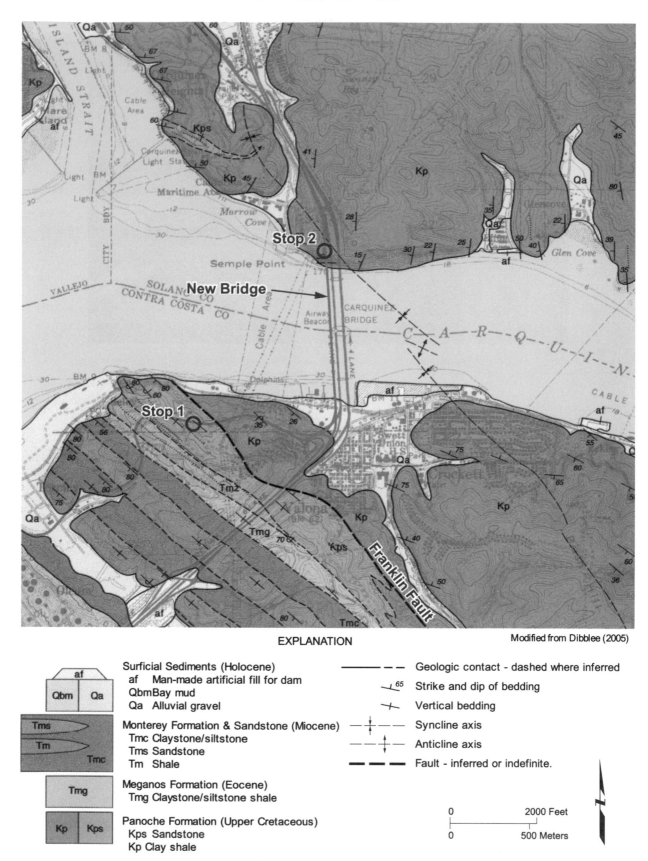

EXPLANATION

Modified from Dibblee (2005)

Surficial Sediments (Holocene)
af — Man-made artificial fill for dam
Qbm — Bay mud
Qa — Alluvial gravel

Monterey Formation & Sandstone (Miocene)
Tmc — Claystone/siltstone
Tms — Sandstone
Tm — Shale

Meganos Formation (Eocene)
Tmg — Claystone/siltstone shale

Panoche Formation (Upper Cretaceous)
Kps — Sandstone
Kp — Clay shale

Geologic contact - dashed where inferred

⌐65 — Strike and dip of bedding

— Vertical bedding

Syncline axis

Anticline axis

Fault - inferred or indefinite.

0   2000 Feet
0   500 Meters

Figure 3. Geologic map of Carquinez Strait area.

was not judged to be a significant hazard. In addition, static and dynamic stability analyses showed that for the observed conditions at the north anchorage, there was a reasonable factor of safety against block sliding on the inferred slide plane.

In the waterway, bedrock is encountered at elevations of –35 m to –40 m, and is overlain by alluvial deposits and bay mud ranging in thickness from a few meters at the north tower to nearly 30 m at the south tower. Some of these alluvial deposits are susceptible to liquefaction during earthquake shaking, and this was accounted for in the evaluation of the soil stiffness and capacity. The bedrock, which is fine-grained sandstone, siltstone, and claystone of the Panoche Formation, is fractured and fairly soft in some locations.

The transition pier and south anchorage were built in reclaimed land, with 3 to 5 m of fill overlying clay at the transition pier, and clay and sand at the south anchorage. Some of the sands at the south anchorage are susceptible to liquefaction, as noted for the towers. Bedrock, which is closely fractured, steeply dipping siltstone and claystone of the Panoche Formation, lies at an elevation of about –22 to –26 m at the transition pier and at an elevation of about –12 to –25 m at the south anchorage.

STOP 2: CARQUINEZ STRAIT BRIDGE PEDESTRIAN AND BICYCLE PLAZA, VALLEJO, CALIFORNIA

Significance of the Site

This location provides access to the north headlands and the bluff on which the north anchorage was built. It also provides an opportunity to walk across the bridge, allowing further inspection of the site and observation of the structure and the cable system, deck, and towers of the bridge. The pedestrian path used to access the location continues across the bridge. The path allows close observation of the structure, including the innovative concrete towers and unusual closed, aerodynamically streamlined, steel box girder roadway.

Accessibility

This is a public site but with limited parking.

Directions

From San Francisco, take I-80 eastbound ~26 mi. After crossing the Carquinez Strait Bridge, exit onto California Highway 29 (in Vallejo), turn left at Maritime Academy Drive, and travel about 0.25 mi and park where possible. Walk ~0.5 mi south on the pedestrian path and stop at the plaza.

Stop Description

The suspension bridge design has a main span of 728 m to provide the required navigation clearance in the north and south channels. The south-side span is relatively short (147 m) to

allow the south transition pier to clear the railroad tracks. The north-side span is longer (181 m) to clear a slide zone and fault in the cliff.

The towers are supported on 3-m-diameter shaft piles. Steel casings were driven through overburden and into the top of the rock, and then an uncased rock socket was drilled below the casing. The rock socket and casing were then reinforced and concreted. Twelve such shafts, with a maximum length of ~90 m, support each tower. The rock strength parameters and side shear resistance determined from the geotechnical investigation were used to define the minimum length of rock socket necessary for the compression, tension, and lateral load demands. The required length for the rock sockets resulted from a performance-based design selected from the results of axial load-deformation analyses.

Reinforced concrete pile caps with precast concrete shells transfer vertical and lateral loads between piles and tower, and provide platforms for construction of the tower shafts. Each of the four pile caps is ~22 × 18 m in plan and 6 m thick. Heavy reinforcement is required for long-term durability and for seismic resistance.

The towers are reinforced concrete portal frames with cellular shafts. The slightly inclined shafts allow clearance for the girder, yet allow the main cables to hang straight. Tied walls and hoop-reinforced corner pilasters were specially developed to meet stringent seismic criteria. They are constant-section as viewed by drivers, and taper in the other direction. This provides optimal performance, aesthetics, and constructability. The tower shafts were built in segments using jump forms.

The south transition pier supports the end of the steel deck girder, houses tie-downs that divert the geometry of the cables to the south anchorage, and supports the end of the south viaduct. It is structurally and architecturally similar to the main towers, with cellular reinforced concrete shafts and cast-in-steel shell pile foundations.

The south cable anchorage transfers the thrust of the cables to the ground via concrete anchor blocks, batter piles, and vertical cast-in-steel shell piles. The splay chambers rise 18 m above ground; the anchor blocks extend ~10 m beneath the ground surface. The subsurface investigations showed highly variable conditions at the south anchorage, which resulted in increased difficulty in construction of the foundation for the anchorage.

The north cable anchorage transfers the thrust of the cables to the ground by direct bearing on the underlying rock, and also serves as a bridge abutment. The concrete anchor blocks and splay chambers are benched into the rock beneath the roadway; only the relatively small saddle housings are exposed. The soft and highly fractured nature of the rock was a significant issue for design and construction of the anchorage, particularly with respect to the deep foundation excavation located between the existing toll booths on Interstate Highway 80 and the Pacific Gas & Electric (PG&E) transmission tower.

Overall, while the rock strength conditions identified in the field exploration program were somewhat lower than anticipated during the preliminary design process, and therefore necessitated some changes for the final design of the foundations, the subsurface conditions were favorable for the large permanent cable thrust loadings of the suspension bridge, and for support of the towers and pier.

The cables carry all loads from the deck to the towers and the ground. They were spun and compacted in the air from individual wires, using a computer-controlled spinning method that is a speed-enhanced evolutionary enhancement of the method used on the Bay and Golden Gate bridges. Steel castings transfer loads to the cables from the vertical suspender ropes, and transfer loads from the cables to the tops of the towers. Splay castings confine the cables in the anchorages.

The suspended superstructure consists of a 1056-m-long closed steel box girder, continuous from the north anchorage to the transition pier at the south, supported along its edges by the suspender ropes. The box girder is 3 m deep × 29 m wide. The edge plate and side plates are shaped to provide an aerodynamically stable cross section. The orthotropic deck of the girder consists of a 16-mm-thick deck plate with 305-mm-deep trapezoidal closed ribs fabricated from 8-mm-thick plates. The deck girder was fabricated in segments in Japan, transported to the site on ships, and hoisted into final position using strand jacks. After all segments were in place, they were welded together to provide the final continuous ribbon of steel.

After the girder was completed, the structure was essentially complete. There were still, however, many construction tasks remaining. These included but were not limited to wrapping and painting the main cables, installing the deck railings and pavement, and making a highway and functional footpath.

The new bridge is a major engineering and construction accomplishment. It brings many "firsts" to the region, to the engineering profession, and to the construction industry; it is (1) the first new toll bridge in the Bay Area since 1980, (2) the first new suspension bridge in the Bay Area since 1937, (3) the first major suspension bridge in the United States since 1973, (4) the first suspension bridge in the United States with an aerodynamic steel deck, (5) the first suspension bridge in the United States with concrete towers, (6) the first suspension bridge in the United States with shaft foundations, and (7) the first suspension bridge in the world with concrete towers in a high seismic zone.

STRUCTURAL QUANTITIES

Structural steel: 12,722,000 kg (14,000 t)
Cable steel: 4,600,000 kg (5060 t)
Structural concrete: 26,580 m³ (31,770 CY)
Reinforcing steel: 4,662,000 kg (5130 t)
3 m diameter concrete piling: 996 m (3300 ft)
2.700 m diameter rock socket: 741 m (2400 ft)
Anchorage piles: 380 ea
Anchorage piles: 12,565 m (41,200 ft)

ACKNOWLEDGMENTS

Owner: California Department of Transportation (Caltrans); Design: Caltrans Engineering Service Center and De Leuw-OPAC-Steinman joint venture; Contractor: FCI/Cleveland Bridge. Additional information is available at the Caltrans District 4 Web site for New Carquinez Bridge: http://www.dot.ca.gov/dist4/carquinez.htm.

REFERENCES CITED

Dibblee, T.F., 2005, Geologic map of the Benicia Quadrangle, Contra Costa and Solano Counties, California: Dibblee Foundation Map No. DF-146, scale 1:24,000.

Geomatrix Consultants and Earth Mechanics, 1999, Foundation Report, Volume 1, Carquinez Bridge and OH Contract No. 59A0007, Contra Costa and Solano Counties, California: Report prepared for De Leuw-OPAC-Steinman, Joint Venture Association, San Francisco, California, August 1999.

Geological Society of America
Field Guide 7
2006

History and pre-history of earthquakes in wine and redwood country, Sonoma and Mendocino counties, California

Suzanne Hecker
U.S. Geological Survey, 345 Middlefield Rd., M.S. 977, Menlo Park, California 94025, USA
Harvey Kelsey
Department of Geology, Humboldt State University, 1 Harpst St., Arcata, California 95521, USA

Contributors: *Hans Abramson Ward,* *Geomatrix Consultants, Inc., 2101 Webster St., Suite 1200, Oakland, California 94612, USA;* ***Julie Bawcom,*** *California Geological Survey, 17501 North Highway 101, Willits, California 95490, USA;* ***John Boatwright,*** *U.S. Geological Survey, 345 Middlefield Rd., M.S. 977, Menlo Park, California 94025, USA;* ***Todd Crampton,*** *Geomatrix Consultants, Inc., 2101 Webster St., Suite 1200, Oakland, California 94612, USA;* ***Wayne Goldberg,*** *City Manager's Office, 100 Santa Rosa Ave., Rm. 10, Santa Rosa, California 95404, USA;* ***Kathryn L. Hanson,*** *Geomatrix Consultants, Inc., 2101 Webster St., Suite 1200, Oakland, California 94612, USA;* ***Victoria E. Langenheim,*** *U.S. Geological Survey, 345 Middlefield Rd., M.S. 989, Menlo Park, California 94025, USA;* ***Mort Larsen,*** *Department of Geology, Humboldt State University, 1 Harpst St., Arcata, California 95521, USA;* ***Gaye LeBaron,*** *Press Democrat, P.O. Box 569, Santa Rosa, California 95402, USA;* ***Darcy K. McPhee,*** *U.S. Geological Survey, 345 Middlefield Rd., M.S. 989, Menlo Park, California 94025, USA;* ***William V. McCormick,*** *Kleinfelder, 2240 Northpoint Parkway, Santa Rosa, California 95407, USA;* ***Robert J. McLaughlin,*** *U.S. Geological Survey, 345 Middlefield Rd., M.S. 973, Menlo Park, California 94025, USA;* ***Craig A. McCabe,*** *U.S. Geological Survey, 345 Middlefield Rd., M.S. 973, Menlo Park, California 94025, USA;* ***David P. Schwartz,*** *U.S. Geological Survey, 345 Middlefield Rd., M.S. 977, Menlo Park, California 94025, USA;* ***Gary Simpson,*** *SHN Consulting Engineers and Geologists, 812 W. Wabash Ave., Eureka, California 95501, USA;* *and* ***Frank H. (Bert) Swan,*** *Consulting Geologist, 240 Laidley Street, San Francisco, California 94131, USA*

OVERVIEW OF THE FIELD TRIP

This guidebook is for a two-day trip: the first part (Day 1) takes place in and near the city of Santa Rosa and on the Rodgers Creek fault in Sonoma County; the second part (Day 2) will go to stops in the town of Willits, on the northern Maacama fault, in Mendocino County.

The Rodgers Creek and Maacama faults are major strands of the San Andreas fault system in northern California. The two faults are separated by a right step and may be considered the northern extension of the Hayward and Calaveras faults, which branch from the San Andreas fault south of the San Francisco Bay area (Fig. 1A). This system of faults accommodates almost a quarter of the total right-slip motion between the Pacific and North American tectonic plates. Slip is released in large, episodic earthquakes and, on some faults, such as the northern Maacama fault, by slow, steady creep.

Keywords: Maacama fault, paleoseismology, fault creep, Rodgers Creek fault, 1906 earthquake, seismic focusing.

OVERVIEW OF DAY 1

Day 1 of this trip highlights destruction from intense ground shaking in Santa Rosa, its likely causes, and efforts to mitigate the hazard. We will also address the record of large earthquakes on the Rodgers Creek fault, which crosses beneath this city. The 1906 earthquake hit Santa Rosa harder per capita than San Francisco (Lawson, 1908), even though Santa Rosa lies ~40 km (25 mi) east of the San Andreas fault.

Day 1 consists of five stops (Fig. 1B). The first and last stops of the day are on the Rodgers Creek fault, which has been estimated to have the greatest probability (17%) of any fault in the San Francisco Bay region of producing a large earthquake in the coming decades (Working Group on California Earth-

Hecker, S., Kelsey, H., AbramsonWard, H., Bawcom, J., Boatwright, J., Crampton, T., Goldberg, W., Hanson, K.L., Langenheim, V.E., Larsen, M., LeBaron, G., McPhee, D.K., McCormick, W.V., McLaughlin, R.J., McCabe, C.A., Schwartz, D.P., Simpson, G., and Swan, F.H., 2006, History and pre-history of earthquakes in wine and redwood country, Sonoma and Mendocino counties, California, *in* Prentice, C.S., Scotchmoor, J.G., Moores, E.M., and Kiland, J.P., eds., 1906 San Francisco Earthquake Centennial Field Guides: Field trips associated with the 100th Anniversary Conference, 18–23 April 2006, San Francisco, California: Geological Society of America Field Guide 7, p. 339–372, doi: 10.1130/2006.1906SF(19). For permission to copy, contact editing@geosociety.org. ©2006 Geological Society of America. All rights reserved.

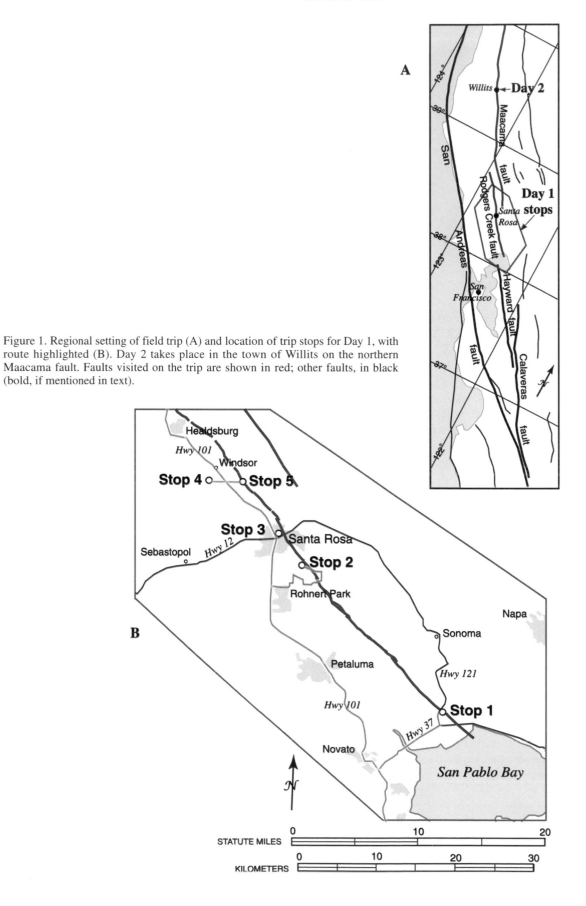

Figure 1. Regional setting of field trip (A) and location of trip stops for Day 1, with route highlighted (B). Day 2 takes place in the town of Willits on the northern Maacama fault. Faults visited on the trip are shown in red; other faults, in black (bold, if mentioned in text).

quake Probabilities, 2003). Both stops provide information from paleoseismic (ancient-earthquake) studies on the timing and frequency of large, surface-faulting earthquakes.

Stop 2, on Taylor Mountain, provides a vantage point from which to describe how fault slip is transferred from the Rodgers Creek fault to the Maacama fault and how deep basin geometries and shallow, unconsolidated sediments may be partly responsible for the unusually strong levels of shaking in Santa Rosa. Stop 3 in downtown Santa Rosa is a four-part stop that provides insight into the disastrous effects of the 1906 earthquake and the 1969 Santa Rosa earthquakes and provides examples of the city's successful efforts to improve the structural safety of its buildings. Stop 4 visits the Shiloh Cemetery north of Santa Rosa, where damage to headstones records a strong level of shaking in 1906.

Stop 1: View of the Southern Rodgers Creek Fault from Atop Roche Carneros Estate Winery: What We've Learned About Recent (and Future) Large Earthquakes (Suzanne Hecker and David P. Schwartz)

Significance of the Site

This hilltop stop near the south end of the Rodgers Creek fault provides a perspective on the setting and expression of the fault trace in this area. Here, we describe geologic studies that show that the most recent large earthquake on the fault probably occurred in the eighteenth century, in the same general time frame as earthquake rupture on the Hayward fault to the south. The time since the most recent earthquake may be equal to the average time between earthquakes on the Rodgers Creek fault, indicating that the next large event may occur in the near future.

Accessibility

There is ample parking in winery parking lot, and during normal business hours, restrooms are available.

GPS Coordinates

38.174°N, 122.450°W.

Directions

From San Francisco, take U.S. Hwy 101 north across the Golden Gate Bridge; continue north for ~20 mi. Go east on Hwy 37 for 7.5 mi to Hwy 121 (Carneros Highway). Go north on Hwy 121 for ~1.5 mi. Roche Winery will be on your right. The winery is the big white building on top of the hill.

Stop Description

A recent study estimates that the Rodgers Creek fault has the highest probability (17%) of any fault in the San Francisco Bay region of generating a large earthquake in the next 30 years (Working Group on California Earthquake Probabilities, 2003). Roche Winery sits within the zone of faulting near the south end of fault-related topography. Evidence of recent activity includes soil color and vegetation lines, closed depressions,

Figure 2. View toward the northwest of Wildcat Mountain, showing where the Rodgers Creek fault cuts across its northeast flank.

linear swales, and deflected drainages. The Rodgers Creek fault forms a bench on the northeast flank of Wildcat Mountain, visible on the horizon to the northwest (Fig. 2). To the southeast, the Rodgers Creek fault disappears beneath mudflats and San Pablo Bay and makes a right step over to the Hayward fault (Fig. 3), which continues to the southeast through the highly urbanized East Bay.

Evidence for the most recent large earthquake on the Rodgers Creek fault was uncovered in trenches excavated at the Triangle G Ranch, ~12 km (7.5 mi) northwest of Roche Winery (Figs. 3–5). Radiocarbon dating of charcoal fragments from deposits displaced by surface rupture indicates that the most recent large earthquake occurred after A.D. 1690, and most likely after A.D. 1715 (Hecker et al., 2005). The absence of accounts of large, damaging earthquakes in the historical record implies that the earthquake occurred before 1824, and possibly before 1776, when Franciscan missions were built in Sonoma and San Francisco, respectively. Also, the evidence from the trenches indicates that the earthquake pre-dates the appearance of non-native pollen, which is associated with the introduction of livestock regionally.

The age of the earthquake identified on the Rodgers Creek fault is similar to the age of a prehistoric rupture documented on the Hayward fault (constrained to A.D. 1640–1776; Hayward Fault Paleoearthquake Group, 1999; Lienkaemper et al., 2002). This general correspondence in timing suggests that segments of the fault system on either side of the Bay may

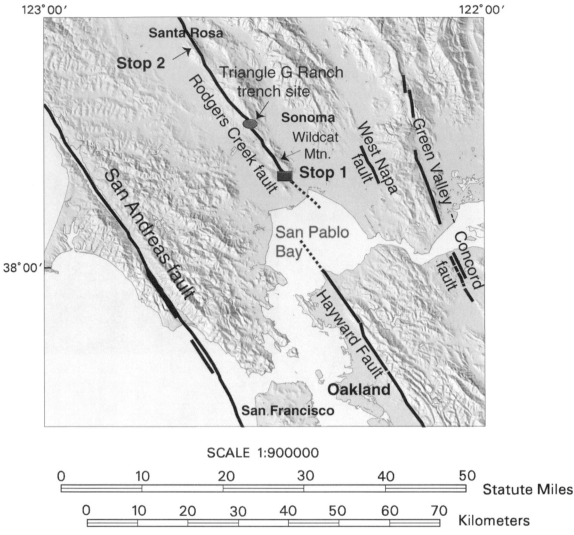

SCALE 1:900000

Figure 3. Shaded relief map of region around Stop 1. Major active faults are in red, dotted where concealed beneath San Pablo Bay. Trench site on the Rodgers Creek fault is shown in Figure 4.

have failed together in a single, major earthquake, or separately in events that occurred within decades of each other (Working Group on California Earthquake Probabilities, 2003; Hecker et al., 2005). Evidence that the Rodgers Creek fault slipped ~2 m (6.5 ft) or more during the earthquake (from measurements of an offset stream channel and debris-flow deposits) implies an earthquake magnitude of ~7.0 or greater (Budding et al., 1991; Hecker et al., 2005).

It has been at least 182 years, and probably between 230 and 291 years, since the last large earthquake on the Rodgers Creek fault. The average time between earthquakes, as estimated from geological data, is thought to be between 131 and 370 years (preferred value, 230 years; Schwartz et al., 1992). Thus, we may be approaching, or may have reached, the average repeat time for large earthquakes on the fault, which indicates that a large event may occur in the near future.

Our next stop will be ~30 km (20 mi) to the northwest, near where the Rodgers Creek fault takes a small right step beneath the city of Santa Rosa and where, to the north, the Rodgers Creek fault is also known as the Healdsburg fault.

Stop 2: Overlook of the Rodgers Creek Fault, Santa Rosa Pull-Apart Basin, and the Santa Rosa Plain from the Peak of Taylor Mountain (Victoria E. Langenheim, Darcy K. McPhee, William V. McCormick, Robert J. McLaughlin, and Craig A. McCabe)

Significance of the Site

Taylor Mountain provides a view of the greater Santa Rosa area, where extensive urbanization has occurred in the flatlands of a pull-apart basin. This basin is a large depression that formed where active fault slip is transferred from the Rodgers

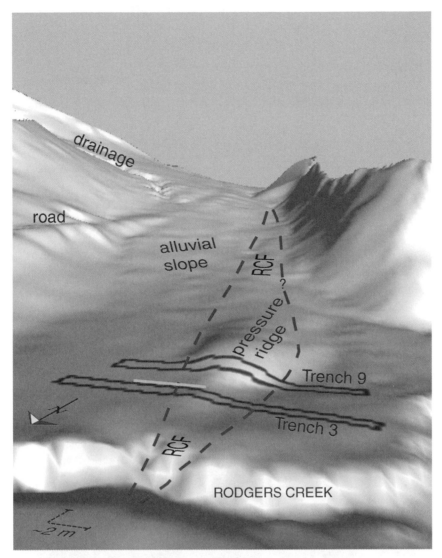

Figure 4. Three-dimensional perspective model (with ~2× vertical exaggeration) of the Triangle G Ranch site looking southeast along the trend of the Rodgers Creek fault (RCF, in red). Trenches show evidence of the most recent earthquake; trench wall marked with blue bar is shown in Figure 5. Figure modified from Hecker et al. (2005).

Creek–Healdsburg fault zone on the southwest side of the basin to the Maacama fault zone on the northeast side of the basin. Significant damage in the city of Santa Rosa was caused by shaking from the 1906 San Francisco earthquake and the 1969 Santa Rosa earthquake sequence. This damage was focused west of the intersection of the Rodgers Creek and Healdsburg faults. Geophysical studies unveil a complex basin configuration beneath the Santa Rosa Plain, which may have influenced the degree of damage in the city of Santa Rosa.

Accessibility

This area is private property and the roads that access Taylor Mountain are owned and maintained by Jackson Family Farms vineyards. Permission to access these roads must always be secured by personal or written request from Jackson Family Farms vineyards. The phone number to their main office in Geyserville is +1-707-433–6341 (5490 Red Winery Road, Geyserville, California 95441).

GPS Coordinates

38.4008°N, 122.6738°W.

Directions

Return to Hwy 101; from the junction with Hwy 37, go north on Hwy 101 for ~30 mi. Take the Golf Course exit, and head east. Go 1.5 mi to Snyder Road, turn left, and go 1 mi to Petaluma Hill Road. Turn right on Petaluma Hill Road and go 1.6 mi to Crane Canyon–Grange Road. Turn left and go 2.7 mi,

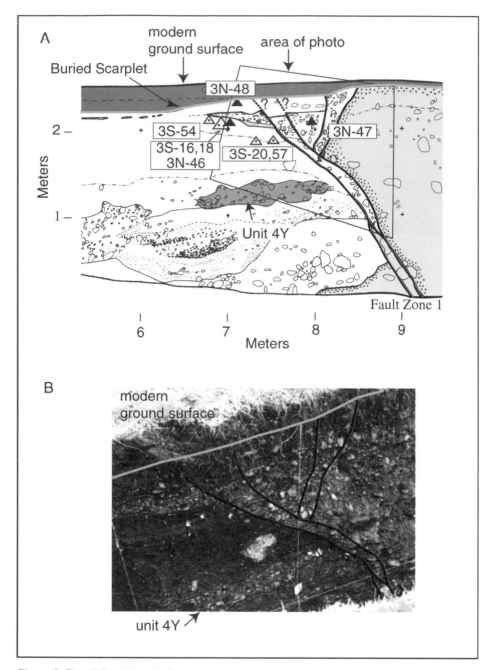

Figure 5. Trench log (A) and photograph (B) of exposure on the northeast side of the pressure ridge (trench 3, southeast wall). Faults are in red; ground surface at the time of the most recent earthquake is in gold. Labeled triangles on trench log mark locations of charcoal samples collected for radiocarbon analysis. Figure modified from Hecker et al. (2005).

then turn left to Jackson Family Farms vineyard. Drive 2.3 mi up the main gravel road to the top of Taylor Mountain. Cross Rodgers Creek fault at 1.4 mi from the vineyard entrance.

Stop Description

The summit of Taylor Mountain is situated just southwest of the Rodgers Creek fault zone (Fig. 6). Linear topography, spring lines, and sag ponds associated with the fault are visible to the

northeast from the top of the mountain, although in places the fault-related topography is obscured by massive landslides that extend from the northeastern slopes of the mountain to Bennett Valley. Rincon Valley, which underlies part of the city of Santa Rosa, and Bennett Valley are visible to the north-northeast from the top of Taylor Mountain (Figs. 6 and 7). These valleys are the expression of a low-lying rhombic basin, called the Santa Rosa pull-apart basin, which is bounded on the northeast by the south-

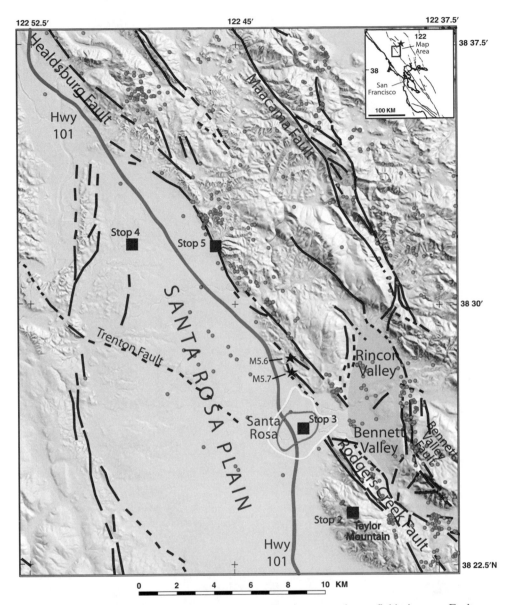

Figure 6. Site map of Taylor Mountain field trip stop. Purple squares denote field trip stops. Faults are in red; earthquake epicenters—green dots; brown stars—epicenters of the 1969 earthquakes (Wong and Bott, 1995). Areas of the 1906 and 1969 earthquake damage are circled in orange and yellow, respectively. The light blue area highlights the Santa Rosa pull-apart basin formed in the right step between the Rodgers Creek and Maacama faults. Earthquake locations indicate active slip deformation partitions between the Rodgers Creek fault and the Maacama fault, and fault-plane solutions indicate right-lateral slip with a prominent component of extension (normal faulting). Red star on index map shows location of Mount St. Helena.

ern Maacama fault zone and on the southwest by the Rodgers Creek fault zone. Geologic investigations (McLaughlin et al., 2005) show that the Maacama, Rodgers Creek, and Healdsburg faults in this area have all slipped at a rate between ~5–6 mm/yr (~0.2 in/yr) since about a million years ago (1 Ma). Other studies show that the Maacama fault has slipped at this same rate since ca. 3.2 Ma, suggesting that the fault system as a whole has maintained a relatively constant slip rate for at least ~3 million years.

During historical large to moderate earthquakes, major shaking damage has occurred just southwest of the pull-apart basin. Catastrophic damage occurred in Santa Rosa as a result of the 1906 San Francisco earthquake, even though the epicenter was ~75 km (45 mi) away and the closest distance to the rupture was ~40 km (25 mi). The shaking and ensuing fire in Santa Rosa, with a population of roughly 7000 at the time, caused the loss of life of about 100 people (LeBaron et al.,

Figure 7. View from Taylor Mountain looking north-northeast into the Santa Rosa pull-apart basin, which lies within Rincon Valley.

1983, p. 200), and the business portion of Santa Rosa was mostly destroyed (Fig. 8; Lawson, 1908; Steinbrugge, 1970).

Santa Rosa was severely shaken by two more earthquakes (M 5.6, M 5.7) near the city on 1 October 1969. These are the two largest events to occur in the northern San Francisco Bay area since the 1906 earthquake. Although these earthquakes were distinctly felt throughout the San Francisco Bay area, it was near the epicenters of the earthquakes in Santa Rosa where the most damage occurred, including millions of dollars of structural damage (Fig. 9; Steinbrugge, 1970).

The damage from both the 1906 and 1969 earthquakes was focused in the same area on the southwest side of the Rodgers Creek–Healdsburg fault zone (Fig. 6). The concentration of significant damage is likely related to at least four factors: (1) geologic structural complexity, (2) the distribution of artificial fills and buried channels, (3) the distribution of water-saturated sediment, and (4) the concentration of buildings and other structures in Santa Rosa. A possible fifth factor may be related to an elevated pulse of seismic energy from the fault rupture, as can be inferred from the distribution of strong shaking in the region

Figure 8. Downtown Santa Rosa looking north along Mendocino Street from 4th Street (A) before the 1906 earthquake and (B) after. The earthquake leveled the business district. (Courtesy of the Sonoma County Museum Collection.)

(Boatwright and Bundock, 2005). Previous investigations in Santa Rosa (Lawson, 1908; Steinbrugge, 1970) have pointed to old filled channels of Santa Rosa Creek and the presence of poorly consolidated fan and terrace materials as probable contributors to the distribution of damage in the Santa Rosa area (see below for additional comments). However, gravity data in the area (Fig. 10) suggests that basin geometry and the thick sedimentary fill of basins beneath the Santa Rosa Plain may also have played a role in focusing this shaking damage. Gravity data can indicate how much sediment, or less dense material, overlies the more dense bedrock in the region. Thus, gravity lows correspond to sedimentary basins. The gravity data indicate that the Santa Rosa Plain has two main basins underneath it, the Windsor basin to the north and the Cotati basin to the south. These basins are roughly 1–2 km (0.6–1.2 mi) deep and are separated by a shallow west-trending bedrock ridge at the latitude of Santa Rosa. The city is located on the northeast corner of the Cotati basin. The most intense earthquake damage coincides with a local depression in the northeast corner of the Cotati basin (Fig. 11), just east of the bedrock ridge, suggesting that seismic energy may have

been focused into this embayment. This hypothesis needs to be tested by simulating the shaking that would be expected given the three-dimensional geometry of the basin.

Subsurface exploration and geotechnical analysis performed by consultants over the past 35 years (Giblin Associates, 2004; Harding-Lawson 1979, 1980, 1987a, 1987b; Kleinfelder, Inc., 2002, 2005) indicate that downtown Santa Rosa, the area hardest hit in the 1906 and 1969 earthquakes, is underlain at the surface by variable thicknesses of old artificial fills (Fig. 12). These old fills were most likely placed to infill old tributaries associated with Santa Rosa Creek, as well as in preparation for early building in the downtown area. Old artificial fills can be typically characterized as loose and uncompacted. Settlement of these old fills during earthquakes, coupled with inadequate building foundations, could have been a major factor in the location and amount of earthquake damage in this area in 1906 and 1969.

Liquefaction caused by ground shaking represents still another potential hazard in Santa Rosa. Geologic mapping (Huffman and Armstrong, 1980) and subsurface exploration

Figure 9. Examples of damage from the 1969 earthquakes in Santa Rosa: partial collapse of brick wall onto car below, Old Courthouse Square (bottom); two-story wood-frame house off its foundations (upper right); chimney damage to wood-frame house (upper left). (Courtesy of the Karl V. Steinbrugge Collection, Earthquake Engineering Research Center.)

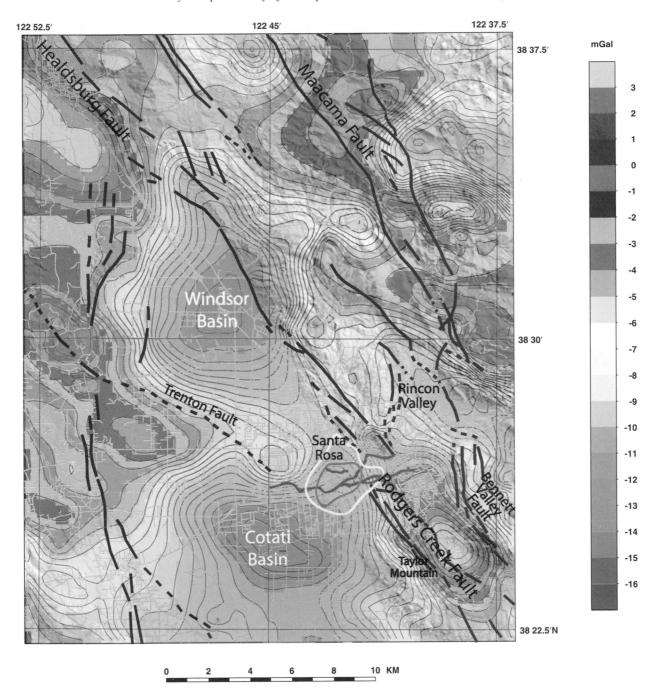

Figure 10. Gravity map overlain on shaded-relief topography of the Santa Rosa Plain and Santa Rosa pull-apart basin. Warm colors indicate gravity highs, or areas where high-density basement rocks are either exposed or close to the surface. Cool colors indicate gravity lows, or areas underlain by thick accumulations of low-density basin fill. Red lines are faults. Orange and yellow lines denote the extent of significant 1906 and 1969 earthquake damage, respectively. Blue lines show the course of stream channels, both modern and filled, through Santa Rosa (Lawson, 1908).

show that the native alluvial (stream) materials beneath the downtown area are thick and highly variable in composition (Fig. 12) and include potentially liquefiable sands (Sowers et al., 1995). Liquefaction occurs when some types of water-saturated sediments (generally loose, cohesionless silts and sands) are strongly shaken in an earthquake. The soils essentially turn into a thick fluid and lose their strength. Santa Rosa may be susceptible to liquefaction because the groundwater table in the downtown area is high, fluctuating between 5 and 15 ft below the ground surface.

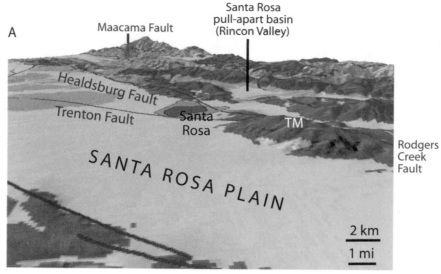

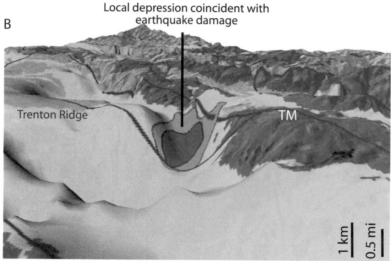

Figure 11. Oblique views to the northeast across the Santa Rosa Plain toward Taylor Mountain (TM) and the city of Santa Rosa. (A) Topography with draped simplified geology, which illustrates the flat surface of the Santa Rosa Plain. (B) Simplified surficial geology draped on the basement surface as defined by inversion of gravity data, illustrating the variation of basin thickness beneath the plain and the local depression that coincides with the 1906 and 1969 earthquake damage, shown in the orange and gold. Gray—young deposits; yellow and brown—Tertiary (2–65 million years old [Ma]) sedimentary rocks; magenta—Tertiary volcanic rocks; green—Mesozoic (older than 65 Ma) basement rocks.

Stop 3: Downtown Santa Rosa: Effects of the 1906 and 1969 Earthquakes and the City's Seismic Retrofit Program (Wayne Goldberg and Gaye LeBaron)

Stop 3A: Old Courthouse Square

Significance of the Site

This site was the location of the county courthouse until it was destroyed in the 1906 earthquake (Fig. 13). The courthouse built in its place was torn down in 1966, as part of the city's redevelopment project. Redevelopment had begun in 1961, but was expanded after the 1969 earthquakes (William Spangle and Associates Inc., 1980). The square is now an urban plaza and serves as a place to reflect on Santa Rosa's earthquake history.

Accessibility

This is a public space with parking adjoining the site on the street and in public garages.

GPS Coordinates

38.4400° N, 122.7139° W.

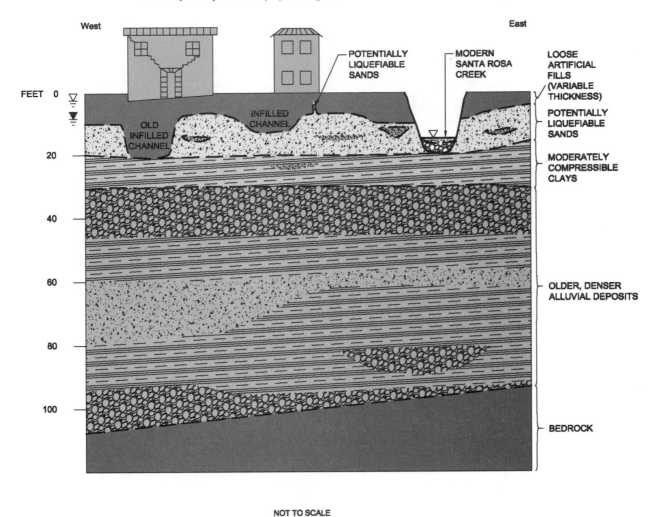

Figure 12. Idealized cross section beneath downtown Santa Rosa showing artificial fills (purple) and stream deposits (yellow).

Directions

Return to Hwy 101 and go north ~5 mi to the downtown Santa Rosa exit. At the foot of the off-ramp, turn right and proceed to the second traffic light. Courthouse Square is at the northeast corner of this intersection.

Stop Description

Here's a perspective on how the 1906 and 1969 earthquakes impacted Santa Rosa:

With the Rodgers Creek–Healdsburg fault running through the center of town, one would expect that the disastrous earthquakes Santa Rosa has experienced would have come from that source, but it was the mighty San Andreas fault, some 25 mi to the west, that produced the havoc of April 1906. It was the poorly known Healdsburg fault that moved, significantly, twice on the night of October 1, 1969, to once again change the face of downtown Santa Rosa. The 1906 jolt, com-

monly known as the San Francisco earthquake, reduced the business district of the 52-year-old community of Santa Rosa to heaps of bricks and crumbled mortar, and no residence escaped damage. In fact, no city in the United States, before or after, was ever so devastated by an earthquake as was Santa Rosa on that spring morning. More than 100 people died that day, in a town of about 7,000. It was the largest per capita percentage of documented deaths in northern California. Most loss of life occurred in the downtown area, which was built mostly of brick. Mindful of the disastrous fires that had swept San Francisco in mid-nineteenth century, Santa Rosa's city fathers had decreed that business buildings should be constructed of brick. Much of the brick was put together with lime mortar made from sand taken from the streams that course through the Santa Rosa Valley. The mortar contained a high percentage of loam and quickly crumbled. Those same streams, creating a high water table, and soft sediments have been blamed for much of the damage done by the "twin" magnitude 5.6 and 5.7 quakes of 1969. Again, it was the downtown area that was affected. This time it was mainly the wood frame structures that twisted and cracked. Deemed unsafe to survive another quake, they were condemned and several

Figure 13. The Sonoma County Courthouse in Santa Rosa before the 1906 earthquake (upper left) and after (bottom). (Photos are courtesy of the Finley Collection/*Press Democrat* and Karl V. Steinbrugge Collection, Earthquake Engineering Research Center, respectively.) The inset (upper right) shows the urban plaza at Old Courthouse Square today.

blocks were cleared. There were no deaths in 1969 and injuries were minimal, thanks to the fact that the streets were clear of pedestrians at 9 p.m. But the clearing of the land, the resulting urban renewal project, the construction of the downtown mall, the lawsuits that delayed rebuilding by a decade, caused considerable economic damage to the community. There are many "survivors" of the 1969 quake left to tell that story. The dramatic tales of the 1906 quake have been preserved in first-person accounts, letters, and newspaper stories of 100 years ago. (Gaye LeBaron, columnist and local historian, for this guide)

Because Santa Rosa experienced extensive damage in 1906 and again in the 1969 earthquakes, the city adopted an aggressive seismic retrofit program in 1970. The program prioritized retrofitting of buildings in three phases, beginning with those of highest occupancy. As the program progressed, the city deferred the requirement for retrofitting smaller buildings until the property was sold. At the time of adoption and for several years following, the seismic safety standards were perhaps the strongest in the state of California and served as a model for other cities many years later when the state adopted retrofitting requirements for unreinforced masonry buildings. The next three stops will examine the seismic retrofit of downtown buildings.

Stop 3B: Russian River Brewing Company

Significance of the Site

This business is an excellent example of a recently retrofitted building (2004). The seismic retrofit measures are fully exposed and visible (Fig. 14).

Accessibility

This is a publicly accessible privately owned building with parking adjoining the site on the street and in public garages.

GPS Coordinates

38.4417°N, 122.7114° W.

Directions

Proceed one block east from Old Courthouse Square to 725 Fourth Street.

Stop Description

This building exemplifies a recent retrofit meeting current seismic codes. It is in a section of the downtown where buildings are built lot line to lot line, so failure of one building jeopardizes the integrity of the adjoining buildings. The retrofit components are exposed and visible, making this a particularly effective example of how seismic stabilization works in a public assembly and microbrewery facility. Cross-bracing is evident, and strapping of brewing equipment can be seen from the public area.

Stop 3C: Barnes & Noble Building

Significance of the Site

The flexibility allowed by the historic-building code was used in retrofitting this classic art deco building. It is an example of how, because of the high costs involved, retrofitting is often accomplished when a property changes ownership. Retrofit measures have been designed to minimally interfere with the original building interior (Fig. 14).

Accessibility

This is a publicly accessible privately owned building, with parking adjoining the site on the street and in public garages.

GPS Coordinates

38.4411°N, 122.7125°W.

Directions

This building is located one block east of Old Courthouse Square at 700 Fourth Street.

Stop Description

This building was originally the main department store (Rosenberg's) in Santa Rosa, which closed when the business could not remain competitive. Following the closure of the store, the building sat vacant for five years and became a haven for the homeless, posing a significant fire and safety hazard. The high cost of a seismic retrofit was a major factor in the building remaining empty, and the owner sought and was granted a demolition permit after environmental review and public hearings. Subsequently, however, the building was purchased and the new owner used the historic-building code to employ construction techniques that achieved the safety objectives of the standard building code while preserving the historic character of the building. It is now fully occupied by Barnes & Noble, Starbucks, and office space. Some components of the seismic retrofit are visible, but do not interfere with the use or appearance of this historic art deco building.

Stop 3D: St. Rose Church and Parish Hall

Significance of the Site

This was the original test case of the seismic retrofit ordinance enacted following the 1969 earthquakes.

Accessibility

This is a privately owned building with parking on adjoining streets.

GPS Coordinates

38.4434°N, 122.7186°W.

Directions

From Old Courthouse Square, proceed north on Mendocino Avenue to 10th Street. Turn left. The address is 398 10th Street.

Stop Description

The St. Rose facilities were the first to be addressed by the city because of high occupancy and unreinforced masonry construction. In the face of strong resistance from the Roman Catholic Diocese of Santa Rosa, the city council upheld the determination that activities in the structures had to be curtailed until seismic stability was achieved.

Stop 4: Damage from the 1906 Earthquake in Shiloh Cemetery: A Measure of Shaking Intensity (John Boatwright)

Significance of the Site

Santa Rosa and Sebastopol (~6 mi southwest of Santa Rosa; Fig. 1B) were severely damaged by the 1906 earthquake. Inspecting rural cemeteries in Sonoma County allows us to detail the spatial extent of the anomalously strong shaking that caused the damage (Boatwright and Bundock, 2005). The 1906 damage to the headstones and monuments in Shiloh Cemetery is readily apparent. The cemetery is well maintained and there is no apparent vandalism.

Figure 14. Examples of seismic retrofit elements in historic buildings of downtown Santa Rosa: Barnes & Noble (top) and the Russian Brewing Company (bottom).

Accessibility

This is a public site with ample parking, but there are no restrooms available.

GPS Coordinates

38.5254°N, 122.8143°W.

Directions

From Santa Rosa, take Highway 101 north for 7 mi, then take the Shiloh Road exit. Turn left on Shiloh Road and go west 1.4 mi. The Shiloh Cemetery is on your right. Turn in at the first entrance to the cemetery and park. The eastern section is the oldest part of the cemetery.

Stop Description

Because broken headstones can be repaired but are almost never replaced, and overturned monuments are usually reset with some misalignment, cemeteries can be used to gauge earthquake shaking. The eastern section of Shiloh Cemetery (the markers on both sides of the entrance from Shiloh Road) amply demonstrates the capacity of cemeteries to act as ground-motion or shaking-intensity indicators. The shaking history of the site is relatively simple: other than the 1906 earthquake, the cemetery has not been severely shaken. The 1969 Santa Rosa earthquakes (M 5.6 and M 5.7; Fig. 6) were relatively small and their impact was felt mainly in Santa Rosa.

To estimate intensity from damaged markers in cemeteries, pre-1906 markers are canvassed and divided into three categories: undamaged, chipped/reset, and broken. Characteristically, headstones will break at the bottom, where the flange fits into the footer. Even if a headstone has been repaired carefully, there is usually some mortar showing (Fig. 15). Similarly, if a monument such as an obelisk has been overturned and reset, it may appear undamaged, but reset monuments are always slightly out of alignment.

Modified Mercalli Intensity (MMI) can be roughly estimated from the percentage of broken and chipped/reset headstones and monuments (Boatwright and Bundock, 2005). At MMI 7, few or no headstones are broken or overturned; at MMI 8, 20%–50% of the headstones and monuments are broken or overturned, and at MMI 9, more than 80% are broken or overturned. At the Shiloh Cemetery, there are 41 broken markers (25%), 17 chipped and/or reset markers (10%), and 103 undamaged markers (65%), which marks it as MMI 8. Most houses nearby would have lost their chimneys, but few, if any, would have been shifted off their foundations.

Stop 5: Paleo-Earthquake Investigations of the Northern Rodgers Creek–Healdsburg Fault at Shiloh Ranch Regional Park (Frank H. [Bert] Swan, Todd Crampton, Hans AbramsonWard, and Kathryn L. Hanson)

Significance of the Site

Fault trenching and detailed topographic surveying within Shiloh Ranch Regional Park provide evidence for three to four large, surface-faulting earthquakes during about the past 1400–1500 years on the northern Rodgers Creek–Healdsburg fault (Swan et al., 2003; Crampton et al., 2004).

Accessibility

This is a public park, with restrooms available and ample parking ($4 fee at park entrance or free parking across the road opposite the park entrance); the northern and southern sites (Fig. 16) are accessible via the hiking trail that extends north along the hill front from the north side of the parking lot (to the right of the restrooms).

GPS Coordinates

38.5257°N, 122.7623°W.

Directions

Go east on Shiloh Road for 2.7 mi. Turn right onto Faught Road; the park entrance is on the left.

Stop Description

Steep westward-flowing drainages at two locations in the park along the range front are offset where they cross the active trace of the Rodgers Creek–Healdsburg fault (Fig. 16). The southern study site lies east of the Ridge Trail, where the trail crosses the first drainage several meters north of the parking lot. The northern site is ~200 m (660 ft) farther to the north, where the trail turns east and climbs into the hills.

The right-lateral stream offset (in which one side of the fault moves to the right relative to the other) and offset terraces at the southern site provide evidence for the location of an active trace of the Rodgers Creek–Healdsburg fault slightly east of the range front. The back edge of a 1–1.5-m-high (3–5 ft) terrace on the north side of the stream is offset at least 13 m (43 ft) along a linear escarpment that trends N35°W (Fig. 17). Presumably, this much displacement was produced by multiple surface-faulting earthquakes. The most recent earthquake along this trace occurred sometime after A.D. 1270, based on a radiocarbon date on charcoal from the faulted terrace deposit, and perhaps before the establishment of a Spanish mission and the beginning of record-keeping in San Francisco in 1776.

The trench (now filled) at the northern site (Figs. 18 and 19) provided evidence for at least three and probably four geologically recent surface-faulting earthquakes. The trench was excavated on a 5-m-high (16.5 ft) terrace across a small sag feature ~60 m (200 ft) south of an offset stream channel. We used such physical evidence as upward fault terminations, fissure infills, and the presence of the sag-fill deposits to identify individual faulting events (Fig. 19). Calibrated radiocarbon dates on charcoal fragments from the sag fill deposits are in correct chronologic sequence and suggest the following event chronology (from youngest to oldest):

• Events 3 and 4(?) likely pre-date the establishment of the Spanish mission in San Francisco (A.D. 1776) and post-date charcoal dated at A.D. 1280–1400;

Figure 15. Examples of pre-1906 headstones in Shiloh Cemetery that were damaged and repaired. The two above broke off at the bottom and were reset using mortar; the one below broke in the middle.

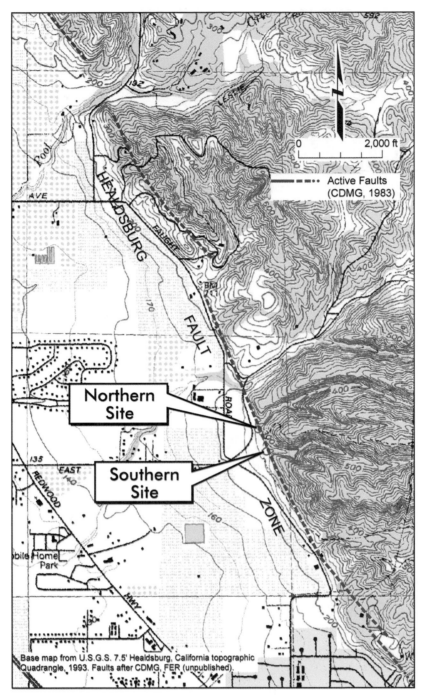

Figure 16. Location of the two sites at the Shiloh Ranch Regional Park, Windsor, California.

- Event 2 pre-dates A.D. 1280–1400 and postdates A.D. 990–1160; and
- Event 1 probably occurred shortly before deposition of the sag fill, which began ca. A.D. 540–660.

The timing of surface-faulting earthquakes along the northern Rodgers Creek–Healdsburg fault is not well constrained compared to most other major faults in the San Andreas fault system in northern California. Nonetheless, there is clear evidence of at least three or four surface-faulting events during about the past 1400–1500 yr. This indicates an average recurrence interval of ~350–500 yr, or less if the record of past events at this site is incomplete. It has been at least 230 years (before 1776) since the last major event along this branch of the San Andreas fault system.

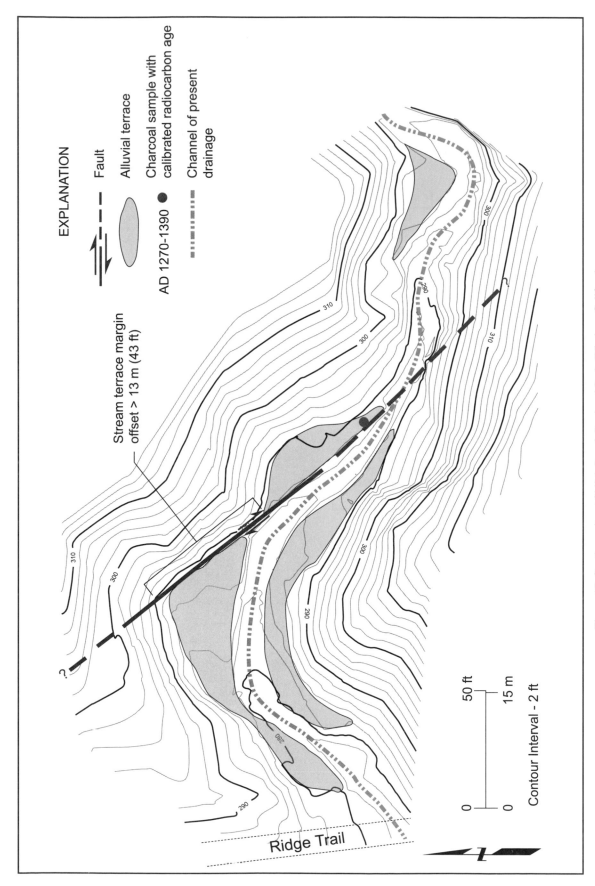

Figure 17. Southern site at Shiloh Ranch Regional Park, Windsor, California.

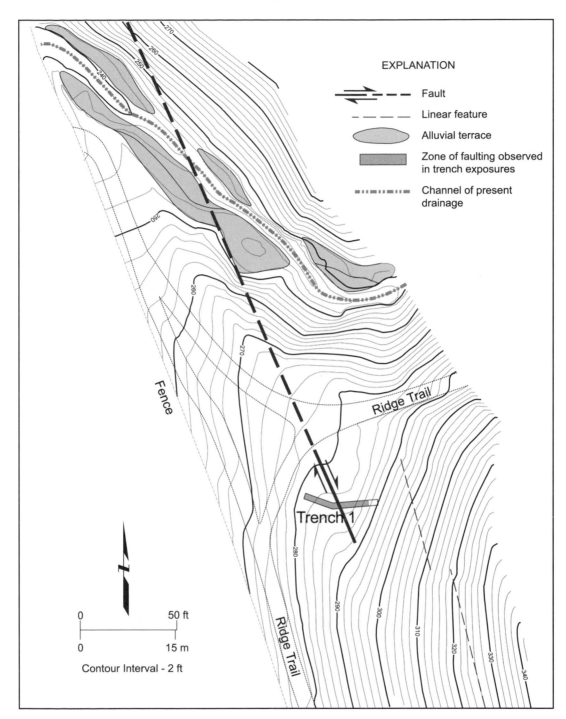

Figure 18. Northern site at Shiloh Ranch Regional Park, Windsor, California.

OVERVIEW OF DAY 2

This field trip on the second day consists of stops at two locations that provide insight into the northern Maacama fault in the Little Lake Valley–Willits area.

The Maacama fault gets its name from a derivative of *Mayacamas*, the name of the mountains that form the divide between the Russian River and Clear Lake. Native Americans on the western slope of these mountains resided in a Yukian Wappo Village, called *Maiya'Kma*, located one mile south of Calistoga (Gudde, 1969; Dawson, 1998). *Mayacamas* means "water going out place."

The northern Maacama fault is the central strand of the three strands that make up the San Andreas fault system in this part of northern California (Fig. 20A). The fault is seismically

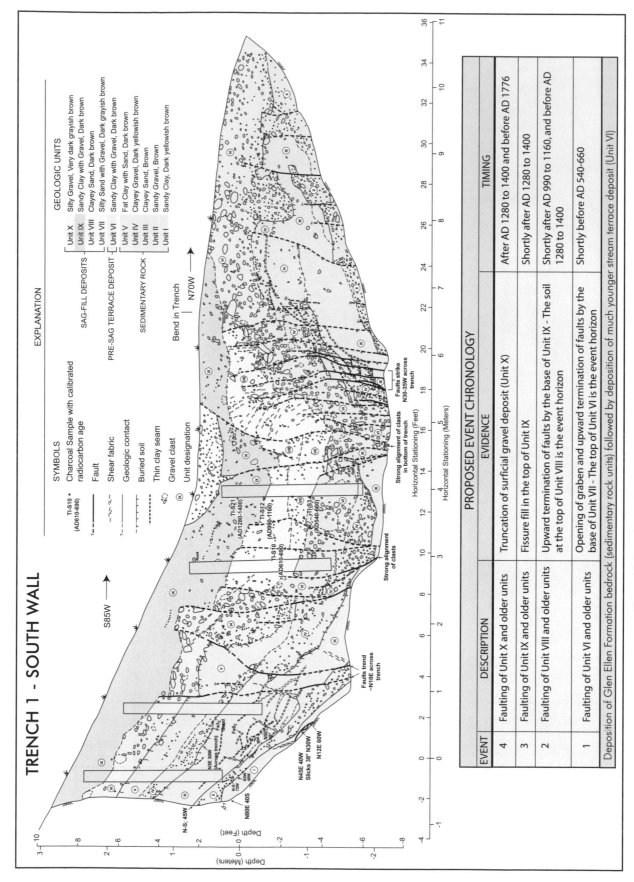

Figure 19. Trench 1 at the northern site at Shiloh Ranch Regional Park.

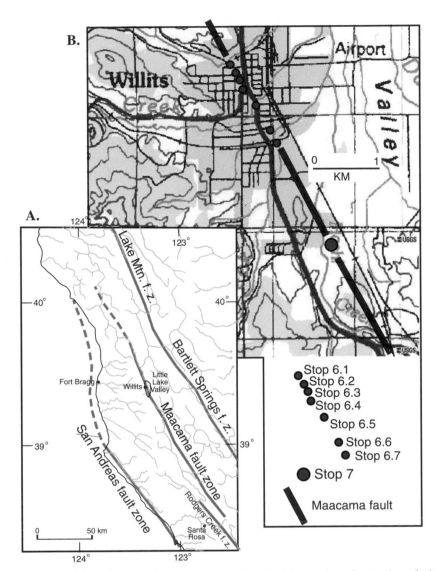

Figure 20. (A) Location map showing the three strands of the northern San Andreas fault system and location of Little Lake Valley and the town of Willits. (B) U.S. Geological Survey (1991) topographic map of the downtown Willits area (100-foot contour interval) showing the seven walking stops for Stop 6 and showing the general location of Stop 7.

active and has documented historic right-lateral offset. For example, the Maacama's far-field geodetically determined strain rate (how much one side of the fault is moving relative to the other as determined by surveying using satellites) is ~14 mm/yr (~0.6 in/yr) (Freymueller et al., 1999), and the fault's measured creep rate (ca. 1991–2001) at two sites (Ukiah and Willits) is ~4–6 mm/yr (~0.2 in/yr) (Galehouse, 2002). Fault creep is persistent slip that is too slow to produce an earthquake.

The first stop is a walking tour of offset cultural features in downtown Willits (Fig. 20B) that provides insight into the deformation patterns characteristic of a creeping strike-slip fault where it cuts through an urbanized setting.

The second stop describes extensive geotechnical and paleoseismological work that has been accomplished at a location

traversed by the Maacama fault that is the proposed site for the new Willits hospital, a senior care center, and a residential subdivision. Discussion at this stop will focus on the techniques used to characterize the location and paleoseismic activity of the Maacama fault.

Stop 6: Walking Tour of Offset Cultural Features in Downtown Willits (Julie Bawcom and Harvey Kelsey)

Significance of the Site

The Maacama fault zone traverses downtown Willits, where creep on the fault is manifest in offset pavement, buildings, and other human constructs. Downtown Willits is one of the best locations in California to see evidence of active fault creep.

Mendocino County, including the town of Willits, suffered significant damage to unreinforced brick buildings during the 1906 earthquake, which ruptured the northern San Andreas fault ~50 km (30 mi) west of Willits. As you walk through town, you will find many old brick buildings still in use. The damage in Willits was described by R.S. Holway in the Lawson earthquake volume published in 1908 (Lawson, 1908, p.187–188): "Brick chimneys were quite generally wrecked. The Buckner Hotel was completely demolished killing the proprietor Mr. Taylor. The stores of the Irvine Muir Company were badly wrecked. Brick walls fell in several other stores, and framed buildings were thrown from their foundations. The valley is an old lake bed with ground water within 3 to 4 feet of the surface in April" (Fig. 21).

Accessibility

This is a public site with parking along residential streets, but there are no restrooms available.

GPS Coordinates

24.5°N, 123.3°W.

Directions

From Santa Rosa, go north on Hwy 101 for ~80 mi to Willits. After entering Willits, continue north to Commercial Street, turn left (west), drive 0.15 mi, and park along this residential street to begin the walking tour (Fig. 20B).

Figure 21. Photograph of Buckner Hotel in Willits, destroyed by shaking during the 1906 earthquake (Lawson, 1908, plate 73B).

Walking Stop 6.1

Begin at the offset sidewalk just west of the intersection of West Commercial and School Street (Figs. 20B and 22). This is the original place that creep was observed and documented in Willits (Harsh et al., 1978). A creep site monitoring station was set up here in November 1991 by Jon Galehouse of San Francisco State University to measure the amount of creep along the

Figure 22. Offset curb, West Commercial Street, at location of creep monitoring site (Stop 6.1).

fault. After 10 years of measurements, the average amount of right-lateral creep along the fault at this location is 6.5 mm/yr (0.26 in/yr) (Galehouse, 2002). The curb and sidewalk were replaced in 1989 and had already moved ~3 cm by 1991.

A sewer line trench excavated along West Commercial Street in May 1994 uncovered both the fault and a bit of Willits history. The trench revealed a layer of organic-rich soil with old nails used for horse shoes—remnants of a late 1800s livery stable. The fault was also exposed in the trench walls as a near-vertical fault zone with dense blue clay gouge.

Walking Stop 6.2

Walk east to School Street, turn right (south), and go to the intersection of School and W. Mendocino Avenue. Notice the tilted telephone pole on the southeast corner of the intersection. Curbs and sidewalks at this location have been replaced every 5–6 yr (1991, 1996, etc.). The creeping fault cuts diagonally through the intersection. Notice the new asphalt patches along the three manhole covers and the four waterline covers. Curbs are offset in both corners.

Continue south, walking across the dirt parking lot toward the two-story blue apartment building. Notice the bulging back wall of the Redwood Empire Cleaners (beige building).

Figure 23. Curb and road damage caused by fault creep at Stop 6.3.

Walking Stop 6.3

Just east of the School Street and Wood Street intersection, near the fire hydrant, notice the offset curbs (Fig. 23) and damage to the blue apartment building walls and sidewalks. The apartments were constructed in the early 1970s before the fault creep was recognized. The creeping fault trace passes through apartments F and G. Cracks in the walls are periodically repaired. Curbs and asphalt have recently been replaced.

Proceed east on Wood Street and turn right (south) onto Highway 101 (referred to as South Main Street in downtown Willits). Notice the historic building on the corner with its unreinforced masonry construction and storefront awning, both of which make it vulnerable to earthquake damage.

Walking Stop 6.4

Continue walking south on South Main Street and turn right on West Valley Street. Walk ~100 ft. Notice the offset curbs near the intersection of West Valley and McKinley Streets and the cracks in the walls and foundations of homes on the southeast side of the intersection. Walk to the back corner of the parking lot at this location behind (west of) the gray office building with a red roof. A pressure ridge that is bulging up diagonally across the parking lot marks the trace of the creeping fault (Fig. 24). The fault was observed in a sewer trench dug at this locality in 1993. The fault zone was ~20 ft wide and was composed of dense blue to brown-red clay surrounded by reddish-brown siltstone; the shear zone was near vertical in the trench, had a strike of N38°W, and was exposed directly below the asphalt (J. Bawcom, field notes). No subgrade was used at this site, which explains the extensive road disruption.

Return to South Main Street, go south for two blocks, and cross over Broaddus Creek Bridge.

Walking Stop 6.5

At the Monroe Street–South Main Street intersection, on the west side of the highway, is a vacant lot that is the former location of the Skunk Motel. Observations taken in July of 1993 noted (J. Bawcom, field notes): "1. the curb was replaced one year ago and the water meter next to the driveway had been replaced three times in the past year; 2. the motel sign and light pole are leaning away from each other; and 3. the motel pool is leaking" (Fig. 25). The motel was removed about two years ago and the pool filled in. On both sides of the highway, unless recently replaced, the curbs and road are warped, and the light pole is tilted.

Backtrack north along South Main Street to the crosswalk and cross to the east side of the highway at South Main and San Francisco Street. Continue south on South Main Street to Flower Street, turn left (east), and stop to look at the parking lot behind (to the east of) the Chevron gas station.

Walking Stop 6.6

Starting in the northwest corner of the parking lot, you can see left-stepping cracks and a slight rise in the asphalt (Fig. 26)

Figure 24. Small pressure ridge developed due to fault creep in parking lot at Stop 6.4.

Figure 25. The Skunk Motel, Willits, in July 1993. Stop 6.5 will inspect damage at the site of the motel; the motel was dismantled in 2003.

that extends to the southeast corner of the building. Deformation caused by the creeping fault has pulled the roof gutters and fascia board away from the structure. Continue walking south, cross Flower Street, and follow the asphalt cracking across the Safeway parking lot in a southeast direction. Stop at the south end of the Safeway store and notice the line of small businesses south of Safeway that form a small strip mall. These buildings are aligned subparallel to the fault, and the concrete slab, brick façade, and roofline of the buildings all show damage or have been recently replaced. If you walk into the Hallmark shop, you will notice a rise in the concrete slab at the entrance.

Continue walking south to the end of the strip mall and across a driveway to a dirt patch and a row of redwood trees along the railroad tracks, our final stop (Fig. 20B).

Walking Stop 6.7

Walk out to view the railroad tracks just east of the Highway 101 road crossing. If you look east you may see right-lateral offset of the railroad tracks (Fig. 27). If the tracks have recently been repaired, the offset may not be visible. These railroad tracks belong to the famous 120-yr-old Skunk Train Railroad. You can catch the train in Willits (near our lunch stop). The

train traverses the Noyo River watershed through redwood forests to the coastal town of Fort Bragg, where the San Andreas fault is located ~5 mi offshore.

The walking tour ends here, and we will shuttle by vehicles to our lunch stop at Willits City Park.

Stop 7: Geotechnical and Paleoseismological Work within the Maacama Fault Zone at the Proposed Site for the New Willits Hospital (Gary Simpson, Mort Larsen, and Harvey Kelsey)

Significance of the Site

From a historical perspective, the significance of this hospital construction site can be traced back to Charles Howard, a San Francisco automobile promoter and owner of the famous racehorse Seabiscuit, who funded the original hospital in Willits. Charles and his wife, Fannie Mae, purchased the Ridgewood Ranch 7 mi south of Willits in 1919 for a summer home. In 1926, the Howards' 15-year-old son, Frankie, rolled a pickup truck while driving on the ranch. Seriously injured, he could not be saved for lack of medical facilities. As a result, Charles Howard funded the construction of the Frank R. Howard

Figure 26. Parking lot of realty building on Flower Street at Stop 6.6 showing left-stepping cracks and bulge in pavement. The left steps form areas of compression and slight uplift in the right-lateral fault.

Figure 27. Looking east from South Main Street at the right lateral offset of the railroad tracks just beyond the railroad bridge over Baechtel Creek (photo taken 5 July 2005). The offset is caused by fault creep, and the tracks have to be realigned periodically.

Memorial Hospital for US$45,000 (Hillenbrand, 2001). It was completed in 1928, with additional wings added in subsequent years. The hospital is not presently up to seismic code and will be replaced by a new hospital at an estimated cost of US$21,000,000. Stop 7 is the site of the proposed hospital.

From a geologic perspective, the hospital site is significant because the Maacama fault crosses the recent (Holocene age) floodplain on which the site is situated. Why propose to build a hospital and a senior care center on this site, part of which is traversed by an active fault? The land had been donated and the proposed new hospital was feasible economically only if the donated land could be utilized. A paleoseismic investigation would determine whether it would be possible to place the footprints of the proposed buildings on portions of the site that are not underlain by or in close proximity to active faults.

The presence of the Maacama fault in geologically youthful sediments at this site allows interpretation of the recent seismic (earthquake) history. Understanding the recent fault history is critical in determining whether the Maacama fault is capable of generating moderate to large surface-rupturing earthquakes, or whether aseismic creep sufficiently relieves fault strain, thus precluding moderate or large earthquakes.

Accessibility

At this time, the hospital site is private property. The property will transition to public ownership once hospital construction is complete.

GPS Coordinates

23.317°N, 123.338°W.

Directions

Baechtel Road forms a "loop" road east of Highway 101 in the southern part of Willits that intersects the highway in two locations. Take either of the two Baechtel Road turnoffs and proceed to the intersection with East Hill Road. Proceed east on East Hill Road (turn left if coming from the north, turn right if coming from the south) ~0.2 mi to a small bridge crossing of Haehl Creek (if you look closely, there are left-stepping cracks marking the fault trace on East Hill Road between Haehl Creek and Baechtel Road). The hospital site occupies the floodplain surface east of Haehl Creek (Fig. 20B), on the right (southern) side of East Hill Road. Until the property transitions to public ownership, the site may be viewed from East Hill Road.

Stop Description

Stop 7 is on the floodplain of Haehl Creek at a site that is diagonally traversed by the Maacama fault (Fig. 28). Active faulting across the site occurs within a relatively narrow zone, typically less than 10 ft wide. The trace of the Maacama fault is expressed across the generally flat floodplain by an ~15-foot-high pressure ridge trending north-northwest (Figs. 28 and 29). The fault traverses the steeper southwestern face of this ridge. There is no geomorphic expression of the fault crossing the flat

portion of the floodplain surface, although any small surface features caused by the fault would have been destroyed long ago by human grading and agricultural activities. A 50-ft-wide left step-over exposed in trenches is present along the fault southeast of the pressure ridge (Fig. 28).

Geotechnical investigation of the proposed Willits hospital at the Haehl Creek site began in 2001, conducted by SHN, a geotechnical consulting firm. Initial trench investigations (SHN, 2003) revealed several important results, including (1) near-surface sediments are middle to late Holocene in age (less than ~8000 yr old); Pleistocene age (less than ~1.8 million years) fine-grained silty clay sediments that have been observed elsewhere in Little Lake Valley are present at a depth greater than 20–25 ft beneath the floodplain; and, (2) the fault is present in Holocene age, stratified sediments. This provided a unique opportunity to conduct research-level investigations of the fault's history and seismic potential through collaboration among SHN consulting geologists and geologists from the U.S. Geological Survey (USGS) and academia (Humboldt State University). Geotechnical studies focused on investigating sites for the three proposed developments: a regional hospital facility, a senior care facility, and a residential subdivision (SHN, 2003, 2004a, 2004b). USGS-funded research focused on evaluating the timing of surface-faulting earthquakes and the slip rate across the fault (Fenton et al., 2002; Larsen et al., 2005). In all, the geotechnical and research investigations have resulted in nearly 4000 ft of paleoseismic trenching, including at least 13 fault crossings (Fig. 28).

Geotechnical investigation of the site was complicated by the great thickness (20–25 ft) of Holocene-age materials beneath the floodplain surface. The state's Alquist-Priolo Earthquake Fault Zone Act (and related legislation for geotechnical investigation of hospitals) requires assessment of the presence or absence of active faulting throughout the Holocene epoch (which began ~11,000 yr ago). As such, pre-Holocene age materials must be investigated in enough detail to determine definitively whether or not they have been affected by fault activity. To answer the critical fault-related questions, a series of large pits was excavated at the site, extending to depths in excess of 30 ft in order to expose pre-Holocene age materials (Fig. 30).

Within the Little Lake Valley, the nature of the sediments being deposited changed noticeably at the time of the Pleistocene-Holocene boundary (~11,000 yr ago). The thick section of Holocene-age sediments consists of mostly silty overbank deposits with periodic coarse sand and gravel channels that were deposited by a high-energy stream. This was found to overlie a section of fine-grained (silty clay–clayey silt) sediment in laterally continuous, tabular beds that were deposited by either a shallow lake or a low-energy river with extensive floodplains that accumulated silty clay during floods (SHN, 2004a, 2004b; Woolace, 2005) (Fig. 31). Several trees (redwood, cottonwood, alder) were encountered in the upper part of the fine-grained section, some in upright growth position, suggesting that forests intermittently developed on floodplain or lake margins. Wood

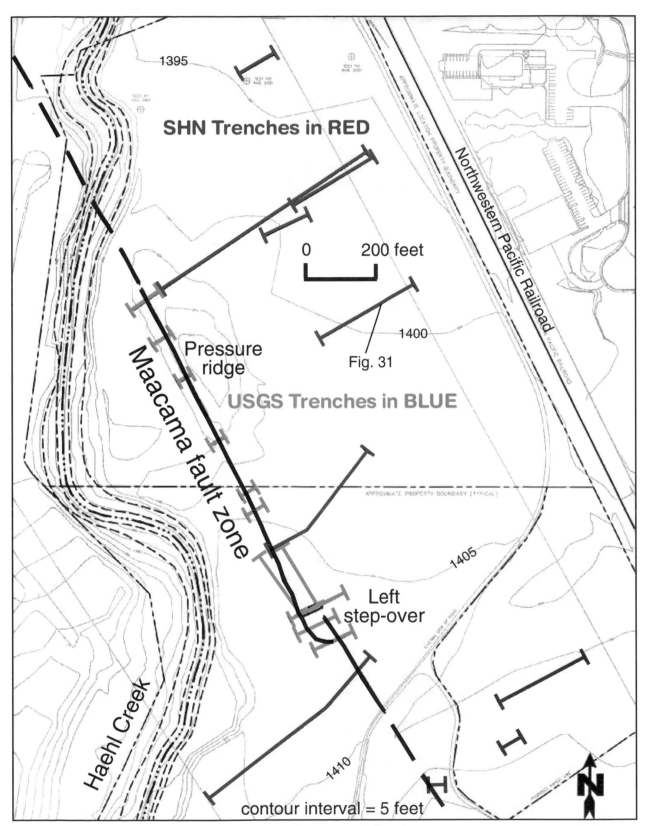

Figure 28. Overview map of the Haehl Creek site (Stop 7) showing locations of fault, pressure ridge, and exploratory trenches. The location of the trace of the Maacama fault across the southern Haehl Creek floodplain is determined by multiple trench exposures; a left step-over of the fault trace also is well defined by trenching.

Figure 29. Photograph of pressure ridge looking to the northwest; the Maacama fault is on the southwest (left) side of the ridge.

Figure 30. Photograph of one of a series of large (>30 ft deep) pits excavated to uncover sediment older in age than 11,000 yr (to prove presence or absence of active faulting through the Holocene epoch).

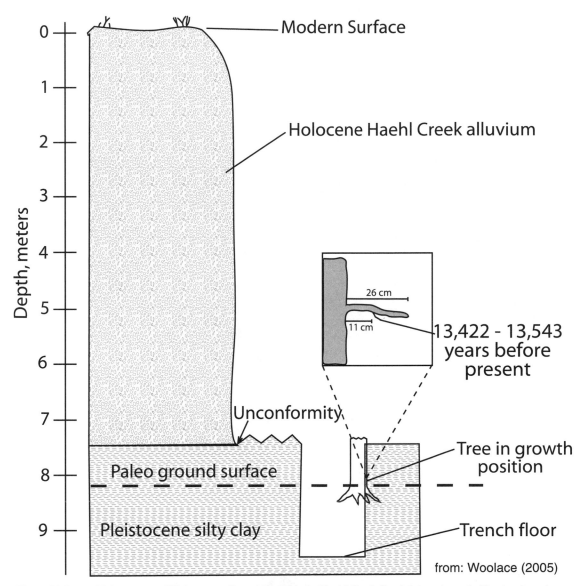

Figure 31. Latest Pleistocene and Holocene sediments beneath the Haehl Creek floodplain, as revealed in trenches, showing sediment type and radiocarbon age information. From Woolace (2005). Location of sketch is shown in Figure 28.

samples from these trees and charcoal samples from other exposures of the silty clay sediments yielded age estimates on the order of 11,350 yr to 22,870 yr before present (Fig. 31). The depositional transition that occurred near the Pleistocene-Holocene boundary in Little Lake Valley was characterized by the development of a higher energy, north-flowing stream system (Haehl Creek) that deposited up to 25 ft of alluvium. In the latest Holocene, Haehl Creek has incised through the entire Holocene section, and currently flows in a narrow, ~20–25-ft-deep arroyo with the latest Pleistocene silty clay sediments exposed at the floor. The cause of this recent incision is unknown.

The late Pleistocene age section is locally warped up along the northeastern side of the fault, where it is present at the ground surface. Up-tilted late Pleistocene silty clay sediments are present in the "core" of the pressure ridge and within the 50-foot-wide left step-over (which, interestingly, is not exposed geomorphically at the ground surface as a ridge).

The initial phase of USGS-funded research resulted in preliminary estimates of the number and timing of recent paleo-earthquakes. Fenton et al. (2002) excavated six trenches on the southwestern face of the pressure ridge and on the adjacent floodplain surface. Structural and stratigraphic relations in the trenches on the pressure ridge suggest at least four, and perhaps five, surface-faulting events during the Holocene. Age dating of charcoal samples from these trenches is on-going, so the results from this effort are likely to be updated in the future.

As part of an in-progress investigation of slip rate across the Maacama fault at the hospital site, Carol Prentice (USGS), Mort Larsen and Harvey Kelsey (Humboldt State University), and Judith Zachariasen (consultant) excavated, in summer 2004, multiple trenches parallel and perpendicular to the fault to provide exposures of paleo-channels on both sides of the fault. Detailed study of these excavations (Larsen et al., 2005) allowed mapping of the paths of two paleo-channels of Haehl Creek where they are offset by the Maacama fault (Fig. 32). The first channel, channel A, is right-laterally offset 4.6 m (15 ft). Based on two radiocarbon ages, the age of the channel is less than or equal to 740–640 yr old, indicating a minimum slip

Figure 32. Offset paleo-channels of Haehl Creek revealed by paleoseismic trenching. Channel A (bottom) is offset 4.6 m (15 ft) and has a preliminary age of 640–740 yr before present (B.P.) and a minimum slip rate of 6–7 mm/yr (0.23–0.27 in/yr). Channel B (top) is offset 27 m (90 ft) and has a preliminary age of 3480–3350 yr B.P. and a minimum slip rate of 8 mm/yr (0.31 in/yr).

rate of ~6 mm/yr (0.23 in/yr). The second and older channel, channel B, is offset right laterally ~27 m (90 ft). Based on one radiocarbon age, channel B is less than or equal to 3480–3350 yr old. From the offset and maximum limiting age, paleoseismologists infer a minimum slip rate for the fault since channel B time of ~8 mm/yr (0.31 in/yr). Because radiocarbon ages are from detrital charcoal that may be older than the age of deposition of the host alluvium, the radiocarbon ages will tend to overestimate the age of the channels. Future dating of more radiocarbon samples may significantly reduce channel ages, which would increase slip-rate estimates.

Preliminary results of the slip rate study are that over the past 700 yr, only fault creep has occurred at the site (given that the creep rate at Commercial Street in Willits, measured since 1991, is 6.5 mm/year (0.26 in/yr) (Galehouse, 2002). However, over the past 3500 yr, the data suggest that the slip rate is greater than the creep rate and therefore we conclude that the overall motion along this fault has included both slow and steady creep and sudden earthquakes with surface rupture (Larsen et al., 2005). The preliminary minimum long-term slip rate at Haehl Creek of ≥8 mm/yr is consistent with the 8–9 mm/yr rates found on the Hayward and Rodgers Creek segments of this fault system to the south and is consistent with the notion that the Maacama fault zone is capable of producing large earthquakes.

The location of active faulting has been adequately defined at all three proposed developments (SHN, 2004a, 2004b), although regulatory review is ongoing at the hospital site. The hospital and senior care center were sited by avoidance of the fault zone; both facilities are located at the edge of the Alquist-Priolo Zone in areas demonstrated to be void of active fault traces. The residential subdivision straddles the fault trace and will be designed such that no structures for human occupancy are located atop any fault traces. Streets and greenbelts will overlie the fault zone.

ACKNOWLEDGMENTS

The investigation of the Shiloh site (Stop 5) was funded under a grant to Geomatrix Consultants Inc. from the U.S. Geological Survey Bay Area Paleoearthquake Program (BAPEX), contract no. 98-7460-6687. We gratefully acknowledge the cooperation of the Sonoma County Board of Supervisors and Shiloh Ranch Regional Park. We thank Jackson Family Farms vineyards for graciously allowing us to access their property for Stop 2, and we thank the Frank R. Howard Memorial Hospital Foundation and Tom Herman for facilitating access to the Maacama fault for Stop 7.

REFERENCES CITED

Boatwright, J., and Bundock, H., 2005, Modified Mercalli Intensity maps for the 1906 San Francisco earthquake plotted in ShakeMap format: U.S. Geological Survey Open-File Report 2005-1135, http://pubs.usgs.gov/of/2005/1135/.

Budding, K.E., Schwartz, D.P., and Oppenheimer, D.H., 1991, Slip rate, earthquake recurrence, and seismogenic potential of the Rodgers Creek fault zone, northern California: Initial results: Geophysical Research Letters, v. 18, no. 3, p. 447–450.

California Division of Mines and Geology (CDMG), 1983, Special Studies zones Map, Healdsburg and Cordelia 7.5 minute quadrangles, scale 1:24,000.

Crampton, T., AbramsonWard, H., Hanson, K., and Swan, F. H., 2004, Preliminary results of paleoseismic investigations of the northern Rodgers Creek–Healdsburg fault at Shiloh Ranch Regional Park, Sonoma County, California (abs.): Seismological Research Letters, v. 74, no. 2, p. 238.

Dawson, A., 1998, The stories behind Sonoma Valley place names from Arrowhead Mountain to Yulupa: Glen Ellen, California, Kulupi Press, 54 p.

Fenton, C.H., Prentice, C.S., Benton, J.L., Crosby, C.J., Sickler, R.R., and Stephens, T.A., 2002, Paleoseismic evidence for prehistoric earthquakes on the northern Maacama fault, Willits, California: Eos, (Transactions, American Geophysical Union), v. 83, no. 47, Fall Meeting supplement, abstract S11B-1143.

Freymueller, J.T., Murray, M.H., Segall, P., and Castillo, D., 1999, Kinematics of the Pacific-North America plate boundary zone, northern California: Journal of Geophysical Research, v. 104, p. 7419–7442, doi: 10.1029/1998JB900118.

Galehouse, J.S., 2002, Data from theodolite measurements of creep rates on San Francisco Bay region faults, California: 1979–2001: USGS Open-File Report 02-225, http://geopubs.wr.usgs.gov/open-file/of02-225/.

Giblin Associates, 2004, Report, soil investigation, White House site mixed-use report, Santa Rosa, California: Giblin Associates, P.O. Box 6172, Santa Rosa, California 95406, USA, unpublished consultant's report, 23 p.

Gudde, E., 1969, California place names, the origins and etymology of current geographical names: Berkeley and Los Angeles, University of California Press, 399 p.

Harding-Lawson Associates, 1979, Soil investigation, 5th and Beaver Streets and Ross and B Streets garages, Santa Rosa, California: Harding-Lawson Associates, 1142 State Farm Drive, Santa Rosa, California 95401, USA, unpublished consultant's report, 38 p.

Harding-Lawson Associates, 1980, Soil investigation, RJV Office Building, 5th and E Streets, Santa Rosa, California: Harding-Lawson Associates, 1142 State Farm Drive, Santa Rosa, California 95401, USA, unpublished consultant's report, 20 p.

Harding-Lawson Associates, 1987a, Geotechnical investigation, parking garage, Seventh and Healdsburg, Santa Rosa, California: Harding-Lawson Associates, 1142 State Farm Drive, Santa Rosa, California 95401, USA, unpublished consultant's report, 34 p.

Harding-Lawson Associates, 1987b, Geotechnical investigation, planned four-story office building, First and Santa Rosa Avenues, Santa Rosa, California: Harding-Lawson Associates, 1142 State Farm Drive, Santa Rosa, California 95401, USA, unpublished consultant's report, 34 p.

Harsh, P.W., Pampeyan, E.H., and Coakley, J.M., 1978, Slip on the Willits fault (abs.): Earthquake Notes, Eastern Section, Seismological Society of America, v. 49, no. 1, p. 22.

Hayward Fault Paleoearthquake Group, 1999, Timing of paleoearthquakes on the northern Hayward fault—preliminary evidence in El Cerrito, California: USGS Open-File Report 99-318, 33 p., http://geopubs.wr.usgs.gov/open-file/of99-318/.

Hecker, S., Pantosti, D., Schwartz, D.P., Hamilton, J.C., Reidy, L.M., and Powers, T.J., 2005, The most recent large earthquake on the Rodgers Creek fault, San Francisco Bay Area: Bulletin of the Seismological Society of America, v. 95, no. 3, p. 844–860, doi: 10.1785/0120040134.

Hillenbrand, L., 2001, Seabiscuit: An American legend: Random House, New York, 339 .

Huffman, M.E., and Armstrong, C.F., 1980, Geology for planning in Sonoma County: California Division of Mines and Geology Special Report 120, 31 p., 8 plates.

Kleinfelder Inc., 2002, Geotechnical investigation report: Moore Building, Santa Rosa, California: Kleinfelder Inc., 2240 Northpoint Parkway, Santa Rosa, California 95407, USA, unpublished consultant's report, 31 p.

Kleinfelder Inc., 2005, Geotechnical investigation report: 730 Third Street (White House site), Santa Rosa, California: Kleinfelder Inc., 2240 Northpoint Parkway, Santa Rosa, California 95407, USA, unpublished consultant's report, 30 p.

Larsen, M., Prentice, C.S., Kelsey, H.M., Zachariasen, J., and Rotberg, G., 2005, Paleoseismic investigation of the Maacama fault at the Haehl Creek site, Willits, California: Geological Society of America Abstracts with Programs, v. 37, no. 4, p. 68.

Lawson, A.C., chairman, 1908, The California earthquake of April 18, 1906: Report of the State Earthquake Investigation Commission: Carnegie Institution of Washington, pub. no. 87, v. I, 451 p., (reprinted in 1969).

LeBaron, G., Blackman, D., Mitchell, J., and Hansen, H., 1983, Santa Rosa. A 19th century town: Santa Rosa, California, Historia Ltd., 224 p.

Lienkaemper, J.J., Dawson, T.E., Personius, S.F., Seitz, G.G., Reidy, L.M., and Schwartz, D.P., 2002, A record of large earthquakes on the southern Hayward fault for the past 500 years: Bulletin of the Seismological Society of America, v. 92, p. 2637–2658, doi: 10.1785/0120000611.

McLaughlin, R.J., Wagner, D.L., Sweetkind, D.S., Sarna-Wojcicki, A.M., Rytuba, J.J., Langenheim, V.E., Fleck, R.J., Jachens, R.C., and Deino, A., 2005, Late Neogene transition from transform to subduction margin east of the San Andreas fault in the wine country of the northern San Francisco Bay area, California, in Stevens, C., and Cooper, J., eds., Field Trip 10 Guide: San Jose, California, Pacific Section, Society for Sedimentary Geology (SEPM), 29 April–1 May 2005 GSA Cordilleran Section–SEPM Pacific Section Joint Meeting, 112 p.

Schwartz, D.P., Pantosti, D., Hecker, S., Okumura, K., Budding, K.E., and Powers, T., 1992, Late Holocene behavior and seismogenic potential of the Rodgers Creek fault zone, Sonoma County, California, in Borchardt, G., Hirschfeld, S.E., Lienkaemper, J.J., McClellan, P., and Wong, I.G., eds., Proceedings of the Second Conference on Earthquake Hazards in the Eastern San Francisco Bay Area: California Division of Mines and Geology Special Publication 113, p. 393–398.

SHN, 2003, Fault rupture hazard evaluation, proposed senior assisted living facility, APNs 007-230-28 and 007-250-18, Willits, Mendocino County, California: SHN Consulting Engineers and Geologists, 812 W. Wabash Ave., Eureka, California 95501, USA, unpublished consultant's report, 12 p., with 8 figures and trench logs.

SHN, 2004a, fault rupture hazard evaluation, proposed Frank R. Howard Memorial Hospital, APN 007-210-15, Willits, Mendocino County, California: SHN Consulting Engineers and Geologists, 812 W. Wabash Ave., Eureka, California 95501, USA, unpublished consultant's report, 14 p., with 9 figures and trench logs.

SHN, 2004b, Fault Rupture Hazard Evaluation, Proposed Residential Subdivision, APN 007–250–27, Willits, California: SHN Consulting Engineers and Geologists, 812 W. Wabash Ave., Eureka, California 95501, USA, unpublished consultant's report, 15 p., with 7 figures and trench logs.

Sowers, J.M., Noller, J.S., and Lettis, W.R., 1995, Maps showing Quaternary geology and liquefaction susceptibility in the Napa Valley, California: U.S. Geological Survey Open-File Report 95-205, 23 p., two sheets, scale 1:100,000.

Steinbrugge, K.V., 1970, Engineering aspects of the Santa Rosa California, earthquakes, October 1, 1969, in Steinbrugge, K.V., Cloud, W.K., and Scott, N.H., The Santa Rosa, California, earthquakes of October 1, 1969: Rockville, Maryland, U.S. Department of Commerce, Coast and Geodetic Survey, p. 1–63.

Swan, F.H., Crampton, T., Abramson, H., and Hanson, K.L., 2003, Paleoseismic investigation of the Rogers Creek–Healdsburg Fault at Shiloh Regional Park, Sonoma County, California: Proceedings of the Hayward Fault Workshop, Eastern San Francisco Bay Area, California, September 19–20, 2003, p. 12.

U.S. Geological Survey, 1991, Willits, California, 7.5' topographic quadrangle: U.S. Geological Survey Map W-1548, plate 6.

William Spangle and Associates Inc., 1980, Land use planning after earthquakes: William Spangle and Associates Inc., 3240 Alpine Road, Portola Valley, California 94028, USA, 24 p., plus appendices.

Wong, I.G., and Bott, J.D., 1995, A new look back at the 1969 Santa Rosa, California, earthquakes: Bulletin of the Seismological Society of America, v. 85, no. 1, p. 334–341.

Woolace, A., 2005, Late Neogene and Quaternary stratigraphy and structure of Little Lake (Willits) Valley, northern Coast Range, California [M.S. thesis]: Arcata, Humboldt State University, 63 p.

Working Group on California Earthquake Probabilities, 2003, Earthquake probabilities in the San Francisco Bay Region: 2002–2031: USGS Open-File Report 03-214, http://pubs.usgs.gov/of/2003/of03-214/.

Geological Society of America
Field Guide 7
2006

A transect spanning 500 million years of active plate margin history: Outline and field trip guide

E.M. Moores
Department of Geology, University of California, Davis, California 95616, USA
J. Wakabayashi
Department of Earth and Environmental Sciences, California State University, Fresno, California 93740, USA
J.R. Unruh
W.L. Lettis & Associates, 1777 Botelho Drive, Suite 262, Walnut Creek, California 95496, USA
S. Waechter
Far West Anthropology Research, Inc., 2727 Del Rio Place , Davis, California 95616, USA

OVERVIEW OF THE FIELD TRIP

A vital lesson of plate tectonics is that there is no validity to any assumption that the simplest and therefore most acceptable interpretation demands a proximal rather than a distant origin.
(Coombs, 1997, p. 763).

This field trip steps back to provide the very long term and large-scale tectonic history that one might call the broader tectonic context of the 1906 San Francisco earthquake. In effect, the field trip follows a cross section of northern California, with stops that illustrate the geologic history of the region. The field guide also discusses several archaeological stops of significance to California's prehistory. The entire field trip is meant to be taken over a period of four days, with overnight stops in Davis and in Quincy. Day one comprises Stops 1–9; Day 2, Stops 10–18; Day 3, Stops 19–28; and Day 4, Stops 29–33.

Northern California geology is the result of an extended history of active plate margin interactions spanning some 500 million years (m.y.). Over the course of this period, countless numbers of large earthquakes of different types no doubt accompanied tens of thousands of kilometers of movement between tectonic plates and microplates that eventually came together to form the rocks of northern California as we see them today.

From ca. 500–18 million years ago (Ma), subduction, a process still active north of Cape Mendocino, dominated the geologic history of northern California. During this period,

several subduction zones and volcanic arcs were active, and subduction zones, whose former positions we will see on our trip, consumed ocean basins thousands of kilometers wide, sweeping together a vast collage of rocks from far-flung locations in the process.

Remnants of the most ancient of these subduction zones and collided blocks (typically called terranes) are preserved in the Sierra Nevada. The most recent subduction history along the North American margin involved the Farallon plate, a plate that lay east of the Pacific plate and was separated from it by a spreading mid-oceanic ridge. The products of this subduction episode are preserved in the rocks of the Coast Ranges, and in the granitic and younger volcanic rocks of the Sierra Nevada (Figs. 1 and 2).

For the past 18 m.y., the plate margin has been dominated by right-lateral faults of a transform plate margin, the most famous of which, the San Andreas fault, produced the 1906 earthquake. The present plate boundary between the Pacific plate on the west and stable North America on the east is a broad one consisting of two active zones: (1) the San Andreas fault system, whose right-lateral faults occupy the California Coast Ranges; and (2) a zone east of the Sierra Nevada including the right-lateral faulting associated with the Walker Lane and the Eastern California Shear Zone, and, east of the Walker Lane, the extensional faults of the Basin and Range province (Fig. 3).

These zones of active faults, shown in Figure 3, are responsible for generating most of the earthquakes in the area traversed by our field trip. The preexisting complexity of the crust resulting from the earlier tectonic history probably influenced

Moores, E.M., Wakabayashi, J., Unruh, J.R., and Waechter, S., A transect spanning 500 million years of active plate margin history: Outline and field trip guide, *in* Prentice, C.S., Scotchmoor, J.G., Moores, E.M., and Kiland, J.P., eds., 1906 San Francisco Earthquake Centennial Field Guides: Field trips associated with the 100th Anniversary Conference, 18–23 April 2006, San Francisco, California: Geological Society of America Field Guide 7, p. 373–413, doi: 10.1130/2006.1906SF(20). For permission to copy, contact editing@geosociety.org. ©2006 Geological Society of America. All rights reserved.

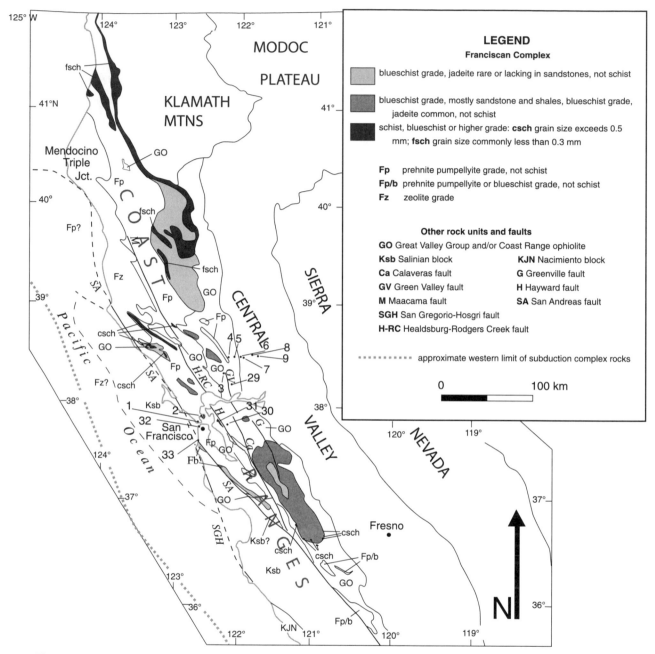

Figure 1. Sketch map of part of the northern Coast Ranges showing major tectonic features and locations of field trip stops.

the development and location of these more recent fault zones, in addition to giving us some exceedingly interesting and complex geology to examine on our trip.

This long and complex history requires a great deal of discussion for complete understanding. In this guide, we present first the stops in sequence, including brief descriptions for each site. To augment these brief discussions, we follow the field trip guide with an Appendix in which we discuss the tectonic development of northern California more fully.

Keywords: California, tectonics, Sierra Nevada, Coast Ranges, Great Valley, neotectonics.

ROCK TYPES ENCOUNTERED ON THIS FIELD TRIP AND THEIR ENVIRONMENTS OF FORMATION

A key element in our analysis is an emphasis on the rocks that are known to have formed in particular geologic environments. Several rocks or rock assemblages are of prime importance:

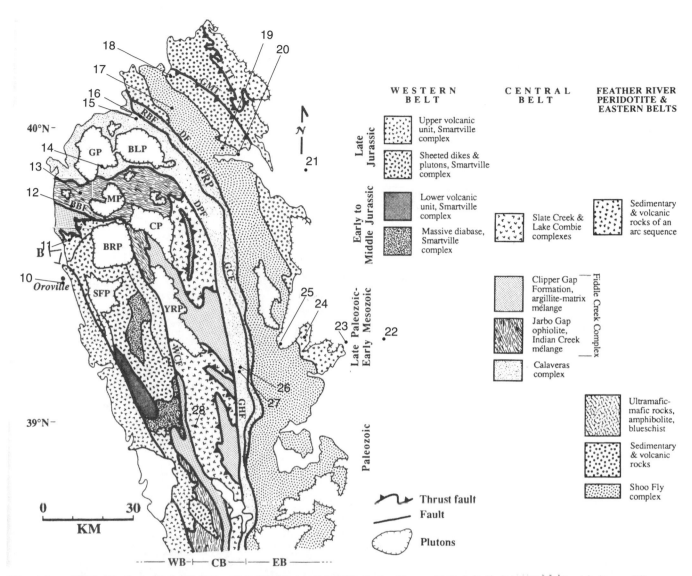

Abbreviations: (Belts): CB= Central Belt, EB=Eastern Belt, WB=Western Belt; FRP= Feather River peridotite belt; (faults):BBF=Big Bend fault zone, DF= Downieville fault, DPF=Dogwood Peak fault,GCF=Goodyear's Creek fault, GHF=Gillis Hill fault, GMT=Grizzly Mtn. fault, RBF=Rich Bar fault, TT=Taylorsville thrust, WCF=Wolf Creek fault; (plutons) BLP=Bucks Lake pluton, CP= Cascade pluton, GP=Grizzly pluton, MP=Merrimac pluton, SFP=Swedes flat pluton, YRP=Yuba Rivers pluton. Adapted from Dilek et al. (1990).

Figure 2. Sketch map of part of the northern Sierra Nevada showing major tectonic features and locations of field trip stops.

Ophiolites

These assemblages of ultramafic rocks (peridotites and/or serpentinized peridotites) and mostly mafic volcanic and plutonic rocks represent ocean crust and mantle formed at spreading centers in the deep ocean. They were emplaced in the continental crust by (1) failed subduction of a continental margin or island arc beneath them, or (2) the scraping off of subduction complex material beneath them (Moores, 1998; and Moores et al., 2000, 2002). An ophiolite marks the edge of a plate beneath

which subduction occurred, and the fault that is present structurally beneath the ophiolite marks the position of a former subduction zone (Wakabayashi, 1999a). Also found beneath some ophiolites are metamorphic rocks that have undergone high-pressure–low-temperature metamorphism consistent with the conditions of metamorphism in subduction zones. The position of former subduction zones, now known as sutures (the scars of formerly existing and now disappeared oceans), represent one of the most important tectonic features of northern California geology. We will view several such sutures on our field trip.

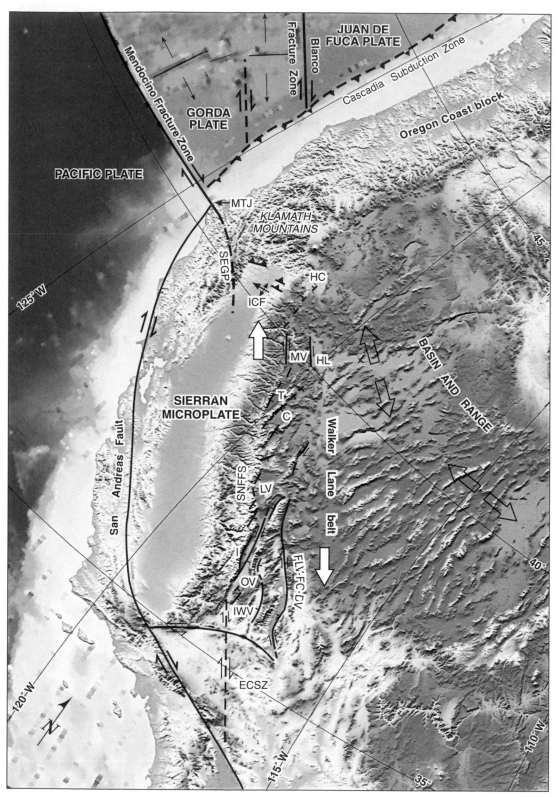

Figure 3. (*this and following page*) Present active tectonic scenario in the western United States. (A) Digital relief map of the Western United States, showing major tectonic features. A—Almanor graben; C—Carson Valley; ECSZ—Eastern California Shear Zone; FLV-FC-DV—Fish Lake Valley–Furnace Creek–Death Valley fault zone; HC—Hat Creek valley; HL—Honey Lake fault; I—Independence fault; ICF—Inks Creek Fold Belt; IWV—Indian Wells Valley; LV—Long Valley; MTJ—Mendocino Triple Junction; MV—Mohawk Valley; OV—Owens Valley; SEGP—southern edge of subducted Gorda Plate; SNFFS—Sierra Nevada Frontal Fault system; T—Tahoe Valley (after Unruh et al., 2003).

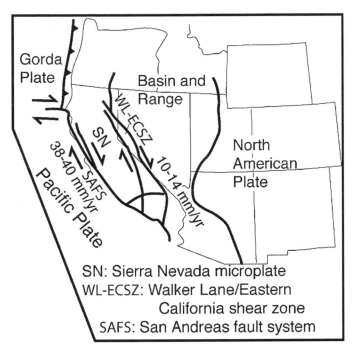

SN: Sierra Nevada microplate
WL-ECSZ: Walker Lane/Eastern
California shear zone
SAFS: San Andreas fault system

Figure 3. (*continued*) (B) Generalized map of the western United States showing the current plate tectonic situation featuring the Pacific plate, the San Andreas fault system, the Sierra Nevada microplate, and the Walker Lane–Eastern California shear zone, with the current understanding of the relative motion between the plates (after Unruh et al., 2003).

Oceanic Volcanic Rocks

These rocks formed in an oceanic setting, either as part of the sea floor formed at a spreading center, as submarine volcanoes on the sea floor, or as part of chains of islands over intra-oceanic subduction zones. They include pillow basalts, which have the distinctive shape of pillows that can only form under water.

Oceanic Sedimentary Rocks

The principal sedimentary rocks of note are called pelagic sediments, mostly thin-bedded siliceous rocks called cherts, sediments that formed so far away from continents that there is essentially no debris from the continents in them. They formed (and form today) by very slow deposition of shells of floating plankton and dust blown off the continents that settles very slowly to the ocean bottom. Marine shales and sandstones are also in this category.

Mélanges

These are chaotic mixtures of igneous, sedimentary, and/or metamorphic rocks of diverse origin in some sort of matrix, usually highly sheared mudstone or serpentine. Mélanges characterize many subduction zones. They also underlie much of the Coast Ranges and parts of the Sierra Nevada and Klamath Mountains.

Our interpretation of many of these oceanic rocks is that they have originated elsewhere and have traveled long distances to become incorporated into the North American continent as plate motions proceeded over the past 200 m.y.

One of the more interesting aspects of the geology that will be demonstrated on this trip is how much we still do not know or do not agree on. There is still much work to do to understand fully the complex series of tectonic interactions that assembled the rocks of California. In fact, it is unlikely that you will find any two geologists who agree completely on any one model of the tectonic events we describe. Even the basic framework of geology in the Sierra Nevada, such as the number of subduction zones, the direction of subduction associated with them, and their ages, remain subjects of inquiry and debate. In other words, geologists have much research to do to understand even the basic history of this complex geologic region.

DAY ONE

Stop 1: Marin Headlands

Significance of the Site

This site displays an excellent exposure of oceanic basalt and red chert of the Marin Headlands terrane in the Franciscan Complex.

Accessibility

This area is publicly accessible. There are no restrooms. Parking is available along the roadside, though it is often crowded, especially during weekends in the summer.

GPS Coordinates

37°.789′N, 122°28.999′W.

Directions

Leave the Moscone Center and drive to the Golden Gate Bridge. The road log begins at 0.0 mi at the Golden Gate Bridge toll plaza.

Cumulative mileage
- 1.4 North end of Golden Gate Bridge.
- 1.9 Exit right at Alexander Avenue.
- 2.1 At the end of the offramp, turn left (westward) at the stop sign, and head under the freeway.
- 2.3 Turn right on Conzelman Road following signs to the Marin Headlands.
- 2.6 Pull into the parking area on the left (south) side of the road.

Stop Description

From the parking area on the Marin Headlands (Fig. 1), on a clear day, we can look across the Golden Gate to San Francisco. We see the city of San Francisco as well as sea cliffs that extend southward from the south abutment of the Golden Gate Bridge. These sea cliffs expose an intra-Franciscan shear zone and a slab of serpentinite, which we will visit on the last day (Day 4) of this field trip. The outcrops across the road from the parking area expose red chert and basalt of the Marin Headlands terrane. As with other tectonic units within the Franciscan Complex, in this region, the terranes are actually tabular rock units that may represent thrust sheets, or nappes (from the French word for sheet). In many places, the chert is faulted against basalt, but locally its original depositional contact on basalt is preserved. Elsewhere in the Marin Headlands, dirty brown-gray sandstone and shale depositionally overly the chert. Metamorphism of these rocks is minor, and igneous and sedimentary features are well preserved (Swanson and Schiffman, 1979; Blake et al., 1984). These rocks probably were buried to a depth of less than 15 km during subduction.

The 80-m-thick chert section of the Marin Headlands was deposited in the deep ocean from 200 to 100 Ma somewhere near the equator, based on studies of the radiolarian fossils (radiolaria are unicellular floating plants that produce a siliceous shell) in the cherts and on paleomagnetic studies (Murchey, 1984). One can see the radiolaria in the rock (best on a freshly broken, wet surface) with a hand lens. These appear as round, somewhat darker dots, set in the dark red-brown matrix of the chert.

The geochemistry of the basalt suggests its formation at an oceanic spreading center (Shervais, 1989). Based on their geochemistry and local field relations, most volcanic rocks within the Franciscan Complex appear to have formed at spreading ridges or were away from the spreading ridge on seamounts or thick volcanic accumulations called oceanic plateaus (Shervais, 1990). Chert deposition in the Marin Headlands unit continued in the open ocean for 100 m.y. as the oceanic plate moved toward the Franciscan subduction zone. Approximately 95 Ma, deposition of the dirty sandstone ("greywacke") on top of the chert occurred as this piece of ocean floor neared the Franciscan trench and was incorporated into the Franciscan Complex (Wahrhaftig, 1984).

Stop 2: Ring Mountain, Tiburon Peninsula

Significance of the Site

This site provides an excellent exposure of Franciscan high-grade tectonic blocks in a disordered unit (mélange) in the highest structural horizon of the Franciscan Complex in the San Francisco Bay Area.

Accessibility

There is a parking lot off the paved road (permission needed for access). No restrooms.

GPS Coordinates

37°54.181′N, 122°28.925′W.

Directions

From Stop 1, carefully turn around and head back toward Highway 101. At the bottom of the hill, turn left at the stop sign. The road curves right and under the Highway 101 overpass.

Cumulative mileage

3.1 Turn right after passing under the freeway, following signs to northbound Highway 101 to Santa Rosa.

8.5 Exit right at Tiburon Blvd.

8.6 Turn right at the end of the offramp onto Tiburon Blvd. and drive eastward.

10.3 Turn left onto Trestle Glen Blvd. (This intersection occurs on a right curve of Tiburon Blvd.)

10.8 Turn left onto Shepherd Way, marked also by signs for the Shepherd of the Hills Lutheran church.

10.9 Turn right off of Shepherd Way into the church parking lot.

Stop Description

Even the nongeologist finds the high-grade metamorphic blocks of Ring Mountain on Tiburon Peninsula exceptionally interesting (these high-grade blocks are coarsely crystalline metamorphic rocks whose minerals indicate high-pressure–low-temperature recrystallization in a subduction zone). **Rockhounds take heed:** This stop is entirely on a protected natural preserve—collecting of rocks is prohibited (one can gawk but not bash or take).

Ring Mountain is probably the best place in the Franciscan Complex to examine high-grade tectonic blocks because of the tremendous variety and number of mineral assemblages. The rocks appear in a serpentinite-matrix mélange that is structurally beneath a sheet of serpentinite (Bero, 2003) and structurally above a stack of coherent Franciscan thrust units or nappes (Blake et al., 1974; Wakabayashi, 1992). Landslides have displaced many of the blocks downslope. The high-grade blocks display metamorphic minerals of several millimeters to several centimeters in size. They include amphibolites (composed of amphibole and other minerals), eclogites (composed of garnet and Na-rich pyroxene, called omphacite), and blueschists (characterized by blue amphibole minerals) that exhibit the oldest ages of metamorphism of any rocks in the Franciscan Complex (Coleman and Lanphere, 1971). Most blocks exhibit an earlier higher temperature (amphibolite grade) metamorphism (Blake et al., 1984; Moore and Blake, 1989). These high-grade blocks constitute but a tiny fraction of Franciscan metamorphic rocks, but they are arresting in appearance. They also record an interesting tectonic history involving high-temperature recrystallization (500–700 °C) followed by deep burial in the Franciscan subduction zone. Some rocks were buried to depths as great as 70 km (Tsujimori et al., 2006), the deepest of any metamorphic rocks found in California.

More widespread sheets of Franciscan metamorphic rocks, which are generally much finer grained (minerals generally tenths of millimeters and smaller) and of lower metamorphic grade, are commonly referred to as coherent blueschists (because of the presence of blue-colored metamorphic minerals) or coherent metamorphic rocks. These blueschists make up a significant part of the Franciscan Complex. Because of their fine grain size, however, they are visually rather disappointing, particularly to geologists who come from areas outside of western California.

From the northwest corner of the church parking lot, take a hiking trail northwest for several hundred meters. After this short hike, you will find yourself on the trail following the crest of the peninsula and will soon see the first of several rocky outcrops on the right. This first outcrop is a typical high-grade block. On this trip, we will have time to view only this block in detail. The block is an amphibolite (a rock with abundant amphibole) containing the minerals garnet and epidote. It preserves a record of progressive metamorphism as the rock was dragged down to great depth during the very earliest stages of subduction.

Stop 3: View of Topographic Escarpment along Green Valley Fault

Significance of the Site

This site provides a view of the easternmost strand of the San Andreas family of strike-slip faults.

Accessibility

This is at a pullout along a paved, public road. No restrooms.

GPS Coordinates

38°21.286′N, 122°12.106′W.

Directions

Leaving Stop 2, we retrace our route back toward Highway 101.

Cumulative mileage

13.1 Turn right off of Tiburon Blvd. onto the onramp for northbound Highway 101 (signed for Eureka). We will stay on northbound 101 until we reach State Highway 37 (SR37).

25.9 Exit right on SR37 (following signs to Vallejo).

33.0 Keep to the right lane in order to stay on SR37.

40.7 Hills at 10–11 o'clock are capped by ca. 4–8 Ma Sonoma volcanics, part of the Coast Range suite of late Cenozoic volcanic rocks. These rocks have been folded so that they are locally steeply dipping. We cross the Rodgers Creek fault on this road, as well as the less well-defined West Napa fault.

45.2 At the intersection of SR37 and SR29, turn left onto SR29. Note: This intersection was under construction in July 2005 and will likely have changed somewhat by the time of the field trip.

52.6 Exit right for Lake Berryessa/downtown Napa.

55.3 At the intersection with SR121, go north toward Lake Berryessa.

56.0 Turn right onto the Silverado trail.

58.4 Keep to the left on Silverado trail.

58.8 Go right on SR121 (Monticello Road) toward Lake Berryessa.

63.8 Park in the small turnout on the right side of the road.

Stop Description

The Green Valley fault is the easternmost strand of the San Andreas system at this latitude. It has at least 20 km of displacement (Wakabayashi, 1999b). The fault disappears into the hills north of here. The road takes a turn northward before descending the NNW-trending, ENE-facing topographic escarpment formed along the fault. This part of the Green Valley fault is near the northern end of the segment of the fault thought to show definitive evidence of Holocene (the past 10,000 years) movement. Existing mapping (Wagner and Bortugno, 1982) shows the Green Valley fault terminating at this location beneath a massive landslide complex over seven miles long and nearly half a mile wide. Unpublished work by consulting geologists indicates that the slide complex consists of initial large block slides, as much as tens of thousands of years old, with superimposed younger block slides and earthflows (slow incoherent downslope earth movements). Some of the younger slides are still active (Turney et al., 1995). It also lies along a belt of seismicity associated with the fault (e.g., Jennings, 1994).

Stop 4: Sedimentary Serpentinite within the Basal Great Valley Group

Accessibility

This is at a pullout along a paved public road. No restrooms (some are nearby, as indicated in directions below).

GPS Coordinates

38°30.485′N, 122°12.858′W.

Directions

Leaving Stop 3, continue northeast on SR121.

Cumulative mileage

67.9 Circle Oaks drive. This subdivision has been constructed, at least in part, on the active landslides of the massive landslide complex. Recurrent sliding had destroyed several houses over the past couple of decades since the subdivision was constructed.

71.1 At the junction with SR128, go left (NW).

74.8 Bridge in active landslide in serpentinite. The western end of the bridge has an adjustable abutment to allow for realignment after movement of the slide (R.A. Matthews, 1991, personal commun.).

76.0 Turn right onto Spanish Flat Road. (There are restrooms in the restaurant at this intersection). Here we pass roadcuts in massive serpentinite that is probably associated with the Coast Range ophiolite (Hopson and Pessagno, 2004).

76.7 We pass roadcuts in Franciscan graywacke and shale.

78.9 Park on the right side of the road.

Stop Description

Here we will view the basal contact of a sedimentary serpentinite unit of the northern Great Valley Group, the Mysterious Valley Formation of Phipps (1984). On the north side of the road (across from the parking area) serpentinite is exposed, some of which is not in place because it has been transported by landslides, such as the landslide on which an electric substation visible to the NE was built. This serpentinite appears somewhat disaggregated, although the slope movement probably influences the appearance of the rock here. We will walk NE along the road for a few hundred feet. The roadcut exposes a contact of serpentinite over shales of the Great Valley Group. The base of the serpentinite unit is marked by a conglomerate that contains gabbro and other mafic (rocks characterized by high Mg and Fe compositions) clasts. This contact indicates that this serpentinite is sedimentary in nature. The sedimentary serpentinite may have originated as serpentinite mud volcano deposits similar to those found in the forearc of the Marianas, overlying an active intra-oceanic subduction zone (Fryer et al., 2000).

Stop 5: Monticello Dam and Basal Upper Cretaceous Section of Great Valley Group

Significance of the Site

This is an excellent and world-famous exposure of the deep-sea fan deposits that characterize the Great Valley Group of the California Coast Ranges.

Accessibility

There is a large public parking area near the dam on SR128. No restrooms. **Note:** Steep cliff; USE CAUTION.

GPS Coordinates

38°30.756′N, 0.22°06.186′W.

Directions

Leaving Stop 4, continue on Spanish Flat Road northeastward 0.1 mi to the driveway to the electric substation.

Cumulative mileage

79.0 Turn around using the substation driveway and return to SR128.

81.9 At the junction with SR128, turn left. For the next several miles, we will drive through shales and sandstones of the Great Valley Group.

86.7 At the junction with SR121, turn left to continue on SR128.

86.8 Roadcut of lower Great Valley Group.

87.2 We can see a greenstone and chert block above the road. This block is surrounded by shale and sandstone matrix and has been mapped as part of the sedimentary mélange known as the Mysterious Valley Formation of Phipps (1984). Unless the base of such a unit is exposed (showing a depositional contact), it is difficult to distinguish a sedimentary mélange unit from a tectonic mélange in the Franciscan Complex (mélanges or chaotic deposits can be either sedimentary or tectonic in origin).

87.6 We pass exposures of the Salt Creek Conglomerate, a well-sorted massive conglomerate within the Great Valley Group.

90.5 We pass through (cross) Wragg Canyon. This geomorphic feature follows the Wragg Canyon fault, the easternmost fault of the San Andreas fault system along this highway. We continue to pass through rocks of the Great Valley Group.

97.2 Pull into a parking area on the left side of the road.

Stop Description

The massive sandstones on the abutments of Monticello dam form the base of the Upper Cretaceous part of the Great Valley Group. The Upper Cretaceous section presents the most voluminous part of the Great Valley Group; this part of the forearc basin strata represents the highest rate of deposition and subsidence (Moxon, 1988). The rapid subsidence that marks this part of the Great Valley Group coincides with the main stage of exhumation of the coherent blueschist facies rocks of the Franciscan Complex. This deposition may have been associated with downward movement on the fault that separated the upper plate of the trench-forearc system (Coast Range ophiolite and Great Valley Group) from the underplated and offscraped Franciscan Complex structurally beneath it (Wakabayashi and Unruh, 1995).

Stop 6: Blackrocks (Putnam Peak Basalt)

Significance of the Site

This site provides a good exposure of columnar jointed landslide blocks of a mid-Tertiary basalt flow that originated NE of the Sierra Nevada.

Accessibility

Find a parking spot on this paved, public road. No restrooms.

GPS Coordinates

38°31.042N, 122°03.361W.

Directions

Leaving Stop 5, continue eastward on SR128 and descend the canyon below Monticello Dam. At 100.3 mi, park in the turnout on the right side of road.

Stop Description

Here we see slide blocks of 15 Ma basalt that represents a part of a unit, the Lovejoy basalt, that we will see more of later in this field trip. The Lovejoy basalt erupted from east of the present Sierra Nevada crest near Honey Lake and flowed westward across what later became the Sierra and the Sacramento Valley (Durrell, 1959). We will see other areas of this basalt later in the trip. The basalt here is called the Putnam Peak basalt and has been correlated with the Lovejoy on the basis of its estimated age and its composition (Siegel, 1988). Recently, detailed measurements of the magnetic properties of these rocks by Coe et al. (2005) also strongly suggest that the Putnam Peak basalt is equivalent to the Lovejoy basalt and that 90% of the Lovejoy basalt erupted within a geologically short period of time, probably a few hundred to a few thousand years. The Lovejoy basalt and other remnants of basalt in the Sierra Nevada have yielded 16 Ma Ar/Ar ages (Page et al. 1995; Garrison, 2004). The Lovejoy basalt is apparently buried beneath post-16 Ma sediments in the Sacramento Valley, whereas in the northern Sierra Nevada caps it ridges. The position of the Lovejoy (Putnam Peak basalt) in these hills along the eastern margin of the Coast Ranges is a product of rock uplift associated with fold and thrust fault development along the eastern Coast Ranges range front (Unruh et al., 1995). Massive landslides were reported from this area during the 1896 Winters-Vacaville earthquakes.

Stop 7: Putah Tuff

Significance of the Site

This site provides an excellent exposure of a young (1.8 Ma) rhyolitic tuff.

Accessibility

Park on the shoulder of this paved, public road. No restrooms.

Directions

Leaving Stop 6, continue eastbound on SR128.

Cumulative mileage

~101.5 Pass roadcuts in the Tehama gravel. These Pleistocene to Recent (£2 Ma) gravels contain clasts of Great Valley and Franciscan rocks, indicating that they were derived principally from source areas to the west. This is the youngest recognized unit of this region. The gravels underlie much of the western part of the Great Valley and probably form the principal aquifers of the western Great Valley. The western Great Valley groundwater is notably hard (because of the dissolving of the carbonate cements in the Great Valley Group rocks), and some levels contain high levels of boron and other elements toxic to many plants.

102.2 Park along the right side of the road.

Stop Description

This 1.8 Ma rhyolitic tuff is probably derived from a volcanic center in the northern Napa valley. The tuff (a product of explosive volcanism) is interlayered with the Tehama gravels and shows evidence of having been reworked by stream action.

Stop 8: Active Fold in Great Valley Surface

Significance of the Site

An example of the active folding that occurs along the western side of the Great Valley (the western margin of the Sierra microplate). The Great Valley is underlain by a thick sequence of oceanic crust and mantle, which in turn lies on the western margin of the continent (see Fig. 4). This dense slab of probably exotic material may account for the low-lying level of the valley, in contrast to the rapidly uplifting Coast Ranges and Sierra Nevada to the west and east, respectively.

Accessibility

Park in the school parking lot. No permission is necessary, but be sensitive to the school activities. There is a bike path here, so watch out for bicycles. No restrooms are available.

GPS Coordinates

38°32.857′N, 121°50.435′W.

Directions

Leaving Stop 7, continue eastbound on SR128 and drive into Winters (a town that was badly damaged in the 1892 earthquake, probably resulting from movement along the basal thrust fault below the Great Valley sequence).

Cumulative mileage

107.7 At the junction with I-505, continue east toward Davis.
110.8 Road 31/32 junction. Continue straight ahead on Road 32.
114.8 Intersection with Road 96. Turn left into the school parking lot.

Stop Description

This modest hill is a fold that resulted from movement on a subhorizontal fault that underlies the western part of the Great Valley (Unruh and Moores, 1992). It represents part of the compressional structures along the western margin of the Sierra Nevada microplate.

Stop 9: Archeological Stop A-1

Significance of the Site

This site provides an example of a pre-European village in the Great Valley.

Accessibility

This stop is in the center of the city of Davis. Street parking is available.

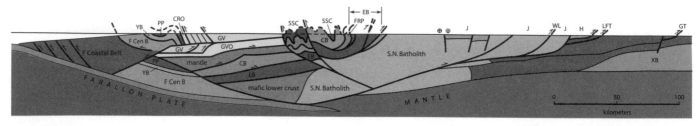

Figure 4. Crustal-scale cross section of the western United States along the approximate line indicated in Figure 1, just prior to San Andreas development. Symbols as in Figure 1, plus: CB—Sierra Nevada Central Belt; EB—Sierra Nevada Eastern Belt; F—Coastal Belt, Franciscan Coastal Belt; CenB—Franciscan Central Belt; GT—Golconda thrust; J—Jurassic rocks; PP—Franciscan Picket Peak unit; S.N.—Sierra Nevada; WL—Walker Lane; XB—North American Precambrian crystalline basement; YB—Franciscan Yolla Bolla unit. Modified after Godfrey and Dilek (2000) and Moores et al., (2002).

Directions

Continue eastward from Stop 8. At 116.9 miles, the intersection with Road 98, the name of Road 31 changes to Russell Blvd. Continue eastward into Davis. Stop 9 is at the intersection of 1st and A streets in Davis.

Stop Description

This is one of several badly disturbed prehistoric village sites on or near the University of California at Davis (UC-Davis) campus. Buried soils along Putah Creek are 4000–6000 years old and at least 2 m below the surface. The oldest archaeological sites are usually found by accident, when excavating for building foundations or pipelines. Sites on the surface in the Davis area are <1000 yr old. Central Davis is located on a topographically high spot. It probably also overlies an active thrust fault.

End of Day 1. The first night of this trip will be a stopover in Davis. Reset mileage to zero for Day 2.

DAY TWO

Stop 10: Overview of Lovejoy Basalt and Late Cenozoic Rock and Surface Uplift of the Sierra Nevada

Significance of the Site

This is an excellent location to view 15 Ma Lovejoy basalt and the tilted surface of the Sierra Nevada.

Accessibility

Park on the pullout alongside State Highway 70, a very busy road. No restrooms.

GPS Coordinates

39°27.636′N, 121°34.918′W.

Directions

Start in downtown Davis. Proceed west on Russell Blvd. to the junction with SR113.

Cumulative mileage

0.0 Proceed north on SR113.

4.8 Exit right at Road 27.

5.1 Turn right at the stop sign at the end of the offramp.

7.0 At the stop sign at Pole Line Road, turn left onto Pole Line Road and head north.

10.7 Cross I-5 and continue north.

14.5 Cross Cache Creek. The creek is the next watershed north of Putah Creek, draining eastward originally into swamps on the west side of the Sacramento River. Canadian fur trappers gave this name to it in the early nineteenth century.

19.0 Rejoin SR113 in Knights Landing. Before the construction of a causeway in 1915 between Davis and Sacramento, in winter one had to come to here in order to gain access to the natural levees of the Sacramento River to travel to Sacramento by land.

19.9 Drawbridge across Sacramento River. Sacramento River was navigable as far north as Red Bluff (~80 mi N) prior to 1860–1884 when hydraulic mining of the Sierra Nevada Eocene Auriferous gravels dumped 1.5 billion cubic yards of material into the valley.

23.4 Sutter (Marysville) Buttes at 10–11 o'clock. This 1–3 Ma andesitic volcanic complex may be either the last occurrence at this latitude of subduction-related volcanism or the first appearance of volcanism related to transform faulting (see Williams and Curtis, 1977).

30.6 Sutter Causeway. This crosses a flood control channel between the Sacramento and Feather Rivers.

36.4 Turn left (northward) onto SR99.

44.8 Entering Yuba City.

46.0 In Yuba City, turn right onto SR20.

47.3 Cross the bridge over Feather River. This is the northernmost river in the Sierra Nevada and the only Sierra stream that crosses the physiographic divide. It is appears to have existed prior to uplift of the Sierra Nevada. As you continue through Marysville, get in the lefthand lane and follow signs for 20E and 70N.

48.4 Turn left onto 9th Street, continuing to follow signs for 20E and 70N.

48.6 Turn left onto SR70. A potential rest stop is at the first stoplight after making this left turn. Continue northward on SR70.

68.3 Gravel piles along the side of the road are the result of gold dredging.

69.7 This is the first view of the gently dipping Lovejoy basalt (Oroville Table Mountain). The foothills beneath the Lovejoy consist of Smartville complex volcanic arc rocks.

71.4 Park on the right side of the highway.

Stop Description

We now see the Lovejoy basalt for the second time on the trip. Here, its gentle westward slope shows the tectonic tilt of the Sierra Nevada. The Lovejoy basalt caps ridges today, but at 16 Ma it flowed down a sediment-covered valley in a low-relief landscape. Some of this old landscape is preserved as low hills (of pre-Cenozoic basement rocks) that are higher than the Lovejoy basalt. The paleo-relief, defined as the difference in elevation between the base of Cenozoic channels and the highest basement adjacent to them, is 100 m or less near the crest of the range in the Feather River watershed, although a few ridges exceed 300 m or so in the lower part of the drainage (Wakabayashi and Sawyer, 2001). Some of the "paleohills" may be visible from this viewpoint as the rounded hills that appear higher than the flat-topped ridges capped by Lovejoy basalt. In general, the northern Sierran landscape at the time of the eruption of the Lovejoy basalt was a very gentle and comparatively featureless surface with a few isolated hills and ridges. We will see more examples of paleo-relief on Day 3 of this field trip.

The Lovejoy basalt also provides a means of estimating late Cenozoic rock uplift of the Sierra Nevada, because the unit spans the range. The reconstruction of the Lovejoy basalt across the Sierra Nevada yields a minimum rock uplift estimate of 1710–1860 m for the crest of the Sierra in the Feather River drainage (Wakabayashi and Sawyer, 2001; Small et al., 1997; Unruh, 1991).

Minor internal deformation of the Sierra is distributed fairly evenly in across the range. There is no preferential concentration of deformation through the metamorphic belts (Wakabayashi and Sawyer, 2000). Although the internal faults have low slip rates (generally hundredths of a mm/yr or slower) and long recurrence intervals between earthquakes (commonly tens of thousands of years or more), these faults are nevertheless a concern for seismic safety of certain critical facilities, such as dams and power plants. The 1975 Richter magnitude 5.7 Oroville earthquake (Hart and Rapp, 1975) alerted the geologic and engineering community to the potential hazard posed by the internal faults.

Stop 11: Foliated Smartville Volcanic Rocks

Significance of the Site

An exposure of the northern part of the 175–185 Ma Smartville Volcanic unit, part of the major collided island arc in the western Sierra Nevada, can be viewed at this site.

Accessibility

Find a parking space along this busy state highway. No restrooms.

GPS Coordinates

39°39.284′N, 121°32.389′W.

Directions

Leave Stop 10 by continuing northward on SR70.

Cumulative mileage

71.6 The first view of Oroville Dam is ahead and to right. This is the "anchor" of the California water project. The Lovejoy basalt caps the ridge ahead.

75.1 Cross Feather River. Restroom facilities are available at the parking lot to the right.

77.4 Here we pass Lovejoy basalt on both sides of us. To the left (west), the Lovejoy dips beneath younger sediments, not to appear again until exposures on the west side of the Sacramento Valley at the Orland Buttes and near Putah Creek (the latter was Stop 7 of Day 1).

80.3 Stay in the right lane at the junction of SR149 and SR70 in order to stay on SR70. The sloping ridge ahead and to the left is capped by ca. 3 Ma volcanic rocks (mainly andesites) of the Tuscan Formation shed from the vicinity of the Sierra crest north of the Feather River canyon. The volcanic center from which the Tuscan issued has been called the Yana volcanic center. From this center to the presently active Lassen area there is a progressive decrease in age (Guffanti et al., 1990).

83.1 Looking at the tilted Tuscan Formation strata ahead and to the left (~10 o'clock) there is a west-down topographic escarpment. This may be fault-related. The Feather River is near a transition in the character of internal Sierra Nevada deformation. The internal faults in the western Sierra have active long-term slip rates of thousandths of millimeters per year, whereas the long-term deformation rates of the most significant structures to the north approach 0.1 mm/yr. The "Chico Monocline" is a west-facing warp in the tilted volcanic rocks that is perhaps the most distinctive feature of this internal deformation (Harwood and Helley, 1987). The actual deformation rate associated with the monocline is difficult to determine because it is hard to be certain how much of the steepening of the volcanic flows occurred before or after their deposition.

85.3 We pass a roadcut of Cretaceous forearc basin deposits (Great Valley Group) on Sierran basement rocks.

86 We see the first exposures of Sierran metamorphic basement. These rocks have been mapped as Jurassic metasediments. Mid-late Jurassic (176–146 Ma) fossils were found 2–5 km north of here in the metamorphosed "Pentz" sandstone.

87.8 Pull to the right and park.

Stop Description

The Smartville is an extensive unit of volcanic and plutonic rocks that represent part of a collided oceanic volcanic arc. It formed ca. 200–170 Ma and collided with the North American continental edge ca. 165–175 Ma. The rock is basaltic andesite (a volcanic rock containing more silica than basalts, but less than average andesites. Modern rocks of such composition form in oceanic regions). This is the northern end of the Smartville block, which forms the western part of the Northern Sierra Nevada (Ricci et al., 1985). The rocks are relatively massive here, but elsewhere they exhibit a NW-trending, NE-dipping foliation (a parting of the rocks caused by preferential orientation of metamorphic minerals). The contact with the Central Belt mélange is locally steeply dipping, but on a kilometer scale it is subhorizontal to SW-dipping with the deformed ophiolitic sequence overlying highly deformed rocks of the Central Belt.

Stop 12: Jarbo Gap Ophiolite

Significance of the Site

This site displays an excellent exposure of fault and intrusive relations in ophiolite rocks possibly indicating an oceanic transform fault zone.

Accessibility

Park at side of paved highway. No restrooms. Use caution: This is a tight roadcut on very busy highway. BE VERY WATCHFUL AND CAREFUL.

Directions to Site

Leaving Stop 11, continue northeastward on SR70.

Cumulative mileage

88.3 Cross a bridge over the West Branch of the Feather River. The rocks are part of the Central Belt of the northern Sierra basement. Cherts in this belt are Triassic to early Jurassic (251–161 Ma), and limestone blocks are Carboniferous to Permian (359–251 Ma). The sedimentary rocks represent a protracted history (~150 m.y.) of open ocean sedimentation. Their presence indicates the subduction and closing of a very large ocean (recall our Marin Headlands stop on Day 1). The span of pelagic depositional ages suggests the subduction of thousands of kilometers of oceanic crust (see age summary and references in Edelman et al., 1989).

89.2 Rest stop, if needed.

90.3 Pass a roadcut of deformed white metachert.

90.5 Pass a roadcut of highly deformed gabbro and serpentinite.

93.9 A the turnoff to Big Bend road, park in a turnout on the right side of SR70 either just before or just past the road intersection. Walk east ~200 m to the roadcut.

Stop Description

We see here a roadcut of sheared and folded serpentinite and mafic breccias intruded by multiple generations of dikes (Dilek et al., 1991). An older dike has yielded a 200 Ma zircon age, whereas a younger dike has a 159 Ma age (Saleeby et al., 1989). Fault lineations in the serpentinite are low-angle and the steps in them suggest predominantly left-lateral movement. Dikes cut these features, which suggests that the deformation took place in an ocean floor setting. The strike-slip indicators in the serpentinite, intrusion of mafic dikes into serpentinite, and the presence of mafic breccias suggest that the rocks formed near or in an oceanic fracture zone (Dilek et al., 1990). These rocks, as well as extensive exposures of gabbro and serpentinite in this area, have been called the Jarbo Gap ophiolite.

Stop 13: Highly Deformed Gabbro, Jarbo Gap Ophiolite

Significance of the Site

This is an exemplary exposure of ophiolitic gabbro that was deformed during crystallization. The structures imply active faulting during magma emplacement and crystallization, possibly in an oceanic transform fault zone.

Accessibility

Park in the pullout along the very busy highway. The outcrop is across road, but textures can be seen in boulders off the right side of the road at this pullout.

GPS Coordinates

39°46.842′N, 121°27.098′W.

Directions

Leave Stop 12 and proceed NE along SR70.

Cumulative mileage

94.9 Alternative parking in case we overshoot the stop.

95.1 Serpentinites in roadcuts through the hamlet of Rock House. Mineral compositions in metamorphic rocks (containing garnet and amphibole) beneath the serpentinite suggest recrystallization at comparatively high pressures (20 or more km depth), whereas the metamorphism of the "upper plate" rocks of the Jarbo Gap ophiolite took place at significantly shallower depths (<15 km) (Wakabayashi and Dilek, 1987). The contrast in metamorphic pressure as well as the spatial distribution of rock types suggests the presence of a subduction zone suture beneath the Jarbo Gap ophiolite.

95.7 Jarbo Gap. We continue downhill passing through impressive exposures of the Jarbo Gap ophiolite. This unit has been highly deformed and has probably been subject to multiple episodes of folding and faulting.

99.8 Small turnout to right. This is an alternative stop in Jarbo Gap ophiolite highly deformed gabbro. The preferred stop (safer) is a half-mile farther.

100.3 Pull into turnout to right.

Stop Description

This gabbro has a prominent high-temperature deformation texture. Minerals (plagioclase and hornblende) are aligned. This fact and the composition of the rocks suggest formation in an oceanic fracture zone, consistent with the interpretation at Stop 13.

Stop 14: Grizzly Pluton–Metamorphic Rock Contact

Significance of the Site

This is an exemplary exposure of a granitic intrusive rock contact.

Accessibility

There is room for parking on the side of very busy paved highway. No restrooms.

GPS Coordinates

39°52.122′N, 121°22.400′W.

Directions

From Stop 13, continue NE along SR70.

Cumulative mileage

101.2 Note that as of July 2005 there is a traffic light here because of construction that has restricted traffic across the bridge to one lane. West end of Pulga Bridge. This high bridge is over a particularly spectacular part of the North Fork Feather River canyon. The walls of the canyon are made up of rocks of the Jarbo Gap ophiolite.

~103 Contact between the ophiolitic and subduction complex rocks with the Grizzly Pluton. This pluton has yielded a radiometric (K/Ar on hornblende) date of 145 Ma (Evernden and Kistler, 1970, corrected for newer decay constants). It is likely part of the early stages of the Sierra magmatism (the Sierra Nevada batholith) that was associated with east-dipping Franciscan subduction. There are a number of hydroelectric power dams on the North Fork Feather River and its tributaries; collectively, these are known as the "Staircase of Power." Diverting water off the stream and running it in a pipe or canal at very low gradient (while the main stream and canyon bottom drop more steeply) then dropping it down to a powerhouse at the canyon bottom generates much of the power. Hydroelectric power generation is very economical and clean compared to other methods of producing electricity, but there are negative effects on the ecosystem of the streams, as well as the obvious aesthetic cost.

107.1 Rest stop, if needed.

107.7 Impressive curved fractures (called sheet exfoliation joints) may be seen in the granitic rock on the right side of the road.

109.1 Just before a tunnel, pull into a small parking area on the right side of the road.

Stop Description

Contact between Grizzly Pluton (a magmatic rock formed at depth within Earth) and metamorphosed pregranitic metavolcanic and metasedimentary (Central Belt) rock.

The impressive granitic canyon and tunnel catches the eye at least as much as the rocks here. At this stop we can see both the granitic rocks as well as metamorphic rocks that consist of amphibolite (probably metamorphosed mafic volcanic rocks) and metamorphosed calcareous-siliceous sedimentary rocks.

Stop 15: Folded Cherts of the Sierra Nevada Central Belt

Significance of the Site

Exemplary exposure of deformed radiolaria-bearing cherts that characterize rocks of the Central Belt of the Sierra Nevada.

Accessibility

Roadside exposure on SR70. No restrooms.

GPS Coordinates

40°00.781′N, 121°11.602′W.

Directions

From Stop 14, continue NE along SR70.

Cumulative mileage

120.4 Metamorphic rocks on the east side of the Bucks Lake pluton. Most of the rocks of the Central Belt consist of argillites (hard very fine grained, siliceous, clay-bearing rocks), oceanic sedimentary rocks (chert and limestone), and metamorphosed basaltic volcanic rocks. They probably formed in a subduction zone.

123.4 Rest stop, if needed.

124.9 We see ahead of us Red Hill, a high mountain composed of ultramafic rock of the Feather River Ultramafic Belt.

125.1 Caribou Junction. This is the confluence of the North Fork Feather River (that flows from the left) and the East Branch North Fork that we will follow upstream as we continue along SR70.

125.8 Pull off to the right into a small turnout.

Stop Description

These are vertically aligned folds in Triassic radiolarian cherts of the Calaveras complex. Detailed information between here and the North Fork Feather River Canyon suggests that these rocks have been deformed more than once. The cherts represent pelagic sediments (compare with Stop 1).

Stop 16: Western Margin of the Feather River Ultramafic Belt

Significance of the Site

This is the western margin of the largest ultramafic body, possibly part of an ophiolite in the Sierra Nevada, some 5–15 km wide and over 100 km long. It is a major tectonic unit of the Sierra Nevada.

Accessibility

Park in the large pullout on the left side of this very busy state highway. Roadcuts are on the left side. Watch out for traffic!

GPS Coordinates

40°00.781′N, 121°11.602′W.

Directions to Site

Continue NE along SR70 from Stop 15. At 127.3 mi, pull into the large parking area on the left side of the road

Stop Description

The Feather River Ultramafic Belt is one of the most enigmatic units in all of California. Why? One reason is that it is an ultramafic and mafic unit of regional extent that is higher in metamorphic grade than units on either side of it. Most ophiolite sheets tend to be of lower metamorphic grade than units structurally beneath them. Another reason this belt is puzzling it that geochronologic data indicate a wide range (over 100 m.y.; ca. 280–380 Ma) of crystallization ages of plutonic rocks and high-grade metamorphism. Just as we stated that no two geologists can agree on the basic elements of Sierran basement geology, so too is it difficult or impossible to find any two geologists who agree on just how the Feather River Ultramafic Belt formed and how it ties into the tectonic history of the Sierra Nevada. At the parking lot and in exposures eastward along SR70, we see serpentinized ultramafic rocks. Looking at a fresh surface of these rocks, you will see a different appearance than is typical of serpentinites. Instead of the soapy appearance associated with most serpentinites, these rocks have a crystalline appearance. Elongate crystals of a Ca- and Mg-bearing amphibole are present, and the sugary appearance of the rest of the rock comes from minerals such as antigorite (Mg-Fe bearing amphibole), talc, and possible pyroxene and olivine. Walking west from the parking lot, we soon come to the western margin of the ultramafic rocks, where they are bordered by amphibolite. The amphibolite is locally garnet-bearing, and a sodic amphibole locally rims calcic amphibole, indicating some blueschist overprint. The garnet amphibolite along the western margin of the ultramafic rocks may represent a "metamorphic sole" that is formed at the inception of subduction beneath young oceanic crust (e.g., Williams and Smyth, 1973;

Jamieson, 1986). If so, it is likely that east-dipping subduction occurred beneath the ultramafic rocks. Blueschist facies rocks are also found west of the amphibolite and the ultramafic rocks south of this area, best exposed in the Downieville area along the Yuba River (Schweickert et al., 1980). Their presence and location also suggests east-dipping subduction beneath the peridotite unit. Possibly the apparent sole, its blueschist overprint, and the neighboring blueschist facies unit, are all related to the same episode of east-dipping subduction.

The amphibolite metamorphism of the ultramafic rocks and associated apparently upper ophiolitic rocks ~20 km south of here, the so-called "Devils Gate ophiolite," suggest fairly deep burial under rather high temperature conditions. This setting is enigmatic.

Stop 17: Shoo Fly Complex Quartzose Sandstone

Significance of the site

This is an exposure of the oldest rocks (400–500 Ma) in the Sierra Nevada, probably exotic to western North America, possibly derived either from the Appalachians or the western margin of Gondwana.

Accessibility

Pullout along very busy SR70. The outcrop is across road from the pullout. Watch out for traffic.

GPS Coordinates

40°01.894′N, 121°00.891′W.

Directions

Leave Stop 16 and resume driving northeastward on SR70.

Cumulative mileage

129.3 Good exposures of unserpentinized peridotite can be found nearby.

131.7 This is the eastern side of the Feather River Ultramafic Belt where it is in tectonic contact with less metamorphosed, multiply-deformed, Triassic(?) mica-rich rocks and limestones that are assigned either to the Cedar Formation (Hietanen, 1973) or to the Arlington Formation (D'Allura et al., 1977).

134.4 Exposure of deformed/foliated Sierra Buttes(?) or Taylor(?) Formation rocks. The Taylor and Sierra Buttes Formations are Devonian volcanic arc rocks that uncomformably overlie the phyllites, cherts, and sandstones of the Ordovician (and older?) Shoo Fly Complex. They represent the oldest subduction-related volcanic rocks in the northern Sierra Nevada. We continue driving eastward through Shoo Fly Complex rocks. The Shoo Fly rocks are the oldest rocks in the Sierra Nevada. They have no known basement. They are multiply deformed, exhibiting an isoclinal (the two sides of the folds are parallel, indicating that the rocks were bent 180°) folding prior to deposition of the overlying Sierra Buttes and Taylor volcanics (Hannah and Moores, 1986).

137.5 Pass an exposure of cherts of the Shoo Fly Complex.

139.4 Pull off on the right side of the road. Watch for traffic.

Stop Description

This metamorphosed quartzose sandstone is thought to have been derived from a continental source (Bond and DeVay, 1980), in a setting similar to the Great Valley. The compositions of minor high-density minerals (M. Mange and J.F. Dewey, 2004, personal commun.) and radiometric ages of zircons from these rocks (Wright and Wyld, 2003, 2006) suggest that they are exotic to western North America, and may have been derived from the western margin of Gondwana (west Africa) or eastern Laurentia (North America) in late Paleozoic time.

Stop 18: Peale Chert, Basalt of Rock Creek and Overview of Quaternary Tectonics of the Area

Significance of the Site

This site shows a view of an important (360–290 Ma) unit of the Sierra Nevada, a view of the North Fork Feather River Canyon, and active faults and Recent basalts that flowed down the canyon.

Accessibility

This will be at a wide spot on a dirt road ~3 mi from SR89. It is on the edge of a very steep canyon. WATCH YOUR STEP! BE CAREFUL!

GPS Coordinates

40°08.590′N, 121°05.694′W.

Directions

Leave Site 17, driving eastward on SR70.

Cumulative mileage

139.9 Pass roadcuts of shiny micaceous metamorphic rocks (phyllites) and cherts of the Shoo Fly Complex. These may be large blocks in mélange.

141.7 At the junction with SR89, turn left onto SR89 and drive along Indian Creek. The exposures are of Shoo Fly phyllites with some pebbly mudstones. We are passing through a change in the dips of the metamorphic structures.

143.6 There is a hot-spring calcium carbonate (travertine) deposit to the right across the creek. This may be part of a line of springs that may be aligned along a Quaternary (<1.8 Ma) fault through this area.

144.9 Sierra Buttes formation exposures followed by Taylor Formation. These rocks are rotated more than 90° (overturned) to the NE.

145.1 At lat 40°00.767′, long 120°57.510′ there is viable parking for a possible Taylor Formation stop. The Taylor in this location consists of thick-bedded basaltic andesite mudflow breccias (fragmental rocks formed by submarine turbid flows).

146 There is a turnout to the left near top of Taylor Formation just west of the rubble of the Peale Formation.

146.9 At lat. 40°04.706′N, long.120°56.07′W, there is a long narrow turnout to right. Roadcuts to the left are in Arlington Formation. These are Permian turbidites that display good relationships between the metamorphic structures and the bedding. The metamorphic structures (the parting of the rock or "cleavage") dips less steeply to the west than the bedding, suggesting that the rocks have been rotated more than 90° (they are "overturned").

147.3 Entering Indian Valley. This is one of the many tectonic basins (many of which are extensional) along the western branch of the Walker Lane that is known as the Mohawk Valley fault zone (Wakabayashi and Sawyer 2000; Unruh et al. 2003).

147.9 Intersection with Taylorsville Road. Continue N on SR89. We cross the Grizzly Mountain fault near the town of Crescent Mills. This east-directed thrust fault places isoclinally folded, foliated, somewhat metamorphosed (greenschist) rocks over little-metamorphosed Paleozoic rocks. The symmetrical mountain at ~3 o'clock is Mount Jura, which is underlain by Jurassic volcanic sediments. The Jurassic rocks underlie the Taylorsville thrust, a fault that places low-mid Paleozoic (488–360 Ma) sedimentary and volcanic rocks over them.

152.8 At the intersection with the road to the Round Valley reservoir, continue straight on SR89. For those running the trip on their own, Round Valley reservoir is a worthwhile side trip. At the small dam, a SW-dipping serpentinite is exposed. This serpentinite is intruded by the 380 Ma Wolf Creek intrusive body (visible later on this trip). In addition to the old serpentinite exposed at Round Valley reservoir, the reservoir basin appears to be the result of a west-down Quaternary fault that has ponded alluvium to the west (upstream) of it.

154+ Driving west from the town of Greenville, pass through bedrock composed of the Sierra Buttes Formation. Some of this low-lying area is covered by rather old soil. Locally, ca. 3 Ma volcanic rocks depositionally overlie this soil (Wakabayashi and Sawyer, 2000).

159.3 The granitic rocks we are passing through are those of the 380 Ma Wolf Creek intrusive body.

161.3 Roadcuts are of 2.4 Ma basalt.

162.1 Enter the town of Canyondam.

162.7 At the intersection with the Westwood Road (SR147), stay straight only very briefly on SR89.

162.7 Turn left onto Seneca Road. As we drive south, we are driving on the surface of the 400 ka Basalt of Westwood.

163.0 At lat. 40°10.133′N, long.121°05.025′W is an alternative stop to view a fault in the Basalt of Westwood.

164.0 At the intersection with Rush Hill motorway, continue on Seneca Road.

164.2 At lat. 40°09.350′N, long.121°05.289′W are outcrops of the Peale Chert.

165.2 Park along the right side of the road.

Stop Description

The Peale chert (upper Peale Formation) exposed in the roadcut ranges in age from lower Mississippian (359 Ma) to lower Permian (271 Ma). Thus this thin unit, <100 m thick where it is well developed, spans an interval of time of ~90 m.y. This fact, the presence of manganese deposits in some localities, and the oceanic nature of the underlying volcanic rocks imply deposition in an ocean basin very far away from a continent for nearly 100 m.y. At this locality, the rocks are rotated more than 90° (overturned) to the NE. Some small folds are also present.

At this stop, we will see a remnant of one of the several basalt flows that flowed into the Almanor basin, then down the North Fork Feather River canyon (see discussion in Wakabayashi and Sawyer, 2000). We see in the roadcut the baked zone in colluvium (slope debris) and overlying ca. 1 Ma basalt. Note the steepness of the basal contact that reflects the buried paleocanyon wall. At this viewpoint we are "downstream" of the Almanor basin from the standpoint of the direction the lavas flowed, yet we are significantly higher than the Almanor basin. The elevation difference we see must be a consequence of faulting. As much as 150 m of vertical movement must have occurred on this fault. In the basin, this basalt would be probably be overlain successively by flows of the ca. 0.6 Ma Basalt of Warner Valley, the ca. 0.4 Ma Basalt of Westwood, and late Quaternary (<10,000 yr) stream deposits that overlie these basalts in the basin. Across the deep canyon of the North Fork Feather River is a flat bench. The canyon walls reveal that this bench is underlain by Basalt of Westwood that overlies Basalt of Warner Valley. The Basalt of Westwood may not have made it much farther downstream than the downstream limit of the bench, for it has not been found downstream of this point.

Across the canyon from the flat bench is a wooded knob (NE of our viewpoint and lower than us). This knob is capped with the Basalt of Warner Valley that overlies the ca. 1 Ma Basalt of Rock Creek. These relationships and the faulting of the Basalt of Westwood on the bench on the northwest (opposite) side of the river also suggest that the Skinner Flat fault may not have started significant movement until after the deposition of the Basalt of Westwood, or the northern tip of faulting has propagated progressively northward since Basalt of Westwood time.

On the wooded knob and the bench across the river, basaltic units still overlie each other in normal stratigraphic fashion. Downstream of these outcrops, starting with the outcrops where we are stopped, an "inverted" topographic series of basalt benches is present, a consequence of successive river downcutting with periods of basalt flowing down the canyon. Inverted topography happens when a volcanic rock flows down a valley. After it cools, it is more resistant to erosion than the surrounding rocks, and what was once a valley, over time becomes a ridge.

Turn and look downstream (it is most convenient to actually hike southeast up a dirt road onto the knoll on the east side of the main road): the river bends around a hill that has two prominent flat surfaces at different elevations. The view from this point has become a bit more difficult with progressive growth of young trees that block the line of sight. The upper flat is underlain by ca. 1 Ma basalt (the same basalt unit we are standing next to). The lower flat is underlain by the ca. 0.6 Ma Basalt of Warner Valley. Similar bench-like remnants exhibiting inverted topographic relationships (oldest benches are highest) are present along the walls of the North Fork Feather River canyon as far downstream as the confluence of the North Fork with the East Branch North Fork. The canyon followed approximately the same course since at least 2.8 Ma, based on the oldest inset volcanic unit. The successive flows down the ancient Feather River canyon permit evaluation of Quaternary faulting as well as rates of canyon down-cutting (incision). Vertical displacement rates on faults are as high as 0.2 mm/yr. The lateral component of movement on these faults is not known, but it is thought to be significant. Collectively, the faults in this area may accommodate up to 2–3 mm/yr of dextral slip (Sawyer and Briggs, 2001).

This entire reach of the North Fork Feather River is now east of the Sierra Nevada crest These faults represent part of a very recent (or ongoing) westward jump of the Frontal Fault System of the Sierra Nevada (Wakabayashi and Sawyer, 2000, 2001).

Directions to Quincy—Stopover at End of Day 2

Leaving Stop 18, there are at least two different ways to turn around. The road log represents one of the possible options.

Cumulative mileage

165.2 At the intersection with Forest Road 26N22, turn around and return to Canyondam.

167.6 At the junction with SR89, turn right and prepare to make an immediate left.

167.6 Turn left (north) onto SR147.

168.0 Turn left into the parking lot of this viewpoint. Here we get a view of Mount Lassen and a potential rest stop. The shoreline down to Lake Almanor below the parking area is very steep because it is a fault scarp of the Eastside fault, the same fault we crossed along the Seneca Road just south of SR89. Across the lake we can see Mount Lassen, the southernmost active volcano of the Cascade volcanic chain that stands over the still-active subduction zone off northern California, Oregon, Washington, and southern British Columbia.

From this parking lot, turn around and head back southward to SR89.

168.5 Junction with SR89; turn left and retrace route to the 89/70 junction.

189.5 Junction with SR70; make a left onto SR70 and drive to Quincy.

199.3 Enter Quincy. Quincy is situated in American Valley, another fault-caused basin along the Eastern Sierra Frontal Fault zone. Here it is called the Mohawk Valley fault zone. As you drop down into the valley, you may be able to see a glaciated gray granitic face to the west of Spanish Peak the Sierra Nevada crest. This is the northern equivalent of the Sierra Nevada eastern front. The glaciated granite face is in part fault-controlled, for an east-down fault lies at its base. A remnant of 15–17 Ma andesitic volcanic rocks (Mehrten Formation) equivalent is present on top of the gentle upland surface above the Spanish Peak escarpment. In common with other areas in the northernmost Sierras, the late Cenozoic deposits are perched atop the highest elevation with few if any adjacent basement exposures attaining higher elevation. Thus the paleorelief of this area is minimal.

End of Day 2. The second night of this trip will be a stopover in Quincy. Reset mileage to zero for Day 3.

DAY THREE

Stop 19: Spring Garden Serpentinite

Significance of the Site
This site provides an excellent exposure of the oldest possibly ophiolitic rocks in the Sierra Nevada.

Accessibility
Park in the turnoff on SR89/70. The roadcut is across this busy highway. Watch for traffic.

GPS Coordinates
39°54.978′N, 120°49.542′W.

Directions
Leave Quincy, driving E on SR70/89.

Cumulative mileage
0.0 Intersection of eastbound SR70/89 and Meadow Valley Road, Quincy.
3.2 Leave Quincy.
7.4 Pull to the right of the road in the turnout.

Stop Description
The outcrops we will examine are on the NE side of the road. This serpentinite is associated with a Na-rich granitic rock that has yielded a 500 Ma age from included zircons (Saleeby et al., 1989). This serpentinite may be correlative with the serpentinite at Round Valley, near Greenville. The serpentinite is thrust over rocks of the Shoo Fly Complex and may indicate the presence of a major suture.

Stop 20: Lovejoy Basalt at Spring Garden

Significance of the Site
This outcrop represents an example of the 15 Ma basalt that is present from the Northern Sierra across to the west side of the Great Valley (see Stops 6 and 11).

Accessibility
Park in a pulloff on this busy highway (SR70/89). Watch for traffic.

Directions
From Stop 19, continue eastbound on SR70. At 11.8 mi, pull into the large turnout/parking area.

Stop Description
This small outcrop exposes Lovejoy basalt, the same unit we saw in the easternmost Coast Ranges and the western foothills of the Sierra near Oroville. To the west, outcrops cap the Sierran crest and ridges westward to where we last saw this unit near Oroville. Between this stop and the Sierran crest are faults that show down-to-the-east displacement. These are branches of the Sierran Frontal fault system–Mohawk Valley fault zone. The source of the Lovejoy is several kilometers east of this stop (Wagner et al., 2000).

Stop 21: Archeological Stop A-2

Significance of the Site
This is a paleo-human site that shows evidence of recurrent climatic stress.

Accessibility
This stop is at or near the L.T. Davis roadside rest stop on SR70, near the town of Truckee. Watch for traffic.

Directions
Continue to drive E on SR70/89 from Stop 20. Stop 20 is near the low divide between the North Fork and Middle Fork Feather River drainages. As we drive eastward on SR70 from this stop, we will soon drop into the Middle Fork Feather River watershed.

Cumulative mileage
23.3 At the junction with SR89, turn right onto SR89 toward Graeagle. As we cross the bridge over the Middle Fork Feather River, we see ahead of us a linear east-facing topographic escarpment. This slope represents the eastern slope of the Sierra Nevada. It is ~1 km high here in

contrast to the 3 km high escarpment in Owens Valley along the southern Sierra. The difference is mainly a product of a larger amount of paleorelief in the southern Sierra Nevada than in the north prior to late Cenozoic uplift (Wakabayashi and Sawyer, 2001). Paleoseismic evidence from the rangefront fault south of here suggests at least two Holocene (<10,000 yr) events, and single event displacements may have been 2–3 m, suggesting large earthquakes (Sawyer et al., 1993).

25.9 Lakes Basin road junction. Keep straight on SR89.

27.4 Junction with road to Clio. Here we see more of the eastern front of the Sierra. The basement rocks in the area are Paleozoic, intruded by a Mesozoic granitic rock. Late Cenozoic volcanic rocks cap the ridges, showing that little paleorelief is present in this area. There are isolated basement highs, or what might be termed "paleopeaks." Sierra Buttes, composed mostly of Devonian arc rocks, is the highest of such paleopeaks, rising nearly 800 m above the nearby base of late Cenozoic deposits (Wakabayashi and Sawyer, 2001).

35.4 We pass through a saddle at 5441′ elevation and descend into Sierra Valley, another fault controlled valley along the Mohawk Valley fault zone.

38.5 Here is a good view of Sierra Valley. Many late Quaternary faults cross this valley, and faulting also defines the base of the mountains bordering the valley on the west.

Stop Description

Recent archaeological work in northern Sierra Valley has uncovered strong evidence for the Medieval warm period and severe droughts between 1000 and 500 before present (B.P.). Pollen studies in nearby Sardine Valley, hydrological studies of the Feather River, and tree-ring studies of the Tahoe region all confirm this climatic anomaly. The archaeological record indicates that the climatic fluctuations of this period caused severe stress on the human population of Sierra Valley, forcing them to make major changes to their adaptive patterns in order to survive. There is abundant evidence from California and across the west that this stress led to increased conflict and warfare and probably contributed to the collapse of great civilizations in Central America and the American Southwest.

Stop 22: Archeological Stop A-3—Alder Hill Prehistoric Basalt Toolstone Quarry

Significance of the Site

This site was one of the main sources of tools for Neolithic native peoples in the Northern Sierra.

Accessibility

This is on SR89, a busy highway. Watch for traffic.

Directions

From Stop 21, continue east on SR70/89.

Cumulative mileage

41.4 At the junction with SR49, turn left onto SR49/89.

42.2 Town of Sattley.

46.6 Turn right in Sierraville onto SR89, leaving SR70. Drive to the intersection of SR89 and Alder Hill road, just north of the town of Truckee.

Stop Description

Alder Hill Prehistoric Basalt Toolstone Quarry. Alder Hill consists of two major basalt flow units between 1.2 and 2.3 Ma. Highway 89 runs through the eastern flow along a prominent fault. This flow consists of a very fine-grained (aphanitic) basalt that was highly desired by prehistoric peoples for stone tools, especially between ~5000 and 1300 yr ago. Alder Hill was one of two primary basalt sources that were systematically relied upon during seasonal use of this area; the other is located ~40 mi northwest of here in the Gold Lake area west of Sierra Valley. Recent archaeological excavations have been conducted at the quarry in advance of residential and recreational development.

Stop 23: Granite of the Sierra Nevada Batholith, View down the Eastern Front of the Northern Sierra

Significance if the Site

This site displays a good exposure of the younger granitic rocks of the Sierra Nevada, as well as a view eastward into the Basin and Range Province, the eastern boundary of the Sierran Microplate, and the location of the dramatic story of the Donner Party (1846).

Accessibility

Parking is available to the right along old U.S. 49, a paved road that is usually plowed to the site. No restrooms.

GPS Coordinates

39°18.999′N, 120°19.548′W.

Directions

From Stop 22, proceed south on SR89 to the intersection with I-80.

Cumulative mileage

69.4 At the junction with I-80, turn right (west) and take I-80 toward Donner Summit.

82.7 A bit after passing Donner Summit, the crest of the Sierra Nevada, exit right at Norden.

82.9 Go left at the stop sign at end of the offramp and head over the freeway.

85.8 Pass an outcrop of Oligocene Valley Springs Formation rhyolite.

86.8 Park in the parking lot at old Donner Summit.

Stop Description

The granitic rocks we see here are part of the Sierra Nevada batholith; this particular pluton has yielded a K/Ar hornblende age of 100 Ma (Evernden and Kistler, 1970, recalculated to newer decay constants). The emplacement of the Sierra Nevada batholith was a consequence of magmatic activity associated with east-dipping Franciscan subduction. In this area, the granitic rocks are discordantly (unconformably) overlain by Oligocene rhyolites of the Valley Springs Formation that are in turn overlain by Miocene Mehrten Formation andesites. This relationship suggests negligible stream incision between Oligocene and Miocene time. In addition, Eocene auriferous gravels locally underlie Valley Springs and Mehrten rocks in other areas of the Sierra (including at Stop 27 on this trip), including near the crest. Collectively these relationships suggest negligible stream incision from Eocene to Miocene time in the Sierra. Had the stream incision been significant, the older deposits would cap higher elevations than the younger ones (because the younger ones would fill channels cut into the bedrock below the older ones). Significant channel cutting (incision) is present within volcanic deposits of the Sierra Nevada. Some channels are eroded through basement rocks, but successively younger channels do not cut below the level of previous volcanic deposits (Bateman and Wahrhaftig, 1966; Huber, 1990; Rood et al. 2004). However, the later fact suggests that the incision is a consequence of clogging of drainages by eruption of volcanic rocks rather than being caused by uplift or climate change (Huber, 1990).

The faulting along the eastern margin of the Sierra migrated westward in Recent geologic time (Henry and Perkins, 2001). Some faulting actually took place in the Sierran crestal region before 10 Ma (Rood et al. 2004). This faulting must not have resulted in rock and surface uplift until sometime after ca. 5 Ma, because no stream incision resulted until then (Wakabayashi and Sawyer, 2001). The earlier Basin and Range faulting simply downdropped blocks to the east relative to sea level without uplifting the footwalls of the normal faults. Faulting of the Sierra produced footwall uplift.

Stop 24: Intrusive Contact of Granitic Rocks and Jurassic Metasediments

Significance of the Site

This is an exemplary exposure of a contact between the main portion of the Sierra Nevada batholith and Jurassic volcanic rocks.

Accessibility

Use the parking lot at the Big Bend Visitor Center. Public restrooms may be available.

GPS Coordinates

39°18.382′N, 120°31.056′W.

Directions

Leaving Stop 23, retrace the route back to I-80.

Cumulative mileage

90.8   Turn onto westbound I-80.
96.6   Exit right at the Big Bend exit.
96.7   Turn left at the stop sign at the end of the offramp.
96.8   Make sharp right turn.
98.0   Stop in parking lot of Big Bend visitor center.

Stop Description

This stop shows the contact between the main part of the Sierra Nevada batholith, which lies mostly east of here. The metamorphosed Jurassic volcanic rocks are part of the "Eastern Belt" of the Sierra Nevada, parts of which we saw at Stops 17, 18, and 19.

Stop 25: Emigrant Gap Vista Point, View of Sierra Nevada Paleorelief

Significance of the Site

This site provides a good example of the old relief of the Sierra Nevada surface that existed at the time of deposition of the youngest volcanic rocks (the 5 Ma Mehrten Formation).

Accessibility

Use the public parking space off I-80. No restrooms.

GPS Coordinates

39°17.958′N, 120°40.372′W.

Directions

Leaving Stop 24, continue westward along the Big Bend road.

Cumulative mileage

98.6   Vertically dipping Jurassic volcanic metasediments.
99.6   Make a left turn toward the freeway.
99.7   Make a right turn onto the onramp for westbound I-80 toward Auburn.
107.9   Exit right for Vista Point and park in the lot.

Stop Description

From this stop, we look northward in the Yuba River drainage. The western part of the vista is dominated by a gently sloping ridgetop that is capped by late Miocene Mehrten Formation andesites. The gentle westward slope, similar to that of the Lovejoy basalt we saw near Oroville, shows the tilt of the Sierra Nevada. Similar volcanic rocks blanketed much of the Sierra north of Sonora Pass, leaving only a few basement highs sticking out above the surface. The youngest volcanic rocks associated with this outpouring are ca. 5 Ma. Thus, the modern-day canyons have been cut since 5 Ma. The canyon depth beneath the Mehrten records incision and relief produced during this time. If we look a bit farther east of this Mehrten-capped ridge, we see that the tilt projects below the tops of some peaks. These peaks are composed of basement rocks, and they are higher than the tops (let alone the bottoms) of the late Cenozoic deposits in the area. Some of them rise over 600 m above the base of the adjacent late Cenozoic paleochannels. These are examples of the paleorelief in this part of the Sierra.

Stop 26: Hydraulic Mining Effects

Significance of the Site

This is an excellent location from which to view the evidence of hydraulic mining in the 1860–1884 period.

Accessibility

This is along a paved, public road in the town of Gold Run.

Directions

From Stop 25, return to westbound I-80.

Cumulative mileage

108.0 Enter westbound I-80.
112.4 Note the California Department of Transportation (Caltrans) maintenance station at the foot of a landslide.
118.2 At the Alta exit sign, Valley Springs Formation rhyolite is visible on the hill to the right.
119.9 Exit right at the Dutch Flat exit.
120.1 Go right at the stop sign at the end of the offramp.
120.2 Go left at Lincoln Avenue.
120.4 Cross the railroad tracks.
121.1 Stop along the road near the railroad tracks. This is a very active railroad. **Watch out for trains—they appear unexpectedly. Stay off the tracks.**

Stop Description

We are on a ridge formed of auriferous (gold-bearing) gravels, an Eocene (50 Ma) river deposit that possibly originated in a Tibet-like highland in present central Nevada. The deposit has been removed to the north and south. Legend has it that the miners tried to buy the land from the railroad, but the Southern Pacific Railroad Company refused to sell. Thus, only this narrow ridge has been preserved. The scale of hydraulic mining can be estimated by looking at the area that has been denuded. Also, the small pine trees in the hydraulically mined area attest to the slowness of recovery of the landscape after mining activity.

Stop 27: Auriferous Gravels and Overlying Mehrten Formation

Significance of the Site

A vertical cliff, representing a hydraulic mining scar of the 50 Ma (Eocene) auriferous gravels, shows their structure and the nature of the clasts. The overlying late Miocene (5 Ma) Mehrten andesites are also visible in the upper part of the cliff.

Accessibility

This site is at a rest stop along I-80. Restrooms are available.

GPS Coordinates

39°10.772′N, 120°51.334′W.

Directions

From Stop 26, retrace the route to I-80 west.

Cumulative mileage

122.2 Return to westbound I-80 (onramp).
123.4 Exit right off of I-80 at the rest stop.
123.7 Park in rest stop parking lot.

Stop Description

Here we see exposures of the Eocene (ca. 50 Ma) auriferous gravels, the base of which was the target of the hydraulic mining effort to recover gold. A few diamonds have also been recovered from the gravels. The source of both the gold and diamonds has not been determined. The Eocene gravels were deposited by streams whose headwaters were far east of the current Sierra Nevada. The gold also originated somewhere east of the Mother Lode Belt because there are gold-bearing gravels east of the Mother Lode. Note at this stop we also see the Mehrten Formation depositionally overlying the gravels, again illustrating the lack of stream incision between Eocene and late Miocene time, testifying to the tectonic quiescence of this area during that time.

Stop 28: Pillow Lavas of the Lake Combie Complex

Significance of the Site

This is an ideal exposure of pillow lavas formed by submarine eruption.

Accessibility

Parking is on the frontage road along I-80. Be careful of traffic.

GPS Coordinates

38°59.034′N, 121°00.366′W.

Directions

From Stop 27, return to westbound I-80.

Cumulative mileage

124.0 Enter the onramp to westbound I-80.
141.8 Exit at the Clipper Gap exit.
142.0 Make a left at the stop sign at the end of the offramp and cross over the freeway.
142.1 Make a left on Applegate Road.
143.4 Pull to the right and park.

Stop Description

These pillows represent submarine oceanic volcanic flows of the Lake Combie ophiolite complex. It is thought to be of early Mesozoic age (250–190 Ma). The pillows are tilted. The bulbous tops point toward N30°E. The Lake Combie Complex is probably older than the Smartville complex to the west (Stop 11) and may be age-equivalent to the Slate Creek ophiolite in the central Sierra to the north, as well as to the Jarbo Gap ophiolite (Stops 12 and 13).

Directions to Davis—Stopover at End of Day 3

From Stop 28, retrace the route to westbound I-80.

Cumulative mileage

144.9 Turn right off Applegate Road to cross over I-80.
145.0 Turn left onto westbound I-80 toward Sacramento.
174.2 At the I-80 and Business 80 junction, keep left on westbound I-80.
182.8 At the I-5/I-80 interchange, keep left and follow the signs for westbound I-80 bound for San Francisco.
197.4 Take the downtown Davis exit.

End of Day 3. The third night of this trip will be a stopover in Davis.

DAY FOUR

Stop 29: Cordelia Fault

Significance of the Site

This is the best exposed San Andreas–related fault zone that we know of in northern California.

Accessibility

There is roadside parking by the roadcut on this busy secondary road. Watch for traffic. No restrooms.

GPS Coordinates

38°15.196′N, 122°08.145′W.

Directions

From the UC-Davis campus, return to I-80 and merge onto I-80 westbound (toward San Francisco). Reset odometer to 0.0 mi. Stay on I-80 for the next 25.6 mi.

Cumulative mileage

4.3 Cross some barely perceptible topography—this little surface wrinkle is Dixon Ridge. It is thought to be the expression of an active buried thrust fault associated with shortening along the boundary between the Coast Ranges and Central Valley—the western boundary of the Sierra Nevada microplate.

18.1 Enter the California Coast Ranges; hills are on both sides of the road. Roadcuts in those hills expose Tertiary (65–1.8 Ma) clastic sediments. We continue through and past Lagoon Valley. Lagoon Valley is a tectonically ponded valley formed as a result of Quaternary (<1.8 Ma) faulting and/or folding in a region of folded Cretaceous (146–66 Ma) sandstones and shales of the Great Valley Group. Stratigraphic layering in the bedrock is evident even as the grass dries in the spring (the grasses are Mediterranean a invasive species, not California natives).
25.6 Exit right on West Texas Street/Rockville Road.
26.1 Turn right on Rockville Road.
28.9 Roadcuts along this road are in Sonoma volcanics (1–6 Ma).
30.1 Stop on right side of road and walk to the road cut.

Stop Description

This is one of the easternmost dextral faults in the San Andreas fault system at this latitude. Some workers consider it a branch of the Green Valley fault. Here the vertical fault zone cuts Sonoma volcanics (1–6 Ma) and exhibits a zone of ground-up rock (gouge) about a meter wide. On some fault surfaces we can see subhorizontal scratches and linear marks, known as slickensides, consistent with the strike-slip movement on the fault. This fault has been active in the late Quaternary (past 100,000 yr), and the southernmost part of the fault displays evidence of movement within the Holocene (past 10,000 yr) (Jennings, 1994).

Stop 30: Orinda Formation and Berkeley Hills Volcanics (Moraga Volcanics)

Significance of the Site

This site offers a fine exposure of continental nonmarine sediments and volcanic rocks that represent a volcanic-sedimentary basin deposit trailing the NW end of the San Andreas fault.

Accessibility

Parking is on a turnout of the road off of SR24. Traffic is occasionally heavy and fast. Be very careful!

GPS Coordinates

37°51.904′N, 122°12.561′W.

Directions

Leaving Stop 29, continue on Rockville Road.

Cumulative mileage

31.7 Turn left onto Green Valley Road from Rockville Road.
34.4 At the intersection with I-80, follow the signs to I-680. Once on I-680, you will be driving south toward Benicia. Stay on I-680 for another 24 mi. The small hill to the right is just west of the Green Valley fault. At ~2 o'clock

is Sulfur Spring Mountain. This is an antiformal (upfold) structure with Great Valley Group rocks on the flanks, and Coast Range ophiolite serpentinite and gabbro in the core, with a small window into Franciscan mélange. Many late Cenozoic (<20 Ma) dikes, probably related to the Sonoma volcanics, intrude the older rocks. All older rocks have undergone severe alteration by hot, salty waters. The interaction of the late Cenozoic hydrothermal systems and the serpentinite resulted in the alteration of much of the serpentinite to "silica carbonate rock," a rock abundant in quartz and calcite, and magnesium carbonate, during the formation of mercury deposits. A mercury mine, the St. John's quicksilver mine, was developed here. One can see many landslide features here. Landslides are abundant throughout areas underlain by both Great Valley Group and Franciscan rocks. Some of the recent commercial development in the surrounding area has resulted in renewed landsliding. The covering up or alteration of landslide features complicates their description and understanding. I-80 itself overlies a slide that has been slowly deforming it.

46.7 Stay on I-680 at this intersection with I-780.

50.9 Looming ahead, we see Mount Diablo, the most prominent topographic landmark in the San Francisco Bay area. The topographic prominence of Mount Diablo results from a rapid surface uplift driven by an active fold and fault structure associated with the active Greenville and Concord faults.

58.6 Exit right on SR24 following signs for Oakland.

66.4 Here we begin to see roadcuts of folded Miocene (23–5 Ma) fluvial gravels, lake deposits, and volcanic rocks. We will view some of these deposits at the next stop.

67.8 Exit right on Fish Ranch Road. This is the last exit before the Caldecott Tunnel.

68.3 Stop and park along the right side of the road.

Stop Description

At this stop, we see the depositional contact of the 9.2–10 Ma Berkeley Hills volcanics on the fluvial gravels of the Miocene (23–10 Ma; Grimisch et al., 1996) Orinda Formation. These rocks record continental nonmarine deposition, different from older marine rocks (Graham et al., 1984). Paleocurrents within the Orinda Formation suggest a source to the west (Graham et al., 1984). Metamorphic fragments at this outcrop have been correlated to the Cazadero area of Sonoma County, suggesting 105–115 km of right slip on the Hayward fault and parallel (presently inactive) strands of the San Andreas fault system that pass between the source area and this outcrop (Dickerman, 1998; Wakabayashi, 1999b). The volcanic rocks of the Berkeley Hills volcanics, like the Sonoma volcanics we viewed earlier on this trip (between Stops 2 and 3 and at Stop 3) resulted from magmatism associated with hot mantle rocks below (Johnson and O'Neil, 1984). These volcanics have also

served as indicators for displacement estimates on San Andreas fault system strands (e.g., Curtis, 1989; McLaughlin et al., 1996; Wakabayashi, 1999b).

Stop 31: El Cerrito Recycling Center: Two Franciscan Coherent Thrust Sheets (Nappes) and the Shear Zone between Them

Significance of the Site

This site displays a fine exposure of the internal structure of Franciscan rocks formed in the subduction zone off North America in the last 150 Ma.

Accessibility

There is public parking at the recycling center. The site is a short walk up a steep hill along a trail. No restrooms.

GPS Coordinates

37°55.121′N, 122°17.994′W.

Directions

Leaving Stop 30, carefully turn around (a large turnout exists across the road from where we parked), then reenter the westbound SR24 and pass through the Caldecott Tunnel.

Cumulative mileage

73.1 Exit right for I-580 bound for San Francisco, keeping to the right lane (to avoid taking eastbound 580 headed for Hayward).

74.2 Exit right for northbound (Sacramento/Berkeley) I-80. After joining I-80, it may be advisable to stay out of the right lanes, which will exit within the next few intersections.

78.6 Stay on Sacramento-bound I-80 through the intersection with I-580.

79.3 Exit right on Central Avenue and, toward the bottom of the ramp, keep right.

79.6 Turn right at the bottom of the ramp onto Central Avenue and proceed east.

80.2 Turn left at San Pablo Avenue and head northward on San Pablo.

80.9 Turn right on Moeser Lane and proceed eastward.

81.2 Turn left on Richmond Avenue.

81.4 Turn right on Schmidt Lane. Drive eastward on Schmidt Lane to near its end.

~81.8 Park in lot. Walk uphill to north.

Stop Description

At this stop, we view one of the finest exposures of a major tectonic contact (fault) found anywhere in California as well as a fine exposure of a mélange of diverse blocks in a sheared-up shale (a so-called "shale-matrix mélange"), all with views of the Golden Gate Bridge and the Marin Headlands. Although this outcrop lies near the active San Andreas and Hayward faults, the structures we will examine probably formed over 70 m.y. ago and are not currently active. Faulting was accompanied by simultaneous growth of metamorphic minerals. From the parking area, we can see the steep quarry walls. The upper part of the walls is tan and the lower part dark. The tan, blocky outcrops are part of a coherent slab of Na-rich pyroxene (jadeite)-bearing metamorphosed sandstone, a metamorphic rock that probably formed at 25 to 30 km depth or more. The dark rocks below are a shale matrix mélange with blocks of sandstone, basalt, and chert. These units are all inclined to the northeast, or into the cliff face, and are structurally above the rocks exposed on the north side of the road and parking area. The sandstone and shale outcrops along Schmidt Lane are less-metamorphosed sandstones. The thin mélange zone exposed in the lower part of the quarry walls is a shear zone that accommodated an estimated 15 km of vertical displacement during thrusting of highly metamorphosed rocks southwestward over the lower grade sandstones.

A hiking trail that leaves the north side of Schmidt Lane heads to a point along the northern margin of the quarry exposure that is near the level of the base of the jadeite-bearing rock. As the hiking trail heads northward away from the quarry, look for a place where you can move eastward onto a bench in the quarry face. Here, on the quarry face, we are right at the base of the jadeite-bearing metamorphosed sandstone unit. Small internal structures within the rock indicate movement toward the SW. Also within the sheared rocks we see dark gray, possibly glassy, layers that may represent congealed frictional melts generated by ancient earthquakes (called pseudotachylites) that occurred when this shear zone was an active fault over 70 m.y. ago and at a depth of at least 20 km.

The sandstone (called a "metagraywacke") has a pronounced planar appearance, but none of the key metamorphic minerals are obvious to the naked eye (their presence must be confirmed by microscopic examination). Although undistinguished in appearance, metamorphosed sandstones such as these constitute the majority of blueschist facies metamorphic rocks in the Franciscan. In other words, most blueschist facies rocks in the Franciscan are neither blue nor schists! (A schist is a metamorphic rock whose minerals are aligned with each other and large enough to see with a magnifying glass. Schists characteristically have a planar parting, similar to slates.) The shear zone we view at this stop provides a clue to the mystery of how rocks that formed at 30 km depths returned to Earth's surface. This topic continues to generate lively debate among researchers (Platt, 1986; Maruyama et al., 1996).

After viewing the basal part of the blueschist-facies metagraywacke, walk southwestward and work your way onto a lower bench in the quarry to view a good exposure of the shale matrix mélange that separates the blueschist-facies and less metamorphosed units. The blocks in the mélange include sandstone, basalt, and chert. Note that the block-in-matrix structure is scale-independent; one can observe this fabric at tens of meters–scale on the quarry face, at meter-scale in outcrop, and on centimeter-scale if we look closely at the matrix of the outcrop (e.g., Medley, 1994). In other words, no matter at what scale one views the mélange, one will find blocks.

This "scale-independent" nature of the mélange is important for engineering geology of much of the Bay Area. Much of the urbanized region is underlain by mélange similar to that which is exposed here. The scale-independent nature of block-matrix relationships in mélange is important for quantitative characterization of such rock units for engineering geologic purposes. The strength of mélange is proportional to the volume proportion of blocks. One must define minimum block dimensions for effective analysis (Medley, 1994, 2001; Medley and Lindquist, 1995).

Stop 32: Baker Beach, Intra-Franciscan Serpentinite and Shale Matrix Mélange

Significance of the Site

This is an excellent beach exposure of internal structure within Franciscan chaotic deposits (mélange).

Accessibility

Use parking along the street in this urban region. Take the short trail down to beach. No restrooms.

GPS Coordinates

37°48.288′N, 122°28.596′W.

Directions

Leaving Stop 31, retrace the route back toward I-80.

Cumulative mileage

83.8 Traveling west on Central Avenue, pass beneath the I-80 overpass and continue westward.

83.9 Turn right onto the onramp for I-580 west and head westward on I-580.

89.7 Richmond Bridge toll plaza.

90.2 To the left is a reddish island. This is Red Rock, a piece of the Marin Headlands unit. The strata on the island dip southwestward, placing it structurally above the sandstones of Point Richmond. These westward-dipping tabular thrust sheets (nappes) are part of the east limb of a large regional downward fold (synform), the axis of which runs along the axis of the Tiburon Peninsula and through Angel Island (Wakabayashi, 1992).

93.2 The large structure at the left is the notorious San Quentin prison.

94.5 Exit right on Sir Francis Drake Blvd. Proceed southwestward on Sir Francis Drake Blvd. When the road becomes a four lane expressway, stay in the left lane.

96.1 Pass the entrance to the Larkspur Landing Ferry terminal on the left and the Larkspur Landing shopping center to the right. Above and north of the shopping center is a condominium/apartment complex built in an old quarry. The quarry walls are in variously disrupted Franciscan sandstone and shale. One can visit these outcrops, although to avoid parking in the private parking space of a resident, it is probably best to walk a few tenths of a mile uphill from the shopping center.

96.4 Turn left onto the onramp for southbound Highway 101. Stay on Highway 101 until across the Golden Gate Bridge.

96.7 Drive through roadcuts of Franciscan coherent sandstone and shale, broken up sandstone and shale, and mélange.

103.8 On the right is a roadcut of well-developed pillow basalts of the Marin Headlands unit. Within two additional miles, we will drive south across the Golden Gate Bridge. While on the bridge, get into the right lane in order to take a right turn immediately after passing through the toll plaza.

107.1 Toll Plaza. Turn immediately to right at first available exit (a very short distance after toll plaza).

107.2 Stop in the space on the right (west) side of the road, and walk to beach.

Stop Description

Here we will view a serpentinite body structurally within the Franciscan in addition to shale matrix mélange and some high-grade tectonic blocks of garnet amphibolite subsequently recrystallized with blueschist minerals. Collectively these rocks are part of the so-called Hunters Point Shear Zone that extends from here to Hunters Point and separates two coherent units (nappes) of the Franciscan: the Alcatraz nappe structurally above, and the Marin Headlands nappe structurally below (Blake et al., 1984; Wakabayashi, 1992). The serpentinite occupies the structurally higher part of the Hunters Point Shear Zone and contains rare gabbro pods. The serpentinite appears coherent rather than disaggregated in the manner of the sedimentary serpentinite we saw earlier on this field trip. The coherent nature of serpentinite and its consistent structural position within the Hunters Point Shear Zone suggest that it comprises a large thrust sheet or series of sheets (Wakabayashi, 2004b).

The rare gabbro pods within the serpentinite appear to have been strongly metamorphosed to amphibole-bearing rocks, probably in a sea-floor setting. The structurally lower part of the mélange zone has a shale matrix. Sandstone is the most common block type in the shale matrix mélange, with fairly common basalt and chert blocks and rare high-grade metamorphic rocks. Serpentinite is rare or absent in the shale matrix mélange except near the contact with the structurally overlying serpentinite. With the exception of the high-grade blocks, the blocks were less metamorphosed. One can observe the shearing in the matrix and its impact on the block margins and see how much tectonism contributed to the fabric we see. At one outcrop, we seem to see extremely fluid-like mixing of a metatuff (a tuff is a volcanic rock formed by an explosive eruption) and shale. Such structures at first glance give the impression of soft sediment deformation, especially since the metamorphic grade is much too low for such

apparently ductility. Such a style of deformation may have resulted from tectonic deformation of hard rock in the presence of high fluid pressure (Jeanbourquin, 2000).

The Hunters Point Shear Zone probably formed ca. 100 Ma. This zone is interesting because it is an example of a ultramafic-bearing structural horizon *within* the Franciscan Complex in contrast to the Coast Range Ophiolite that structurally overlies the Franciscan. Intra-Franciscan serpentinite may have been scraped off of the subducting plate and may have originated as topographic highs of mantle rock exposed at the sea floor (Coleman, 2000).

A walk along Baker Beach affords a great opportunity to look at details of the rocks of the Franciscan complex. Many of the exposures at the base of the cliff are not in place, having slid down the cliff face to some extent, but a few exposures appear to be in place. The blocks here are similar to the high-grade blocks viewed at Tiburon Peninsula (Stop 2, Day 1).

Stop 33: Fort Funston and the Merced Formation

Significance of the Site

This site provides a view of the relationship between extensional structure (pull-apart basin) and the 1906 epicenter.

Accessibility

There is a public parking lot along the beach. It is a short trail walk to the beach. No restrooms.

Directions

From Stop 32, continue driving on Merchant to a stop sign at Lincoln Blvd.

Cumulative mileage

107.3 Turn right (southward) onto Lincoln Blvd. This road hugs the top of the cliffs and heads southward, then curves westward.

108.6 Turn left onto 25th Avenue shortly after this westward (right) curve.

109.2 Turn right onto Geary. Geary continues west and then curves southward. After taking a few curves above some sea cliffs, the road becomes the Great Highway.

114.1 Pull into the oceanside parking lot and drive as far south in the parking lot as you can before parking. Depending on the winter coastal erosion, the access and availability of parking spaces in this area is variable.

Stop Description

Walk south along the beach to see cliffs composed of the Pleistocene (1.8 Ma–10,000 yr old) Merced Formation and uncomformably (discordantly) overlying Colma Formation. This stop has long been a favorite of field trips focusing on the nature of the sedimentary rocks. Recently, these classic outcrops have received more attention because of their involvement in local tectonics. These outcrops are situated directly east of the San Andreas fault, which passes through the sea cliffs south of this stop at a location partly masked by landslides and is offshore to the west at this stop. To the north, opposite and west of the Golden Gate, the submerged San Andreas fault has two overlapping branches (Zoback et al. 1999; Bruns et al., 2002). Zoback et al. (1999) suggested that the 1906 earthquake nucleated at this overlap; the 1906 epicenter is considered to be just offshore our stop.

At this stop, we will see dips of up to ~60° in the Merced Formation. The part of the Merced examined here is all younger than ca. 600 ka. These sediments are interpreted to have been deposited in a nearshore or shelf environment in a basin in which subsidence kept pace with sedimentation (Clifton et al., 1988). The deformation of the Merced Formation here is a result of active shortening (Kennedy and Caskey, 2001); the outcrops have been subjected to a reversal in tectonic environment, from extension and deposition to uplift, erosion, and shortening probably beginning sometime in the late Pleistocene (125–10 ka) (Wakabayashi et al., 2004, Stoffer, 2005).

End of Day 4; end of trip.

APPENDIX: TECTONIC SKETCH OF NORTHERN CALIFORNIA

In this brief introduction, we will first present a simplified tectonic history based on Moores et al. (2002) that emphasizes the pre-Cenozoic ("basement") history (ca. 500–65 million years ago [Ma]—Part A). Following the review of pre-Cenozoic history, we will review Cenozoic geologic history (65 Ma to the present—Part B). Further details are in the individual site descriptions and the road log. For simplicity we present much of the description of tectonic evolution of this part of the western margin of North America by considering a cross sectional view. We recognize that strike-slip motion has affected and continues to affect the western part of the United States and that the region also exhibits marked variations from north to south in the region.

Appendix Part A—Paleozoic-Mesozoic Tectonic History: Cross Sectional and Map Views of General Tectonic Elements

Figure 5 shows a generalized map of the western U.S. margin in California and neighboring regions. Two maps are shown. Figure 5A shows the position of selected key elements at present. Figure 5B is a sketch that restores Cenozoic Basin and Range extension and ~200 km of Cretaceous right-lateral faulting (Lewis and Girty, 2001). Figure 4 shows a generalized cross section of the region of discussion. The cross section is a composite section based upon Wakabayashi and Unruh (1995), Godfrey and Dilek (2000), and more recent data, as presented in the following. We describe the elements of this cross section from west to east, approximately along a sector at 39–40° N latitude.

The cross section shows east-directed, west-dipping thrust faults, of a variety of ages, beneath the Coast Ranges, the Cen-

tral Valley, the Sierra Nevada, and the eastern part of the Sierra Nevada Batholith. Figure 6 shows a listing of selected tectonic events in the region.

Franciscan Complex

Rocks of the Franciscan Complex comprise much of the basement of the California Coast Ranges. The Franciscan Complex formed during the most recent subduction episode in California, a chapter in geologic history that spanned the period of 165 Ma to 20 Ma at the latitude of our field trip. The Franciscan formed from materials scraped off the top of an eastward-subducting oceanic plate (Ernst, 1970).

The Franciscan was offscraped from a downgoing oceanic plate subducting beneath oceanic crust now exposed as the Coast Range ophiolite. The Coast Range ophiolite is depositionally overlain by the sandstones and shales of the Great Valley Group that represent deposits from a large forearc basin that lay between the Franciscan subduction complex and trench to the west and the active magmatic arc to the east. The intrusive rocks associated with this magmatic arc are now exposed as the Sierra Nevada Batholith.

Franciscan rock units include trench sediments derived from the continent (now sandstones and shales), as well as more-traveled pieces that represent the top of the subducted oceanic crust (cherts, limestones, basalts). The offscraping process that formed the Franciscan Complex has resulted in considerable deformation of these rocks. A significant part of the Franciscan consists of chaotic units known as "mélanges" (after a French word meaning "mixture"). These geologic units consist of a sheared matrix of shale and/or serpentinite with included blocks of a wide range of rock types; they differ dramatically with the "layer cake" stratigraphy one associates with areas such as the Grand Canyon (Hsü, 1968, Maxwell, 1974). Mélanges are thought to represent fault zones, and some of them may have originated as submarine landslides, known as olistostromes (e.g., Cloos, 1984; Cowan, 1985). Franciscan Complex researchers commonly refer to non-mélange units as "coherent" to distinguish them from mélange units. The large-scale structure of the Franciscan can be generalized as a series of low-angle fault-bounded coherent sheets or "nappes" stacked upon each other and separated from each other by mélange (or fault) zones (Wakabayashi, 1992, 1999c).

Unlike a stratigraphic sequence of rocks, the major units of the Franciscan are all fault-bounded. The age at which rocks were incorporated into the Franciscan generally becomes progressively younger structurally downward. This age decrease from east to west is consistent with the model of progressive offscraping in which each successive unit is shingled beneath the previous as subduction proceeds. It is important to realize that in a subduction complex the age of incorporation may have little to do with the age of formation. For instance, the oldest rocks in the Franciscan, from the standpoint of origin, are the basalts of the Marin Headlands and related units that formed ca. 200 Ma at a mid-oceanic spreading center and were incorpo-

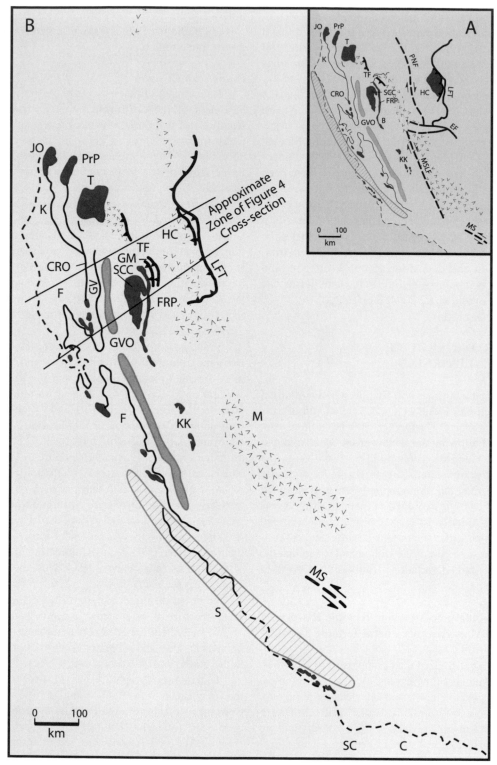

Figure 5. Tectonic sketch map of part of the U.S. Pacific margin, showing selected principal tectonic features, major ophiolite complexes (dark shading), the Great Valley ophiolite (light shading), and the Salinian block (cross-hatched). B—Bear Mountains ophiolite; C—Catalina schist; CRO—Coast Range Ophiolite; EF—Excelsior fault; F—Franciscan; FRP—Feather River Peridotite; GM—Grizzly Mountain thrust; GV—Great Valley sequence; GVO—Great Valley ophiolite; JO—Josephine ophiolite; HC—Humboldt complex; K—Klamath Mountains; KK—Kings Kaweah ophiolite; LFT—Luning Fencemaker thrusts; M—Mojave block; MS—Mojave Sonora megashear; MSLF—Mojave Snow Lake Fault; PNF—Pine Nut fault; PrP—Preston Peak ophiolite; S—Salinian block; SC—Santa Cruz Island; SCC—Smartville, Slate Creek, and Jarbo Gap ophiolites; T—Trinity ophiolite. (A) Present configuration. (B) Palinspastic map with displacement on PNF-MSLF removed. Modified after Moores et al., (2002).

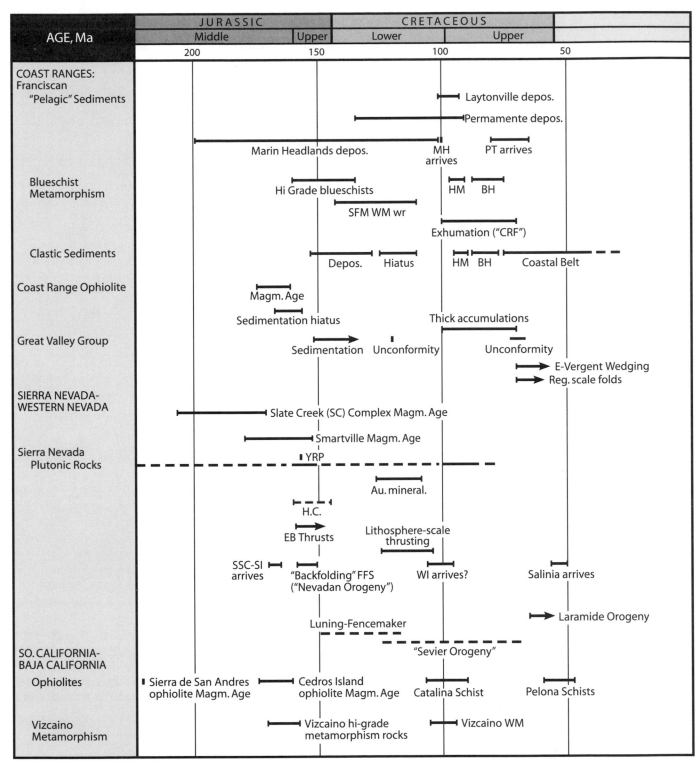

Figure 6. Generalized time-space diagram of features along the North American Cordilleran margin. Symbols as in Figures 1 and 2, plus: am—amphibolite facies metamorphism; bls—blueschist-facies metamorphism; BH—Burnt Hills unit of the Franciscan Complex; "CRF"—Coast Range fault; dr—dextral-reverse (thrust) faults; FFS—Foothill Fault System of Sierra Nevada; H.C.—Humboldt complex. Franciscan units: HM—Hull Mountain unit; MH—Marin Headlands terrane; PT—Permanente terrane. SC—Slate Creek complex of Sierra Nevada; SFM—South Fork Mountain schist of the Klamaths; SI—Stikine-Intermontane superterrane; sr—sinistral-reverse faulting; WI—Wrangell-Insular superterrane; WM—white mica, used for age determination; wr—whole rock samples used for radiometric age determination; YRP—Yuba Rivers pluton in the northern Sierra Nevada.

rated into the Franciscan Complex ca. 95 Ma. In contrast, the first rocks incorporated into the subduction complex are "high-grade" (formed at great depth and pressure) metamorphic blocks that mark the beginning of Franciscan subduction ca. 165 Ma and whose basaltic parents probably formed ca. 170 Ma (Saha et al., 2005). Thus the formational age of exposed Franciscan rocks at the latitude of our field trip range from ca. 200 Ma to perhaps 50 Ma, whereas the incorporation ages (that track the time of subduction itself) range from ca. 165 Ma to 20 Ma (Wakabayashi, 1999c).

About a third of the exposed Franciscan was buried to sufficient depths (>20 km) during the subduction process to cause metamorphic minerals to form at high pressure and low temperature. These minerals are commonly blue in color, so that these rocks are known as "blueschists" (Ernst, 1970). Such rocks are crucial evidence that more than half the rocks were buried to 15 km or more in the subduction zone and subsequently exhumed.

North of the San Francisco Bay region, the Franciscan complex has traditionally been divided into three principal belts, the Eastern, Central, and Coastal Belts, become younger in incorporation age from east to west and from structurally highest to lowest (e.g., Berkland et al., 1972; Blake et al., 1988; Fig. 3). In the cross section, the three belts are shown modified after the reconstruction of Wakabayashi and Unruh (1995).

As mentioned above, there was considerable variation from north to south along the paleo-plate boundary. The three-belt division does not continue south of the San Francisco Bay region. Furthermore the chronology associated with Franciscan tectonic events does not apply in southern California. For example, the Catalina schist offshore of southern California (for example on Catalina Island) includes high-temperature metamorphic rocks that indicate that subduction began there at ca. 115 Ma, ~50 million years after Franciscan subduction began (Anczkiewicz et al., 2004). The Pelona-Orocopia schists of southern California and Arizona may record initiation of a different subduction zone at 60–65 Ma (Moores et al., 2002).

Coast Range–Great Valley Ophiolite

The oceanic crust remnant known as the Coast Range ophiolite structurally overlies the Franciscan Complex. In general the ophiolite stratigraphically underlies the Great Valley Group forearc basin strata, although the contact is complicated by faulting in some places (Hopson et al., 1981; McLaughlin et al., 1988). Geophysical evidence indicates that beneath the Great Valley itself, a slab of oceanic crust and mantle underlies the buried Great Valley sediments (the so-called Great Valley ophiolite) (Godfrey and Klemperer, 1998; Godfrey et al., 1997). Most exposures of the ophiolite comprise one or more of the following rock types: serpentinite, gabbro, quartz diorite, diabase, basalt, and felsic volcanic rocks (Hopson et al., 1981). The age of the Coast Range ophiolite is ca. 165–172 Ma (Hopson et al., 1996; Shervais et al., 2005; Pessagno et al., 2000).

In exposures, faults are present everywhere below and in

some places above the Coast Range Ophiolite. The fault beneath the ophiolite is commonly called the Coast Range Fault (Worrall, 1981; Jayko et al., 1987); north of San Francisco, along the eastern margin of the Coast Ranges, the fault at the base of the Great Valley Group is the Stony Creek fault (Lawton, 1956; Chuber, 1962). The Coast Range ophiolite displays no penetrative deformation and records negligible history of subduction-related metamorphism (Hopson et al., 1981).

The ophiolitic (oceanic crust and mantle) rocks beneath the Central Valley in turn overly continental crust and mantle belonging to the Sierra Nevada. Thus, the Central Valley possesses two crust-mantle boundaries (this boundary is called the Moho discontinuity). The presence of two Mohos and the high density of the oceanic rocks help explain the long-standing enigma of the existence of the low-lying Central Valley basin surrounded on all sides by rising regions—the Coast Ranges, the Klamath Mountains, the Sierra Nevada, and the Tehachapis.

Great Valley Group

The Great Valley Group is a thick sequence (>10 km) of sandstones and shales that were deposited in a so-called "forearc" region between the Franciscan subduction zone and the Sierran magmatic "arc." The largest exposures of Great Valley Group forearc basin strata are present along the western margin of the Central Valley. Other significant exposures are present in the interior of the Coast Ranges. These sandstones and shales generally range in age from early Jurassic to latest Cretaceous, spanning ca. 150 to 65 Ma (e.g., Moxon, 1988). Cenozoic (<65 Ma) sandstones and shales, volcanic rocks, and poorly consolidated sediments overlie the Great Valley Group (e.g., Bartow, 1990). Jurassic and Cretaceous rocks were deposited by slurry-like sediment-bearing turbid flows coming from the edge of the continent and deposited in deep water on oceanic crust of the Coast Range ophiolite. Sedimentary rocks thus formed are called "turbidites." Turbidites characterize the Great Valley sediments. As with Coast Range ophiolite, the Great Valley Group lacks significant recrystallization and "penetrative" deformation. The "classic" view of the Coast Range ophiolite and Great Valley Group held that they behaved somewhat passively above the subduction zone as Franciscan rocks accumulated below (e.g., Dickinson and Seely, 1979) Several subsequent studies, however, indicated that faulting associated with both extension and shortening affected these two units at various times (e.g., Wentworth et al., 1984; Wakabayashi and Unruh, 1995; Unruh et al., 1995).

A major west-dipping, east-directed thrust fault was rooted in (merges with) the subduction zone and displaced Franciscan, Coast Range Ophiolite, and Great Valley Group rocks eastward (Figs. 3 and 5; Unruh and Wakabayashi, 1995) This thrusting was in the opposite sense of the subduction zone and began in the latest Cretaceous–early Tertiary (ca. 80–65 Ma), just after a period of thick accumulation of Great Valley sediments. It corresponds to a major break in deposition (unconformity) in the Great Valley Group (Peterson, 1967a, 1967b). Most exhumation (unroofing) of Franciscan metamorphic rocks from depths of 25–30 km or more to depths of 15 km or less probably occurred as a result of east-directed thrusting. The west-dipping (so-called "east-vergent" thrust system was reactivated in Pliocene time (5–2 Ma) and is still active. This renewed activity has given rise to steep dips in the Plio-Pleistocene (5 Ma to 10,000 yr old) strata along the western Central Valley margin and to significant seismicity. The 1892 Winters-Vacaville and 1983 Coalinga earthquakes (Unruh and Moores, 1992; Unruh et al., 1995) probably resulted from activity on these thrust faults along the western margin of the Great Valley.

Sierra Nevada

In the northern Sierra Nevada, rocks older than the intrusion of the Sierra Nevada granitic rocks are grouped into four generally recognized belts. From west to east, these belts are

1. The **Western Jurassic Belt** consists of andesitic (comparable in composition to Mount Shasta) volcanic rocks, shallow and related intrusive ("plutonic") rocks, and sedimentary rocks. The belt extends some 200 km southward from the northern end of the Sierra Nevada (e.g., Schweickert, 1981; Beard and Day, 1987). North of I-80, this belt consists of the Smartville complex, part of a 185–160 Ma oceanic-island arc that formed above an intra-oceanic subduction zone that was separate from the subduction zone along the California margin. The Smartville complex in turn developed on older (200–220 Ma) oceanic crust now represented in the Sierra Nevada by exposures of serpentinite, gabbro, and various dikes (Saleeby et al., 1989; Bickford and Day, 2001; Dilek and Moores, 1992, Dilek et al., 1991).

2. The **Central Belt** consists of the 225–175 Ma Jarbo Gap and Slate Creek ophiolites, made up of serpentinite, gabbro, diabasic dikes, basaltic breccias, and volcanic rocks, the youngest units of which correlate with the oceanic crust beneath the Smartville Complex. A Mesozoic chert-argillite (a dark, hard rock made up of firmly cemented, poorly bedded mud rocks) unit with disordered and discontinuous beds (a so-called "chaotic" unit) contains blocks of Carboniferous-Permian (360–250 Ma) limestones that possibly formed on top of volcanoes beneath the ocean (seamounts). Ophiolitic rocks sit in thrust contact above the chert-argillite sequence in places, but elsewhere the latter are intruded by rocks of the ophiolite. The thrust contact between the ophiolitic rocks (Slate Creek ophiolite and related rocks) and the chert-argillite sequence is intruded by a 165 Ma pluton (Edelman and Sharp, 1989). This fact indicates that the thrusting of the Slate Creek ophiolite over the chert-argillite occurred before 165 Ma (middle Jurassic). Ophiolitic remnants are common within and along the Central Belt's western margin but not in its eastern part. This fact implies that the chaotic chert-argillite unit and included blocks of the Central Belt formed in a *west*-dipping subduction zone (Moores, 1970; Moores and Day, 1984). Some workers have proposed that the Cen-

tral Belt actually comprises two subduction complexes, the western part of which was associated with west-dipping subduction and the eastern part with east-dipping subduction (e.g., Moores, 1970; Schweickert and Cowan, 1975).

3. The **Feather River complex** and associated **Devils Gate ophiolite** form a 6–10-km-wide zone that extends for >100 km from the north end of the Sierra Nevada. The belt contains basalts, diabase, and gabbros (now metamorphosed to amphibole-containing rocks, "amphibolites"), and ultramafic rocks (fresh peridotites and serpentinites). Magmatic rocks exhibit two ages: an earlier Devonian age (416–359 Ma), and a later Carboniferous age (ca. 300–320 Ma (Saleeby et al., 1989). Metamorphic rocks in the Feather River Belt range in age from 240 to 390 Ma (Devonian-Triassic; reviewed in Hacker and Peacock, 1990). Coarsely crystalline metamorphic rocks containing garnet and amphibole, including blue amphiboles, border the ultramafic rocks on the west and appear to dip eastward beneath them. This relationship suggests that east-dipping subduction occurred beneath the Feather River complex (e.g., Hacker and Peacock, 1990). Such a subduction zone would coincide with the east-dipping subduction zone along the eastern margin of the Central Belt proposed by Moores (1970) and Schweickert and Cowan (1975).

4. The **Eastern Belt** is a thick sequence of metamorphosed sedimentary and volcanic rocks with a few granitic intrusive bodies and ranges in age from early Paleozoic to Jurassic (542–146 Ma). The lowermost unit is the lower Paleozoic Shoo Fly complex, containing fault-bounded slices of quartz-rich turbidites, mafic volcanics, a fault zone containing several slivers of serpentinite, and a mélange containing blocks of chert and Ordovician (488–444 Ma) limestone (Hannah and Moores, 1986; Harwood 1992). These rocks have been deformed more than once. Early east-northeast–trending "isoclinal" folds (folds where both sides are parallel to each other, indicating that the layers have been bent ~180°) are present in these rocks (Varga and Moores, 1981). The largest serpentinite exposure is only a few hundred meters thick in outcrop, but gravity and magnetic data indicate that it becomes several kilometers thick at depth (Griscom *in* Blake et al., 1989). The turbidites and mélange may represent a lower Paleozoic subduction complex. The serpentinite may represent remnants of an ophiolite that was emplaced over the Shoo Fly rocks in mid-late Devonian time (398–360 Ma; Varga and Moores, 1981). Discordantly (or "unconformably") overlying the Shoo Fly rocks are three volcanic complexes: (1) the Devonian-Mississippian (416–318 Ma) units of the Sierra Buttes, Taylor, Elwell, Keddie, and Peale Formations, interpreted as the remnants of a chain of oceanic volcanoes formed above an intra-oceanic subduction zone; (2) the Permian–Triassic (299–200 Ma) units of the Robinson, Reeve, Arlington, and Cedar Formations also may represent an oceanic volcanic sequence similarly formed above an oceanic subduction zone; and (3) a Jurassic (200–146 Ma) Mount Jura and Milton sequences that may represent rem-

nants of a volcanic chain that formed above a subduction zone near to or along the continental margin (e.g., Hannah and Moores, 1986). These units all feature andesitic (a volcanic rock more silica-rich than a basalt) volcanic rocks, including submarine lavas with pillowforms and fragmental volcanic rocks derived from volcanic explosions. For much of the length of their exposure, the rocks are primarily older in the west and younger in the yeast ("east-facing"). In addition, they have been tilted more than 90° to the east from their original horizontal orientation. Near the northern end of the Sierra Nevada, however, the rocks are highly folded and deformed by east-directed thrust faults. Along the western margin of the Eastern Belt, an enigmatic sequence of Devonian(?)-Jurassic (416–146 Ma) rocks crop out that show affinities with rocks in the Klamath Mountains (Harwood, 1992; Jayko, 1988, 1990; Hannah and Moores, 1986).

Three major fault blocks are present in the Eastern Belt. These fault blocks are separated from each other by east-directed (west-dipping) thrust faults (Fig. 5). The degree of deformation in Eastern Belt rocks increases in complexity from east to west. In the east, post–Shoo Fly rocks are generally unfoliated (that is, their metamorphic minerals are not formed parallel to each other) and little metamorphosed. To the west, however, post–Shoo Fly rocks progressively become very intensely folded as one approaches the contact with the Feather River peridotite. In addition, the rocks become more metamorphosed and the minerals thus formed are aligned, producing a preferential plane of parting in the rocks, or "cleavage." This cleavage dips westward in the east but gradually becomes east-dipping as one approaches the Feather River Peridotite.

The Sierra Nevada granitic batholith intrudes the rocks described above. On Figure 4, the batholith is shown modified from Godfrey and Dilek (2000). The general structural relations described by Day et al. (1985) suggest that the main early Mesozoic structures in the Sierra Nevada consist of east-directed thrust faults and folds, subsequently modified by west-directed faults. Accordingly, structures are depicted on the cross section as both west-dipping and east-dipping, respectively (Fig. 4). The early east-directed faults are interpreted to dip westward beneath the Central Belt, Western Belt, and Great Valley, consistent with geophysical and geochemical data (Godfrey and Klemperer, 1998; Godfrey et al., 1997; Bickford and Day, 2001; Ducea, 2001). These fault geometries also conform with those displayed by seismic data collected by the Consortium for Continental Reflection Profiling (COCORP) Project in a traverse across the northern Sierra Nevada (Nelson et al., 1986).

Significant tectonic and magmatic events for the Sierra Nevada on Figure 5 include the age of the Slate Creek and Smartville complexes (Bickford and Day, 2001), the Yuba Rivers pluton (Bickford and Day, 2001), gold mineralization of the Mother Lode (Böhlke, 1999), the Humboldt complex ages (Dilek and Moores, 1995), age of Eastern Belt thrusts (Hannah and Moores, 1986), lithosphere-scale thrusting

(Ducea 2001), and apparent times of arrival of the Smartville/Slate Creek ophiolites.

Parts of the western Sierra Nevada were affected by pronounced deformation and recrystallization associated with east-over-west thrust faulting and left-lateral or "sinistral" shearing from 151 to 123 Ma (Paterson et al., 1987; Tobisch et al., 1989; Wakabayashi, 1992). Conversely, shear zones in the Sierra Nevada batholith display west-directed (east-over-west) and right-lateral (or "dextral") movement. These zones have an age of ca. 100–85 Ma (e.g., Renne et al., 1993; Tobisch et al., 1995). These complex, contradictory deformations relatively late in Sierra Nevada history probably are related to complex history of Franciscan subduction along the California margin.

Many of these fault zones are present in the western part of the Sierra Nevada. They formed the conduits for hot fluids that deposited gold-bearing quartz veins in the so-called "Mother Lode district" of the Sierra Nevada. Accordingly, the faults are variously called the Mother Lode or the Foothill Fault system.

Archipelago Style of Orogeny

An archipelago is a group of islands in a sea or an ocean. Island groups such as the Aleutians, the Greater Antilles, the Philippines, Indonesia, or the Marianas are modern examples of archipelagoes (e.g., Hall, 1996). These examples are chains of islands that involve active subduction of one oceanic plate beneath another. As subduction proceeds along a continental margin, it would not be surprising if one or more oceanic archipelagoes were swept against the continent and the remnants preserved there as subduction proceeded. These remnants have a geology that is different from the rocks adjoining them. It has become common to call such regions with different geology a "terrane." A terrane is a region with a specific geologic history, separated by faults from surrounding regions with their own different geologic history. They began their existence in different locations and migrated separately, coming together at various times, and then becoming attached to the western margin of the continent at different times. This complex history can be read in a study of the geology of the individual and combined terranes.

Terranes are abundant in both the Franciscan Complex of the Coast Ranges and the Sierra Nevada as well as its possible equivalents to the north and south. Indeed, some "superterranes," amalgamations of several separate terranes, are now part of our vocabulary in trying to describe the tectonic events along the western margin of North America.

Moores (1998) proposed a model for an "archipelago" style of orogenic development, involving convergence and collision of already complexly deformed oceanic island arcs or collections of "terranes" or "superterranes" during Mesozoic and Cenozoic time along the western margins of North America and northern South America. Figure 7 shows a generalized tectonic sketch map and cross section for early Jurassic time, just prior to one collision in mid Jurassic time (ca. 185–160 Ma). A volcanic arc on the North American continent gives way to the

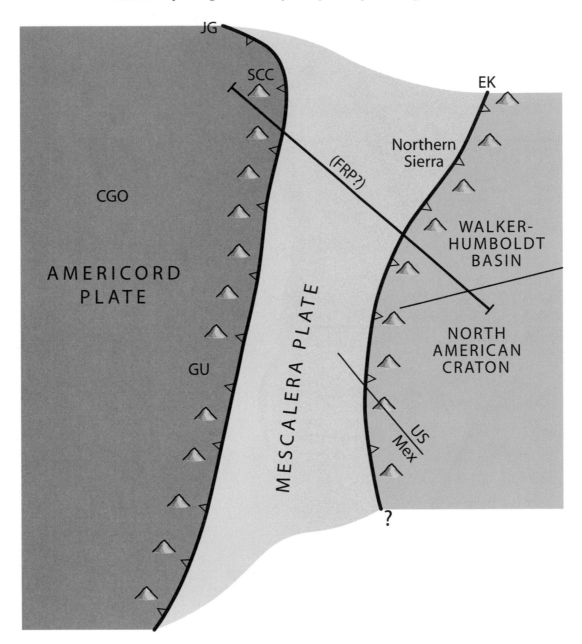

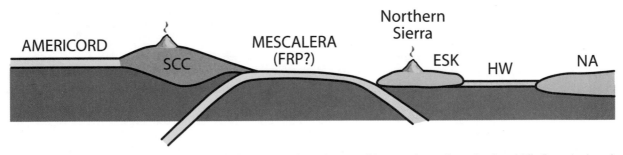

Figure 7. Generalized sketch map (top) and cross section (bottom) illustrating possible tectonic configuration in middle Jurassic time, just prior to collision of an oceanic-island arc with the North American continent. CGO—Coast Range–Great Valley ophiolites; EK—Eastern Klamath Belt; ESK—Eastern Klamath, Eastern Sierra Nevada Belts; FRP—Feather River Peridotite; GU—Guerrero terrane, Mexico; HW—Walker-Humboldt basin; JG—Jarbo Gap ophiolite; NA—North American continent. Mescalera plate after Dickinson and Lawton (2001).

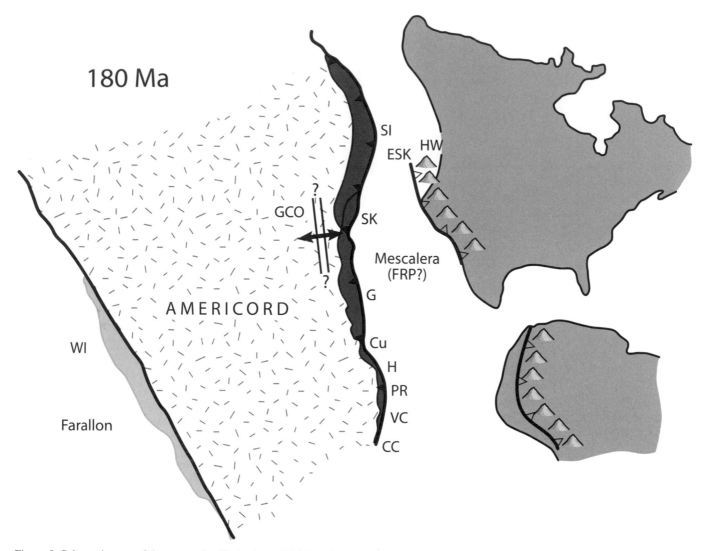

Figure 8. Schematic map of the eastern Pacific basin at 180 Ma (mid-Jurassic). C—Cuba; CC—Cordillera Central of Colombia; ESK—Eastern Sierra and Klamath Belts; FRP—Feather River peridotite; G—Guerrero terrane; GCO—Great Valley–Coast Range ophiolites; H—Hispaniola; HW—Humboldt-Walker basin; PR—Puerto Rico; SI—Stikine Intermontane superterrane; SK—Sierra Nevada Central and Western Belts and related rocks in Klamath Mountains; VC—Venezuelan Coast Ranges; WI—Wrangell-Insular superterrane. Modified after Moores et al. (2002, their Figure 6). See text for discussion.

NW to an Alaska Peninsula–like extension in the northern Sierra Nevada and western Nevada, separated from the continental interior by the oceanic Walker-Humboldt basin in western Nevada. An oceanic-island arc represented by the Jarbo Gap, Smartville–Slate Creek ophiolites, and similar rocks now in Mexico (the Guerrero terrane) and in the Caribbean (Cuba, Hispaniola, Puerto Rico) and in northern South America (Venezuelan Coast Ranges, NW Colombia) is separated from the North American margin by a plate that was consumed on both its margins. This plate may be the oceanic "Mescalero plate" of Dickinson and Lawton (2001). This plate has essentially disappeared as a result of subduction, leaving only a few small pieces that were scraped off this subducting plate.

Implicit in this model are two ideas:

1. Much of western North America is oceanic in origin and became attached to the continent at various times in the past; and
2. Many of the major Caribbean islands originated in the Pacific Ocean.

We interpret the thrust-faults at the base of these ophiolite complexes to represent major sutures (former position of subduction zones and/or disappeared oceans). The subduction zone dipped west beneath the colliding arc, as shown in Figure 7. The Central Belt rocks were likely scraped off a subducting plate.

The fault west of and beneath the Feather River peridotite, the largest body of ultramafic rocks in the Sierra Nevada, represents a major east-dipping suture, illustrated in Figure 7 as the east-dipping subduction zone.

West of the colliding oceanic arc is an entirely oceanic plate, called the Amerced plate. It subsequently subducted beneath North America prior to the arrival of the next major archipelago—now preserved as the so-called Wrangell-Insular Superterrane. This model for plate evolution is similar to that proposed by Ingersoll (2000).

Tectonic Reconstructions of North American–Northern South American Margins

We present here two cartoons modified after Moores et al. (2002) that elaborate on the "archipelago" style of deformation. Figure 8 shows a possible reconstruction ca. 180 Ma. On the west, the Farallon plate bordered the Wrangell-Insular superterrane, a group of exotic rocks present from southern Alaska to Vancouver Island, which at this time was an active island arc in the approximate position shown (Debiche et al., 1987; Stamatakos et al., 2001). A separate, now-disappeared, oceanic plate, the "Americord" plate, separated the Wrangell-Insular superterrane from the Stikine-Intermontaine superterrane. The latter consisted of a series of exotic blocks now in British Columbia and Yukon, Canada, and possible continuations to the south—the rocks in the Klamath Mountains, the Sierra Nevada Central and Eastern Belts, the Guerrero terrane of Mexico, major Caribbean islands, and exotic terranes of northern South America. The Mescalera plate separated the Stikine-Intermontane superterrane from continental North and South America. Note that two plates separate North and South America from the Farallon plate. As mentioned above, the Farallon plate is the plate that most recently has been subducting beneath North America, producing the Franciscan. Remnants of it are present off the Pacific Northwest (producing the Cascade volcanoes) and south of the mouth of the Gulf of California (producing the volcanoes of Mexico and Central America). The spreading center producing the Great Valley–Coast Range ophiolite is shown as within the Americord plate, a hypothetical plate that separated the Stikine-Intermontane and Wrangell-Insular Superterranes.

Figure 9 shows a possible scenario at 40 Ma. Detailed discussion of the evolution of this scenario is beyond the scope of this field guide (see Moores et al., 2002, for a fuller exposition). Suffice it to say, however, that the hypothesis implies a record of a complex intersection of North America with two major archipelagoes, the Wrangell-Insular and Stikine-Intermontane, and their continuations through time. Many features are shown. Of particular interest are the two superterranes already mentioned. Also note that the model shows the origin of the major Caribbean islands as parts of the Stikine-Intermontane terrane migrated eastward in the gap between North and South America.

Appendix Part B—Post-Batholithic Rocks

After intrusion of the Sierra Nevada granites at depths of several to many kilometers, the region now occupied by the Sierra Nevada was uplifted and eroded down to a gently undu-

lating plane. This erosion episode probably occurred prior to ca. 80 Ma (late Cretaceous). On this erosion surface was deposited several rock units:

1. Great Valley Group: Rocks of the uppermost Great Valley Group (84–65 Ma) are present along the westernmost margin of the Sierra Nevada, notably near Chico, Oroville, and Folsom. These rocks dip gently westward and overly steeply tilted older Sierra Nevada rocks. They were deposited between the time represented by Figures 8 and 9.

2. Auriferous gravels (56–34 Ma): A sequence of gold-bearing gravels and sands, ca. 50 Ma (Eocene) are present in many places in the Sierra Nevada. These gravels probably were formed by sediment-choked rivers flowing westward from a highland in the present area of Nevada, before the present Sierra Nevada mountains formed, approximately at the time of Figure 9. The highland in Nevada may have been as high as present-day Tibet (Dilek and Moores, 1999). These rocks contain significant amounts of gold. They were the object of hydraulic mining from ca. 1860–1885. Hydraulic mining is a process in which whole streams are diverted into ditches and then through pipes to emerge in large nozzles, called "monitors" or "dictators." In the 25 or so years in which this method was practiced, some 1.5 to 2 billion cubic yards of debris were washed off the Sierra into the Great Valley, changing the nature of the streams, especially the Feather, Yuba, American, and Sacramento Rivers, and reducing the size of the San Francisco–San Pablo–Suisun Bay (Bateman and Wahrhaftig, 1966; Durrell, 1966, and references therein).

3. A series of 15–30 Ma volcanic rocks of various abundances of silica. These rocks are thought to be the product of magmas formed over descending lithospheric slab during late-stage subduction along the California margin.

4. A basalt unit of ca. 15–17 Ma, present in the northern Sierra. This unit is exposed in the eastern Sierra near Blairsden, in the western Sierra near Oroville, and along the eastern side of the Coast Ranges between Vacaville and Winters. This basalt may be related to similar rocks in north-central Nevada and in eastern Oregon and Washington.

5. A series of volcanic rocks of mostly andesitic (intermediate silica contents; similar to Mount Shasta) of ca. 5–15 Ma (Wagner et al., 2000). These rocks are also thought to represent the products of subduction along the California margin. Along the Sierra crest they were erupted during faulting. Thus they are probably coeval with initiation of uplift of the present Sierra Nevada.

Basin and Range

The Basin and Range province of North America is a zone of north-trending ranges and intervening valleys that extends from British Columba to northern Mexico. This region is generally interpreted as an area where the continent is extending at 1–2 cm/yr (see Fig. 1; Unruh et al., 2003). The Sierra Nevada marks the western margin of the Basin and Range province.

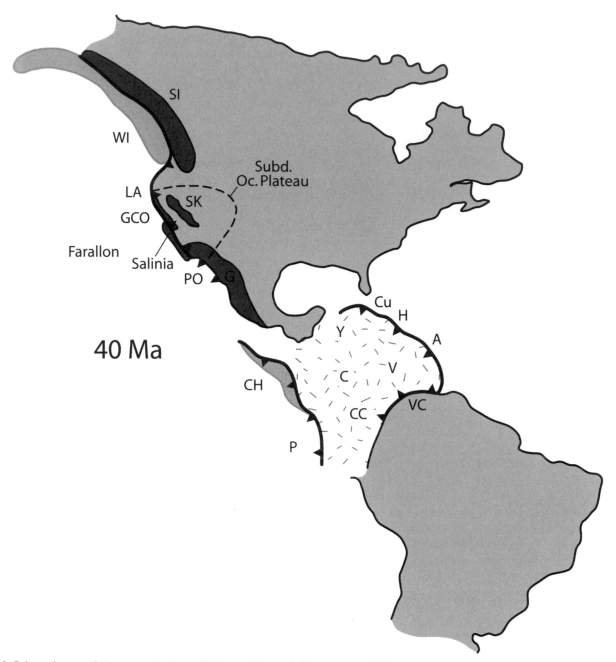

Figure 9. Schematic map of the eastern Pacific at 40 Ma (mid-Eocene) (Moores et al., 2002). Symbols as in Figure 8. The area labeled "subducted oceanic plateau" would have represented a highland, reminiscent of present-day Tibet.

At the latitude of the cross section, the Sierra Nevada batholith extends into the Basin and Range. The eastern side of the batholith is shown involved in east-directed thrust faults, which we associate with west-dipping crustal-scale seismic reflectors of Allmendinger et al. (1987). West-dipping thrust faults along the Walker Lane and other parts of western Nevada are modified after Dilek et al. (1988), Godfrey and Dilek (2000), and Dilek and Moores (1993). The timing of these thrusts is not clear, although they must be post Jurassic, pre-late Tertiary (146–3 Ma).

To reiterate, the latest episode of subduction along the continental margin of this part of California began ca. 140 Ma, before arrival of the latest archipelago, and ended ca. 20 Ma as the East Pacific Rise intersected the subduction zone (Atwater, 1970). The combination of the spreading ridge and offsetting fracture zone (to become the San Andreas fault system) produced two "triple junctions" (points where three plates meet) that migrated in opposite directions along the California margin as the spreading ridge was consumed. To the south, the Rivera triple junction migrated southeastward and is now located south of the mouth of the Gulf of California (Sea of Cortez), while to the north, the Mendocino triple junction migrated northwestward.

As these triple junctions migrated away from each other a transform plate boundary lengthened between them (Atwater, 1970). The transform plate margin of western North America is a broad one with deformation in two main areas (Argus and Gordon, 1991): (1) the San Andreas fault system of dextral (right-lateral) strike-slip faults that accommodates ~80% of the dextral plate motion between the North American and Pacific plates; and (2) dextral slip and extension east of the Sierra Nevada, including the Walker Lane and Basin and Range extension; this area accommodates the remaining 20% of plate motion. *In other words, you cannot point to any single fault and call it THE plate boundary.* In the following discussion, it is important to remember that the slip (displacement) rate of a fault is generally proportional to the energy released in earthquakes along it per unit time, so the higher the slip rate of a fault, the more seismic hazard it poses.

Between the two active deformation zones is a region of relatively low seismic activity, now called the **Sierra Nevada microplate** (see Fig. 3) that comprises the Sierra Nevada and the Central Valley. The boundary between the Sierra Nevada microplate and the deformation to the east is the system of prominent east-down "dip-slip" normal and dextral-normal "oblique-slip" faults that marks the eastern escarpment of the Sierra Nevada. These faults are commonly referred to as the Sierra Nevada Frontal Fault system. Dextral faulting along the eastern margin of the Sierra Nevada actually accommodates higher slip rates than the more visually spectacular normal faults. A combination of strike-slip and extensional faulting may characterize the Sierra Nevada Frontal Fault system (Unruh et al. 2003). This zone marks the eastern boundary of the Sierra Nevada microplate. Its western boundary is a region of folds and thrust faults along the Central Valley–Coast Range boundary (Namson and Davis, 1988; Unruh et al., 1995). Estimated slip rates on the microplate's eastern boundary are as much as 3 mm/yr, whereas along its western margin slip rates are 0.5–1 mm/yr (Unruh et al., 1995).

Dextral faults of the San Andreas fault system are the most active faults of the plate boundary (see Fig. 3B), and they have been the source of major earthquakes within historic times, including the 1906 San Francisco earthquake on the San Andreas fault itself. In the San Francisco Bay area, active slip from the San Andreas fault in central California has split into several strands including the Peninsula San Andreas fault, ~17 mm/yr; the Hayward fault, ~9 mm/yr; the Calaveras fault, ~6 mm/yr; and the Greenville fault, ~3 mm/yr (Hall et al., 1999; Lienkaemper et al., 1991; Kelson et al., 1996; Sawyer and Unruh, 2002). In central California, the San Andreas fault is slipping at a rate of ~35 mm/yr. The San Gregorio fault may accommodate 5 mm/yr or more of slip (Weber and Lajoie, 1980; Simpson et al., 1998). It merges with the San Andreas fault north of the Golden Gate, and the slip rate of the northern

San Andreas fault is thus the sum of Peninsula San Andreas and San Gregorio slip (Niemi and Hall, 1992; Prentice, 1989). Shortening of a few tenths of millimeters per year occurs within the Coast Ranges, as well as on their eastern margin. An exception is Mount Diablo. It is a compressional structure that accommodates a transfer of slip from the Greenville to the Concord fault. Mount Diablo appears to be shortening at a rate comparable to the dextral rate on the Greenville fault (~3 mm/yr), and it is uplifting rapidly (at about the same rate), producing the most prominent topographic landmark in the San Francisco Bay area (Unruh and Sawyer, 1997, 2001; Sawyer, 1999).

The pattern of slip distribution along the dextral plate boundary has thus been fairly complex in time and space. Historically, ~800 km of dextral slip has accumulated along the Pacific–North American plate boundary since 29 Ma (the inception of the San Andreas fault system), of which 540–590 km took place on the San Andreas fault system strands (Atwater and Stock, 1998). The 540–590 km of slip may include the following displacement amounts on faults in the San Francisco Bay area (from west to east): 45–95 km on offshore faults, 175–185 km on the San Gregorio fault, 22–36 km on the Peninsula San Andreas fault, 70–130 km on now-dormant faults between the San Andreas and Hayward faults, 37–60 km on the Hayward fault, 30–50 km on largely dormant faults between the Hayward and Calaveras faults, 60–70 km on the Calaveras fault, and 12 km on the Greenville and related faults (Wakabayashi, 1999b).

In the Coast Ranges, Eocene to Miocene (56–5 Ma) marine sedimentary rocks overlie basement rocks of the Franciscan, Coast Range Ophiolite, and the Great Valley Group. The older of these sequences represent the younger equivalents of the Great Valley Group. The younger deposits (Miocene, 23–5 Ma) were associated with pull-apart or extensional basins that developed along the faults of the San Andreas transform plate margin (e.g., Graham et al., 1984). Most deposits have been folded and locally some have also been displaced by thrust faults (e.g., Aydin and Page, 1984; Zoback et al., 1999; Wakabayashi et al., 2004). In addition to the marine rocks, Oligocene-Miocene to Quaternary (34 to <2 Ma) volcanic rocks are also present. These rocks range in composition from basalts to rhyolites. They have been associated with thermal activity in the mantle that followed the cessation of subduction (Johnson and O'Neil, 1984; Cole and Basu, 1995).

Only minor active faulting is present within the Sierran microplate; these faults commonly have slip rates of hundredths to thousandths of millimeters per year (Wakabayashi and Sawyer, 2000). As mentioned above, the Sierra Nevada basement is locally discordantly (uncomformably) overlain by essentially undeformed Cenozoic rocks of Eocene to Quaternary age (56–<2 Ma; Bateman and Wahrhaftig, 1966). The oldest of these are the Eocene (56–34 Ma) auriferous gravels (e.g., Böhlke, 1999), followed by the Oligocene (34–23 Ma) rhyolites of the Valley Springs Formation, and the andesites of the Miocene-Pliocene (23–5 Ma) Mehrten Formation (Bateman and Wahrhaftig, 1966); the latter are related to the last stages of subduction prior to establishment of the transform plate boundary. Younger basaltic and andesitic units cover the northernmost Sierra (Guffanti et al., 1990; Harwood and Helley, 1987). The Cenozoic deposits allow evaluation of the tectonic and geomorphic processes that have given rise to the shape of the Sierra Nevada we see today (e.g., Bateman and Wahrhaftig, 1966; Huber, 1981, 1990; Unruh, 1991; Wakabayashi and Sawyer, 2001). The present northern Sierra Nevada topography is primarily a product of late Cenozoic (0–5 Ma) surface uplift (Unruh, 1991; Wakabayashi and Sawyer, 2001), although this is a controversial subject that is still undergoing discussion (e.g., House et al., 1998; Small and Anderson, 1995; see discussion in Wakabayashi and Sawyer, 2001).

ACKNOWLEDGMENTS

Over the years, many people have added to our understanding of this notable and complex region. Especially memorable are our exchanges with W.S. Alvarez, B.C. Burchfield, G.A. Davis, Y. Dilek, C. Durrell, W.G. Ernst, W.L. Lettis, J.G. Liou, J.C. Maxwell, D.R.H. O'Connell, C.S. Riebe, T.L. Sawyer, R. Schweickert, R.W. Twiss, D.L. Wagner, and C. Wahrhaftig.

REFERENCES CITED

Allmendinger, R.W., Hauge, T.A., Hauser, E.C., Potter, C.J., Klemperer, S.L., Nelson, K.D., Knuepfer, P.L.K., and Oliver, J., 1987, Overview of the COCORP 40 degrees N transect, Western United States; the fabric of an orogenic belt: Geological Society of America Bulletin, v. 98, p. 308–319, doi: 10.1130/0016-7606(1987)98<308:OOTCNT>2.0.CO;2.

Anczkiewicz, R., Platt, J.P., Thirlwall, M.F., and Wakabayashi, J., 2004, Franciscan subduction off to slow start: Evidence from high-precision Lu-Hf garnet ages on high-grade blocks: Earth and Planetary Science Letters, v. 225, p. 147–161, doi: 10.1016/j.epsl.2004.06.003.

Argus, D.K., and Gordon, R.G., 1991, Current Sierra Nevada–North America motion from very long baseline interferometry: Implications for the kinematics of the western United States: Geology, v. 19, p. 1085–1088.

Atwater, T., 1970, Implications of plate tectonics for the Cenozoic tectonic evolution of western North America: Geological Society of America Bulletin, v. 81, p. 3513–3536.

Atwater, T., and Stock, J., 1998, Pacific-North America plate tectonics of the Neogene southwestern United States: An update: International Geology Review, v. 40, p. 375–402.

Adyin, A., and Page, B.M., 1984, Diverse Pliocene-Quaternary tectonics in a transform environment, San Francisco Bay region, California: Geological Society of America Bulletin, v. 95, p. 1303–1317, doi: 10.1130/0016-7606(1984)95<1303:DPTIAT>2.0.CO;2.

Bartow, J.A., 1990, The late Cenozoic evolution of the San Joaquin Valley, California: U.S. Geological Survey Professional Paper 1501, 40 p.

Bateman, P.C., and Wahrhaftig, C., 1966. Geology of the Sierra Nevada, in Bailey, E.H., ed., Geology of northern California: California Division of Mines and Geology Bulletin 190, p. 107–172.

Beard, J.S., and Day, H.W., 1987, The Smartville intrusive complex, northern Sierra Nevada, California: the core of a rifted volcanic arc: Geological Society of America Bulletin, v. 99, p. 779–791, doi: 10.1130/0016-7606(1987)99<779:TSICSN>2.0.CO;2.

Berkland, J.O., Raymond, L.A., Kramer, J.C., Moores, E.M., and O'Day, M., 1972, What is Franciscan?: Bulletin of the American Association of Petroleum Geologists, v. 56, p. 2294–2302.

Bero, D.A., 2003, Geology of the Tiburon Peninsula, Marin County, California: Geological Society of America Abstracts with Programs, v. 35, no. 6, p. 640.

Bickford, M.E., and Day, H.W., 2001, Tectonic setting of the Smartville and Slate Creek complexes, northern Sierra Nevada, California: evidence for zircon geochronology and common Pb studies: Geological Society of America Abstracts with Programs, v. 33, no. 6, p. A-208.

Blake, M.C., Jr., Howell, D.G., and Jayko, A.S., 1984, Tectonostratigraphic terranes of the San Francisco Bay Region, in Blake, M.C., Jr., ed., Franciscan geology of northern California: Pacific Section, Society of Economic Paleontologists and Mineralogists, v. 43, p. 5–22.

Blake, M.C., Jr., Jayko, A.S., McLaughlin, R.J., and Underwood, M.B., 1988, Metamorphic and tectonic evolution of the Franciscan Complex, northern California, in Ernst, W.G., ed., Metamorphism and crustal evolution of the western United States: Englewood Cliffs, New Jersey, Prentice-Hall, Rubey Volume VII, p. 1035–1060.

Blake, M.C., Bruhn, R.L., Miller, E.L., Moores, E.M., Smithson, S.B., and Speed, R.C., 1989, Continental-Ocean Transect C-1 Mendocino triple junction to North American craton: Geological Society of America, Decade of North American Geology.

Blake, M.C., Jr., Bartow, J.A., Frizzell, V.A., Jr., Schlocker, J., Sorg, D., Wentworth, C.M., and Wright, R.H., 1974, Preliminary geologic map of Marin, and San Francisco counties and parts of Alameda, Contra Costa and Sonoma Counties, California: U.S. Geological Survey Miscellaneous Field Study Map MF-574, scale 1:62,500.

Böhlke, J.K., 1999, Mother Lode gold, in Moores, E.M., Sloan, D., and Stout, D.L., 1999, Classic cordilleran concepts: A view from California: Geological Society of America Special Paper 338, p. 55–67.

Böhlke, J.K., 1999, Mother Lode gold, in Moores, E.M., Sloan, D., and Stout, D.L., eds., Classic Cordilleran concepts: A view from California: Geological Society of America Special Paper 338, p. 55.

Bond, G.C., and DeVay, J., 1980, Pre-upper Devonian quartzose sandstones in the Shoo Fly Formation, northern California—Petrology, provenance, and implications for regional tectonics: The Journal of Geology, v. 88, p. 285–308.

Bruns, T.R., Cooper, A.K., Carlson, P.R., and McCulloch, D.S., 2002, Structure of the submerged San Andreas and San Gregorio fault zones in the Gulf of Farralones off San Francisco, CA, from high-resolution seismic reflection data, in Parsons, T., ed., Crustal structure of the coastal and marine San Francisco Bay region: U.S. Geological Survey Professional Paper 1658, p. 79–119.

Chuber, S., 1962, Late Mesozoic stratigraphy of the Elk Creek-Fruto area, Glenn County, California [Ph.D. dissertation]: Stanford University, 115 p.

Clifton, H.E., Hunter, R.E., and Gardner, J.V., 1988. Analysis of eustatic, tectonic, and sedimentologic influences on transgressive and regressive cycles in the late Cenozoic Merced Formation, San Francisco, California, in Paola, C., and Kleinspehn, K.L., eds., New perspectives of basin analysis: New York, Springer-Verlag, p. 109–128.

Cloos, M., 1984, Flow mélanges and the structural evolution of accretionary wedges, in Raymond, L., ed., Mélanges: Their nature, origin, and significance: Geological Society of America Special Paper 198, p. 71–80.

Coe, R.S., Stock, G.M., Lyons, J.J., Beitler, B., and Bowen, G.J., 2005, Yellowstone hotspot volcanism in California? A paleomagnetic test of the Lovejoy flood basalt hypothesis: Geology, v. 33, p. 697–700; doi: 10.1130/G21733.1.

Cole, R.B., and Basu, A., 1995, Nd-Sr isotopic geochemistry and tectonics of ridge subduction and middle Cenozoic volcanism in western California: Geological Society of America Bulletin, v. 107, p. 167–179, doi: 10.1130/0016-7606(1995)107<0167:NSIGAT>2.3.CO;2.

Coleman, R.G., 2000, Prospecting for ophiolites along the California continental margin, in Dilek, Y.D., Moores, E.M., Elthon, D., and Nicolas, A., eds., Ophiolites and oceanic crust: New insights from field studies and the Ocean Drilling Program: Geological Society of America Special Paper 349, p. 351–364.

Coleman, R.G., and Lanphere, M.A., 1971, Distribution and age of high-grade blueschists, associated eclogites, and amphibolites from Oregon and California: Geological Society of America Bulletin, v. 82, p. 2397–2412.

Coombs, D.S., 1997, A note on the terrane concept, based on an introduction to the Terrane '97 conference, Christchurch, New Zealand, February 1997: American Journal of Science, v. 297, p. 763–764.

Cowan, D.S., 1985, Structural styles in Mesozoic and Cenozoic mélanges in the Western Cordillera of North America: Geological Society of America Bulletin, v. 96, p. 451–462, doi: 10.1130/0016-7606(1985)96<451:SSIMAC>2.0.CO;2.

Curtis, G.H., 1989. Late Cenozoic volcanic rocks of the central Coast Ranges, *in* Wahrhaftig, C., and Sloan, D., eds., Geology of San Francisco and vicinity: International Geological Congress Field Trip Guidebook T105: Washington, D.C., America Geophysical Union, p. 33–35.

D'Allura, J., Moores, E.M., and Robinson, L., 1977, Paleozoic rocks of the northern Sierra Nevada: Their structural and paleogeographic implications, *in* Stewart, J.H., Stevens, C.H., and Fritsche, A.E., eds., Paleozoic paleography of the western United States: Pacific Section, Society of Economic Paleontologists and Mineralogists, Pacific Coast Paleogeography Symposium 1, p. 395–408.

Day, H.W., Moores, E.M., and Tuminas, A.C., 1985, Structure and tectonics of the northern Sierra Nevada: Geological Society of America Bulletin, v. 96, p. 436–450, doi: 10.1130/0016-7606(1985)96<436:SATOTN>2.0.CO;2.

Debiche, M.G., Cox, A., and Engebretson, D., 1987, The motion of Allochthonous terranes across the North Pacific basin: Geological Society of America Special Paper 207, 49 p.

Dickinson, W.R., and Lawton, T.F., 2001, Carboniferous to Cretaceous assembly and fragmentation of Mexico: Geological Society of America Bulletin, v. 113, p. 1142–1160, doi: 10.1130/0016-7606(2001)113<1142:CTCAAF>2.0.CO;2.

Dickinson, W.R., and Seely, D.R., 1979, Structure and stratigraphy of fore-arc regions: American Association of Petroleum Geologists Bulletin, v. 63, p. 2–31.

Dickerman, S., 1998, Paleogeographic significance of granitic, high temperature metamorphic, and blueschist clasts in conglomerates of the Upper Miocene Contra Costa Group, Alameda and Contra Costa Counties, California (abs.): Eos (Transactions, American Geophysical Union), v. 79, no. 46 (Fall Meeting Supplement), p. F807.

Dilek, Y., and Moores, E.M., 1992, Island-arc evolution and fracture zone tectonics in the Mesozoic Sierra Nevada, California, and implications for transform offset of the Sierran/Klamath convergent margins (U.S.A.), *in* Bartholomew, M.J., Hyndman, D.W., Mogk, D.W., and Mason, R., eds., Characterization and comparison of ancient (Precambrian-Mesozoic) continental margins—Proceedings of the 8th International Conference on Basement Tectonics, Butte, Montana, USA: Dordrecht, Kluwer, p. 166–86.

Dilek, Y., and Moores, E.M., 1993, Across-strike anatomy of the Cordilleran orogen at 40°N latitude: Implications for Mesozoic paleogeography of the western United States, *in* Dunne, G.C., and McDougall, K.A., eds., Mesozoic paleogeography of the western United States—II: Los Angeles, Pacific Section, Society for Sedimentary Geology (SEPM), p. 333–346.

Dilek, Y., and Moores, E.M., 1995, Geology of the Humboldt igneous complex, Nevada, and tectonic implications for the Jurassic magmatism in the Cordilleran orogen, *in* Busby, C., and Miller, D.M., eds., Jurassic magmatism and tectonics of the North American Cordillera, R.L. Armstrong Memorial Volume: Geological Society of America Special Paper 299, p. 229–248.

Dilek, Y., and Moores, E.M., 1999, A Tibetan model for the early Tertiary western United States: Journal of the Geological Society [London], v. 156, p. 929–941.

Dilek, Y., Moores, E.M., and Erskine, M.C., 1988, Ophiolitic thrust nappes in western Nevada: Implications for the Cordilleran orogen: Journal of the Geological Society [London], v. 145, p. 969–975.

Dilek, Y., Thy, P., Moores, E.M., and Grundvig, S., 1990. Late Paleozoic–early Mesozoic oceanic basement of a Jurassic arc terrane in the northwestern Sierra Nevada, California, *in* Harwood, D, and Miller, M.M., eds., Paleozoic and early Mesozoic paleogeographic relations: Sierra Nevada, Klamath Mountains, and related terranes: Geological Society of America Special Paper 255, p. 351–370.

Dilek, Y., Thy, P., and Moores, E.M., 1991, Episodic dike intrusions in the northwestern Sierra Nevada, California: implications for multistage evolution of a Jurassic arc terrane: Geology, v. 19, p. 180–184, doi: 10.1130/0091-7613(1991)019<0180:EDIITN>2.3.CO;2.

Ducea, M., 2001, The California arc: thick granitic batholiths, eclogitic residues, lithospheric-scale thrusting, and magmatic flare-ups: GSA Today, v. 11, no. 11, p. 4–10, doi: 10.1130/1052-5173(2001)011<0004:TCATGB>2.0.CO;2.

Durrell, C., 1959, The Lovejoy Formation of northern California: California Publications in Geological Sciences, v. 34, p. 193–220.

Durrell, C., 1966, Tertiary and Quaternary geology of northern Sierra Nevada: California Division of Mines and Geology Bulletin 190, p. 185–197.

Edelman, S.H., and Sharp, W.D., 1989, Terranes, early faults, and pre-Late Jurassic amalgamation of the western Sierra Nevada metamorphic belt: Geological Society of America Bulletin, v. 101, p. 1420–1433, doi: 10.1130/0016-7606(1989)101<1420:TEFAPL>2.3.CO;2.

Edelman, S.H., Day, H.W., Moores, E., and Zigan, S.M., Murphy, T., and Hacker, B.R., 1989, Structure across a Mesozoic ocean-continent suture zone in the northern Sierra Nevada, California: Geological Society of America Special Paper 227, 56 p.

Ernst, W.G., 1970, Tectonic contact between the Franciscan mélange and the Great Valley Sequence, crustal expression of a Late Mesozoic Benioff Zone: Journal of Geophysical Research, v. 75, p. 886–902.

Evernden, J.F., and Kistler, R.W., 1970. Chronology of emplacement of Mesozoic batholith complexes in California and western Nevada: U.S. Geological Survey Professional Paper 623. 28 p.

Fryer, P., Lockwood, J.P., Becker, N., Phipps, S., and Todd, C.S., 2000, Significance of serpentine mud volcanism in convergent margins, *in* Dilek, Y., Moores, E.M., Elthon, D., and Nicolas, A., eds., Ophiolites and oceanic crust: New insights from field studies and the Ocean Drilling Program: Geological Society of America Special Paper 349, p. 35–51.

Garrison, N.J., 2004, Geology, geochronology and geochemistry of the mid-Miocene Lovejoy flood basalt, northern California [M.S. thesis]: Santa Barbara, University of California, 106 p.

Godfrey, N., and Dilek, Y., 2000, Mesozoic assimilation of oceanic crust and island arc into the North American continental margin in California and Nevada: Insights from geophysical data: Geological Society of America Special Paper 349, p. 365–382.

Godfrey, N.J., and Klemperer, S.L., 1998, Ophiolitic basement to a forearc basin and implications for continental growth: The Coast Range–Great Valley ophiolite, California: Tectonics, v. 17, p. 558–570, doi: 10.1029/98TC01536.

Godfrey, N.J., Beaudoin, B.C., Klemperer, S.L., and the Mendocino Working Group, 1997, Ophiolitic basement to the Great Valley forearc basin, northern California, from seismic and gravity data: Implications for crustal growth at the North American continental margin: Geological Society of America Bulletin, v. 109, p. 1536–1562, 10.1130/0016-7606(1997)109<1536:OBTTGV>2.3.CO;2.

Graham, S.A., McCloy, C., Hitzman, M., Ward, R., and Turner, R., 1984, Basin evolution during change from convergent to transform continental margin in central California: American Association of Petroleum Geologists Bulletin, v. 68, p. 233–249.

Grimsich, J.L., Scott, G.R., Swisher, C.C., III, and Curtis, G.H., 1996, Paleomagnetism and $^{40}Ar/^{39}Ar$ dating of the Miocene Contra Costa Group, Berkeley Hills, California (abs.): Eos (Transactions, American Geophysical Union), v. 77, no. 46 (Fall Meeting Supplement), p. F165.

Guffanti, M., Clynne, M.A., Smith, J.G., Muffler, L.J.P., and Bullen, T.D., 1990, Late Cenozoic volcanism, subduction, and extension in the Lassen region of California, southern Cascade range: Journal of Geophysical Research, v. 95, p. 19,453–19,464.

Hacker, B.R., and Peacock, S.M., 1990, Comparison of the Central Metamorphic Belt and Trinity terrane of the Klamath Mountains with the Feather River terrane of the Sierra Nevada, *in* Harwood, D.S., and Miller, M.M., eds. Paleozoic and early Mesozoic paleogeographic relations: Sierra Nevada, Klamath Mountains, and related terranes: Geological Society of America Special Paper 255, p. 75–92.

Hall, R., 1996, Reconstructing Cenozoic SE Asia, *in* Hall, R., and Blundell, D., eds., Tectonic evolution of Southeast Asia: London, Geological Society Special Publication 106, p. 153–184.

Hall, N.T., Wright, R.H., and Clahan, K., 1999, Paleoseismic studies of the San Francisco Peninsula segment of the San Andreas fault zone near Woodside, California: Journal of Geophysical Research, v. 104, p. 23,215–23,236, doi: 10.1029/1999JB900157.

Hamilton, W.B., 1969, Mesozoic California and underflow of the Pacific mantle: Geological Society of America Bulletin, v. 80, p. 2409–2430.

Hannah, J.L., and Moores, E.M., 1986, Age relationships and depositional environments of Paleozoic strata, northern Sierra Nevada, California: Geological Society of America Bulletin, v. 97, p. 787–797, doi: 10.1130/0016-7606(1986)97<787:ARADEO>2.0.CO;2.

Harwood, D.S., 1992, Stratigraphy of Paleozoic and lower Mesozoic rocks in the northern Sierra terrane, California: U.S. Geological Survey Bulletin 1957, 78 p.

Harwood, D.S., and Helley, E.G., 1987, Late Cenozoic tectonism of the Sacramento Valley, California: U.S. Geological Survey Professional Paper 1359.

Hart, E.W., and Rapp, J.S., 1975, Ground rupture along the Cleveland Hill fault, *in* Sherburne, R.W., and Hauge, C.J., eds., Oroville, California, earthquake 1 August 1975: California Division of Mines and Geology Special Report 124, p. 61–72.

Henry, C.D., and Perkins, M.E., 2001, Sierra Nevada-Basin and Range transition near Reno, Nevada: Two-stage development at 12 and 3 Ma: Geology, v. 29, p. 719–722, doi: 10.1130/0091-7613(2001)029<0719:SNBART>2.0.CO;2.

Hopson, C.A., and Pessagno, E.A. Jr., 2004, Tehama-Colusa serpentinite mélange; a remnant of Franciscan Jurassic oceanic lithosphere, Northern California, *in* Ernst, W.G., ed., Serpentine and serpentinites; mineralogy, petrology, geochemistry, ecology, geophysics, and tectonics: Columbia, Maryland, Bellwether Press, Geological Society of America International Book Series 8, p. 301–336.

Hopson, C.A., Mattinson, J.M., and Pessagno, E.A., Jr., 1981, The Coast Range ophiolite, western California, *in* Ernst, W.G., ed., The geotectonic development of California: Englewood Cliffs, New Jersey, Prentice-Hall, p. 419–510.

Hopson, C.A., Pessagno, E.A., Jr., Mattinson, J.M., Luyendyk, B.P., Beebe, W., Hull, D.M., Munoz, I.M., and Blome, C.D., 1996, Coast Range ophiolite as paleoequatorial mid-ocean lithosphere: GSA Today, v. 6, no. 2, p. 3–4.

House, M.A., Wernicke, B.P., and Farley, K.A., 1998, Dating topography of the Sierra Nevada, California, using apatite (U-Th)/He ages: Nature, v. 396, p. 66–69, doi: 10.1038/23926.

Hietanen, A., 1973, Geology of the Pulga and Bucks Lake quadrangles. U.S. Geological Survey Professional Paper 731, 65 p.

Hsü, K.J., 1968, Principles of mélanges and their bearing on the Franciscan-Knoxville paradox: Geological Society of America Bulletin, v. 79, p. 1063–1074.

Huber, N.K., 1981, Amount and timing of late Cenozoic uplift and tilt of the central Sierra Nevada, California-evidence from the upper San Joaquin river basin: U.S. Geological Survey Professional Paper 1197, 28 p.

Huber, N.K., 1990, The late Cenozoic evolution of the Tuolumne River, central Sierra Nevada, California: Geological Society of America Bulletin, v. 102, p. 102–115, doi: 10.1130/0016-7606(1990)102<0102:TLCEOT>2.3.CO;2.

Ingersoll, R.I., 2000, Models for origin and emplacement of Jurassic ophiolites of northern California, Geological Society of America Special Paper 349, p. 395–402.

Jamieson, R.A., 1986, PT paths from high temperature shear zones beneath ophiolites: Journal of Metamorphic Geology, v. 4, p. 3–22.

Jayko, A.S., 1990, Stratigraphy and tectonics of Paleozoic arc-related rocks of the northernmost Sierra Nevada, California; the eastern Klamath and northern Sierra terranes. Geological Society of America Special Paper 255, p. 307–323.

Jayko, A.S., 1988, Paleozoic and Mesozoic rocks of the Almanor 15′ quadrangle, Plumas County: U.S. Geological Survey Open File Report 88-757, scale 1:48,000.

Jayko, A.S., Blake, M.C., Jr., and Harms, T., 1987, Attenuation of the Coast Range ophiolite by extensional faulting, and the nature of the Coast Range "thrust," California: Tectonics, v. 6, p. 475–488.

Jeanbourquin, P., 2000, Chronology of deformation of a Franciscan mélange near San Francisco (California, USA): Eclogae Geologicae Helvetiae, v. 93, p. 363–378.

Jennings, C.W., 1977, Geologic Map of California: California Division of Mines and Geology, scale 1:750,000.

Jennings, C.W., 1994, Fault activity map of California and adjacent areas: California Division of Mines and Geology, California Geologic Map Series, Map No. 6, scale 1: 750,000.

Johnson, C.M., and O'Neil, J.R., 1984, Triple junction magmatism: A geochemical study of Neogene volcanic rocks in western California: Earth and Planetary Science Letters, v. 71, p. 241–262, doi: 10.1016/0012-821X (84)90090-6.

Kelson, K.I., Simpson, G.D., Lettis, W.R., and Haradan, C., 1996, Holocene slip rate and recurrence of the northern Calaveras fault at Leyden Creek, northern California: Journal of Geophysical Research, v. 101, p. 5961–5975, doi: 10.1029/95JB02244.

Kennedy, D.G., and Caskey, S.J., 2001. Fault propagation folding along the Serra thrust fault and evidence for late Pleistocene onset of transpression along the San Andreas fault, northern San Francisco Peninsula, California: Eos (Transactions, American Geophysical Union), v. 82, no. 47 (Fall Meeting Supplement), p. F934.

Lawton, J.E., 1956, Geology of the north half of the Morgan Valley quadrangle and the south half of the Wilbur Springs quadrangle, California [Ph.D. dissertation]: Stanford, California, Stanford University, 365 p.

Lewis, J.G., and Girty, G.H., 2001, Tectonic implications of a petrographic and geochemical characterization of the lower to middle Jurassic Sailor Canyon formation, northern Sierra Nevada, California: Geology, v. 29, p. 627–630, doi: 10.1130/0091-7613(2001)029<0627:TIOAPA>2.0.CO;2.

Lienkaemper, J.J., Borchardt, G., and Lisowski, M., 1991, Historic creep rate and potential for seismic slip along the Hayward fault, California: Journal of Geophysical Research, v. 96, p. 18,261–18,283.

Maruyama, S., Liou, J.G., and Terabayashi, M., 1996, Blueschists and eclogites of the world and their exhumation: International Geology Review, v. 485–594.

Maxwell, J.C., 1974, Anatomy of an orogen: Geological Society of America Bulletin, v. 85, p. 1195–1204, doi: 10.1130/0016-7606(1974)85<1195:AOAO>2.0.CO;2.

McLaughlin, R.J., Sliter, W.V., Sorg, D.H., Russell, P.C., and Sarna-Wojcicki, A.M., 1996, Large-scale right-slip displacement on the east San Francisco Bay region fault system, California: Implications for location of late Miocene to Pliocene Pacific plate boundary: Tectonics, v. 15, p. 1–18, doi: 10.1029/95TC02347.

McLaughlin, R.J., Blake, M.C., Jr., Griscom, A., Blome, C.D., and Murchey, B., 1988, Tectonics of formation, translation and dispersal of the Coast Range ophiolite of California: Tectonics, v. 7, p. 1033–1056.

Medley, E.W., 1994, The engineering characterization of mélanges and similar block-in-matrix (bimrocks) [Ph.D. thesis]: Berkeley, University of California.

Medley, E.W., 2001, Orderly characterization of chaotic Franciscan mélanges: Felsbau, v. 19, p. 20–33.

Medley, E.W., and Lindquist, E.S., 1995, The engineering significance of the scale-independence of some Franciscan mélanges in California, USA, *in* Daemen, J.K., and Schultz, R.A., eds., Proceedings of the 25th US Rock Mechanics Symposium: Rotterdam, Balkema, p. 907–914.

Moore, D.E., and Blake, M.C., Jr., 1989, New evidence for polyphase metamorphism of glaucophane schist and eclogite exotic blocks in the Franciscan Complex: California and Oregon: Journal of Metamorphic Geology, v. 7, p. 211–228.

Moores, E.M., 1970, Ultramafics and orogeny, with models of the U.S. Cordillera and the Tethys: Nature, v. 228, p. 837–842, doi: 10.1038/228837a0.

Moores, E.M., 1998, Ophiolites, the Sierra Nevada, "Cordilleria," and orogeny along the Pacific and Caribbean margins of North and South America: International Geology Review, v. 40, p. 40–54.

Moores, E.M., and Day, H.W., 1984, An overthrust model for the Sierra Nevada: Geology, v. 12, p. 416–419, doi: 10.1130/0091-7613(1984)12<416:OMFTSN>2.0.CO;2.

Moores, E.M., Kellogg, L.H., and Dilek, Y., 2000, Tethyan ophiolites, mantle convection, and tectonic "Historical Contingency": A resolution of the "Ophiolite Conundrum," *in* Dilek, Y., Moores, E.M., Elthon, D., and Nicolas, A., eds., Proceedings of the Ophiolite Penrose Conference: Geological Society of America Special Paper 349, p. 312.

Moores, E.M., Wakabayashi, J., and Unruh, J.R., 2002, Crustal-scale cross-section of the U.S. Cordillera, California and beyond, its tectonic significance, and speculations on the Andean Orogeny: International Geology Review, v. 44, p. 479–500.

Moxon, I., 1988, Sequence stratigraphy of the Great Valley in the context of convergent margin tectonics, *in* Graham, S.A., ed., Studies of the geology of the San Joaquin Basin: Pacific Section, Society for Sedimentary Geology (SEPM), v. 60, p. 3–28.

Murchey, B.M., 1984, Biostratigraphy and lithostratigraphy of chert in the Franciscan Complex, Marin Headlands block, California, *in* Blake, M.C., Jr., ed., Franciscan geology of Northern California: Pacific Section, Society of Economic Paleontologists and Mineralogists, v. 43, p. 23–30.

Namson, J., and Davis, T., 1988, Structural transect of the western Transverse Ranges, California: Implications for lithospheric kinematics and seismic risk evaluation: Geology, v. 16, p. 675–679, doi: 10.1130/0091-7613(1988)016<0675:STOTWT>2.3.CO;2.

Nelson, K.D., Zhu, T.F., Gibbs, A., Harris, R., Oliver, J.E., Kaufman, S., Brown, L., and Schwickert, R.A., 1986, COCORP deep seismic reflection profiling in the northern Sierra Nevada, California: Tectonics, v. 5, p. 321–333.

Niemi, T.M., and Hall, N.T., 1992, Late Holocene slip rate and recurrence of great earthquakes on the San Andreas fault in northern California: Geology, v. 20, p. 195–198, doi: 10.1130/0091-7613(1992)020<0195:LHSRAR>2.3.CO;2.

Page, W.D., Sawyer, T.L., and Renne, P.R., 1995, Tectonic deformation of the Lovejoy Basalt, a late Cenozoic strain gage across the northern Sierra Nevada and Diamond Mountains, *in* Page, W.D., ed., Quaternary geology along the boundary between the Modoc Plateau, southern Cascades and northern Sierra Nevada: Friends of the Pleistocene Pacific Cell Field Trip, San Francisco, 368 p.

Paterson, S.R., Tobisch, O.T., and Radloff, J.K., 1987, Post-Nevadan deformation along the Bear Mountains fault zone: Implications for the Foothills terrane, central Sierra Nevada, California: Geology, v. 15, p. 513–516, doi: 10.1130/0091-7613(1987)15<513:PDATBM>2.0.CO;2.

Pessagno, E.A., Jr., Hull, D.M., and Hopson, C.A., 2000, Tectonostratigraphic significance of sedimentary strata occurring within and above the Coast Range ophiolite (California Coast Ranges) and the Josephine ophiolite (Klamath Mountains), northwestern California, Geological Society of America Special Paper 349, p. 383–394.

Peterson, G.L., 1967a, Upper Cretaceous stratigraphic discontinuity: Northern California and Oregon, American Association of Petroleum Geologists Bulletin, v. 51, p. 558–568.

Peterson, G.L., 1967b, Lower Cretaceous stratigraphic discontinuity in northern California and Oregon: American Association of Petroleum Geologists Bulletin, v. 51, p. 864–872.

Phipps, S.P., 1984, Ophiolitic olistostromes in the basal Great Valley sequence, Napa County, northern California Coast Ranges: Geological Society of America Special Paper 198, p. 103–125.

Platt, J.P., 1986, Dynamics of orogenic wedges and the uplift of high-pressure metamorphic rocks: Geological Society of America Bulletin, v. 97, p. 1037–1053, doi: 10.1130/0016-7606(1986)97<1037:DOOWAT>2.0.CO;2.

Prentice, C.S., 1989, Earthquake geology of the northern San Andreas fault near Point Arena, California [Ph.D. dissertation]: Pasadena, California Institute of Technology, 252 p.

Renne, P.R., Tobisch, O.T., and Saleeby, J.B., 1993, Thermochronologic record of pluton emplacement, deformation, and exhumation at Courtwright shear zone, central Sierra Nevada, California: Geology, v. 21, p. 331–334, doi: 10.1130/0091-7613(1993)021<0331:TROPED>2.3.CO;2.

Ricci, M.P., Moores, E.M., Verosub, K.L., and McClain, J.S., 1985, Geologic and gravity evidence for thrust emplacement of the Smartville ophiolite: Tectonics, v. 4, p. 539–546.

Rood, D.H., Busby, C.J., and Wagner, D.L., 2004, USGS EDMAP study of the Tertiary volcanic stratigraphy and structure of the Sonora Pass region, central Sierra Nevada, California: Geological Society of America Abstracts with Programs, v. 36, no. 4, p. 94.

Saha, A., Basu, A.R., Wakabayashi, J., and Wortman, G.L., 2005, Geochemical evidence for subducted nascent arc from Franciscan high-grade tectonic blocks: Geological Society of America Bulletin, v. 117, no. 9/10, doi: 10.1130/B25593.1.

Saleeby, J.B., Shaw, H.F., Niemeyer, S., Moores, E.M., and Edelman, S.H., 1989, U/Pb, Sm/Nd, and Rb/Sr, geochronogical and isotopic study of northern Sierra Nevada ophiolitic assemblages, California: Contributions to Mineralogy and Petrology, v. 102, p. 205–220, doi: 10.1007/BF00375341.

Sawyer, T.L., 1999, Assessment of contractional deformation rates of the Mt. Diablo fold and thrust belt, eastern San Francisco Bay Region, Northern California: Reston, Virginia, Final Technical Report, U.S. Geological Survey National Earthquake Hazards Reduction Program, Award No. 98-HQ-GR-1006, 53 p.

Sawyer, T.L., and Briggs, R., 2001, Kinematics and late Quaternary activity of the Mohawk Valley fault zone, *in* Adams, K., et al., contributors, Northern Walker Lane and northeast Sierra Nevada: Friends of the Pleistocene Pacific Cell Field Trip Guide, October 12–14, 2001, p. 49–62.

Sawyer, T.L., and Unruh, J.R., 2002. Paleoseismic investigation of the Holocene slip rate on the Greenville fault, eastern San Francisco Bay area, California: Reston, Virginia, Final Technical Report, U.S. Geological Survey National Earthquake Hazards Reduction Program, Award No. 00HQGR0055.

Sawyer, T.L., Page, W.D., and Hemphill-Haley, M.A., 1993, Recurrent late Quaternary surface faulting along the southern Mohawk Valley fault zone, NE California: Geological Society of America Abstracts with Programs, v. 25, no. 5, p. 142.

Schweickert, R.A., 1981, Tectonic evolution of the Sierra Nevada range, *in* Ernst, W.G., ed., The geotectonic development of California: Englewood Cliffs, New Jersey, Prentice-Hall, p. 87–131.

Schweickert, R.A., and Cowan, D.S., 1975, Early Mesozoic tectonic evolution of the western Sierra Nevada, California: Geological Society of America Bulletin, v. 86, p. 1329–1336, doi: 10.1130/0016-7606(1975)86<1329:EMTEOT>2.0.CO;2.

Schweickert, R.A., Armstrong, R.L., and Harakal, J.E., 1980, Lawsonite blueschist in the northern Sierra Nevada: Geology, v. 8, p. 27–31, doi: 10.1130/0091-7613(1980)8<27:LBITNS>2.0.CO;2.

Shervais, J.V., 1989, Geochemistry of igneous rocks from Marin Headlands, *in* Wahrhaftig, C., and Sloan, D., eds., Geology of San Francisco and vicinity: Washington, D.C., American Geophysical Union, International Geological Congress Field Trip Guidebook T105, p. 40–41.

Shervais, J.W., 1990, Island arc and ocean crust ophiolites; contrasts in the petrology, geochemistry and tectonic style of ophiolite assemblages in the California Coast Ranges, *in* Malpas, J., Moores, E., Panayiotou, A., and Xenophontos, C., eds., Ophiolites oceanic crustal analogues: Proceedings of the Symposium 'Troodos 1987': Nicosia, Cyprus, Geological Survey Department, Ministry of Agriculture and Natural Resources, p. 507–520.

Shervais, J.W., Murchey, B.L., Kimbrough, D.L., Renne, P.R., and Hanan, B., 2005, Radioisotopic and biostratigraphic age relations in the Coast Range Ophiolite, northern California: Implications for the tectonic evolution of the Western Cordillera: Geological Society of America Bulletin, v. 117, p. 633–653, doi: 10.1130/B25443.1.

Siegel, J.H., 1988, Stratigraphy of the Putnam Peak Basalt and correlation to the Lovejoy Formation, California [M.S. thesis]: Hayward, California State University, 119 p.

Simpson, G.D., Lettis, W.R., and Randolph, C.E., 1998, Slip rate of the northern San Gregorio fault near Seal Cove, California (abs.): Eos (Transactions, American Geophysical Union), v. 79, no. 45 (Fall Meeting Supplement), p. F611.

Small, E.E., and Anderson, R.S., 1995, Geomorphologically driven late Cenozoic rock uplift in the Sierra Nevada, California: Science, v. 270, p. 277–280.

Small, E.E., Anderson, R.S., Repka, J.L., and Finkel, R., 1997, Erosion rates of alpine bedrock summit surfaces deduced from in situ ^{10}Be and ^{26}Al: Earth and Planetary Science Letters, v. 150, p. 413–425, doi: 10.1016/ S0012-821X(97)00092-7.

Stamatakos, J.A., Trop, J.M., and Ridgway, K.D., 2001, Late Cretaceous paleogeography of Wrangellia; paleomagnetism of the MacColl Ridge Formation, southern Alaska, revisited: Geology, v. 29, p. 947–950, doi: 10.1130/0091-7613(2001)029<0947:LCPOWP>2.0.CO;2.

Stoffer, P.W., 2005, The San Andreas fault in the San Francisco Bay area, California: A geology fieldtrip guidebook to selected stops on public lands: U.S. Geological Survey Open File Report 2005-1127, 133 p., http://pubs.er.usgs.gov/pubs/ofr/ofr20051127.

Swanson, S.E., and Schiffman, P., 1979, Textural evolution and metamorphism of pillow basalts from the Franciscan Complex, western Marin County, California: Contributions to Mineralogy and Petrology, v. 69, p. 291–299, doi: 10.1007/BF00372331.

Tobisch, O.T., Paterson, S.R., Saleeby, J.B., and Geary, E.E., 1989, Nature and timing of deformation in the Foothills terrane, central Sierra Nevada, California, and its bearing on orogenesis: Geological Society of America Bulletin, v. 101, p. 401–413, doi: 10.1130/0016-7606(1989)101<0401: NATODI>2.3.CO;2.

Tobisch, O.T., Saleeby, J.B., Renne, P.R., McNulty, B., and Tong, W., 1995, Variations in deformation fields during the development of a large-volume magmatic arc, central Sierra Nevada, California: Geological Society of America Bulletin, v. 107, p. 148–166, doi: 10.1130/0016-7606(1995)107<0148:VIDFDD>2.3.CO;2.

Tsujimori, T., Matsumoto, K., Wakabayashi, J., and Liou, J.G., 2006, Franciscan eclogite revisited: Reevaluation of P-T evolution of tectonic blocks from Tiburon Peninsula, California, *in* Mogessie, A., and Proyer, A., eds., International Eclogite Conference 7th Special Volume (in press).

Unruh, J.R., 1991, The uplift of the Sierra Nevada and implications for late Cenozoic epeirogeny in the western Cordillera: Geological Society of America Bulletin, v. 103, p. 1395–1404, doi: 10.1130/0016-7606(1991)103<1395:TUOTSN>2.3.CO;2.

Unruh, J.R., and Moores, E.M., 1992, Quaternary blind thrusting in the southwestern Sacramento Valley, California: Tectonics, v. 11, p. 192–203.

Unruh, J.R., and Sawyer, T.L., 1997, Assessment of blind seismogenic sources, Livermore Valley, eastern San Francisco Bay region: Reston, Virginia, Final Technical Report, U.S. Geological Survey, National Earthquake Hazards Reduction Program, Award No. 1434-95-G-2611.

Unruh, J.R., and Sawyer, T.L., 2001, Structure, late Cenozoic development, and seismic potential of the Mt. Diablo anticline: Guidebook, American Seismological Society of America 2001 Annual Meeting Field Trip, April 21, 2001, 15 p.

Unruh, J.R., Loewen, B.A., and Moores, E.M., 1995, Progressive arcward contraction of a Mesozoic-Tertiary fore-arc basin, southwestern Sacramento Valley, California: Geological Society of America Bulletin, v. 107, p. 38–53, doi: 10.1130/0016-7606(1995)107<0038:PACOAM>2.3.CO;2.

Unruh, J., Humphrey, J., and Barron, A., 2003, Transtensional model for the Sierra Nevada frontal fault system, eastern Sierra: Geology, v. 31, p. 327–330, doi: 10.1130/0091-7613(2003)031<0327:TMFTSN>2.0.CO;2.

Varga, R.J., and Moores, E.M., 1981, Age, origin and significance of an unconformity that predates island-arc volcanism in the northern Sierra Nevada: Geology, v. 9, p. 512–518, doi: 10.1130/0091-7613(1981)9 <512:AOASOA>2.0.CO;2.

Wagner, D.L., and Bortugno, E.L., compilers, 1982, Geologic map of the Santa Rosa Quadrangle, California: California Division of Mines and Geology, Regional Geologic Map Series, scale 1:250,000.

Wagner, D.L., Saucedo, G.J., and Grose, T.J., 2000, Tertiary volcanic rocks of the Blairsden area, northern Sierra Nevada, California, *in* Brooks, E.R., and Dida, L.T., eds. Field guide to the geology and tectonics of the northern Sierra Nevada: California Division of Mines and Geology Special Publication 122, p. 155–172.

Wahrhaftig, C., 1984, Structure of the Marin Headlands block, California: A progress report, *in* Blake, M.C., ed., Franciscan Geology of Northern California: Pacific Section, Society of Economic Paleontologists and Mineralogists, v. 43, p. 31–50.

Wakabayashi, J., 1992, Nappes, tectonics of oblique plate convergence, and metamorphic evolution related to 140 million years of continuous subduction, Franciscan Complex, California: Journal of Geology, v. 100, p. 19–40.

Wakabayashi, J., 1999a, Subduction and the rock record: Concepts developed in the Franciscan Complex, California, *in* Sloan, D., Moores, E.M., and Stout, D. eds., Classic Cordilleran concepts: A view from California: Geological Society of America Special Paper 338, p. 123–133.

Wakabayashi, J., 1999b, Distribution of displacement on, and evolution of, a young transform fault system: The northern San Andreas fault system, California: Tectonics, v. 18, p. 1245–1274, doi: 10.1029/1999TC900049.

Wakabayashi, J., 1999c, The Franciscan Complex, San Francisco Bay area: A record of subduction processes, *in* Wagner, D.L., and Graham, S. A., eds., Geologic field trips in northern California: California Division of Mines and Geology Special Publication 119, p. 1–21.

Wakabayashi, J., 2004b, Contrasting settings of serpentinite bodies, San Francisco Bay area, California: Derivation from the subducting plate vs. mantle hanging wall: International Geology Review, v. 46, p. 1103–1118.

Wakabayashi, J., and Dilek, Y., 1987, An alpine-style collision in the northern Sierra Nevada, California: structural and metamorphic evidence: Eos (Transactions, American Geophysical Union), v. 68, no. 44, p. 1474.

Wakabayashi, J., and Sawyer, T.L., 2000, Neotectonics of the Sierra Nevada and the Sierra Nevada–Basin and Range transition, California, with field trip stop descriptions for the northeastern Sierra Nevada, *in* Brooks, E.R., and Dida, L.T., eds., Field guide to the geology and tectonics of the northern Sierra Nevada: California Division of Mines and Geology Special Publication 122, p. 173–212.

Wakabayashi, J., and Sawyer, T.L., 2001, Stream incision, tectonics, uplift, and evolution of topography of the Sierra Nevada, California: Journal of Geology, v. 109, p. 539–562, doi: 10.1086/321962.

Wakabayashi, J., and Unruh, J.R., 1995, Tectonic wedging, blueschist metamorphism, and exposure of blueschist: are they compatible?: Geology, v. 23, p. 85–88, doi: 10.1130/0091-7613(1995)023<0085:TWBMAE>2.3.CO;2.

Wakabayashi, J., Hengesh, J.V., and Sawyer, T.L., 2004, Four-dimensional transform fault processes: progressive evolution of step-overs and bends: Tectonophysics, v. 392, p. 279–301, doi: 10.1016/j.tecto.2004.04.013.

Weber, G.E., and Lajoie, K.R., 1980, Map of Quaternary faulting along the San Gregorio fault zone, San Mateo and Santa Cruz counties, California: U.S. Geological Survey Open-File Report 80-907, scale: 1:24,000, sheet 1 of 3.

Wentworth, C.M., Blake, M.C. Jr., Jones, D.L., Walter, A.W., and Zoback, M.D., 1984, Tectonic wedging associated with emplacement of the Franciscan assemblage, California Coast Ranges, in Black, M.C. Jr., ed., Franciscan geology of northern California: Los Angeles, California, Pacific Section, Society of Economic Paleontologists and Mineralogists, v. 43, p. 163–173.

Williams, H., and Curtis, G.H., 1977, The Sutter Buttes of California: A study of Plio-Pleistocene volcanism: University of California Publications in the Geological Sciences, v. 116, 56 p.

Williams, H., and Smyth, R., 1973, Metamorphic aureoles beneath ophiolite suites and Alpine peridotites: Tectonic implications with west Newfoundland examples: American Journal of Science, v. 273, p. 594–621.

Worrall, D.M., 1981, Imbricate low-angle faulting in uppermost Franciscan rocks, south Yolla Bolly area, northern California: Geological Society of America Bulletin, v. 92, p. 703–729, doi: 10.1130/0016-7606(1981)92<703:ILFIUF>2.0.CO;2.

Wright, J.E., and Wyld, S.J., 2003, Appalachian, Gondwanan, Cordilleran interactions: A new geodynamic model for the Paleozoic tectonic evolution of the North American Cordillera: Geological Society of America Abstracts with Programs, v. 34, no. 7, p. 557.

Wright, J.E., and Wyld, S.J., 2006, Gondwanan, Iapetan, Cordilleran interactions: A geodynamic model for the Paleozoic tectonic evolution of the North American Cordillera, *in* Monger, J., Enkin, R., and Haggert, J., eds., Paleogeography of western North America: Constraints on large-scale latitudinal displacements: Geological Association of Canada Special Paper (in press).

Zoback, M.L., Jachens, R.C., and Olson, J.A., 1999, Abrupt along-strike change in tectonic style: San Andreas fault zone, San Francisco Peninsula: Journal of Geophysical Research, v. 104, p. 10,719–10,742, doi: 10.1029/1998JB900059.

GLOSSARY OF TERMS

accelerogram The record produced by an accelerometer, a type of seismometer that measures the acceleration of the ground due to the passage of seismic waves.

accretionary Increasing in size by addition of external material.

aggrading stream A stream that is actively building up its channel because it is being supplied with a greater sediment load than it can carry.

alluvial fan A fan-shaped deposit of alluvium formed at the base of hills as the velocity of a stream decreases.

alluvial plain A gently sloping plain consisting of material eroded out of nearby hills.

alluvium Sediment deposited by a stream.

aseismic Movement without earthquakes; an area not subject to earthquakes.

base isolation A system that decouples a structure from the ground motion of an earthquake, dampening the transmission of seismic energy to the structure.

basement rocks The rocks underlying the rocks of interest to a particular study in a given area.

bedrock Solid rock that underlies soil.

cistern A tank for catching or holding water.

clastic Pertaining to sedimentary rocks composed of broken fragments of other, preexisting rocks.

collector A horizontal member of the lateral-force-resisting system that collects lateral forces and transfer transfers them to the principal members of the lateral-force-resisting system.

colluvium Loose soil or rock fragments collected at the base of a slope due to transport by gravity.

concretion A concentration of cementing minerals that have precipitated locally, usually around an organic nucleus such as a fossil.

cornice A horizontal decorative molding that crowns or completes the top of a building.

coseismic Occurring at the time of an earthquake.

creep *See* fault creep.

creeping strand A creeping fault strand is one that slowly but continuously moves at the surface.

cupola A domed roof or ceiling.

dead load The permanent load applied to a structure or foundation (permanent weight of the structure).

deformation Alteration of the form or shape of earth materials due to tectonic forces.

dextral See *right lateral*.

differential settlement Uneven settling; commonly refers to buildings not uniformly sinking into filled land.

dip-slope A hillslope that conforms roughly to the angle and direction of dip of the underlying rock unit.

elastometric Polymers that have the elastic properties of natural rubber.

en echelon fractures A set of cracks that are arranged in an overlapping pattern so that each crack is oriented obliquely to the overall linear trend of the set.

epicenter The location on Earth's surface directly above the source of an earthquake.

estuarine Relating to an estuary such as the San Francisco Bay.

expansion coupling A sleeve-like joint that allows movement between the ends of adjoining segments of a pipe or conduit.

fault creep Slow fault movement that occurs without an earthquake.

fault offset Displacement of rock or a structure by fault movement.

fault scarp A steep slope formed by movement along a fault.

fault strand One of several branches of a fault.

fault trace A fault line.

fission-track studies A method of calculating the age of rocks that contain Uranium.

fluvial deposits River or stream sediments.

Franciscan rocks The bedrock of most of the Coast Ranges; in San Francisco it is comprised predominantly of sandstone, chert, or serpentinite.

geodetic Relating to measurements of the size and shape of Earth and the precise location of points on its surface.

geomorphic Relating to Earth's surface features.

geomorphology The branch of geology that studies landscapes and landforms at the surface of Earth.

gouge Ground-up rock within a fault zone.

graben An elongate basin between two high-angle normal faults.

groundwater Water present in the spaces in sediment and rock below the ground's surface.

Holocene The past ~10,000 calendar years of geologic time.

impost blocks A transitional member in the construction of an arch that receives and distributes the thrust at the end of an arch.

inertial forces The tendency of matter to remain at rest or, if moving, to continue moving in the same direction at the same speed unless affected by an outside force.

intensity of an earthquake (see also *Mercalli intensity*) The measure of the effects of an earthquake at a given location due to ground shaking.

isolation valves Shut-off valves located along a pipeline for the purpose of isolating a pipeline segment (such as at a fault crossing).

kips A unit of measure equal to thousands of pounds.

knocker A large resistant rock within a mélange.

landslide plane See *slide plane*.

landslide toe The lowest part of a landslide, which commonly overrides the existing surface.

lateral-force–resisting system The collection of structural members that resist lateral forces, typically generated by wind or seismic events, on the structure.

leveling grout Historically, a mixture of cement, sand, and enough water to make a stiff mixture placed between a foundation and column base to provide a complete bearing surface for the column base.

liquefaction (a) Ground failure due to water saturated sediment and fill liquefying during ground shaking in earthquakes. (b) The change from a solid to a liquid, such as when water-saturated sand is shaken in an earthquake and behaves as a liquid.

live load A variable or moving weight added to the dead load of a structure.

magnitude of an earthquake (M) A measure of the energy released by an earthquake.

mass wasting The downslope transport of material under the force of gravity.

mat foundation A concrete structural (reinforced and thickened) slab that extends across the footprint of a structure and supporting that structure.

maximum credible earthquake The largest earthquake anticipated on a particular fault.

maximum probable earthquake The largest earthquake expected with a particular probability during a particular time period.

mélange An unordered or chaotic mixture of rock materials, consisting of small to very large blocks in a ground-up matrix.

Mercalli Intensity (or Modified Mercalli Intensity, MMI) An index to rate the strength of ground shaking at a particular location based on the nature of the damage to structures.

Mesozoic The era of geologic time from about 225 to about 65 million years ago.

metasedimentary Said of a sedimentary rock that has been metamorphosed.

metavolcanic Said of a volcanic rock that has been metamorphosed.

monoclinal flexure A single limb fold formed by draping or uplift of stratified deposits over the tip of a buried fault.

neo-classical architecture Architecture designed with deliberate imitation of Greco-Roman buildings.

offset curb A jog in a curb that crosses perpendicular to a creeping fault. When standing on the southwest side of the Hayward fault, the curb on the northeast side of the fault appears to have moved to the right.

ophiolitic An assemblage of rocks believed to represent a fragment of oceanic crust.

orthotropic deck A bridge deck that consists of a collage of steel plates welded together and supported by ribs welded to framing members, overlain by an integrated driving surface. Orthotropic decks are particularly valued for their seismic performance.

oxidized zone Soil that has yellowish to reddish colors due to the "rusting" or oxidation of the iron in soil solutions percolating through geologic materials that are above the water table.

paleoliquefaction Prehistoric movement of fine sands showing evidence of turning to quicksand and being pressurized during an earthquake.

paleosol A fossil soil; a soil that formed on a landscape in the past with distinctive morphological features resulting from a soil-forming environment that no longer exists at the site.

palinspastic map A map showing geologic features restored as nearly as possible to their original geographic positions before deformation due to folding and/or fault displacement.

percentile (84th or 95th) non-exceedance The level at which 84% (or 95%) of the occurrences will not exceed the target value.

period or building period The time between oscillations of a swinging object, such as a pendulum. The fundamental period of a structure is the dominant period of the structure.

Pleistocene The period of Earth's history from 1.6 million to 10,000 years ago.

plutonic Pertaining to an igneous rock that formed at great depth.

poorly engineered fill Artificial fill with engineering properties that have not been designed or tested.

pressure ridge A landform created due to the shortening of the land surface, usually between two fault traces.

reduced zone Soil that has gray to olive colors due to the lack of oxygen that normally would cause oxidation at the surface of the earth. The continuous presence of water prevents oxidation beneath the water table.

resonance In earthquakes, when a building vibrates at the same frequency as the earthquake—this leads to rhythmic amplification of the movement of the structure, which can cause enormous damage.

Richter Scale The numerical scale measuring the strength or magnitude of an earthquake.

rift valley A valley formed by a down-dropped block between two faults. This term is also sometimes used to describe a valley formed as a result of motion along a strike-slip fault.

right-lateral fault A fault with lateral movement along which the side opposite to the viewer appears to move to the right.

Rocklin granite Granite quarried from the Rocklin quarries east of Sacramento.

rupture trace The trace of a fault on the ground surface after an earthquake.

sag pond A shallow depression filled with water typically found along a strike-slip fault where fault motion has impounded drainage.

sandstone Sedimentary rock composed of sand-sized grains that have been compacted and cemented together.

scarp A break in slope caused by fault movement.

seismic Relating to earthquakes.

seismic base shear The lateral force imparted to a building due to a seismic event.

seismogram The record, usually on paper, made by a seismograph.

seismograph An instrument that records seismic waves.

seismometer The sensor part of a seismograph, usually a suspended pendulum.

shale Sedimentary rock composed of clay and silt-sized particles compacted together.

shear Deformation that results when two sides of a fault slide past each other.

shear forces Forces acting perpendicular to the longitudinal axis of a structural member.

shear wall A wall that is part of the lateral-force–resisting system that resists lateral forces principally through shear deformation.

shotcrete Sprayed concrete or mortar.

silicic volcanics Volcanic rocks with high silica content.

slickensides Polished surfaces produced by rock rubbing against rock under pressure.

slide plane The sheared, nearly flat-lying contact between a landslide and the material it has overridden; the surface over which a landslide moves.

slip rate The rate of movement along a fault.

strike-slip fault A fault on which the movement is dominantly horizontal (parallel to the fault's strike).

swale A narrow linear depression commonly associated with strike-slip faults.

tectonic Referring to movements of the crust.

tension The state or condition of being pulled apart.

tension-only plate diagonals Diagonal truss web members that are flat plate–shaped and are designed to act in tension only.

Tertiary The period of geologic time between 65 and 1.8 million years ago.

topographic Referring to the relief and contours of an area.

unreinforced masonry Brick- or stone-work lacking structural support.

water table The upper surface of water-saturated sediment or rocks below the ground.

wave-cut platform A horizontal or gently sloping surface cut by waves near the shoreline.

GSA Field Guides

Interior Western United States: GSA Field Guide 6

edited by Joel L. Pederson and Carol M. Dehler, 2005

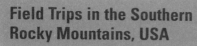

NEW!

The 2005 GSA Annual Meeting in Salt Lake City provided a large and diverse terrain for field trips—from the Basin and Range to the Rocky Mountains, from the Snake River Plain, across the Colorado Plateau, to the Mojave Desert. This volume contains 22 field trip articles. All combine the latest research with useful road logs to spectacular and often classic geologic settings. The regional tour has a core of structure and stratigraphy-paleontology contributions, and is rounded off with volcanic, glacial, lacustrine, fluvial geomorphology, neotectonic, geologic hazard, and geoarchaeology articles.

FLD006, 524 p., ISBN 0-8137-0006-X
$45.00, **member price $36.00**

Field Trips in the Southern Rocky Mountains, USA

edited by Eric P. Nelson and Eric A. Erslev, 2004

The Front Range of the Rocky Mountains and the High Plains preserve an outstanding record of geological processes from Precambrian through Quaternary times. With energy and mineral resources, geological hazards, water issues, geoarchaeological sites, and famous dinosaur fossil sites, the Front Range and adjacent High Plains region provide ample opportunities for field trips focusing on our changing world. The chapters in this field guide all contain technical content as well as a field trip log describing field trip routes and stops. Of the 25 field trips offered at the 2004 GSA Annual Meeting, 14 are described in the guidebook, covering a wide variety of geoscience disciplines, with chapters on tectonics (Precambrian and Laramide), stratigraphy and paleoenvironments (e.g., early Paleozoic environments, Jurassic eolian environments, the K-T boundary, the famous Oligocene Florissant fossil beds), economic deposits (coal and molybdenum), geological hazards, and geoarchaeology.

FLD005, 234 p., ISBN 0-8137-0005-1
$30.00, **member price $24.00**
REDUCED PRICE!

Western Cordillera and Adjacent Areas

edited by Terry W. Swanson, 2003

This volume includes guides for 15 of the field trips held in conjunction with the 2003 GSA Annual Meeting in Seattle. Topics covered include Glacial Lake Missoula and the Clark Fork Ice Dam; the Sauk Sequence in western Utah; the geology of wine in Washington state; the Columbia River basalt and Yakima Fold Belt; Alpine glaciation of the North Cascades; and recent geoarchaeological discoveries in central Washington. Quaternary geology of Seattle, engineering geology in the central Columbia Valley, and the tephrostratigraphy and paleogeography of southern Puget Sound also are covered, as are trips to the central Cascade Range and the White River.

FLD004, 284 p. ISBN 0-8137-0004-3, softcover
$45.00, (sorry, no additional discounts)

INQUA 2003 Field Guide Volume: Quaternary Geology of the United States

edited by Don J. Easterbrook, 2003

Much of the landscape in the United States was shaped by climatic events during the Quaternary, especially the erosion and deposition in the Pleistocene. The wealth of Quaternary features found in the U.S. includes continental ice sheet glaciation, alpine glaciation, marine shorelines, marine deposits, faulting, tectonic uplift, effects of isostatic rebound, pluvial lakes, large-scale eolian deposits, the world's largest geothermal area, and much more. This volume contains 17 guides with contributions from 97 authors across the country, from Alaska and the west coast to New England, including much new, previously unpublished information. Each guide includes specific sites with interpretations of the features to be seen and discussions of critical issues.

FLDINQ01, 438 p. ISBN 0-945920-50-4
$45.00 (sorry, no additional discounts)

GSA SALES AND SERVICE
P.O. Box 9140 • Boulder, Colorado 80301-9140, USA
+1.303.357.1000, option 3 • Toll free: +1.888.443.4472
Fax: +1.303.357.1071

THE GEOLOGICAL SOCIETY OF AMERICA